esa S. Stover
rd-winning author and instructional designer

Microsoft

W9-AZE-016

Microsoft®
Project
Version 2002
INSIDE
OUT

PUBLISHED BY
Microsoft Press
A Division of Microsoft Corporation
One Microsoft Way
Redmond, Washington 98052-6399

Library of Congress Cataloging-in-Publication Data
Stover, Teresa S.
    Microsoft Project Version 2002 Inside Out / Teresa S. Stover.
        p. cm.
    Includes index.
    ISBN 0-7356-1124-6
    1. Microsoft Project.   2. Project management--Computer programs.   I. Title.

    HD69.P75 S76   2002
    658.4'04'02855369--dc21   2002075340

Printed and bound in the United States of America.

1 2 3 4 5 6 7 8 9   QWT   7 6 5 4 3 2

Distributed in Canada by H.B. Fenn and Company Ltd.

A CIP catalogue record for this book is available from the British Library.

Microsoft Press books are available through booksellers and distributors worldwide. For further informa-
tion about international editions, contact your local Microsoft Corporation office or contact Microsoft
Press International directly at fax (425) 936-7329. Visit our Web site at www.microsoft.com/mspress.
Send comments to *mspinput@microsoft.com*.

Acquisitions Editor: Kong Cheung
Project Editor: Aileen Wrothwell; Sandra Haynes
Series Editor: Sandra Haynes

Body Part No. X08-24258

To Craig, my best friend.

Contents At A Glance

Contents At A Glance

Table of Contents

Part 2

Developing the Project Plan

Chapter 3

Starting a New Project

Chapter 4

Viewing Project Information

newfeature!

Chapter 5
Scheduling Tasks   127

Chapter 6
Setting Up Resources in the Project   163

Chapter 7
Assigning Resources to Tasks 189

Chapter 8
Planning Resource and Task Costs 217

Chapter 9
Checking and Adjusting the Project Plan 231

Part 3
Tracking Progress   279

Chapter 10
Saving a Baseline and Updating Progress   281

Chapter 11
Responding to Changes in Your Project   309

Chapter 15
Exchanging Information Between Project Plans

411

Part 6
Integrating Microsoft Project with Other Programs

427

Chapter 16
Exchanging Information with Other Applications

429

Chapter 21

newfeature!

Managing Your Team Using Microsoft Project Web Access

505

Customizing the Microsoft Project Interface   641

Automating Your Work with Macros   657

Standardizing Projects Using Templates   671

Chapter 29
Managing Project Files   **685**

Part 10
Programming Custom Solutions   **703**

Chapter 30
Understanding the Visual Basic Language   **705**

newfeature!

Acknowledgments

With many of us feeling sometimes that this project was jinxed, getting *Microsoft Project Inside Out* to print was a Herculean task. But…we did it. Heartfelt gratitude goes to the following:

The team at Microsoft Press: Kong Cheung, Sandra Haynes, Alex Blanton, Aileen Wrothwell, Wendy Zucker, and Robert Lyon. Their high standards, along with their compassion, reap beautiful results.

Claudette Moore at Moore Literary Agency. She combines excellent insight and problem solving with an encouraging and positive touch.

Joyce Cox's team at Online Training Solutions, Inc. (please see their credits following the index): Aaron L'Heureux, Martin Stillion, Nancy Depper, Nealy White, Liz Clark, R.J. Cadranell, Lisa Van Every, and Jan Bednarczuk. They make me look good.

My co-writers on this project (please read their biographies following the index): Ken Speer, for steadiness and perseverance under difficult circumstances. Stephen T. Adams, for challenging me to maintain ever-higher standards. James Scott, for facing challenges with admirable enthusiasm and adaptability. Bonnie Biafore, for redefining the phrase "hit the ground running."

The American Red Cross, for being there to provide emergency food, clothing, and shelter for individuals shattered by natural and manmade disasters, and for including me on their disaster action team. I get a lot more than I give, including the opportunity to do something other than sit at a computer and contemplate project management.

My family, who inspire me to live life to the fullest: Richard, Ai Soon, Lester, Pauline, Denise, Monique, and Katie Remhof; and Betty and Stub Stover. And of course, Craig Stover, husband extraordinaire, for still making me laugh after all these years.

We'd Like to Hear from You!

Our goal at Microsoft Press is to create books that help you find the information you need to get the most out of your software.

The INSIDE OUT series was created with you in mind. As part of an effort to ensure that we're creating the best, most useful books we can, we talked to our customers and asked them to tell us what they need from a Microsoft Press series. Help us continue to help you. Let us know what you like about this book and what we can do to make it better. When you write, please include the title and author of this book in your e-mail, as well as your name and contact information. We look forward to hearing from you.

How to Reach Us

E-mail:	nsideout@microsoft.com
Mail:	Inside Out Series Editor
	Microsoft Press
	One Microsoft Way
	Redmond, WA 98052

Note: Unfortunately, we can't provide support for any software problems you might experience. Please go to http://support.microsoft.com *for help with any software issues.*

About the CD

The companion CD that ships with this book contains many tools and resources to help you get the most out of your Inside Out book.

What's On the CD

Your Inside Out CD includes the following:

- **Microsoft and Third-Party Tools and Add-Ins.** In this section, you'll find many great tools, utilities, demos, and trial software for your use.

- **Author Extras.** This section includes files the author selected for you to install and use as additional reference material.

- **Office Tools on the Web.** Here you'll find complete descriptions and links to official Microsoft Office resources online.

- **Complete eBook and Sample Chapters.** In this section you'll find the entire electronic version of this title as well as a set of sample chapters from other Inside Out books.

The companion CD provides detailed information about the files on this CD, and links to Microsoft and third-party sites on the Internet. All the files on this CD are designed to be accessed through Microsoft Internet Explorer (version 5.01 or higher). Executable applications are included for some Microsoft add-ins and some third-party add-ins.

> **note** Please note that the third-party software and links to third-party sites are not under the control of Microsoft Corporation and Microsoft is therefore not responsible for their content, nor should their inclusion on this CD be construed as an endorsement of the product or the site. Please check third-party Websites for the latest version of their software.
>
> Software provided on this CD is in English language only and may be incompatible with non-English language operating systems and software.

Using the CD

To use this companion CD, insert it into your CD-ROM drive. If AutoRun is not enabled on your computer, click on Index.htm in the WebSite folder in the root of the CD.

> **important** This book also contains a trial version of the Microsoft Project 2002 Standard software. This software is fully functional, but it expires 60 days after you install it. You should not install the trial version if you have already installed the full version of either Microsoft Project 2002 Standard or Professional edition.

System Requirements

Following are the minimum system requirements necessary to run the CD:

- Microsoft Windows 95 or higher operating system (including Windows 98, Windows Millennium Edition, Windows NT 4.0 with Service Pack 3, Windows 2000, or Windows XP)
- 266-MHz or higher Pentium-compatible CPU
- 64 megabytes (MB) RAM
- 8X CD-ROM drive or faster
- 46 MB of free hard disk space (to install the eBook files)
- Microsoft Windows–compatible sound card and speakers
- Microsoft Internet Explorer 5.01 or higher
- Microsoft Mouse or compatible pointing device

> **note** System requirements may be higher for the add-ins available on the CD. Individual add-in system requirements are specified on the CD. An Internet connection is necessary to access the hyperlinks in the Office Tools on the Web section. Connect time charges may apply.

Support Information

Every effort has been made to ensure the accuracy of the book and the contents of this companion CD. For feedback on the book content or this companion CD, please contact us by using any of the addresses listed in the "We'd Like to Hear From You" section.

Microsoft Press provides corrections for books through the World Wide Web at *http://www.microsoft.com/mspress/support/*. To connect directly to the Microsoft Press Knowledge Base and enter a query regarding a question or issue that you may have, go to *http://www.microsoft.com/mspress/support/search.htm*.

For support information regarding Windows XP, you can connect to Microsoft Technical Support on the Web at *http://support.microsoft.com/*.

Conventions and Features Used in this Book

This book uses special text and design conventions to make it easier for you to find the information you need.

Text Conventions

Convention	Meaning
Abbreviated menu commands	For your convenience, this book uses abbreviated menu commands. For example, "Click Tools, Track Changes, Highlight Changes" means that you should click the Tools menu, point to Track Changes, and click the Highlight Changes command.
Boldface type	**Boldface** type is used to indicate text that you enter or type.
Initial Capital Letters	The first letters of the names of menus, dialog boxes, dialog box elements, and commands are capitalized. Example: the Save As dialog box.
Italicized type	*Italicized* type is used to indicate new terms.
Plus sign (+) in text	Keyboard shortcuts are indicated by a plus sign (+) separating two key names. For example, Ctrl+Alt+Delete means that you press the Ctrl, Alt, and Delete keys at the same time.

Design Conventions

newfeature!

This text identifies a new or significantly updated feature in this version of the software.

InsideOut

These are the book's signature tips. In these tips, you'll get the straight scoop on what's going on with the software—inside information about why a feature works the way it does. You'll also find handy workarounds to deal with software problems.

tips   Tips provide helpful hints, timesaving tricks, or alternative procedures related to the task being discussed.

Troubleshooting

Look for these sidebars to find solutions to common problems you might encounter. Troubleshooting sidebars appear next to related information in the chapters. You can also use the Troubleshooting Topics index at the back of the book to look up problems by topic.

Cross-references point you to other locations in the book that offer additional information about the topic being discussed.

 This icon indicates information or text found on the companion CD.

cautions   Cautions identify potential problems that you should look out for when you're completing a task or problems that you must address before you can complete a task.

notes   Notes offer additional information related to the task being discussed.

Sidebars

The sidebars sprinkled throughout these chapters provide ancillary information on the topic being discussed. Go to sidebars to learn more about the technology or a feature.

Part 1

Project Fundamentals

Chapter 1

Introducing Microsoft Project 2002

Consider this scenario: You are a product manager of a small startup company. In addition to handling research, development, material procurement, marketing, and staff development, you have been assigned the responsibility of being the project manager of the launch of your company's newest product next year.

Consider a second scenario: You are a project management professional who manages projects for several departments in your corporation at any given time. You are responsible for managing thousands of tasks, hitting hundreds of deadlines, and assigning scores of resources. You need to plan and monitor each project, work with different managers, and make the best use of team members—some of whom might work on only one project, and others might be shared among several of your projects.

As these two scenarios illustrate, project management is a process and a discipline that can be one of many tasks in your job description or the full focus of your career.

Numerous industries rely on sound project management for their success:

- Construction
- Computer system deployment
- Engineering
- Events planning
- Filmmaking
- Logistics
- Publishing
- Software development

Effective project management is vital at the start of a project when you're determining what needs to be done, when, by whom, and for how much money. Effective project management is also essential after you kick off the project, when you are continually controlling and managing the project details. You frequently analyze the project—tracking the schedule, the budget, resource requirements, and the scope of tasks. In addition, you're managing the level of quality in the project, planning for risks and contingencies, and communicating with the members of the project team as well as upper management or customers.

Throughout this intricate process of planning and tracking your project, Microsoft Project 2002 is a valuable assistant—a software tool that can help you manage the many responsibilities associated with your project. Many software applications can help you work toward producing a specific result that you can print, publish, or post. Although it's true that you use Microsoft Project to set up a project schedule and print reports that reflect that schedule, Microsoft Project goes beyond just the printed outcome. It helps you brainstorm, organize, and assign your tasks as you create your plan in the planning phase. Microsoft Project then helps you track progress and control the schedule, your resources, and your budget during the execution phase. All this so you can achieve your real objective—to successfully achieve the goals of your project on schedule and under budget.

Using This Book

This book is designed for intermediate to advanced computer users who manage projects. Even if you have never used Microsoft Project or managed a project before, this book assumes you have experience with Microsoft Windows and at least a couple of programs in Microsoft Office, such as Microsoft Word, Microsoft Excel, and Microsoft Outlook.

- If you are completely new to project management and Microsoft Project, this book will give you a solid grounding in the use of Microsoft Project as well as standard project management practices and methodologies. It will help you understand the phases of project management, including the controlling factors in the project life cycle.

- If you're an experienced Microsoft Project user, this book will help you better understand the inner workings of Microsoft Project, so you can use it more effectively to do what you need it to do. This book also introduces the new features of Microsoft Project 2002, giving you ideas as to whether and how you can use those features.

- If you're an experienced project manager, this book integrates common project management practices with the use of the software tool. This helps you see how you can use Microsoft Project to carry out the project management functions you're accustomed to.

Chapter 1: Introducing Microsoft Project 2002

Whether you're a new project manager or a seasoned project management professional, this book will help you work with Microsoft Project as a facilitator for your project's processes and phases. Read the chapters and parts you feel are appropriate for your needs right now. Familiarize yourself with the topics available in the other chapters. Then as you continue to manage your projects with Microsoft Project, keep the book within arm's reach so you can quickly find the answers to questions and problems as they come up. As you master your current level of knowledge, use this book to help you get to the next level, whether it's working with multiple projects at one time, customizing Microsoft Project, or programming Microsoft Project functions to automate repetitive activities. This book is your comprehensive Microsoft Project reference, in which you can quickly find answers and then get back to work on your project plan. The book is organized into the following parts:

Part 1. Project Fundamentals. If you want a primer on project management in general or Microsoft Project in particular, read the chapters in this part. Here you'll find an overview of Microsoft Project, including what's new in Microsoft Project 2002. There's an overview of project management processes and how Microsoft Project facilitates those processes. You'll also find a discussion of the various kinds of people involved in your project, as well as some keys to successful project management.

Part 2. Developing the Project Plan. Everything you need to know about starting a new project and creating a new project plan is found here. You'll get details about working with the Microsoft Project workspace, scheduling tasks, setting up resources, assigning resources to tasks, establishing costs, and adjusting the project plan to be an accurate model of your project's reality.

Part 3. Tracking Progress. After you've created the perfect project plan, you're ready to execute it. To keep the project plan working for you, it needs to be up to date. This part provides details about setting and working with baselines so you can track and compare your progress toward deadlines. It covers important aspects of updating and tracking costs as well as adjusting the schedule, resource workload, and costs to reflect ongoing changes in your project.

Part 4. Reporting and Analysis. Microsoft Project provides a wide range of options for setting up and printing views and reports. This part outlines these methods—from simply printing your current view to designing a custom report and publishing it to the Web. This part also describes how you can export data to Excel for calculation and other analysis, as well as how you can use earned value data to analyze progress and costs.

Part 5. Managing Multiple Projects.   As a project manager, it's likely that you're managing more than one project at a time. This part explains the concepts and practices of master projects, subprojects, and resource pools. It also explains how you can exchange information between different project plans, copy or link information, and leverage customized views, reports, groups, and other Microsoft Project elements you might have created.

Part 6. Integrating Microsoft Project with Other Programs.   Microsoft Project is designed to work effortlessly with other programs. You can copy, embed, link, hyperlink, import, and export information. This part describes these methods in detail and also devotes chapters to the specific integration techniques for working with Excel and Outlook.

Part 7. Collaborating as a Team.   Microsoft Project helps facilitate collaboration. You can exchange project-related messages with members of your resource team. You can assign tasks, obtain task progress updates, and receive status reports through your company's own e-mail system or through Microsoft Project Server and Web Access, the latest generation of Microsoft Project Central. This part discusses these team collaboration solutions.

Part 8. Managing Projects Across Your Enterprise.   If you are working with Microsoft Project Professional 2002 and Microsoft Project Server, you and your organization have access to the new enterprise features. This part describes how you can use the enterprise features to standardize and customize Microsoft Project and project management throughout your organization. It also covers enterprise resource management and executive summaries.

Part 9. Customizing and Managing Project Files.   With Microsoft Project, you can create and customize your own views, tables, groups, reports, formulas, toolbars, dialog boxes, macros, and more. This part covers the details of these custom elements. This part also discusses methods for closing a project at the end of its life cycle and continuing to use what you've learned by creating templates that can become the basis for the next project of its kind. In addition, this part details project file management issues, including file locations, backups, and multiple versions.

Part 10. Programming Custom Solutions.   You have access to a number of programming tools that will help you fully customize and automate Microsoft Project to meet your specific requirements. This part provides the information you need about the programming tools, including a primer on Visual Basic, using the Visual Basic Editor, creating VBA macros, and working with the Microsoft Project Database.

Part 11. Appendixes.   This part includes ancillary information you'll find useful in your work with Microsoft Project. For example, you'll find installation guidelines, a reference of Microsoft Project fields, and a list of online resources to expand your knowledge of Microsoft Project and project management.

Throughout the book, you'll find tips providing shortcuts or alternate methods for doing certain tasks. The Inside Out tips give you information about known issues or idiosyncrasies with Microsoft Project and possible methods of working around them. There are also Troubleshooting tips, which alert you to common problems and how to avoid or recover from them.

This book is designed to be referenceable, so you can quickly find the answers you need at the time you have the question. The comprehensive table of contents is a good starting point. Another excellent place to start finding your solution is in one of the two indexes at the end of the book. You can use the special Troubleshooting index to solve specific problems. Use the master index to help you find the topics you're looking for when you need them.

Using Microsoft Project—an Overview

Microsoft Project is a specialized database that stores and presents thousands of pieces of data related to your project. Examples of such data include tasks, durations, links, resource names, calendars, assignments, costs, deadlines, and milestones.

These pieces of information interrelate and affect each other in a myriad of ways. Underlying this project database is the scheduling engine, which crunches the raw project data you enter and presents the calculated results to you (see Figure 1-1 on the next page). Examples of such calculated results include the start and finish dates of a task, resource availability, the finish date of the entire project, and the total cost for a resource or for the project.

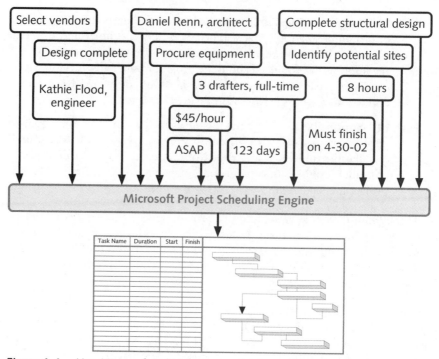

Figure 1-1. Use Microsoft Project as your database of project management information.

You can then manipulate and display this calculated information in various views to analyze the planning and progress of your project. This information helps you make decisions vital to the project's success.

You can also communicate your progress and provide the feedback necessary to keep your team and other stakeholders informed of essential project information create and print reports for status meetings or distribution to stakeholders, and print or publish certain views or reports to your team's Web site.

Microsoft Project 2002 Editions

With Microsoft Project 2002, you have a choice of two editions: Microsoft Project Standard 2002 and Microsoft Project Professional 2002.

Chapter 1: Introducing Microsoft Project 2002

Microsoft Project Standard 2002 is the basic desktop edition of Microsoft Project, and it is the updated version of Microsoft Project 2000. It supports project management as well as online team collaboration. It includes all the essential features to support management at the individual or workgroup level. These features include:

- Task scheduling
- Tracking
- Team collaboration
- Resource management
- Reporting
- Customization

With this substantial set of features, you can start planning, managing, and reporting your project information "out of the box"—that is, immediately upon installation (see Figure 1-2).

With Microsoft Project Standard, you can plan and track your project and resources as your stand-alone desktop tool.

With e-mail or Microsoft Project Server and Web Access, you and your team members can communicate and update project information electronically.

You can manage multiple projects and share resources among projects.

Figure 1-2. Develop and execute your project plan with Microsoft Project Standard 2002.

Part 1: Project Fundamentals

Microsoft Project Professional 2002 provides everything that Microsoft Project Standard 2002 does. In addition, with this new edition, project management is now fully scalable across multiple departments and divisions in a corporation or other enterprise (see Figure 1-3).

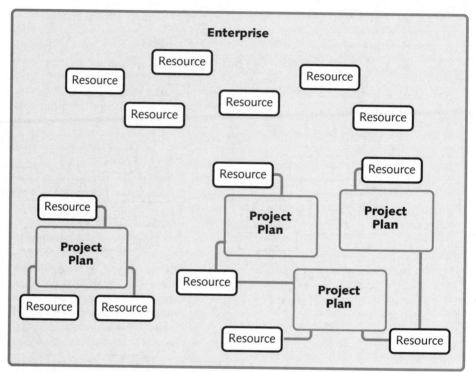

Figure 1-3. Develop and execute multiple project plans with Microsoft Project Professional 2002.

Microsoft Project Professional includes the following features:

- Global templates, enterprise fields, and other elements, enabling a system administrator to standardize and customize the use of Microsoft Project for the way your enterprise manages projects.

- The ability to choose and manage resources from the pool of a specific group or the entire company. You can see resource availability across multiple projects and have Microsoft Project automatically find resources that will appropriately fill project team requirements.

- High-level overviews of all the projects taking place throughout the organization. With the new enterprise capabilities of Microsoft Project Professional 2002, all information is gathered, organized, and reported consistently throughout the organization, providing a complete and accurate picture of all projects.

Project Server and Web Access

Microsoft Project Server is the separately licensed companion program that can accompany either Microsoft Project Standard 2002 or Microsoft Project Professional 2002. Microsoft Project Server provides for team collaboration among project managers, team members, and other stakeholders.

Project managers use Microsoft Project to enter, store, and update project information. They can then send project information, such as assignments or task updates, to specific team members through Microsoft Project Server.

Team members and other associated stakeholders in the project can view and work with the information held in Microsoft Project Server through the use of a Web-based user interface called Microsoft Project Web Access. Not only can team members review their assigned tasks and other project information in Microsoft Project Web Access, they can add tasks, update progress information, and send status reports through Project Server. This ultimately updates the project plan being maintained by the project manager.

Microsoft Project Server and Microsoft Project Web Access are the updated version of Microsoft Project Central, which you might have used with Microsoft Project 2000.

> For more information about installing Microsoft Project Standard 2002, Microsoft Project Professional 2002, Microsoft Project Server, or Microsoft Project Web Access, see Appendix A.

What's New in Microsoft Project 2002

The biggest news in Microsoft Project 2002 is the recognition that project managers don't go it alone. In addition to making Microsoft Project easier to use in a variety of ways, the commitment to substantive team collaboration and project management across an entire enterprise most characterizes this new release.

This section summarizes the new features in Microsoft Project Standard 2002 and Microsoft Project Professional 2002. Cross-references indicate where these new features are covered in more detail elsewhere in the book. In those locations, the discussion is marked with the New Feature icon.

newfeature!
What's New in Microsoft Project Standard 2002

This new version includes a new Project Guide, enhanced task assignment and tracking, improved views, and easier integration with other applications.

Using the Project Guide

The Project Guide is a new interactive interface element in Microsoft Project that helps you work through your project from the standpoint of project management processes

Chapter 1

and goals. This complements the existing menus and toolbars, which allow you to approach your project plan from a strictly feature-oriented point of view.

The Project Guide is a pane on the left side of the screen that provides topics, instructions, and controls that assist your current work in your plan (see Figure 1-4). For example, while you're working in the Gantt Chart, the Project Guide displays the Tasks guide. This guide contains topics directly related to entering and scheduling tasks. If you then switch to a resource view, the Project Guide displays the Resources guide, now presenting topics and controls related to entering and assigning resources.

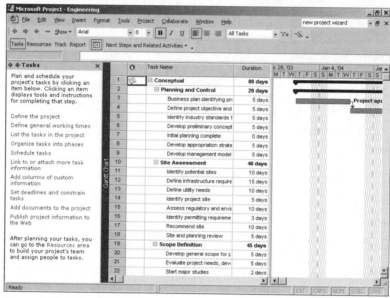

Figure 1-4. The Project Guide is on the left side of the screen.

The Project Guide also includes the Project Guide toolbar just above the Project Guide pane. Use the buttons on this toolbar to display any Project Guide list or topic you want to see. You can view the Tasks, Resources, Track, or Report lists, display any topic on those lists, and toggle the display of the Project Guide pane on or off.

> For more information about the Project Guide, see "Learning As You Go," later in this chapter.

The Project Guide also includes new wizards to help automate certain processes:

- The Define The Project Wizard helps you create a new project plan, either from scratch or from an existing template (see Figure 1-5). This wizard integrates all the tasks you need to create a new project: entering basic project information, setting team collaboration options, adding supporting documentation, and saving the project file.

Chapter 1: Introducing Microsoft Project 2002

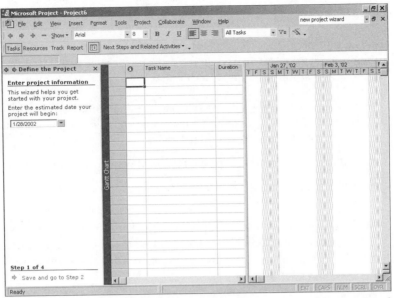

Figure 1-5. Start creating your plan with the Define The Project Wizard.

● The Project Working Times Wizard simplifies the methods of specifying and changing working days and hours, nonworking days and hours, and time units. You can use the Project Working Times Wizard for the project as a whole, in alternative calendars such as a weekend shift, and for specific resources.

● The Setup Tracking Wizard determines how you will collect and enter progress information about tasks. Based on the information you provide, the Setup Tracking Wizard designs a tracking view for your specific purposes.

Assigning Resources to Tasks

More information is instantly available to help you assign resources to tasks, for example:

● Direct guidance is provided regarding how a new resource assignment will affect task scheduling, taking into account whether the task is effort-driven.

● When assigning resources, you can now search or filter for resources with the necessary skill set. You can also review resources' availability to work on your project.

For more information about assigning resources, see Chapter 7, "Assigning Resources to Tasks."

Tracking Task Progress

Microsoft Project's new tracking improvements enable you to do more while tracking progress, do it more easily, and obtain more of the specific information you need. With these tracking improvements, you can now:

- Save up to 11 complete baseline plans and ten interim plans. In Microsoft Project 2000, you could only save a single baseline and ten interim plans (saving only the Start and Finish dates).

- Control how your baseline data is rolled up into summary tasks.

- Enter the actual percent complete or percent work complete data in fewer, more efficient steps.

- Reschedule work that hasn't been completed, and have the constraints remain as you originally set them, rather than being automatically rescheduled as before. You can also choose any reschedule date you want—past, present, or future.

- Use the status date with greater flexibility and see different views of your progress information. You also have choices regarding how completed and remaining progress information should be presented relative to the status date you select.

- Use the new earned value fields available. These are schedule performance index (SPI), to complete performance index (TCPI), cost performance index (CPI), cost variance percent (CV%), and schedule variance percent (SV%). You can calculate earned value data based on any of 11 saved baselines.

> For more information about baselines, updating progress, rescheduling the project, and working with the status date, see Chapter 10, "Saving a Baseline and Updating Progress." For more information about earned value analysis, see Chapter 13, "Analyzing Project Information."

Viewing Project Information

You can do and see more in certain types of views. With the improved view features, you can now:

- Group information with the same type of colored banding used in Gantt Chart groups in the Network Diagram. You can show indicator icons in Network Diagram nodes and directly edit task information in nodes.

- Group assignments in the Task Usage and Resource Usage views. You can get a summary of grouped information in a usage view and include totals when printing usage views.

● Display a third timescale for more detailed calendar breakdowns in any view showing a timescale, such as the Gantt Chart, the usage views, and other graphical views.

● Display two timescaled views in separate panes as a combination view, for example, the Gantt Chart in the upper pane and the Resource Usage view in the lower pane. In such a view, the timescaled portions of the two views line up with one another. Full editing is available in both upper and lower panes.

> For more information about working with Microsoft Project views, see Chapter 4, "Viewing Project Information."

Integrating Microsoft Project with Other Applications

Exchanging project information between different applications increases your flexibility and enables you to work with a variety of team members using a variety of tools. With Microsoft Project 2002 integration enhancements, you can now:

● More easily exchange information between Microsoft Project and other applications by using the Import/Export Mapping Wizard. When you begin to save your project information to Microsoft Access, Excel, XML, or another file format, the wizard helps you set up your export map. Likewise, when you begin to open project information from another file format, the wizard helps you set up your import map.

● Exchange information between Microsoft Project and Excel more easily.

● Use the new Excel Task List template to quickly start a new project's task list. Gather and compile Excel task lists from others on the team using the preformatted Excel template with worksheets for tasks, resources, and assignments. Then, without having to create an import map, you can easily open the task list in Microsoft Project and continue to build the project from there.

● Easily import a task list from Outlook into Microsoft Project using the new Import Outlook Tasks dialog box. The task list is imported directly to become task rows in Microsoft Project.

● Work with Microsoft Project tables in a similar way to Excel spreadsheets.

● Use Smart Tags, which are indicators that alert you to a particular calculation or other result of the interaction of tasks, resource, and assignment information in your project plan. These Smart Tags also give you options for reacting to this information.

> For more information about working with Excel, see Chapter 17, "Integrating Microsoft Project with Microsoft Excel." For more information about working with Outlook, see Chapter 18, "Integrating Microsoft Project with Microsoft Outlook."

Customizing Microsoft Project

New features allow for increased customization of Microsoft Project to fit the way you and your team need to work. The customization features include:

- The enhanced Microsoft Project OLE DB (object linking and embedding database) provider, which gives you access to more project details. These include timephased data, additional tables, and extended properties for data access pages. Also improved are scalability, reliability, and the ability to work with Microsoft Office Web components.

- A COM add-in, which enables you to create, view, and edit data access pages from within Microsoft Project.

- XML (extensible markup language) available as a file format for importing, exporting, and saving your files.

> For more information, see Chapter 32, "Working with Microsoft Project Data."

What's New in Microsoft Project Server and Web Access

Microsoft Project Server and Web Access is the next generation of Microsoft Project Central, introduced with Microsoft Project 2000 and designed to facilitate communication of task assignments and progress among members of a project team.

> For more information, see Chapter 21, "Managing Your Team Using Microsoft Project Web Access."

What's New for the Project Manager

There are substantial changes to this team collaboration method as it affects the project manager. Using new features, you can now:

- Use the new Collaborate tab on the Options dialog box to configure the interface with Microsoft Project Server. Likewise, the new Collaborate menu improves upon the old Workgroup menu, with better options for exchanging project information with your team.

- View information in your Microsoft Project Web Access pages directly within Microsoft Project.

- Review, group, and filter summarized updates and task requests with the new Manager Transactions page.

- Standardize the format of the new, streamlined timesheet in Microsoft Project Web Access to choose the way you prefer time to be reported and to simplify reporting for team members.

- Create and manage a simple task list through a new Tasks page in Web Access. You can also open this list in Microsoft Project.

- Enable multiple project managers to track tasks and resources in a single project.

- Collect a comprehensive history of unique resource comments, compiled from task notes in Microsoft Project.

What's New for the Team Member

Team members and other stakeholders who used Microsoft Project Central will be able to take advantage of better guidance, improved views and functions, and increased functionality throughout Microsoft Project Web Access. Team members can now:

- Use wizard-like instructions and controls in the left pane to assist with managing task lists, delegating tasks, reporting, and viewing overall project information.

- Manage their notifications and reminders through the Access Transaction page.

- Save a view with their own grouping or filtering applied. They can also group on multiple hierarchies, apply colors to groups, display splits in the Gantt Chart view, and use additional AutoFilters.

- See change indicators when data in a field has changed since the last update.

- Send separate task updates for each separate project they're working on.

- Take advantage of improved delegation capabilities, particularly for task selection and notification. This is particularly useful for resource managers and group leads.

- Update Microsoft Project Web Access views and status reports from Microsoft Outlook. Team members can also include Web Parts on the Outlook Digital Dashboard.

Managing Project Documents and Team Issues

SharePoint Team Services is the new Microsoft Office team collaboration tool. You can integrate SharePoint Team Services with Microsoft Project Server and Web Access to manage project-related documents and to track issues that the team needs to be aware of.

The document library serves as a valuable repository in Microsoft Project Server for documents generated throughout the project life cycle. Team members can access the document library through Microsoft Project Web Access.

With the issue tracker, team members can enter issues, assign ownership, track progress, record resolutions, and create related reports, all for storage on Microsoft Project Server and accessible through Microsoft Project Web Access.

Administering Microsoft Project Server and Web Access

Microsoft Project Server includes functionality to make project system administration tasks easy and manageable, as follows:

- Microsoft Project Server administration is more flexible, with additional views, functionality, roles, and permissions.

- Microsoft Project Server information can now be accessed over the Internet.

- Microsoft Project Server supports load balancing for Web servers and clustering for database servers. This facilitates the handling of the large volumes of activity likely in larger organizations.

- Microsoft Project Server has ActiveX controls that enable the Microsoft Project Web Access interface to be more easily programmed, allowing greater extensibility and customization.

The New Enterprise Solution in Microsoft Project Professional 2002

With Microsoft Project Professional 2002, project management is now scalable across multiple departments and groups in a corporation or other enterprise. This enterprise solution provides for a powerful coordinating entity among all the departments working on their individual projects. Powerful reporting, analysis, and resource management capabilities are made possible through this top-down coordination.

Managing Resources Across an Enterprise

You can access, assign, and manage resources to leverage the many skill sets available throughout the enterprise. Microsoft Project Enterprise can provide up-to-date information about the availability and utilization of thousands of resources in an enterprise as follows:

- Multiple servers can be used for different sets of enterprise projects and resources to take full advantage of the information resources in the enterprise.

- All resource assignments throughout the enterprise are visible to project managers, resource managers, and other authorized stakeholders. This provides accurate information regarding resource availability. Resource assignments can be checked out, edited, and checked in again.

- The Resource Substitution Wizard analyzes the skills needed by a project, matches them with skills possessed by resources in the enterprise, and determines their availability. This builds an optimized team for a project's assignments.

Chapter 1: Introducing Microsoft Project 2002

- The Team Builder helps you find resources throughout the enterprise who have the right skills and availability to work on your project. Filter and query the enterprise resource database to fine-tune your project for the right resources.

- Resource availability graphs enable project managers to quickly identify when and why resources might be underallocated or overallocated.

Customizing to Your Enterprise Standards

Standardize and customize the use of Microsoft Project for the way your enterprise specifically does business, as follows:

- Tailored fields, calendars, views, modules, and other consistent Microsoft Project elements are applied throughout all projects in the Enterprise global template. Individual project templates are also available in the Enterprise database.

- Your organization's system administrator for projects can use enterprise custom fields and create formulas, outlines, and pick lists for skill codes or titles. Project management efforts can therefore be tailored to the specific processes of the organization.

Reporting and Analyzing Your Enterprise Project Activities

All information can be gathered, organized, and reported consistently across the organization to provide an accurate picture of all projects.

With Portfolio Modeler, you can create multiple versions of the same plan to model what-if scenarios: comparing, analyzing, and experimenting with different versions to help decide on the best course of action.

With Portfolio Analyzer, executives and functional managers see spreadsheet or graphical summaries of a set of projects and resources in their organization. They can see these enterprise projects, including any combination of project codes, task codes, resource codes, and time periods. Through analyzing project performance and resource utilization from this standardized data across all projects, management can make informed decisions in support of enterprise priorities and initiatives.

For more information about Enterprise reporting and analysis, see Chapter 24, "Using Enterprise Features to Manage Projects."

Learning As You Go

As you work in your project plan, you can quickly get assistance when you need it. This section details the different types of information accessible to you from within Microsoft Project.

newfeature!
Working with the Project Guide

The Project Guide is the new side pane and toolbar in Microsoft Project that provides assistance as you work through the project management goals in your plan. The Project Guide is interactive; it takes note of your current view and your current activities and presents a list of relevant topics.

When you click one topic, for example, a wizard might appear in the Project Guide, asking you questions about the activity you want to carry out. As you answer the questions, the wizard pulls together your answers and executes the task automatically, without your having to search and complete the appropriate dialog boxes in the appropriate views.

---

tip   **Temporarily turn off the Project Guide**

Show/
Hide
Project
Guide

If you're concerned about the real estate that the Project Guide is taking up on your screen, you can temporarily turn the Project Guide off and then turn it on again whenever you like. Click the Close button in the Project Guide pane, or click the Show/Hide Project Guide button on the Project Guide toolbar. When you want it back, click the button again.

When you click another topic, you might find concise text about how to carry out the activity. Or you might click a control in the Project Guide and the activity will be done for you on the spot.

For information about how to customize the Project Guide to include your own project management information, see Chapter 26, "Customizing the Microsoft Project Interface."

As you move from task views to resource views, the Project Guide switches from task-related topics to resource-related topics. There are also groups of topics for tracking and reporting. When you click the Next Steps And Related Activities button on the Project Guide toolbar, you can review the entire process. This helps you see what you've done and what you might need to do next.

InsideOut

In previous versions of Microsoft Project, the view bar was displayed on the left side of the window and online Help automatically opened on the right. Now the Project Guide takes up a fair amount of real estate on the screen. Although the Project Guide includes wizards and controls, there's some overlap with online Help. Decide for yourself whether it's useful to you. If you never want to use the Project Guide, click Tools, Options, and then click the Interface tab. Clear the Display Project Guide check box.

Chapter 1: Introducing Microsoft Project 2002

Getting Online Help for Your Project Goals

The Project Map is an innovative concept in online Help, which provides Help procedures and concepts relevant to the stage of project planning you're in now (see Figure 1-6).

To open the Project Map, click Help, Getting Started, Project Map.

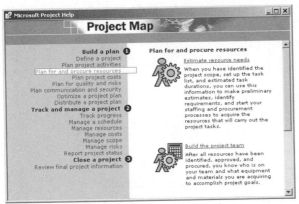

Figure 1-6. Get help for stages in project planning with the Project Map.

The Project Map indicates the three major phases of the project management process: Build A Plan, Track And Manage A Project, and Close A Project. Under each of the phases are goals, for example, Plan For And Procure Resources, Manage Costs, and Review Final Project Information.

When you click the name of a goal, the goal topic appears to the right of the Map. In that goal topic is an overview of the goal and links to the procedural and conceptual Help topics that help you achieve this goal. Wherever you are in the project management process, you can find the related Help topics for that stage. This helps you manage your project successfully, and also helps you get the most out of Microsoft Project as a facilitator to your project management.

When opened, procedural Help topics appear in the Help pane that is docked along the right edge of the Microsoft Project window (see Figure 1-7 on the next page). This enables you to read the procedure while carrying it out in your plan.

In goal topics as well as procedural topics, sometimes you'll be asked to make a choice between various courses of action. When you choose one, the Help information after that point interactively changes to reflect your choice. This way you always see just the Help you need without having to wade through extraneous information.

Part 1: Project Fundamentals

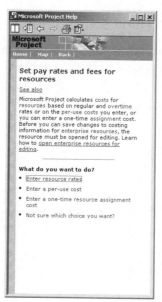

Figure 1-7. Find your specific help topic in a Help procedure.

Asking Specific Questions of the Office Assistant

---

tip   **Ask a question**

Instead of using the Office Assistant, you can get help from the Ask A Question box in the upper-right corner of the Microsoft Project window. Type your question in the box, and then press Enter. A list of related Help topics appears. Click the topic you want to see, and it appears. Unlike the Office Assistant, the Ask A Question box is always present but never in the way.

---

tip   **Keep the Office Assistant at the ready**

You can keep the Office Assistant open in your workspace. Just drag it to an out-of-the-way corner until you need it again. When you want to ask another question, click it or press F1, and the window will appear.

Rather than going through a particular structure of ordered goals and topics, it's often faster to just ask a direct question and get a direct answer. If you prefer to get your Help that way, use the Office Assistant. To use the Office Assistant:

Chapter 1: Introducing Microsoft Project 2002

Project Help

1 On the Standard toolbar, click the Microsoft Project Help button.

2 In the Office Assistant window, type your question, and then click Search.

3 Review the list of topics that appears, and click the one that matches what you're looking for.

The topic appears in the Help pane.

> **tip** **Hide the Office Assistant temporarily**
>
> If you'd like to hide the Office Assistant temporarily, on the Help menu, click Hide The Office Assistant. When you need it again, just press the Microsoft Project Help button or F1 again, and it will appear.

InsideOut

If you find the Office Assistant annoying and don't want to use it, you can turn it off permanently. In the Office Assistant window, click Options. In the Options dialog box, clear the Use The Office Assistant check box, and then click OK. Then clicking the Microsoft Project Help button or pressing F1 will display the Help Home page in the Help pane.

Finding Reference Information

In addition to the procedural and conceptual Help topics, a robust set of reference Help is available.

To access reference Help, click Help, Reference. The following types of reference Help are available:

- Microsoft Project Specifications
- Templates
- Using Microsoft Project If You Have A Disability
- Using Multilingual Features In Microsoft Project
- "All About" Help Topics
- Fields Reference
- Glossary
- Toolbars and Shortcut Menus
- Mouse and Keyboard Shortcuts
- Troubleshooting

23

- Views, Tables, Filters, And Groups
- Visual Basic For Applications

More reference information is available on the Internet; the links to the appropriate Web sites are found in the Reference Help pane:

- The Microsoft Project Resource Kit
- The Microsoft Project Software Development Kit

Getting Help within Dialog Boxes

While working in your project plan, if you're trying to figure out what a certain control in a dialog box does, you can get a ScreenTip, which is a short definition of the control.

To see a ScreenTip in a dialog box:

1 Click the question mark icon in the upper right corner of the dialog box. The mouse pointer changes to a question mark.

2 Click the box, option, check box, or other control that you want information about to see the ScreenTip (see Figure 1-8).

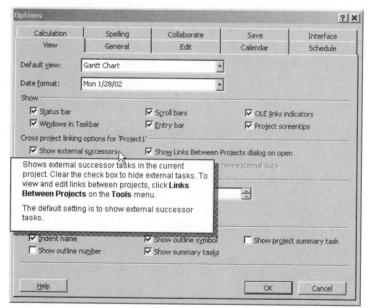

Figure 1-8. ScreenTips help familiarize you with dialog box options.

3 After reading it, click the ScreenTip to dismiss it.

Some of the more complex dialog boxes have a Help button as well. This button opens a topic in the Help pane describing the details and uses of the dialog box.

Understanding Projects and Project Management

You use a word processing program to create a text document. You use a spreadsheet program to calculate sales data. You use a publishing program to design and lay out a brochure. In these cases, the application helps you create the end result.

With Microsoft Project, this isn't so. While Microsoft Project helps you create a *project plan*, the actual project is being executed by you and your team, who are carrying out the tasks to fulfill the overarching goals of the project. It's up to you to track and control the actual project, using the project plan as your essential road map. When effectively maintained, the project plan provides an accurate picture of what's currently going on, what's happened in the past, and what will happen in the future.

This chapter describes project basics and the phases of the project management process. It also outlines how Microsoft Project fits into the world of your project. You'll understand how you can use Microsoft Project as your project information system, that is, the essential tool for modeling your project and helping you efficiently and successfully manage it.

If you're new to project management, read this entire chapter. If you're an experienced project manager but new to Microsoft Project, skip ahead to the section in this chapter titled "Facilitating Your Project with Microsoft Project."

Understanding Project Management Basics

Although it might overlap with other types of management, project management is a specific management process.

What Is a Project?

There are two types of work performed by organizations: operations and projects. An *operation* is a series of tasks that are routine, repetitive, and ongoing throughout the life of the organization. Operations are typically necessary to sustain the business. Examples of operations are accounts receivable, employee performance reviews, shipping and receiving, and factory production. Employee performance reviews might take place every six months, for example, and although the names and circumstances of employees and supervisors might change, the process of preparing and conducting employee reviews is always the same. In addition, it's expected that there will continue to be employee reviews throughout the life of the organization.

On the other hand, *projects* are not routine or ongoing. That is, projects are unique and temporary, and often implemented to fulfill a strategic goal of the organization. A project is a series of tasks that will culminate in the creation or completion of some new initiative, product, or activity by a specific end date. Some project examples include an office move, a new product launch, the construction of a building, and a political campaign. It is never the same project twice—for example, this year's product launch is different from last year's product launch. There's a specific end date in mind for the launch, after which the project will be considered complete. After the project is complete, a new and unique product will be on the market.

Projects come in all sizes. One project might consist of 100 tasks, another 10,000. One project might be implemented by a single resource, another by 500. One project might take two months to complete; another might take ten years. There can be projects within projects, linked together with a master project consolidating them all. These sub-projects, however, are all unique and temporary, and all have a specific outcome and end date.

What Is Project Management?

Project management is the coordinating effort to fulfill the goals of the project. The project manager, as the leader of the project team, is responsible for this effort and its ultimate result. Project managers use knowledge, skills, tools, and methodologies to:

- Identify the goals, objectives, requirements, and limitations of the project.
- Coordinate the different needs and expectations of the various project stakeholders, including team members, resource managers, senior management, customers, and sponsors.

Chapter 2: Understanding Projects and Project Management

- Plan, execute, and control the tasks, phases, and deliverables of the project based on the identified project goals and objectives.

- Close the project when completed and capture knowledge accrued.

Project managers are also responsible for balancing and integrating competing demands to implement all aspects of the project successfully, as follows:

- **Project scope.** Outlining the specific work to be done for the project.

- **Project time.** Specifying the finish date of the project as well as any interim deadlines for phases, milestones, and deliverables.

- **Project cost.** Indicating the project costs and budget.

- **Project human resources.** Signing on the team members who will carry out the tasks of the project.

- **Project procurement.** Acquiring the material and equipment resources with which to carry out project tasks.

- **Project communications.** Conveying assignments, updates, reports, and other information with team members and other stakeholders.

- **Project quality.** Specifying the acceptable level of quality for the project goals and objectives.

- **Project risk.** Analyzing potential project risks and response planning.

Chapter 2

InsideOut

Microsoft Project supports many, but not all, of the management areas associated with project management. For example, it provides only minimal support for project procurement, and very little support for project quality and project risk.

The solution is to use Microsoft Project in conjunction with other tools and resources. Use Microsoft Project to provide the initial information you need. Then use other tools and resources as needed to more fully handle responsibilities specifically associated with procurement, quality, or risk. Finally, come full circle with Microsoft Project by adding notes to tasks or resources, inserting related documents, or linking to other locations.

For example, use Microsoft Project to help estimate your initial equipment and material resource requirements. Work through your organization's procurement process, and compile the relevant data. Add notes to the resources or tasks in your project plan, making the information easily referenceable. Use a tool such as Microsoft Excel, or another program especially designed for this purpose, to help track the depletion of materials to the point where reorder becomes necessary. Even though Microsoft Project can't manage every aspect of your project, it can still be the repository for all related information.

Balancing scope, time, and money is often among the biggest responsibilities of the project manager (see Figure 2-1).

Figure 2-1. Use the project triangle as a way to think about the project's priorities.

If you increase the scope, the time or money side of the triangle will also be increased. If you need to reduce time, that is, bring in the project finish date, you might need to decrease the scope or increase the cost through the addition of resources.

note There's some debate about how to accurately describe the key controlling elements that make up a project. Some believe it's best described as a triangle—the three sides representing time, money, and resources. Others say it's a square—with scope, time, money, and resources being the four sides, each one affecting the others. This book approaches money and resources as synonymous in this context, because resources cost money. Adding resources adds money, and the only thing you'd need more money for would be resources. So in this book, the project is conceptualized as a triangle with the three sides being scope, time, and money/resources.

Project Management Practices:
Balancing and Integrating Competing Demands

Depending on the priorities and standards set for your project and by your organization, certain demands carry more weight than others in your project. Knowing these priorities and standards will help you make sound decisions about the project as issues arise. Although scope, time, and cost tend to be the most prevalent demands, the following is the full list of project controls:

- Scope
- Time
- Cost

- Human resources
- Procurement
- Communications

- Quality
- Risk

For information about working with the project triangle during the planning phase, see Chapter 9, "Checking and Adjusting the Project Plan." For information about working with the project triangle during the controlling phase, see Chapter 11, "Responding to Changes in Your Project."

Understanding the Project Management Process

It might seem daunting when you realize that as a project manager, you're responsible for such a tremendous balancing act. However, this responsibility can be broken down into four manageable phases:

1 Initiating and planning the project

2 Executing the project

3 Controlling the project

4 Closing the project

Most of the chapters in this book are structured with these four phases in mind. For each phase, you use Microsoft Project in specific ways. There are also standard project management practices for each phase. Throughout this book, the Microsoft Project processes and project management practices are described in the context of the relevant project phase.

The Project Management Process

These are the four phases of the project management process, as well as the key elements within each phase:

● **Initiating and planning the project:**
Examine the big picture
Identify the project's milestones, deliverables, and tasks
Develop and refine the project schedule
Identify skills, equipment, and materials needed

● **Executing the project:**
Have assigned resources execute the project
Save a baseline plan for comparison
Track progress on tasks

● **Controlling the project:**
Analyze project information
Communicate and report

● **Closing the project:**
Identify lessons learned
Create a project template

Planning the Project

You're ready to begin the planning phase after an authoritative stakeholder has decided to implement this project with you as the project manager. The outcome of this planning phase will be a workable project plan and a team ready to start working the project. When planning the project, you:

Look at the big picture.   Before you get too far into the nuts and bolts of planning, you need a comprehensive vision of where you're going with your project. You shape this vision by first identifying the project goals and objectives. This helps you set the scope of the project. You learn the expectations, limitations, and assumptions for this project, and they all go into the mix. You also identify possible risks and contingency plans for the project.

Identify the project's milestones, deliverables, and tasks.   Subdivide the project into its component tasks and then organize and sequence the tasks to accurately reflect the project scope.

Develop and refine the project schedule.   To turn the task list into a workable project schedule, specify task durations and relate tasks to each other. You can create task dependencies, that is, a model of how the start of one task depends on the completion of another task, for example. If you have any specific deadlines for deliverables, you can enter those as task constraints. At that point, Microsoft Project can start to calculate a realistic schedule for tasks in particular and the project as a whole. With this plan, you can accurately forecast the scope, schedule, and budget for the project. You can also determine which resources are needed, how many, and at what time.

Identify skills, equipment, and materials needed.   After the tasks are identified, you can determine the skills, equipment, and materials needed to carry out the work for those tasks. You obtain the needed resources and assign them to the appropriate tasks. You can now calculate when the project can be completed and how much it will cost. If it looks like you're exceeding the allowable deadline or budget, you can make the necessary adjustments.

For more detailed information about planning the project, see the chapters in Part 2, "Developing the Project Plan."

Executing the Project

The second phase of the project management process is execution. At this point, you have your project plan in hand. The tasks are scheduled and the resources are assigned. Everyone's at the starting gate waiting for you to say "Go!"

You give the word, and the project moves from the planning phase to the execution and controlling phase. In the course of executing the project, you:

Save a baseline plan for comparison.   To get good tracking information, keep a copy of certain project plan information in hand so you can compare your plan to actual progress as the project moves along.

Monitor the resources as they carry out their assigned tasks.   As the project manager, you keep an eye on their progress in completing their tasks.

Track task progress.   You can track progress in terms of percent complete, how long a task takes from beginning to end, or how many hours a resource spends on a task. As you gather this information, you can see whether tasks will be finished on time. You can also gather information about costs of resources, tasks, and the project as a whole.

> For more information about tracking progress, see Chapter 10, "Saving a Baseline and Updating Progress."

Controlling the Project

While your project team is executing the tasks, you're making sure the project stays within the prescribed deadline and budget while maintaining the scope outlined in the project goals. In project management, this is referred to as "controlling the project." In the controlling phase, you monitor all task activities, compare the plan to actual progress, and make adjustments as needed. To control the project, you do the following:

Analyze project information.   Analyze the information you're gathering and use this analysis to solve problems and make decisions. Often, you need to decide how to recover a slipped schedule or a budget overrun. Sometimes you're in the happy position of deciding what to do with extra time or money.

> For more information about controlling the project, see Chapter 11, "Responding to Changes in Your Project."

Communicate and report. Throughout the execution of the project, you will be in constant communication with your team members and other stakeholders. You need to keep upper management, customers, and other stakeholders informed of any potential problems, new decisions, and your overall progress.

> For more information about views and reports, see Chapter 12, "Reporting Project Information."

Closing the Project

In the final phase of the project, you have successfully fulfilled the goals of the project and it's now complete. Before you move on to the next project, it's a good idea to capture the knowledge you gained from this one. When closing the project, you:

Identify lessons learned. Work with your project team and conduct a "post-mortem" meeting to learn what went well and what could be improved.

Create a project template. Save the project plan along with tasks, duration metrics, task relationships, resource skills, and the like, so the next time you or someone else manages a similar project, your wheel will not need to be reinvented.

> For more information about closing the project, see Chapter 28, "Standardizing Projects Using Templates."

Facilitating Your Project with Microsoft Project

Because a project involves a myriad of tasks, resources, assignments, dates, and more, it's clear that you need some kind of tool to help you keep track of the details. Using a spreadsheet or word processing program, you could create a table that lists your tasks, durations, start and finish dates, and assigned resources. In fact, that might very well get you started. But it's likely that you'll end up working harder than you have to in an attempt to make the tool work right. Such a table would not be able to:

- Calculate the start and finish dates for you.

- Indicate whether assigned resources are actually available.

- Inform you if assigned resources are underallocated or overworked.

- Alert you if you have an upcoming deadline.

- Calculate how much of the budget you've spent so far.

- Draw your project tasks as a Gantt chart or network diagram so you can get a visual picture of your project.

To do this and more, you can create a similar table in Microsoft Project. You can then use the project database, schedule calculation, and charting capabilities to help facilitate your project management processes (see Figure 2-2).

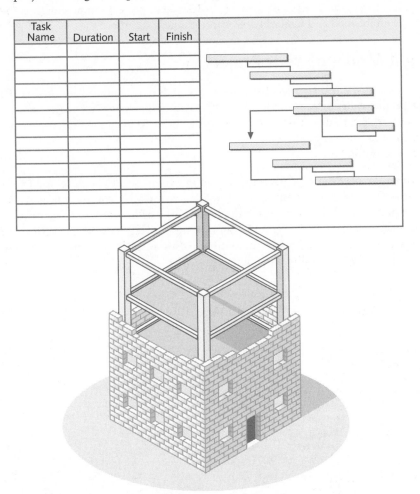

Figure 2-2. The project plan helps you manage your project.

Although Microsoft Project can't negotiate a more reasonable finish date, it can help you determine what you have to sacrifice to make that date. Although Microsoft Project won't complete a difficult and time-consuming task for your team, it will help you find extra time in the schedule or additional resources for that task. And although Microsoft Project can't motivate an uninspired team member, it can tell you if that team member is working on critical tasks that will affect the finish date of the entire project.

Chapter 2

33

In short, Microsoft Project can help you facilitate all phases of the project management process, from developing your scope, modeling your project schedule, and tracking and communicating progress, to saving knowledge gained from the closed project. Furthermore, with Microsoft Project Professional, project management standards can be established and disseminated throughout your enterprise.

Creating a Model of Your Project

You can use Microsoft Project to create a model, or blueprint, of your project. This model reflects the reality of your project. You enter your tasks, resources, assignments, and other project-related information into Microsoft Project. You can then organize and manage the copious and very detailed bits of project information that otherwise can be quite overwhelming.

With all the necessary information stored in Microsoft Project, the exact project information you need at any given time is always available at your fingertips. You can manipulate and analyze this information in various ways to solve problems and make decisions to successfully manage the project. As you take action and move forward in your project, you update information in Microsoft Project so that it continues to reflect reality (see Figure 2-3).

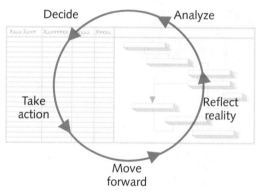

Figure 2-3. Model your project's reality.

Specifically, in the planning phase, you use Microsoft Project to:

Create your phases, milestones, and task list.   Microsoft Project uses your task list as the basis for the project database it creates for you. You can organize tasks within phases or subtasks within summary tasks so you can break your project down into manageable segments.

Estimate task durations.   One task might take 2 hours to complete; another might take 4 days. Microsoft Project uses these durations to help build your schedule.

Chapter 2: Understanding Projects and Project Management

Link tasks with their appropriate relationships to other tasks.   Often, a task cannot begin until a previous task has been completed. For example, for an office move project, you would schedule the "Design office space" task before the "Order new furniture" task. The two tasks would be linked, because the second task cannot be done until the first task is complete. Microsoft Project uses these task relationships to build your schedule. The durations and task relationships are also shown in the Gantt Chart and Network Diagram views of your project.

Enter any imposed deadlines or other date constraints.   If you know you must be out of your current office space by the end of August, for example, you would work with that date as one of the important constraints of your project. Microsoft Project schedules according to such constraints, and informs you if there's a conflict between a constraint and the durations or task relationships you have also set.

Set up the resources and assign them to tasks.   Not only does Microsoft Project keep track of which resources are assigned to which tasks, it also schedules work on assignments according to the resource's availability and lets you know if a resource is overloaded with more tasks than can be accomplished in the resource's available time.

Establish resource costs and task costs.   You can specify hourly or monthly rates for resources. You can specify per-use costs for resources and other costs associated with tasks. Microsoft Project calculates and adds these costs so you can get an accurate view of how much your project will cost to execute. You can often use this as a basis for the project budget.

Adjust the plan to achieve a targeted finish date or budget amount.   Suppose your project plan initially shows a finish date that's two months later than required or a cost that's $10,000 more than the allocated budget. You can make adjustments to scope, schedule, cost, and resources in order to bring the project plan in line. While working through your inevitable project tradeoffs, Microsoft Project will recalculate your schedule automatically until you have the result you need.

In the execution and control phases of the project, use Microsoft Project to:

Save the baseline plan.   For comparison and tracking purposes, you need to take a snapshot of what you consider your baseline project plan. As you update task progress through the life of the project, you can compare current progress with your original plan. This gives you valuable information about whether you're on track with the schedule and your budget.

Project Management Terminology

The following is a list of project management-related terms:

Baseline.   A snapshot of key project information for tasks, such as their start dates, finish dates, durations, and costs. With baseline information, you have a means of comparison against actual progress on tasks.

Constraints.   A specific date associated with a specific task. A date constraint dictates that a task must be finished by a certain date, for example, or started no earlier than a certain date.

Deliverable.   A tangible outcome, result, or item that must be produced to mark the completion of a project or a project phase. Often the deliverable is subject to approval by the project sponsor or customer.

Dependency.   The reliance of one task upon another. When one task cannot start or finish until a related task starts or finishes, the tasks are dependent upon one another. Also referred to as a *task relationship*.

Gantt Chart.   A graphic representation of a project. The left half of a Gantt chart is a table listing task names and other task-related information. The right half of the Gantt chart is a bar chart along a timeline in which each bar represents a task, its start and finish date, and its duration. Links to other tasks can also be represented.

Milestone.   A significant event in the project, often the completion of a major deliverable or phase. Milestones are represented as part of a project's task list.

Network Diagram.   A graphic representation of a project, characterized by nodes representing tasks and link lines showing the relationship among the tasks. Also sometimes called a PERT (program evaluation and review technique) chart.

Phase.   A grouping of tasks that represents a major stage in the life cycle of the project. The outcome of a phase is typically a major deliverable.

Scope.   The specific work that needs to be done in a project to deliver the product or service.

Stakeholders.   Individuals or organizations who have a vested interest in the outcome of the project and who can influence those project outcomes. Stakeholders include the project manager, members of the project team, the sponsoring organization, and customers.

Task Dependency.   The linkage of one task to another. When one task cannot start or finish until a related task starts or finishes, the tasks are linked, or related. Also referred to as a *task relationship* or *link*.

Update actual task progress.   With Microsoft Project, you can update task progress by entering percent complete, work complete, work remaining, and more. As you enter actual progress, the schedule is automatically recalculated.

Compare variances between planned and actual task information. Using the baseline information you saved, Microsoft Project presents various views to show your baseline against actual and scheduled progress, along with the resulting variances. For example, if your initial project plan shows that you had originally planned to finish a task on Thursday but the resource actually finished it on Monday, you'd have a variance of three days in your favor.

Review planned, actual, and scheduled costs.   In addition to seeing task progress variances, you can compare baseline costs against actual and currently scheduled costs and see the resulting cost variances. Microsoft Project can also use your baseline and current schedule information for earned value calculations you can use for more detailed analyses.

Adjust the plan to respond to changes in scope, finish date, and budget. What if you get a directive in the middle of the project to cut $5,000 from your budget? Or what if you learn that you must bring the project in a month earlier to catch a vital marketing window? Even in the midst of a project, you can adjust scope, schedule, cost, and resources in your project plan. With each change you make, Microsoft Project will recalculate your schedule automatically.

Report on progress, costs, resource utilization, and more.   Using the database and calculation features of Microsoft Project, you can generate a number of built-in reports. For example, there are reports for project summary, milestones, tasks starting soon, over-budget tasks, resource to-do lists, and many more. You can modify built-in reports to suit your own needs or create custom reports entirely from scratch.

In the closing phase of the project, use Microsoft Project to:

Capture actual task duration metrics.   If you track task progress throughout the project, you end up with solid, tested data for how long certain tasks actually take.

Capture successful task sequencing.   Sometimes you're not sure at the outset of a project whether a task should be done sooner or later in the process. With the experience of the project behind you, you can see whether your sequencing worked well.

Chapter 2

37

Save a template for the next project of this kind. Use your project plan as the boilerplate for the next project. You or other project managers will have a task list, milestones, deliverables, sequence, durations, and task relationships already in place that can be easily modified to fit the requirements of the new project.

You can also use Microsoft Project to work with multiple projects, and even show the task or resource links among them.

> For more information about using Microsoft Project to plan your project, see the chapters in Part 2, "Developing the Project Plan."

In the course of modeling your project in this way, Microsoft Project serves as your project information system. Microsoft Project arranges the thousands of bits of information in various ways so you can work with it, analyze your data, and make decisions based on coherent and soundly calculated project management information. This project information system carries out three basic functions:

- It stores project information including tasks, resources, assignments, durations, task relationships, task sequences, calendars, and more.

- It calculates information including dates, schedules, costs, durations, critical path, earned value, variances, and more.

- It presents views of information you're retrieving. You can specify the views, tables, filters, groups, fields, or reports, depending on what aspect of your project model you need to see.

Working with Your Team through Microsoft Project

In addition to helping you create your project plan, Microsoft Project helps with resource management, cost management, and team communications.

With Microsoft Project resource management features, you can:

- Enter resources in the Microsoft Project resource list.

- Enter resources from your organization's e-mail address book.

- Maintain a reusable pool of resources available across multiple projects.

- Specify skills required for a task, and have Microsoft Project search for available resources with those skills.

Chapter 2: Understanding Projects and Project Management

- Schedule tasks according to assigned resources' availability.

- Check for resource overload or underutilization and make adjustments accordingly.

> For more information about managing resources, see Chapter 6, "Setting Up Resources in the Project," and Chapter 7, "Assigning Resources to Tasks."

With Microsoft Project's cost management features, you can:

- Enter resource rates including multiple rates for different task types.

- Enter fixed costs for tasks.

- Estimate costs for the project while still in the planning phase.

- Compare planned cost variances to actual cost variances.

- View cost totals for tasks, resources, phases, and the entire project.

> For more information about setting and managing costs, see Chapter 8, "Planning Resource and Task Costs" and Chapter 11, "Responding to Changes in Your Project."

Your communications requirements might be as simple as printing a Gantt chart or resource list for a weekly status meeting. On the other hand, you might need to electronically exchange task updates with your resources every day and publish high-level project information to your company's intranet.

With Microsoft Project, you can communicate with others in just the way you need. You can:

- Print a view as it looks on your screen.

- Generate and print a predesigned report.

- Create a custom view or report.

- Exchange task assignments and updates with your team members through your organization's e-mail system.

- Exchange task assignments, updates, and status reports with your team members through Microsoft Project Server and Microsoft Project Web Access.

- Allow team leads to delegate tasks to other team members.

- Track issues through SharePoint Team Services, Microsoft Project Server, and Microsoft Project Web Access.

- Publish views or the entire project through Microsoft Project Server and Microsoft Project Web Access for review by team members, senior management, customers, and other stakeholders.

Using Microsoft Project In Your Enterprise

You can use Microsoft Project Professional as a means for standardization across your enterprise. Through the customization of numerous elements including views, filters, groups, fields, and formulas, a template can be designed that reflects your organization's project management methodology. This customization and design is done by a *project system administrator*. This project system administrator is typically the person who sets up and manages the installation of Microsoft Project for your organization. The project system administrator knows the requirements of project management and the features of Microsoft Project well enough to design custom solutions, and is often a programmer or other information technology professional.

When your project system administrator designs a common enterprise project template, all project managers in the organization can then work with the same customized project elements that support organizational initiatives. In addition, senior managers can review summary information from multiple projects throughout the organization.

For more information about enterprise capabilities, see Part 8, "Managing Projects Across Your Enterprise."

Understanding Project Stakeholders

Every project has a set of stakeholders associated with it. Project stakeholders are individuals or organizations who are somehow connected to the project and can influence the project's outcome. As the project manager, you need to be able to work with different types of stakeholders in various ways. A stakeholder can:

- Be actively involved in the work of the project.

- Exert influence over the project and its outcome (also known as *managing stakeholders*).

- Have a vested interest in the outcome of a project.

There are a variety of stakeholder categories, each supported in its own way by Microsoft Project. The categories are:

Project manager.   Microsoft Project directly supports the project manager with its scheduling, tracking, and communication capabilities.

Team members.   These stakeholders executing the project are supported minimally through e-mail communication with their project manager. In a more comprehensive manner, team members are supported through Microsoft Project Web Access, in which they can view their assigned tasks, send and receive task updates, send status reports, and review the project as a whole.

Chapter 2: Understanding Projects and Project Management

Team leads.   Team leads can use Microsoft Project Web Access to delegate and manage tasks.

Project resource manager.   A resource manager might work in concert with the project manager to help acquire and maintain necessary resources. Through Microsoft Project Web Access, a resource manager can analyze resource utilization information.

Senior managers, executives, or sponsors.   People who lead the organization in implementing the project or supply the project budget or other resources can use Microsoft Project Web Access to review high-level project summaries. In an enterprise environment, executives can review a summary comparing multiple projects being carried out throughout the organization. Such individuals are also known as *managing stakeholders.*

InsideOut

Other possible stakeholders include customers or end users. There's no direct Microsoft Project support for such stakeholders. However, you could provide them with Microsoft Project Web Access or periodically publish a view designed for them on a Web site.

For more information about Microsoft Project Web Access, see Chapter 21, "Managing Your Team Using Microsoft Project Web Access." For more information about publishing project information, see Chapter 12, "Reporting Project Information."

Managing stakeholders can influence the planning processes of a project and help set the expectations and assumptions of the project. Sometimes the expectations of different stakeholders conflict with one other. It's the job of the project manager to balance and reconcile these conflicts well before project execution begins.

Managing stakeholders might also impose new requirements during the execution phase of a project, requiring adjustments to the finish date, budget, or scope. Even if this happens in the midst of the execution phase of a project, you can use Microsoft Project to adjust the project to respond to the new demands.

Keys to Successful Project Management

Being well-versed in project management processes and using a powerful tool like Microsoft Project puts you well ahead in the project management game. For an even greater edge toward a successful project, follow these guidelines:

Develop the goals and objectives.   Know the overarching goals as well as the specific, measurable objectives of your project. These are your guiding principles.

Learn the scope.   Know the scope (including tasks, quality, deliverables) of your project and exactly what is expected of it. The scope includes how much you're doing (quantity) and how well you're doing it (quality).

Know your deadlines.   Find out any deadlines—final as well as interim milestone and deliverable deadlines. If these deadlines are up to you to suggest, lucky you. But often this isn't your luxury. Often you might propose one reasonable date only to have upper management or your customers suggest another, not-so-reasonable date. The sooner you learn of these dates, the better you can plan for them by adjusting the scope, the budget, and the resources.

Know your budget.   If the project finish date is not your limitation, the budget might very well be. Again, it might be up to you to tell upper management how much the proposed project will cost. But it's also likely that the budget will be imposed upon you, and you'll need to be able to fulfill the goals of the project within a very specific and unrelenting dollar amount. Again, the sooner you know the real budget of the project, the more realistic and accurate your plan can be. You can adjust scope, time, and resources in order to meet the budget.

Find the best resources.   Gather input about who the best candidates for certain tasks are so you can get the best resources. Although the more experienced resources will likely be more expensive, they'll also be more likely to complete tasks more quickly and with a higher level of quality. Likewise with equipment or material resources. Determine the acceptable level of quality for the project, balance this with your budget constraints, and procure the best you can get.

Enter accurate project information.   You can enter tasks and durations, link them together, and assign them to resources, making it seem like you have a real project plan. But suppose the data you entered doesn't reflect the real tasks that will be done, how much time resources will really be spending on these tasks, and what needs to be done before each task can start. Then all you have is a bunch of characters and graphics on a screen or in an impressive-looking report. You don't have a project plan at all. The "garbage-in-garbage-out" maxim applies. As you're planning the project, draw upon previous experience with a similar type of project. Solicit input from resources already earmarked for the project—they can provide excellent information about which tasks need to be done, how long they take, and how tasks relate to each other.

Chapter 2: Understanding Projects and Project Management

Adjust the project plan to meet requirements.   Look at the plan's calculated finish date and the total cost. See if these match your limitations for project deadline or budget. If they do not, make the necessary adjustments. This must all be done before you actually start the project—probably even before you show the project plan to any of your managing stakeholders.

Save a baseline and go.   After you have a project plan that solidly reflects reality, take a "snapshot" of the plan, and begin the execution phase. This snapshot is called the baseline. It will be the means for determining whether you're on track and how far you might have strayed if you need to recover the schedule later.

Track progress.   Many project planners take it only this far: They enter and calculate all the tasks, durations, relationships, and resources to where they can see a schedule and budget. They say "go" and everyone charges, but the plan is left behind. As project variables change (and they always do), the project plan is now useless as a blueprint for managing the project. If you want the project plan to be useful from the time you first enter, assign, and schedule tasks until the time you close the project on time and on budget, you need to maintain the project plan as a dynamic tool that accompanies you every step of the way. Maintaining the plan means tracking progress information. Suppose a task planned for 5 days takes 10 days instead. You can enter that the task actually took 10 days and the schedule will be recalculated. Your plan will still work and you'll still be able to see when succeeding tasks should be completed.

Make necessary adjustments.   As project variables change during the execution phase, you can see if an unplanned change affects key milestones, your resources' schedule, your budget, or your project finish date. If it does, you can take steps well ahead of time to make the necessary adjustments and avert the impending crisis. Use the power of Microsoft Project to recalculate the project plan when actual project details vary from the plan. Then you can analyze the plan, decide on the best course of action to keep the project on track, and take action. This action might be within the project plan or outside the confines of the plan, in the real world of the real project itself.

Communicate.   Make sure your team members know what's expected of them. Pay attention when they alert you to potential problems with their tasks. Keep upper management and customers informed of your progress and of any changes to the original plan.

Close the completed project and capture information.   When a project goes well, we're often so happy that we don't think to capture all the information we should. When a project is completed with much difficulty, sometimes we're just relieved that we're done with it and can't wait to get on with the next project and forget about this unhappy nightmare. But whether a project is simple or difficult, a radiant success or a deplorable failure, there's always much to be learned. Even if you're not involved in any other projects of this type, other people might be. It's important to record as much information about the project as possible. Narrative and evaluative information can be captured through a postmortem or "lessons learned" document. Project information such as tasks, resources, durations, relationships, and calendars can be captured in a project plan itself. If the project went very well, you can even save your project plan as a template to be used for future such projects, thereby enabling future project managers to benefit from your hard-won experience.

Part 2

Developing the Project Plan

Starting a New Project

In the planning phase of a new project, you do a substantial amount of work to set the stage. You define the big picture and get stakeholder approval for the project, in terms of the product or service you're creating as well as the overall project scope.

After this vision is in place, you're ready to create your project blueprint—the project plan—using Microsoft Project. You create a new project file, and enter foundation information.

Then you begin to break down your project goals and objectives into the actual phases, milestones, and tasks that form the backbone of your project information system. You sequence the phases and tasks, and organize them into a hierarchy that maps to your project.

If your project or organization has more specialized or advanced requirements, you can use work breakdown structure codes which organize your task list by each deliverable.

You can add your supporting documentation, such as the vision or strategy document, to the project plan. Likewise, you can add other supplementary information like notes or hyperlinks to individual tasks, milestones, and phases. All this information makes your project plan the central repository of all project information.

Focusing the Project Vision

Although you might already have a clear picture in your mind of what your project is about and what it will be when it is complete, it might still be a little fuzzy, at least around the edges. It's not uncommon for other stakeholders to have a clear vision when you're not sure if you get it just yet.

47

And don't be surprised if one stakeholder's expectations seem clear enough but another stakeholder's expectations sound entirely contradictory.

The challenge at this very important starting point is to clearly define the project, without ambiguity, so that everyone involved is talking about the same project, the same expectations, and the same results. Defining the vision clearly at the beginning will prevent redirection (and the attendant wasted effort) in the middle of the project or disappointment at the end.

So how do you create a vision? You work with key stakeholders such as the customers, potential users, sponsors, executives, and project team members to get their project expectations. You might have to reconcile conflicting views and opposing agendas. Throughout this process, you'll identify the goals of the project as well as their measurable objectives. You'll identify project assumptions, spell out potential risks, and make contingency plans for those risks. You'll also identify known limitations, such as budget, time, or resources.

By the time you finish this high-level project planning and get the necessary approval, everyone involved will know exactly what they're signing up for.

Defining Scope

The product's scope determines the vision of the product you're creating and the project that will create it. As your project is executed and issues arise, you use the scope document to help you make decisions. The scope document is your guideline for whether or not the direction you're considering is really the job of this project or not.

If you don't stay focused on the scope, you're likely to experience "scope creep," in which you end up spending time, money, and resources on tasks and deliverables that are not part of the project.

That's not to say that scope can't change during the course of a project. Business conditions, design realities, budgets, time, resource availability, and many other factors can make it necessary to change project scope midway through. Nonetheless, your scope document helps you manage those changes so that you change in the proper direction—in line with your organization's overall strategy, the product's reason for being, and the project's goals.

Understanding Product Scope and Project Scope

There are two types of scope: product scope and project scope. First you define the product scope, unless it has already been defined for you. The *product scope* specifies the features and functions of the product that will be the outcome of the project. The product scope might well be part of the product description in your charter. The product can be tangible, such as the construction of a new office building or the design of a new aircraft. The product can also be the development of a service or event, for example, deployment of a new computer system or implementation of a new training initiative.

Regardless of the type of product, the product scope indicates the specifications and parameters that paint a detailed picture of the end result. For example, the product scope of the construction of a new office building might include square footage, number of stories, location, and architectural design elements.

The *project scope* specifies the work that must be done to complete the project successfully, according to the specifications of the associated product scope. The project scope defines and controls what will and will not be included in the project. If there will be multiple phases of product development, the project scope might specify which phase this project is handling. For example, a computer system deployment project might specify that its scope encompasses the infrastructure development and installation of the new computer system, but not the documentation and training for new system users. Or it might specify that the project is handling all aspects of the product from concept through completion of the final phase.

Developing the Scope Statement

To define the project scope and communicate it to other key stakeholders, you develop the scope statement. Depending on your organization's planning processes, some elements of the scope statement might be defined very early, perhaps even before you have been assigned as project manager. Other elements might be defined just before you begin identifying and sequencing the project's tasks. Your scope statement should include the following:

Project justification. The scope statement should define the business need or other stimulus for this project. This justification will provide a sound basis for evaluating future decisions, including the inevitable tradeoffs.

Product description. The scope should characterize the details of the product or service being created. The project justification and product description together should formulate the goals of the project.

Project constraints or limitations. The scope should include any limiting factors to the project. Factors that can limit a project's options include a specific budget, contractual provisions, a precise end date, and so on.

> **note** Because we use the term *constraints* throughout this book to mean task constraints, in this chapter we're using the term *limitations* to refer to overall project constraints.

Project assumptions. The scope should list any elements considered to be true, real, or certain—even when they might not be—for the sake of being able to continue developing the project plan and moving forward. By their nature, assumptions usually carry a degree of risk. For example, if you don't know whether the building for a commercial construction project will be 10,000 or 15,000 square feet, you have to assume one or the other for the sake of planning. The risk is that the other choice might end up being correct. You can adjust the plan after the facts are known, but other project dependencies might already be in place by then.

note Although the project justification and product description are typically broad statements that remain unchanged through the iterative planning process, that's not necessarily the case with project limitations and assumptions. As the scope becomes more tightly defined, the limitations and assumptions come to light and are better exposed. Likewise, as you continue down the road in the planning process, the entire project scope tends to become more and more focused.

Project deliverables. The scope should list the summary-level subproducts created throughout the duration of the project. The delivery of the final subproject deliverable marks the completion of the entire project. This list might bring into focus major project phases and milestones, which will be valuable when you start entering tasks into your project plan.

Project objectives. The scope should enumerate the measurable objectives to be satisfied for the project to be considered successful. The objectives map to the deliverables and are driven by the project goals, as described by the project justification and product description. To be meaningful, the project objectives must be quantifiable in some way, for example, in terms of a specific dollar amount, a specific timeframe, a specific value, or a specific level of quality.

note Your scope statement might also address other project planning issues such as communications, quality assurance, and risk management. The scope statement can define the reporting requirements and the collaboration tools to be implemented. The scope statement can also specify the minimum level of quality acceptable, define the potential risks associated with the itemized limitations and assumptions, and stipulate methods of countering the risks.

Product scope and project scope are intricately linked. The project scope relies on a clear definition of the product scope. The project scope is fulfilled through the completion of work represented in the project plan. Likewise, product scope is fulfilled by meeting the specifications in the product requirements.

With the draft of the scope statement in hand, you have a document you can use to clearly communicate with other project stakeholders. This draft helps you flush out any cross-purposes, mistaken assumptions, and misplaced requirements. As you continue to refine the scope statement, the project vision is honed to the point where all the stake-holders should have a common understanding of the project. And because all the stakeholders participated in the creation of the vision, you can feel confident that everyone understands exactly what they're working toward when you begin to execute the project plan.

Creating a New Project Plan

You're now at the point where you can start Microsoft Project and actually create your project plan. When you create a new project file, you first decide whether you're schedul-ing from a start date or finish date. You set your overall project calendar that the tasks will be scheduled against. If you like, you can attach project documentation such as your all-important scope statement and possibly other project-related documents.

Creating a Project File

To start creating your new project plan, you simply start Microsoft Project and choose whether you're creating a new project from scratch or from a template.

> If you haven't installed Microsoft Project yet, refer to Appendix A, "Installing Microsoft Project 2002," for installation details and guidelines.

To start Microsoft Project, click the Windows Start menu. Point to programs, and then click Microsoft Project. Microsoft Project starts (see Figure 3-1 on the next page).

> **tip** Depending on how you've customized your setup, you might also be able to open Microsoft Project from an icon on your Windows desktop.

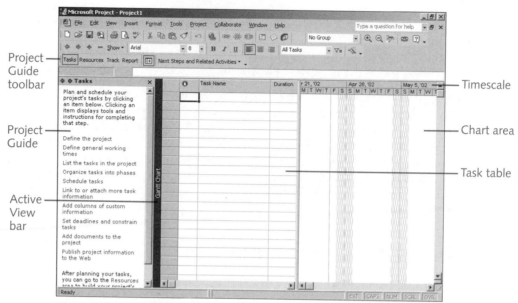

Figure 3-1. A blank project file appears in Microsoft Project.

The Microsoft Project workspace is called the *view*, and the view that comes up by default when you first open Microsoft Project is the Gantt Chart. The Gantt Chart is a *combination view*; it has a task table on the left side and the chart with Gantt bars on the right.

> For more information about working with views such as the Gantt Chart and others, see Chapter 4, "Viewing Project Information."

You can use the blank project file to start creating your project plan from scratch. If you prefer to do this, skip to the next section, "Scheduling from a Start or Finish Date."

You can also create a new project from a template. A *template* is a type of project file that contains existing project information that helps you start your project more quickly. The template usually contains a list of tasks, already sequenced and organized. The task list might be further detailed with phases, milestones, and deliverables. There might be additional task information in the template as well, such as task durations and task dependencies. You can use this task list as the basis for your project. You can add, remove, and rearrange tasks and adapt the task information as needed to correspond to your project requirements. A template can also include resource information, customized views, calendars, reports, tables, macros, option settings, and more.

The template file has an extension of *.mpt*, indicating that it is the Microsoft Project template file type. When you open and modify a template file, by default it is saved as a normal *.mpp* (Microsoft Project plan) file.

> For more information about file types and project file management, see Chapter 29, "Managing Project Files."

Chapter 3

Templates can be generated from the following sources:

- The set of templates built in to Microsoft Project reflecting various types of products or services in different industries.

  These templates are provided with Microsoft Project 2002 and are based on widely accepted industry standards for projects of these types:

General use templates	Commercial construction
	Engineering
	Home move
	Infrastructure deployment
	New business
	New product
	Office move
	Project office
	Residential construction
Software-related project templates	Microsoft Active Directory deployment
	Microsoft Exchange 2000 deployment
	Microsoft Office XP corporate deployment
	Microsoft SharePoint Portal Server deployment
	Microsoft Windows XP deployment
	MSF Application development
	Software development
	Software localization

- Any previous projects you have saved as project template files.

> For more information about using completed projects as templates, see Chapter 28, "Standardizing Projects Using Templates."

- The enterprise global template available if you're working in an enterprise environment with Microsoft Project Professional. This project template is set up by the enterprise project administrator, and includes customized elements that reflect the project standards for your organization. These elements can include a set of customized views, tables, fields, and more.

> For more information about the enterprise global template, see Chapter 24, "Using Enterprise Features to Manage Projects."

- The templates that are standard to project management within your specific industry. Professional organizations, standards organizations, and industry groups might have resources, possibly on their Web sites, that include such templates.

Creating a New Project with a Template

To create a new project from a template, follow these steps:

1 Click File, New.

2 In the Project Guide (the left pane), under New From Template, click the
General Templates link.

3 In the Templates dialog box, click the Project Templates tab (see Figure 3-2).

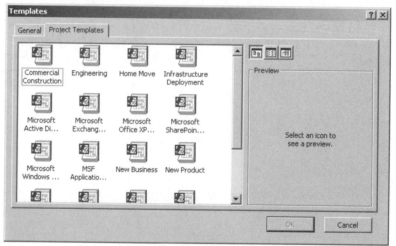

Figure 3-2. The Project Templates tab lists all templates provided with Microsoft
Project.

4 Click the project template you want to use, and then click OK (see Figure 3-3).

The first time you choose a template, Microsoft Project might need to install
it. This just takes a few moments.

54

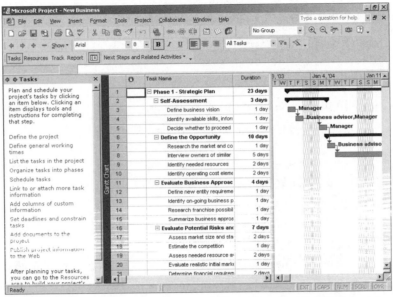

Figure 3-3. A new project file is created based on the chosen template.

---

tip Additional templates are continually being added to the Microsoft Project Web site. To see these templates, in the New Project page of the Project Guide, click the Templates On Microsoft.com link.

InsideOut

Looking for the old New dialog box? It's been replaced by the New Project pane of the Project Guide. This is true even if you close the Project Guide pane and completely turn off the Project Guide.

Click Tools, Options, and then click the Interface tab. Clear the Display Project Guide check box. On the General tab, you can also clear the Show Startup Task Pane check box. Still, when you click File, New, the New Project side pane appears. This pane provides everything the New dialog box used to have.

Creating a New Project from an Existing Project

If you have an existing project that you want to use as a starting point for your new project, you can simply copy and modify it for your current purposes. To do this, follow these steps:

Open

1 On the Standard toolbar, click Open.

2 Browse to the existing project file, and then click Open.

---

new feature!

Use the New Project Wizard

The New Project Wizard can walk you through the setup of your new project and complete the necessary dialog boxes quickly for you. To set up a new project by using the New Project Wizard:

1 Create your new project file, either from a blank project or from a template.

2 In the Project Guide, open the Tasks side pane by clicking the Tasks button on the Project Guide toolbar.

The Project Guide side pane is similar to the task pane in Microsoft Office XP applications.

3 Click the Define The Project link. The New Project Wizard starts in the side pane.

4 Enter the estimated start date for your project, and then click the Save And Go To Step 2 link.

5 Continue working through the New Project Wizard, clicking the Save And Go To link at the bottom of the pane after each step.

6 When you finish with the New Project Wizard, click the Define General Working Times link, and work through the Project Working Times Wizard.

Saving Your New Project

Whether you are creating a new project from scratch, from a template, or from an existing project file, your next step is to save your new project. To do this:

1 Click File, Save As.

---

tip **Saving a new project**

Save

If you're creating a new project from scratch or from a template, you can simply click the Save button on the Standard toolbar to open the Save As dialog box.

56

2 In the Save As dialog box, choose the drive and folder in which you want
to save the new project.

3 In the File Name box, enter a descriptive name for your project, and then
click the Save button.

Scheduling from a Start or Finish Date

Your first decision affecting how your project will be scheduled is whether you want
to schedule your project from a start date or from a finish date. Often, you have a finish
date in mind, but you can still schedule from the start date and then make sure you hit
the targeted finish date. You'll get more predictable results when you schedule from a
start date.

For example, suppose you set up a project with 100 tasks. You specify task durations
and sequence, link the tasks in the order they are to be done, and indicate whether any
tasks have specific dates by which they must be completed. Tasks that do not require
a specific start or finish date are scheduled to be done as soon as possible. Using task
durations, links, and date constraints, Microsoft Project schedules the first task to start
on your project start date and the remaining tasks from that point forward until the
last task is completed. If that last task is done on a date that is too late for your project
requirements, you can adjust the duration and sequencing as well as the scope and
resources assigned to bring in the finish date where you need it to be.

However, you might know the project finish date but not when your project will begin
because you're receiving work from another source that could be delayed. Or the project
management methodology you use might require you to schedule from a finish date.

InsideOut

If you must schedule from the finish date, be aware that your task constraints and leveling tools will behave differently than in a project that is scheduled from the start date.

For more information about task constraints, see "Scheduling Tasks to Achieve Specific
Dates" on page 147. For more information about resource leveling, see "Balancing Resource
Workloads" on page 253.

Consider that same project of 100 tasks. In a project scheduled from the finish date,
any tasks that do not require a specific date are scheduled to be done as late as possible,
rather than as soon as possible. Microsoft Project schedules the last task to be finished
on your project finish date and works backwards from that point until the first task
is started. If that first task is scheduled before the current date or too early for your
project requirements, you can make schedule and project adjustments.

To set up your project plan to be scheduled from the project start date, follow these steps:

1 Click Project, Project Information. The Project Information dialog box appears (see Figure 3-4).

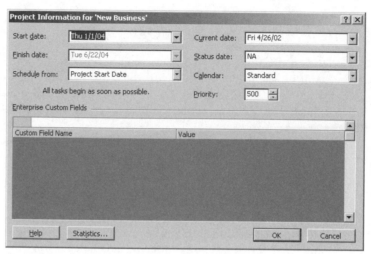

Figure 3-4. Use the Project Information dialog box to specify settings for the entire project.

2 In the Start Date box, enter the project start date. By default, the Start Date box shows today's date.

3 In the Schedule From box, click Project Start Date.

Leave the Project Finish Date box as is. Microsoft Project will calculate this date for you later.

To set up your project plan to be scheduled from the project finish date, follow these steps:

1 Click Project, Project Information.

2 In the Schedule From box, click Project Finish Date.

3 In the Finish Date box, enter the project finish date.

Leave the Project Start Date box as is. Microsoft Project will calculate this date for you later.

Setting Your Project Calendar

Your project calendar sets the working days and times for your project and its tasks, and by default, for any resources working on your project. That is, the project working times calendar indicates when your organization typically works on project tasks and when it's off work. By setting your project calendar, you're establishing one of the fundamental methods for scheduling the tasks in your project.

Working with Base Calendars in Microsoft Project

Microsoft Project comes with three *base calendars*. These base calendars are like calendar templates that you can apply to a set of resources, a set of tasks, or the project as a whole.

Standard
Working time is set to Monday through Friday, 8:00 A.M. until 5:00 P.M., with an hour off for lunch from noon until 1:00 P.M. each day. This is the default base calendar used for the project, for tasks, and for resources.

Night Shift
Working time is set to an 11:00 P.M. until 8:00 A.M. night shift, five days a week, with an hour off for lunch from 3:00 A.M. until 4:00 A.M. each morning. This base calendar is generally used for resources who work a graveyard shift. It can also be used for projects that are carried out only during the night shift.

24 Hours
Working time is set to midnight until midnight seven days a week; that is, work never stops. This base calendar is typically used for projects in a manufacturing situation, for example, which might run two or three back-to-back shifts every day of the week.

You can modify the base calendar in any way you need. To modify an existing base calendar, follow these steps:

1 Click Tools, Change Working Time.

2 In the For box, click the name of the base calendar you want to modify (see Figure 3-5).

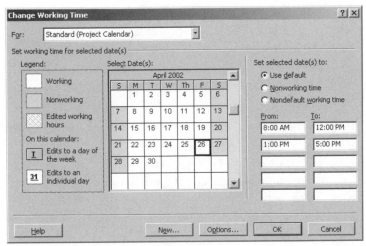

Figure 3-5. Use the Change Working Time dialog box to modify a base calendar.

3 To change the working time of a single day, click that day.

If you're changing working time to nonworking time, select the Nonworking Time option.

If you're changing the working time to something other than the default, select the Nondefault Working Time option. Then change the times in the From and To boxes as needed.

4 To change the working time of a particular day of each week, click the day heading. For example, click the M heading to select all Mondays. Select the Nonworking Time or Nondefault Working Time option, and then change the times in the From and To boxes as needed.

5 To change the working time of a day in another month, scroll down in the Select Dates box until you see the correct month. As before, click the Nonworking Time or Nondefault Working Time option, and then change the working times as needed. This is a good method for setting holidays as nonworking time.

6 When you finish changing the selected base calendar, click OK.

To create a new base calendar, follow these steps:

1 Click Tools, Change Working Time.

2 Click the New button. The Create New Base Calendar dialog box appears (see Figure 3-6).

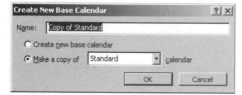

Figure 3-6. You can create a new base calendar from scratch or adapt it from an existing one.

3 In the Name box, type the name you want for the new base calendar, for example, *Swing Shift*.

4 Select the Create New Base Calendar option if you want to adapt your calendar from the Standard base calendar.

Select the Make A Copy Of option if you want to adapt the new calendar from a different base calendar, such as the Night Shift calendar. Click the name of the existing calendar you want to adapt and click OK.

5 Make the changes you want to the working days and times of individual days or of a particular day of every week, as needed.

6 When finished with your new base calendar, click OK.

60

Applying a Base Calendar to the Project Calendar

If you're going to use the Standard base calendar as your project calendar, you don't need to do much because the Standard calendar is the project calendar by default. Just make sure to modify the Change Working Times dialog box to reflect your team's working times and days off, as well as any holidays you'll all be taking.

If you want to use a different base calendar, you must select it as your project calendar. Follow these steps:

1 Click Project, Project Information.

2 In the Calendar box, select the name of the base calendar.

3 Click OK.

Calendars in Microsoft Project

Microsoft Project uses three types of calendars as tools for scheduling the project.

Project calendar	Governs when tasks are scheduled to be worked on and when resources are scheduled to work on assigned tasks.
Resource calendar	Governs when resources are scheduled to work on assigned tasks. One group of resources (for example, day shift resources) can be assigned to a different base calendar than another group of resources (for example, swing shift resources). Each resource can have his or her own individual resource calendar, which can reflect special work schedules, personal days off, and vacation time. By default, the resource calendar is the Standard calendar.
Task calendar	Governs when tasks are scheduled to be worked on. As a rule, tasks are scheduled according to the project calendar and the calendars of any assigned resources. However, sometimes a task has special scheduling requirements that are different from the norm. For example, a task might be carried out by a machine running 24 hours a day. In such a case, it's useful for a task to have its own calendar.

You can use any of the three base calendars (Standard, Night Shift, or 24 Hours) as the basis for the project calendar, resource calendars, or task calendars.

All three of these calendars can easily be customized for specialized working days and times. If you need to apply a common working schedule to a group of resources or a set of tasks and it isn't built in to Microsoft Project already, you can create your own base calendar.

For more information about the task calendar, see "Working with Task Calendars" on page 158. For more information about the resource calendar, see "Setting Resource Working Time Calendars" on page 176.

Chapter 3

Attaching Project Documentation

You can make Microsoft Project the central repository for all your important project documentation. For example, you might want to attach or link your scope statement to your project plan, as well as other documents like the needs analysis, market study, and product specifications.

Showing the Project Summary Task

The first step for adding planning documentation to your project is displaying the project summary task. Not only will this task eventually provide summary date and cost information for the project as a whole, it can serve as the location for your attached or linked planning documents. To display the project summary task, follow these steps:

1 Click Tools, Options, and then click the View tab.

2 Under Outline Options, select the Show Project Summary Task check box.

3 Click OK. A summary task appears in Row 0 of the Gantt Chart (see Figure 3-7).

Figure 3-7. Use the project summary task to attach or link planning documents.

Copying a Planning Document into Your Project File

You can include documents created in other programs within Microsoft Project. Although this can significantly increase your file size, you'll know that all your project information is stored in one place.

Task Information

Insert Object

1 With the project summary task selected, click Task Information on the Standard toolbar, and then click the Notes tab.

2 On the Notes tab, click the Insert Object button.

3 In the Insert Object dialog box, select the Create From File option, and then click the Browse button.

4 In the Browse dialog box, select the project-planning document you want to attach or embed into your project file. Click the Insert button.

5 Back in the Insert Object dialog box (see Figure 3-8), select the Display As Icon check box.

6 Click OK. The document's icon appears in the Notes area of the Summary Task Information dialog box (see Figure 3-9).

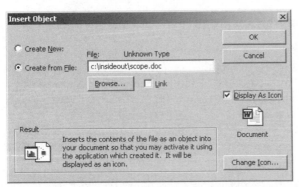

Figure 3-8. The selected document will be embedded in your project plan.

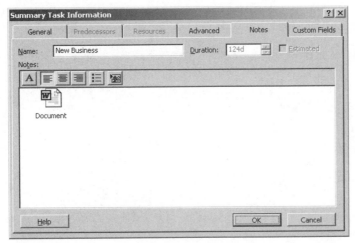

Figure 3-9. You can double-click the icon to open the document.

7 In the Summary Task Information dialog box, click OK. The Notes indicator appears in the Gantt Chart (see Figure 3-10).

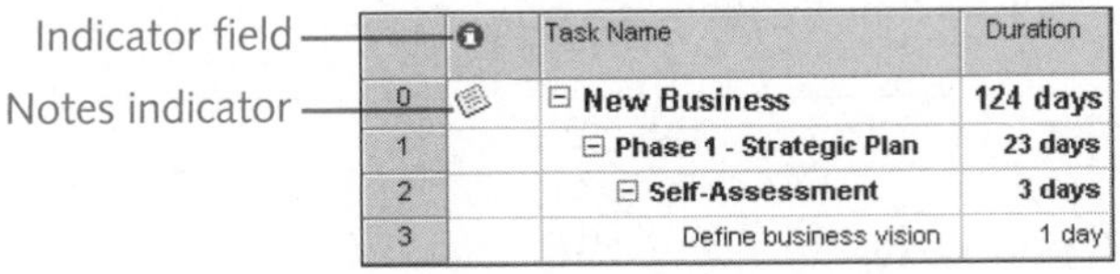

Indicator field ——
Notes indicator ——

	ⓘ	Task Name	Duration
0	🗒	⊟ **New Business**	**124 days**
1		⊟ **Phase 1 - Strategic Plan**	**23 days**
2		⊟ **Self-Assessment**	**3 days**
3		Define business vision	1 day

Figure 3-10. When you store something in a Notes tab, the Notes indicator appears in the corresponding row of the Gantt Chart.

Now whenever you need to review the document, just double-click the Notes indicator to open the Notes tab of the Summary Task Information dialog box. Then double-click the document icon.

For more information about embedding, see "Embedding Information" on page 437.

Chapter 3

63

Hyperlinking a Planning Document to Your Project File

You can also hyperlink to a document from Microsoft Project. Hyperlinking is a preferred method when you want to keep your file size trimmer and you know that your project plan and associated planning documents will always be in the same place. It's also a very efficient method for opening associated documents quickly. To insert a hyperlink, follow these steps:

Insert
Hyperlink

1 With the project summary task selected, click Insert Hyperlink on the Standard toolbar.

2 In the Text To Display box, type a descriptive name for the document to which you are linking, for example, *Project Scope Statement*.

3 Find and select the project planning document you want to link to your project file (see Figure 3-11).

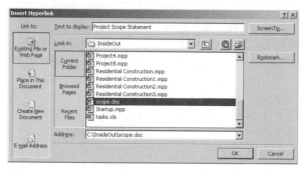

Figure 3-11. The path and name of the selected document appear in the Address box.

Hyperlink
indicator

4 Click OK. The Hyperlink indicator appears in the Indicators field of the Gantt Chart.

Now whenever you need to review the document, just click the Hyperlink indicator. The document opens in its own application window.

> For more information, see "Hyperlinking Information" on page 447.

One more method for keeping all project documents together is to use the *document library*. If you use Microsoft Project Server and Microsoft Project Web Access with SharePoint Team Services, you can set up and maintain a document library. This way, all your team members and other stakeholders can view the documents through their Web browsers.

> For more information about setting up a document library with SharePoint Team Services, see "Tracking Issues and Storing Documents" on page 526.

64

Entering Tasks

When your project file is set up, you're ready to enter tasks.

> **note** If you're working with a template or a copy of an existing project plan, you already have tasks in place. In this case, you can skip this section.

There are several approaches you can take to fill in the Gantt Chart. The following are some examples:

Brainstorming.   Enter tasks as you think of them, without regard to sequence or grouping of related tasks. You can always move and organize later.

Sequential.   Think through the project from beginning to end, and enter tasks sequentially.

Phases.   Think of the overall phases of the project. For example, in a commercial construction project, you might enter the phases of Procurement, On-Site Mobilization, Site Grading, Foundations, Steel Erection, and so on. After those phases are in place, you can add tasks and subtasks beneath them.

Milestones and deliverables.   Consider what the project is producing in terms of the milestones and deliverables. Enter those as tasks, and then add tasks and subtasks beneath them to flesh out the project. Your scope statement can be a valuable guide in this process.

Team collaboration.   Ask team members to list the tasks they believe will be necessary to the areas under their responsibility. (You must have team members already in place and available.) This can be done informally, for example, through e-mail. Team members can submit tasks and their estimated durations in a Microsoft Excel spreadsheet, which you can later import into Microsoft Project. If you're using Microsoft Project Server, team members can send you tasks from Microsoft Project Web Access, and then you can incorporate them automatically into your project plan.

For more information about creating new tasks through automated team collaboration, see "Assigning Tasks" on page 515.

Expert consultation.   Ask known experts what tasks are needed for various aspects of the project. This is particularly useful if you're the manager of a project in which you're not necessarily an expert. This happens frequently enough, and it's not necessarily a bad thing, but you will need dependable experts to help provide reliable task information. Even if you're well versed in the project knowledge area, you might not know all the necessary details for each phase. Experts can come from within your own group, from stakeholders, from other groups or project managers within your organization, or from colleagues in your profession or industry.

65

Project Management Practices: Activity Definition

The stage of the project management process in which you're entering tasks is often referred to as activity definition. This is the point in the planning phase in which the planning team identifies the specific activities, or tasks, that must be done to produce the project deliverables and meet the project objectives as specified in the scope statement.

Activity definition is typically done with the guidance provided in the scope statement and the work breakdown structure (WBS). The deliverables, or work packages, described in the WBS are divided and subdivided into smaller tasks that can be better managed and controlled in the project.

> For more information about work breakdown structures in Microsoft Project, see "Setting Up Your Work Breakdown Structure" later in this chapter.

In some organizations, the project management methodology dictates that the WBS is developed first and the task list is developed next. Other organizations develop both at the same time.

In any case, the task list must include all activities that will be performed in the project, but it does not include any activities that are not required as part of the project scope. Each task should be descriptive enough to communicate to responsible team members what is required by the task.

Adding Tasks to Your Project Plan

To enter tasks directly into your project plan, follow these steps:

1 Make sure you're working in the Gantt Chart. You can see the name of the current view in the Active View bar that runs vertically along the left side of the view. If it doesn't say *Gantt Chart*, click View, Gantt Chart.

> For more information about views, see Chapter 4, "Viewing Project Information."

2 Type the name of the task in the Task Name field.

3 Press Enter or your down arrow key to move to the next row. The task name isn't recorded and other commands remain unavailable until you press Enter.

> For more information about entering durations, links, and start and finish dates, see Chapter 5, "Scheduling Tasks."

Tips for Entering Tasks

Keep the following in mind when entering tasks:

- Don't be overly concerned about sequence when first entering tasks. You can worry about that after you have a "first draft" of tasks in place.

- Enter duration estimates either at the same time you enter your new tasks or later. The default duration estimate is 1 day, and estimates are formatted with a question mark to remind you that they are not confirmed yet.

- Don't enter a start or finish date in the Start or Finish fields in the Gantt Chart, although it might be tempting to do so. In most cases, you'll want Microsoft Project to calculate those dates for you, based on other task information you'll be entering.

- Name the task with sufficient description to communicate to team members and stakeholders what the task is about. A task called simply *Review* or *Edit* might not be enough information.

- Decide whether you want the context of the task to be understood if it's ever separated (by being in a separate view, report, filter, or grouping, for example) from its surrounding tasks. For example, you might have several tasks in different phases for "Administer contracts." But one task might relate to procurement, one to the architects, and another one to the builders.

- Note whether you have sets of tasks that are repeated in different phases of the project. You might want to give them more general names so you can copy and paste these sets of tasks under their respective phases, instead of repeatedly typing them individually.

InsideOut

By default, the Gantt Chart table includes the Task Name, Duration, Start, Finish, Predecessors, and Resource Names fields as columns. A natural impulse when entering tasks is to enter project information into each of these fields. However, you can get yourself into some trouble if you enter dates in the Start and Finish fields. Not only would you be struggling to calculate start and finish dates for each task while Microsoft Project could more easily do it for you, but you'd be putting undue restrictions on your schedule, and possibly creating scheduling conflicts.

The best approach is to enter the task names first, and then the durations if you know them. Leave the Start and Finish fields as they are for now, and let Microsoft Project calculate them for you as you add other project information. The Predecessors field will be filled in for you when you start creating links between tasks. At that point, with durations and links in place, Microsoft Project will calculate the Start and Finish dates. If you then need to constrain the dates, you can edit them as you need.

newfeature!
Importing Tasks from an Excel Worksheet

Many project managers do well by having others on the team develop a task list of their specific areas of responsibility. A great way to automate this process is to have these individuals use Microsoft Excel to create their task lists, and then import the worksheets into the Microsoft Project Gantt Chart.

The standard Excel importing process involves mapping the Excel columns to the corresponding Project columns to ensure that the right information ends up in the right places in your Gantt Chart task table. In Microsoft Project 2002, a new Excel Task List template is set up for this very purpose.

To use Excel and the Excel Task List template on the same computer on which Microsoft Project is installed, follow these steps:

1 Start Microsoft Excel.

2 Click File, New.

3 In the New Workbook task pane, click General Templates. The Templates dialog box appears.

4 Click the Spreadsheet Solutions tab.

5 Double-click Microsoft Project Task List Import Template. The template creates a new file with columns that correspond to the default Gantt Chart in Microsoft Project (see Figure 3-12).

6 Enter tasks and other task information as needed, and then save the file.

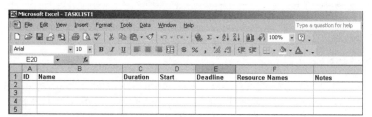

Figure 3-12. Share the Excel Task List template with your team to help build your project plan.

> **note** If you're working with a version of Microsoft Excel 2000 or earlier, you can still use the Microsoft Project Task List Import template. Open Excel, and then click File, New. Click the 1033 or Spreadsheet Solutions tab. Double-click the Microsoft Project Task List Import Template.

When you're ready to import the task list into your project plan, follow these steps:

1 Open the project plan.

2 On the Standard toolbar, click Open.

3 Go to the location on your computer or network where the Excel task list is saved.

4 In the Files Of Type list, click Microsoft Excel Workbooks (*.xls). The task list appears in the list of folders and files.

5 Click the task list workbook, and then click Open. The Import Wizard appears.

6 Click Next.

7 Click Project Excel Template, and then click Next.

8 Specify whether you want to import the file as a new project, append the tasks to the currently active project, or merge the data into the active project. Then click Finish. The tasks are imported into Microsoft Project as you specified.

9 If you need to provide this template to others on your team, by default, it's located in the C:\Program Files\Microsoft Office\Templates\1033 folder. Those who want to use this template should copy this file to the same location on their computers.

> For more information about using Microsoft Project with other applications, see "Importing and Exporting Information" on page 441, and Chapter 17, "Integrating Microsoft Project with Microsoft Excel."

Chapter 3

Entering Recurring Tasks

You might have certain tasks that need to be scheduled at regularly occurring intervals. For example, you might have a project team meeting every Thursday morning. You might need to gather information and generate a resource management report the first Monday of each month. Instead of entering the same task every week or every month throughout the span of the project, you can enter a recurring task. To do this, follow these steps:

1 Make sure you're working in the Gantt Chart. If necessary, click View, Gantt Chart.

2 In the Task Name field, click the row below where you want the recurring task to appear.

3 Click Insert, Recurring Task.

4 In the Recurring Task dialog box, type the name of the recurring task in the Task Name field, for example, *Generate resource management report* (see Figure 3-13).

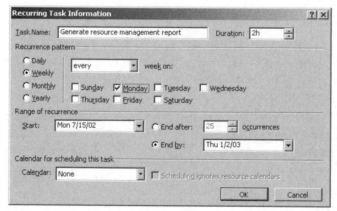

Figure 3-13. Specify the name and scheduling details of your recurring task.

5 Under Recurrence Pattern, specify how often the task is to be scheduled, that is, daily, weekly, or monthly.

6 Specify the details of when the task is to take place during that frequency, for example, every other Thursday or the first Monday of every month.

7 Under Range Of Recurrence, specify when the recurring task is to begin and end.

Recurring indicator

8 When finished, click OK. The recurring task is marked with a recurring task indicator. It's represented with a summary task with all occurrences of the task as subtasks.

---

tip Review the recurrence pattern and range by resting your pointer over the recurring task indicator. Double-click the recurring task to open the Recurring Task dialog box.

Troubleshooting

You're entering project information in Gantt Chart view, and your menus and toolbars have all gone gray

When you're in the middle of entering a task or any other task information in a Gantt Chart, the menus and toolbars become temporarily unavailable and are therefore grayed out.

Finish entering the task by pressing Enter. If you want to do something to that task, click it to select it again, and then choose the command or button you want.

Sequencing and Organizing Tasks

With the Gantt Chart in your project file now full of tasks, it's time to put these tasks in a logical order. It's also time to make sure to add any forgotten tasks or to delete duplicated ones.

Moving Tasks

To move a task from one row to another, follow these steps:

1 In the table portion of the Gantt Chart, select the entire task row by clicking the gray row heading, which includes the task number.

71

2 With your mouse pointer still over the row heading (the pointer should appear as a black crosshair), drag the task to the location in the Gantt Chart where you want to place it. A gray line along the row border follows your mouse movements, indicating where the task will be inserted when you release the mouse button.

3 Release the mouse button to insert the task in the new location.

Inserting Additional Tasks

To add a new task to other existing tasks, follow these steps:

1 In the table portion of the Gantt Chart, click the row below where you want the new task to be inserted.

2 Click Insert, New Task.

> **tip**   You can also simply press the Insert key.

3 Type the name of the new task, and then press Enter.

Copying Tasks

You can copy one or more tasks to use as the basis for other tasks. The following list describes the various copy techniques:

Copy Cell

Copy a single task name.   Click in the Task Name field, and then click Copy Cell on the Standard toolbar. Click the Task Name field in a blank row, and then click Paste.

Paste

Copy multiple adjacent task names.   Click the first task name you want to select, hold down the Shift key, and then click the last task name. All task names between the first and last are selected. Click Copy Cell. Click the first Task Name field where you want the selected tasks to be pasted, and then click Paste.

You can also simply drag to select the tasks. If you want to copy the selected tasks to empty rows directly under a particular task, drag the fill handle in the lower right corner of the cell into those empty rows (see Figure 3-14).

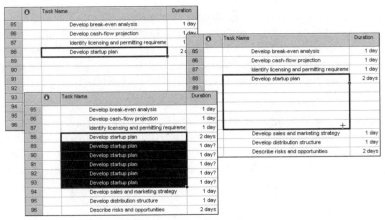

Figure 3-14. Copy tasks using the fill handle.

Copy multiple nonadjacent task names. Click the first task name you want to select, hold down the Ctrl key, and then click any additional task names you want to add to the selection (see Figure 3-15). Click Copy Cell. Select the Task Name field where you want the selected tasks to start to be added, and then click the Paste button. The tasks are added in the order that you selected them.

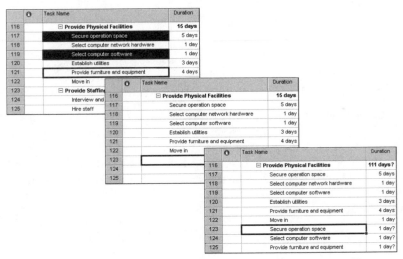

Figure 3-15. Copy multiple task names at once to save yourself some keyboard entry.

Chapter 3

73

Copy a single task and its task information. Click the row heading of the task you want to copy. This selects the entire task and its associated information. Click Copy Cell. To add the task into an empty row, select the row, and then click Paste. To insert the task between two existing tasks, select the lower task (below where you want the pasted task to appear), and then click Paste.

Copy multiple adjacent tasks and their task information. Click the row heading of the first task you want to copy. Hold down the Shift key, and then click the row heading of the last task (see Figure 3-16). Click Copy Cell. Click the Task Name field where you want the selected tasks to start to be added, and then click Paste.

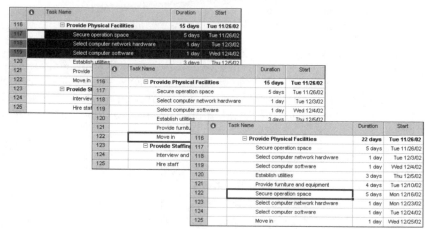

Figure 3-16. Copy multiple tasks along with all their associated information.

Copy multiple nonadjacent tasks and their task information. Click the row heading of the first task you want to copy. Hold down the Ctrl key, and then click the row headings of all the tasks you want to copy. Click Copy Cell. Click the first Task Name field where you want the selected tasks to be added. Click Paste. The tasks are added in the order that you selected them.

Deleting Tasks

To delete a task you don't need, select the row heading, and then press the Delete key.

newfeature! In previous versions of Microsoft Project, when you clicked a task name and pressed the Delete key, the entire task row was deleted. Now the Delete indicator appears in the Indicators column, enabling you to choose whether to delete the entire task or just the task name (see Figure 3-17).

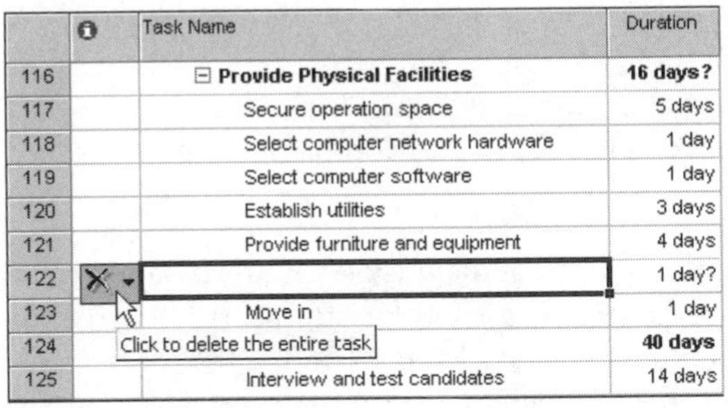

	ⓘ	Task Name	Duration
116		⊟ **Provide Physical Facilities**	**16 days?**
117		Secure operation space	5 days
118		Select computer network hardware	1 day
119		Select computer software	1 day
120		Establish utilities	3 days
121		Provide furniture and equipment	4 days
122	✕ ▾		1 day?
123		Move in	1 day
124		Click to delete the entire task	**40 days**
125		Interview and test candidates	14 days

Figure 3-17. Click the down arrow next to the Delete indicator to choose what you want to delete.

If you want to delete the entire task, click the indicator. If you simply want to clear the task name, press Enter or click elsewhere in the view.

Organizing Tasks into an Outline

Your task list now has some order and sequence applied. You're ready to organize the tasks into a structure representing the hierarchy of tasks from the broader perspective to the deep and detailed perspective where real work will actually take place.

A task at a higher outline level than other tasks is called a summary task. The tasks beneath that summary task are called subtasks (see Figure 3-18 on the next page). Summary tasks typically represent phases in a project. For example, in a new business startup project, you might have summary tasks for developing the strategic plan, defining the business opportunity, planning for action, and proceeding with the startup plan.

75

Summary task — Subtasks — Summary tasks —

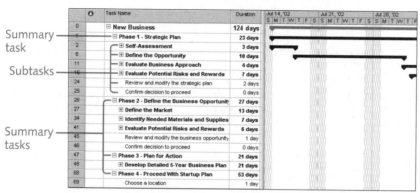

Figure 3-18. Use summary tasks and subtasks to combine related tasks into manageable chunks.

The subtasks under those phases could be actual tasks that are assigned to resources. Or they could be another set of summary tasks. For example, the "Define the business opportunity" summary task could have subtasks like "Define the market," "Identify needed materials and supplies," and "Evaluate potential risks and rewards." These subtasks in turn can be summary tasks to still more subtasks. You can have up to nine outline levels.

Many project managers use the outline levels to correspond to their work breakdown structure, in which the lowest-level subtask corresponds to the work package.

For more information about work breakdown structures in Microsoft Project, see "Setting Up Your Work Breakdown Structure" later in this chapter.

As you create the outline structure in your task list, you might find that you need to refine the task list even more by inserting, moving, and deleting tasks.

All your tasks are initially at the first outline level. To make a summary task, you need to indent subtasks beneath it. The following list describes various outlining techniques:

Indent

Make a task a subtask. Click the task. On the Formatting toolbar, click Indent. The task is indented, and the task above it becomes its summary task. Summary tasks are highlighted in bold in the table portion of the Gantt Chart and are marked with a black bar spanning the summary tasks in the chart portion of the Gantt Chart.

Create a subtask under a subtask.   Click a task under a subtask. Click Indent twice. It's now in the third outline level, as a subtask of a subtask.

Move a subtask to a higher level.   Click a subtask, and then click Outdent.

Outdent

Indent several tasks at one time.   Drag the mouse pointer down several adjacent tasks to select them, and then click Indent. Use the Ctrl key to select several nonadjacent tasks at once, and then click Indent. This also works for tasks that will become subtasks to different summary tasks.

Show the tasks at a specified outline level.   If you want tasks only at the first and second outline levels to be visible throughout your entire project plan, for example, on the Formatting toolbar, click Show, and then click Outline Level 2. You can select any outline level you want. You can also click All Subtasks to see all outline levels.

Show
Subtasks

Hide or show the subtasks for a selected summary task.   Next to each summary task is a plus or minus sign. The plus sign indicates that there are hidden subtasks for this summary task. Click the plus sign, and the subtasks appear. The minus sign indicates that the subtasks are currently displayed. Click the minus sign, and the subtasks will be hidden.

Hide
Subtasks

You can also use Show Subtasks and Hide Subtasks on the Formatting toolbar to do the same thing.

Summary tasks show rolled-up task information that is an aggregate of the information in the associated subtasks. For example, if there are four subtasks, each with a duration of 2 days, the summary task shows the total of 8 days. You can also see rolled-up summary information for costs, start dates, finish dates, and more.

You can also display a summary task for the project as a whole. To do this, follow these steps:

1 Click Tools, Options.

2 On the View tab, under Outline options, select the Show Project Summary Task check box.

With a project summary task, you can see rolled-up summary information for the project as a whole.

Chapter 3

Setting Up Your Work Breakdown Structure

Many project managers and organizations use a *work breakdown structure (WBS)* as an essential element of their project management methodology. Similar to the outline structure of your project task list, the WBS is a hierarchical chart view of deliverables in the project in which each level down represents an increasingly detailed description of the project deliverables. The levels each have their own code sets, such as 2.1.3.a. Levels in the hierarchy represent summary tasks, subtasks, work packages, and deliverables. You can define a project's scope and develop its task lists with the WBS.

An industry, application area, or organization experienced with a particular type of project tends to have WBSs developed to represent the life cycles of their typical types of projects, for example, the design of a new vehicle or the construction of an office building.

Understanding Work Breakdown Structure Codes

Each item and level in a work breakdown structure is described by a unique WBS code. Each digit in the code typically represents a level in the structure's hierarchy, such as 2.1.4.3 or 5.B.c.3. A WBS code like 1.2.3 might represent the third deliverable for the second activity in the first phase of the project.

> **note** In some industries or application areas, the work breakdown structure is also known as the *project breakdown structure,* or *PBS.*

In Microsoft Project, any outline structure you set up for your tasks is assigned a set of unique outline numbers. The outline number for the first summary task is 1. The outline number for the first subtask under the first summary task is 1.1 (see Figure 3-19).

Outline numbers ⌐   ⌐ Default WBS codes

🛈	Outline Number	WBS	Task Name	Duration
1	**1**	**1**	⊟ **Phase 1 - Strategic Plan**	**23 days**
2	**1.1**	**1.1**	⊟ **Self-Assessment**	**3 days**
3	1.1.1	1.1.1	Define business vision	1 day
4	1.1.2	1.1.2	Identify available skills, information and su	1 day
5	1.1.3	1.1.3	Decide whether to proceed	1 day
6	**1.2**	**1.2**	⊟ **Define the Opportunity**	**10 days**
7	1.2.1	1.2.1	Research the market and competition	1 day
8	1.2.2	1.2.2	Interview owners of similar businesses	5 days
9	1.2.3	1.2.3	Identify needed resources	2 days
10	1.2.4	1.2.4	Identify operating cost elements	2 days
11	**1.3**	**1.3**	⊟ **Evaluate Business Approach**	**4 days**
12	1.3.1	1.3.1	Define new entity requirements	1 day

Figure 3-19. The outline number specifies the task's position in your project plan's task outline hierarchy.

By default, Microsoft Project creates WBS codes that are derived from these outline numbers. You cannot change the code scheme of the outline numbers. However, if you and your organization have a specific WBS coding scheme, you can change the WBS numbering. The following lists some things to keep in mind about WBS codes:

- You can only have one set of WBS codes. However, if you use additional coding schemes, you can create up to ten sets of outline codes and then sort or group your tasks by those codes.

> **note** Certain project management methodologies use other structured and hierarchical codes that can describe your project from different viewpoints. Examples include the *organizational breakdown structure (OBS)*, the *resource breakdown structure (RBS)*, and the *bill of materials (BOM)*.

For more information about outline codes, see "Working with Outline Codes" on page 631.

- You can include ordered numbers, uppercase letters, and lowercase letters as part of your custom WBS code format. You can also include unordered characters in the code format.

- You can automatically generate your custom WBS codes for tasks as you add them.

Setting Up Work Breakdown Structure Codes

To set up your custom WBS code scheme, follow these steps:

1 Click Project, WBS, Define Code.

2 If you use a prefix, or *code mask,* for the project in front of the WBS code to distinguish it from other projects using the same code format, enter that prefix in the Project Code Prefix box.

3 In the Sequence field in the first row, select whether the first digit of the code (representing the first level of the hierarchy) is an ordered number, ordered uppercase letter, ordered lowercase letter, or unordered character.

4 In the Length field in the first row, specify whether there is a length limit for the first code.

5 In the Separator field in the first row, specify the character that separates the first and second code.

6 Repeat the process in the Sequence field in the second row. Continue these steps until all the levels of your custom WBS code are set up (see Figure 3-20).

As you enter the code mask for each succeeding level, the Code Preview box shows an example of the code.

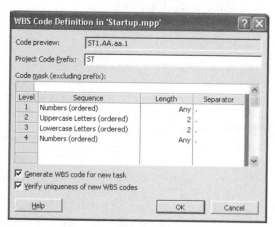

Figure 3-20. Define your organization's WBS code format.

7 When finished, click OK. The WBS codes for your tasks are reset to conform to your custom structure (see Figure 3-21).

	❶	Outline Number	WBS	Task Name	Duration
1		1	ST1	⊟ Phase 1 - Strategic Plan	**23 days**
2		1.1	ST1.AA	⊟ Self-Assessment	**3 days**
3		1.1.1	ST1.AA.aa	Define business vision	1 day
4		1.1.2	ST1.AA.ab	Identify available skills, information and su	1 day
5		1.1.3	ST1.AA.ac	Decide whether to proceed	1 day
6		1.2	ST1.AB	⊟ Define the Opportunity	**10 days**
7		1.2.1	ST1.AB.aa	Research the market and competition	1 day
8		1.2.2	ST1.AB.ab	Interview owners of similar businesses	5 days
9		1.2.3	ST1.AB.ac	Identify needed resources	2 days
10		1.2.4	ST1.AB.ad	Identify operating cost elements	2 days
11		1.3	ST1.AC	⊟ Evaluate Business Approach	**4 days**
12		1.3.1	ST1.AC.aa	Define new entity requirements	1 day

Figure 3-21. Your newly defined WBS codes replace the default WBS codes derived from the outline numbers.

Chapter 3

InsideOut

You can use the Microsoft Project Gantt Chart to set up and rearrange your tasks according to your custom work breakdown structure. If you use Microsoft Visio 2000 or later, you can take this a step further and use Visio's charting features for your WBS structure. You can then display project information in a Visio WBS chart. This is done with the Visio WBS Chart Wizard, which is a Microsoft Project Component Object Model (COM) add-in.

Download the Visio WBS Chart Wizard from the Microsoft Project Web site (*http://go.microsoft.com/fwlink/?LinkId=4325*). The Visio WBS Chart Wizard is also provided on the CD that comes with this book.

To create a Microsoft Visio WBS chart from your project tasks:

1 On the Visio WBS Chart toolbar, click Visio WBS Chart Wizard. If the toolbar is not showing, on the View menu, point to Toolbars, and then click Visio WBS Chart.

2 Click Launch Wizard.

3 Follow the instructions to create the Visio WBS Chart. This will create a chart for all tasks, or for all tasks based on a selected outline level.

You can also create a chart for specific selected tasks. To do this, click Apply Task Selection View. In the Visio WBS Chart Task Selection view, select the tasks you want to include in the chart by clicking Yes in the Include In WBS Chart field for that task. On the Visio WBS Chart toolbar, click Visio WBS Chart Wizard, click Launch Wizard, and follow the steps.

Adding Supplementary Information to Tasks

You can annotate an individual task by adding notes. You can also provide documentation or references in support of a task by linking it to other documents or Web sites.

To add a note to a task, follow these steps:

1 Click the task, and then click Task Information on the Standard toolbar.

Chapter 3

81

2 Click the Notes tab.

3 In the Notes area, type the note.

4 When finished, click OK.

You can insert an entire document as a note associated with an individual task. For more information, see "Copying a Planning Document into Your Project File" earlier in this chapter.

You can also hyperlink from a task to a document on your computer or on a Web site. For more information, see "Hyperlinking a Planning Document to Your Project File" earlier in this chapter.

Viewing Project Information

To plan, track, and manage your project with Microsoft Project, you enter a variety of detailed information regarding tasks, resources, assignments, durations, resource rates, and more. Microsoft Project in turn takes your information and does calculations to create even more information, including start dates, finish dates, costs, and remaining work. Over 400 pieces of information are available for tasks, resources, and assignments. The more tasks, resources, and assignments you have in your project, and the more custom capabilities you use, the more these pieces of information are multiplied.

There's no way you could look at this mass of project information at one time and work with it in any kind of meaningful or efficient way. To solve this problem, Microsoft Project organizes and stores the information in a *database*. All information associated with an individual task, for example, is a single *record* in that database. Each piece of information in that record is a separate *field* (see Figure 4-1 on the next page).

When you need to look at or work with a particular set of information, you choose a particular *view* to be displayed in the Microsoft Project workspace. A view filters the project information in a specific way according to the purpose of the view, and then presents that layout of information in the Microsoft Project workspace so you can easily work with it. There are over 20 views available in Microsoft Project.

You can rearrange the project information presented in a view. You can sort information in many views by name, date, and so on. You can group information, for example, by complete versus incomplete tasks. You can filter information to see only the information you want, for example, tasks that are assigned to a particular resource. These concepts and techniques are all presented in this chapter.

83

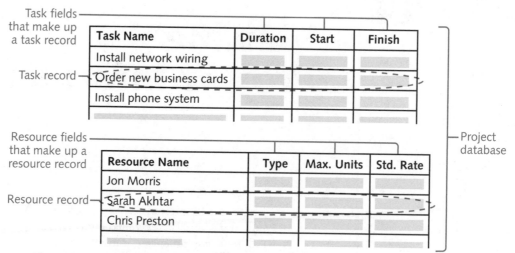

Task fields that make up a task record

Task record

Task Name	Duration	Start	Finish
Install network wiring			
Order new business cards			
Install phone system			

Resource fields that make up a resource record

Resource record

Resource Name	Type	Max. Units	Std. Rate
Jon Morris			
Sarah Akhtar			
Chris Preston			

Project database

Figure 4-1. Each task represents a single record in your project database, with all associated information represented by individual fields.

Understanding Project Information Categories

The means for organizing, managing, and storing the thousands of pieces of project information is the Microsoft Project database. There are three major categories in the project database:

- Task information
- Resource information
- Assignment information

When you start entering project information, typically you enter tasks and associated information such as duration, date constraints, deadlines, and task dependencies. These all fall under the task information category.

Then you enter resource names and associated information such as standard rate, overtime rate, and working times calendar. These all fall under the resource information category.

As soon as you assign a resource to a task, you create an assignment, which is the intersection of task and resource. Information associated with an assignment includes the amount of work, the assignment start and finish dates, the cost for the assignment, and so on. These fall under the assignment information category.

> **note** There are also three subcategories of project information: task-timephased, resource-timephased, and assignment-timephased. These are covered in "Working with Usage Views" later in this chapter.

Understanding these three categories is important when viewing project information. There are task views, resource views, and assignment views. The individual fields that make up all views are also classified as task, resource, or assignment fields, and can only be seen in their respective views. Likewise, there are filters and groups designed for task views and other filters and groups designed for resource views.

> For more information about working with your Microsoft Project database, see Chapter 32, "Working with Microsoft Project Data."

Accessing Your Project Information

You access information in your Microsoft Project database by selecting a specific view to be displayed in your Microsoft Project workspace. There are more than 20 views built in to Microsoft Project; some views have to do with tasks, others with resources, and still others with assignments. Some views are a spreadsheet of tables and columns. Others are graphs or forms. Other views are a combination; for example, the Gantt Chart is a combination of a sheet and a graph.

You can switch tables in a view, and add and remove fields shown in a view, and so modify these views to present your project information exactly the way you need.

Using Views

When you first start using Microsoft Project, typically the first view you use is the Gantt Chart, which is the default view. Here you enter tasks, durations, and task relationships. Typically, the second view you need is the Resource Sheet, in which you enter resource information. As you continue to plan your project, your requirements become more sophisticated, and you find you need other views. For example, you might need to see all your tasks with their current percent complete, along with the critical path. Or you might need a graph showing a particular resource's workload throughout April and May.

> **tip** **Change the default view**
>
> To change the view that opens when you first open Microsoft Project and create a new project file, click Tools, Options, and in the Options dialog box, click the View tab. In the Default View box, click the view that you want to appear by default whenever you create a new project file.
>
> This setting only changes the view for any new project files. For an existing project file, the last view shown when you saved and closed the file is the one that appears when you open it again.

> For more information about other view options, see "Arranging Your Microsoft Project Workspace" later in this chapter.

85

The most commonly used views are available on the View menu. All views are available on the More Views submenu. To switch to a different view, follow these steps:

1 Click View, and then review the top half of the menu to see if the view you want is listed.

2 If it is listed, click its name. If the view is not listed, click More Views. The full list of available Microsoft Project views appears (see Figure 4-2).

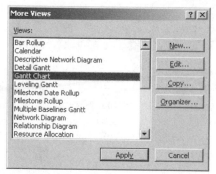

Figure 4-2. The More Views dialog box lists all available views in alphabetical order.

3 Double-click the view you want. It appears in your Microsoft Project workspace, replacing the previous view.

Keep in mind that when you switch from one view to another, you're not changing the data; you're just getting a different look at the data in your project database.

If you display the *View bar*, you can use it to quickly switch views. To show the View bar:

1 Click View, View Bar. The View bar appears on the far left edge of the Microsoft Project window (see Figure 4-3). The same views that appear on the View menu are listed on the View bar.

2 Click a view's name or icon to switch to that view. If you can't see the view's name, click the arrow at the bottom of the list to see more views.

If the view isn't listed on the View bar, click More Views to see the full list.

---

tip   **Switch views with Active View bar**

To hide a showing View bar, click View, View Bar.

When the View bar is hidden, a blue vertical bar appears between the Project Guide side pane and the current view. This *Active View* bar shows the name of the current view. To change the current view, right-click the Active View bar. If the view you want appears in the shortcut menu, click it. Otherwise, click More Views to display the More Views dialog box, and then click the view you want.

86

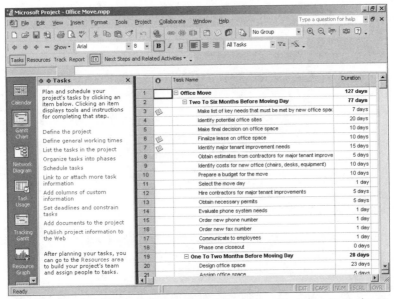

Figure 4-3. The View bar lists icons for the same views shown in the View menu.

InsideOut

The most commonly used views are listed on the View menu and the View bar. But these might not be *your* most commonly used views. For example, you might use the Task Entry view and the Detail Gantt daily, and you don't want to click More Views every time you need it.

You can add your frequently used views to the View menu and View bar. Click View, More Views. Click the view you want to add to the View menu, and then click Edit. The View Definition dialog box appears. Select the Show In Menu check box.

You can use this technique to remove views you never use from the View menu and View bar as well. Simply select the view, click Edit, and clear the Show In Menu check box.

You can also rearrange the order of views listed. The task views are listed first, in alphabetical order, and then the resource views are listed in alphabetical order. In the More Views dialog box, click the view you want to rearrange, and then click Edit. In the Name box, add a number in front of the name, and that will bring it to the top of its respective list. Prefix all the displayed views with a sequential number, and they'll appear in the order you want.

> **note** You can fully customize your views and create entirely new views. For more information, see "Customizing Views" on page 586.

You can think of Microsoft Project views in the following categories:

- Gantt charts
- Network diagrams
- Graph views
- Sheet views
- Usage views
- Forms
- Combination views

Working with Gantt Charts

Gantt charts are a special type of combination view used extensively in project management. The left side of a Gantt chart contains a sheet view and the right side contains a bar graph along a timescale (see Figure 4-4).

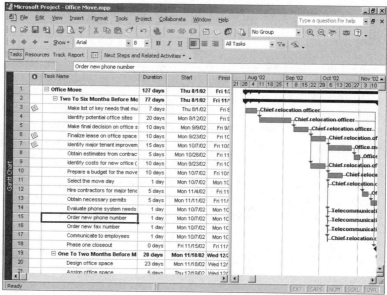

Figure 4-4. A Gantt chart shows task information in the sheet portion of the view, and the corresponding bar graph shows the task's duration, start and finish dates, and task relationships.

Table 4-1 describes the Microsoft Project Gantt charts.

Table 4-1. Microsoft Project Gantt Charts

Type of Gantt chart	How you can use it
Bar Rollup (task view)	View summary tasks with labels for all subtasks. Use the Bar Rollup view with the Rollup_Formatting macro to see all tasks concisely labeled on summary Gantt bars. For more information about macros, see Chapter 27, "Automating Your Work with Macros."
Detail Gantt (task view)	View tasks and associated information in a sheet and slack and slippage for tasks over time in a bar graph on a time-scale. Use the Detail Gantt to check how far a task can slip without affecting other tasks. For more information about adjusting the schedule, see Chapter 9, "Checking and Adjusting the Project Plan."
Gantt Chart (task view)	View tasks and associated information in a sheet, and tasks and durations over time in a bar graph on a timescale. Use the Gantt Chart to enter and schedule a list of tasks. This is the view that appears by default when you first start Microsoft Project. For more information about starting new projects, see "Creating a New Project Plan" on page 51.
Leveling Gantt (task view)	View tasks, task delays, and slack in a sheet, and the before and after effects of the Microsoft Project leveling feature. Use the Leveling Gantt to check the amount of task delay caused by leveling. For more information about leveling, see "Balancing Resource Workloads" on page 251.
Milestone Date Rollup (task view)	View summary tasks with labels for all subtasks. Use the Milestone Date Rollup view with the Rollup_Formatting macro to see all tasks concisely labeled with milestone marks and dates on summary Gantt bars. For more information about macros, see Chapter 27, "Automating Your Work with Macros."
Milestone Rollup (task view)	View summary tasks with labels for all subtasks. Use the Milestone Rollup view with the Rollup_Formatting macro to see all tasks concisely labeled with milestone marks on the summary Gantt bars. For more information about macros, see Chapter 27, "Automating Your Work with Macros."

(continued)

Chapter 4

Table 4-1. *(continued)*

Type of Gantt chart	How you can use it
Multiple Baselines Gantt (task view)	View different colored Gantt bars for the first three baselines (Baseline, Baseline1, and Baseline2) on summary tasks and subtasks in the chart portion of the view. Use the Multiple Baselines Gantt to review and compare the first three baselines you saved for your project. For more information about baselines, see Chapter 10, "Saving a Baseline and Updating Progress."
PA_Expected Gantt (task view)	View your schedule's expected scenario based on durations calculated from PERT analysis. For more information about schedules, see Chapter 5, "Scheduling Tasks."
PA_Optimistic Gantt (task view)	View your schedule's best-case scenario based on durations durations calculated from PERT analysis. For more information about durations, see "Setting Task Durations" on page 128.
PA_Pessimistic Gantt (task view)	View your schedule' worst-case scenario, based on durations calculated from PERT analysis. For more information about durations, see "Setting Task Durations" on page 128.
Tracking Gantt (task view)	View tasks and task information in a sheet, and a chart showing a baseline and scheduled Gantt bars for each task. Use the Tracking Gantt to compare the baseline schedule with the actual schedule. For more information about baselines, see Chapter 10, "Saving a Baseline and Updating Progress."

You can change the look and content of bars on a Gantt chart. You can:

- Change the pattern, color, and shape of the Gantt bar for a selected task.
- Change the text accompanying the Gantt bar for a selected task.
- Change the format and text for all Gantt bars of a particular type.
- Change the text style for all Gantt bars of a particular type.
- Change the layout of links and bars on a Gantt chart.
- Change the gridlines in the view.

> For more information about making these changes, see "Formatting a Gantt Chart View" on page 589.
>
> To change the timescale in a Gantt Chart, see "Working with Timescales" later in this chapter.
>
> You can also change the content or look of the sheet portion of a Gantt chart. For details, see "Working with Sheet Views" later in this chapter.
>
> You can print views with the content and format you set up in the Microsoft Project window. For more information, see "Setting Up and Printing Views" on page 340.

Working with Network Diagrams

Network diagrams are a special type of graph view that presents each task and associated task information in a separate box, or *node*. The nodes are connected by lines that represent task relationships. The resulting diagram is a flowchart of the project. Network Diagram views (see Figure 4-5) are also referred to as PERT (Program Evaluation and Review Technique) charts.

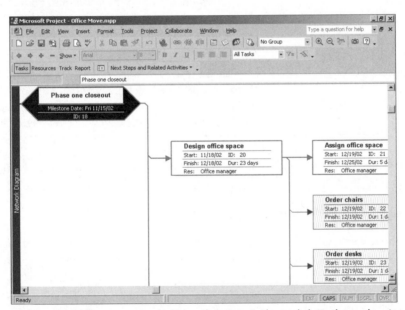

Figure 4-5. You can enter, edit, and review tasks and their dependencies in the Network Diagram view.

Table 4-2 describes the Microsoft Project network diagram views.

Table 4-2. Microsoft Project Network Diagram Views

Type of Network diagram	How you can use it
Descriptive Network Diagram (task view)	View all tasks and task dependencies. Use the Descriptive Network Diagram to create and fine-tune your schedule in a flowchart format. This view is similar to the regular Network Diagram, but the nodes are larger and provide more details. For more information about task dependencies, see "Establishing Task Dependencies" on page 139.
Network Diagram (task view)	Enter, edit, and review all tasks and task dependencies. Use the Network Diagram to create and fine-tune your schedule in a flowchart format. For more information about task dependencies, see "Establishing Task Dependencies" on page 139.
Relationship Diagram (task view)	View the predecessors and successors of a single selected task. In a large project, use this task view to focus on the task dependencies of a specific task. For more information about task dependencies, see "Establishing Task Dependencies" on page 139.

To learn about modifying the content or format of a Network diagram, see "Customizing Views" on page 586.

Working with Graph Views

Graph views are views that present project information with some type of pictorial representation that more readily communicates the data (see Figure 4-6).

Table 4-3 describes the Microsoft Project graph views.

Table 4-3. Microsoft Project Graph Views

Type of graph view	How you can use it
Calendar (task view)	View tasks and durations for a specific week or range of weeks in a monthly calendar format (see Figure 4-7). For more information about tasks, see Chapter 5, "Scheduling Tasks."
Resource Graph (resource view)	View resource allocation, cost, or work over time for a single resource or group of resources at a time. Information is displayed in a column graph format (see Figure 4-6). For more information about the project plan, see Chapter 9, "Checking and Adjusting the Project Plan."

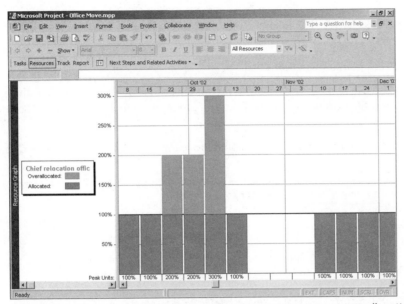

Figure 4-6. One use of the Resource Graph is to review resource allocation levels.

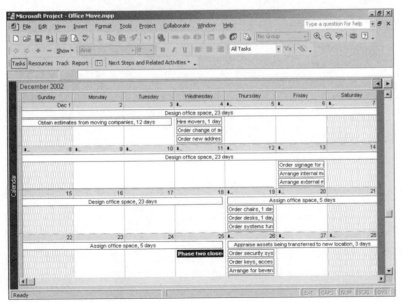

Figure 4-7. In the Calendar view, you can quickly see which tasks are scheduled on particular days, weeks, or months.

You can change the type of information being shown in the Resource Graph. To do this, follow these steps:

1 Click Format, Details.

2 The Details submenu lists the various categories of information that the Resource Graph can chart. These categories include Work, Percent Allocation, and Cost.

3 Click the category of information you want charted on the Resource Graph.

> For information about modifying the format of the Resource Graph or Calendar view, see "Customizing Views" on page 586.

Working with Sheet Views

Sheet views are spreadsheet-type views that are divided into columns and rows, and in which each individual field is contained in a cell (see Figure 4-8).

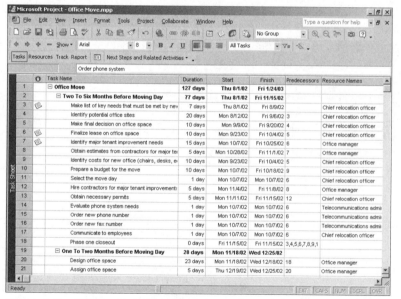

Figure 4-8. Use the Task Sheet to enter tasks and durations, and to review calculated start and finish dates.

The Microsoft Project sheet views are described in Table 4-4.

Table 4-4. Microsoft Project Sheet Views

Type of sheet view	How you can use it
PA_PERT Entry Sheet (task view)	Enter your schedule's best-case, expected-case, and worst-case scenarios for a task's duration in preparation of calculating the most probable duration using PERT analysis. This analysis helps you consider and reconcile disparities between different task estimates. For more information about durations, see "Setting Task Durations" on page 128.
Resource Sheet (resource view)	Enter, edit, and review resource information in a spreadsheet format. For more information about resources, see Chapter 6, "Setting Up Resources in the Project."
Task Sheet (task view)	Enter, edit, and review task information in a spreadsheet format. For more information about starting new projects, see "Creating a New Project Plan" on page 51.

For information about modifying the content or format of a sheet view, see "Customizing Views" on page 586.

Working with Usage Views

Usage views are combination views in which the left side is a sheet view and the right side is a timesheet. With the timescale, the timesheet can show work, cost, availability, and other data broken out by time, or *timephased* (see Figure 4-9).

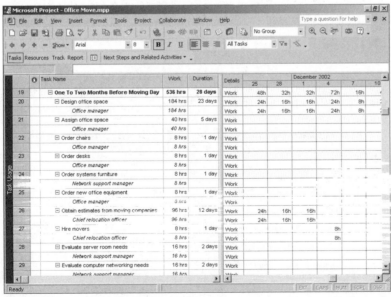

Figure 4-9. Display the Task Usage view to review assignments by task.

The Microsoft Project usage views are described in Table 4-5.

Table 4-5. Microsoft Project Usage Views

Type of usage view...	How you can use it
Resource Usage (assignment view)	Review, enter, and edit assignments by resource. In the sheet portion of the Resource Usage view, each resource is listed with the tasks to which they're assigned. In the timesheet portion of the view, information such as work or costs for the resource and the assignment is listed according to the timescale, for example, by week or by month. For more information about resource assignments, see Chapter 7, "Assigning Resources to Tasks."
Task Usage (assignment view)	Review, enter, and edit assignments by task. In the sheet portion of the Task Usage view, each task is listed with the resources that are assigned to it. In the timesheet portion of the view, information such as work or costs for the task and the assignment is listed according to the timescale, for example, by day or by week. For more information about resource assignments, see Chapter 7, "Assigning Resources to Tasks."

Because the timesheet portion of the usage views breaks down information from certain fields and from specific time periods, there are three subcategories to the major field categories of tasks, resources, and assignments. These subcategories are:

- Task-timephased
- Resource-timephased
- Assignment-timephased

You can review task-timephased and assignment-timephased fields in the timesheet portion of the Task Usage view. You can review resource-timephased and assignment-timephased fields in the timesheet portion of the Resource Usage view.

You can also change the timephased fields shown in the timesheet portion of a usage view. To do this, follow these steps:

1 Click Format, Details.

2   The Details menu lists the different timephased fields that the timesheet portion of the usage view can display, for example, Actual Work, Baseline Work, and Cost. Any fields currently displayed are noted with a check mark.

3   Click the field you want to add to the timesheet. Another row of timephased information is added to the timesheet for each task.

4   To remove a row of information from the timesheet, click Format, Details, and then click the item you want to remove.

For information about modifying the format of a usage view, see "Customizing Views" on page 586.

Working with Forms

Forms are specialized views that include text boxes and grids in which you can enter and review information in a way similar to a dialog box (see Figure 4-10).

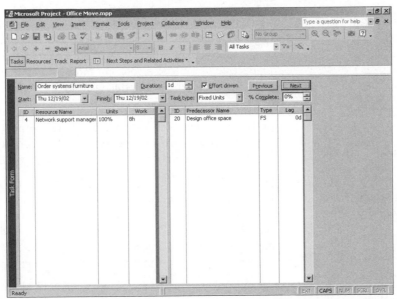

Figure 4-10. This Task Form shows fundamental information about the task, along with information about assigned resources and predecessor tasks.

The Microsoft Project forms are described in Table 4-6.

Table 4-6. Microsoft Project Forms

Type of form	How you can use it
Resource Form (resource view)	Enter, edit, and review all resource, task, and schedule information about a selected resource, one resource at a time. The grid area can show information about the resource's schedule, cost, or work on assigned tasks. It is most useful when used as part of a combination view. For more information about resource assignments, see Chapter 7, "Assigning Resources to Tasks."
Resource Name Form (resource view)	Enter, edit, and review the selected resource's schedule, cost, or work on assigned tasks. The Resource Name Form is a simplified version of the Resource Form. For more information about resource assignments, see Chapter 7, "Assigning Resources to Tasks."
Task Details Form (task view)	Enter, edit, and review detailed tracking and scheduling information about a selected task, one task at a time. The grid area can show information about assigned resources, predecessors, and successors. For more information about tasks, see Chapter 5, "Scheduling Tasks."
Task Form (task view)	Enter, edit, and review information about a selected task, one task at a time. The grid area can show information about the task's assigned resources, predecessors, and successors. For more information about tasks, see Chapter 5, "Scheduling Tasks."
Task Name Form (task view)	Enter, edit, and review the selected task's assigned resources, predecessors, and successors. The Task Name Form is a simplified version of the Task Form. For more information about tasks, see Chapter 5, "Scheduling Tasks."

You can change the categories of information shown in a form view. To do this, follow these steps:

1 On the View menu, click More Views to display the More Views dialog box. In the dialog box, click the form you want to view. Click the Apply button.

2 Right-click the blank area on the form. A shortcut menu appears, which shows different types of information that can be shown in the form. A check mark appears next to the information currently shown in the form.

3 Click the information you want to display in the form. You can choose only one item from the shortcut menu at a time.

Working with Combination Views

Combination views are groupings of two views in a split screen. Typically, the information in one portion of the split screen controls the content in the other portion (see Figure 4-11).

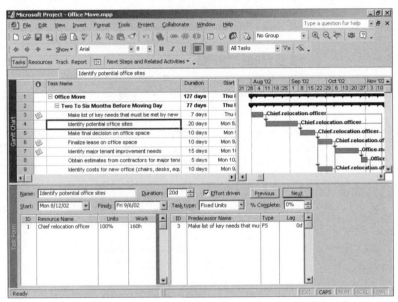

Figure 4-11. When you click a task in the upper Gantt Chart portion of the Task Entry view, the task, assignment, and predecessor information for that selected task appear in the lower Task Form portion of the view.

The other Microsoft Project combination views are described in Table 4-7 on the next page.

99

Table 4-7. **Microsoft Project Combination Views**

Type of combination view	How you can use it
Task Entry (task view)	Enter, edit, and review detailed information about the task selected in the Gantt Chart. The Gantt Chart appears in the upper portion of the view, and the Task Form appears in the lower portion. The information shown in the Task Form corresponds with the task selected in the Gantt Chart. For more information about tasks, see Chapter 5, "Scheduling Tasks."
Resource Allocation (resource view)	Review and resolve resource overallocations. The Resource Usage view appears in the upper portion of the view, and the Leveling Gantt appears in thelower portion. The information shown in the Leveling Gantt corresponds with the resource or assignment selected in the Resource Usage view. For more information about leveling, see "Balancing Resource Workloads" on page 253.

You can create a combination view by simply splitting the view. For example, if you split the Gantt Chart view, the Task Form appears in the lower pane, giving you the Task Entry view. If you split the Resource Sheet, the Resource Form appears in the lower pane.

The split bar is located in the lower-right corner of the Microsoft Project window, just below the vertical scroll bar. To split a view, drag the split bar up to about the middle of the view, or wherever you want the split to occur. Or click Window, Split.

To remove the split and return to a single view, double-click the split bar. Or click Window, Remove Split.

To modify a combination view, simply modify one component of the combination view as if it were in its own view.

For more information about views, see "Customizing Views" on page 586.

Troubleshooting

You can't get the combination view to be a single view again

In a combination view such as Task Entry or Resource Allocation, one of the two views always has focus, that is, it's the currently active view. When you switch to another view, only the active view switches.

Before switching to another view, make the combination view a single view. To do this, click Window, Remove Split. Or double-click the split bar—the gray dividing bar between the two views. Then switch to the other view.

newfeature!
Working with Timescales

Many Microsoft Project views, including Gantt charts and usage views, use a timescale to indicate time in the project. The timescale appears above the chart or timesheet area of a view. You can display up to three timescales (see Figure 4-12), each timescale in a *tier*. The highest tier shows the broadest period of time, and the lowest tier shows the most detailed period of time. For example, you can show days within weeks within months, or you can show weeks within quarters. The default timescale is two tiers: days within weeks.

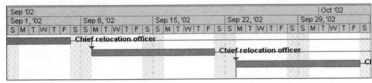

Figure 4-12. You can zoom your timescales up or down while you're working.

To set your timescale options, follow these steps:

1 Show a view that contains a timescale, for example, the Gantt Chart, the Task Usage, or the Resource Graph.

2 Click Format, Timescale. The Timescale dialog box appears.

3 The Timescale dialog box has four tabs: Top Tier, Middle Tier, Bottom Tier, and Non-Working Time. The Middle Tier tab is displayed by default. In the Show box, click the number of timescale tiers you want to display (one, two, or three).

4 In the Units box, specify the time unit you want to display at the middle tier, for example, quarters, months, or weeks.

Chapter 4

5 In the Label box, click the format in which you want to display the time unit, for example, Mon Jan 28, '02; Mon January 28; or Mon 1/28.

6 If you chose to display more than one tier, click the Top Tier and/or Bottom Tier tabs and repeat steps 4 and 5.

Using Tables

Any sheet view, including the sheet portion of any Gantt chart or usage view, has a default table defined for it. You can change the table for these types of views. Or you can modify an existing table to add, change, or remove the fields in the columns.

Views that use Tables

Table 4-8 shows the default table for each view.

Table 4-8. Default Table Views

View	Default table	View	Default table
Bar Rollup	Rollup Table	PA_PERT	PA_PERT Entry Entry Sheet
Detail Gantt	Delay	PA_Pessimistic Gantt	PA_Pessimistic Case
Gantt Chart	Entry	Resource Allocation	Usage (Resource Usage view) Delay (Leveling Gantt view)
Leveling Gantt	Delay	Resource Sheet	Entry
Milestone Date Rollup	Entry	Resource Usage	Usage
Milestone Rollup	Rollup Table	Task Entry	Entry
Multiple Baselines Gantt	Entry	Task Sheet	Entry
PA_Expected Gantt	PA_Expected Case	Task Usage	Usage
PA_Optimistic Gantt	PA_Optimistic Case	Tracking Gantt	Entry

102

Table 4-9 lists a description of the task tables and their default fields.

Table 4-9. Task Tables and Their Default Fields

Information displayed	Default fields included
Baseline	
Specific baseline values reflecting the schedule as originally planned.	ID, Task Name, Duration, Baseline Start, Baseline Finish, Baseline Work, and Baseline Cost
Constraint Dates	
The specific task constraint types for each task, along associated dates if applicable. You can use these fields to review or change the constraint type and date.	ID, Task Name, Duration, Constraint Type, Constraint Date
Cost	
Cost information for each task, helping you analyze various types of cost calculations.	ID, Task Name, Fixed Cost, Fixed Cost Accrual, Total Cost, Baseline, Variance, Actual, and Remaining
Delay	
Information to help you determine how long it will take to complete your tasks given the resources you have and the amount of time they have for a given task.	ID, Indicators, Task Name, Leveling Delay, Duration, Start, Finish, Successors, and Resources
Earned Value	
Earned value information that compares the relationship between work and costs based on a status date.	ID, Task Name, BCWS, BCWP, ACWP, SV, CV, EAC, BAC, and VAC.
Earned Value Cost Indicators	
Earned value information, including the ratio of budgeted to actual costs of work performed.	ID, Task Name, BCWS, BCWP, CV, CV%, CPI, BAC, EAC, VAC, and TCPI.

newfeature!

(continued)

Table 4-9. *(continued)*

Information displayed	Default fields included
Earned Value Schedule Indicators	
Earned value information, including the ratio of work performed to work scheduled.	ID, Task Name, BCWS, BCWP, SV, SV%, and SPI.
Entry	
The most fundamental information regarding tasks. This table is most useful for entering and viewing the most essential task information.	ID, Indicators, Task Name, Duration, Start, Finish, Predecessors, Resource Names, and % Complete.
Export	
A wide range of fields from which to export task fields to other applications.	ID, Unique ID, Task Name, Duration, Type, Outline Level, Baseline Duration, Predecessors, Start, Finish, Early Start, Early Finish, Late Start, Late Finish, Free Slack, Total Slack, Leveling Delay, % Complete, Actual Start, Actual Finish, Baseline Start, Baseline Finish, Constraint Type, Constraint Date, Stop, Resume, Created, Work, Baseline Work, Actual Work, Cost, Fixed Cost, Baseline Cost, Actual Cost, Remaining Cost, WBS, Priority, Milestone, Summary, Rollup, Text1–10, Cost1–3, Duration1–3, Flag1–10, Marked, Number1–5, Subproject File, Contact, Start1–5, and Finish1–5.
Hyperlink	
Hyperlink information to associate linked shortcuts with your tasks.	ID, Indicators, Task Name, Hyperlink, Address, and SubAddress.
PA_Expected Case	
Expected scheduling information based on PERT analysis.	ID, Indicators, Task Name, Expected Duration, Expected Start, and Expected Finish.
PA_Optimistic Case	
The best-case scheduling information based on PERT analysis.	ID, Indicators, Task Name, Optimistic Duration, Optimistic Start, and Optimistic Finish.
PA_PERT Entry	
The most probable duration information for a project based on PERT analysis.	ID, Task Name, Duration, Optimistic Duration, Expected Duration, and Pessimistic Duration.

newfeature!

Table 4-9. *(continued)*

Information displayed	Default fields included
PA_Pessimistic Case	
The worst-case scheduling information based on PERT analysis.	ID, Indicators, Task Name, Pessimistic Duration, Pessimistic Start, and Pessimistic Finish.
Rollup Table	
General task information that appears after you run the Rollup_Formatting macro.	ID, indicators, Task Name, Duration, Text Above, Start, Finish, Predecessors, Resource Names.
Schedule	
Detailed scheduling information, which can help you see when a task is scheduled to begin and how late it can actually begin without jeopardizing the project's finish date.	ID, Task Name, Start, Finish, Late Start, Late Finish, Free Slack, and Total Slack.
Summary	
Overview project information to analyze durations, dates, progress, and costs.	ID, Task Name, Duration, Start, Finish, % Complete, Cost, and Work.
Tracking	
Actual progress and cost information, as contrasted with scheduled or baseline information.	ID, Task Name, Actual Start, Actual Finish, % Complete, Physical % Complete, Actual Duration, Remaining Duration, Actual Cost, and Actual Work.
Usage	
The most fundamental task schedule information.	ID, Indicators, Task Name, Work, Duration, Start, and Finish.
Variance	
Gaps between baseline start and finish dates and the actual start and finish dates, enabling a comparison between your original planned schedule and actual performance.	ID, Task Name, Start, Finish, Baseline Start, Baseline Finish, Start Variance, and Finish Variance.
Work	
A variety of measurements for analyzing the level of effort for each task.	ID, Task Name, Work, Baseline, Variance, Actual, Remaining, and % Work Complete.

Chapter 4

Table 4-10 lists a description of all resource tables and their default fields.

Table 4-10. Resource Tables and Their Default Fields

Information displayed	Default fields included
Cost	
Cost information about resources in a project.	ID, Resource Name, Cost, Baseline Cost, Cost Variance, Actual Cost, and Remaining.
Earned Value	
Earned value information that compares the relationship between work and costs based on a status date.	ID, Resource Name, BCWS, BCWP, ACWP, SV, CV, EAC, BAC, and VAC.
Entry	
The most essential information regarding resources. This table is most useful for entering and viewing fundamental resource information.	ID, Indicators, Resource Name, Type, Material Label, Initials, Group, Maximum Units, Standard Rate, Overtime Rate, Cost/Use, Accrue At, Base Calendar, Code, and Material.
Entry – Material Resources	
The most essential information about consumable material resources.	ID, Indicators, Resource Name, Type, Material Label, Initials, Group, Standard Rate, Cost/Use, Accrue At, and Code.
Entry – Work Resources	
The most essential information about work (people and equipment) resources.	ID, Indicators, Resource Name, Type, Initials, Group, Maximum Units, Standard Rate, Overtime Rate, Cost/Use, Accrue At, Base Calendar, and Code.
Export	
A wide range of fields from which to export task fields to other applications.	ID, Unique ID, Resource Name, Initials, Maximum Units, Standard Rate, Overtime Rate, Cost Per Use, Accrue At, Cost, Baseline Cost, Actual Cost, Work, Baseline Work, Actual Work, Overtime Work, Group, Code, Text1–5, and Email Address.
Hyperlink	
Hyperlink information to associate linked shortcuts with your resources.	ID, Indicators, Resource Name, Hyperlink, Address, and SubAddress.

Table 4-10. *(continued)*

Information displayed	Default fields included
Summary	
Overview resource information.	ID, Resource Name, Group, Maximum Units, Peak, Standard Rate, Overtime Rate, Cost, and Work.
Usage	
The most essential assignment scheduling information.	ID, Indicators, Resource Name, and Work.
Work	
A variety of methods for analyzing work, or the level of effort, for resources and their assigned tasks.	ID, Resource Name, % Complete, Work, Overtime, Baseline, Variance, Actual, and Remaining.

Changing the Table in a View

To switch to a different table, follow these steps:

1 Display the view containing the table you want to change. This could be the Task Sheet, Resource Sheet, Gantt Chart, Task Usage view, and so on.

2 Click View, Table.

3 If the table is listed on the submenu, click it. If the table is not listed on the submenu, click More Tables (see Figure 4-13), and then double-click the table you want.

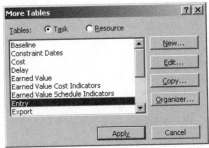

Figure 4-13. The More Tables dialog box contains the full list of built-in tables.

The table is replaced by the table you clicked.

Chapter 4

> **note** If a task view is currently displayed, task tables are listed. If a resource view is currently displayed, resource tables are listed. You cannot apply a resource table to a task view, and vice versa.

Modifying a Table

Suppose the Entry task table provides all the information you need except baseline values. You can easily add another column to any table. You can just as easily remove superfluous columns. There are also certain changes you can make to the columns themselves.

> **note** When working with columns in a table, you're working with fields in your project database. Fields are discussed in more detail in "Using Fields," later in this chapter.

To add a column to a table, follow these steps:

1 Display the view and table to which you want to add a new column.

2 Right-click the column heading to the left of where you want the new column to be inserted, and then click Insert Column. The Column Definition dialog box appears.

> **tip** You can also open the Column Definition dialog box (see Figure 4-14) by clicking the column heading and then clicking Insert, Column.

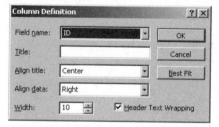

Figure 4-14. You can also open the Column Definition dialog box by clicking a column heading and then pressing the Insert key.

3 In the Field Name box, click the field representing the information you want in the new column.

> **tip** With the Field Name box selected, you can just type the first letter of the field's name to scroll close to its name in the list.

Troubleshooting

The field you're looking for is not in the Field Name list

When you display a task view and table, only task fields are listed in the Column Definition dialog box. Likewise, when you display a resource view and table, only resource fields are listed. Assignment fields are available only in the Task Usage and Resource Usage views.

To remove a column from a table, follow these steps:

1 Display the view and table from which you want to remove a column.

2 Right-click the heading of the column you want to remove, and then click Hide Column.

tip **Remove a column**

You can also remove a column by selecting the column heading and then clicking Edit, Hide Column. Or simply select the column heading and press the Delete key.

The column is removed. The field still exists in the database, however, and can be displayed again in this or other tables.

tip **Hide a column temporarily**

You can also hide a column in your table while keeping it in place. Position your mouse pointer over the right edge of the column heading border. The mouse pointer changes to a black crosshair. Drag the right border past the column's left border. The column disappears.

To show the column again, position your mouse pointer on the edge where your column is hidden. Drag to the right, and your column appears again.

To use this method, you need to know where you hid the column, because there's no visual indication that it's there.

You can change the title of the column to something other than the actual field name. You can also modify the column text alignment and the column width. To modify a column, follow these steps:

1 Display the view and table containing the column you want to modify.

2 Double-click the heading of the column you want to change. The Column Definition dialog box appears.

109

3 To change the field information appearing in the column, click the field you want in the Field Name list.

4 To change the title of the column heading, type a new title in the Title box.

5 Use the Align Title list to change the alignment of the column title.

6 Use the Align Data list to change the alignment of the field information itself.

7 Click a number in the Width box to change the column width.

---

tip   **Change the column width by dragging**

You can also change the column width directly on the table. Click the column's heading to select the column. Then move the mouse pointer to the right edge of the column until the pointer changes to a black crosshair. Drag to the right to widen the column. Drag to the left to make the column narrower. Double-click the edge to widen the column to the same size as the longest entry in the column.

You can move a column to another location in the table simply by dragging. To move a column, follow these steps:

1 Display the view and table containing the column you want to move.

2 Click the heading of the column you want to move.

3 With the black crosshair mouse pointer over the column heading, drag to the new location for the column. As you drag, a gray line moves with the mouse pointer to indicate where the column will be inserted when you release the mouse button.

---

note In addition to adding and removing columns in existing tables, you can also create entirely new tables. For more information about tables, see "Customizing Tables" on page 610.

Using Fields

Fields are the smallest piece of data in the vast collection of information that makes up your project database. For example, one task comprises a single record in this database. This record consists of a number of task fields, such as the task name, duration, start date, finish date, assigned resource, deadline, and more.

Whether you see them in a view or not, there are numerous fields for your tasks, resources, and assignments, as well as the project as a whole.

For more information about the project database, see Chapter 32, "Working with Microsoft Project Data."

Some fields are entered by you, such as task name and duration. Other fields are calculated for you by Microsoft Project, such as start date, finish date, and total cost. Still other fields can either be entered by you or calculated by Microsoft Project.

You're already familiar with the different field categories:

- Task fields
- Resource fields
- Assignment fields
- Task-timephased fields
- Resource-timephased fields
- Assignment-timephased fields

The timephased fields break down field information, such as work, costs, and availability, by time periods. This gives you more information you can work with in your project. In the Task Usage and Resource Usage views, for example, you can see task cost by day or resource work by week. You can break either of those down further into the component assignments. The timephased fields also give you more tools for analysis, through earned value calculations.

For more information about earned value analysis, see "Analyzing Progress and Costs Using Earned Value" on page 381.

Another way that fields are categorized is by *data type*. The data type indicates how a field can be used, for example, as a currency-type field, or a date-type field. The field data types are:

Currency. Information is expressed as a cost.

Date. Information is expressed as a date.

Duration. Information is expressed as a span of time.

Enumerated. Information is selected from a list of predefined choices.

Indicator. Information is shown as graphical indicators about a task, resource, or assignment.

Integer. Information is expressed as a whole number.

Outline code. Information is defined with a custom tag for tasks or resources that enables you to show a hierarchy of tasks in your project.

Percentage/Number. Information is displayed as a value that can be expressed as either a percentage or decimal number, such as 100 percent or 1.00.

Text. Information is expressed as unrestricted characters of text.

Yes/No. Information is set to either Yes or No, that is, a Boolean or True/False value.

Chapter 4

Fields make up your project database, the whole of which you might never view. Fields are also seen throughout your project plan. You see field information in:

- Columns in a table.
- Rows in a timesheet.
- Information in a network diagram node.
- Gantt bars and associated text in a Gantt chart.
- Fields in a form view.
- Fields in a dialog box.

Some of these, like columns in a table and rows in a timesheet, you can change to suit your needs. Others, like the fields in a form view or dialog box, are fixed.

newfeature!
You can create your own custom fields and add them to tables in your views. There are custom fields you can define for currency, dates, durations, finish dates, start dates, text, numbers, outline codes, and more. With Microsoft Project Professional, there's an additional set of enterprise custom fields as well, so an enterprise can design a robust set of fields that standardizes how the enterprise manages projects.

> For more information about defining custom fields, see "Customizing Fields" on page 613. For a complete list of fields, see Appendix B, "Field Reference."

Learn More about Microsoft Project Fields

You can immediately get comprehensive information about any field in a table. Position your mouse pointer over the column heading, and a ToolTip pops up containing a link to online Help for this field. Click the link, and a Help topic appears.

Duration	↓ Start	Finish
10 days	Start	ri 9/20/02
10 days	M Help on Start	ri 10/4/02
15 days	Mon 10/7/02	Fri 10/25/02

You can also get lists of field categories and find information about fields by following these steps:

1 Click Help, Reference. Click the Fields Reference link.

2 At the bottom of the Help pane, click one of the links, for example, See A List Of Field Types. Several types of fields are listed.

3 Click one of the field types, for example, Duration Fields. A comprehensive list of fields of that type appears (see Figure 4-15).

4 Click a field name, and its Help topic appears (see Figure 4-16).

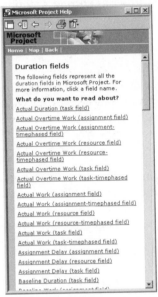

Figure 4-15. This Help topic provides links for all duration fields throughout Microsoft Project.

Figure 4-16. The Fields Reference Help topics each contain comprehensive information about the field.

These online Help topics about the fields contain the following information:

- Data type (duration, cost, text, and so on)
- Entry type (entered, calculated, or both)
- Description (a general overview of the field's function)
- How Calculated (for calculated fields)
- Best Uses (the purpose of the field)
- Example (how this field might be used to facilitate a project plan)
- Remarks (any additional information)

Chapter 4

113

Rearranging Your Project Information

The ability to switch from one view to another, to switch tables in a sheet view, and to add or remove fields in a view gives you tremendous versatility in how you see your project information. You can take it a step further by sorting, grouping, and filtering the information in a view.

Sorting Project Information

By sorting information in a table, you can arrange it in alphabetical or numerical order by a particular field. For example, you might sort your tasks by start date so you can see tasks that are due to start next week. Or you might sort your tasks by duration so you can see the tasks with the longest durations and how you might break them up and bring in the project finish date.

You can also sort resources. For example, in the Resource Sheet, you might have originally entered all resources as they came on board. But it might be easier for you to manage if they were in alphabetical order. You can easily sort by the resource name. Better yet, you can sort by department or group name, and then by resource name.

To sort items in a sheet view, follow these steps:

1 Display the sheet view whose information you want to sort.

2 Click Project, Sort.

3 In the submenu that appears, commonly used sort fields are presented. For example, if you're working in the Gantt Chart with the default Entry table applied, you can sort by Start Date, Finish Date, Priority, Cost, or ID. If you're working in the Resource Sheet with the default Entry table applied, you can sort by Cost, Name, or ID.

4 If you want to sort by a different field than what's presented in the submenu, click Sort By. The Sort dialog box appears (see Figure 4-17).

5 Under Sort By, click the name of the field you want to sort by, and then specify whether you want the sort to be ascending (lowest to highest) or descending (highest to lowest). If you want to sort within the sort, add another field in one or both of the Then By boxes.

6 Make sure that the Permanently Renumber check box is cleared. You will likely want to clear this check box in the majority of the cases. However, if you really want this sort to be permanent and you're certain that you won't ever want to return to the original order of the tasks or resources, go ahead and select this check box. The ID numbers for the tasks or resources are changed, and the tasks or resources will be sorted by order of the ID numbers when you don't have any other sort order applied.

7 Click Sort.

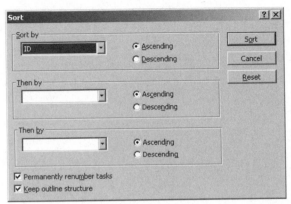

Figure 4-17. Use the Sort dialog box to choose the fields you want to sort by.

InsideOut

If you select the Permanently Renumber Tasks or Permanently Renumber Resources check box for the current sort operation, the check box remains selected for your subsequent sort operation. That's true whether your next sort operation is for resources or tasks. This can be a problem if you want to do a temporary sort—which is likely to be the case most of the time—and you're not in the habit of looking at that check box.

To prevent unwittingly jumbling up your project plan, whenever you do a permanent renumber sort, immediately open the Sort dialog box again, clear the Permanently Renumber check box, and then click Reset.

To return a sorted sheet view to its original order, click Project, Sort, and then click By ID.

Grouping Project Information

Think of grouping as a more sophisticated kind of sorting, in which a graphical layout is applied to the sheet to segregate the groupings you've chosen. For example, suppose you group your task sheet by complete and incomplete tasks. Tasks that are 0 percent complete (not started yet) are grouped first, and marked by a yellow band (see Figure 4-18 on the next page). Tasks that are 1-99 percent complete (in progress) are grouped next, also bounded by a yellow band. Tasks that are 100 percent complete are grouped last.

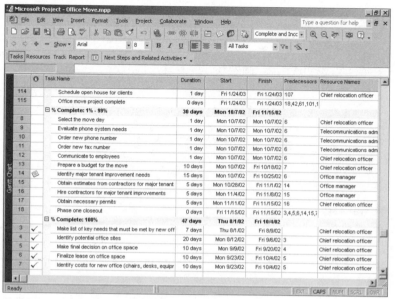

Figure 4-18. Groups graphically separate categories of information in a view.

The grouping band shows the title of the group, for example, Percent Complete: 0% or 100% Complete. Where appropriate, the grouping band also rolls up information summarized from the group, such as total duration for the grouping, the earliest start date for all tasks in the grouping, the latest finish date for all tasks in the grouping, and so on.

Built-in Task Groups

All built-in task groups appear on the Group By submenu on the Project menu when a task view is showing. The following is a complete list of these built-in task groups:

- Complete And Incomplete Tasks
- Constraint Type
- Critical
- Duration
- Duration Then Priority

- Milestones
- Priority
- Priority Keeping Outline Structure
- TeamStatus Pending

You can also group resources in a resource sheet. For example, you might want to group resources by their department or code or by resource type (work or material).

newfeature!

You can also group nodes in the Network Diagram view (see Figure 4-19).

To group task or resource information in a sheet view or Network Diagram, follow these steps:

1 Display the view whose information you want to group.

Built-in Resource Groups

All built-in resource groups appear on the Group By submenu on the Project menu when a resource view is showing. The following is a complete list of these built-in task groups:

- Assignments Keeping Outline Structure
- Complete And Incomplete Resources
- Resource Group
- Response Pending
- Standard Rate
- Work vs. Material Resources

2 Click Project, Group By.

3 In the submenu that appears, click the grouping you want.

To remove a grouping, click Project, Group By, and then click No Group.

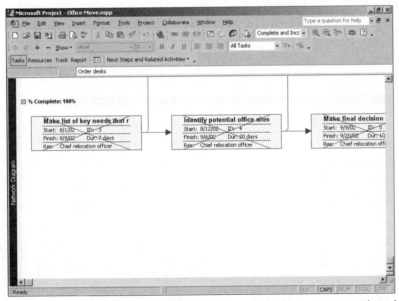

Figure 4-19. Nodes are collected and rearranged when you group them by a particular category.

---

tip **Use the Group By tool on the Standard toolbar**

You can also use the Group By tool on the Standard toolbar. With a sheet view displayed, click the grouping you want to apply.

When you want to restore the view to its original order, click the arrow in the Group By tool and select No Group.

Chapter 4

> **note** You can customize built-in groups and create entirely new groups as well. You can also group by fields, including custom outline codes that you create. For more information about groups, see "Customizing Groups" on page 620.

Filtering Project Information

When you filter a view, you're excluding information you don't need to see so you can focus on what you do need to see. For example, if you want to see only tasks that use a particular resource so you can more closely analyze the workload, you can apply the Using Resource filter. Or if you're about to attend a status meeting and you want to discuss tasks that are either in progress or not started, you can apply the Incomplete Tasks filter to a task sheet.

Built-in Task Filters

The most commonly used task filters appear on the Filtered For submenu of the Project menu. All built-in filters are accessible in the More Filters dialog box. The following is a complete list of the built-in task filters:

- Completed Tasks
- Confirmed
- Cost Greater Than
- Cost Overbudget
- Created After
- Critical
- Date Range
- In Progress Tasks
- Incomplete Tasks
- Late/Overbudget Tasks Assigned To
- Linked Fields
- Milestones
- Resource Group
- Should Start By
- Should Start/Finish By
- Slipped/Late Progress

- Slipping Tasks
- Summary Tasks
- Task Range
- Tasks With A Task Calendar Assigned
- Tasks With Attachments
- Tasks With Deadlines
- Tasks With Estimated Durations
- Tasks With Fixed Dates
- Tasks/Assignments With Overtime
- Top Level Tasks
- Unconfirmed
- Unstarted Tasks
- Update Needed
- Using Resource In Date Range
- Using Resource
- Work Overbudget

You can also apply filters to a resource sheet. If you want to examine all resources that are running over budget, for example, you can apply the Cost Overbudget filter. Or if you want to see only your material resources, you can apply the Resources – Material filter to a resource sheet.

Built-in Resource Filters

The most commonly used resource filters appear on the Filtered For submenu of the Project menu. All built-in filters are accessible in the More Filters dialog box. The following is a complete list of the built-in resource filters:

- Confirmed Assignments
- Cost Greater Than
- Cost Overbudget
- Date Range
- Group
- In Progress Assignments
- Linked Fields
- Overallocated Resources
- Resource Range
- Resources – Material
- Resources – Work

- Resources With Attachments
- Resources/Assignments With Overtime
- Should Start By
- Should Start/Finish By
- Slipped/Late Progress
- Slipping Assignments
- Unconfirmed Assignments
- Unstarted Assignments
- Work Complete
- Work Incomplete
- Work Overbudget

To filter information in a view, follow these steps:

1 Display the view whose information you want to filter. You can filter information in all views.

2 Click Project, Filtered For.

3 If the filter you want is listed on the submenu, click it. If the filter is not in the submenu, click More Filters, and then find and click it in the More Filters dialog box (see Figure 4-20). Click Apply.

Figure 4-20. The More Filters dialog box lists all built-in filters.

4 Some filters require you to enter more information. For example, if you choose the Should Start/Finish filter, you'll need to enter start and finish dates and click OK.

> **tip** **Apply a highlighting filter**
>
> By default, the filters exclude tasks or resources that do not meet the conditions of the filter. If you prefer, you can have the filter highlight tasks or resources that do meet the filter conditions. Click Project, Filtered For, More Filters. Click the filter you want, and then click the Highlight button.

To remove a filter and show all tasks or all resources again, click Project, Filtered For, and then click All Tasks.

> **tip** **Use the Filter tool on the Formatting toolbar**
>
> You can also use the Filter tool on the Formatting toolbar. Display the view you want to filter, then use the tool to click the filter you want to apply. When finished, click the arrow in the Filter tool and select All Tasks.

Using AutoFilter, you can quickly filter by a value in a particular field. To do this, follow these steps:

AutoFilter

1 Display the sheet view whose information you want to autofilter.

2 On the Formatting toolbar, click AutoFilter. The AutoFilter arrows appear in each column heading in the sheet view.

Duratio	Start	Finish	Predecesso
127 days	Thu 8/1/02	Fri 1/24/03	
77 days	Thu 8/1/02	Fri 11/15/02	
7 days	Thu 8/1/02	Fri 8/9/02	

3 Click the arrow in the column whose information you want to filter by, and then click the value you want to filter by.

For example, suppose you are displaying the Gantt Chart with the Entry table applied. If you want to filter for all tasks scheduled to start next month, click the AutoFilter arrow in the Start column, and then click Next Month.

When an AutoFilter is applied, the column heading changes color.

4 To show all tasks or resources again, click the AutoFilter arrow in the applied column heading, and then click All.

The AutoFilter arrows remain in the column headings for all views throughout your project plan until you turn AutoFilter off. With AutoFilter on, you can always quickly filter tasks or resources in a sheet, which can be very convenient. If you want to turn AutoFilter off, click the AutoFilter button again.

120

Troubleshooting

Some of your project information is missing

It's easy to apply a filter, work with your project information for a while, and then forget that the filter is applied. Then when you look for certain tasks or resources that you know are there, you can't see them.

Check whether a filter is applied. Click the Project menu and look at the Filtered For command. If it says Filtered For: All Tasks or All Resources, you know you're seeing it all. If it says Filtered For: Critical, for example, you know you have a filter applied. Click All Tasks or All Resources to show your information again.

When you have an AutoFilter applied, the Project menu might still indicate that you're showing all tasks or resources. If the Project menu indicates that you're displaying everything but you're not, check whether AutoFilter is on. If it is, review your column headings and find the one that's blue. Click the arrow, and then click All to show all tasks or resources.

note You can customize built-in filters and create entirely new filters as well. For more information, see "Customizing Filters" on page 624.

Learn More about Microsoft Project Views, Tables, Filters, and Groups

In Microsoft Project online Help, you can get more information about all available views, tables, filters, and groups. To do this, follow these steps:

1 Click Help, Reference. Click the Views, Tables, Filters, And Groups link.

2 Click links to select the categories and topics you want.

Arranging Your Microsoft Project Workspace

The more you work with Microsoft Project, the stronger your preferences become about various workspace options. You can make changes to the Microsoft Project workspace that will persist across your working sessions with the project plan as well as to other projects you create. For example, you can reset which view should be the default when you first start a new project plan. You can also show or hide different elements in the default Microsoft Project window. In making these changes, you can set up your Microsoft Project workspace to be the most efficient for your own working methods.

On the other hand, sometimes you need to rearrange the workspace temporarily to accomplish a specific task. For example, sometimes you need to see the same window in two different panes. You can arrange open windows to do this. You can also easily switch among multiple open projects.

Setting Your Default View

The Gantt Chart is the default view that appears whenever you start Microsoft Project or create a new project file. This is because the Gantt Chart is the view used by most project managers. However, if a different view is your favorite, you can make that one the default view. To do this, follow these steps:

1 Click Tools, Options.

2 Click the View tab.

3 In the Default View box, click the name of the view you want as your default view.

InsideOut

Setting the default view does not control the view that appears when you open an existing project plan. When you open an existing project plan, it displays the last view you were working with when you closed it. If you want your project plan to open in a particular view each time, make sure you end your working session in that view.

Showing and Hiding Workspace Elements

Certain workspace elements are displayed by default in your Microsoft Project workspace. To expand your working area, you can hide elements you don't use much. You can still use these elements when you need them. This also frees up more space if you want to add a different element in its place.

Table 4-11 lists the workspace elements you can show or hide, along with the procedure for doing so.

Table 4-11. **Workspace Elements**

Workspace element	How to display or hide it
Project Guide	Click Tools, Options. On the Interface tab, under Project Guide Settings, select or clear the Display Project Guide check box.
View bar	Click View, View Bar.
Online Help	Click Help, Contents And Index. Click the Hide button to hide the left pane of the Help window. Arrange the Microsoft Project window so that the Help window is docked right next to it. To hide the Help window, simply click its Close button.
Toolbars	Click View, Toolbars, and then click the name of the toolbar you want to show or hide.
Entry bar (the bar above the view)	Click Tools, Options. On the View tab, under Show, select or clear the Entry Bar check box.
Scroll bars	Click Tools, Options. On the View tab, under Show, select or clear the Scroll Bars check box.
Status bar (the bar below the view)	Click Tools, Options. On the View tab, under Show, select or clear the Status Bar check box.

Splitting a Window

You might be familiar with the Split function in Microsoft Excel or Microsoft Word, in which you can divide the window into two panes and scroll each pane independently. In Microsoft Project, this function can be useful when you need to see different parts of the same Microsoft Project view. Perhaps you want to see different parts of the same view in a split screen because you're modeling a new section of a project on an existing section further up the view. Or maybe you want to see two different views at the same time.

The problem is that when you split a screen in Microsoft Project (using Window, Split), a form appears, giving you a combination view. You can switch to a different view, but the lower view is designed to show information relevant to the information selected in the upper view.

The solution is to open a second instance of the same window, and then arrange them side by side in your Microsoft Project window. To see two independent panes of your project plan at the same time, follow these steps:

1 Click Window, New Window. In the New Window dialog box, click the name of your project plan, and click OK. This opens a second instance of your project plan. The two instances are marked in the title bar with a "1" and "2," indicating that these are separate windows of the same project. Any changes you make in one window are simultaneously made in the other.

2 Click Window, Arrange All. All open project plans are tiled in your project window (see Figure 4-21).

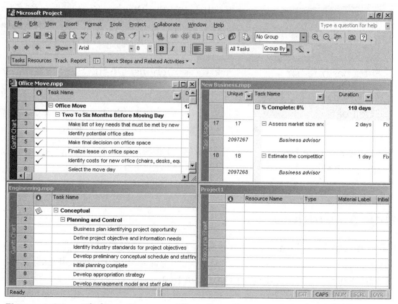

Figure 4-21. Clicking Arrange All makes all open projects visible.

3 If you have other project plans open besides the two you want to work with, either close them or select each one and click Window, Hide. When only the two instances of the project plan are displayed, click Window, Arrange All again. The two open projects are tiled horizontally, one above and the other below (see Figure 4-22). Now you can scroll the two windows independently of each other, and also look at different views independently.

---

tip   **Hide toolbars temporarily to add space**

To give yourself more working space while viewing two project windows at one time, hide a toolbar or two. Click View, Toolbars, and then click the name of the checked toolbar you want to hide. By default, the Standard, Formatting, and Project Guide toolbars are showing.

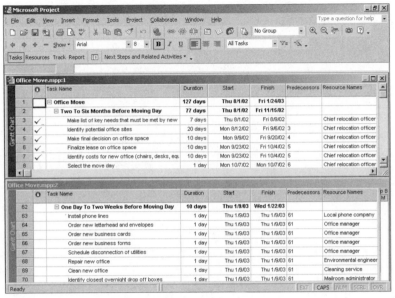

Figure 4-22. You can independently scroll or change views in the two tiled project windows.

Switching among Open Projects

If you have multiple projects open at the same time, there are several ways to switch among them. You can:

- Click the project's button on the Windows taskbar.
- Press Alt+Tab to cycle through all open programs and windows.
- Press Ctrl+F6 to cycle through all open projects.

---

tip   **Multiple Project files on a single Windows taskbar button**

By default, multiple open Microsoft Project files are represented as individual buttons on the Windows taskbar. You can change this so that there's just a single Microsoft Project button on the taskbar, regardless of the number of open project files. Click Tools, Options, and then click the View tab. Clear the Windows In Taskbar check box.

Scheduling Tasks

You've developed your task list, and it's sequenced and outlined. Perhaps it has a work breakdown structure applied. You have a good task list, but you don't have a schedule…yet.

Although there are many knowledge areas (including scope management, cost management, and resource management) that contribute to successful project management, time management is most related to development of your project schedule—your roadmap for completing tasks, handing off deliverables, passing milestones, and finally, achieving the goals of your project in a timely manner.

To develop an accurate and workable schedule that truly reflects how your project will run, you need to:

- Enter task durations.

- Identify the relationships, or dependencies, among tasks.

- Schedule certain tasks to achieve specific dates when necessary.

When you've done these three things, you begin to see the basic outline of a real project schedule. You have not yet added and assigned resources, which further influence the schedule. Nor have you refined the project plan to make the project finish date and costs conform to your requirements. However, at this point, you can start to see how long certain tasks will take and how far into the future the project might run.

To learn about adding and assigning resources, see Chapter 7, "Assigning Resources to Tasks." For information about refining your project, see Chapter 9, "Checking and Adjusting the Project Plan."

There are scheduling cues at your disposal to help keep you focused and on track as you and your team work your way through the project. You can:

- Create reminders that will alert you as deadlines are approaching.

- Add milestones to your schedule as conspicuous markers of producing a deliverable, completing a phase, or achieving another major event in your project.

- Apply a calendar to a task that is independent of the project calendar or the calendars of resources assigned to the task, so that the task can be scheduled independently.

Setting Task Durations

Your task list is entered, sequenced, and outlined (see Figure 5-1).

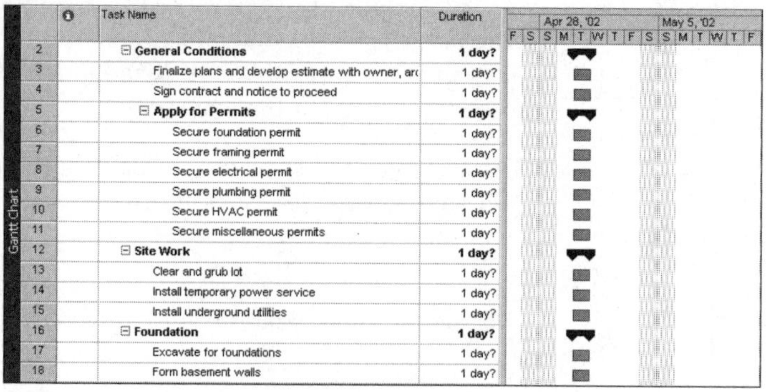

Figure 5-1. Your project schedule displays all tasks starting on the project start date, each with an estimated duration of 1 day.

To create a realistic schedule, you can start by entering the amount of working time you believe each task will take to complete, that is, the task *duration*. As soon as you enter a task, Microsoft Project assigns it an estimated duration of 1 day, just to have something to draw in the Gantt Chart. You can easily change that duration.

Entering accurate durations is very important to creating a reliable project schedule. Microsoft Project uses the duration of each task to calculate the start and finish dates for the task. If you will be assigning resources, the duration is also the basis for the amount of work for each assigned resource.

Developing Reliable Task Durations

As the project manager, you can start by entering a broad duration estimate based on your experience. Then you can refine the estimate by soliciting input from others who are more directly involved or experienced with the sets of tasks. There are four possible sources for developing reliable task durations, as follows:

Team knowledge.   Suppose you're managing a new business startup project and you already have your team in place. The business advisor can provide durations for tasks such as creating a market analysis, researching the competition, and identifying the target market niche. The accountant can provide durations for tasks such as forecasting financial returns, setting up the accounting system, and obtaining needed insurance. Team members ready to work on the project can also provide duration estimates for tasks based on their previous experience as well as their projection of how long they expect the tasks to take for this particular project.

Expert judgment.   If you don't have a team in place yet from whom you can get durations, or if you want reliable input from disinterested professionals in the field, you might call upon experts such as consultants, professional associations, or industry groups. These can help you establish task durations.

Project files.   Similar projects that have been completed can be an excellent source of durations. If Microsoft Project files are available, you can see the initial durations. If the project manager had tracked actuals diligently throughout the life of the project, you'll have valuable information about how long certain tasks actually took, as well as any variances from their planned durations.

Industry standards.   Historical duration information for tasks typical to an industry or discipline is sometimes available commercially through professional or standards organizations. You can adapt such information for tasks and durations to fit the unique requirements of your project.

You might use a combination of these methods to obtain durations for all the tasks in your project. It's often very useful to have durations based on established metrics. For example, knowing both the industry standard for the number of hours it takes to develop certain types of architectural drawings and the number of those drawings you'll need will help you determine a reasonable duration.

Project Management Practices: Building in a Buffer

Building in a duration *buffer* is a method that many project managers use as a contingency against project risk. Some say that the durations should be as "real" and accurate as possible, already taking into account any possible risk. Others say it just isn't realistic to believe you can account for all possible problems in the planning phase. To build in a buffer, also known as *reserve time*, you can do one or more of the following:

- Add a percentage of the duration itself as a buffer to each duration. For example, if a duration estimate is 10 days, adding 10 percent of that as a buffer would make the duration 11 days.
- Add a fixed number of work periods (hours, days, or weeks) to each duration.
- Add a "buffer task" close to the end of the project, with a duration that represents a percentage of the total project duration.
- Add a buffer task close to the end of the project, with a duration that represents a fixed work period, for example, two weeks.

The reserve time can later be reduced or eliminated as more precise information about the project becomes available. For example, suppose you initially entered a duration of 5 days to set up the accounting system. Then later, more concrete information indicates that it will actually take 8 days. You can "transfer" that time from your buffer without pushing out your project finish date.

Understanding Estimated vs. Confirmed Durations

Any value in the Duration field that's followed by a question mark is considered a duration estimate. Technically, all planned durations are only estimates, because you don't know how long a task takes until it's completed and you have an actual duration. However, the question mark indicates what you might consider an "estimate of a duration estimate." Estimated durations are calculated into the schedule the same as confirmed durations. They simply serve as an alert that a duration is still somewhat of a guess.

tip **Turn off estimated durations**

If you have no use for the estimated durations question mark, you can turn it off. Click Tools, Options, and then click the Schedule tab. Clear the Show That Tasks Have Estimated Durations check box. Also, clear the New Tasks Have Estimated Durations check box.

By default, a duration estimate of 1 day is entered for any newly added task (*1d?*). Use this value as a flag to indicate that the duration still needs to be entered for this task. You can also enter a question mark (?) after a duration, for example, *2w?*. Use this value as a flag to indicate that the duration is still under consideration, and might be changed after you receive more information. When you remove the question mark from a duration, the duration is confirmed, that is, you're now confident of this duration.

---

tip **Rearrange your view by estimated durations**

You can sort, group, or filter tasks by whether a task has an estimated or confirmed duration. For more information, see "Rearranging Your Project Information" on page 114.

Entering Durations

You can enter duration in different time period units, as follows:

- Minutes (m or min)
- Hours (h or hr)
- Days (d or dy)
- Weeks (w or wk)
- Months (mo or mon)

---

note Whether you type "h," "hr," or "hour" in your duration entry, by default Microsoft Project enters "hr." You can change which abbreviation of the time unit appears in the Duration field. Click Tools, Options, and then click the Edit tab. In each of the fields under View Options For Time Units, set the abbreviation of the time unit you want to see. This setting applies to that project file only. If you want it to apply to all new projects you create, click the Set As Default button.

You can use different duration units throughout your plan. One task might be set with a duration of 2w, and another task might be set for 3d.

---

tip **Specify the time unit you use most often**

If you don't specify a duration unit, by default Microsoft Project assumes the unit is days, and automatically enters "days" after your duration amount. If you want the default duration unit to be something different, like hours or months, you can change it. Click Tools, Options, and then click the Schedule tab. In the Duration Is Entered In box, select the time unit you want as the default.

Chapter 5

131

To enter a duration, follow these steps:

1. Display the Gantt Chart.
2. In the Duration field for each task, type the duration, for example, *1w* or *4d*.
3. If a duration is an estimate, add a question mark after it, for example, *1w?* or *4d?*.
4. Press Enter. The Gantt bar is drawn to represent the time period for the task (see Figure 5-2). In addition, the Finish field is recalculated for the task. Microsoft Project adds the duration amount to the Start date to calculate the Finish date.

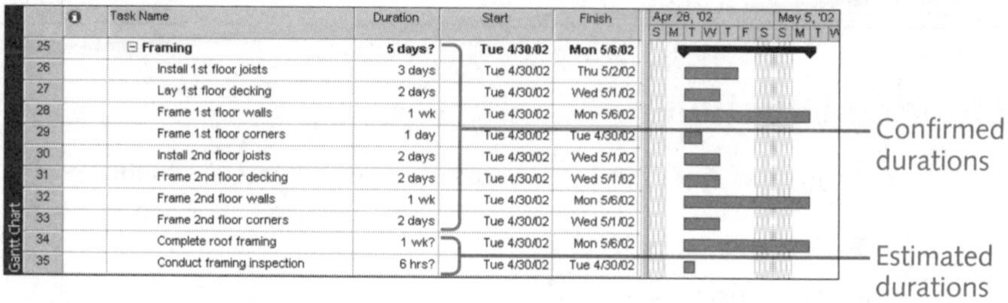

	Task Name	Duration	Start	Finish
25	**Framing**	**5 days?**	**Tue 4/30/02**	**Mon 5/6/02**
26	Install 1st floor joists	3 days	Tue 4/30/02	Thu 5/2/02
27	Lay 1st floor decking	2 days	Tue 4/30/02	Wed 5/1/02
28	Frame 1st floor walls	1 wk	Tue 4/30/02	Mon 5/6/02
29	Frame 1st floor corners	1 day	Tue 4/30/02	Tue 4/30/02
30	Install 2nd floor joists	2 days	Tue 4/30/02	Wed 5/1/02
31	Frame 2nd floor decking	2 days	Tue 4/30/02	Wed 5/1/02
32	Frame 2nd floor walls	1 wk	Tue 4/30/02	Mon 5/6/02
33	Frame 2nd floor corners	2 days	Tue 4/30/02	Wed 5/1/02
34	Complete roof framing	1 wk?	Tue 4/30/02	Mon 5/6/02
35	Conduct framing inspection	6 hrs?	Tue 4/30/02	Tue 4/30/02

Figure 5-2. Confirmed as well as estimated durations are drawn with the Gantt bars.

> **tip** In a Gantt chart, you can also drag the right edge of a Gantt bar to change the task duration.

> **tip** You can change the estimated durations of multiple tasks to confirmed durations. Select all the tasks containing estimated durations. On the Standard toolbar, click Task Information, and then click the Advanced tab. Clear the Estimated check box.

Chapter 5

Understanding How Durations Affect Scheduling

When you enter a duration, the task is scheduled according to its assigned calendar. Initially, this is the project calendar. When resources are assigned, the task is scheduled according to the resource's working times calendar. If a task calendar is applied, the task is scheduled according to the task's working times calendar.

For more information about task calendars, see "Working with Task Calendars" later in this chapter.

For example, suppose you enter a 2d duration for the "Create market analysis plan" task, and the task starts Monday at 8:00 A.M. Based on the default Standard working times calendar and its options, Microsoft Project counts the 16 working hours in the 2-day duration to arrive at a finish date of Tuesday at 5:00 P.M.

> **note** Until you set task dependencies by linking predecessors and successors, the Start date of all your tasks is the same as the project start date by default.
>
> You can make any new tasks adopt the current date as the start date. Click Tools, Options, and then click the Schedule tab. In the New Tasks list, click Start On Current Date.
>
> In a schedule-from-finish project, the Finish date of all your tasks is the same as the Project finish date.

> **note** If you're working in a schedule-from-finish task and you enter a duration, Microsoft Project subtracts the duration amount from the Finish date to calculate the Start date.

If you want a task to take a set amount of time regardless of any working times calendars, you can enter an *elapsed duration*. This can be useful for tasks such as "Paint drying" or "Cement curing" that can't be stopped after they've started or that are independent of project schedules or resource assignments. Elapsed durations are scheduled 24 hours a day, 7 days a week, until finished. That is, one day is always considered 24 hours long (rather than 8 hours), and one week is always 7 days (rather than 5 days). To specify an elapsed duration, simply enter an "e" before the duration unit, for example, "3ed" for three elapsed days (see Figure 5-3).

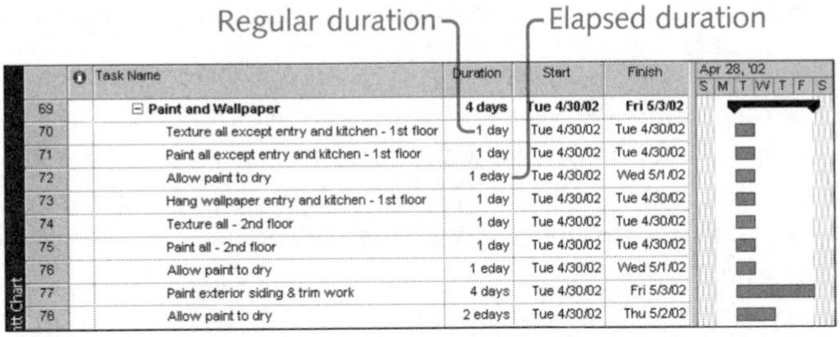

Figure 5-3.   Regular durations are scheduled according to applied working time calendars, whereas elapsed durations are based on 24 hours per day, 7 days per week.

For regular durations, we need a way to specify the number of working hours in a day and week, the number of working days in a month, and so on. This way, when we specify 2 weeks as a duration, for example, we can be assured that this means the same thing as 80 hours, or 10 days. To set these options, follow these steps:

1 Click Tools, Options, and then click the Calendar tab (see Figure 5-4 on the next page).

Chapter 5

133

You can also click Tools, Change Working Time, and then click the Options button.

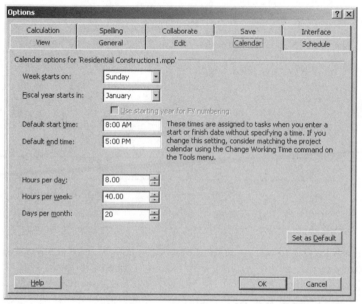

Figure 5-4. On the Calendar options tab, you can specify the details of your working time units, including the hours, days, and weeks.

2 Select the options on this tab to reflect the way your team works.

The Default Start Time (8:00 A.M.) and Default End Time (5:00 P.M.) are assigned to tasks when you enter a start or finish date without specifying a time.

The Hours Per Day, Hours Per Week, and Days Per Month values serve as your time unit specifications when needed. If you specify that a task has a duration of 1 month, does that mean 20 days or 30 days? These settings are used in conjunction with the working times calendars to dictate how your tasks are scheduled.

Calculating Your Most Probable Duration

In the course of researching task duration information, you might get conflicting results. Maybe the team member who's going to carry out a major task says it's going to take 3 weeks. Perhaps an expert stakeholder says it should take 2 weeks. And maybe the industry standard states that the same task should take 4 weeks. These are large discrepancies and they're all coming from credible sources. How do you schedule a task with three possible durations?

Or maybe you have a single reliable duration or a duration range like 2 weeks +/- 10 percent for all tasks in your task list, and you want your project plan to model a best-case scenario, a worst-case scenario, and an expected scenario for all durations. This way you can learn the earliest possible project finish date, the latest possible date, and the most probable finish date.

Troubleshooting

You set the calendar for 20 hours per week but the tasks are still being scheduled for 40 hours per week

Or you thought you set the calendar for 8:00 A.M. to 12:00 P.M., for the project to be scheduled only in the mornings, but the tasks are still being scheduled 8:00 A.M. to 5:00 P.M.

Sometimes the Calendar options tab confuses more readily than it assists. The Hours Per Day, Hours Per Week, and Days Per Month settings can easily be misinterpreted to make us think we're using them to set the schedule for the project. What we're actually doing is setting start and end times and specifying how duration entries are to be converted to assignment work.

Suppose you want to specify that work on this project is to be scheduled only in the mornings, from 8:00 A.M. until 12:00 P.M. To affect actual task scheduling in this way, you'd need to edit the working times for each day in the Change Working Time calendar. The Default Start Time only specifies the time that Microsoft Project should enter if you enter a start date without a corresponding start time. The Default End Time only specifies the time that Microsoft Project should enter if you enter a finish date without a corresponding finish time.

Also, suppose you want to specify that work on this project is to be scheduled only 20 hours per week because your team is working on another project at the same time. If you enter *20* in the Hours Per Week box, and then enter a duration of 2 weeks, that is scheduled as 40 hours—according to the project calendar. That means if the project's working times calendar is still set for Monday through Friday, 8:00 A.M. through 5:00 P.M., the 2 weeks is scheduled as two sets of 20 hours back to back, resulting in "2 weeks" taking place in 1 actual week in your schedule—probably not what you intended.

The solution is to make the corresponding change in the working times calendar. Set the working and nonworking times in the Change Working Time calendar so that there are 20 hours of working time per week. Then when you enter 2 weeks as a duration, the first 20 hours will be scheduled in the first week, and the second 20 hours will be scheduled in the second week.

The settings in the Calendar Options tab also determine how durations are translated into work time units when you assign resources to tasks.

135

To help resolve discrepancies or to model alternative scenarios, you can run a *PERT analysis*. PERT (Program Evaluation and Review Technique) analysis uses a weighted average of optimistic, pessimistic, and expected durations to calculate task durations and therefore the project schedule. This can be an effective risk management tool. It can also help if you're working out a project proposal or estimating time, cost, or resource requirements.

caution When you run a PERT analysis, the resulting calculated values in the Optimistic Duration, Expected Duration, and Pessimistic Duration fields will be stored in the custom fields Duration1, Duration2, and Duration3, respectively. In addition, the resulting optimistic start and finish dates are stored in the custom fields Start1 and Finish1. The expected start and finish dates are stored in the custom fields Start2 and Finish2. The pessimistic start and finish dates are stored in the custom fields Start3 and Finish3. Any values in any of these custom fields are overwritten by the results of the PERT analysis. This can be significant if you were storing interim plan information in these fields.

For more information about interim plans, see "Saving Additional Baselines" on page 288. For more information about using custom fields, see "Customizing Fields" on page 613.

To set up a PERT analysis, follow these steps:

1 Click View, Toolbars, PERT Analysis.

2 On the PERT Analysis toolbar, click PERT Entry Sheet.

PERT Entry Sheet

3 For each task, enter the optimistic, expected, and pessimistic durations in the appropriate fields (see Figure 5-5).

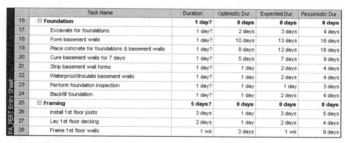

	Task Name	Duration	Optimistic Dur.	Expected Dur.	Pessimistic Dur.
16	⊟ **Foundation**	**1 day?**	**0 days**	**0 days**	**0 days**
17	Excavate for foundations	1 day?	2 days	3 days	4 days
18	Form basement walls	1 day?	10 days	13 days	16 days
19	Place concrete for foundations & basement walls	1 day?	8 days	12 days	16 days
20	Cure basement walls for 7 days	1 day?	5 days	7 days	9 days
21	Strip basement wall forms	1 day?	1 day	2 days	4 days
22	Waterproof/Insulate basement walls	1 day?	1 day	2 days	4 days
23	Perform foundation inspection	1 day?	1 day	1 day	3 days
24	Backfill foundation	1 day?	1 day	2 days	4 days
25	⊟ **Framing**	**5 days?**	**0 days**	**0 days**	**0 days**
26	Install 1st floor joists	3 days	1 day	3 days	5 days
27	Lay 1st floor decking	2 days	1 day	2 days	4 days
28	Frame 1st floor walls	1 wk	3 days	1 wk	9 days

Figure 5-5. Use the PERT Entry Sheet to specify the optimistic, expected, and pessimistic durations for each task.

If you do not expect a duration for a particular task to vary at all, enter the same value in all three fields.

4 On the PERT Analysis toolbar, click Calculate PERT.

Calculate PERT

136

The estimated durations are calculated, and the results change the value in the Duration field (see Figure 5-6).

		Task Name	Duration	Optimistic Dur.	Expected Dur.	Pessimistic Dur.
	15	Install underground utilities	1 day?	0 days	0 days	0 days
	16	⊟ **Foundation**	**13 days?**	**10 days**	**13 days**	**16 days**
	17	Excavate for foundations	3 days?	2 days	3 days	4 days
	18	Form basement walls	13 days?	10 days	13 days	16 days
	19	Place concrete for foundations & basement walls	12 days?	8 days	12 days	16 days
	20	Cure basement walls for 7 days	7 days?	5 days	7 days	9 days
	21	Strip basement wall forms	2.17 days?	1 day	2 days	4 days
	22	Waterproof/insulate basement walls	2.17 days?	1 day	2 days	4 days
	23	Perform foundation inspection	1.33 days?	1 day	1 day	3 days
	24	Backfill foundation	2.17 days?	1 day	2 days	4 days
	25	⊟ **Framing**	**5.5 days?**	**4 days**	**5 days**	**10 days**
	26	Install 1st floor joists	3 days?	1 day	3 days	5 days
	27	Lay 1st floor decking	2.17 days	1 day	2 days	4 days
	28	Frame 1st floor walls	1.07 wks	3 days	1 wk	9 days

Figure 5-6. The recalculated durations based on the PERT analysis replace the values in the Duration field for each task.

InsideOut

The PERT method is seldom used to calculate task durations these days. Another, more commonly used method, and the one on which the standard Microsoft Project calculations are based, is the CPM (Critical Path Method). In the CPM method, project duration is forecasted by analyzing which sequence of project activities has the least amount of scheduling flexibility. An early start and early finish are calculated, as are the late start and late finish.

For more information about the critical path method, see "Working with the Critical Path and Critical Tasks" on page 233.

You can review Gantt charts using each of the three sets of durations, as follows:

Optimistic
Gantt

- For the optimistic durations, click Optimistic Gantt on the PERT Analysis toolbar (see Figure 5-7).

		ⓞ	Task Name	Opt Dur	Opt Start	Opt Finish	Apr 28, '02 S M T W T F S	May 5, '02 S M T W T F
	16		⊟ **Foundation**	**10 days**	Tue 4/30/02	Mon 5/13/02		
	17		Excavate for foundations	2 days	Tue 4/30/02	Wed 5/1/02		
	18		Form basement walls	10 days	Tue 4/30/02	Mon 5/13/02		
	19		Place concrete for foundation	8 days	Tue 4/30/02	Thu 5/9/02		
	20		Cure basement walls for 7 da	5 days	Tue 4/30/02	Mon 5/6/02		
	21		Strip basement wall forms	1 day	Tue 4/30/02	Tue 4/30/02		
	22		Waterproof/insulate basemen	1 day	Tue 4/30/02	Tue 4/30/02		
	23		Perform foundation inspectior	1 day	Tue 4/30/02	Tue 4/30/02		
	24		Backfill foundation	1 day	Tue 4/30/02	Tue 4/30/02		
	25		⊟ **Framing**	**4 days**	Tue 4/30/02	Fri 5/3/02		
	26		Install 1st floor joists	1 day	Tue 4/30/02	Tue 4/30/02		
	27		Lay 1st floor decking	1 day	Tue 4/30/02	Tue 4/30/02		
	28		Frame 1st floor walls	3 days	Tue 4/30/02	Thu 5/2/02		

Figure 5-7. The Optimistic Gantt shows the optimistic durations for the PERT Analysis.

Chapter 5

137

Expected
Gantt

Pessimistic
Gantt

- For the expected durations, click Expected Gantt on the PERT Analysis toolbar.

- For the pessimistic durations, click Pessimistic Gantt on the PERT Analysis toolbar.

InsideOut

Set PERT
Weights

Sometimes the PERT analysis results appear to be skewed or exaggerated. You can adjust how Microsoft Project weights duration estimates for the PERT analysis. On the PERT Analysis toolbar, click Set PERT Weights. Change the number in at least two of the three fields: Optimistic, Expected, and Pessimistic—so that the sum of all three numbers equals 6 (see Figure 5-8). Then enter the durations in the PERT Entry Sheet as described above, and finally click Calculate PERT.

By default, the PERT weights are 1-4-1, that is, heavily weighted toward the expected duration, and lightly and equally weighted for the pessimistic and optimistic durations. Although 1-4-1 is the standard PERT weighting, 1-3-2 can build in a little more pessimism for better risk management.

Figure 5-8. Use the Set PERT Weights dialog box to change the weighting of optimistic, expected, and pessimistic durations for the PERT Analysis calculation.

---

tip   **Use your PERT analysis to check how you're progressing**

A good use of the PERT analysis is for a quick check of how your project is going. Has your critical path or resource leveling pushed the project schedule beyond your worst-case PERT analysis? If so, this can tell you it's time to replan your project.

Establishing Task Dependencies

Now task durations are entered in your Gantt Chart (see Figure 5-9).

		O	Task Name	Duration	Start	Finish	Apr 28, '02 S M T W T F S	May 5, '02 S M T W T
	16		⊟ **Foundation**	**13 days**	**Tue 4/30/02**	**Thu 5/16/02**		
	17		Excavate for foundations	3 days	Tue 4/30/02	Thu 5/2/02		
	18		Form basement walls	13 days	Tue 4/30/02	Thu 5/16/02		
	19		Place concrete for foundations & bas	12 days	Tue 4/30/02	Wed 5/15/02		
	20		Cure basement walls for 7 days	7 days	Tue 4/30/02	Wed 5/8/02		
	21		Strip basement wall forms	2 days	Tue 4/30/02	Wed 5/1/02		
	22		Waterproof/insulate basement walls	2 days	Tue 4/30/02	Wed 5/1/02		
	23		Perform foundation inspection	1 day	Tue 4/30/02	Tue 4/30/02		
	24		Backfill foundation	2 days	Tue 4/30/02	Wed 5/1/02		
	25		⊟ **Framing**	**4 days**	**Tue 4/30/02**	**Fri 5/3/02**		
	26		Install 1st floor joists	2 days	Tue 4/30/02	Wed 5/1/02		
	27		Lay 1st floor decking	2 days	Tue 4/30/02	Wed 5/1/02		

Figure 5-9. Durations are graphed in the Gantt Chart, and all tasks start on the project start date.

The next step in creating your schedule is to link tasks that are dependent upon each other. Often, one task cannot begin until a previous task has been completed. Sometimes several tasks are dependent upon the completion of one task. Sometimes several tasks must finish before a single later task can begin. You can link the previous, or *predecessor* task to its succeeding, or *successor* task, and thereby set up the *task dependency* between the two.

---

note A task dependency is also referred to as a *task relationship* or a *link*.

With your task dependencies and durations in place, your project plan really starts to look like a real schedule, and you can start to see possible start dates and finish dates, not only for the individual tasks, but also for major phases, milestones, and the project as a whole. When you create a link between two tasks, Microsoft Project calculates the successor's start and finish dates based on the predecessor's start or finish date, the dependency type, the successor's duration, and any associated resource assignments. There's still more information and refinement to be done, but you're getting closer to a schedule you can work with.

Creating the Finish-to-Start Task Dependency

The most typical link is the finish-to-start task dependency. With this link, the predecessor task must finish before the successor task can begin. To link tasks with the finish-to-start task dependency, follow these steps:

1 Display the Gantt Chart.

You can set task dependencies in any task sheet, but you can see the effects of the links immediately in the Gantt Chart.

Chapter 5

2   In the task sheet, select the two tasks you want to link. Drag from the predecessor to the successor task if they are right next to each other. If they are not adjacent tasks, click the predecessor, hold down the Ctrl key, and then click the successor.

Link Tasks

3   On the Standard toolbar, click Link Tasks.

The tasks are linked in the chart portion of the Gantt Chart. In addition, the Predecessor field of the successor task lists the task number for its predecessor (see Figure 5-10).

	ⓘ	Task Name	Duration	Start	Finish
25		⊟ Framing	22 days	Tue 4/30/02	Wed 5/29/02
26		Install 1st floor joists	2 days	Tue 4/30/02	Wed 5/1/02
27		Lay 1st floor decking	2 days	Thu 5/2/02	Fri 5/3/02
28		Frame 1st floor walls	4 days	Mon 5/6/02	Thu 5/9/02
29		Frame 1st floor corners	1 day	Fri 5/10/02	Fri 5/10/02
30		Install 2nd floor joists	2 days	Mon 5/13/02	Tue 5/14/02
31		Frame 2nd floor decking	2 days	Wed 5/15/02	Thu 5/16/02
32		Frame 2nd floor walls	3 days	Fri 5/17/02	Tue 5/21/02
33		Frame 2nd floor corners	2 days	Wed 5/22/02	Thu 5/23/02
34		Complete roof framing	3 days	Fri 5/24/02	Tue 5/28/02
35		Conduct framing inspection	1 day	Wed 5/29/02	Wed 5/29/02

Figure 5-10.   Linked tasks in the Gantt Chart.

---

tip   **Link multiple tasks at once**

You can link multiple tasks at one time, as long as they all have the same type of task dependency. Select all the tasks that are to be linked, either by dragging them or by clicking them while holding down the Ctrl key. On the Standard toolbar, click Link Tasks.

---

tip   **Set multiple links to a single task**

You can have multiple links to and from a single task. One task might be the predecessor for several other tasks. Likewise, one task might be the successor for several tasks. There's no difference in how you set the links. Select the two tasks and click Link Tasks on the Standard toolbar. Or select the successor, and then set the predecessor and link type on the Predecessors tab in the Task Information dialog box.

---

tip   **Link tasks by dragging between Gantt bars**

In the chart portion of the Gantt Chart, drag from the middle of the predecessor Gantt bar to the middle of the successor Gantt bar. Before you drag, be sure that you see a crosshair mouse pointer. This creates a finish-to-start task dependency between them.

Understanding the Dependency Types

Although the finish-to-start task dependency is the most common, there are four types of dependencies, as follows:

Finish-to-start (FS).   As soon as the predecessor task finishes, the successor task can start.

Finish-to-finish (FF).   As soon as the predecessor task finishes, the successor task can finish.

Start-to-start (SS).   As soon as the predecessor task starts, the successor task can start.

Start-to-finish (SF).   As soon as the predecessor task starts, the successor task can finish. This type of link is rarely used, but still available if you need it.

---

tip   **Link tasks with the Project Guide**

You can use the Project Guide to help you set task dependencies. On the Project Guide toolbar, click the Tasks button. In the Project Guide pane, click the Schedule Tasks link. Read the information, and use the controls provided to link tasks. When finished, click the Done link.

---

tip   **Automatically link tasks**

By default, when you move a task from one location to another in your task sheet, or when you insert a new task, that task is automatically linked like its surrounding tasks. You can control this setting. Click Tools, Options, and then click the Schedule tab. Select or clear the Autolink Inserted Or Moved Tasks check box.

Chapter 5

To apply a task dependency, follow these steps:

1 Display the Gantt Chart or other view with a task sheet.

2 Select the task that is to become the successor in the dependency you will be setting.

3 On the Standard toolbar, click Task Information.

You can also simply double-click a task to open the Task Information dialog box.

4 Click the Predecessors tab (see Figure 5-11).

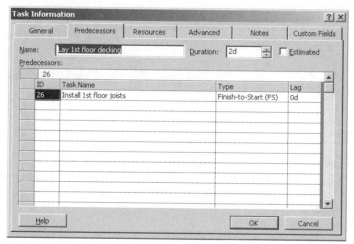

Figure 5-11. Use the Predecessors tab in the Task Information dialog box to set different types of task dependencies.

5 Click the first blank row in the Task Name field, and then click the down arrow. The list of tasks in the project appears.

6 Click the task that is to be the predecessor to the current task.

7 Click the Type field, and then select the type of task dependency: Finish-to-Start (FS), Start-to-Start (SS), Finish-to-Finish (FF), Start-to-Finish (SF), or None.

---

tip   **Change the task link directly in the Gantt Chart**

You can also apply the Finish-to-Start task link to a pair of tasks, and then quickly change the link on the chart portion of the Gantt Chart. Double-click the task link line on the chart. The Task Dependency dialog box appears. In the Type box, change the dependency type, and then click OK.

142

tip **Link between projects**

Not only can you link tasks within one project, you can link tasks in different projects. For more information, see Chapter 15, "Exchanging Information Between Project Plans."

Overlapping Linked Tasks by Adding Lead Time

One way to make your project schedule more efficient is to overlap linked tasks where possible. Suppose you have a task that can't begin until a previous task is finished. You realize that the predecessor doesn't actually have to be finished—after it's 50 percent complete, the successor can begin. The successor essentially gets a 50 percent head start, hence the term *lead time*. For example, "Construct walls" is the predecessor to "Plaster walls." Although plastering cannot be done until the walls are constructed, the final wall does not need to be constructed before plastering of the first wall can begin. You can set an amount of lead time for the "Plaster walls" task.

Lead time is expressed as a negative value. It can be a percentage of the predecessor, for example, *-25%*. Or, it can be a specific time period, for example, *-4d* or *-1ew*.

To enter lead time for a linked task, follow these steps:

1 Display the Gantt Chart or other view with a task sheet.

2 Select the successor task that is to have the lead time.

3 On the Standard toolbar, click Task Information.

4 In the Task Information dialog box, click the Predecessors tab.

5 In the Lag field for the existing Predecessor, type the amount of lead time you want for the successor. Use a negative number, and enter the lead time as a percentage or duration amount.

tip **Enter lead time directly in the task sheet**

You can also enter lead time in the sheet portion of the Gantt Chart. Click in the Predecessors field for the successor task. The field should already contain the Task ID of the predecessor task. After the Task ID, enter the code representing the link type, and then enter the amount of lead time. For example, *9FS-1 day*, or *14FF-20%*.

143

Chapter 5

Delaying Linked Tasks by Adding Lag Time

Suppose you have a pair of tasks with a finish-to-start link. And then you realize that the successor really can't start when the predecessor is finished—there needs to be some additional delay. This is usually the case when something needs to happen between the two tasks that isn't another task. For example, suppose the "Order equipment" task is the predecessor to the "Install equipment" task. Although the equipment cannot be installed until after the equipment is ordered, it still cannot be installed immediately after ordering. Some *lag time* is needed to allow for the equipment to be shipped and delivered. In such a case, the successor needs to be delayed, and you can enter lag time in the schedule to accurately reflect this condition.

Just like lead time, lag time can be a percentage of the predecessor, for example, *75%*. Or it can be a specific time period, for example, *16h* or *3ed*. Unlike lead time, however, lag time is expressed as a positive number.

> **note** Don't confuse the delay afforded by lag time with *assignment delay*. With lag time, the delay is from the end of the predecessor to the beginning of the successor task. With assignment delay, there is a delay from the task start date to the assignment start date.

> For more information about adjusting assignments using delay, see "Adjusting Assignments" on page 261.

To enter lag time for a linked task, follow these steps:

1 Display the Gantt Chart or other view with a task sheet.

2 Select the successor task that is to have the lag time.

3 On the Standard toolbar, click Task Information.

4 In the Task Information dialog box, click the Predecessors tab.

5 In the Lag field for the existing Predecessor, type the amount of lag time you want for the successor. Use a positive number, and enter the lag time as a percentage or duration amount.

> **tip** **Enter lag time directly in the task sheet**
>
> You can also enter lag time values in the sheet portion of the Gantt Chart. Click in the Predecessors field of the successor task. The field should already contain the Task ID of the predecessor task. After the Task ID, enter the code representing the link type, and then enter the amount of lag time. For example, *9FS+1 day*, or *14FF+20%*.

Changing or Removing Links

To change or remove an existing task dependency, follow these steps:

1 Display the Gantt Chart or other view with a task sheet.

2 Select the successor task whose link you want to change.

3 On the Standard toolbar, click Task Information.

4 In the Task Information dialog box, click the Predecessors tab.

5 Click in the Type field for the predecessor you want to change, and then select the type of task dependency you want it to be: Finish-to-Start (FS), Start-to-Start (SS), Finish-to-Finish (FF), Start-to-Finish (SF), or None. If you select None, the link is removed entirely.

Troubleshooting

You're trying to remove just the predecessor link from a task, but the successor link is removed at the same time

Unlink
Tasks

When you click a task and then click Unlink Tasks, all links are removed—predecessor, successor, and any multiples. As a result, the scheduling of this task returns to the project start date or a start date entered as a constraint.

To remove just a single predecessor, click the task, and then click Task Information on the Standard toolbar. In the Task Information dialog box, click the Predecessors tab. Click the task name of the predecessor you want to delete, and then press the Delete key.

Reviewing Task Dependencies

When needed, the following three views can give you a closer look at the task dependencies in your project:

- The Gantt Chart shows task dependencies with link lines between the Gantt bars. In fact, all Gantt chart views show task dependencies this way.

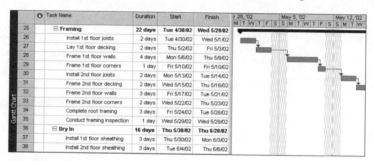

- The Network Diagram shows each task as an individual node, with link lines between them.

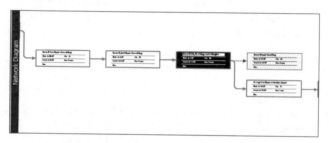

- The Relationship Diagram shows the predecessors and successors of a single selected task.

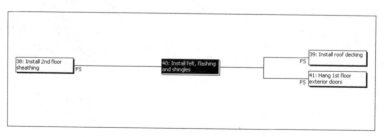

Chapter 5

Scheduling Tasks to Achieve Specific Dates

With task dependencies established, your project schedule is taking shape and looking more and more realistic (see Figure 5-12).

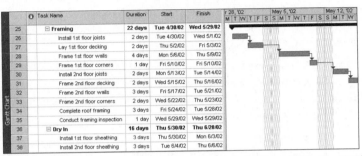

Figure 5-12. With durations entered and tasks linked, the Gantt Chart is starting to show meaningful information.

With working times calendars, durations, and task dependencies in place, Microsoft Project has the information needed to schedule your project from start to finish. By default, Microsoft Project schedules each task to start "As Soon As Possible."

However, you might have additional dates to consider. For example, maybe certain pivotal supplies will not be ready for use in the project until after April 6. Perhaps an important review meeting is taking place on June 29 that will set the stage for work toward the final milestones. Maybe one of your deliverables is a presentation at a key professional conference held on August 22.

To schedule around these important dates, you can set a *constraint*, which is a restriction on the start or finish date of a task. All tasks have a constraint applied—at the very least, the default "As Soon As Possible" constraint. The As Soon As Possible constraint indicates that the task should be scheduled according to its working times calendars, duration, task dependencies, and any resource assignments—without regard to any specific date.

Understanding Constraint Types

The As Soon As Possible constraint is applied by default to all tasks in a project scheduled from the start date. In a project scheduled from the finish date, the As Late As Possible constraint is applied. The As Soon As Possible and As Late As Possible constraints are considered flexible constraints.

> **note** Different types of constraints are applied in certain situations depending on whether you're working with a project scheduled from the start date or from the finish date. For example, entering a date in the Start field of a project scheduled from the start date causes a Start No Earlier Than constraint to be applied. Doing the same thing in a project scheduled from the finish date causes a Start No Later Than constraint to be applied.

147

When a task needs to be scheduled in relation to a specific date, there are additional constraints you can apply, each of which is associated with a date. The following is a list of all the date constraints you can use to refine your project schedule:

Start No Earlier Than (SNET). A moderately flexible constraint that specifies the earliest possible date that a task could begin. For projects scheduled from a start date, this constraint is automatically applied when you enter a start date for a task.

Finish No Earlier Than (FNET). A moderately flexible constraint that specifies the earliest possible date that this task could be completed. For projects scheduled from a start date, this constraint is automatically applied when you enter a finish date for a task.

Start No Later Than (SNLT). A moderately flexible constraint that specifies the latest possible date that this task could begin. For projects scheduled from a finish date, this constraint is automatically applied when you enter a start date for a task.

Finish No Later Than (FNLT). A moderately flexible constraint that specifies the latest possible date that this task could be completed. For projects scheduled from a finish date, this constraint is automatically applied when you enter a finish date for a task.

Must Start On (MSO). An inflexible constraint that specifies the exact date when a task must begin. Other scheduling controls such as task dependencies become secondary to this requirement.

Must Finish On (MFO). An inflexible constraint that specifies the exact date on which a date must be completed. Other scheduling controls such as task dependencies become secondary to this requirement.

InsideOut

If you enter a date in the Start field (in a project scheduled from the start date), the Start No Earlier Than constraint is applied. The Finish date is recalculated based on the new Start date and the existing duration.

If you then enter a date in the Finish field of the same task, the constraint changes to Finish No Earlier Than. The Start date remains as you set it, but the duration is recalculated to reflect the difference between your entered Start and Finish dates.

Always be aware that any dates you enter will change the As Soon As Possible or As Late As Possible constraints to something more inflexible. If you enter both the Start and Finish dates for a task, Microsoft Project will recalculate the duration.

Project Management Practices: Working with Date Constraints

When developing your project schedule, you might contend with one of two major categories of date constraints: externally imposed dates and milestone dates.

An externally imposed date reflects situations outside the project that influence the project schedule. Examples include the following:

- Shipment of material needed for the project
- A market window for a new product
- A product announcement date at a trade conference
- Weather restrictions on outdoor activities
- A special event important to the project but scheduled by forces outside the project

You can reflect externally imposed dates as constraints on the tasks they affect. You can also add a task note as a reminder of the source of this date.

Milestone dates are typically dates set internally. As the project manager, you might set them yourself as goals to work toward. The project sponsor, customer, or other stakeholder might request certain dates for certain milestones, deliverables, or events being produced by the work of your project. You can set constraints on milestones as well as on regular tasks.

Changing Constraints

Remember, tasks always have a constraint applied—even if it's just As Soon As Possible or As Late As Possible. So we never think of *adding* or *removing* constraints. When making a change, we're typically changing a constraint from a flexible one to a more inflexible one, or vice versa.

There are several methods of changing constraints, as follows:

- In the Gantt Chart or similar view with a task sheet, type or select dates in the Start or Finish fields. In a project scheduled from the start date, this causes a Start No Earlier Than or Finish No Earlier Than constraint to be applied. In a project scheduled from the finish date, this causes a Start No Later Than or Finish No Later Than constraint to be applied.

● In any task view, select the task whose constraint you want to change, and then click Task Information on the Standard toolbar. In the Task Information dialog box, click the Advanced tab (see Figure 5-13). In the Constraint Type box, click the constraint type you want to apply to this task. If applicable, enter the date in the Constraint Date box.

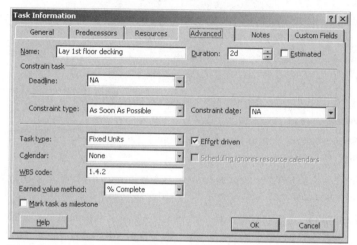

Figure 5-13. On the Advanced tab of the Task Information dialog box, you can set constraints, deadlines, milestones, and task calendars.

● On the Project Guide toolbar, click the Tasks button. In the Project Guide pane, click the Set Deadlines And Constrain Tasks link. Read the information under Constrain A Task, and use the controls that are provided to set constraints.

● In the Gantt Chart or other view with a task sheet, apply the Constraint Dates table. Click View, Table, More Tables. In the More Tables dialog box, click Constraint Dates, and then click the Apply button (see Figure 5-14). In the Constraint Type field, click the constraint type you want to apply to this task. If applicable, enter the date in the Constraint Date box.

	Task Name	Duration	Constraint Type	Constraint Date
25	⊟ **Framing**	**22 days**	**As Soon As Possible**	**NA**
26	Install 1st floor joists	2 days	Start No Earlier Than	Thu 8/8/02
27	Lay 1st floor decking	2 days	As Soon As Possible	NA
28	Frame 1st floor walls	4 days	As Soon As Possible	NA
29	Frame 1st floor corners	1 day	Must Finish On	Tue 8/20/02
30	Install 2nd floor joists	2 days	As Soon As Possible	NA
31	Frame 2nd floor decking	2 days	As Soon As Possible	NA
32	Frame 2nd floor walls	3 days	As Soon As Possible	NA
33	Frame 2nd floor corners	2 days	As Soon As Possible	NA
34	Complete roof framing	3 days	Finish No Later Than	Thu 9/5/02
35	Conduct framing inspection	1 day	As Soon As Possible	NA

Figure 5-14. Apply the Constraint Dates table to review or change constraint types and dates.

---

tip   **Change constraints for multiple tasks at once**

Select all the tasks that will have the same constraint applied. Drag across adjacent tasks to select them, or hold down Ctrl while clicking nonadjacent tasks. On the Standard toolbar, click Task Information, and in the Multiple Task Information dialog box, click the Advanced tab. Change the Constraint Type, and if applicable, the Constraint Date. Click OK. The constraint is changed for all selected tasks.

This works best if you're changing date constraints to As Soon As Possible or As Late As Possible, because it's rare that multiple tasks would have the same constraint date.

Troubleshooting

You can't delete a constraint

By their nature, constraints are not deleted. A constraint is applied to every task. If you're thinking of deleting a constraint, what you probably want to do is change it from a date constraint like Must Start On or Finish No Later Than to a flexible constraint like As Soon As Possible.

Double-click the task to open the Task Information dialog box, and then click the Advanced tab. In the Constraint Type box, click As Soon As Possible or As Late As Possible.

Working with Flexible and Inflexible Constraints

There are three levels of flexibility associated with task constraints: flexible, moderately flexible, and inflexible.

The flexible constraints are As Soon As Possible and As Late As Possible. These constraints work with task dependencies to schedule a task as soon or as late as the task dependency and other scheduling considerations will accommodate. These are the default constraints, and allow Microsoft Project maximum flexibility in calculating start and finish dates for the tasks. For example, a task with an ASAP constraint and a finish-to-start dependency will be scheduled as soon as the predecessor task finishes.

The moderately flexible constraints (Start No Earlier Than, Start No Later Than, Finish No Earlier Than, and Finish No Later Than) have a range of dates to work within. That is, the task is restricted to starting or finishing before or after the date you choose. This provides some room for flexibility, even though a date is in place. For example, a task with a Start No Later Than constraint for November 14 and a finish-to-start dependency to another task can begin any time its predecessor is finished up until November 14, but it cannot be scheduled after November 14.

The inflexible constraints, Must Start On and Must Finish On, have an absolute single date that the schedule must accommodate. This means that other scheduling considerations must fall by the wayside if necessary to meet this date. By default, constraints take precedence over task dependencies when there's a conflict between the two. For example, a task with a Must Finish On constraint for April 30 and a finish-to-start dependency to another task will always be scheduled for April 30, regardless of whether the predecessor finishes on time.

InsideOut

If you set a moderately flexible constraint such as Start No Earlier Than, or an inflexible constraint such as Must Finish On, you run the risk of a conflict with task dependencies. Suppose the "Hang wallpaper" task has a Must Finish On constraint for June 25. Because of various delays, the task's finish-to-start predecessor task, "Texture walls," actually finishes on June 29.

This creates a scheduling conflict. According to the task dependency, you can't hang wallpaper until the walls are textured, which won't finish until June 29. But according to the constraint, the wallpaper must be hung by June 25.

By default, where there's a conflict like this between a task dependency and a constraint, the constraint takes precedence. In this case, there would be 4 days of *negative slack*, which essentially means that the predecessor task is running 4 days into the time allotted to the successor task. You might see a Planning Wizard message regarding this, especially if you're still in the planning phase and are setting up tasks with such a conflict before actual work is even reported.

To resolve this, you can change the constraint to a more flexible one, like Finish No Earlier Than. You can change the Must Finish On date to a later date that will work. You can also change the scheduling precedence option. If you want task dependencies to take precedence over constraints, click Tools, Options. In the Options dialog box, click the Schedule tab. Clear the Tasks Will Always Honor Their Constraint Dates check box.

Reviewing Constraints

With the right constraints in place, you have the beginnings of a schedule. The Gantt Chart can provide a great deal of information about your constraints and other scheduling controls.

You can sort tasks by Start Date, Finish Date, Constraint Type, or Constraint Date. You can group tasks by Constraint Type. You can filter tasks by the Should Start By date or the Should Start/Finish By date.

These can provide overviews of the big picture of start and finish dates across many tasks at a time. If you want to review details, you can review the Task Information dialog box for a task. The General tab includes the scheduled start and finish dates, and the Advanced tab includes the constraint type and constraint date.

You can apply the Task Entry view. The task details for any task you select in the Gantt Chart in the upper pane are shown in the Task Form in the lower pane. The default Resources & Predecessors details show task dependencies as well as any lead or lag time (see Figure 5-15).

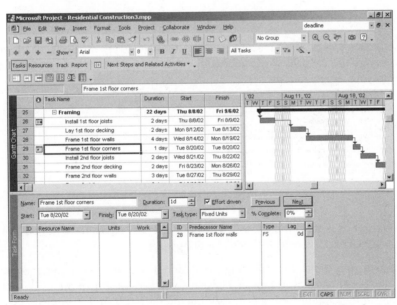

Figure 5-15. With the Task Entry view, you can review details of an individual task selected in the Gantt Chart.

Chapter 5

newfeature! Getting Scheduling Feedback

After you have assigned tasks to resources, Microsoft Project 2002 employs Microsoft Office XP Smart Tags technology to provide scheduling feedback. When you make certain kinds of changes that affect scheduling, such as changes to duration, start date, or finish date, a green triangle might appear in the corner of the edited cell in a Gantt chart, task sheet view, or usage view.

2 days	Tue 4/2/02
2 days	Wed 4/3/02
2 days	Fri 4/5/02

Scheduling feedback triangle

When you move your mouse pointer over the cell containing the feedback indicator, the Smart Tag icon appears.

	2 days	Tue 4/2/02
⬦	2 days	Wed 4/3/02
	2 days	Fri 4/5/02

Smart tag icon

Click the Smart Tag icon. A message explains the scheduling ramifications of your edit. The message usually gives you the opportunity to change the edit so that the result is closer to your expectation.

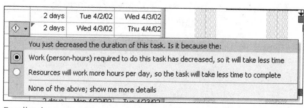

Feedback message

The indicator appears in the cell as long as the edit is available for an Undo operation. After you make a new edit, the indicator disappears.

Unlike Microsoft Office XP Smart Tags, you cannot change or create your own feedback messages in Microsoft Project. However, you can turn them off. Click Tools, Options. In the Options dialog box, click the Interface tab, and then clear any of the check boxes under Show Indicators And Options Buttons.

> For more information about feedback indicators in resource assignments, see "Changing Resource Assignments" on page 206.

Setting Deadline Reminders

Suppose you want a task or milestone to be completed by a certain date, but you don't want to limit the schedule calculations by setting a constraint. Set a *deadline* instead. A deadline appears as an indicator on your Gantt Chart as a target or goal, but does not affect the scheduling of your tasks.

To set a deadline, follow these steps:

1 Select the task for which you want to set a deadline.

2 On the Standard toolbar, click Task Information.

3 In the Task Information dialog box, click the Advanced tab.

4 In the Deadline box, enter or select the deadline date.

The deadline marker appears in the chart area of the Gantt Chart (see Figure 5-16). Repeat Steps 1-4 to change or remove a deadline if necessary. If you're removing a deadline, select the date and press the Delete key.

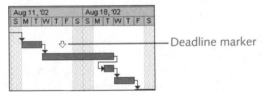
———Deadline marker

Figure 5-16. The deadline does not affect scheduling but simply provides a guideline for important dates.

---

tip **Use the Project Guide to set deadlines**

On the Project Guide toolbar, click the Tasks button. In the Project Guide pane, click the Set Deadlines And Constrain Tasks link. Read the information under Set A Deadline, and use the controls provided to set deadlines.

You can show deadlines in your task sheet as well, by adding the Deadline field as a column. To do this, follow these steps:

1 Right-click the column heading to the right of where you want your new Deadline column to be inserted, and then click Insert Column.

  Or you can click the column heading, and then click Insert, Column.
  The Column Definition dialog box appears.

2 In the Field Name box, click Deadline. You can type the first one or two letters to go straight to it in the list.

The Deadline field shows any deadline dates that have already been set, and "NA" for tasks without deadlines. You can enter deadlines directly in this field.

If the schedule for a task moves beyond its deadline date, either because of normal scheduling calculations or because of actual progress information entered, an alert appears in the Indicators field, specifying that the task is scheduled to finish later than its deadline (see Figure 5-17).

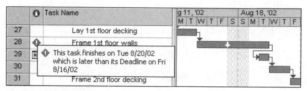

Figure 5-17. If a deadline is going to be missed, the deadline indicator provides the details.

You can set deadlines for summary tasks as well as individual tasks. If the summary task's deadline conflicts with the finish dates of any of the subtasks, the deadline indicator specifies a missed deadline among the subtasks. You can also set deadlines for milestone tasks as well as for normal tasks.

InsideOut

There are two instances in which a deadline can indeed affect task scheduling. The first is if you enter a deadline that falls before the end of the task's total slack, the total slack is recalculated using the deadline date rather than the task's late finish date. If the total slack reaches 0, the task becomes critical.

The second is if you set a deadline on a task with an As Late As Possible constraint. Suppose the task is scheduled to finish on the deadline date. However, if any predecessors slipped, the task could still finish beyond its deadline.

For more information about the critical path, slack, and late finish dates, see "Working with the Critical Path and Critical Tasks" on page 233.

Creating Milestones in Your Schedule

You can designate certain tasks as *milestones* in your project plan. Having milestones flagged in your project plan and visible in your Gantt Chart helps you see when you've achieved another benchmark. Milestones often indicate the beginning or ending of major phases or the completion of deliverables in your project. As you complete each milestone, you come ever closer to completing the project. Milestones are also excellent reporting points.

A milestone, as such, has no additional calculation effect on your schedule. However, you typically link a milestone to other tasks. You might also set a date constraint on a milestone.

The simplest method for entering a milestone is to create the task, worded like a milestone, for example, "First floor construction complete," and enter a duration of 0. Any task with a 0 duration is automatically set as a milestone. The milestone marker and date are drawn in the chart area of the Gantt Chart (see Figure 5-18).

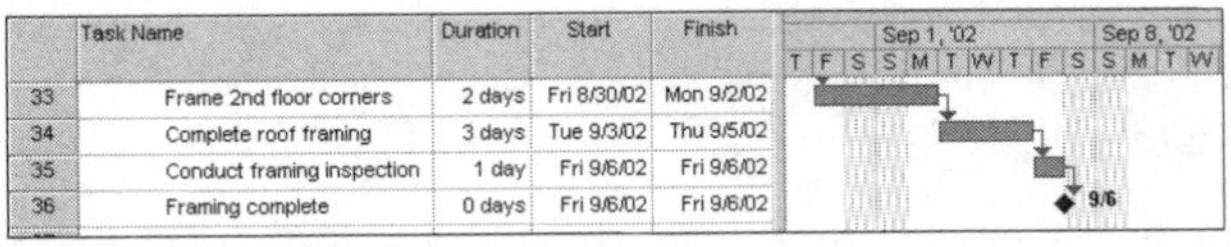

	Task Name	Duration	Start	Finish
33	Frame 2nd floor corners	2 days	Fri 8/30/02	Mon 9/2/02
34	Complete roof framing	3 days	Tue 9/3/02	Thu 9/5/02
35	Conduct framing inspection	1 day	Fri 9/6/02	Fri 9/6/02
36	Framing complete	0 days	Fri 9/6/02	Fri 9/6/02

Figure 5-18. Microsoft Project interprets any task with a 0 duration as a milestone.

However, a milestone does not have to have a 0 duration. You might want to make the final task in each phase a milestone, and these are real tasks with real durations. To change a regular task into a milestone, follow these steps:

1. Select the task you want to become a milestone.
2. On the Standard toolbar, click Task Information.
3. In the Task Information dialog box, click the Advanced tab.
4. Select the Mark Task As Milestone check box.

The Gantt bar for the task changes to the milestone marker in the chart area of the Gantt Chart (see Figure 5-19).

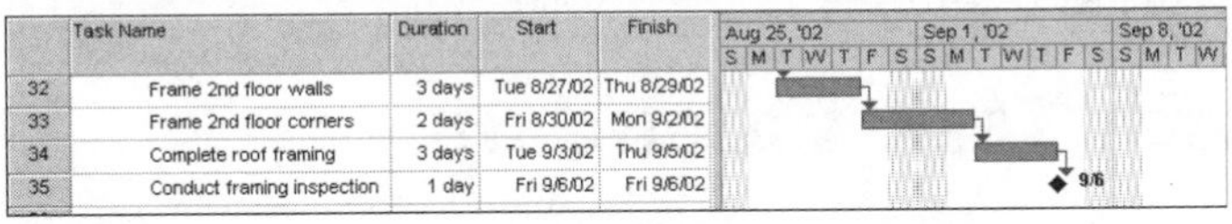

	Task Name	Duration	Start	Finish
32	Frame 2nd floor walls	3 days	Tue 8/27/02	Thu 8/29/02
33	Frame 2nd floor corners	2 days	Fri 8/30/02	Mon 9/2/02
34	Complete roof framing	3 days	Tue 9/3/02	Thu 9/5/02
35	Conduct framing inspection	1 day	Fri 9/6/02	Fri 9/6/02

Figure 5-19. You can set any task as a milestone.

Chapter 5

InsideOut

By default, milestones markers are set to appear on their Start date. Suppose you have a 4-day task with a Start date of December 12 and a Finish date of December 16. If you change this task to a milestone, the duration, start date, and finish dates remain the same. However, the Gantt bar for the task in the chart area of the Gantt Chart changes to a milestone marker on December 12. This can be misleading because there's no longer anything drawn to show the end of the task.

You can change the bar style for the milestone marker. By default, the style is drawn "From Start To Start." You can change it to be "From Finish To Finish." Click Format, Bar Styles. In the grid, click in the From field for the Milestone style, and then click Finish. Click in the To field for the Milestone style, and then click Finish. This will cause the milestone marker to sit on the Finish date (see Figure 5-20).

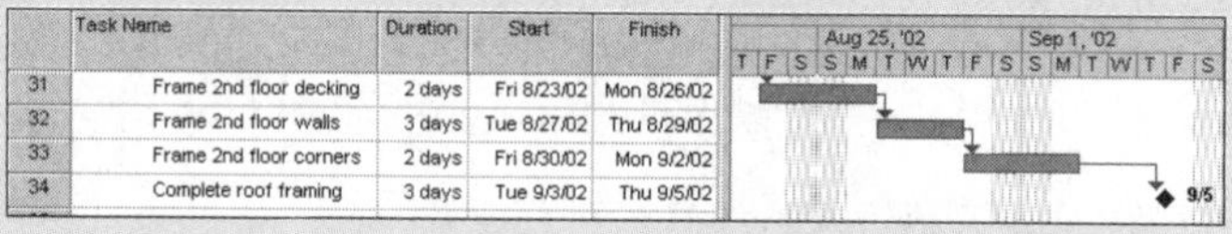

Figure 5-20. You can change the milestone marker to appear on the Finish date rather than the Start date.

Or you can change the bar style to include a bar showing duration, with the milestone marker at the end of the bar. In the Bar Styles dialog box, click the Appearance field for the Milestone style. Below the grid, under Middle, enter a shape, pattern, and color for the Gantt bar you want to represent the milestone bar. Under End, enter the shape, type, and color for the end marker for the milestone Gantt bar. In the grid, change the From field to Start and the To field to Finish. This will give you a Gantt bar showing the duration of the milestone task as well as a symbol to mark the end of the task and completion of the milestone (see Figure 5-21).

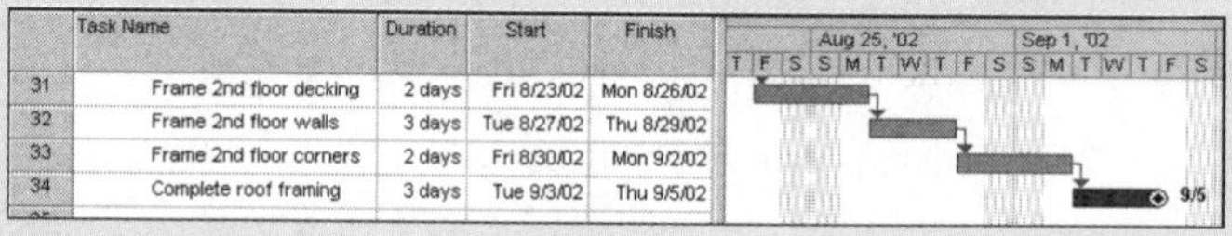

Figure 5-21. You can create a milestone Gantt bar to show the milestone's duration as well as its end point.

Working with Task Calendars

The scheduling of your tasks is driven by task duration, task dependencies, and constraints. It's also driven by the project calendar. If your project calendar dictates that work is done Monday through Friday, 8:00 A.M. until 5:00 P.M., initially that's when your tasks are scheduled.

For more information about calendars, see "Setting Your Project Calendar" on page 58.

158

However, if a task is assigned to a resource who works Saturday and Sunday, 9:00 A.M. until 9:00 P.M., the task is scheduled for those times instead. That is, the task is scheduled according to the assigned resource's working times calendar, rather than the project calendar.

Sometimes you have a task that needs to be scheduled differently from the working times reflected in the project calendar or the assigned resource calendars. For example, you might have a task that specifies preventive maintenance on equipment at specified intervals. Or you might have a task being completed by a machine running 24 hours a day. In any case, the task has its own working time, and you want it to be scheduled according to that working time rather than the project or resource working time so it can accurately reflect what's really happening with this task.

Creating a Base Calendar

Microsoft Project comes with three *base calendars*. These base calendars are like calendar templates that you can apply to the project as a whole, a set of resources, or in this case, a set of tasks. The three base calendars are described in Table 5-1.

Table 5-1. Base Calendar Types

Calendar type	Description
Standard	Working time is set to Monday through Friday, 8:00 A.M. until 5:00 P.M., with an hour off for lunch from 12:00 P.M. until 1:00 P.M. each day. This is the default base calendar used for the project, for tasks, and for resources.
Night Shift	Working time is set from 11:00 P.M. until 8:00 A.M. five days a week, with an hour off for lunch from 3:00 A.M. until 4:00 A.M. each morning. This base calendar is generally used for resources who work a graveyard shift. It can also be used for projects that are carried out only during the night shift.
24 Hours	Working time is set to 12:00 A.M. until 12:00 A.M. seven days a week, that is, work never stops. This base calendar is typically used for projects in a manufacturing situation, for example, which might run two or three back-to-back shifts every day of the week.

note If you are running Project Server, the Night Shift and 24 Hours calendars are available only to administrators.

Chapter 5

If you want to apply a task calendar, you often need to create a special base calendar for the purpose. To create a new base calendar, follow these steps:

1 Click Tools, Change Working Time.

2 Click the New button. The Create New Base Calendar dialog box appears (see Figure 5-22).

Figure 5-22. Create a new base calendar to set a unique working times schedule for a specific task.

3 In the Name box, type the name you want for the new base calendar, for example, "Equipment Maintenance."

4 Select Create New Base Calendar if you want to adapt your calendar from the Standard base calendar.

Select Make A Copy Of if you want to adapt the new calendar from a different existing base calendar, such as the Night Shift. Select the name of the existing calendar you want to adapt.

5 Click OK.

6 Make the changes you want to the working days and times for individual days or entire days of the week, as needed.

7 When finished with your new base calendar, click OK.

Assigning a Base Calendar to a Task

To assign a base calendar to a task, follow these steps:

1 Select the task to which you want to assign a base calendar.

2 On the Standard toolbar, click Task Information.

3 In the Task Information dialog box, click the Advanced tab.

4 In the Calendar box, click the name of the calendar you want to assign to this task. All base calendars are listed, including ones you have created yourself.

A calendar indicator appears in the Indicator column. If you rest your mouse pointer over the indicator, a ScreenTip displays the name of the assigned calendar (see Figure 5-23). Follow this same procedure to change to a different task calendar, or to remove the task calendar.

	🛈	Task Name	Duration
69		⊟ **Paint and Wallpaper**	**17 days**
70	🗓	Texture all except entry and kitchen - 1st floor	1 day
71	🗓	The calendar 'Night Shift' is assigned to the task. hen - 1st floor	1 day
72		chen - 1st floor	1 day
73		Texture all - 2nd floor	1 day

Figure 5-23. Assign a calendar to a task to schedule it independently from the project or resource calendars.

Troubleshooting

You've assigned a task calendar, but it's not scheduling tasks in all the times it should

The task probably also has a resource assigned, and the resource calendar is conflicting with what you want the task calendar to accomplish.

When you assign a task calendar, it takes the place of the project calendar. However, suppose resources are assigned to the task as well. Resources are all associated with their own resource calendars, as well. Although a resource's calendar might be the same as the project calendar, it might be customized for the resource's specific working times.

When resources are assigned, the task is scheduled not just for the working times indicated in the task calendar. Instead, by default, Microsoft Project schedules the task according to the common working times between the task calendar and the resource calendar.

For example, suppose the 24-hour base calendar is assigned to a task that's also assigned to a resource who works Friday through Sunday, 9:00 A.M. until 7:00 P.M. The only times the two calendars have in common are Friday through Sunday, 9:00 A.M. until 7:00 P.M., so by default, those are the only times when work will be scheduled for this task.

If you want the resource calendar to be ignored on a task, open the Task Information dialog box for the task, and click the Advanced tab. Select the Scheduling Ignores Resource Calendars check box.

Chapter 5

Setting Up Resources in the Project

As soon as you're assigned as manager of the project, you might already have certain resources in mind whom you know would be right for this project. As the scope becomes more defined, and you develop the task list along with the milestones and deliverables, you're likely to have even more ideas. If you have specific people in mind, you might start inquiring about their availability. You might also start investigating sources, specifications, and prices for material and equipment.

By the time you develop the durations of the tasks, you have very concrete information in front of you—you now know exactly which tasks need to be done and what kinds of resources you need to do them.

There might be a team in place already—the full-time members of a department who are waiting to sink their teeth into a good project. There might be no team at all, and you'll have to hire some people and contract others. Or you might have a core staff, but for this project you'll need to contract additional temporary workers to fill out the skills needed for the team.

You can add the names of resources who will be working on this project as you acquire them. These might be the names of actual people. Or these might be generic resource names that describe the skills and competencies needed to fulfill the task. Where applicable, you can also enter the names of equipment or material resources that will also help implement the project. You can also enter additional resource information, such as availability, cost, and notes.

How Many Resources Do You Need?

Although you know the tasks that need to be done and the kinds of resources you need to do them, you might not know *how many* of a particular type of resource you need just yet.

Here's the process: First you identify the tasks that need to be done. Second you identify the resources needed to do those tasks. Third you assign resources to the tasks. At that point, you can see if the resulting schedule meets your target date or target budget.

You need to have tasks in place to find out how many resources you need. You also need resources to assign to those tasks to create an accurate schedule and cost estimate. After assigning resources, if the schedule calculates a finish date later than the target finish date, you might have to go back and add more resources to your team. Or if the project costs are over budget and you haven't even started work yet, you might have to forgo additional resources or scramble to replace expensive resources with less expensive ones.

As you can see, tuning your project plan to get the right number of resources to meet your schedule, costs, and workload requirements is an iterative process. You might need to go through several cycles of refinement before you arrive at the perfect plan.

For more information about refining the project plan to meet a target date or budget, see Chapter 9, "Checking and Adjusting the Project Plan."

Understanding the Impact of Resources in the Project Plan

Resources carry out the work of your project. However, with your tasks defined and scheduled, why is it necessary to actually specify resources in your project plan? You could just print the schedule and tell people which tasks they're responsible for: Here are your due dates, now go make it happen.

This might seem like a simple way of managing a project, but if you do it this way, you'd miss out on the immense scheduling, tracking, and communication capabilities provided by Microsoft Project. By adding resources to your project, you can:

- Increase the accuracy of your schedule. In addition to scheduling according to the project calendar, durations, task dependencies, and constraints, when you assign resources, Microsoft Project adds the working times and availability of your resources into the scheduling calculations.

- Know ahead of time whether any resources are overloaded with too much work in the allotted time. You can also see whether anyone is underallocated and shift responsibilities accordingly as you refine your schedule. Later, when work is being done and you're getting progress information on each task, you can find bottlenecks or any new overallocations or underallocations due to shifts in the schedule.

● Track progress according to resource work. Your resources can tell you how much time they've spent on their tasks for a given week and how much more time they will need. This can help you make any necessary adjustments to keep the project moving in the right direction. This also helps you capture historical information that will be invaluable for future projects.

● Track the use, cost, and consumption of materials in your project. This can help you monitor your budget performance as well as give you advance notice as to when you need to reorder supplies.

● Exchange task assignments, task updates, progress information, and status reports with your resources, either through e-mail communication or Microsoft Project Server and Microsoft ProjectWeb Access.

● Make sure that all tasks are assigned to a responsible and accountable resource, so nothing inadvertently slips through the cracks to be forgotten until it's too late.

Adding Work Resources to the Project

The following types of resources can accomplish work on your tasks:

● People

● Equipment

● Materials

Microsoft Project consolidates these three into two resource types. *Work resources* consist of people and equipment, which use time as a measure of effort on a task. *Material resources* are consumable supplies, which use quantity as a measure of effort on a task.

> For more information about material resources, see "Adding Material Resources to the Project," later in this chapter.

Add resources to your project simply by entering their names into your project plan. To automate the process, you can select resource names from your company's e-mail address book. If you have a resource list in an Excel workbook, you can import it into your project plan. After your resources are in place, you can add information, including their availability, costs, notes, and more.

Chapter 6

165

Project Management Practices: Staffing Management

Ongoing operations such as accounts payable or shipping and receiving always need to be staffed "forever." In projects, however, that's not the case. Because projects have a specific beginning and ending point, there's a definite starting point when you begin to need resources. There also a definite ending point when resources will no longer be needed because the project is complete. In between the start and finish dates, there are likely to be ramp-up and ramp-down periods. These ramp-up and ramp-down periods can often take place at a variety of times for different phases or functions.

Given this condition of project staffing, it's important to have a clear sense of when you actually need people to work on projects, what you need them for, at what point you will not need them anymore, and what happens to them after that point.

A staffing management plan is considered a subset of your project plan. It describes when and how your human resources will be brought on and taken off your project team. An excellent way to develop your staffing management plan is to develop your task list and preliminary schedule using generic resources to determine your staffing needs based on the tasks and schedule.

Adding Resource Names Manually

To add resources to your project by simple data entry, follow these steps:

1 Click View, Resource Sheet to switch to the Resource Sheet view (see Figure 6-1).

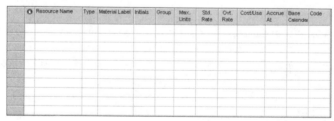

Figure 6-1. Enter Resource information on the Resource Sheet.

2 Make sure the Entry table is applied. Click View, Table, Entry.

3 In the first Resource Name field, type a resource name, and press Enter.

4 Enter the names of other resources in the same way.

If a piece of equipment will be integral to the successful completion of a task, enter its name as a work resource, just as you would a human resource.

---

tip **Sort your resource names**

When you have all the resources entered, you might want to sort them in a particular order and have them stay in that order. In the Resource Sheet, click Project, Sort, Sort By. In the Sort By field, click the field you want the resources sorted by, for example, Name, or Group. Select the Permanently Renumber Resources check box, and then click OK. This makes this particular order permanent because it renumbers the Unique ID for each resource.

Whenever you select the Permanently Renumber Resources check box and click OK, it's a very good idea to open the Sort dialog box again and clear the check box. This way, the next time you sort your resources, you won't inadvertently renumber the resources again.

You can enter the actual names of resources or you can enter a *generic resource*. A generic resource is a title or other similar description of the resource rather than an actual name, for example, Accountant, Marketing Specialist, Sales Representative (see Figure 6-2).

ⓘ	Resource Name	Type	Material Label	Initials	Group	Max. Units	Std. Rate	Ovt. Rate	Cost/Use	Accrue At	Base Calendar
1	Sarah Akhtar	Work		S		1	$0.00/hr	$0.00/hr	$0.00	Prorated	Standard
2	Beth Parsons	Work		B		1	$0.00/hr	$0.00/hr	$0.00	Prorated	Standard
3	Mike Nash	Work		M		1	$0.00/hr	$0.00/hr	$0.00	Prorated	Standard
4	Jose Lugo	Work		J		1	$0.00/hr	$0.00/hr	$0.00	Prorated	Standard
5	Designer	Work		D		1	$0.00/hr	$0.00/hr	$0.00	Prorated	Standard
6	Project Engineer	Work		P		1	$0.00/hr	$0.00/hr	$0.00	Prorated	Standard
7	Drafter	Work		D		1	$0.00/hr	$0.00/hr	$0.00	Prorated	Standard

Figure 6-2. Use either actual resource names or generic categories of resources to get started.

As you bring resources into the project, you can either leave the generic names or you can replace the generic names with the actual names. Whenever you change resource names in the Resource Sheet, the names are changed on the assigned tasks automatically.

Troubleshooting

You have duplicate resource names, and information is being tracked separately for each instance

Whether you enter actual names or generic names, be aware that Microsoft Project allows duplicate entries of the same name. Through the use of a unique identifier (Unique ID) for each resource record you enter, the duplicate entries appear unique to the Microsoft Project database. The problem is that when you assign tasks to a duplicated resource, you might assign some tasks to one instance of the resource and

(continued)

Chapter 6

> **Troubleshooting** *(continued)*
>
> other tasks to another instance. Microsoft Project tracks the resource and assignment information as if they are separate resources, and your information therefore is skewed.
>
> If you've entered a long list of resources, it's a good idea to sort the resource list and review the sorted list to check for duplicates. In the Resource Sheet, click Project, Sort, By Name.

> **tip** **Mark generic resources and automatically substitute them**
>
> If you're using Microsoft Project Professional with Microsoft Project Server and the enterprise features, you can mark generic resources as such. The Resource Substitution Wizard can then search throughout the enterprise resource pool to find the resources with the skill set and availability you need. When the right resource is found, the Resource Substitution Wizard replaces the generic resource with the real resource who can now work on your project.
>
> For information about the Resource Substitution Wizard and the Team Builder, see Chapter 24, "Using Enterprise Features to Manage and Participate in Projects."

Estimate Resource Requirements Using Generic Resources

Entering generic resources is very helpful when you want Microsoft Project to help you estimate which resources and how many of a type of resource you need to meet your project finish date within a targeted budget. Enter your generic resources in the Resource Sheet, and then assign them to tasks.

For more information about assigning resources, see Chapter 7, "Assigning Resources to Tasks."

Check the calculated project finish date to see if you need additional resources to meet the targeted project finish date. Check the total project costs to see if you need to change your resource mix to meet your budget.

When you have finished tweaking your project plan to meet your requirements, you'll know which resources you need.

Adding Resources from Your E-Mail Address Book

If Microsoft Project is installed on the same computer as your company's Microsoft Exchange e-mail connection, you can add resources to your project plan from the e-mail address book. To do this, follow these steps:

1 Click Insert, New Resource From, Address Book.

If the Choose Profile dialog box appears, click the profile name for your e-mail system.

The Select Resources dialog box appears.

2 Click the resources you want, and then click the Add button to add the selected resources to your project plan.

You can add all resources contained in a group or distribution list. Add the name of the group to your list, just as you would add an individual resource. When you click the Add button, Microsoft Project will ask whether you want to expand the group to list the individual resources in the project plan.

---

tip   **Add resources from Microsoft Project Server**

If you're connected to Microsoft Project Server to use the enterprise features, Microsoft Project Web Access, or both, you have access to all existing resources identified in the server. Click Insert, New Resource From, Microsoft Project Server.

Using Resource Information from Microsoft Excel

Suppose you have a list of resources in a Microsoft Excel workbook. You can easily use it to populate your project's Resource Sheet. You can copy information or you can import the file.

To copy a resource list from an Excel workbook, follow these steps:

1 Open the Excel workbook that contains the resource list.

2 Select the resource names. On the Standard toolbar in Excel, click Copy.

3 Open the project plan. If necessary, click View, Resource Sheet.

4 In the Resource Name column, click the cell where you want to begin inserting the copied resources.

5 On the Standard toolbar in Microsoft Project, click Paste.

Chapter 6

169

newfeature!

You can also use the Microsoft Project Plan Import Export Template to import resources from Excel to Microsoft Project. The standard Excel importing process involves mapping the Excel columns to the corresponding Microsoft Project columns to ensure that the right information ends up in the right locations in your Resource Sheet. In Microsoft Project 2002, the new Microsoft Project Plan Import Export Template is set up to enter more detailed resource information in the format needed by Microsoft Project. To do this, make sure that Excel and the Microsoft Project Plan Import Export Template are installed on the same computer as Microsoft Project, and then follow these steps:

1 Start Microsoft Excel.

2 Click File, New.

3 In the New Workbook task pane, click General Templates. The Templates dialog box appears.

4 Click the Spreadsheet Solutions tab.

5 Double-click Microsoft Project Plan Import Export Template. The template creates a new file with columns that correspond to the most commonly used fields in Microsoft Project.

6 At the bottom of the workbook window, click the Resource_Table tab.

7 Enter resources and any other resource information in the columns provided (see Figure 6-3). Save the file.

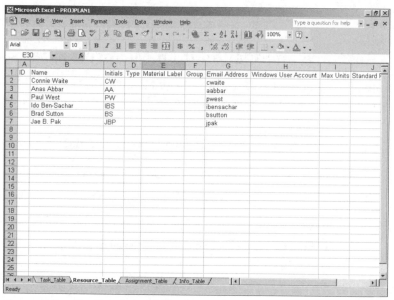

Figure 6-3. The Resource_Table sheet of the Microsoft Project Plan Import Export Template in Excel contains the most commonly used resource fields.

Chapter 6

Add Resources Using the Project Guide

You can also use the Project Guide to help add resources to your project plan. It can walk you through the steps to enter resources manually, to add them from your company address book or directory, or from Microsoft Project Server. To add resources using the Project Guide:

1 On the Project Guide toolbar, click Resources.

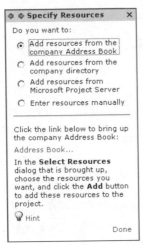

2 In the Project Guide pane, click the Specify People And Equipment For The Project link.

3 Read the succeeding panes, and make choices as directed (see Figure 6-4).

Figure 6-4. Make the choices you want, follow any directions, and click the controls provided. The Project Guide walks you through the process.

note If you're working with a version of Microsoft Excel 2000 or earlier, you can still use the Microsoft Project Plan Import Export template. Open Excel, and then click File, New. Click the 1033 or Spreadsheet Solutions tab. Double-click the Microsoft Project Plan Import Export Template.

When you're ready to import the resource list into your project plan, follow these steps:

1 If necessary, open the project plan.

2 On the Standard toolbar, click the Open button.

3 Go to the location on your computer or network where the Excel workbook is saved.

4 In the Files Of Type list, click Microsoft Excel Workbooks (*.xls). The task list appears in the list of folders and files.

5 Click the task list workbook, and then click the Open button. The Import Wizard appears (see Figure 6-5).

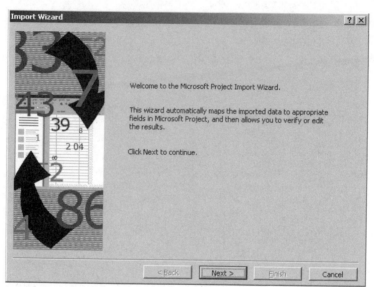

Figure 6-5. The Import Wizard helps you import the resource information from your Excel workbook into your project plan.

6 Click the Next button.

7 Click Project Excel Template, and then click the Next button.

8 Specify whether you want to import the file as a new project, append the resources to the currently active project, or merge the data into the active project, and then click the Finish button (see Figure 6-6).

For more information about using Microsoft Project with other applications, see "Importing and Exporting Information" on page 441, and Chapter 17, "Integrating Microsoft Project with Microsoft Excel."

For more information about adding resources to your project plan from a shared resource pool file, see "Sharing Resources Using a Resource Pool" on page 402. For more information about adding resources from the Enterprise resource pool, see Chapter 24, "Using Enterprise Features to Manage Projects."

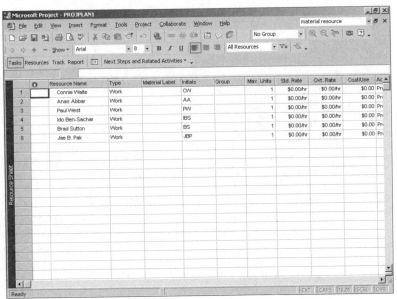

Figure 6-6. The resource information is imported into Microsoft Project as you specified.

Specifying Resource Availability

Suppose most of your resources will be working full time on your project. But you have two part-timers—one available half time, and the other available three out of the five working days.

You can specify this kind of resource availability by setting the resource's *maximum units*, also referred to as *resource units*. The full-time resources are each available at 100 percent units. The half-time resource is available at 50 percent units. The other part-timer is available at 60 percent resource units. When you assign resources to tasks, those tasks are scheduled according to that resource's availability.

Here's another scenario: suppose you have three engineers, two architects, and four drafters, all working a full-time schedule. Instead of naming them individually, you decide you want to name your resources by their functions and consolidate them into a single resource representing multiple individuals. You can do that with resource units as well. The three engineers together are available at 300 percent, the two architects at 200 percent, and the four drafters at 400 percent.

If you have three full-time drafters and one half-time drafter, your *Drafters* resource is available at 350 percent resource units.

To enter resource units, simply type the percentage in the Max. Units field in the Resource Sheet (see Figure 6-7 on the next page).

	ⓘ	Resource Name	Type	Material Label	Initials	Group	Max. Units
1		Kim Yoshida	Work		K		100%
2		Katherine Inman	Work		K		100%
3		Adam Stein	Work		A		100%
4		Tristan Randall	Work		T		100%
5		Daniel Penn	Work		D		100%
6		Carol Philips	Work		C		50%
7		Lani Ota	Work		L		60%
8		Engineers	Work		E		300%
9		Architects	Work		A		200%
10		Drafters	Work		D		350%

Figure 6-7. You can enter resource units when you enter resource names, or come back to it later. The default for the Max. Units field is 100%.

Now suppose your staffing plan specifies that you'll start the project life cycle needing four drafters. After three months, you'll only need three drafters. Two months later, you'll only need one. To specify variable resource quantity or availability over time, follow these steps:

1 In the Resource Sheet, click the resource whose resource units you want to adjust.

Resource
Information

2 On the Standard toolbar, click Resource Information. Or simply double-click the resource name. The Resource Information dialog box appears. Make sure the General tab is displayed (see Figure 6-8).

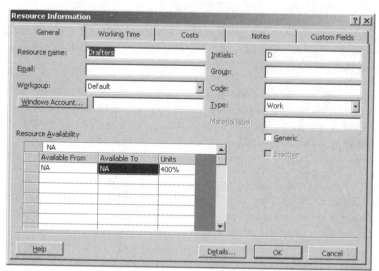

Figure 6-8. Use the Resource Information dialog box to enter detailed information about an individual or consolidated resource.

Chapter 6

3 Under Resource Availability, enter the first date range for the resource's units specification. That is, enter the beginning date, the ending date, and the resource units that will be available during those dates. For example, in the first row under Available From, enter 1/6/03. Under Available To, enter 3/28/03. Under Units, enter 400%.

4 In the second row, enter the second date range for the resource's units specification. For example, enter 3/31/03 under Available From. Enter 6/27/03 under Available To. Then enter 300% under Units.

5 Continue in this manner until your entire resource availability specification is set. For example, enter 6/30/03 under Available From. Enter 8/29/03 under Available To, and 100% under Units (see Figure 6-9).

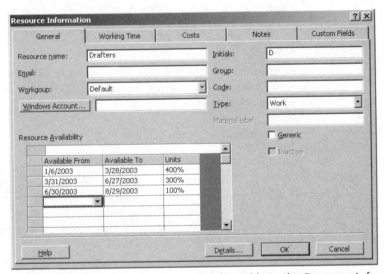

Figure 6-9. Use the Resource Availability table in the Resource Information dialog box to specify multiple levels of resource units throughout the project.

---

tip **Switch units from percentage to decimal**

By default, resource units are expressed as a percentage. You can have them expressed as a decimal if you prefer. Click Tools, Options, and then click the Schedule tab. In the Show Assignment Units As A box, select Decimal. Now instead of 100 percent, one full-time resource will be shown as having 1 max unit.

Adding Material Resources to the Project

Any supplies that are integral to completing tasks can be added to your project plan as a material resource. Examples of such material resources might be steel for a building structure, roofing material for a home, bricks for a landscaping project, and so on. You might have a task "Lay brick sidewalk," to which a bricklayer is assigned for a certain amount of time. You can also assign a quantity of bricks to the task. The bricklayer and the bricks are both essential resources to the completion of the task.

To enter a material resource, follow these steps:

1 Display the Resource Sheet with the Entry table applied.

2 In the first available Resource Name field, type the name of the material resource, for example, *Bricks*, and then press Enter.

3 In the Type field, select Material.

4 In the Material Label field, enter the unit of measurement for the material. This will differ depending on the nature of the material. It might be tons, yards, feet, cartons, and so on.

When you specify that a resource is a material rather than a work resource, be aware of the following points:

- Resource units (or maximum units) and the associated variable availability are not applicable to material resources. You'll specify units, for example, 50 yards, or 100 feet per day, when you assign the material resource to a task. With these assignment units, you'll be able to track the usage of materials and possibly the depletion rate of materials.

For more information about material resource assignments, see "Assigning Material Resources to Tasks" on page 203.

- Resource calendars are not available for material resources.

- Workgroup fields, such as E-mail, Workgroup, and Windows Account are not available for material resources. The Overtime field is also disabled.

Setting Resource Working Time Calendars

With resource units (maximum units), you're able to specify resource availability in terms of part-time, full-time, or the number of individuals or machines available. Another means of specifying resource availability is through the resource's working time calendar, also known as simply the *resource calendar*. The resource calendar is basically a project calendar that can be customized to reflect the individual resource's specific working times. Because the resource calendar indicates when a resource is available to work on assigned tasks, it affects the manner in which tasks are scheduled.

Viewing a Resource Calendar

As soon as you create a resource, the project calendar is assigned by default as the resource's working time calendar. To view a resource's working time calendar, follow these steps:

1 Display the Resource Sheet or other resource view.

2 Click the resource whose working time calendar you want to view.

3 On the Standard toolbar, click Resource Information.

4 In the Resource Information dialog box, click the Working Time tab. The working time calendar for the selected resource appears (see Figure 6-10). By default, it's identical to the project calendar until you change it. The Base Calendar field indicates which base calendar is the origin of the resource calendar.

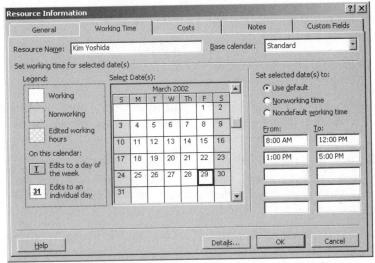

Figure 6-10. Use the Working Time tab in the Resource Information dialog box to view or modify an individual resource's working times. These are the days and times when assigned tasks can be scheduled for this resource.

> **note** Microsoft Project comes with three *base calendars*: Standard, Night Shift, and 24 Hours. These base calendars are like calendar templates that you can apply to a set of resources, a set of tasks, or the project as a whole.

Modifying a Resource Calendar

You can change an individual resource's calendar to reflect a different work schedule from others on the project team. For example, most everyone on your team might work Monday through Friday, 8:00 A.M. until 5:00 P.M. But suppose one team member works just three days a week, and another team member works weekend nights. You can change their resource calendars to fit their actual work schedules. This way, their assigned tasks will only be scheduled when they're actually available to work on them.

You can also update resource calendars to reflect vacation time, personal time off, sabbaticals, and so on. Updating the resource calendars helps keep your schedule accurate. To modify a resource's working time calendar, follow these steps:

1   Display the Resource Sheet or other resource view.

2   Double-click the resource whose working time calendar you want to modify. The Resource Information dialog box appears.

3   Click the Working Time tab.

4   To change the working time of a single day, click that day.

    If you're changing working time to nonworking time, select the Nonworking Time option.

    If you're changing the working time to something other than the default, select the Nondefault Working Time option. Then change the times in the From and To boxes as needed.

5   To change the working time of a particular day of each week, click the day heading. For example, click the M heading to select all Mondays. Select the Nonworking Time or Nondefault Working Time option, and then change the times in the From and To boxes as needed.

6   To change the working time of a day in another month, scroll down in the Select Dates box until you see the correct month. As before, select the Nonworking Time or Nondefault Working Time option, and then change the working times as needed.

7   When finished, click OK.

Creating a New Base Calendar for Resources

If you find you're making the same modifications to individual resource calendars repeatedly, you might do well by creating an entirely new base calendar and applying it to the applicable resources. If you have a group of resources who work a different schedule, for example, a weekend shift or "four-tens," create a new base calendar, and apply it to those resources. To create a new base calendar:

1 Click Tools, Change Working Time.

2 Click the New button. The Create New Base Calendar dialog box appears (see Figure 6-11).

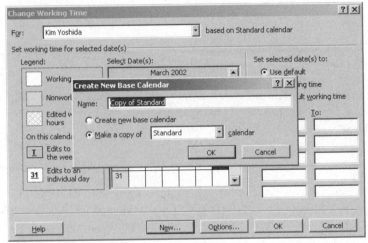

Figure 6-11. You can create a new base calendar from scratch or adapt it from an existing one.

3 In the Name box, type the name you want for the new base calendar, for example, *Weekend Shift*.

4 Select the Create New Base Calendar option if you want to adapt your calendar from the Standard base calendar.

Select the Make A Copy Of option if you want to adapt the new calendar from a different base calendar, such as the Night Shift. Click the name of the existing calendar you want to adapt, and click OK.

5 Make the changes you want to the working days and times of individual days or of a particular day of every week, as needed.

6 When finished with your new base calendar, click OK.

When you create a new base calendar, it becomes available in any of the three calendar applications—project calendar, task calendar, or resource calendar. To assign the new base calendar to a resource, follow these steps:

1 Display the Resource Sheet or other resource view.

2 Double-click the resource to whom you want to assign the new base calendar. The Resource Information dialog box appears.

3 Click the Working Time tab.

Chapter 6

4 In the Base Calendar field, select the base calendar you want to apply to the selected resource.

5 Make any additional changes to the calendar as needed for this resource. These changes apply only to the selected resource. They do not change the original base calendar.

InsideOut

You cannot change the base calendar for multiple resources at once. You have to select each resource individually, and then change his or her calendar. The fastest way to do this is to work in the Resource Sheet. For each resource, select the new calendar in the Base Calendar field.

You can also set your resource working times using the Project Guide. On the Project Guide toolbar, click Resources. In the Project Guide pane, click the Define Working Times For Resources link. Read the succeeding panes, and make choices as directed (see Figure 6-12).

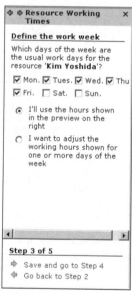

Figure 6-12. The Resource Working Times pane of the Project Guide assists you through the process of setting resource calendars.

> **tip** **Specify availability for equipment resources**
>
> You can enter resource units with varying availability and a customized resource calendar for equipment resources just as you can for human resources because they are both considered work resources. Setting equipment working times and availability can be useful to account for other projects using the same equipment at different times. It can also be useful to schedule downtime for preventive maintenance.

Adding Detailed Resource Information

Along with the basic resource information like the resource name, type, units, and calendar, you can add supplementary information to either work or material resources. This can include additional fields of resource information, notes, or hyperlinks.

Working with Supplemental Resource Fields

To add initials, group designations, or a code to a resource, enter that information in the appropriate field in the Resource Sheet or on the General tab in the Resource Information dialog box. The following list provides examples of how you might use these fields:

Initials. If you want a resource's initials rather than his or her entire name to appear in any field in your project plan, enter the initials in the Initials field in the Resource Sheet or on the General tab in the Resource Information dialog box.

Group. Use the Group field to specify any categories of resources that might be useful for sorting, grouping, or filtering. For example, you can specify the department the resources come from, like Product Development or Marketing. If you are using contracted resources, you can enter their company's name in the Group field. Or you can use the Group field to specify the resource's title or skill set, for example, Engineer, Architect, or Designer.

> **note** You cannot assign a group name to a task. The group simply provides more information about a resource so you can sort, group, or filter resources.

Code. Enter any code meaningful to you or your company in the Code field. This can be any alphanumeric designation you want. In fact, you could use it the way you use the Group field. You can enter job codes or skill codes, for example. Like the Group field, you can then sort, group, or filter on these codes.

Chapter 6

> **note** You can create and assign resource outline codes to your resources. This can be useful when you want to apply a Resource Breakdown Structure, for example, or any other code-based hierarchical or outline structure to your resources. You can then group by your outline codes to see the resources displayed in that structure.

> For more information about outline codes, see "Working with Outline Codes" on page 631.

Cost-related fields are an important part of the Resource Sheet. The Resource Information dialog box also includes a Cost tab.

> For more information about resource cost information for both work and material resources, see "Planning Resource Costs" on page 218.

Other tables containing different collections of resource fields are available. To apply a different table to the Resource Sheet, follow these steps:

1 Display the Resource Sheet.

2 Click View, Table. Click the table you want.

If the table you want is not listed, click More Tables. Click the table in the list (see Figure 6-13), and then click Apply.

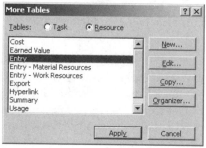

Figure 6-13. Apply any table that fits what you're trying to do.

There are a myriad of additional resource fields you can add to your Resource Sheet. To add a new field to your current table, follow these steps:

1 Click the column heading to the right of where you want the new column to be inserted.

2 Click Insert, Column, or simply press the Insert key. The Column Definition dialog box appears.

3 In the Field Name box, select the field you want to add. The fields listed are all resource fields. You can quickly move to a field by typing the first letter of its name.

To hide a field you don't need, follow these steps:

1 Click the column heading you want to hide.

2 Click Edit, Hide Column, or simply press the Delete key. The column is hidden. However, the information is not deleted. It's still in the database and can be shown again whenever you display its column.

---

tip   **Hide a column by making it very narrow**

You might frequently hide and insert certain columns, for example, when you print a view for presenting at a status meeting. If you're getting tired of constantly deleting and then inserting these columns, you can just make them very narrow. Position your mouse pointer on the right edge of the heading for the column you want to hide. When the pointer becomes a black crosshair, drag to the left to narrow the column until the contents cannot be seen.

If you drag past the left column edge, the column will be completely hidden, although still actually there.

When you're ready to display the narrow column again, drag the edge of the column heading to the right until you can read the contents of the column.

There's no indication that a column you hid completely is there—you just have to remember.

Adding Initials of Assigned Resources to the Gantt Bar

By default, the full resource name appears next to the Gantt bars in the Gantt Chart, displaying the resources assigned to this task. To help make your Gantt Chart look a little less cluttered, or to enable you to fit more task details in a small space, set a resource's initials as text next to a Gantt bar instead of the full name.

For more information about resource assignments, see Chapter 7, "Assigning Resources to Tasks."

To change the text style of your Gantt bar to include resource initials rather than the full resource name, follow these steps:

1 In the Resource Sheet, make sure that all resources have initials identified for them. It doesn't necessarily have to be their actual initials—it can be a short name, their first or last name, a nickname, or whatever you want.

2 Click View, Gantt Chart.

(continued)

Adding Initials of Assigned Resources to the Gantt Bar *(continued)*

3 Click Format, Bar Styles.

4 In the table area of the Bar Styles dialog box, make sure the Task row is selected.

5 In the lower half of the dialog box, click the Text tab.

6 By default, *Resource Names* appears in the Right field.

7 Click the Right field, and then click Resource Initials (see Figure 6-14). Click OK.

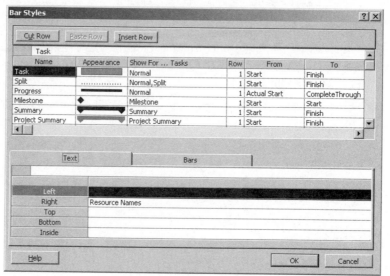

Figure 6-14. Use the Text tab in the Bar Styles dialog box to change the text that appears with the selected Gantt bar.

The resource initials you defined replace the full resource names next to the Gantt bars in the chart (see Figure 6-15).

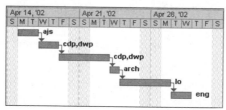

Figure 6-15. Resource initials replace the full resource names next to the Gantt bars.

Chapter 6

Specifying Workgroup Information

If you're going to communicate project information electronically with resources, you might need to complete one or more of the following fields on the General Tab in the Resource Information dialog box:

E-mail. Specifies the resource's e-mail address. This is essential if you are exchanging e-mail messages or project files with team members. If the resource is outside your company, that is, using a different e-mail system than you, be sure to specify the full e-mail address, for example, *someone@microsoft.com.*

> For more information about communicating project information through e-mail, see Chapter 18, "Integrating Microsoft Project with Microsoft Outlook," and Chapter 20, "Collaborating Using E-Mail."

Workgroup. Specifies the workgroup method for this resource. The choices are Microsoft Project Server, E-mail Only, None, or Default. To set the default workgroup choice, click the Collaborate menu, click Collaboration Options, and then in the Collaborate Using list, click your default workgroup method.

Windows Account. Authenticates the resource through Microsoft Project Server. The Windows Account button finds the resource's user account in the local address book and places it in that resource's Windows User Account field. Having the resource's user account information identifies the Microsoft Windows users to Microsoft Project Server. To use this button, click the Collaborate menu, and then click Collaboration Options. In the Microsoft Project Server URL box, enter a valid URL.

> For guidelines on setting up Microsoft Project Server options, see Appendix A, "Installing Microsoft Project 2002."

Adding a Note Regarding a Resource

You can add comments regarding a resource by adding notes. Notes might include information about the skills or experience of the resource or anything you believe is pertinent to this resource working on this project. To add a note to a resource, follow these steps:

1   Display the Resource Sheet or other resource view.

2   Click the resource name, and then on the Standard toolbar, click Resource played (see Figure 6-16 on the next page).

Resource Notes

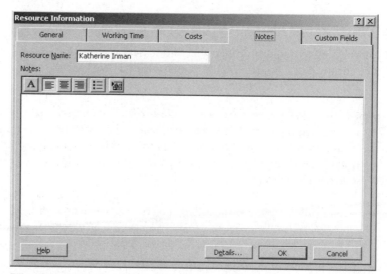

Figure 6-16. Enter relevant notes about a resource in the Notes tab of the Resource Information dialog box. You can also attach outside documents in the Notes tab.

3 In the Notes area, type the note.

4 When finished, click OK.

The Note indicator appears next to the resource name in the Indicators field of the Resource Sheet. You can double-click this icon when you want to read the note.

Hyperlinking to Resource Information

If there's a document or Web site relevant to a resource, you can create a hyperlink to reference it. This is a very efficient method of opening associated documents quickly. To insert a hyperlink, follow these steps:

1 Display the Resource Sheet or other resource view.

2 Click the resource to which you want to link an outside document or Web page.

3 On the Standard toolbar, click Insert Hyperlink.

4 In the Text To Display box, type a descriptive name for the document to which you are linking, for example, *Quarterly Goals*.

5 Find and select the document or site you want to link to your project file
   (see Figure 6-17).

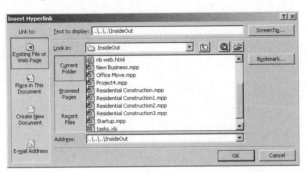

Figure 6-17. The path and name of the selected document appear
in the Address box.

6 Click OK. The Hyperlink indicator appears in the Indicators field
   of the Resource Sheet (see Figure 6-18).

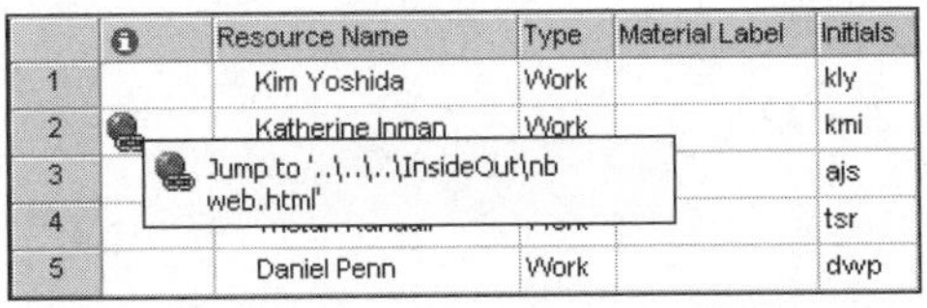

	ⓘ	Resource Name	Type	Material Label	Initials
1		Kim Yoshida	Work		kly
2	🔗	Katherine Inman	Work		kmi
3		Jump to '..\..\..\InsideOut\nb web.html'			ajs
4		Trotan Randall	Work		tsr
5		Daniel Penn	Work		dwp

Figure 6-18. Position your mouse pointer over the Hyperlink indicator
to read the link. Click the indicator to jump to the link's location.

Whenever you need to review the target of the hyperlink, just click the Hyperlink
indicator. The contents open in their own application window.

You can use the Project Guide to help you add notes or hyperlinks to resources.
On the Project Guide toolbar, click Resources. In the Project Guide pane, click the Link
To Or Attach More Resource Information link. Read the succeeding panes and make
choices as directed.

Assigning Resources to Tasks

You have tasks. You have resources. Now you need to match them up. Tasks + resources = assignments. With human, equipment, and material resources assigned to tasks, Microsoft Project can create a project schedule that reflects not only the project calendar, task durations, dependencies, and constraints, but also the calendars and availability of assigned resources.

Assigning Work Resources to Tasks

When you assign a work resource, you are attaching the resource name to a task and then indicating how much of the resource's total availability is to be devoted to this task.

When you first add a resource to the project plan, through the use of maximum units (also known as *resource units*), you specify how available this resource will be to this project. For example, if the resource is available full time on the project, say, 40 hours a week, you would probably specify that the resource has 100 percent resource units. If another resource is available 20 hours a week, you would probably specify that this resource has 50 percent resource units. If you have three of the same type of resource, for example, three graphic designers, you could indicate that there are 300 percent resource units.

When you assign these resources to tasks, you take the idea of availability a step further by using *assignment units*. With resource units, you specify resource availability to the project as a whole. With assignment units, you specify resource availability to the specific task to which the resource is assigned.

189

Project Management Practices: Assigning the Right Resources to Tasks

As the project manager, you consider several factors when deciding whom to assign to which tasks. One of the most important factors is the resource's skill set, competencies, and proficiencies. His or her ability to carry out the assigned task is essential to the success of the task. You can set up your resources in Microsoft Project so that you can find and assign resources based on their skill set.

Another important factor is the resource's availability. If the perfect resource is 100 percent committed to another project during the same timeframe as your project, you won't be able to use this resource. Microsoft Project can help you find resources that are available to work on your project.

There are other factors as well:

Experience.   Have the resources you're considering for the assignment done similar or related work before? How well did they do it? Perhaps you can use this assignment as an opportunity to pair a more experienced team member with a less experienced one. This can set up a mentoring situation in which both team members can benefit, and in which your team is strengthened in the long run.

Enthusiasm.   Are the resources you're considering personally interested in the assignment? In many cases, a resource with less experience but more enthusiasm can be more effective than a seasoned but bored resource.

Team dynamics.   Do certain tasks require several resources to work together? If so, are the resources you're considering likely to work well together? Do they have a history of conflicts with each other? Do certain team members have good synergy with one another?

Speed.   Is alacrity important to your project, all other things being equal? Some resources work faster than others. This can be a function of experience. Or it can be a function of working style or level of quality. Determine how important speed is to your project, and assign tasks accordingly.

Cost.   Are you hiring contractors for the project? If you have specific budget limitations, cost is definitely a factor. Sometimes the rework required by an inexpensive resource can negate any cost savings. Conversely, sometimes more expensive resources can be a bargain, especially if they work faster than the norm.

Quality.   What are your quality standards for the project? Try to assign resources who can match those standards.

For example, one resource might be available full time to perform one task. When that's finished, she'll be assigned full time to the next task, and so on. Upon assigning this resource to the task, you therefore indicate 100 percent assignment units for this resource.

InsideOut

Because resource units and assignment units are both called "units," they can be confusing. They're related but different. It would be nice if they had names that were a little more different and a little more descriptive. But they're vital to our assignment scheduling and they're what we have to work with. So we need to keep them straight in our minds.

The Max. Units field applies to resources. Think of this kind of unit as *resource units*. The value you enter in the Max Units field tells Microsoft Project how much of a particular resource you have, whether it's half of full time (50 percent), full time (100 percent), or three full-time equivalents (300 percent).

The Units field applies to assignments. Think of this kind of unit as *assignment units*. The value you enter in the Units field tells Microsoft Project how much of the resource you can use to work on this specific assignment.

Both kinds of units can be expressed in either percentages or decimals.

You might have another full-time resource, however, who's spending 40 percent of his time on one task and 60 percent of his time on another task taking place at the same time. For the first task, you'd specify 40 percent assignment units, and for the second task, 60 percent. The assignment units specify the percentage of the full 100 percent resource units being used for the task in question.

Now take the case of a half-time resource (50 percent resource units) who's spending all available time on one task. The maximum assignment units you can have for this resource is 50 percent. If this resource is spending half her time on one task and half on another, the assignment units would be 25 percent for each task.

Finally, let's look at the case of the three graphic artists whose resource units are 300 percent. When you start to assign tasks to a *consolidated resource* like this, Microsoft Project does not assume you want to use all three on one task. You can, but the default assignment units are 100 percent. You can change it to anything up to 300 percent.

> **tip** **Switch assignment units from percentage to decimal**
>
> By default, assignment units are expressed as a percentage. You can express them as a decimal if you prefer. Click Tools, Options, and in the Options dialog box, click the Schedule tab. In the Show Assignment Units As A box, click Decimal. Now a resource working full time on an assignment will be shown as having 1 assignment unit instead of 100 percent. This setting also changes how maximum units are displayed in the Resource Sheet.

Creating Work Resource Assignments

By creating an assignment, you specify both the resources assigned to a task and their associated assignment units. Using the Assign Resources dialog box, you can assign one resource to a task, multiple resources to a task, or multiple resources to multiple tasks. To assign a work resource to a task, follow these steps:

1 In the Gantt Chart or other task sheet, click the task to which you want to assign resources.

Assign
Resources

2 On the Standard toolbar, click Assign Resources. The Assign Resources dialog box appears (see Figure 7-1).

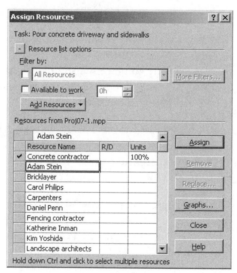

Figure 7-1. Use the Assign Resources dialog box to specify which resources are to be assigned to which tasks, and for how much of their available time.

3 In the dialog box, click the name of the work resource you want to assign to the task, and then click the Assign button.

192

The resource name moves to the top of the Resources list in the table and a default percentage appears in the Units field for the resource. For individual resources, the default assignment units are the same as the resource's maximum units. For consolidated resources with more than 100 percent maximum units, the default assignment units are 100 percent.

4 Review the Units field to make sure it's appropriate for this assignment.

5 If you want to assign a second resource, click that resource name, and then click the Assign button. Modify the Units field as necessary. If you change the Units field, you need to press Enter or click another field. This ends the edit mode for the field, sets your change, and makes the Assign button available.

---

tip **Assign multiple resources in one operation**

You can select all resources to be assigned to a task and assign them at once. Click the first resource, hold down Ctrl, and then click all other resources. Click the Assign button.

---

6 Repeat Step 5 for all resources you want to assign to the selected task.

7 To assign resources to a different task, click the next task for which you want to make assignments. You don't have to close the Assign Resources dialog box to select a different task.

8 Repeat steps 3–6 to assign resources to all tasks as necessary.

9 When finished assigning resources to tasks, click the Close button.

---

tip **Keep the Assign Resources dialog box open as long as you like**

Unlike other dialog boxes, you can switch back and forth between the task sheet and the Assign Resources dialog box. It's handy to keep it open while you're working out all the details you need to finish making your assignments.

Adding and Assigning Resources at the Same Time

Suppose you want to assign a specific resource to a task but that resource isn't listed in the Assign Resources dialog box because you haven't added him or her to your Resource Sheet yet. You can add new resources to your project plan while working in the Assign Resources dialog box and then immediately assign the newly added resource to tasks. You can then go to the Resource Sheet and complete any detailed resource information you want. To add new resources in the Assign Resources dialog box, follow these steps:

1 In the Gantt Chart or other task sheet, click the task to which you want to assign resources.

193

2 On the Standard toolbar, click Assign Resources to display the Assign Resources dialog box.

3 In the Resources table, type the resource name in the next available blank Resource Name field.

4 Click the Assign button. The resource name moves to the top of the Resources list in the table, and 100% appears in the Units field for the resource.

5 Adjust the assignment units if necessary. Assign any additional tasks you want.

6 When finished, click the Close button.

7 Click View, Resource Sheet. The new resources you added are listed. Modify any field as necessary, such as Group, Max. Units, Calendar, and so on.

---

tip   **Add resource information from the Assign Resources dialog box**

Double-click any resource name in the Assign Resources dialog box and the Resource Information dialog box appears. Enter detailed resource information as appropriate.

You can add an entire group of resources from your e-mail address book, Windows server, or Microsoft Project Server to the Assign Resources dialog box, just as you can in the Resource Sheet. To add resources from a server, follow these steps:

1 With the Gantt Chart or other task sheet open, click Assign Resources on the Standard toolbar.

newfeature!

2 In the Assign Resources dialog box, click the Add Resources button.

If you don't see the Add Resources button (see Figure 7-2), click the + Resource List Options button. The dialog box expands to include the Add Resources button.

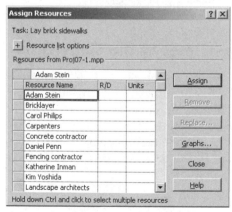

Figure 7-2.   Click the – Resource List Options button to collapse the Assign Resources dialog box. Click the + Resource List Options button to expand it.

3 Click From Active Directory if you are working with a Windows Server and want to add resources from the Active Directory.

Click From Address Book if you want to add resources from your e-mail program's address book.

Click From Microsoft Project Server if you want to add the resources who are listed as Project Server and Web Access users.

4 Click the resources you want, and then click the Add button to add the selected resources to the Assign Resources dialog box.

5 After the resources are added, you can immediately assign them to tasks.

Filtering for Resources

In addition to filtering for resources in the Assign Resources dialog box, you can filter for tasks and assignments using particular resources. To do this, follow these steps:

1 Display the task or assignment view in which you want to filter for certain assignments, for example, the Gantt Chart or Resource Usage view.

2 Click Project, Filtered For, Using Resource.

3 In the Using Resource dialog box, click the name of the resource whose assignments you want to see.

To filter for a resource's assignments within a particular date range, do the following:

1 Display the task or assignment view in which you want to filter.

2 Click Project, Filtered For, More Filters.

3 In the More Filters dialog box, click Using Resource In Date Range, and click the Apply button.

4 In the Using Resource In Date Range dialog box, enter the name of the resource whose assignments you want to see, and then click OK.

5 Enter the beginning of the date range you want to see, and then click OK.

6 Enter the end of the date range you want to see, and then click OK.

To see all tasks or assignments again, click Project, Filtered For, All Tasks.

newfeature!
Finding the Right Resources for the Job

You can use the Assign Resources dialog box to narrow your list of resources to only those who meet the criteria needed for the tasks you're assigning. You can filter the resource list to show only those resources who belong to the Marketing department, for example, or only those resources who have a particular job code or skills definition. This is an instance when using resource fields like Group or Code comes in handy.

195

If you create and apply resource outline codes, you can also filter for a particular outline code level.

To find resources that meet certain criteria, follow these steps:

1 With the Gantt Chart or other task sheet open, click Assign Resources on the Standard toolbar.

2 In the Assign Resources dialog box, select the check box next to the Filter By box.

If you don't see the Filter By box, click the + Resource List Options button. The dialog box expands to include the Filter By box.

3 In the Filter By list, click the filter that applies to the type of resource you want to find. For example, Group or Resources – Work.

For additional filters, click the More Filters button.

Any filter that requires additional information includes an ellipsis (…) after its name. Click the filter, and then in the dialog box that appears, enter the requested information, and click OK.

As soon as you select a filter, the list in the Resources table changes to show only those resources that meet the filter's criteria (see Figure 7-3).

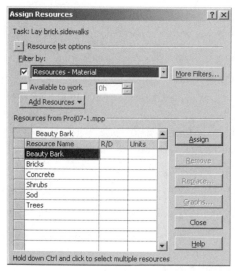

Figure 7-3. By filtering your resource list, you can choose from a set of targeted resources that meet the criteria for the tasks you are currently assigning.

4 Assign resources to tasks as usual.

5 When you want to review the full list of resources again, click All Resources in the Filter By list, or simply clear the Filter By check box.

InsideOut

There is no built-in resource filter for Code or Outline Code. You can create your own filters by clicking New in the More Filters dialog box, and then specifying the field name, test, and value for the filter. For example, you can create a filter that finds all resources that have a Code field greater than 9100. Or you can create a filter that finds all resources that have an Outline Code equal to 1200-B.

For more information about creating custom filters, see "Customizing Filters" on page 624.

Defining a Resource Skill Set

If you set up a resource field that defines certain skill sets, you can use the Assign Resources dialog box to filter for resources with specific skills. For example, you can use the Group field in the Resource Sheet to specify the type of resource, for example, "Writer," "Editor," "Designer," or "Programmer." To assign writing tasks, you can filter for Writer in the Group field. To assign programming tasks, you can filter for Programmer in the Group field. This can be especially useful if you have a large number of resources.

Other fields you can use to define skill sets include Code and Outline Code. You can also use custom fields such as Text1 or Number1 to specify skills descriptions or numbers.

For more information about working with custom fields, see "Customizing Fields" on page 613.

note If you're using Microsoft Project Professional with Microsoft Project Server and the enterprise features, you can use the Resource Substitution Wizard and Team Builder to search throughout the enterprise resource pool to find the resources with the skill set and availability you need.

For information about the Resource Substitution Wizard and the Team Builder, see Chapter 24, "Using Enterprise to Manage and Participate in Projects."

You can filter your resources to see only those who actually have enough time available for more work. For example, suppose you've assigned all your resources to tasks. Then you add several more tasks and you want to assign only resources who have time for them. To filter for resources with a certain amount of available time, follow the steps on the next page.

1 With the Gantt Chart or other task sheet open, click Assign Resources on the Standard toolbar.

2 In the Assign Resources dialog box, select the Available To Work check box.

If you don't see the Available To Work check box, click the + Resource List Options button. The dialog box expands to include the Available To Work check box.

In the Available To Work box, enter the amount of time needed for the task you're about to assign. For example, if you need a resource with 4 days of available time, enter *4d* in the box.

As soon as you enter the amount of time, the list in the Resources table changes to show only those resources who have the specified availability.

3 Assign resources to tasks as usual.

4 When you want to see the full list of resources again, simply clear the Available To Work check box.

Troubleshooting

Your Filter By or Available To Work boxes are dimmed

It might look like the Filter By box and its More Filters button are unavailable to you because they're dimmed. They don't look available until you select the check box next to the Filter By box.

The same applies to the Available to Work box. It's dimmed until you select the Available To Work check box.

Selecting the check boxes is necessary because it helps you specify what kind of resource filter you want to apply. You can apply a filter only, or an availability check only. Or you can combine the two—applying a filter to find only those resources who meet the filter criteria *and* have a certain amount of available time.

You can review graphs of resource availability from the Assign Resources dialog box. This can help you decide which work resource should be assigned to a task. To review the resource availability graph, follow these steps:

1 With the Gantt Chart or other task sheet open, click Assign Resources on the Standard toolbar.

2 In the Assign Resources dialog box, click the work resource whose availability graph you want to view. Note that availability does not apply to material resources.

3 Click the Graphs button. The Resource Availability Graph for the selected resource appears (see Figure 7-4). By default, the work graph is displayed.

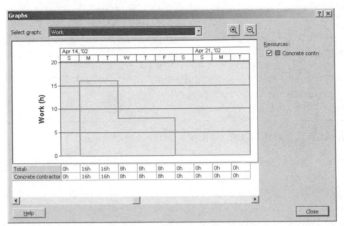

Figure 7-4. In the Work version of the Resource Availability Graph, you can review the selected resource's current workload over time.

4 To change the field on which the graph is based, click Remaining Availability or Assignment Work in the Select Graph list. The Work graph shows the total work for all the selected resource's assignments. The Assignment Work graph breaks down the work on the currently selected tasks in relation to the selected resource's total work assigned (see Figure 7-5). The Remaining Availability graph shows when the selected resource has any available time for more assignments.

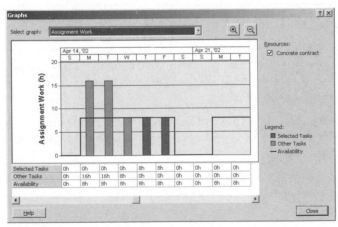

Figure 7-5. With the Assignment Work version of the Resource Availability Graph, you can compare the workload of selected tasks with those of other tasks.

5 To change the timescale for the graph, click the Zoom In or Zoom Out buttons. The Zoom In button provides a closer look at a shorter time period. For example, it can change the graph from a view of weeks to a view of days. The Zoom Out button provides an overview of availability over a longer time period. For example, it can change the graph from a view of weeks to a view of months.

6 When finished reviewing the graph, click the Close button. The Assign Resources dialog box appears again.

---

tip   **Review availability graphs for multiple resources at a time**

Select multiple resources in the Assign Resources dialog box and then click the Graphs button. The Resource Availability Graph shows graphs for each resource at the same time, using different colors for each resource. In the upper-right corner of the graph window, clear the check box for any resource whose graph you want to hide.

Understanding Assignment Calculations

Work is the amount of time it takes a resource to complete a task. As soon as you assign a resource to a task, the duration is translated into work. A simple example: If you have a task with a 3-day duration and you assign a single full-time resource to it, that resource now has an assignment with 24 hours of work spread across three days (assuming default calendar settings).

Translate Duration to Work Amounts

You can control how Microsoft Project translates duration to work amounts. By default, if you specify a 1-day duration, Microsoft Project translates this to 8 hours of work. However, if you want 1 day to mean 6 hours, to account for non-project work, you can change your calendar options.

Click Tools, Options, and in the Options dialog box, click the Calendar tab. Change the settings in Hours Per Day, Hours Per Week, or Days Per Month, as needed to fit your requirements.

If you want the project or resource calendar to reflect the changes you made to the duration to work-amount settings, be sure to change the appropriate working time calendars to match.

For more information about changing the project calendar, see "Setting Your Project Calendar" on page 58. For information about resource calendars, see "Setting Resource Working Time Calendars" on page 176.

If you assign two full-time resources to that same 3-day task, both resources are assigned 24 hours of work, also spread across 3 days (see Figure 7-6). When you assign multiple resources *initially*, Microsoft Project assumes that you intend for the resources to have the same amount of work across the original task duration.

	ⓘ	Task Name	Work	Duration	Details	Apr 14, '02 S	M	T	W	T
1		⊟ Lay brick sidewalk	24 hrs	3 days	Work		8h	8h	8h	
		Bricklayer	24 hrs		Work		8h	8h	8h	
2		⊟ Install fence	48 hrs	3 days	Work		16h	16h	16h	
		Kim Yoshida	24 hrs		Work		8h	8h	8h	
		Tristan Randall	24 hrs		Work		8h	8h	8h	

Figure 7-6. In the first task with a single resource assigned, the total work is 24 hours. In the second task with two resources assigned, the total work is 48 hours.

Troubleshooting

You assign two resources to a task, but the work is doubled rather than halved

When you assign multiple resources *initially*, Microsoft Project assumes that you intend for the same amount of work to be applied to all assigned resources across the time span represented by the task duration.

If you want the duration to be reduced because multiple resources are assigned, set the duration accordingly. Or start by assigning just one resource at first. Then assign the additional resources in a separate operation. As long as the task is not a *fixed-duration task*, the duration will be reduced based on the number of additional resources added.

The calculations for work and duration can change if you assign one resource *initially*, and then *later* assign a second resource. This might also be true if you initially assign two resources, and later remove one of them.

For more information about these schedule recalculations, see "Changing Resource Assignments" later in this chapter.

---

tip   **Specify the work time unit you use most often**

If you don't specify a work unit, by default Microsoft Project assumes the unit to be hours, and automatically enters "hrs" after your work amount. You can change the default work unit if you like. Click Tools, Options, and then click the Schedule tab. In the Work Is Entered In box, select the time unit you want as the default.

You can see the amount of work assigned to resources in either the Task Usage or Resource Usage views. The Task Usage view shows assignments by tasks (see Figure 7-7 on the next page). The information for each assignment is rolled up, or summarized, in the row representing the task. To switch to the Task Usage view, click View, Task Usage.

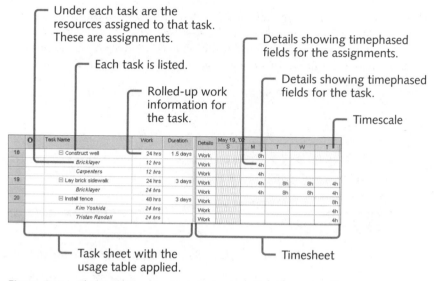

Under each task are the resources assigned to that task. These are assignments.

Each task is listed.

Rolled-up work information for the task.

Details showing timephased fields for the assignments.

Details showing timephased fields for the task.

Timescale

Task sheet with the usage table applied.

Timesheet

Figure 7-7. The Task Usage view shows task duration as well as assignment work.

The Resource Usage view shows assignments by resources (see Figure 7-8). The information for each assignment is rolled up, or totaled, in the row representing the resource. To switch to the Resource Usage view, click View, Resource Usage.

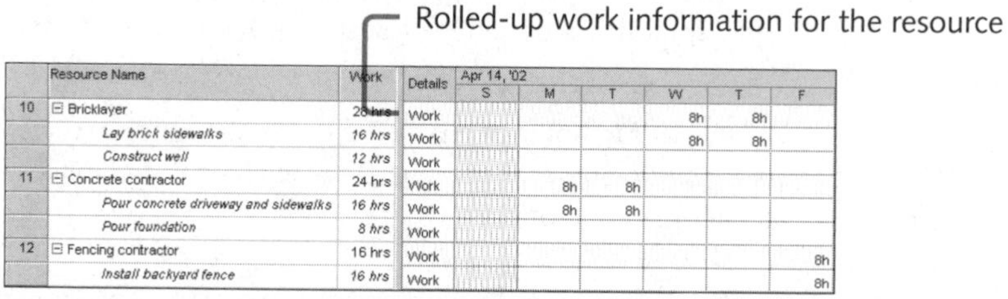

Rolled-up work information for the resource

Figure 7-8. The Resource Usage view focuses on resource and assignment work.

Either Usage view is great for reviewing assignment information. Which one you use depends on whether you want to see assignments within the context of tasks or resources.

The Usage views are the only two views in which you can see detailed assignment information. From these two views, you can also access the Assignment Information dialog box (see Figure 7-9). Just double-click the assignment whose information you want to see.

202

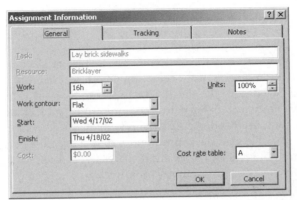

Figure 7-9. You can open the Assignment Information dialog box by double-clicking an assignment in the Task Usage or Resource Usage views.

---

tip   **Add a note about an assignment**

Assignment Notes

In the Task Usage or Resource Usage view, click the assignment, and click Assignment Notes on the Standard toolbar. The Notes tab in the Assignment Information dialog box appears. Enter the note, and click OK when finished. The Notes icon appears in the Indicators column of the Usage view.

Assigning Material Resources to Tasks

When you assign a material resource, you are attaching the material resource name to a task and then indicating the quantity of material to be used in fulfilling this task.

Material resources are supplies consumed in the course of fulfilling a task. As with work resources, there are units of measurement to specify how much of the resource is available to carry out the task. With work resources, this measurement is time—number of hours or days, for example. With materials, however, the measurement, and therefore the material resource assignment units, is quantity. When you assign a material resource to a task, you specify the quantity of resource that this task will consume.

For example, suppose you have a landscaping project that includes the "Lay down beauty bark" task. The material resource for this task is obviously beauty bark. Because beauty bark is measured in cubic yards, you would have set the material's unit of measurement, or label, as *cubic yards* when you added beauty bark as a material resource in the Resource Sheet. Now when you assign beauty bark as a material resource to the "Lay down beauty bark" task, you can specify the assignment units as 6, to indicate 6 cubic yards of beauty bark.

Other examples of material labels include tons, linear feet, packages, cartons, pounds, crates, and so on.

The quantity of material consumed in the course of performing a task can be fixed or variable, based on duration. That is, if the same amount of material will be used whether the task takes 2 days or 2 weeks, the material is said to have a *fixed material consumption*. However, if more material will be used if the duration increases and less material used if the duration decreases, the material is said to have a *variable material consumption*. To specify variable material consumption, enter a per-time period specification in the assignment Units field. For example, 1/week or 3/day. This will be translated with the material's label, for example, 1 ton/week, or 3 yards/day.

InsideOut

You would think that a material with a variable consumption rate could be set as such in the Label field of the Resource Sheet. Not so. You can enter any string you want in the Label field, including something like *yards/day*. But when you assign the material to a task, the expected per-day calculations will not be made.

To specify the variable consumption rate, always specify it in the Units field in the Assign Resources dialog box rather than in the Label field in the Resource Sheet.

To assign a material resource to a task, follow these steps:

1 In the Gantt Chart or other task sheet, click the task to which you want to assign a material resource.

2 On the Standard toolbar, click Assign Resources.

3 In the Assign Resources dialog box, click the name of the material resource you want to assign to the task, and then click the Assign button.

The material resource name moves to the top of the Resources list in the table, and the label appears in the Units field, defaulting to a quantity of 1, for example, *1 yards*.

4 Change the *1* in the Units field to the correct quantity for this assignment, for example, *3 yards* (see Figure 7-10).

If you change the Units field, you need to press Enter or click another field. This ends the edit mode for the field, sets your change, and makes the Assign button available.

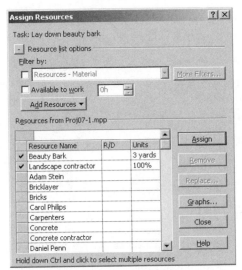

Figure 7-10.   Change the default of 1 unit to the appropriate quantity of material to be used to complete the selected task.

5   If necessary, change the material from the default fixed consumption rate to variable consumption rate (see Figure 7-11). After the material's label, enter a slash and time period abbreviation, for example, *3 yards/d*.

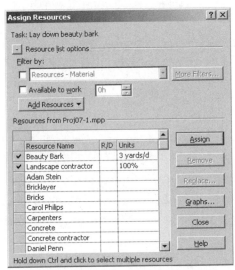

Figure 7-11.   Use the standard time period abbreviations (h, d, w, and so on) to specify the quantity per time period for a material resource with a variable consumption rate.

6 If you want to assign another resource to the selected task, click the name, and then click the Assign button. Modify the Units field as necessary.

You can assign material and work resources in the same operation.

7 To assign material resources to a different task, click the next task to which you want to assign a material resource. You don't have to close the Assign Resources dialog box to select a different task.

8 When finished assigning resources to tasks, click the Close button.

Changing Resource Assignments

There are three ways you can change resource assignments:

- You can add more resources to the existing resources assigned to a task.

- You can replace one resource with another.

- You can remove a resource from a task.

To add more resources to the existing ones initially assigned to a task, follow these steps:

1 In the Gantt Chart or other task sheet, click the task to which you want to add more resources.

2 On the Standard toolbar, click Assign Resources. The Assign Resources dialog box appears, showing a check mark next to the names of resources already assigned.

3 Click the name of the resource you want to add to the task, and then click the Assign button.

The resource name moves to the top of the Resources list in the table, and the default percentage appears in the Units field for the resource.

4 Review the Units field and make sure it's appropriate for this assignment.

If you change the Units field, you need to press Enter or click another field. This ends the edit mode for the field, sets your change, and makes the Assign button available.

5 When finished working with resource assignments, click the Close button.

206

newfeature! In the task sheet, you'll see that the task has been updated to include the new resource. You'll also see the green feedback triangle in the task cell. Position your mouse pointer over the triangle and the Smart Tag icon appears in the Indicators field. Click the Smart Tag icon. A menu appears (see Figure 7-12).

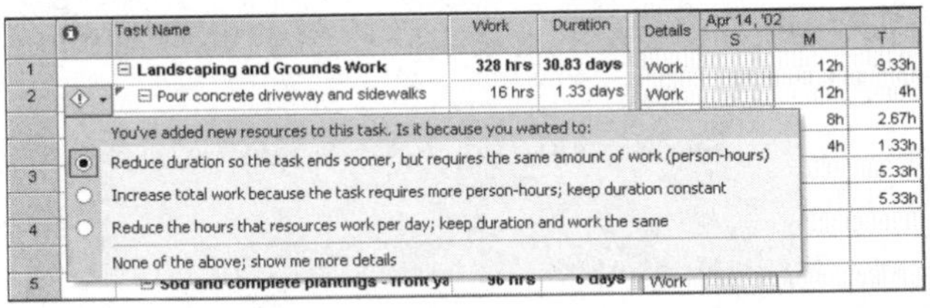

Figure 7-12. The Smart Tag informs you of the ramifications of adding a resource to the task. These results are based on the task type.

The Smart Tag disappears as soon as you carry out another operation and therefore cannot undo the previous operation.

To replace one resource with another, follow these steps:

1 In the Gantt Chart or other task sheet, click the task to which you want to add more resources.

2 On the Standard toolbar, click Assign Resources. The Assign Resources dialog box appears, showing a check mark next to the names of resources already assigned.

3 Click the name of the assigned resource you want to replace, and then click the Replace button. The Replace Resource dialog box appears, showing the same resources that are displayed in the Assign Resources dialog box, according to any filters you might have applied.

4 Click the name of the replacement resource, and then click OK.

The name of the replacement resource moves to the top of the Resources list in the table, and the default percentage appears in the Units field for the resource.

5 Review the Units field and make sure it's appropriate for this assignment.

6 When finished adding resources, click the Close button.

To remove a resource assignment, follow these steps:

1 In the Gantt Chart or other task sheet, click the task from which you want to remove a resource.

2 On the Standard toolbar, click Assign Resources. The Assign Resources dialog box appears, showing a check mark next to the names of resources already assigned.

3 Click the name of the assigned resource you want to remove, and then click the Remove button.

4 When finished working with resource assignments, click the Close button.

---

note When you remove a resource assignment, you're only removing the assignment, not the resource itself. The resource is still assigned to other tasks, and is available for assignment to other tasks.

In the task sheet, you'll see that the task has been updated to exclude the deleted resource. If there were multiple resources assigned and you removed one of them but left others intact, you'll also see the green feedback triangle in the task cell. Position your mouse pointer over the triangle and the Smart Tag icon appears in the Indicators field. Click the Smart Tag icon. A menu appears (see Figure 7-13).

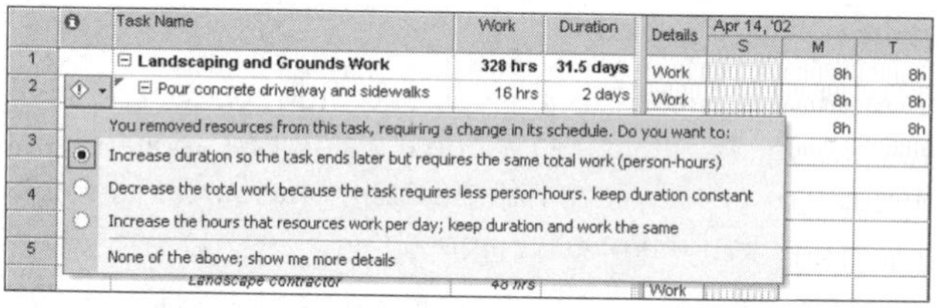

Figure 7-13. The Smart Tag informs you of the ramifications of removing a resource from the task. These results are based on the task type.

---

tip **Use the Task Information dialog box to assign or change resources**

As an alternative to the Assign Resources dialog box, you can double-click a task to open the Task Information dialog box and then click the Resources tab (see Figure 7-14). Although the Task Information dialog box doesn't have all the options of the Assign Resources dialog box, you can still assign, replace, and remove assigned resources, as well as set the assignment units.

208

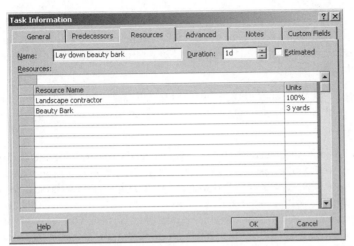

Figure 7-14. Use the Resources tab in the Task Information dialog box to create or modify resource assignments.

---

tip **Turn off Smart Tags**

Smart Tags provide feedback for users who are still getting used to the ways Microsoft Project schedules tasks. This feedback helps users understand the impact of scheduling changes being made.

If you understand the impact of your scheduling changes, you might not need Smart Tags, so you can turn them off. To do this, click Tools, Options, and in the Options dialog box, click the Interface tab. Under Show Indicators And Option Buttons For, clear the Resource Assignments and the Edits To Work, Units Or Duration check boxes.

Controlling Changes with Effort-Driven Scheduling

When you assign an additional resource to a task that already has assigned resources, by default, the amount of work scheduled for each assigned resource decreases. Likewise, when you remove a resource from a task, leaving at least one remaining resource assigned, by default, the amount of work scheduled for each remaining assigned resource increases.

This is a function of *effort-driven scheduling*, which dictates that as more resources are added, there is less work for each resource to perform, although the total work to be performed by all resources stays constant. If resources are removed, each remaining resource needs to do more work, again, with the total work remaining constant.

The results of effort-driven scheduling operate in conjunction with the task type. If the task type is set to fixed units or fixed work, adding resources decreases the duration. If the task type is set to fixed duration, adding resources decreases the units for each assigned resource.

By default, effort-driven scheduling is enabled for all tasks. This makes sense because in the majority of cases the primary reason for adding resources to a task is to bring in its finish date.

However, you might have certain tasks whose work should not change regardless of the addition or removal of assigned resources. For example, you might have a 4-day document review task. You want all resources assigned to have 4 days to review the document. Suppose you realize later that you forgot a resource who also needs to review the document. When you add this resource to the task, you wouldn't want the work to be reduced—you still want everyone to have 4 days. Because each resource is reviewing different aspects of the document, it isn't the type of task that can be completed more quickly if more resources are added.

To turn off effort-driven scheduling for selected tasks, follow these steps:

1 In the Gantt Chart or other task sheet, click the task for which you want to turn off effort-driven scheduling.

If you want to turn off effort-driven scheduling for several tasks at one time, click the first task, hold down Ctrl, and then click the other tasks you want.

2 On the Standard toolbar, click Task Information.

3 In the Task Information dialog box, click the Advanced tab.

4 Clear the Effort Driven check box.

To turn off effort-driven scheduling for all new tasks in this project plan, follow these steps:

1 Click Tools, Options, and in the Options dialog box, click the Schedule tab.

2 Clear the New Tasks Are Effort Driven check box.

Chapter 7

---

tip **Use Smart Tag feedback when adding or removing resources**

When you add or remove resources assigned to a task, the Smart Tag feedback icon appears so that you'll get the scheduling results you want. Click the Smart Tag icon to read your options, and then make any changes you want. If you click Show Me More Details, the Customize Assignment pane in the Project Guide appears.

Controlling Schedule Changes with Task Types

Adding or removing resources after the initial assignment can change the task and assignment scheduling based on whether the task is effort driven.

The scheduling for a task or assignment can also change when one of the following items is changed:

- Task duration
- Assignment units
- Work

Duration, units, and work are interrelated and interdependent (see Figure 7-15). When you change one of the three, at least one of the others is affected. For example, by default, if you revise duration, work is recalculated. If you revise assignment units, duration is recalculated.

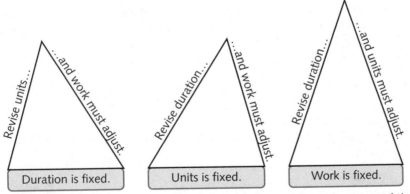

Figure 7-15. When you change one of the three elements, at least one of the others is affected, which changes your task or assignment scheduling.

You need to be able to control how the schedule is affected when you change duration, assignment units, or work. This control is the *task type*. Think of the task type like the one anchor among the three elements of duration, units, and work. When you make a change, the task type dictates which of the three elements must remain fixed and which of the other two can flex to accommodate the change. Therefore, the three task types are as follows:

- Fixed Units
- Fixed Duration
- Fixed Work

Which one you choose for your project and your individual tasks has to do with how you develop your project and the scheduling rules you have in mind as you set your task durations and assign your resources.

---

tip   **Use Smart Tag feedback when you change scheduling controls**

When you change units, work, or duration, the Smart Tag feedback icon appears so that you'll get the scheduling results you want. Click the Smart Tag icon to read your options, and then make any changes you want. If you click Show Me More Details, the Customize Assignment pane in the Project Guide appears.

Understanding the Fixed Units Task Type

When you assign a resource to a task, you specify the assignment units in the Units field of the Assign Resources dialog box. You can see the units in the chart portion of the Gantt Chart (see Figure 7-16). By default, the units appear with the resource name next to the Gantt bar if it's anything other than 100 percent.

Figure 7-16.   Assignment units other than 100 percent are shown next to the relevant Gantt bars.

The Fixed Units task type dictates that the percentage of assignment units on an assignment should remain constant regardless of changes to duration or work. This is the default task type. This is most appropriate in most cases. If you increase task duration, Microsoft Project shouldn't force you to find another resource, or force a 50 percent resource to work 100 percent on the assignment.

Changes to a Fixed Unit task have the following results:

- If you revise the duration, work also changes, and units are fixed.
- If you revise work, duration also changes, and units are fixed.
- If you revise units, duration also changes, and work is fixed.

Understanding the Fixed Work Task Type

When you assign a resource to a task, the task's duration is translated into work. You can see the amount of work in the Task Usage or Resource Usage view.

The Fixed Work task type dictates that the amount of work on an assignment should remain constant regardless of changes to duration or units.

Changes to a Fixed Work task have the following results:

- If you revise the duration, units also change, and work is fixed.
- If you revise units, duration also changes, and work is fixed.
- If you revise work, duration also changes, and units are fixed.

Understanding the Fixed Duration Task Type

When you create a task, you specify the task's duration in the Duration field of the Gantt Chart or other task sheet. The Gantt bar for the task is drawn according to the duration you set.

The Fixed Duration task type dictates that the task duration should remain constant, regardless of changes to units or work.

Changes to a Fixed Duration task have the following results:

- If you revise units, work also changes, and duration is fixed.
- If you revise work, units also change, and duration is fixed.
- If you revise the duration, work also changes, and units are fixed.

Changing the Task Type

As you gain more experience working with Microsoft Project, you'll see the impact of the schedule recalculations engendered by the changes you make. You can control the way changes to the resource assignments of tasks are made by choosing a default task type and you can make occasional exceptions when needed.

213

By default, all tasks are Fixed Units. To change the task type of selected tasks, follow these steps:

1 In the Gantt Chart or other task sheet, click the task for which you want to change the task type.

If you want to change the task type for several tasks at one time, click the first task, hold down Ctrl, and then click the other tasks you want.

Task
Information

2 On the Standard toolbar, click Task Information.

3 In the Task Information dialog box, click the Advanced tab.

4 In the Task Type box, click the task type you want to apply to the selected tasks.

To set the default task type for all new tasks in this project plan, follow these steps:

1 Click Tools, Options, and in the Options dialog box, click the Schedule tab.

2 In the Default Task Type box, click the task type you want to apply to all new tasks.

All the tasks in your schedule can have the same task type, or they can be intermixed.

Contouring Resource Assignments

When you assign a resource to a task, typically the work time allotted for the task is spread equally across the task duration. For example, if Pat is the only resource assigned full-time to a 4-day task, Pat is assigned 8 hours of work in each of the 4 days.

If you want to adjust how the hours are assigned, however, you can shape the work amounts. You can assign 1 hour on the first day, 2 hours on the second day, 5 hours on the third day, 8 hours on the fourth and fifth day, 5 hours on the sixth day, 2 hours on the seventh day, and 1 hour on the eighth day. You still have 32 hours of work, but the duration has stretched to 8 days. The assignment is shaped like a bell: It has a ramp-up period, a full-on period, and a ramp-down period. A shape applied to the work is called a work *contour* (see Figure 7-17).

Chapter 7

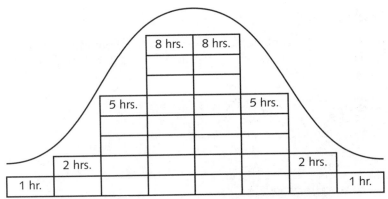

Figure 7-17. Apply the Bell work contour to shape the work amounts to reflect ramp-up, peak, and ramp-down periods, in the shape of a bell.

You can apply this shape by adjusting work amounts for the assignment in the time-sheet portion of the Task Usage view. Or you can apply the built-in bell contour, which converts the default flat contour into different shapes of time, such as back loaded, front loaded, early peak, and more.

The available built-in work contours are:

- Flat (the default)

- Early Peak

- Back Loaded

- Late Peak

- Front Loaded

- Bell

- Double Peak

- Turtle

To apply a built-in work contour to an assignment, follow these steps:

1 Display the Task Usage or Resource Usage view so you can see assignments.

2 Click the assignment to which you want to apply a work contour, and then click Assignment Information. The Assignment Information dialog box appears.

Assignment
Information

215

3 If necessary, click the General tab.

4 In the Work Contour box, click the work contour you want to apply (see Figure 7-18). Work for the assignment is redistributed in the shape of the selected contour.

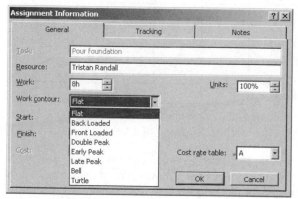

Figure 7-18. Use the General tab in the Assignment Information dialog box to set work contours.

You can also reshape the work for an assignment manually by editing work amounts in the timesheet portion of the Usage view. When you do this, an icon appears in the Indicators column, alerting you to the fact that work amounts have been edited.

 Any assignment with a work contour applied shows the specific contour icon in the Indicators field of the Task Usage or Resource Usage view.

---

tip **Apply a work contour to material resources**

You can also apply a work contour to material resources. In this case, the quantity of material used is distributed over the task span according to the selected contour.

Planning Resource and Task Costs

Microsoft Project can help you plan, forecast, and track costs associated with the performance of the project. The bulk of your costs is likely to be generated by the resources assigned to tasks. There might also be costs directly associated with tasks.

The starting point is to enter unit resource costs and any fixed costs for tasks. As resources are assigned to tasks, Microsoft Project calculates these unit costs to forecast the cost for each assignment, resource, task, and the project as a whole.

Use this cost estimate to develop your project's budget. Or if the budget has already been imposed, see whether the project plan is in line with the realities of the budget. If not, you can make the necessary adjustments.

Cost planning involves estimating your costs and setting your budget, which is the subject of this chapter. If necessary, you can adjust the project plan to conform to the budget. As soon as you start executing the project, you start tracking and managing costs. At that point, you can compare actual costs to your original planned costs and analyze any variances between the two.

For information about tracking costs, including setting cost baselines and entering actual costs, see Chapter 10, "Saving a Baseline and Updating Progress." For information about managing costs, see "Monitoring and Adjusting Costs" on page 320. For more information about adjusting the project plan to conform to the budget, see "Reducing Project Costs" on page 249.

Working with Costs and Budgeting

Project cost management is one of the many knowledge areas, or disciplines, required for a successful project execution. Simply put, effective project cost management ensures that the project is completed within the approved budget. Processes associated with project cost management include:

Resource planning.   After you've determined the types and quantities of resources needed for the project, you can estimate costs for those resources. You obtain work resources by hiring staff through human resources processes. You obtain contract staff, material resources, and equipment resources through procurement processes. You then enter those resources into your project plan and assign them to tasks.

Cost estimating.   *Top-down cost estimating* is the practice of using the actual cost of a previous, similar project as the basis for estimating the cost of the current project. *Bottom-up cost estimating* involves estimating the cost of individual tasks and then summarizing those estimates to arrive at a project cost total. The estimate should take into consideration labor, materials, supplies, and any other costs. With Microsoft Project, you can see the planned costs of resources, as well as the fixed costs associated with tasks. Microsoft Project can total all costs to give you a reliable estimate of how much it will cost to implement the project.

Cost budgeting.   The budget can allocate certain amounts to individual phases or tasks in the project. Or the budget can be allocated to certain time periods when the costs will be incurred. The cost estimate and the project schedule, with the scheduled start and finish dates of the different phases, tasks, milestones, and deliverables, are instrumental to developing the project budget.

Cost control.   This process controls changes to the project budget. Cost control addresses the manner in which cost variances will be tracked and managed, and how cost information will be reported. A cost management plan can detail cost control procedures and corrective actions.

Planning Resource Costs

The key to planning project costs is entering resource costs. The majority of your costs comes from resources carrying out their assignments. When you enter resource cost rates and assign resources to tasks, those resource cost rates are multiplied by the work on assignments. The result is the cost of the assignment.

You can set costs for work resources as well as material resources. Cost rates can be variable, such as $40/hour, or $200/ton. Or they might be a fixed per-use cost, such as $300 per use.

Setting Costs for Work Resources

You can set pay rates for work resources. When these resources are assigned to tasks, Microsoft Project multiplies the pay rates by the amount of assigned work to estimate the planned cost for the assignment. You can also set per-use costs for work resources. If a resource has different costs for different types of assignments or during different periods of time, you can enter multiple costs for one resource.

---

tip   **Enter costs when entering resources**

You can enter cost information for resources at the same time you add resources to the project. Simply complete all the fields in the Resource Sheet at the same time.

Specifying Variable Work Resource Costs

To set pay rates for work resources, follow these steps:

1 Click View, Resource Sheet.

2 If the Entry table is not already applied to the Resource Sheet, click View, Table, Entry.

Project Management Practices: Procurement Management

When you need to hire contract staffing or use vendors for certain phases of your project, procurement management comes into play. Procurement is also necessary when you need to purchase materials and equipment from selected suppliers.

You use procurement planning to identify which project requirements are best satisfied by purchasing products or services outside the project organization. Through procurement planning, you decide what you need, how much you need, when you need it, and who you're purchasing it from.

The procurement process includes the following:

- Bid solicitation planning
- Bid solicitation
- Vendor selection
- Contract administration
- Contract closing

Because contracting and procurement are specialized knowledge areas, it's best to get experts enlisted and involved on the project team as soon as possible.

219

3 Make sure the work resource is set up. It should be designated as a Work resource in the Type field.

> For more information about setting up work resources, see "Adding Work Resources to the Project" on page 165.

4 In the Std. Rate field for the first work resource, enter the resource's standard pay rate, for example, $30/hour, or $400/day.

5 If the resource is eligible for overtime, enter the resource's overtime pay rate in the Ovt. Rate field.

> **tip** **Set default rates**
>
> You can set a default standard rate and overtime rate for all work resources. Click Tools, Options, and then click the General tab. Enter values in the Default Standard Rate and Default Overtime Rate boxes. This ensures that there's an estimated value in the work resource rate fields. This can help you estimate project costs in broad terms until you have all your actual resources and rates added to the project.

> **note** If you're working with Microsoft Project Professional in an enterprise environment, you can update enterprise resource cost information. However, you must first check the resource out from Microsoft Project Server. Only one user at a time with the proper permissions can check out a resource and update resource information.
>
> > For more information about working with enterprise resources, see Chapter 24, "Using Enterprise Features to Manage Projects."

InsideOut

Microsoft Project does not automatically assign the overtime pay rate when a resource's work exceeds 8 hours in a day or 40 hours in a week. Although it seems like this would be the expected behavior, Microsoft Project can't make that assumption. If it did, you might end up with higher costs than you actually incurred.

For the overtime rate to be used, you must specify overtime work in addition to regular work for the resource. For example, if a person is scheduled to work 50 hours in a week, which includes 8 hour of regular work and 2 hours of overtime work per day, you should assign 10 hours of regular work per day, and designate 2 hours of it as overtime work. The cost of the hours specified as overtime work is then calculated with the overtime rate you entered for the resource.

For more information about working with overtime, see "Balancing Resource Workloads" on page 253.

Specifying Fixed Work Resource Costs

Some work resources incur a cost each time you use them. This *per-use cost* might be instead of or in addition to a cost rate, and is often associated with equipment. It's a set, one-time fee for the use of the resource. For example, rental equipment might have a delivery or setup charge every time it's used, in addition to its day rate.

Per-use costs never depend on the amount of work to be done. They're simply one-time costs that are incurred each time the resource is used.

To specify a per-use cost, follow these steps:

1 Click View, Resource Sheet.

2 If the Entry table is not already applied to the Resource Sheet, click View, Table, Entry.

3 In the Cost/Use field for the work resource, enter the resource's per-use cost, for example, $100.

---

tip **Set options for how currency is displayed**

You can set the currency symbol, the placement of the symbol to the number, and the number of digits after the decimal point. Click Tools, Options, and then click the View tab. Enter the options you prefer in the fields under Currency Options. The changes apply to your current project plan.

Setting Costs for Material Resources

To set resource costs, follow these steps:

1 Click View, Resource Sheet.

2 If the Entry table is not already applied to the Resource Sheet, click View, Table, Entry.

3 Make sure the material resource is set up in your Resource Sheet. It should be designated as a material resource in the Type field and have a unit of measurement, such as yards, tons, feet, and so on, in the Material Label field.

For more information about setting up material resources, see "Adding Material Resources to the Project" on page 176.

4   In the Std. Rate field for the material resource, enter the cost per unit. For example, if you have a material resource that is measured in tons, and each ton of this material costs $300, enter $300 in the Std. Rate field.

5   If there's a per-use cost for the material, such as a setup fee or equipment rental fee associated with using the material, enter it in the Cost/Use field.

Setting Multiple Costs for a Resource

Suppose you know that certain work resources will get a 5 percent raise on September 1. Maybe the contract for an equipment resource stipulates a discount for the first month of use, and then the cost returns to normal for the second month and beyond. Or perhaps a resource has one rate for one type of work, and another rate for another type of work. You can specify different costs at different times by using the *cost rate tables*. To specify different costs, follow these steps:

1   In the Resource Sheet, click the work or material resource for which you want to specify multiple cost rates.

2   On the Standard toolbar, click Resource Information.

3   In the Resource Information dialog box, click the Costs tab (see Figure 8-1).

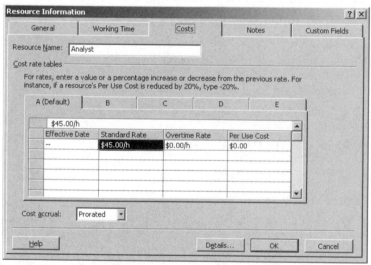

Figure 8-1.   Use the cost rate tables in the Resource Information dialog box to specify up to 25 different resource rates.

4 On the A (Default) tab, you see the standard rate, overtime rate, and per-use cost you might have already entered in the Resource Sheet.

5 To specify a change in rate after a certain period of time, click in the next blank Effective Date field, and enter the date the change is to take effect. Enter the cost changes as applicable in the Standard Rate, Overtime Rate, and Per Use Cost fields (see Figure 8-2).

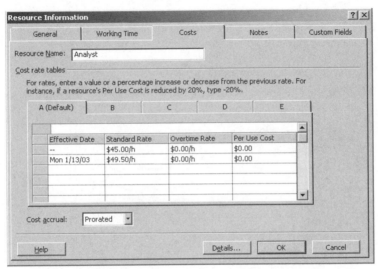

Figure 8-2. If new costs are to take effect on a certain date, add the date and costs in the A (Default) cost rate table.

6 To specify different costs based on different types of activities, enter the different costs in a different tab, such as B or C. Click the B tab, for example, and enter the Standard Rate, Overtime Rate, and Per Use Cost for the other activity as applicable. When you assign this resource to a task that uses the different rates, you can specify them with the assignment.

---

tip   **Specify rate changes in percentages**

If a percentage rate change goes into effect on a certain date, you can have Microsoft Project calculate the new rate for you. Enter the date in the Effective Date field, and then in the Standard Rate, Overtime Rate, or Per Use Cost fields, enter the percentage change, for example, +10% or -15%. The actual rate representing that change is immediately calculated and entered in the field.

Cost Rate Table A for resources is applied to the resource's assignments by default. If you've defined a different cost rate table for another category of work, specify which cost rate table is to be used for the assignment. To do this, follow these steps:

1 Assign the resource to the task using the Assign Resources dialog box.

2 Click View, Task Usage or View, Resource Usage to switch to an assignment view.

3 Click the assignment that needs a different cost rate table applied, and then click Assignment Information on the Standard toolbar.

4 In the Assignment Information dialog box, click the General tab.

5 In the Cost Rate Table list, click the cost rate table you want to apply to this assignment (see Figure 8-3).

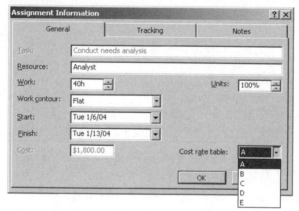

Figure 8-3. Select which cost rate table should be used for this assignment in the Assignment Information dialog box.

Setting Cost Accrual

The point in time when costs are incurred, or charged, is the *cost accrual method*. You can have costs incurred at the beginning of the assignment or after the end of the assignment. Or you can have the costs *prorated* across the time span of the assignment, which is the default method. Specifying the cost accrual method is important for budget cash flow planning.

To specify the cost accrual method, follow these steps:

1 Click View, Resource Sheet.

2 If the Entry table is not already applied to the Resource Sheet, click View, Table, Entry.

3 In the Accrue At field for the work or material resource, click the method: Start, Prorated, or End.

You can also specify the cost accrual method on the Costs tab in the Resource Information dialog box. Although different resources can have different cost accrual methods, you cannot set different cost accrual methods for different cost rate tables.

Planning Fixed Task Costs

Most of your costs are associated with resources and are calculated based on resource rates and assigned work. However, sometimes you have a cost associated with a task that's independent of any resource. In this case, you can enter a fixed cost for a task. Examples might include printing costs associated with the completion of a document deliverable or the travel costs associated with a milestone conference or event. To enter a fixed cost for a task, follow these steps:

1 Display the Gantt Chart or other task sheet.

2 Click View, Table, Cost. The Cost table with the Fixed Cost and Fixed Cost Accrual fields is applied to the task sheet (see Figure 8-4).

	Task Name	Fixed Cost	Fixed Cost Accrual	Total Cost
25	⊟ **Development**	**$0.00**	**Prorated**	**$15,840.00**
26	Review functional specifications	$0.00	Prorated	$480.00
27	Identify modular/tiered design parameters	$0.00	Prorated	$480.00
28	Assign development staff	$0.00	Prorated	$480.00
29	Develop code	$0.00	Prorated	$7,200.00
30	Developer testing (primary debugging)	$0.00	Prorated	$7,200.00
31	Development complete	$0.00	Prorated	$0.00

Figure 8-4. Apply the Cost table to enter fixed costs for tasks.

3 In the Fixed Cost field for the task, enter the cost.

4 In the Fixed Cost Accrual field, specify when the cost should be accrued— at the beginning of the task, at the end, or prorated throughout the duration of the task. The planned fixed cost for the task is added to the planned cost for the task based on assigned resources, and is shown in the Total Cost field.

---

tip **Set the default fixed cost accrual method**

To set the default fixed cost accrual method, click Tools, Options, and then click the Calculation tab. In the Default Fixed Costs Accrual list, select your preferred accrual method. This applies only to fixed costs for tasks but not resource costs.

You can also enter a fixed cost for the project as a whole. To do this, follow these steps:

1 Display the Gantt Chart or other task sheet.

2 Click View, Table, Cost. The Cost table is applied.

225

3 Click Tools, Options, and in the Options dialog box, click the View tab.

4 Under Outline Options, select the Show Project Summary Task check box, and then click OK. The project summary task row appears at the top of the view (see Figure 8-5).

	Task Name	Fixed Cost	Fixed Cost Accrual	Total Cost
0	⊟ **Software Development**	**$0.00**	**Prorated**	**$63,740.00**
1	⊟ **Scope**	**$0.00**	**Prorated**	**$1,240.00**
2	Determine project scope	$0.00	Prorated	$200.00
3	Secure project sponsorship	$0.00	Prorated	$400.00
4	Define preliminary resources	$0.00	Prorated	$320.00
5	Secure core resources	$0.00	Prorated	$320.00
6	Scope complete	$0.00	Prorated	$0.00
7	⊟ **Analysis/Software Requirements**	**$0.00**	**Prorated**	**$5,220.00**

Figure 8-5. Add the project summary task to add a fixed cost for the project.

5 In the Fixed Cost field for the project summary task, enter the fixed cost for the project.

6 In the Fixed Cost Accrual field, specify when the cost should be accrued—at the beginning of the project, at the end, or prorated throughout the duration of the project. The planned fixed cost for the project is added to all other costs calculated for assignments and tasks throughout the project. This total is shown in the Total Cost field of the project summary task.

Reviewing Planned Costs

The planned costs for your project become reliable figures that you can use for a budget request or a project proposal when the following information is entered in your project plan:

● All required work and material resources, even if they're just generic resources

● Costs rates and per-use costs for all work and material resources

● All tasks, complete with reliable duration estimates

● Assignments for all tasks

● Any fixed costs for tasks

After this information has been entered, you can review planned assignment costs, resource costs, task costs, and total project costs.

226

Reviewing Assignment Costs

You can review assignment costs by applying the Cost table to the Task Usage or Resource Usage view, as follows:

1 Click View, Task Usage or View, Resource Usage, to display one of the assignment views.

2 Click View, Table, Cost. The Cost table is applied to the view (see Figure 8-6).

Task Name	Fixed Cost	Fixed Cost Accrual	Total Cost	Details		M	T	W
7	⊟ **Analysis/Software Requirements**	**$0.00**	**Prorated**	**$5,220.00**	Work		8h	8h	8h
8	⊟ Conduct needs analysis	$0.00	Prorated	$1,800.00	Work				
	Analyst			*$1,800.00*	Work				
9	⊟ Draft preliminary software specificat	$0.00	Prorated	$1,080.00	Work		8h	4h	
	Analyst			*$1,080.00*	Work		8h	4h	
10	⊟ Develop preliminary budget	$0.00	Prorated	$640.00	Work			4h	8h
	Project manager			*$640.00*	Work			4h	8h
11	⊟ Review software specifications/bud	$0.00	Prorated	$340.00	Work				
	Project manager			*$160.00*	Work				
	Analyst			*$180.00*	Work				

Figure 8-6. Apply the Cost table to the Task Usage view to see assignment costs.

In the Task Usage view, you can see individual assignment costs, as well as the total cost for each task. In the Resource Usage view, you can see individual assignment costs with the total cost for each resource.

You can review timephased costs by adding cost details to the timesheet portion of the Task Usage or Resource Usage view, as follows:

1 Display either the Task Usage or Resource Usage view.

2 Click Format, Details, Cost. The Cost field is added to the Work field in the timesheet portion of the view (see Figure 8-7).

Task Name	Fixed Cost	Fixed Cost Accrual	Total Cost	Details		T	F
11	⊟ Review software specifications/budget with team	$0.00	Prorated	$340.00	Work		8h	
					Cost		$340.00	
	Project manager			*$160.00*	Work		4h	
					Cost		$160.00	
	Analyst			*$180.00*	Work		4h	
					Cost		$180.00	
12	⊟ Incorporate feedback on software specifications	$0.00	Prorated	$360.00	Work			8h
					Cost			$360.00
	Analyst			*$360.00*	Work			8h
					Cost			$360.00

Figure 8-7. Review assignment costs over time by adding the Cost field to the Task Usage or Resource Usage timesheet.

Zoom In Zoom Out

To see more or less time period detail, click the Zoom In or Zoom Out buttons on the Standard toolbar.

Reviewing Resource Costs

You can review resource costs to see how much each resource is costing to carry out assigned tasks. To get total costs for a resource's assignments, add the Cost field to the Resource Sheet, as follows:

1 Click View, Resource Sheet.

2 Click the column heading to the right of where you want to insert the Cost field.

3 Click Insert, Column.

4 In the Field Name list, click Cost, and then click OK. The Cost field is added to the table and shows the total planned costs for all assignments for each individual resource.

You can sort, filter, and group resources by cost. In the Resource Sheet with the Cost field added, you can rearrange the view by cost information as follows:

● Click Project, Sort, By Cost.

To return your Resource Sheet to its original order, click Project, Sort, By ID.

● Click Project, Filtered For, More Filters. Click Cost Greater Than, and then click the Apply button. Enter an amount, and then click OK.

To see all resources again, click Project, Filtered For, All Resources.

● Click Project, Group By, Standard Rate.

To ungroup your resources, click Project, Group By, No Group.

Reviewing Task Costs

You can review task costs to see how much each task will cost to carry out. This cost is the sum of all the costs of resources assigned to this task, as well as any fixed costs for tasks. To view total costs for tasks, do the following:

1 Display the Gantt Chart or other task sheet.

2 Click View, Table, Cost.

3 Review the Total Cost field to see the cost for each task.

There are two built-in reports you can run that show planned costs. To generate the Budget report, do the following:

1 Click View, Reports.

2 Double-click Costs.

3 Double-click Budget.

The Budget report appears (see Figure 8-8).

Task Name	Fixed Cost	Fixed Cost Accrual	Total Cost
	Budget Report as of Wed 4/3/02 Software Development		
Develop code	$0.00	Prorated	$7,200.00
Developer testing (primary debugging)	$0.00	Prorated	$7,200.00
Develop Help system	$0.00	Prorated	$4,800.00
Develop user manuals	$0.00	Prorated	$4,800.00
Develop training materials	$0.00	Prorated	$4,200.00
Conduct needs analysis	$0.00	Prorated	$1,800.00
Develop functional specifications	$0.00	Prorated	$1,800.00
Obtain user feedback	$0.00	Prorated	$1,600.00

Figure 8-8. The Budget report shows the task name, fixed costs, and total planned costs.

4 To print the report, click the Print button.

To generate the Cash Flow report, do the following:

1 Click View, Reports.

2 Double-click Costs.

3 Double-click Cash Flow.

The Cash Flow report appears (see Figure 8-9).

	3/31/02	4/7/02	4/14/02
	Cash Flow as of Wed 4/3/02 Software Development		
Software Development			
Scope			
Determine project scope	$200.00		
Secure project sponsorship	$400.00		
Define preliminary resources	$320.00		
Secure core resources	$320.00		
Scope complete			
Analysis/Software Requirements			
Conduct needs analysis	$540.00	$1,260.00	
Draft preliminary software specifications		$540.00	$540.00
Develop preliminary budget			$640.00
Review software specifications/budget with team			$340.00
Incorporate feedback on software specifications			$360.00

Figure 8-9. The Cash Flow report shows planned costs by task, with totals for tasks and for weekly periods.

4 To print the report, click the Print button.

For more information about reports, see "Setting Up and Printing Reports" on page 343.

229

You can sort and filter tasks by cost. In the Gantt Chart or other task sheet, rearrange your view by cost information as follows:

- Click Project, Sort, By Cost.

  To return your task list to its sort original order, click Project, Sort, By ID.

- Click Project, Filter For, More Filters. Click Cost Greater Than, then click the Apply button. Enter an amount, and then click OK.

  To see all tasks again, click Project, Filter For, All Tasks.

Reviewing the Total Planned Cost for the Project

You can see the total planned cost for the entire project. This cost is the sum of all task costs, as well as any fixed costs you might have entered for the project. To see the total cost for the project, add the Project Summary Task to the Gantt Chart or other task sheet, as follows:

1. Display the Gantt Chart or other task sheet.

2. Click View, Table, Cost. The Cost table is applied.

3. Click Tools, Options, and in the Options dialog box, click the View tab.

4. Under Outline Options, select the Show Project Summary Task check box, and then click OK. The project summary task row appears at the top of the view. The total project cost is displayed in the Total Cost field.

Another way to see the total project cost is in the Project Statistics dialog box. To display the Project Statistics dialog box, follow these steps:

1. Click Project, Project Information.

2. Click the Statistics button. The Project Statistics dialog box appears (see Figure 8-10).

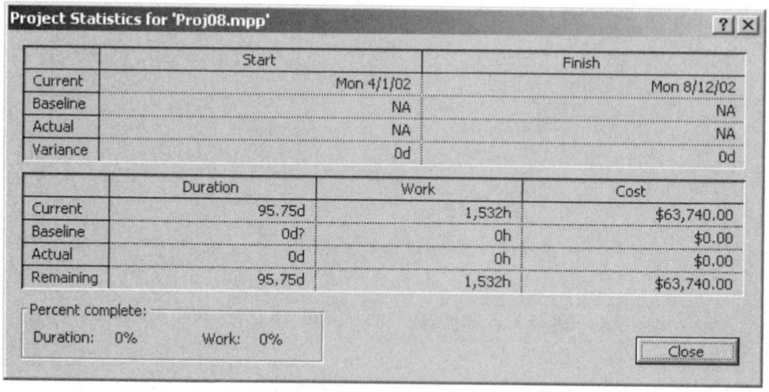

Project Statistics for 'Proj08.mpp'

	Start			Finish
Current		Mon 4/1/02		Mon 8/12/02
Baseline		NA		NA
Actual		NA		NA
Variance		0d		0d

	Duration	Work	Cost
Current	95.75d	1,532h	$63,740.00
Baseline	0d?	0h	$0.00
Actual	0d	0h	$0.00
Remaining	95.75d	1,532h	$63,740.00

Percent complete:
Duration: 0%   Work: 0%

Figure 8-10. The Project Statistics dialog box shows the overall project cost, as well as the project start and finish dates, total duration, and total work.

Checking and Adjusting the Project Plan

In a perfect world, you'd define the project scope, schedule tasks, assign resources, and presto! The project plan would be finished and ready to execute.

In reality, however, this is rarely the case. After you've scheduled tasks and assigned resources, you generally need to check the results and see if they meet expectations and requirements. Ultimately, you might need to answer one or all of the following questions to your satisfaction and to the satisfaction of your managing stakeholders:

- Will the project be finished on time?
- Is the project keeping to its budget?
- Do the resources have the appropriate amount of work?

If you get the wrong answers to any of these questions, you need to adjust your project plan until you get the right answers. For example, if the finish date is too far away, you can add more resources to major tasks.

After you make such adjustments, you'll need to check the project plan again. Adding resources to tasks might bring in the finish date but it also might add cost if you hired additional resources or authorized overtime. And if you assigned more tasks to existing resources, those resources might be overallocated.

To save time as well as money, you might decide to cut certain tasks, a deliverable, or a phase. But if this means you're cutting project scope, you'll probably need to get approval from your managing stakeholders.

This relationship between time, money, and scope is sometimes referred to as the *project triangle* (see Figure 9-1). When you change one side of the triangle, it affects at least one of the other sides of the triangle.

Figure 9-1. Managing your project requires balancing time, money, and scope.

You need to know which side of the triangle is your most important consideration. Is it schedule—you definitely have to finish by November 14? Is it budget—there is absolutely $264,300 for this project, and not a penny more? Is it scope—it is imperative that each and every task in your project plan be implemented? Only one side of the triangle can be "absolute." The other two sides must be flexible so you can adjust the project plan to hit that one absolute.

Depending on which side of your project triangle is your absolute, you might adjust your project plan to do one of the following:

- Bring in the project finish date
- Reduce project costs
- Cut project scope

Although not strictly a part of your project triangle, it's likely that you're also going to check resource workloads. Resources are the biggest part of your project costs. If any resources are overallocated, you might be facing more overtime than your budget will allow. If resources are grossly overallocated, you run the risk that the tasks won't be done on time and the entire project will slip. If any resources are underallocated, you might be paying more for resources than you should, which also affects your budget.

After you've made your adjustments and balanced your project triangle to meet the project requirements, you'll be ready for stakeholder buyoff. After you have buyoff, you'll be ready to start the execution phase of the project.

Sources of Your Project Scope, Finish Date, and Budget

Your project scope, finish date, and budget can be imposed on you for various reasons, depending on the type of project and the specific situation. The following are a few examples:

- You are a seller or potential subcontractor bidding on a project whose scope has been defined in the Request For Proposal (RFP). You need to provide the full scope, but your costs and finish date must be competitive with other bidders. If possible, you'd like to include value-added items to give your proposal an advantage while still making a good profit.

- You are a subcontractor and you have been awarded the contract based on a proposal including broad assumptions of scope, finish date, and cost. Having taken this risk, now you must create a detailed project plan that will actually implement that finish date, cost and scope.

- You've been assigned as project manager of a project within your company. The scope, budget, or finish date have been handed down as one or more of the project assumptions. Your success is predicated upon your ability to implement the project within those limitations.

- You've been assigned as project manager of a project within your company. You and other stakeholders developed the scope to a fair level of detail. It's up to you to propose the budget and finish date for the project.

- You are the project manager and you've balanced your project triangle the way you believe is best. However, after you submitted the project plan for client review, certain new project requirements or limitations surfaced. You have to readjust the project triangle to take the new limitations or requirements into account.

Working with the Critical Path and Critical Tasks

In most projects, there are multiple sets of tasks, which have task relationships with one another, taking place at any one time. In an office move project, for example, the facilities manager and her team might be researching new office sites and then working out the lease terms. At the same time, the office manager and his team might be ordering new office furniture and equipment and then arranging for movers. These two sets of activities are not dependent on each other and use different sets of resources. Therefore, they can be scheduled on parallel tracks. There can be any number of sets of tasks on these parallel tracks, or *paths*, depending on the size and complexity of the project, as well as the number of resources involved.

At any time, there's one task that has the latest finish date in the project. This task, along with its predecessors, dictates the finish date of the project as a whole. The finish date of this path is critical to the finish date of the project itself; therefore we call it the *critical path*. In turn, the tasks that make up each step along the critical path are called the *critical tasks*. Because the critical path dictates the finish date of the project, in project management we pay a tremendous amount of attention to it.

> **note** The term "critical task" only refers to tasks that are on the "critical path." These terms reflect the scheduling of the tasks, not their relative importance. There can be very important tasks that don't happen to be on the critical path.

In the planning phase, you identify a particular critical path. After you begin the execution phase and actual progress begins to be reported, the critical path might change from one set of linked tasks to another. For example, task progress is likely to differ in various ways from the original schedule. Perhaps one task in the critical path finishes early but a task in a second path is delayed. In this case, the second path might become the critical path if that is now the path with the latest finish date in the project.

If you need to bring in the finish date, one of the most effective things you can do is focus on the critical path. If you can make critical tasks along that path finish sooner, you can make the project itself finish sooner.

> For more information about strategies to bring in a project's finish date, see "Bringing In the Project Finish Date," later in this chapter.

Understanding Slack Time and Critical Tasks

Many tasks have some amount of scheduling buffer—an amount of time that a task can slip before it causes a delay in the schedule. This scheduling buffer is called *slack*, or *float*. The following describes the two types of slack:

- *Free slack* is the amount of time a task can slip before it delays another task, typically its successor task.

- *Total slack* is the amount of time a task can slip before it delays the project finish date.

> **note** Sometimes you run into a situation in which you have *negative slack*, that is, the opposite of slack time. An example of negative slack would be when a successor task is due to begin before the predecessor is finished. This can happen when the task duration of a predecessor task conflicts with a successor task that must begin on a date specified by an assigned constraint, for example.

Because critical tasks cannot slip without delaying the project finish date, critical tasks have no slack and tasks with no slack are critical.

If a noncritical task consumes its slack time, it usually causes its successor to use some or all of its total slack time. The task becomes a critical task and causes its successor tasks to become critical as well.

Maybe you don't want just those tasks with total slack of 0 to be critical. For example, perhaps you want your critical tasks to be those that still have 1 day of slack. In this case, you can change the definition of a critical task. To do this, follow these steps:

1 Click Tools, Options, and in the Options dialog box, click the Calculation tab.

2 Enter your preference for a critical task in the Tasks Are Critical If Slack Is Less Than Or Equal To box (see Figure 9-2).

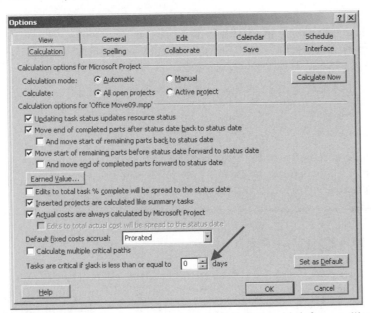

Figure 9-2. Specify the amount of slack that should define a critical task in your project plan.

To see how much free slack and total slack each task has, you can apply the Schedule table to a task sheet, as follows:

1 Click View, Gantt Chart. Or display any other task sheet you want.

2 Click View, Table, Schedule. The Schedule table is applied (see Figure 9-3 on the next page). You might need to drag the vertical divider to the right to see some of the columns in this table.

Task Name	Start	Finish	Late Start	Late Finish	Free Slack	Total Slack
11	⊟ Acquire new furniture and equipment	Mon 4/15/02	Tue 5/7/02	Thu 4/18/02	Fri 5/10/02	3 days	3 days
12	Assess furniture and equipment requirer	Mon 4/15/02	Thu 4/18/02	Thu 4/18/02	Tue 4/23/02	0 days	3 days
13	Research furniture	Fri 4/19/02	Mon 4/22/02	Wed 4/24/02	Thu 4/25/02	0 days	3 days
14	Research equipment	Tue 4/23/02	Fri 4/26/02	Fri 4/26/02	Wed 5/1/02	0 days	3 days
15	Order furniture	Mon 4/29/02	Wed 5/1/02	Thu 5/2/02	Mon 5/6/02	0 days	3 days
16	Order equipment	Thu 5/2/02	Mon 5/6/02	Tue 5/7/02	Thu 5/9/02	0 days	3 days
17	Schedule delivery for furniture and equip	Tue 5/7/02	Tue 5/7/02	Fri 5/10/02	Fri 5/10/02	3 days	3 days

Figure 9-3.   The Schedule table shows free slack and total slack, as well as late start and late finish dates.

Understanding the Critical Path Method (CPM)

Schedules are developed from task sequences, durations, resource requirements, start dates, and finish dates. Various mathematical methods are used to calculate project schedules.

The *Critical Path Method*, or *CPM*, is the technique that underlies Microsoft Project scheduling. The focus of CPM is to analyze all series of linked tasks in a project and determine which series has the least amount of scheduling flexibility, that is, the least amount of slack. This becomes designated as the critical path.

Four date values are part of the slack calculation for each task:

- Early start
- Early finish
- Late start
- Late finish

The difference between the late start and early start dates is compared, as is the difference between late finish and early finish. The smaller of the two differences becomes the value for total slack.

Viewing the Critical Path

The easiest way to see the critical path in a Gantt chart is to click View, Tracking Gantt. The Tracking Gantt highlights the critical path in red in the chart portion of the view (see Figure 9-4). The Entry table is applied by default to the Tracking Gantt, just as in the regular Gantt Chart.

You can also use the Gantt Chart Wizard, which will format the chart portion of any Gantt Chart view to highlight the critical path. To do this, follow these steps:

1 Click View, Gantt Chart.

If you want to modify another Gantt chart view, such as the Leveling Gantt or Tracking Gantt, display that view instead.

Gantt Chart
Wizard

2 On the Formatting toolbar, click Gantt Chart Wizard.

236

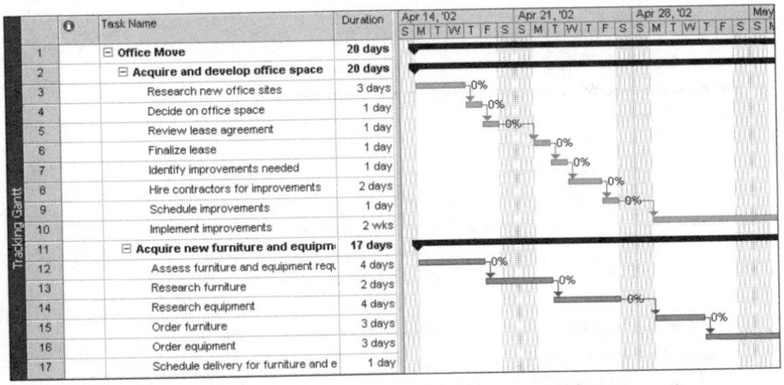

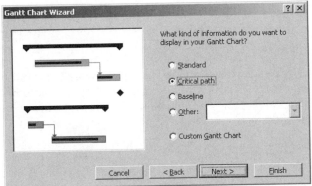

Figure 9-4.   The Tracking Gantt highlights the critical path.

3   On the first page of the Gantt Chart Wizard, click Next.

4   On the second page, select the Critical Path option (see Figure 9-5).
Then click Next.

Figure 9-5.   To highlight the critical path Gantt bars, select the Critical
Path option.

5   On the third page, select the option for the text you want to accompany the
Gantt bars, such as resources, dates, and so on. Click Next.

6   On the fourth page, select whether you want the link lines for task dependencies to show. Click Next.

7   On the final page, click the Format It button.

Microsoft Project formats your Gantt Chart according to your specifications.

8   Click the Exit Wizard button to view your new Gantt Chart format, which
displays red Gantt bars for critical tasks (see Figure 9-6 on the next page).

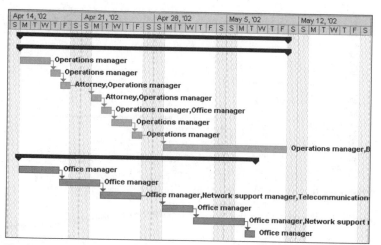

Figure 9-6. Use the Gantt Chart Wizard to instantly highlight critical path tasks.

InsideOut

The Gantt Chart Wizard is convenient for quickly changing the Gantt bar format of certain types of tasks. However, if you use the wizard to do your formatting, you could lose certain standard Gantt bar formatting that you might want to preserve. For example, the Deadline bar style is lost.

If you want to see only critical tasks in a Gantt chart view, switch to the Detail Gantt or Tracking Gantt.

If you want to highlight critical tasks in the Gantt Chart, customize the bar styles.

For more information, see "Customizing Views" on page 586.

Although displaying the Detail Gantt or using the Gantt Chart Wizard can display the Gantt bars for the critical path at a glance, you can also look at the details for individual critical tasks. The following list details different methods for viewing critical tasks:

Display the Detail Gantt. To do this, click View, More Views, Detail Gantt. This view shows the critical path tasks in red Gantt bars. By default, the Delay table is applied to the sheet portion of the view.

Review the Critical Tasks report. To do this, click View, Reports. Double-click Overview, and then double-click Critical Tasks.

Group tasks by critical and noncritical tasks. (see Figure 9-7) To do this, click Project, Group By, Critical. To return tasks to their original order, click Project, Group By, No Group.

Task Name		Start	Finish	Late Start	Late Finish
⊟ **Critical: No**		**Mon 4/15/02**	**Tue 5/7/02**	**Thu 4/18/02**	**Fri 5/10/02**
12	Assess furniture and equipment requiremer	Mon 4/15/02	Thu 4/18/02	Thu 4/18/02	Tue 4/23/02
13	Research furniture	Fri 4/19/02	Mon 4/22/02	Wed 4/24/02	Thu 4/25/02
14	Research equipment	Tue 4/23/02	Fri 4/26/02	Fri 4/26/02	Wed 5/1/02
15	Order furniture	Mon 4/29/02	Wed 5/1/02	Thu 5/2/02	Mon 5/6/02
16	Order equipment	Thu 5/2/02	Mon 5/6/02	Tue 5/7/02	Thu 5/9/02
17	Schedule delivery for furniture and equipme	Tue 5/7/02	Tue 5/7/02	Fri 5/10/02	Fri 5/10/02
19	Select move day	Mon 4/15/02	Mon 4/15/02	Fri 5/3/02	Fri 5/3/02
20	Research moving companies	Tue 4/16/02	Thu 4/18/02	Mon 5/6/02	Wed 5/8/02
21	Decide on moving company	Fri 4/19/02	Fri 4/19/02	Thu 5/9/02	Thu 5/9/02
22	Review moving contract	Mon 4/22/02	Mon 4/22/02	Fri 5/10/02	Fri 5/10/02
⊟ **Critical: Yes**		**Mon 4/15/02**	**Fri 5/10/02**	**Mon 4/15/02**	**Fri 5/10/02**
3	Research new office sites	Mon 4/15/02	Wed 4/17/02	Mon 4/15/02	Wed 4/17/02
4	Decide on office space	Thu 4/18/02	Thu 4/18/02	Thu 4/18/02	Thu 4/18/02
5	Review lease agreement	Fri 4/19/02	Fri 4/19/02	Fri 4/19/02	Fri 4/19/02
6	Finalize lease	Mon 4/22/02	Mon 4/22/02	Mon 4/22/02	Mon 4/22/02
7	Identify improvements needed	Tue 4/23/02	Tue 4/23/02	Tue 4/23/02	Tue 4/23/02

Figure 9-7. Use the Critical grouping to group critical tasks together and noncritical tasks together.

Filter for critical tasks. To do this, click Project, Filtered For, Critical. Only critical tasks are shown. To show all tasks again, click Project, Filtered For, All Tasks.

Use the Project Guide. To do this, on the Project Guide toolbar, click Report. Click the See The Project's Critical Tasks link. The view changes to a Critical Tasks Gantt generated by the Project Guide. Additional information is provided in the Project Guide side pane.

> Report

Working with Multiple Critical Paths

By default, you have one path through your project that constitutes your critical path. However, if you like, you can display multiple critical paths. It can be helpful to see different networks of tasks throughout your project, for example, for different phases or parallel efforts. To do this, follow these steps:

1 Click Tools, Options, and in the Options dialog box, click the Calculation tab.

2 Select the Calculate Multiple Critical Paths check box.

To create multiple critical paths, Microsoft Project changes the calculation of the critical path so that any task without a successor becomes a critical task. That is, its late finish date is set to be the same as its early finish date. This gives the task 0 slack, which in turn makes it a critical task. Any series of predecessors before this final task becomes a critical path. Hence this provides multiple critical paths.

This calculation contrasts with that of a single critical path, in which a task without a successor has its late finish date set to the project finish date. This gives the task slack and therefore makes it a noncritical task.

239

Bringing In the Project Finish Date

A time-constrained project is one in which the project finish date is the most important factor in your project plan. Although you still need to balance budget constraints and satisfy the project scope, the finish date reigns supreme over those other considerations.

If your project plan calculates that your finish date will be beyond your all-important target finish date, focus on the critical path. Shorten the critical path, and you bring in the finish date.

Viewing Finish Dates and the Critical Path

Before you analyze the critical path, you just need to see your bottom line—what's the project finish date? Follow these steps:

1 Click Project, Project Information.

2 In the Project Information dialog box, click the Statistics button. The Project Statistics dialog box appears. The current, or scheduled, finish date appears in the Finish column (see Figure 9-8).

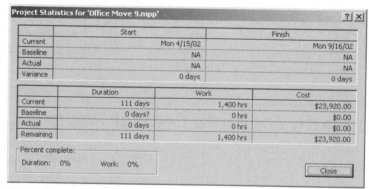

Figure 9-8. The Project Statistics dialog box shows overall project information—project start date, project finish date, total duration, total work, and total cost.

Another way to keep your eye on the project finish date at all times is to add the project summary task row, as follows:

1 Click Tools, Options, and in the Options dialog box, click the View tab.

2 Select the Show Project Summary Task check box.

240

The project summary task appears at the top of any task sheet view, including the Gantt Chart (see Figure 9-9). Task information is rolled up for the entire project and its summary total displayed in the project summary row. Specifically, the Finish field in the project summary row shows the latest finish date in the project.

	❶	Task Name	Duration	Start	Finish
0		⊟ Office Move 9	111 days	Mon 4/15/02	Mon 9/16/02
1		⊟ Office Move	111 days	Mon 4/15/02	Mon 9/16/02
2		⊟ Acquire and develop office space	20 days	Mon 4/15/02	Fri 5/10/02
3		Research new office sites	3 days	Mon 4/15/02	Wed 4/17/02
4		Decide on office space	1 day	Thu 4/18/02	Thu 4/18/02
5		Review lease agreement	1 day	Fri 4/19/02	Fri 4/19/02

Figure 9-9. The Project Summary row rolls up task information to display the totals for the entire project.

To see the critical path, click View, Tracking Gantt.

For more information about viewing the critical path, see "Viewing the Critical Path," earlier in this chapter.

By viewing the finish date or the critical path, you'll easily see whether you're hitting your target finish date. If you need to bring in the finish date, you might want to focus on the critical tasks. You can filter your task sheet to show only critical tasks by clicking Project, Filtered For, Critical. To show all tasks again, click Project, Filtered For, All Tasks.

What If You Have More Time Than Needed for the Project?

You reviewed your finish date and got a happy surprise—you have more time available than your schedule says you need. What to do? It depends, of course, on the type of project, the situation, and the amount of surplus time. You can:

- Use the extra time as buffer against potential risks.
- Add scope. Add tasks you were hoping to include but thought you wouldn't have the time. Build in a higher level of quality. Increase quantities being produced, if applicable to your project.
- Use the extra time to save money. For example, you might be able to be able to hire two designers instead of three and have those two designers carry out the design tasks in the longer available time.
- Inform your manager or client that you'll be able to complete the project sooner than expected.

Checking Your Schedule Assumptions

If you've determined that you need to bring in the finish date, look first at the schedule itself. Make sure that all the scheduling controls you put into place are accurate and required. The fewer controls you impose, the more flexibility Microsoft Project can have with scheduling, and that added flexibility can give you an earlier finish date. In the Gantt Chart or other task sheet, review and update the following:

- Date constraints
- Durations
- Task dependencies
- Task calendars

You can look at all tasks in the project, but to affect the finish date you need only make adjustments to critical tasks. If you shorten the sequence of critical path tasks to the point where a different sequence is now the critical path, check to see if that path finishes before your target finish date. If it does, switch your focus to that new critical path until you achieve the planned project finish date you need.

> **note** If you change aspects of your schedule to bring in the finish date, the good news is that you probably won't adversely affect your project triangle. That is, adjusting your schedule to meet your schedule requirements only affects the schedule side of the triangle. Costs and scope will probably stay as they are.

Checking and Adjusting Date Constraints

First look at any date constraints you've set in your schedule, particularly for your critical tasks. This is where you can potentially make a significant impact on your finish date. To look at the constraints you've applied, follow these steps:

1 Display the Gantt Chart or other task sheet.

2 Click View, Table, More Tables.

3 In the More Tables dialog box, click Constraint Dates, and then click Apply. The table shows the constraint type and constraint dates for all tasks.

If you have the tasks sorted by Task ID, that is, in their outline sequence, you can review constraints for each task within the context of its surrounding tasks. If you like, you can sort the tasks by constraint type, as follows:

1 Apply the Constraint Dates table to the Gantt Chart or other task sheet.

2 Click Project, Sort, Sort By.

3 In the Sort By dialog box, click Constraint Type, and then click Sort. The tasks are sorted by constraint type so you can see where you might have applied a Must Finish On or Start No Later Than constraint, for example. You can also see their associated dates.

To see only the constraints for critical tasks, follow these steps:

1 Apply the Constraint Dates table to the Gantt Chart or other task sheet.

2 Click Project, Filtered For, Critical. Only critical tasks are shown.

When you want to see all tasks again, click Project, Filtered For, All Tasks.

Make sure that the constraint types and dates you have applied are truly necessary. Wherever you can, change a date constraint to a flexible one like As Soon As Possible or As Late As Possible. Even changing an inflexible date constraint such as Must Start On or Must Finish On to a moderately flexible date constraint such as Start No Later Than or Finish No Earlier Than can improve your schedule. To change the constraint, do the following:

1 Apply the Constraint Dates table to the Gantt Chart or other task sheet.

2 Click the Constraint Type field, click the arrow, and then click the constraint you want in the list.

---

tip **Changing all constraints at one time**

Maybe you applied too many date constraints to too many tasks and you just want to start fresh. Select all tasks in the project either by dragging them or by clicking the Select All box just above the row 1 heading in the upper-left corner of the table. On the Standard toolbar, click Task Information. In the Task Information dialog box, click the Advanced tab. In the Constraint Type box, click As Soon As Possible or As Late As Possible. The constraints on all selected tasks are changed.

For more information about constraints, see "Scheduling Tasks to Achieve Specific Dates" on page 147.

Checking and Adjusting Task Dependencies

The second place to check your schedule for critical path-shortening opportunities is your task dependencies. A Gantt chart is the best view for reviewing task dependencies and their impact on your schedule. View the Tracking Gantt or Detail Gantt so you can see critical tasks highlighted. Focusing on the task dependencies of critical tasks will help you bring in the finish date.

Specifically, examine whether the task dependencies are required. If two tasks don't really depend on each other, remove the link. Or consider whether two tasks can begin at the same time. If so, you can change a finish-to-start dependency to a start-to-start dependency. Change a task dependency as follows:

1 Click the successor task.

2 On the Standard toolbar, click Task Information.

3 In the Task Information dialog box, click the Predecessors tab.

4 To change the link type, click in the Type field for the predecessor. Click the arrow, and then click the link type you want in the list.

To remove the link entirely, click anywhere in the predecessor row, and press the Delete key.

---

tip **Removing all links**

If you want to start over with your task dependency strategy, you can remove all links in the project. Be sure that this is really what you want to do because it can erase a lot of the work you've done in your project plan.

Unlink
Tasks

Click the Select All box just above the row 1 heading in the upper-left corner of the table. On the Standard toolbar, click Unlink Tasks. All links on all tasks are removed.

For more information about task dependencies, see "Establishing Task Dependencies" on page 139.

Checking and Adjusting Durations

After adjusting date constraints and task dependencies, if the finish date is still beyond your target, look at task durations. However, be aware that it's risky to be too optimistic about durations, especially if you used reliable methods such as expert judgment, past project information, industry metrics, or PERT analysis to calculate your current durations.

You can look at durations in the Gantt Chart or most task sheets. If you have the tasks sorted by Task ID, that is, in their outline sequence, you can review durations for each task within the context of its surrounding tasks. However, if you like, you can sort tasks by duration so you can see the longer durations first. These longer durations might have more buffer built in so they might be a good place to trim some time. To sort tasks by duration, follow these steps:

1 Display the Gantt Chart with the Entry table applied, or display another task sheet that includes the Duration field.

2 Click Project, Sort, Sort By. The Sort dialog box appears.

3 In the Sort By list, click Duration, and then click Sort. The tasks are sorted by duration.

4 To see only the durations for critical tasks, click Project, Filtered For, Critical. When you want to see all tasks again, click Project, Filtered For, All Tasks.

5 To change a duration, simply type the new duration into the task's Duration field. The schedule is recalculated with the new duration.

For more information about duration, see "Setting Task Durations" on page 128.

Project Management Practices: Duration Compression

There are two commonly used methods in project management of shortening a series of tasks without changing the project scope. These two *duration compression* methods are as follows:

Crashing the schedule.   The schedule and associated project costs are analyzed to determine how a series of tasks, like the critical path, can be shortened, or *crashed*, for the least additional cost.

Fast tracking.   Tasks normally done in sequence are rescheduled to be done simultaneously. For example, starting to build a prototype before the specifications are approved.

By their nature, both of these methods are risky. It's important to be aware that these methods can increase cost or increase task rework.

tip   **Check and adjust assigned task calendars**

Task calendars can be applied to tasks that can be scheduled beyond the normal project working times calendar. However, sometimes a task calendar indicates a specific frequency with which a task is performed. Examine tasks with their own task calendars to make sure they're accurately reflecting reality and not holding up progress.

Tasks with task calendars assigned display a calendar icon in the Indicators column next to the task name. Place the mouse pointer over the icon to see more information.

For more information about task calendars, see "Working with Task Calendars" on page 158.

245

Adjusting Resource Settings to Bring in the Finish Date

Another way to bring in the finish date is to adjust your resource settings. You can check that the resource availability affecting assigned task scheduling is accurate. You can also add resources to tasks to decrease task duration. Be aware that increasing resource availability as well as adding resources to tasks usually means an increase in costs.

Checking and Adjusting Resource Availability

The more availability your resources have, the sooner their assigned tasks can be completed. For example, a 4-day task assigned to a resource who works a regular 5-day week will be completed in 4 days. The same 4-day task assigned to a resource who works a 2-day week will be completed in 2 weeks. For resources assigned to critical tasks, review and update the following:

- Resource calendars
- Resource (maximum) units
- Assignment units

The Task Entry view is best for checking these three items. Apply the view, set the Task Form to show the resource information you need, and filter for critical tasks, as follows:

1 Click View, More Views. In the More Views dialog box, click Task Entry, and then click Apply.

2 To view critical tasks, click in the Gantt Chart (upper) portion of the view. Click Project, Filtered For, Critical. Only critical tasks are displayed.

   You can also click View, Tracking Gantt. Critical tasks are shown in red.

3 Click in the Task Form (lower) portion of the view. Click Format, Details, Resource Work (see Figure 9-10).

4 Click a critical task in the Gantt chart portion of the view. The resources assigned to the selected task are listed in the Task Form portion of the view.

5 To check the resource calendar for this assigned resource, double-click the resource name. The Resource Information dialog box appears. Click the Working Time tab. Check the working times set for this resource and make sure they're correct.

> For more information about resource calendars, see "Setting Resource Working Time Calendars" on page 176.

6 To check resource units, click the General tab in the Resource Information dialog box. Under Resource Availability, check the resource units and associated dates if applicable, and make sure they're correct.

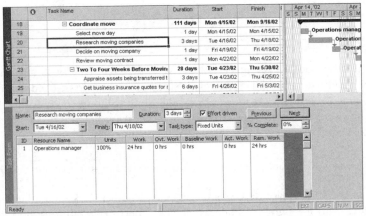

Figure 9-10. The Task Entry view is now set up to check resource and assignment availability.

For more information about resource units, see "Specifying Resource Availability" on page 173.

7 To check assignment units, review the Units field next to the resource name in the Task Form, and make sure the setting is correct.

For more information about assignment units, see "Assigning Work Resources to Tasks" on page 189.

Adding Resources to Decrease Duration

A key method of shortening the critical path and bringing in the project finish date is adding resources to critical tasks in such a way that it decreases the task's duration. For example, two people working together might be able to complete a development task in half the time it takes either of them individually. For this to be the case, the tasks must be either fixed-units and effort-driven, or fixed-work. They cannot be fixed-duration tasks, for obvious reasons.

With fixed-units effort-driven scheduling, which is the default for tasks in Microsoft Project, when you assign an additional resource to a task that already has assigned resources, the amount of work scheduled for each assigned resource decreases. Likewise, when you remove a resource from an effort-driven task, the amount of work scheduled for each assigned resource increases.

The same is true for fixed-work tasks, which are effort-driven by definition. When you add or remove resources (that is, assignment units) on a fixed-work task, duration changes but work remains fixed, of course.

For more information about effort-driven scheduling, see "Controlling Changes with Effort-Driven Scheduling" on page 209. For more information about task types, see "Controlling Schedule Changes with Task Types," on page 211.

Project Management Practices: The Right Resources for Critical Tasks

Having overallocated resources assigned to critical tasks can push out your finish date. If you level overallocated resources, their assignments are rescheduled to when they have time to do them. As much as possible, shift assignments to evenly distribute the resource workload and ensure that resources working on critical tasks are not overallocated.

For more information about leveling, see "Leveling Assignments," later in this chapter.

If you have an overallocated resource assigned to critical tasks and an underallocated resource with the right skills and availability, you can switch to or add the underallocated resources to the critical tasks to shorten their durations.

Also, check that the fastest and more experienced resources are assigned to the longer or more difficult critical tasks. Although this might or might not actually reduce the duration, it significantly reduces the risk of critical tasks needing rework or being otherwise delayed.

note You can also adjust scope to bring in the finish date.

For more information about cutting scope, see "Changing Project Scope" later in this chapter.

To check the task type of an individual task, follow these steps:

1 In a task sheet, such as the Gantt Chart, double-click the task.

2 In the Task Information dialog box, click the Advanced tab.

3 Review the Task Type list and the Effort Driven check box. Make any changes necessary.

You can add the task type and effort-driven fields to a task sheet so you can see the scheduling methods for all tasks at a glance, as follows:

1 Display the task sheet to which you want to add the new columns.

2 Click the column heading to the right of where you want the new column to be inserted.

3 Click Insert, Column.

4 In the Field Name box, select Type.

Type "ty" to move quickly to the Type field in the list.

5 Click OK, and the task types are shown in the task sheet. You can use this field to quickly change task types.

6 Follow steps 1-5 to add the Effort Driven field to the task sheet. This field displays Yes or No, indicating whether the task is effort driven.

When you assign additional resources to your fixed-units and effort-driven or fixed-work critical tasks, the duration of those critical tasks is reduced and therefore the length of the critical path is reduced.

> **note** Be aware that as you add resources to critical tasks, you run the risk of reduced productivity. There might be additional overhead associated with bringing on additional resources. More support might be needed to get those resources up to speed on the tasks, and you might lose whatever time savings you thought you might gain. Take care to add resources who are experienced enough to hit the ground running so your efforts don't backfire on you.

Reducing Project Costs

A budget-constrained project is one in which costs are the most important factor in the project plan. Although you still need to balance schedule requirements and satisfy the project scope, the costs are at the forefront of your decision-making processes as you plan and execute the project.

If your project plan calculates that your total costs are above the allowed budget, you need cost-cutting strategies. Your best strategies will involve cutting resources because resources and costs are virtually synonymous in projects. As described in the previous section, when you want to bring in the finish date, you focus on tasks in the critical path. In the same way, when you want to cut costs, you focus on resources to gain the biggest cost savings.

Viewing Project Costs

Review your cost picture first, compare it with your budget, and then make any necessary adjustments. To review total project costs using Project Statistics, do the following:

1 Click Project, Project Information.

2 In the Project Information dialog box, click the Statistics button. The Project Statistics dialog box appears. The current or scheduled total project cost appears in the Cost column.

249

You can also see the total project cost in the Project Summary Task and Cost table, as follows:

1 Display the Gantt Chart or other task sheet.

2 Click View, Table, Cost. The Cost table is applied.

3 Click Tools, Options, and in the Options dialog box, click the View tab.

4 Under Outline Options, select the Show Project Summary Task check box, and then click OK. The project summary task row appears at the top of the task sheet. The total project cost, as currently scheduled, is displayed in the Total Cost field.

Two cost reports can help you analyze project costs, as follows:

Budget report. Click View, Reports. Double-click Costs, and then double-click Budget (see Figure 9-11). The Total Cost column is a summary of the resource costs and fixed costs for each task.

Budget Report as of Sun 4/14/02
Office Move 9

ID	Task Name	Fixed Cost	Fixed Cost Accrual	Total Cost
10	Implement improvements	$0.00	Prorated	$3,200.00
25	Get business insurance quotes for new s	$0.00	Prorated	$1,200.00
63	Inventory existing office furniture (general	$0.00	Prorated	$1,000.00
65	Inventory existing furniture by office	$0.00	Prorated	$1,000.00
5	Review lease agreement	$0.00	Prorated	$960.00
6	Finalize lease	$0.00	Prorated	$960.00
3	Research new office sites	$0.00	Prorated	$960.00
20	Research moving companies	$0.00	Prorated	$960.00
12	Assess furniture and equipment requirem	$0.00	Prorated	$800.00
14	Research equipment	$0.00	Prorated	$800.00
8	Hire contractors for improvements	$0.00	Prorated	$640.00
22	Review moving contract	$0.00	Prorated	$640.00
15	Order furniture	$0.00	Prorated	$600.00
16	Order equipment	$0.00	Prorated	$600.00
37	Plan for disposal of old office equipment	$0.00	Prorated	$600.00

Figure 9-11. Run the Budget report to view costs for each task.

Cash Flow report. Click View, Reports. Double-click Costs, and then double-click Cash Flow (see Figure 9-12). This report forecasts the funding needed for each period of time, enabling you to see whether budgeted costs will be exceeded at a particular point.

Cash Flow as of Sun 4/14/02
Office Move 9

	4/14/02	4/21/02	4/28/02
Office Move 9			
Office Move			
Acquire and develop office space			
Research new office sites	$960.00		
Decide on office space	$320.00		
Review lease agreement	$960.00		
Finalize lease		$960.00	
Identify improvements needed		$520.00	
Hire contractors for improvements		$640.00	
Schedule improvements		$320.00	
Implement improvements			$1,800.00

Figure 9-12. Run the Cash Flow report to see cost forecasts by time period.

You can sort a sheet view by costs. To review task or resource costs in order of amount, do the following:

1   Display a task sheet or resource sheet, depending on whether you want
    to see costs by resource or by task.

2   Click View, Table, Cost.

3   Click Project, Sort, By Cost.

    To return to the original sort order, click Project, Sort, By ID.

You can also filter a sheet view to display only tasks or resources that have costs
exceeding a specified amount. To do this, follow these steps:

1   Display a task sheet or resource sheet, depending on whether you want
    to see costs by resource or by task.

2   Click View, Table, Cost.

3   Click Project, Filtered For, More Filters.

4   In the More Filters dialog box, click Cost Greater Than, and then click Apply.

5   In the Cost Greater Than dialog box, enter the amount (see Figure 9-13).

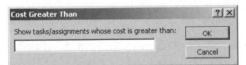

Figure 9-13. To see only those tasks or assignments that have a scheduled
cost exceeding a certain amount, enter the amount in this dialog box.

To see all tasks or all resources again, click Project, Filtered For, All Tasks
or All Resources.

What If You Have More Money Than You Need?

If you investigate your total project costs and discover that you have more budget
than costs, you have some decisions to make. Depending on the type of project, the
situation, and the amount of extra budget, you can:

- Reserve the buffer. Use the extra funding as insurance against potential risks.

- Add resources. Use the money to hire resources and take some of the load
  off overallocated resources or bring in the finish date.

- Add scope. Add tasks you were hoping to include but thought you wouldn't
  have enough money. Build in a higher level of quality. If applicable, increase
  quantities being produced.

- Inform your manager or client that you'll be able to complete the project well
  under budget.

Checking Your Cost Assumptions

If you find that your scheduled costs are higher than your budget, first review the individual costs themselves. Check the resource rates as well as fixed costs for tasks and make sure they're accurate.

To check resource rates, review the Resource Sheet with the Entry table applied. With the default fields in the Entry table, you can see each resource's standard rate, overtime rate, and cost per use.

To check fixed costs for tasks, review a task sheet such as the Gantt Chart with the Cost table applied. The Fixed Cost field displays any costs associated with the tasks that are independent of resource costs.

Adjusting the Schedule to Reduce Costs

If many of your resource costs are based on time periods such as an amount per hour or per day, you might be able to cut costs if you can reduce task durations. For example, suppose you have a 2-day fixed-units task assigned to a $100/hour resource. By default, this resource is assigned to 16 hours of work, for a cost of $1600. If you reduce the duration to 1 day, the work is reduced to 8 hours, and the cost is reduced to $800.

When you reduce task duration in a fixed-units or fixed-duration task, the amount of work is also reduced. However, if you reduce duration for a fixed-work task, work stays the same and assignment units increase. In this case, resource costs would not be reduced.

> For more information about changing durations, see "Checking and Adjusting Durations" earlier in this chapter.

Adjusting Assignments to Reduce Costs

Another way to reduce work and therefore cut costs is to reduce work directly. In effect, you're cutting the amount of time that resources are spending on assigned tasks.

The manner in which a work reduction affects your task and resource scheduling depends on the individual task types. When you decrease work in a fixed-units or fixed-work task, duration is reduced. When you decrease work in a fixed-duration task, units are decreased.

To change work amounts for individual resources, display the Task Usage view or Resource Usage view, and edit the Work field for the assignment.

Strategies for Reducing Resource Costs

The following are suggestions for reducing resource costs by adjusting assignments:

- If you have assignments with multiple resources assigned, reduce the work for the more expensive resources and assign the work to less expensive resources. By shuffling work around on an assignment, you won't risk changing duration or units inadvertently.

- If you have resources with the same skills and availability, replace the more expensive work or material resources with less expensive ones. Although this can introduce some risk into your project, it can also ensure that you're using your expensive resources where you really need them.

- If you have resources with the same skills and availability, replace slower work or equipment resources with faster ones. If one resource is faster than another, you might save money even if the faster resource's rate is higher.

- If you have material resources whose costs are based on assignment units, for example, 3 tons or 100 yards, decrease the assignment units; that is, use less of the material.

note You can also adjust scope to cut costs.

For more information about cutting scope, see "Changing Project Scope" later in this chapter.

Balancing Resource Workloads

Sometimes the use of resources is the most important limitation on a project. In the resource-constrained project, you need to make sure that all the resources are used well, doing the right tasks, and neither underallocated nor overallocated. That is, you need to examine workloads and allocations and fix any problems you find. You still need to keep your eye on the schedule and your costs, but in this type of project, schedule and costs are secondary to resource utilization.

Balancing resource workloads isn't really part of the project triangle. However, you can adjust scope—add or remove tasks—to balance workload. You can also adjust the schedule—split or delay tasks until resources have time to work on them. Finally, you can adjust costs—add more money to pay for additional resources to help balance the workload.

InsideOut

Although resource management is typically a large part of the project manager's job, it's important to keep in mind that the primary job of Microsoft Project is to schedule and track tasks. Traditionally, the resource management functions of Microsoft Project have been more rudimentary. However, Microsoft Project 2002 has more features devoted to resource management than past versions. The new resource availability features attest to this, as do the continuing improvements in team collaboration and delegation capabilities through Microsoft Project Server and Web Access. The Resource Substitution wizard, enterprise resource pool, Team Builder, and other enterprise resource features available through Microsoft Project Professional have taken resource management in projects to a higher level.

Viewing Resource Workloads

When you analyze resource workloads, you're actually reviewing how resources are assigned. The optimum situation is when all resources in your project are assigned at their full availability, no more and no less, throughout their time on the project.

Troubleshooting

Tasks scheduled at the same time are causing overallocations

You influence how tasks and assignments are scheduled by specifying resource availability through their working time calendars, resource units (maximum units), and assignment units. Within those limitations, however, Microsoft Project might still schedule multiple tasks for the same time frame. This can cause overallocations.

For example, suppose there's a resource with a working time calendar specifying that she works on this project only on Tuesdays. When you assign a task to her, that task is scheduled to accommodate the fact that work will be done only on Tuesdays. When you assign a 5-day task to her, by default, this assignment will take 40 hours, which will stretch across 5 weeks.

Likewise, suppose there's another resource who works half-time. His resource units are 50 percent. When you assign a task to him, by default, his assignment units are also 50 percent. So by default, a 5-day task does not translate to 40 hours in a week, but rather 20 hours.

However, if you have two 1-day tasks assigned to the same resource at the same time, both assignments will be scheduled for the resource at the same time, and therefore that resource will be overallocated.

You can resolve overallocations by following the strategies outlined in "Adjusting Assignments" and "Leveling Assignments," both later in this chapter.

254

However, there might be resources for whom you are not able to fill every hour. These resources are said to be *underallocated*. You might have to pay for these resources' time even when they're not directly implementing project tasks.

There might be other resources who consistently have more work than time. These resources are *overallocated*. Such a situation represents risk to the project. If there's more work than available time, it's highly probable that deadlines will be missed, quality will suffer, or costs will increase.

At this point in the project, just before work actually begins, you can look at scheduled underallocations and overallocations, make the necessary changes to maximize your resource contributions, and reduce your risk from overallocation. The goal is to balance the workload as much as possible so that you're not wasting resource dollars and burning out a handful of key resources.

InsideOut

Task views do not indicate when resources are overallocated. This can be a problem because you're assigning tasks in a task view. Even the Assign Resources dialog box doesn't give an indication unless you apply the Available To Work filter.

To see which resources have too much work assigned, switch from a task view to a resource view. Overallocated resources are highlighted in red.

To see which tasks have overallocated resources assigned, add the Overallocated column to a task sheet. To do this, click the column heading to the left of where you want to insert the Overallocated column. Click Insert, Column. In the Field Name box, click Overallocated. This is a Yes/No field. Any tasks that have overallocated resources assigned will display a Yes. You can sort by the Overallocated field so you can better focus on balancing the assignments for those tasks. Be aware that even resources overallocated by a couple hours in just one week will be marked as overallocated.

You can use one of several Microsoft Project views to review how much work is assigned to a resource in any selected time period, as follows:

Resource Graph.   Click View, Resource Graph (see Figure 9-14 on the next page). In the default Peak Units format, the Resource Graph displays how much the resource is being utilized, in terms of maximum units, for the time period specified in the timescale.

To see resource allocation information by different measures, click Format, Details, and then pick a different format such as Overallocation or Percent Allocation.

To change the timescale, click the Zoom In or Zoom Out buttons.

255

To see information for a different resource, press the Page Down or Page Up buttons.

The graph shows work units for this resource.

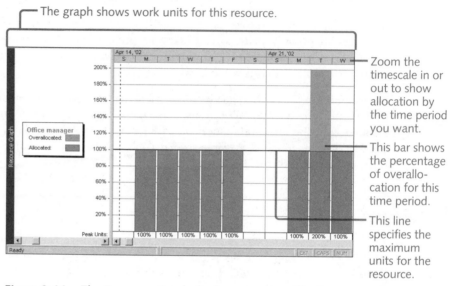

Zoom the timescale in or out to show allocation by the time period you want.

This bar shows the percentage of overallocation for this time period.

This line specifies the maximum units for the resource.

Figure 9-14. The Resource Graph displays resource utilization, one resource at a time.

Resource Usage View. Click View, Resource Usage. Each resource is listed with all assigned tasks (see Figure 9-15). The timesheet portion of the view shows how work is allocated over the selected time period. As in all resource views, overallocated resources are shown in red. In the timesheet portion, any work that exceeds the resource availability for the time period is also shown in red.

	ⓘ	Resource Name	Work	Details	Apr 14, '02 S	M	T	W	T	F
1	◈	⊟ Operations manager	200 hrs	Work		16h	16h	16h	16h	16h
		Research new office sites	24 hrs	Work		8h	8h	8h		
		Decide on office space	8 hrs	Work					8h	
		Review lease agreement	8 hrs	Work						8h
		Finalize lease	8 hrs	Work						
		Identify improvements needed	8 hrs	Work						
		Hire contractors for improvemen	16 hrs	Work						
		Schedule improvements	8 hrs	Work						
		Implement improvements	80 hrs	Work						
		Select move day	8 hrs	Work		8h				
		Research moving companies	24 hrs	Work			8h	8h	8h	
		Decide on moving company	8 hrs	Work						8h
2	◈	⊟ Attorney	24 hrs	Work						8h
		Review lease agreement	8 hrs	Work						8h
		Finalize lease	8 hrs	Work						
		Review moving contract	8 hrs	Work						
3	◈	⊟ Office manager	660 hrs	Work		8h	8h	8h	8h	8h
		Identify improvements needed	8 hrs	Work						
		Assess furniture and equipment	32 hrs	Work		8h	8h	8h	8h	

Figure 9-15. The Resource Usage view can help you notice periods of overallocation.

Resource Allocation view.   Click View, More Views, and in the More
Views dialog box, click Resource Allocation. This is a combination view,
with the Resource Usage view in the upper portion of the view and the Leveling Gantt in the lower portion (see Figure 9-16).

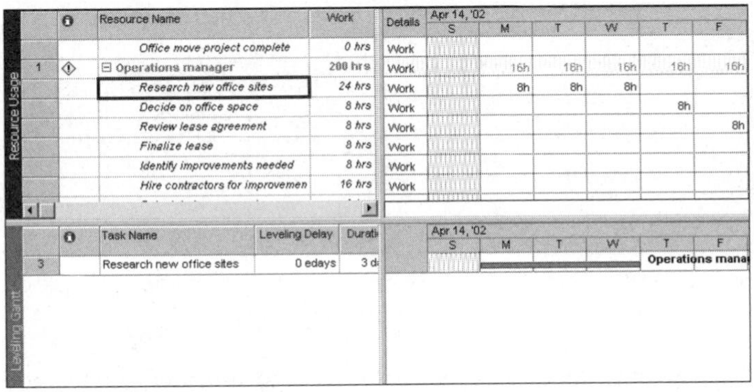

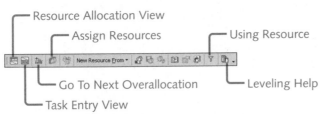

Figure 9-16.   The Leveling Gantt portion displays details about the tasks
assigned to the resource selected in the Resource Usage view.

---

tip   **Use the Resource Management toolbar to find overallocated resources**

Click View, Toolbars, Resource Management. The Resource Management toolbar
(see Figure 9-17) includes a variety of functions that help you work with your resources.
As you're analyzing resource overallocations, click the Go To Next Overallocation
button to find and review the assignments for each overallocated resource in turn.

┌─ Resource Allocation View
│   ┌─ Assign Resources   ┌─ Using Resource

[toolbar icons] New Resource From ▾

│   └─ Go To Next Overallocation   └─ Leveling Help
└─ Task Entry View

Figure 9-17.   The Resource Management toolbar includes a variety of functions that
help you work with your resources.

---

note   When you want to switch to another view from a combination view, remember to
remove the split in the window. Click Window, Remove Split, or double-click the split
bar. When you switch to the view you want, it'll appear in the full screen.

Resource Form.   With a resource sheet view displayed, such as the Resource
Sheet or Resource Usage view, click Window, Split. The Resource Form
appears in the lower portion of the view with the resource sheet in the
upper portion (see Figure 9-18 on the next page).

257

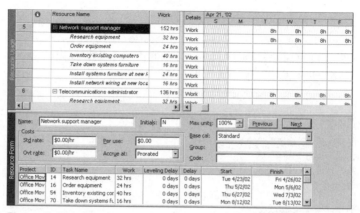

Figure 9-18. The Resource Form displays details about the resource selected in the upper portion of the view.

Another means of seeing how your resources are allocated is by running assignment-related reports, as follows:

Who Does What When report. Click View, Reports. Double-click Assignments, and then double-click Who Does What When. This report displays the amount of work for each resource by day and by assignment (see Figure 9-19).

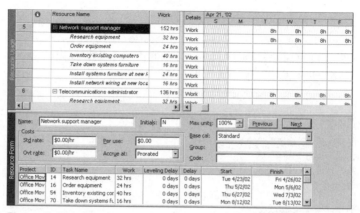

Figure 9-19. Run the Who Does What When report to see assignment details by day.

Overallocated Resources report. Click View, Reports. Double-click Assignments, and then double-click Overallocated Resources. This report displays only overallocated resource information (see Figure 9-20). If there are no overallocated resources, no report is generated.

Overallocated Resources as of Sun 4/14/02
Office Move 9

ID	Resource Name / Task Name	Units	Work	Delay	Start	Finish
◆	**Attorney**		24 hrs			
5	Review lease agreement	100%	8 hrs	0 days	Fri 4/19/02	Fri 4/19/02
6	Finalize lease	100%	8 hrs	0 days	Mon 4/22/02	Mon 4/22/02
22	Review moving contract	100%	8 hrs	0 days	Mon 4/22/02	Mon 4/22/02
◆	**Office manager**		560 hrs			
7	Identify improvements needed	100%	8 hrs	0 days	Tue 4/23/02	
12	Assess furniture and equipment requirements	100%	32 hrs	0 days	Mon 4/15/02	
13	Research furniture	100%	16 hrs	0 days	Fri 4/19/02	
14	Research equipment	100%	32 hrs	0 days	Tue 4/23/02	
15	Order furniture	100%	24 hrs	0 days	Mon 4/29/02	
16	Order equipment	100%	24 hrs	0 days	Thu 5/2/02	

Figure 9-20. Run the Overallocated Resources report to see assignment information about units and work for each overallocated resource.

Resource Usage report. Click View, Reports. Double-click Workload, and then double-click Resource Usage. This report displays the amount of work each week by resource and assignment. Totals are included for the resource, assignment, and week (see Figure 9-21).

Resource Usage as of Sun 4/14/02
Office Move 9

	4/14/02	4/21/02	4/28/02	5/5/02	5/12/02
Operations manager	80 hrs	40 hrs	40 hrs	40 hrs	
Research new office sites	24 hrs				
Decide on office space	8 hrs				
Review lease agreement	8 hrs				
Finalize lease		8 hrs			
Identify improvements needed		8 hrs			
Hire contractors for improvements		16 hrs			
Schedule improvements		8 hrs			
Implement improvements			40 hrs	40 hrs	
Select move day	8 hrs				
Research moving companies	24 hrs				
Decide on moving company	8 hrs				
Attorney	8 hrs	16 hrs			
Review lease agreement	8 hrs				
Finalize lease		8 hrs			
Review moving contract		8 hrs			
Office manager	40 hrs	56 hrs	80 hrs	48 hrs	16 hrs
Identify improvements needed		8 hrs			
Assess furniture and equipment requirements	32 hrs				
Research furniture	8 hrs	8 hrs			

Figure 9-21. Run the Resource Usage report to see assignment details by week.

Reports are particularly useful for resource management meetings or team status meetings. Remember that you can also print views for dissemination.

You can also filter a view to get a closer look at task allocation, as follows:

- In a resource sheet like the Resource Usage view, click Project, Filtered For, Overallocated Resources.
- In a task sheet like the Gantt Chart, click Project, Filtered For, Using Resource. Enter the name of the resource whose tasks you want to see.
- When you want to see all resources or tasks again, click Project, Filtered, For, All Resources or All Tasks.

> **tip**   **Use the Project Guide to review resource allocation**
>
> On the Project Guide toolbar, click Report. Click the See How Resources' Time Is Allocated link. The view changes to a combination view including the Resource Usage view and Gantt Chart. Additional information is provided in the Project Guide side pane.

What If You Have More Resources Than You Need for the Project?

If you have more resources than needed for the project, you need to determine whether this is a help or a hindrance. Depending on the type of project, the situation, and the number of extra resources, you can do one of the following:

- If the underallocated resources have the same skills and availability as other resources that are overallocated, you can use them to balance the workload.

- Even if you have no overallocations, consider assigning multiple resources to tasks to shorten the schedule.

- If you can't use the resources, find another project for them. Having extra people without work can get in the way of progress on the project. It can also cost you money unnecessarily.

Adjusting Resource Availability

If you find that resources are overallocated or underallocated, check with the resources to see if their availability can be modified to reflect how they're needed on the project. For example, if a full-time resource is consistently 50 percent underallocated throughout the life of the project, you might consider changing his units to 50 percent and making him available as a 50 percent resource on another project. Or if a part-time resource is consistently 20 percent overallocated, ask her if she could add more time to her availability on the project.

To change resource units, in a resource sheet, double-click the resource name to open the Resource Information dialog box. Click the General tab. In the Resource Availability table, specify the units in the Units field. If necessary, enter the starting and ending dates of the new levels of availability.

To change a resource's working time calendar, click the Working Time tab in the Resource Information dialog box. Make the necessary changes to increase or decrease the resource's working time on the project.

Adjusting Assignments

You can shift assignments around to fix overallocations and underallocations. This assumes, however, that you have resources with similar skills and availability who can fulfill the necessary tasks.

If you can't add or replace resources to take the burden off overallocated resources, you might be able to delay tasks or assignments until the resources have time to work on them. Or you can simply add overtime work to account for the overallocation.

Adding More Resources to Tasks

You can add underallocated resources to tasks to assist overallocated resources. Depending on the task type, you can distribute the work or the assignment units among the assigned resources, thereby balancing the workload better.

> For more information about adding resources to tasks, including the impact of effort-driven scheduling and the different task types, see "Adjusting Resource Settings to Bring in the Finish Date" earlier in this chapter.

Replacing Overallocated Resources

You can replace an overallocated resource on an assignment with an underallocated one as long as they have the same skills and availability. To replace a resource on a task, do the following:

1 In a task sheet such as the Gantt Chart, select the task for which you want to replace resources.

2 On the Standard toolbar, click Assign Resources.

3 In the Assign Resources dialog box, click the resource you want to replace. The currently assigned resources have check marks next to their names.

4 Click the Replace button. The Replace Resource dialog box appears (see Figure 9-22).

Figure 9-22. Use the Replace Resource dialog box to remove one resource and add a different one in a single operation.

5 Click the resource you want to add to the task, and then click OK.

6 In the Assign Resources dialog box, click Close. The old resource is replaced with the new one.

Delaying a Task or Assignment

You can delay a task or assignment until the assigned resource has time to work on it, as follows:

Leveling delay. This is a *task delay*—the amount of time that should pass from the task's scheduled start date until work on the task should actually begin. This delays all assignments for the task. *Leveling delay* can also be automatically calculated and added by the Microsoft Project leveling feature.

> For more information about leveling, see "Leveling Assignments" later in this chapter.

> **note** Don't confuse lag time with task delay. Lag time is the amount of time to wait after the predecessor is finished (or has started, depending on the link type) before a successor task should start.
>
> > For more information about lag time, see "Delaying Linked Tasks by Adding Lag Time" on page 144.

Assignment delay. This is the amount of time that should pass from the task's scheduled start date until the assignment's scheduled start date.

Because it's best to delay within available slack time, review the tasks or assignments in context of their slack time and then add delay as time is available. Otherwise, you could push out the finish date of the task or even of the project if it's a critical task. To check available slack, do the following:

1 Click View, More Views. In the More Views dialog box, click Resource Allocation, and then click Apply.

2 Click the Resource Usage portion of the view, and then click the resource or assignment for which you want to examine slack and possibly delay.

3 Click the Leveling Gantt portion of the view.

4 Click View, Table, Schedule.

5 Review the Free Slack and Total Slack fields to find tasks that have slack (see Figure 9-23).

6 Also review the chart portion of the Leveling Gantt. The thin bars to the right of the regular Gantt bars show any available slack (see Figure 9-24).

262

	Task Name	Start	Finish	Late Start	Late Finish	Free Slack	Total Slack
5	Review lease agreement	Fri 4/19/02	Fri 4/19/02	Mon 8/26/02	Mon 8/26/02	0 days	91 days
6	Finalize lease	Mon 4/22/02	Mon 4/22/02	Tue 8/27/02	Tue 8/27/02	0 days	91 days
7	Identify improvements needed	Tue 4/23/02	Tue 4/23/02	Wed 8/28/02	Wed 8/28/02	0 days	91 days
8	Hire contractors for improvements	Wed 4/24/02	Thu 4/25/02	Thu 8/29/02	Fri 8/30/02	0 days	91 days
9	Schedule improvements	Fri 4/26/02	Fri 4/26/02	Mon 9/2/02	Mon 9/2/02	0 days	91 days
10	Implement improvements	Mon 4/29/02	Fri 5/10/02	Tue 9/3/02	Mon 9/16/02	18.2 wks	18.2 wks
19	Select move day	Mon 4/15/02	Mon 4/15/02	Mon 4/15/02	Mon 4/15/02	0 days	0 days

Figure 9-23. Use the Schedule table in the Resource Allocation view to find available slack in which to add task delay.

This thin bar indicates available slack.

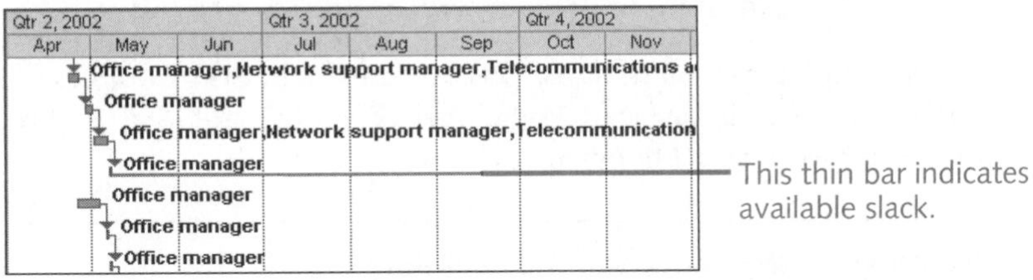

Figure 9-24. Use the Leveling Gantt portion of the Resource Allocation view to find available slack in which to add task delay.

After you've found tasks with slack that you can use, add leveling delay as follows:

1 With the Resource Allocation view open, click the Leveling Gantt portion of the view.

2 Click View, Table, More Tables. In the More Tables dialog box, click Delay, and then click Apply.

3 In the Resource Usage portion of the view, click the assignment whose task you want to delay.

4 In the Leveling Gantt portion of the view, enter the amount of time you want to delay the task in the Leveling Delay field.

If you want to delay an individual assignment for a task that has multiple resources assigned, add assignment delay instead of leveling delay, as follows:

1 With the Resource Allocation view open, click the Resource Usage portion of the view.

2 Click the column heading to the right of where you'd like to insert the Assignment Delay column.

3 Click Insert, Column.

4 In the Field Name box, click Assignment Delay.

5 In the Assignment Delay field of the assignment you want to delay, enter the length of the delay. This indicates how much time after the task's start date the resource is to wait before starting work on this assignment.

263

Specifying Overtime Work to Account for Overallocations

Often, you can't reassign overallocated work to other resources or delay a task until later. In this case, overtime might be the answer.

Microsoft Project does not automatically assign overtime or the associated overtime pay rate when a resource's work exceeds your definition of a normal workday, for example, 8 hours, or a normal workweek, for example, 40 hours. You need to specify overtime work, in addition to total work, for the resource.

For example, suppose a resource is assigned to 10 hours of work in a day. You can specify 2 of those hours as overtime work. The work still totals 10 hours, but 8 hours are regular work and 2 hours are overtime.

---

tip   **Regular work, overtime work, and total work**

When working with overtime, it's important to keep your work terminology straight, otherwise it can get confusing. The Work field is actually *total work*, that is, the total amount of time that this resource is assigned to this task.

When you add overtime on an assignment, that amount is stored in the Overtime Work field, and the (total) Work amount stays the same.

There's another field, Regular Work, which contains the amount of regular (non-overtime) work, based on your amount of total work and overtime work, according to the following calculation:

Regular Work + Overtime Work = (total) Work.

You can add the Regular Work field to a sheet view if you want to see the amount of regular work schedules for a resource, in relation to overtime work and (total) work.

To specify overtime work for overallocated resources, first set up a view containing overtime work fields, as follows:

1 Click View, Resource Usage.

2 Click the column heading for the Work field.

3 Click Insert, Column.

4 In the Field Name box, click Overtime Work. Click OK. The Overtime Work field is added to the Resource Usage view.

5 Click Format, Detail Styles. The Detail Styles dialog box appears (see Figure 9-25).

264

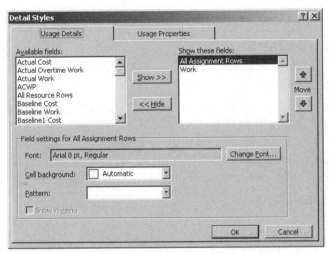

Figure 9-25. Use the Detail Styles dialog box to add another row of timephased information to the timesheet portion of the Resource Usage or Task Usage view.

6 In the Available Fields box, click Overtime Work, and then click Show. The Overtime Work field appears in the Show These Fields box. Click OK. The Overtime Work field is added to the timesheet portion of the view (see Figure 9-26).

	0	Resource Name	Overtime Work	Work	Details		20	23	26	29	Ma
3	◇	⊟ Office manager	0 hrs	568 hrs	Work		8h	32h	16h	48h	
					Ovt. Work						
		Identify improvements needed	0 hrs	8 hrs	Work			8h			
					Ovt. Work						
		Assess furniture and equipment	0 hrs	32 hrs	Work						
					Ovt. Work						
		Research furniture	0 hrs	16 hrs	Work		8h				
					Ovt. Work						
		Research equipment	0 hrs	32 hrs	Work			24h	8h		
					Ovt. Work						
		Order furniture	0 hrs	24 hrs	Work					24h	

Figure 9-26. Add the Overtime Work field to the sheet and timesheet portion of the Resource Usage view.

---

tip **Adding the Regular Work field**

You might also find it helpful to add the Regular Work field to the sheet portion of the Resource Usage view. Click the Work field, and then click Insert, Column. In the Field Name box, click Regular Work, and then click OK.

265

Chapter 9

To specify overtime work for overallocated resources, follow these steps:

1 In the Resource Usage view containing the Overtime Work field, find the first overallocated resource (highlighted in red) for whom you want to add overtime work.

2 Under the overallocated resource, review the assignments and the hours in the timesheet portion of the view. Find the assignments that are contributing to the overallocated work amounts.

3 In the sheet portion of the view, in the Overtime Work field for the assignment, enter the amount of overtime you want to designate.

You do not change the work amount because the overtime work amount is a portion of the total work. The amount you enter in the Overtime Work field is distributed across the time span of the assignment, which you can see in the timesheet portion of the view. For example, if an assignment spans 3 days, and you enter 6 hours of overtime, an amount of overtime is added to each day for the assignment.

In the timesheet portion of the view, you can view how the overtime work you enter is distributed across the assignment's timespan. However, you cannot edit the amount of overtime in the individual time periods.

4 Repeat this process for any other assignments causing the resource to be overallocated.

When you enter overtime work, the duration of the task is shortened. Overtime work is charged at an overtime rate you enter for the resource, either in the Resource Sheet or in the Resource Information dialog box. The resource name is still shown in red as overallocated, but now you've accounted for the overallocation using overtime.

Splitting Tasks

Sometimes a resource needs to stop working on one task, start work on a second task, and then return to the first task. This can happen, for example, when an overallocated resource needs to work on a task with a date constraint. In this situation, you can split a task. With a *split task*, you can schedule when the task is to start, stop, and then resume again. Just as with delay, splitting a task can ensure that resources are working on tasks when they actually have time for them.

> **note** In a split task, the task duration is calculated as the value of both portions of the task, not counting the time when the resource is working on something else. However, if you split a task with an elapsed duration, the duration is recalculated to include the start of the first part of the task through the finish of the last part of the task.

To split a task, follow these steps:

1 Display the Gantt Chart by clicking View, Gantt Chart.

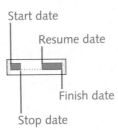

Split Task

2 On the Standard toolbar, click Split Task. Your mouse pointer changes to the split task pointer.

3 In the chart portion of the view, position your mouse pointer on the Gantt bar of the task you want to split, on the date when you want the split to occur.

4 Drag the Gantt bar to the date when you want the task to resume (see Figure 9-27).

Start date

Resume date

Finish date

Stop date

Figure 9-27. Drag the Gantt bar to represent when the task stops and when it resumes again.

You can split the task multiple times. Click Split Task on the Standard toolbar to activate each new split.

To remove the split in a split task, drag a portion of the Gantt bar so that it touches another portion.

---

tip **Split a task after work has started**

After you begin the execution and tracking phase of the project, you can also split a task on which a resource has started working.

For more information, see "Rescheduling the Project" on page 306.

---

note You can also adjust scope to balance the workload.

For more information about cutting scope, see "Changing Project Scope" later in this chapter.

Leveling Assignments

The previous sections described how you can delay and split tasks to balance or *level* resource assignments. Microsoft Project can balance the workload for you with the leveling feature. The leveling feature adds delay and splits in your project plan according to specifications that you set.

Chapter 9

267

You can have Microsoft Project level assignments whenever you give the command. You also have the option to keep the leveling feature on all the time. If you leave leveling on all the time, whenever you change the schedule in some way, Microsoft Project levels assignments at that time.

InsideOut

It's a great idea to have Microsoft Project automatically schedule assignments only when the resources actually have time available. However, if you set up automatic leveling, your schedule will be recalculated every time you make a change. If you have a large or complex project file, you might find that this constant recalculation slows down work in your project file.

One way around this is to turn on automatic leveling and turn off automatic recalculation. To do this, click Tools, Options, and in the Options dialog box, click the Calculation tab. For Calculation Mode, select the Manual option. Any time you want Microsoft Project to recalculate values in your project based on scheduling changes you've made, press the F9 key, which calculates all open projects. (If you want to calculate just the active project, press Shift+F9.) Whenever you've made changes that require calculation, the status bar will say "Calculate."

The other solution is to have Microsoft Project level resources only when you give the command. Click Tools, Level Resources. Make sure the leveling options are what you want, and click the Level Now button.

An advantage to directing when Microsoft Project levels is that you can immediately review the results of leveling in the Leveling Gantt and undo the operation if you don't like the results.

Note that leveling does not reassign tasks or units. Also, leveling only works on actual work resources—that is, material resources and generic resources are not leveled.

When you level resources, you carry out some or all these major process steps, which are detailed in the following sections.

Setting Leveling Priorities

You can set a priority for each task if you like. The priority levels range from 0, the lowest priority, to 1000, the highest. All tasks start with a default priority of 500, that is, they are all equal in priority. Microsoft Project uses the task priority setting as a leveling criteria. If you have certain tasks that are so important that you never want the leveling feature to split or delay them, you would set them for a priority of 1000, which ensures that Microsoft Project will never level resources using that task. You might have other tasks that, although important, enjoy more potential flexibility as to when they can be completed. Those you can set with a lower priority, like 100. This gives Microsoft Project the flexibility it needs to effectively level resource assignments.

To change the priority of an individual task, do the following:

1 In the Gantt Chart or other task sheet, double-click the task whose priority you want to change from the default of 500.

2 In the Task Information dialog box, click the General tab.

3 In the Priority box, enter the number representing the priority you want for this task.

InsideOut

Although it seems that priorities can help influence Microsoft Project's scheduling decisions throughout your project, priorities are actually only used in the context of leveling. When Microsoft Project is determining whether to split or delay one task versus another in order to level resources, it can use priority as one of its criterion, in addition to the other criteria you have set in the Resource Leveling dialog box.

You can still set up your own uses of priorities. You can sort and group tasks by priority. You can also create a filter to see only tasks above a certain priority.

Suppose there are ten tasks throughout your project that you want to set with a higher priority than the average. You can select those tasks, and then change their priority in one operation, as follows:

1 In the Gantt Chart or other task sheet, select all the tasks whose priority you want to change to the same number. To select adjacent tasks, click the first task, hold down the Shift key, and then click the last task. To select non-adjacent tasks, click the first task, hold down the Ctrl key, and then click each task you want to include.

2 On the Standard toolbar, click Task Information.

3 In the Multiple Task Information dialog box, click the General tab.

4 In the Priority box, enter the number representing the priority you want for all selected tasks.

You can add the Priority field to a task sheet and change the priority for tasks individually throughout the sheet. To do this, follow these steps:

1 In the Gantt Chart or other task sheet, click the column to the right of where you want the new Priority column to be inserted.

2 Click Insert, Column.

3 In the Field Name box, click Priority, and then click OK. The Priority column appears in your sheet (see Figure 9-28).

	ⓘ	Task Name	Duration	Priority	Start
3		Research new office sites	3 days	500	Mon 4/15/02
4		Decide on office space	1 day	500	Thu 4/18/02
5		Review lease agreement	1 day	500	Fri 4/19/02
6		Finalize lease	1 day	500	Mon 4/22/02
7		Identify improvements needed	1 day	500	Tue 4/23/02
8		Hire contractors for improvements	2 days	500	Wed 4/24/02
9		Schedule improvements	1 day	500	Fri 4/26/02

Figure 9-28. Type or select the priority you want in the Priority field.

4 For any task whose priority should be other than the default, enter the number in the Priority field.

---

tip **How many levels of priority do you need?**

Having 1000 levels of priority might seem like overkill, but the number of levels you use depends on what you're trying to do with your project, and how much control you want to wield over the leveling process.

If you feel you only need 10 levels of priority, use 0, 100, 200, 300, and so on as your priorities. Or use 495 through 505.

If you only need three priorities—low, medium, and high, for example, use 0, 500, and 1000. Or use 499, 500, and 501.

Remember, however, that tasks with a priority of 1000 are never leveled.

Leveling Resources using Standard Defaults

You use the Resource Leveling dialog box to set your leveling preferences and give the command to level. The default settings of the dialog box work for the majority of resource leveling needs. It's a good idea to try leveling with those settings first and see how they work for you. Then you'll have a better idea as to the kinds of controls you want to impose on the leveling operation. Follow these steps to level resources using the default settings:

1 If you want to level selected resources only rather than all resources, switch to a resource sheet and select the resource(s) you want to level.

To select multiple adjacent resources, drag from the first to the last resource.

To select multiple nonadjacent resources, click the first resource, hold down the Ctrl key, and then click each of the others.

2 Click Tools, Level Resources. The Resource Leveling dialog box appears (see Figure 9-29).

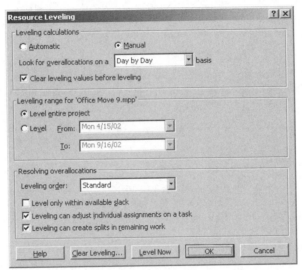

Figure 9-29. You can do a standard leveling operation using the defaults or you can set your own options.

3 Click the Level Now button.

4 If you had resources selected, the Level Now dialog box appears (see Figure 9-30). Select the Entire Pool or Selected Resources option, and then click OK.

Figure 9-30. Specify whether you want to level all or selected resources.

This dialog box does not appear if you had a task selected. In that case, all resources are leveled for the entire project.

Your resources are leveled according to the default dialog box settings.

To see the changes that leveling has made, see "Checking the Results of Leveling" later in this chapter.

Chapter 9

271

InsideOut

By default, Microsoft Project levels on a day-by-day basis. That means even if resources are assigned just one hour over their availability as determined by their resource calendar or maximum units, their assignments will be leveled.

You might think this is somewhat nit-picky, and maybe you'd rather not split tasks or add delays unless there are larger overallocations. In this case, open the Resource Leveling dialog box, and under Leveling Calculations, change the Day By Day setting to Week By Week or Month By Month.

Setting Leveling Options

If you've leveled your project a few times and want to take more control over how Microsoft Project levels, click Tools, Level Resources, and then change the options you want in the Resource Leveling dialog box. The following describes the available options:

Calculate automatically or manually. Under Leveling Calculations, select the Automatic option if you want Microsoft Project to level resources whenever you make a change that affects scheduling. Select the Manual option if you only want resources leveled when you give the Level Now command. If you select the Automatic option, clear the Clear Leveling Values Before Leveling check box to improve performance.

Specify the overallocation leveling time period. Resources are considered overallocated if they have even one hour of work scheduled beyond their availability as determined by their resource calendars and maximum units. You can set the time period at which leveling is triggered with the Look For Overallocations On A Basis box. By default, the time period basis is a day. This means that if resources are overallocated by a minute or hour within a day, they'll be leveled. If you set the overallocation leveling time period basis to the week, then resources that are scheduled for more work than can be accomplished by their weekly availability will be leveled. The choices are Minute By Minute, Day By Day (the default), Week By Week, and Month By Month.

Clear leveling. The Clear Leveling Values Before Leveling check box is selected by default. This specifies that any delays previously entered as a result of leveling, or as a result of manually entering leveling delay, are to be cleared before the next leveling operation is performed. The Clear Leveling button does the same thing. Use the check box if you're about to level again and you want to start fresh. Use the button if you're not planning to level right now but want to remove any leveling delay from your project plan.

Level certain tasks or the entire project. Under Leveling Range, you can specify that only those tasks falling within a date range you enter should be leveled. This can be particularly useful in projects that take place over a long period of time or that are subject to many changes. The default is for all tasks in the project to be leveled.

Set the order of leveling operations. The first part of the leveling process is to determine which tasks are causing overallocations. Then Microsoft Project works through the project, splitting tasks and adding delays to remove the overallocation. You can control the order in which Microsoft Project levels through the project by setting the leveling order. By default, Microsoft Project uses the Standard leveling order, which looks at task relationships, slack, start dates, priorities, and constraints to determine whether and how tasks should be leveled. If you choose the ID Only leveling order, Microsoft Project delays tasks with the higher ID numbers before considering any other criteria. If you choose the Priority, Standard leveling order, Microsoft Project first looks at any priorities you've set, and then at all the factors of the Standard leveling order.

Level within available slack. By default, the Level Only Within Available Slack check box is cleared. Select this check box if you need to ensure that leveling will not push out the finish date. However, unless your project has a fair amount of built-in slack, if this check box is selected, you might not see many changes to your project.

Adjust individual assignments on a task. By default, the Leveling Can Adjust Individual Assignments On A Task check box is selected. This controls adjustments to when a resource works on a task, independent of other resources working on the same task.

Create splits in remaining work. By default, the Leveling Can Create Splits In Remaining Work check box is selected. This means that not only can leveling split tasks that haven't started yet, it can also split tasks that are currently in progress.

When you've changed the leveling options to your satisfaction, level the resources in your project plan by clicking the Level Now button.

InsideOut

If you level tasks in a project scheduled from the finish date, negative delay values are applied from the end of the task or assignment. This causes the task or assignment's finish date to happen earlier.

Also, if you switch a project to be scheduled from the finish date from one to be scheduled from the start date, any leveling delays and splits are removed.

Troubleshooting

Leveling delay you've entered manually has disappeared

Suppose you've entered leveling delay to delay tasks manually. When you use the Microsoft Project leveling feature, by default, any previously entered leveling delay is removed. This is true whether the delay was entered automatically or manually.

To prevent manual leveling delay from being removed in the future, always clear the Clear Leveling Values Before Leveling check box in the Resource Leveling dialog box. And don't click the Clear Leveling button.

You might also consider entering assignment delay rather than leveling delay when manually entering delay values. Whereas leveling delay values delay all assignments on a task, assignment delay values delay individual assignments. Therefore, it might be a little more cumbersome and repetitious to enter initially, but you never have to worry about losing the values to a new leveling operation.

To get your leveling back, click Edit, Undo. This will reverse the leveling operation only if it's the very last operation you've done in your project. Otherwise you might need to enter the leveling delay again or use a backup project file.

For more information about manually entering delay, see "Delaying a Task or Assignment" earlier in this chapter.

Checking the Results of Leveling

To see the changes made to your project plan as a result of leveling, use the Leveling Gantt. Display the Leveling Gantt as follows:

1 Click View, More Views.

2 In the More Views dialog box, click Leveling Gantt.

The Gantt bars in this view display the task schedule as it looked before the leveling operation in addition to the task schedule as it looks after leveling so you can compare the changes made (see Figure 9-31). It also shows any new task delays and splits.

Troubleshooting

Microsoft Project performance has slowed since you last leveled

You probably set resource leveling to Automatic. Every time you make a scheduling change that affect assignments, Microsoft Project automatically levels resources. Although this is a nice feature, and often what we expect Microsoft Project to do for us, in larger or more complex projects, this can significantly slow down performance.

There are three ways to resolve this. In the Resource Leveling dialog box, select the Manual option under Leveling Calculations. Then click Level Now whenever you want resources to be leveled.

Another way to resolve this is to maintain automatic leveling but turn off automatic calculation. Click Tools, Options, and in the Options dialog box, click the Calculation tab. Under Calculation Options, select the Manual option. Now whenever you make schedule changes, your schedule won't be recalculated until you come back to this tab and click the Calculate Now button, or press F9 to calculate all open projects or Shift+F9 to calculate only the active project.

Here's the third method for improving performance. If you want to keep automatic leveling as well as automatic calculation, clear the Clear Leveling Values Before Leveling check box in the Resource Leveling dialog box. This can help improve performance because previous leveling values are not cleared before the new leveling is done.

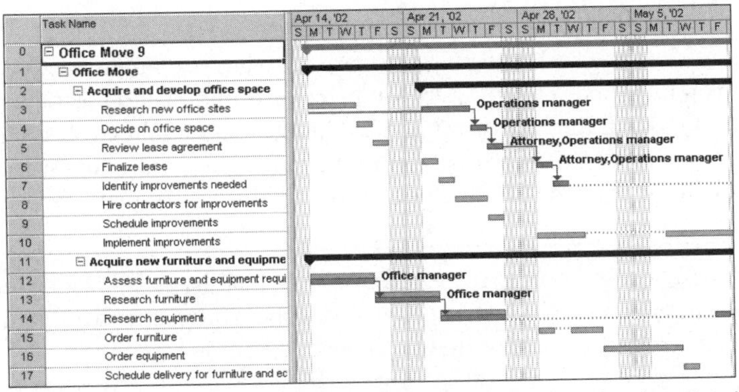

Figure 9-31. The chart portion of the view shows what leveling has done with your schedule, in terms of task delays and splits.

If you don't like the results of leveling, click Tools, Level Resources, and then click Clear Leveling.

> **tip** **Switch to the Leveling Gantt before leveling**
>
> If you go to the Leveling Gantt first and then level your project, you can see the results immediately in the Leveling Gantt. If you don't like the results, you can click Edit, Undo to reverse the changes made by leveling.

Troubleshooting

You told Microsoft Project to level your resources but nothing changed

You set up all your options in the Resource Leveling dialog box and then clicked OK. But if leveling is set to Manual, nothing will happen in your project plan. In the Manual leveling mode, your resources will not be leveled until you click the Level Now button. Therefore, instead of clicking OK, click the Level Now button, and your resources will be leveled.

Another alternative is to select the Automatic leveling option. In this case, as soon as you click OK, Microsoft Project levels your project plan. In addition, every time you make a scheduling change that affects assignments, Microsoft Project levels resources again.

Changing Project Scope

In the course of checking and adjusting your project plan, you might need to cut scope. For example, you might need to cut tasks you perceive as optional to meet the finish date. To bring project costs in line with your allotted budget, you might cut tasks associated with increased quality or quantity that you think you can live without. Or maybe you need to cut an entire phase or deliverable in order to alleviate resource overallocation.

> **note** Your task list is likely based on the scope statement that all the stakeholders, including customers, originally approved. If you need to cut scope, you might have to go back and obtain stakeholder approval for these changes.

To delete a task, simply click its row heading, and press the Delete key. You can also delete a summary task that represents an entire phase or group of related tasks. To delete a summary task, click its row heading, and press the Delete key. A message appears and warns you that deleting the summary task will delete all of its subtasks as well. Click OK to confirm that you want to do this.

Reviewing the Impact of Changes

When you've adjusted your project plan to bring in your finish date, reduce costs, or balance your workload, check that you've succeeded in hitting your target. Look at the Project Statistics dialog box or review the project summary task as described earlier in this chapter.

When you're content with one aspect of your project plan, such as your finish date, it's a good idea to see if you've "broken" any other aspect of your project, such as your costs. Keep an eye on your finish date, total project costs, and resource allocation, while always remembering your highest priority of the three. Continue to adjust and balance until all aspects of the project are just the way you want it.

Obtaining Buyoff on the Project Plan

Typically, before you even start Microsoft Project, you have a defined scope for the project. This scope drives the development of deliverables, milestones, phases, and tasks. This scope was also probably developed in conjunction with various stakeholders.

If you've been forced to cut scope as a result of adjusting the project plan to meet finish date, cost, or resource requirements, you need to go back to those stakeholders and get their approval for your scope changes.

You might need to justify your changes and specify the tradeoffs that are being made to meet the finish date, reduce costs, or balance workload to a reasonable level. You can also point out that the scope is now defined more precisely, based on the project limitations. With this more precise definition, you've lowered potential risks. The plan is solid and realistic. The project is less apt now to incur unexpected delays or costs or other changes that can disrupt the project, cause rework, or lower productivity.

As soon as you obtain the buyoff from your stakeholders, you have officially completed the planning phase of your project. You're finally ready to tell your team "Go!" and enter the execution phase of the project.

Part 3

Tracking Progress

279

Chapter 10

Saving a Baseline and Updating Progress

By now you've completed the planning phase of your project. The scope is set, along with the project goals and objectives. The tasks and deliverables are scheduled. The budget is approved, and you've procured the necessary human, equipment, and material resources. Your project plan reflects all these details and has been signed off by upper management or by your customers.

After all this, you're ready to charge forward with your team and actually start doing the work prescribed by the project. You are now leaving the planning phase and entering the execution phase.

The execution phase consists of four major activities:

Tracking. You track progress on tasks so you know when tasks are actually completed by their assigned resources.

Analyzing. You examine any differences between your original plan and how it's actually progressing. You monitor the differences in schedule or cost to anticipate any potential problems.

Controlling. You take any necessary corrective actions to keep the project on a steady course toward completion by its deadline and on its budget.

Reporting. You keep stakeholders informed. Whether you're providing the big picture to your team members or presenting high-level progress information to executives, you're regularly reporting various aspects of project information.

Are You a Charter or a Tracker?

Some project managers set up a project plan, painstakingly enter tasks, and create a schedule with meticulously accurate durations, task dependencies, and constraints. They acquire and assign exactly the right resources and calculate costs to the last penny. However, after they have their plan perfected, they execute the project and leave the project plan behind. What started out as an excellent roadmap of the project is now little more than a bit of planning history.

To be an effective project manager, take your project plan with you as you move to the execution phase of your project. Maintain the plan and enter actual progress information. By tracking progress in this way, your schedule and costs are updated so you know what to expect as you work through the weeks and months of your project. By doing that, you can use the power of Microsoft Project to calculate variances between your original plan and your current schedule, to do *earned value* analyses, and to generate reports you can share at status meetings.

Most importantly, you'll always have the up-to-date details you need at your fingertips. If you need to make an adjustment to the plan, either to recover a slipping phase or to respond to a directive to cut 10 percent of the project budget, Microsoft Project can serve as your project management information system and help you make those adjustments.

You used Microsoft Project in the planning phase to organize, schedule, and budget your project. Now you can use it in the execution phase to enter progress information, analyze performance, and generate status reports. With a close eye on progress and performance, you can adjust the project plan as necessary to ensure that your scope, schedule, costs, and resources are all balanced the way you need them to be.

To execute your project with Microsoft Project, you need to do two things: save baseline information on your project as planned and enter progress information as your resources start to complete tasks. With both baseline and progress information in hand, you can use the power of Microsoft Project to execute your project toward a successful outcome.

Saving Original Plan Information Using a Baseline

The project plan, having been adjusted to perfection, is considered your *baseline*. Think of it as your *original* plan. It represents the most ideal balance between scope, schedule, and cost.

The project plan, at this point in time, is also your *scheduled* plan. Think of it as your *current* plan. This is the only point in the project when the original plan and the current plan are exactly the same.

This is true because the current project plan is fluid. As soon as you enter progress information such as one task's actual start date or another task's percent complete, your project plan is recalculated and adjusted to reflect the new information from those *actuals*.

For example, suppose Task A has a scheduled finish date of May 3. It's linked with a finish-to-start task dependency to Task B, so Task B's scheduled start date is also May 3. However, Task A finishes 2 days early on May 1. So after entering the actual finish date of Task A, the scheduled start date of Task B changes to May 1. The scheduled start dates of any other successor tasks are recalculated as well.

This constant recalculation is essential for you to always know where your project stands in the current reality. But what if you want to know what your original start dates were? What if you want to compare the original baseline plan with the *current schedule* to analyze your progress and performance?

The answer is to save baseline information. By saving a baseline, you're basically taking a snapshot of key scheduling and cost information in your project plan at that point in time, that is, before you enter your first actuals and the scheduled plan begins to diverge from the original baseline plan. With fixed baseline information saved, you'll have a basis for comparing the current or actual project plan against your original baseline plan.

The difference between baseline and current scheduled information is called a *variance*. Baselines, actuals, and variances are used in a variety of ways, including earned value analysis, to monitor project schedule and cost performance. In fact, you cannot perform earned value analyses at all unless you have first saved a baseline.

Saving a baseline is not the same as saving the entire project plan. When you save a baseline, you save the following specific fields for all tasks, resources, and assignments:

- Cost, in the Baseline Cost field
- Duration, in the Baseline Duration field
- Finish, in the Baseline Finish field
- Start, in the Baseline Start field
- Work, in the Baseline Work field

These are the fields that will give you a good basis for schedule and budget performance as you execute your project.

Saving a Baseline

To save the first set of baseline information for your project plan, follow these steps:

1 Click Tools, Tracking, Save Baseline. The Save Baseline dialog box appears (see Figure 10-1).

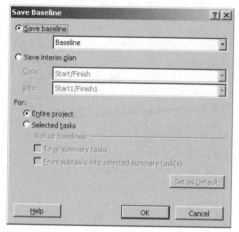

Figure 10-1. Use the Save Baseline dialog box to save up to 11 baselines or up to 10 interim plans.

2 Make sure the Save Baseline option is selected.

3 Under the Save Baseline option, make sure that Baseline is selected.

4 Under For, make sure the Entire Project option is selected.

5 Click OK.

What if you save a baseline and later add another set of additional tasks? Even after you save the baseline initially, you can still add tasks to it, as follows:

1 In the Gantt Chart or another task sheet, select the tasks that you want to add to the baseline.

2 Click Tools, Tracking, Save Baseline to display the Save Baseline dialog box. Make sure the Save Baseline option is selected.

3 Under the Save Baseline option, make sure that Baseline is selected. The Baseline box lists the date you last saved the baseline.

If you want to add tasks to a different baseline, for example, Baseline 1 or Baseline 2, click that baseline in the list.

4 Under For, select the Selected Tasks option.

newfeature! The Roll Up Baselines check boxes become available when you select the Selected Tasks option (see Figure 10-2). This ensures that the summarized baseline data shown in summary tasks are accurate and rolled up the way you expect.

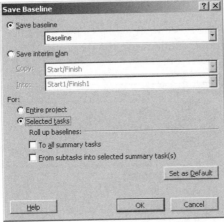

Figure 10-2. When you save a baseline for selected tasks, you can choose how to update the corresponding baseline data on summary tasks.

5 Select the check box that reflects how you want the baseline information of the selected task to be rolled up to summary tasks.

By default, after the initial baseline is saved, a summary task is not updated when a subtask is modified, added, or deleted.

If you want the selected tasks to be rolled up to all associated summary tasks, select the To All Summary Tasks check box.

If you want the selected tasks to be rolled up only to a selected summary task, select the From Subtasks Into Selected Summary Task(s) check box.

6 Click OK, and then click Yes to confirm that you want to change the existing baseline.

---

tip **Overwrite existing baseline information**

When saving a baseline, click the name of the baseline that has a Last Saved date. Under For, select Entire Project or Selected Tasks to specify whether you want to overwrite the baseline information of the entire project or only of selected tasks. The current schedule information in your project plan overwrites the baseline information in the selected baseline.

Chapter 10

Reviewing Baseline Information

After you've saved baseline information, you can review it in various ways. Initially, baseline information is identical to the scheduled information. As your team starts to complete work on the project, the two might diverge. It's this divergence, and the amount of it, that you'll be interested in as you monitor and control the project.

The following lists methods of reviewing baseline information:

Apply the Tracking Gantt.   Click View, Tracking Gantt. The Tracking Gantt shows the baseline Gantt bars underneath the scheduled Gantt bars (see Figure 10-3).

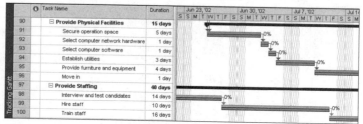

Figure 10-3.   The Tracking Gantt shows baseline start, duration, and finish in its Gantt bars, in relation to the scheduled Gantt bars.

Apply the Baseline table to a task sheet.   Click View, Table, More Tables, and in the More Tables dialog box, click Baseline. This table shows baseline information for duration, start, finish, work, and cost (see Figure 10-4). This table is also useful if you want to edit baseline information.

	Task Name	Baseline Dur.	Baseline Start	Baseline Finish	Baseline Work	Baseline Cost
90	⊟ Provide Physical Facilities	15 days	Wed 6/26/02	Tue 7/16/02	120 hrs	$10,760.00
91	Secure operation space	5 days	Wed 6/26/02	Tue 7/2/02	40 hrs	$5,000.00
92	Select computer network hardware	1 day	Wed 7/3/02	Wed 7/3/02	8 hrs	$640.00
93	Select computer software	1 day	Thu 7/4/02	Thu 7/4/02	8 hrs	$640.00
94	Establish utilities	3 days	Fri 7/5/02	Tue 7/9/02	24 hrs	$1,680.00
95	Provide furniture and equipment	4 days	Wed 7/10/02	Mon 7/15/02	32 hrs	$2,240.00
96	Move in	1 day	Tue 7/16/02	Tue 7/16/02	8 hrs	$560.00
97	⊟ Provide Staffing	40 days	Mon 6/10/02	Fri 8/2/02	320 hrs	$22,400.00
98	Interview and test candidates	14 days	Mon 6/10/02	Thu 6/27/02	112 hrs	$7,840.00
99	Hire staff	10 days	Fri 6/28/02	Thu 7/11/02	80 hrs	$5,600.00
100	Train staff	16 days	Fri 7/12/02	Fri 8/2/02	128 hrs	$8,960.00

Figure 10-4.   The Baseline table shows many of the baseline fields.

---

tip   **Editing a baseline**

Technically, a baseline field should never be edited. The baseline information is a snapshot of the project plan information at a particular point in time. When you change a baseline field, you're probably changing a variance or results of an earned value analysis.

If you need different values in baseline fields because of changed circumstances, save a new baseline, for example, Baseline 1 or Baseline 2. You can retain the values in your original baseline and choose which baseline is to be used for earned value analyses.

Add baseline fields to an existing table.   You might like to add a baseline field next to the equivalent scheduled field in, for example, the Entry table (see Figure 10-5). You can add the Baseline Duration field next to the Duration field and the Baseline Start field next to the Start field. Click Insert, Column. In the Field Name box, click the baseline field you want to add. The names of all baseline fields begin with the word "Baseline."

	Task Name	Baseline Duration	Duration	Baseline Start	Start	Baseline Finish	Finish
90	⊟ **Provide Physical Facilities**	**15 days**	**15 days**	**Wed 6/26/02**	**Wed 6/26/02**	**Tue 7/16/02**	**Tue 7/16/02**
91	Secure operation space	5 days	5 days	Wed 6/26/02	Wed 6/26/02	Tue 7/2/02	Tue 7/2/02
92	Select computer network hardware	1 day	1 day	Wed 7/3/02	Wed 7/3/02	Wed 7/3/02	Wed 7/3/02
93	Select computer software	1 day	1 day	Thu 7/4/02	Thu 7/4/02	Thu 7/4/02	Thu 7/4/02
94	Establish utilities	3 days	3 days	Fri 7/5/02	Fri 7/5/02	Tue 7/9/02	Tue 7/9/02
95	Provide furniture and equipment	4 days	4 days	Wed 7/10/02	Wed 7/10/02	Mon 7/15/02	Mon 7/15/02
96	Move in	1 day	1 day	Tue 7/16/02	Tue 7/16/02	Tue 7/16/02	Tue 7/16/02
97	⊟ **Provide Staffing**	**40 days**	**40 days**	**Mon 6/10/02**	**Mon 6/10/02**	**Fri 8/2/02**	**Fri 8/2/02**
98	Interview and test candidates	14 days	14 days	Mon 6/10/02	Mon 6/10/02	Thu 6/27/02	Thu 6/27/02
99	Hire staff	10 days	10 days	Fri 6/28/02	Fri 6/28/02	Thu 7/11/02	Thu 7/11/02
100	Train staff	16 days	16 days	Fri 7/12/02	Fri 7/12/02	Fri 8/2/02	Fri 8/2/02

Figure 10-5.   Showing baseline fields next to the equivalent scheduled fields can help you see at a glance whether and how much of a variance exists.

---

tip   **Review current and baseline summary information**

Open the Project Statistics dialog box to compare current schedule information with baseline information in terms of Start, Finish, Duration, Work, and Cost. Click Project, Project Information. In the Project Information dialog box, click the Statistics button.

Troubleshooting

You see nothing in the baseline fields

Baseline fields are empty until you save a baseline. If you add baseline fields to a table, apply the Baseline table, or show the Tracking Gantt before you have saved a baseline, you'll see no information. Click Tools, Tracking, Save Baseline, and then click OK. The baseline fields will now be populated.

For more information about using baseline information to analyze variance and monitor progress, see Chapter 11, "Responding to Changes in Your Project." For more information about earned value, see "Analyzing Progress and Costs Using Earned Value" on page 381.

Chapter 10

Saving Additional Baselines

Sometimes you track your project for a period of time and then a big change occurs. Maybe your company undergoes a major shift in priorities. Maybe an emergency project comes up that takes you and your resources away from this project. Maybe funding was stalled and then started up again. In such cases, your original baseline might not be as useful a tool as it once was. And although you don't want to replace it entirely, you would like to use another, more up-to-date baseline for your everyday tracking requirements.

Even if nothing catastrophic happened to your project, you might still have good uses for multiple baselines. In addition to taking that snapshot at the beginning of your execution phase, you might want to take another snapshot at the end of each month or each quarter. This can show more exact periods of time when you experienced greater variances between baseline and scheduled information.

newfeature!

With Microsoft Project 2002, you can save up to 11 different baselines. If you use earned value analyses, you can use one of 11 baselines for the earned value calculations.

To save an additional baseline, do the following:

1 Click Tools, Tracking, Save Baseline.

2 Make sure the Save Baseline option is selected.

3 In the Save Baseline list, click Baseline 1, for example (see Figure 10-6).

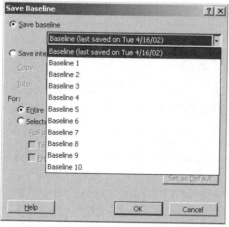

Figure 10-6. To save an additional baseline, choose any of the baselines in the list.

If a baseline has a Last Saved date after it, you've already saved information in that baseline. If you select one of those, you'll overwrite the previous baseline information with current schedule information.

4 Under For, make sure the Entire Project option is selected.

> **tip** **View multiple baseline Gantt bars**
>
> Using the Multiple Baselines Gantt, you can view Gantt bars reflecting different baselines. This can give you a visual representation of schedule changes from one set of baseline information to another. Click View, More Views, and then click Multiple Baselines Gantt. Each baseline is represented as a different color Gantt bar.

Project Management Practices: Working with the Baseline

The schedule baseline is the approved project schedule. This baseline has been adjusted and refined to the point where it meets the scope, the targeted finish date, and the budget of the project. The baseline has been deemed technically feasible given available resources. The baseline has been approved as the plan of record by the managing stakeholders.

This baseline plan is a component of the overall project plan. It provides the basis for measuring the schedule and cost performance of the project. In turn, any variances found can drive decisions about whether corrective actions should be taken and what those corrective actions should be.

In the course of project execution, if the schedule variance becomes very large, perhaps because of major scope changes or lengthy delays, *rebaselining* might be needed to provide realistic information from which to measure performance. Historically, rebaselining has been a painful decision for project managers using Microsoft Project because until now, only one set of baseline information could be saved. With Microsoft Project 2002, however, the project manager can save up to 11 baselines. There should always be a single baseline, however, which serves as the definitive baseline to be used for analysis and authoritative historical data.

Saving Additional Scheduled Start and Finish Dates

In addition to saving up to 11 baselines, you can also save up to 10 different sets of start and finish dates, or *interim plans*. These are like mini-baselines. Instead of saving the full set of schedule information such as duration, work, cost, and so on, an interim plan only saves the current start and finish dates and stores them in the custom Start1-10 and Finish1-10 fields.

To save an interim plan, follow these steps:

1 Click Tools, Tracking, Save Baseline.

2 Select the Save Interim Plan option.

3 By default, the Copy box displays *Start/Finish*. This indicates that the dates in the currently scheduled Start and Finish fields will be saved as this interim plan. You can copy from a different set of Start and Finish fields. In the Copy list, click the set you want.

4 By default, the Into box displays *Start1/Finish1*. This specifies where the start and finish dates of this interim plan will be stored. You can copy the start and finish fields into a different set of Start and Finish fields. In the Into box, click the set you want.

5 Under For, click Entire Project or Selected Tasks.

newfeature!

You can copy start and finish dates from other baselines into an interim plan. This can be useful if you have an old baseline you want to reuse but you want to retain the start and finish dates. To do this, click the old baseline in the Copy list, and then click the set of Start and Finish fields in the Into list.

You can also copy start and finish dates from an interim plan to one of the baselines. This can be useful if you've used interim plans as a substitute for baselines in the past. Now that multiple baselines are available, you can take advantage of them using your interim plan information. To do this, in the Copy list, click the interim plan containing the start and finish dates. Then in the Into list, click the baseline to which you want the information to be moved.

InsideOut

Interim plans seem to be a vestige of previous versions of Microsoft Project in which only one baseline was available. Interim plans were a mere "bone" thrown to project managers who really needed multiple baselines. With interim plans, at least multiple sets of Start and Finish dates could be saved.

Now finally we have multiple baselines, so interim plans don't seem to have much use anymore. They need to stick around, however, for those project managers who are updating project plans created in previous versions of Microsoft Project.

Interim plans might also be useful for project managers who like to create periodic snapshots, maybe once a month or once a quarter. With 11 baselines, you might run out of baseline fields in less than a year. With 10 interim plans, you have more fields to work with, even if they are limited to just the start and finish dates.

Clearing a Baseline

You can clear baseline and interim plan fields, as follows:

1 Click Tools, Tracking, Clear Baseline. The Clear Baseline dialog box appears.

2 Select the Clear Baseline Plan or Clear Interim Plan option.

3 In the corresponding box, click the name of the sets of fields you want to clear, for example, Baseline 3, or Start5/Finish5.

4 Select the Entire Project or Selected Tasks option.

The selected fields are cleared.

Updating Task Progress

So the resources are digging into their assignments and progress is being made. At regular intervals, you want to record their progress in Microsoft Project. Depending on how much time you want to spend entering progress information (and how much time you want your team members to spend doing that), you can choose a simple, high-level method, a comprehensive, detailed method, or something in between.

Entering actual progress information into Microsoft Project ensures that you'll always know how the project's going. You can keep an eye on the critical path and your budget. You can monitor key tasks and know exactly when you'll be handing off an important deliverable. With actual information coming into your project plan, you can also anticipate potential problems and take corrective actions as necessary.

If you're using Microsoft Project Server with Web Access, updating task progress can become highly automated. You set up the types of progress information you want to receive from your team members, and that information is integrated with the assignments in the timesheet that team members use in Microsoft Project Web Access. Every week, or however often you specify, team members send you an update regarding their actual progress toward completing tasks. You can have the progress information automatically integrated into your project plan or you can review the information before incorporating it.

For more information about exchanging task updates using Microsoft Project Web Access, see Chapter 21, "Managing Your Team Using Microsoft Project Web Access."

Chapter 10

Chapter 10

Project Management Practices: Scope and Quality Verification

As you meet milestones in your project and hand off deliverables, be sure to obtain formal acceptance of the project scope from the appropriate stakeholders, for example, the sponsor or customer. The sponsor reviews the deliverables and signs off that they're completed to his or her satisfaction.

At the same time, the sponsor should also check the correctness, or quality standards, of the work results.

It's important to have this acceptance process at various interim stages throughout the project, for example, for each deliverable, or at the end of each major phase, rather than waiting until the end of the project.

You can also exchange task update messages with your team members through e-mail, although the features are more limited.

For more information about using e-mail for team collaboration, see Chapter 20, "Collaborating Using E-Mail."

Whether you're exchanging updates electronically, getting a status update in a weekly meeting, or making the rounds to hear team members' progress, you can enter the following actual progress information in your project plan:

- Percent complete
- Actual duration and remaining duration
- Actual start and actual finish
- Percent work complete
- Actual work complete and remaining work
- Actual work complete by time period

tip   **Collect progress information to set future benchmarks**

When you enter actuals in your project plan, you're not just keeping your project on track. You're also building historical information that you'll be able to use as metrics for other similar project plans. You're tracking solid, tested data about how long these tasks actually take.

When you enter one piece of status information, often other pieces of information are calculated by Microsoft Project. Certainly the schedule and costs are automatically recalculated.

---

tip **Turn automatic calculation on or off**

By default, Microsoft Project recalculates information in your project plan as soon as you make a change that warrants recalculation. Such changes include assigning a resource, linking tasks, adding a cost, and so on.

If your project plan is very large or complex, you might find that constant recalculation slows down system performance. You can have Microsoft Project calculate your changes only when you give the command. To do this, click Tools, Options, and in the Options dialog box, click the Calculation tab. Under Calculation Mode, select the Manual option.

Whenever you make a change that requires a calculation, the word "Calculate" appears in the status bar. Press F9 to calculate all open projects. Press Shift+F9 to calculate just the active project.

Choosing the Best Method of Entering Actuals

There are several methods of tracking actual progress information in your project plan. How do you decide which method to use?

The first consideration is the level of detail you need. Your managing stakeholders might expect you to report at a certain level of detail at the weekly status meetings. Or you might need reliable historical information from this project because it's serving as a benchmark for similar future projects.

The second consideration is time. Are you going to have time to enter detailed progress information, or are you going to be so busy managing the project and perhaps working on your own assigned tasks that you won't be able to keep track of everything with an adequate amount of detail? What about your team members? Are they going to be too stretched to complete an electronic or paper timesheet? If you're using Microsoft Project Server and Web Access, certain processes are automated for you, but they might still take time for your team members.

The third consideration is whether you've assigned resources to tasks in your project plan. Obviously, resources will carry out the tasks one way or the other. But if you've chosen not to include resources in your project plan, you have fewer available tracking methods.

Tracking Task Progress through Your Collaboration Method

If you're collaborating with your team members using Microsoft Project Server and Web Access or using e-mail, you can tailor the fields shown in the team members' electronic timesheet. Depending on the progress information you want to track, you might want to add any of the following fields to the team members' timesheet:

- % Work Complete
- Actual Duration
- Actual Finish
- Actual Start
- Actual Work Complete
- Remaining Duration
- Remaining Work

Although these fields involve task progress, you can add any task or assignment field available in Microsoft Project. The timesheet becomes part of the periodic task update that the team members send you.

> For more information about setting up your timesheet options for e-mail collaboration, see Chapter 20, "Collaborating Using E-Mail." For more information about setting up Microsoft Project Web Access options, see Chapter 21, "Managing Your Team Using Microsoft Project Web Access."

Using one primary method of tracking actuals does not prevent you from using other methods for other tasks. Although you might achieve more consistent results if you stick to one method, sometimes other tasks simply lend themselves to a different type of progress information. Certain tasks are so important that you want to track them very closely. You can do that—you're never locked into a single tracking method.

Using the Tracking Toolbar

Many of your tracking functions are available on the Tracking toolbar (see Figure 10-7). To display the Tracking toolbar, click View, Toolbars, Tracking.

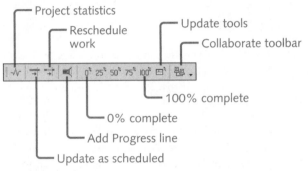

Figure 10-7. The Tracking toolbar includes buttons for setting percent complete, updating multiple tasks at once, and more.

The following list describes the functions available on the Tracking toolbar:

Project Statistics. Opens the Project Statistics dialog box, which shows the current, baseline, actual, variance, and remaining information for overall project start, finish, duration, work, and cost.

Update As Scheduled. Enters actual information to show that the selected tasks are proceeding exactly as planned. This is a shortcut to using the Update Project dialog box with the default settings.

Reschedule Work. Reschedules the entire project to start any uncompleted work after the current date. This is a shortcut to using the Update Project dialog box to reschedule uncompleted work.

Add Progress Line. Changes your cursor to a selection tool for you to select the status date for the progress line. Click the date in the chart portion of the Gantt Chart, and the progress line is drawn according to that date. This is a shortcut to using the Progress Lines dialog box.

0% Complete through 100% Complete. Enters actual progress for the selected tasks to the selected percent complete. This is a shortcut to using the Update Tasks dialog box.

Update Tasks. Opens the Update Tasks dialog box.

Collaborate Toolbar. Displays the Collaborate toolbar, which you can use to publish assignments, update project progress, request progress information, and use various features associated with e-mail collaboration, Microsoft Project Server and Web Access, and enterprise projects.

Updating Progress Using Task Scheduling Controls

You can update progress by entering actual information from task scheduling controls such as percent complete, duration, start date, and finish date. You can use these methods whether or not resources are assigned in Microsoft Project.

Updating the Project as Scheduled

Probably the easiest method of entering tracking information is to provide information to Microsoft Project that shows that your project is going exactly according to plan. You can use today's date or another date as the reference *complete through* date. With this method, tasks are updated as follows:

● Any tasks with a scheduled finish date before your complete through date are shown as completed on that scheduled date. In other words, your scheduled finish dates become your actual finish dates up to today's date or whichever date you specify.

● Any tasks with a scheduled start date before your complete through date (and a finish date after your date) are shown to be in progress through that date.

● Any tasks with a scheduled start date after your complete through date are untouched.

To update the project as scheduled, follow these steps:

1 Click Tools, Tracking, Update Project. The Update Project dialog box appears (see Figure 10-8).

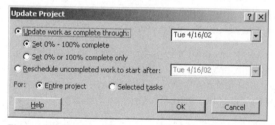

Figure 10-8. Update your project as scheduled through a specified date.

2 Make sure that the Update Work As Complete Through option is selected.

3 Enter the complete through date in the box. By default, today's date appears.

4 Select the Set 0% - 100% Complete option if you want Microsoft Project to calculate whether the task is not started, 100% complete, or in progress.

If a task's scheduled start date is after your complete through date, the task remains 0% complete.

If a task's scheduled finish date is before your complete through date, the task is set to 100% complete.

If a task's scheduled start date is before your complete through date and the scheduled finish date is after your complete through date, Microsoft Project calculates a percent complete value (see Figure 10-9).

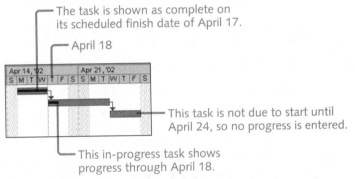

The task is shown as complete on its scheduled finish date of April 17.

April 18

This task is not due to start until April 24, so no progress is entered.

This in-progress task shows progress through April 18.

Figure 10-9. If your complete through date is April 18 and you want the Update Project function to calculate current progress of completed and in-progress tasks, your Gantt Chart will show progress bars looking like this.

5 Select the Set 0% or 100% Complete Only option if you want in-progress tasks to remain at 0% (see Figure 10-10). That is, any tasks whose scheduled finish date is after your complete through date would not have any progress entered for them.

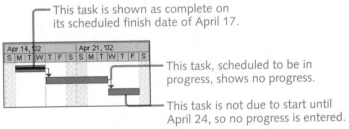

This task is shown as complete on its scheduled finish date of April 17.

This task, scheduled to be in progress, shows no progress.

This task is not due to start until April 24, so no progress is entered.

Figure 10-10. If you want the Update Project function to display in-progress tasks as 0% complete, this is the result when your complete through date is April 18.

You can use this method to update the entire project or selected tasks. Select the Entire Project or Selected Tasks option to specify your choice.

Entering Percent Complete

Another relatively simple method of tracking task progress is to specify percent complete. When you enter percent complete, Microsoft Project calculates actual duration and remaining duration.

To enter percent complete for one or more tasks, do the following:

1 In a task sheet view, such as the Gantt Chart or Tracking Gantt, select the task(s) whose percent complete you want to update.

2 On the Standard toolbar, click Task Information.

3 In the Task Information dialog box, click the General tab.

4 In the Percent Complete box, enter the percent complete that applies to all selected tasks.

The tasks are updated to reflect the percent complete. In the Gantt Chart, the percent complete is represented as a thin black line within Gantt bars (see Figure 10-11).

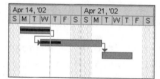

Figure 10-11. Gantt bars display how much of the task has been completed.

---

tip **Use the Tracking toolbar to update percent complete**

| 50% Complete | To display the Tracking toolbar, click View, Toolbars, Tracking. Click the tasks whose percent complete you want to update. Click the 0%, 25%, 50%, 75%, or 100% buttons as appropriate. |

---

note By default, when you enter percent complete for a task, this percentage is distributed evenly across the actual duration of the task. You can change this to distribute to the status date instead. Click Tools, Options. On the Calculation tab of the Options dialog box, select the Edits To Total Task % Complete Will Be Spread To The Status Date check box.

Chapter 10: Saving a Baseline and Updating Progress

Entering Actual Duration

If you enter the actual duration of a task, Microsoft Project calculates the percent complete. You can change remaining duration if necessary.

To enter actual duration of one or more tasks, do the following:

1 In a task sheet view, such as the Gantt Chart or Tracking Gantt, select the task(s) whose actual duration you want to update.

2 Click Tools, Tracking, Update Tasks. The Update Tasks dialog box appears (see Figure 10-12).

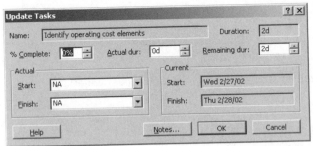

Figure 10-12. Use the Update Tasks dialog box to enter different types of progress information for one or more selected tasks.

3 In the Actual Dur box, enter the actual duration value.

4 If you expect the task to take more or less time than currently scheduled, update the remaining duration in the Remaining Dur box.

note By default, when you enter progress information for tasks, Microsoft Project automatically calculates the actual and remaining work and cost for assigned resources. This is the case when you update Percent Complete, Actual Duration, or Remaining Duration of tasks or assignments.

If you prefer to enter values for actual and remaining work and cost yourself rather than have Microsoft Project calculate it for you based on entered task progress, you can turn this option off. Click Tools, Options. On the Calculation tab, clear the Updating Task Status Updates Resource Status check box.

Entering Actual Start and Actual Finish

When you enter actual start and finish dates for tasks, you can better monitor the finish date of the project as whole, especially when working with critical tasks. When you enter an actual start date, the scheduled start date changes to match the actual start date. Likewise, when you enter an actual finish date, the scheduled finish date changes to match the actual finish date.

To enter an actual start or finish for one or more tasks, do the following:

1 In a task sheet view, such as the Gantt Chart or Tracking Gantt, select the task(s) whose actual start or finish you want to update.

2 Click Tools, Tracking, Update Tasks.

3 Under Actual, enter the actual start date in the Start box or the actual finish date in the Finish box.

The scheduled start and finish dates are shown under Current.

Troubleshooting

Your scheduled start and finish dates change when you enter actuals

When you enter actual start or actual finish dates, your scheduled (current) start or finish dates change to match. This is essential so that you can see any effects the change might have on the rest of your schedule. For example, if Task A was scheduled to finish on May 15 but it finished on May 20 instead, you'd need to know how its successor Task B is now scheduled. This is especially important if these are critical tasks.

If you want to keep your scheduled start and finish dates for comparison purposes, save a baseline or interim plan before you enter the actuals. With a baseline, not only can Microsoft Project can remember the original start and finish dates, but it can also calculate the differences between the original and scheduled information. These differences are stored in the Variance fields, which are empty until you save a baseline and start entering progress information.

Design a Custom Tracking View

Track

Use the Tracking Setup Wizard in the Project Guide to help you set up a custom tracking view tailored to work-related progress information and how you're receiving it. The Tracking Setup Wizard facilitates your tracking efforts whether progress information comes in automatically through Microsoft Project Server and Web Access or you're entering information manually. Either way, the Tracking Setup Wizard helps you set up the tracking of work-related progress information.

To start the Tracking Setup Wizard, click Track on the Project Guide toolbar, and then click the Prepare To Track The Progress Of Your Project link. Read the information in the Project Guide side pane and work through the steps, clicking the Save And Go To link at the bottom of the page when you're ready to move to the next step (see Figure 10-13). When finished, click the Save And Finish link.

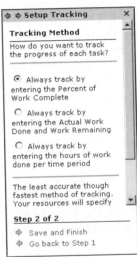

Figure 10-13. The Project Guide walks you through the steps for setting up a custom tracking field.

When you want to enter progress information, click Track on the Project Guide toolbar. Click the Incorporate Progress Information Into The Project link. Your custom view appears and the Project Guide side pane provides guidelines and controls to help you through the process.

You can also access your custom tracking view on the View menu.

Chapter 10

Updating Progress Using Resource Work

If resources are assigned in Microsoft Project, you can update progress information based on *work* for the task or the assignment. Work doesn't exist in your project plan unless you assign resources, at which time task duration is translated into assignment work time. Work can be further divided among multiple assigned resources, depending on the task type. Updating progress using work can be more precise than updating with percent complete or actual duration.

The following work tracking methods are listed in order from the quickest and simplest to the most sophisticated.

---

new feature! Updating Progress Around the Status Date

As you enter actual progress, you can choose the status date to be the reference point for actual and remaining portions of the task. Changing the status date can be helpful if you received actuals on Friday but you don't enter them into the project plan until the next Wednesday. If you were to use Wednesday's date as the status date, some of your actuals could be skewed. By default, the status date is the current date, that is, today. To set the status date, do the following:

1 Click Project, Project Information.

2 In the Status Date box, enter the status date you want to use for the actual progress information you're about to enter.

You have additional options about how actual progress is to be entered in your project plan. Click Tools, Options, and in the Options dialog box click the Calculation tab. Under Calculation Options for your project file, a series of four check boxes provides options for handling actual and remaining task information in your schedule in relation to the status date. These options are as follows:

- Move End Of Completed Parts After Status Date Back To Status Date
- And Move Start Of Remaining Parts Back To Status Date
- Move Start Of Remaining Parts Before Status Date Forward To Status Date
- And Move End Of Completed Parts Forward To Status Date

Entering Percent Work Complete

If resources are assigned in Microsoft Project, you can enter their reports of what percentage of work they've completed so far. To enter percent work complete for a task, follow these steps:

1 Display a task sheet view, such as the Tracking Gantt or Task Usage view.

2 Apply the Work table. Click View, Table, Work.

3 In the % W. Comp. field of the task you want to update, enter the value of percent work complete.

Follow these steps to enter percent work complete of an assignment:

1 Display the Task Usage view.

2 Select the assignment (the resource name beneath the task) whose percent work complete you want to update.

If you want to update several assignments at once with the same percent work complete, select them all.

3 On the Standard toolbar, click Assignment Information.

4 In the Assignment Information dialog box, click the Tracking tab (see Figure 10-14).

5 In the % Work Complete box, enter the value.

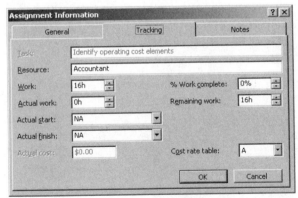

Figure 10-14. Use the Tracking tab in the Assignment Information dialog box to update progress for an assignment.

Chapter 10

Part 3: Tracking Progress

If entering percent work complete is going to be your primary method of updating progress information, use the Project Guide to create a custom tracking view. A view similar to the Tracking Gantt is created with the % Work Complete field added as a column in the sheet portion of the view (see Figure 10-15).

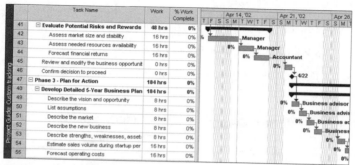

Figure 10-15. The Project Guide can create a custom view for updating percent work complete, which is considered the quickest method of entering work-related actuals.

Entering Actual Work Complete and Remaining Work

If resources are assigned in Microsoft Project, you can enter their reports of actual work completed. If they believe that there is more or less work (than originally scheduled) remaining to be done, you can adjust remaining work as well.

If you have multiple resources assigned to a task and you enter actual work completed for the task, the work amounts are evenly distributed among the assigned resources. To enter total amounts for actual work completed on a task, do the following:

1 Display a task sheet, such as the Task Usage view or Tracking Gantt.

2 Click View, Table, Work.

3 If necessary, drag the divider bar to see the Actual (work) field (see Figure 10-16).

Task Name	Work	Baseline	Variance	Actual	Remaining	% W. Comp.	Details	M
16 ⊟ Evaluate Potential Risks and Rewards	80 hrs	80 hrs	0 hrs	0 hrs	80 hrs	0%	Work	8h
17 ⊟ Assess market size and stability	16 hrs	16 hrs	0 hrs	0 hrs	16 hrs	0%	Work	8h
Business advisor	_16 hrs_	_16 hrs_	_0 hrs_	_0 hrs_	_16 hrs_	_0%_	Work	8h
18 ⊟ Estimate the competition	8 hrs	8 hrs	0 hrs	0 hrs	8 hrs	0%	Work	
Business advisor	_8 hrs_	_8 hrs_	_0 hrs_	_0 hrs_	_8 hrs_	_0%_	Work	
19 ⊟ Assess needed resource availability	16 hrs	16 hrs	0 hrs	0 hrs	16 hrs	0%	Work	
Business advisor	_16 hrs_	_16 hrs_	_0 hrs_	_0 hrs_	_16 hrs_	_0%_	Work	

Figure 10-16. Use the Work table to update actual work on a task.

4 In the Actual (work) field of the task you want to update, enter the actual work value.

The values in the Remaining (work) and % W. Comp fields are recalculated.

Chapter 10: Saving a Baseline and Updating Progress

To enter total amounts of actual work completed on an assignment, do the following:

1 Display the Task Usage view.

2 Click View, Table, Work.

3 If necessary, drag the divider bar to see the Actual (work) field.

4 In the Actual (work) field of the assignment (the resource name under the task) you want to update, enter the actual work value.

The values in the Remaining (work) and % W. Comp fields for the assignment are recalculated.

---

tip   **Update actual work in the Assignment Information dialog box**

You can also double-click the assignment to open the Assignment Information dialog box. Click the Tracking tab. Update the value in the Actual Work box. This is also a good method of updating actual work for multiple assignments if they all have the same value.

If entering actual work is going to be your primary method of updating progress information, use the Project Guide to create a custom tracking view. A view similar to the Tracking Gantt is created with the Tracking table applied. This method is considered a happy medium—moderately detailed and moderately time-consuming.

Entering Actual Work Complete by Time Period

The most comprehensive method of updating actual progress information is to enter actual work on assignments by time period. This is the smallest unit of information you can enter because you're entering information about the assignment, and you're probably entering hours worked in a day.

With this method, you're using the timesheet portion of the Task Usage view to enter actuals. To do this, follow these steps:

1 Display the Task Usage view.

2 Click Format, Details, Actual Work. The timesheet portion of the view changes to include Act. Work as a row under (scheduled) Work.

3 If you want to show rolled-up actual work totals for assignments, apply the Work table to the sheet portion of the view. Click View, Table, Work (see Figure 10-17 on the next page).

Task Name	Work	Baseline	Variance	Details	M	T	W
16	⊟ Evaluate Potential Risks and Rewards	80 hrs	80 hrs	0 hrs	Work	8h	8h	8h
					Act. Work			
17	⊟ Assess market size and stability	16 hrs	16 hrs	0 hrs	Work	8h	8h	
					Act. Work			
	Business advisor	*16 hrs*	*16 hrs*	*0 hrs*	Work	8h	8h	
					Act. Work			
18	⊟ Estimate the competition	8 hrs	8 hrs	0 hrs	Work			8h
					Act. Work			
	Business advisor	*8 hrs*	*8 hrs*	*0 hrs*	Work			8h
					Act. Work			

Figure 10-17. Use the Task Usage view to enter daily values of actual work on assignments.

4 In the Act. Work field of the assignment and the day, enter the actual work value.

If you want to enter actual work for different time periods, click Zoom Out or Zoom In on the Standard toolbar.

If entering actual work by time period is going to be your primary method of updating progress information, use the Project Guide to create a custom tracking view. A view similar to the Task Usage view is created with the Act. Work field added as a row in the timesheet portion of the view and the Work and Actual Work fields added as columns in the sheet portion of the view.

Rescheduling the Project

Suppose you and your team started executing a project a few months ago. Some tasks were completed and some were in progress when your team's efforts were redirected onto a different urgent priority. Now you're all back to work on this project again, ready to pick up where you left off.

What do you do with your project plan? The scheduled dates of tasks you need to work on now are two months old. Do you have to readjust all the tasks to align them with the current calendar?

No, you just need to reschedule incomplete tasks for the current date. Microsoft Project will shift any incomplete tasks forward to a date you specify, and you can continue forward from there (see Figure 10-18).

note In a situation like this, it might be a good idea to save a new baseline. Keep the old one, but use the new baseline for your everyday variance measurements.

Chapter 10: Saving a Baseline and Updating Progress

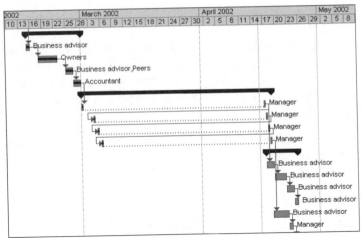

Figure 10-18. This project stalled in early March, and then was rescheduled to continue in mid-May.

To reschedule uncompleted tasks, follow these steps:

1 Click Tools, Tracking, Update Project.

2 Select the Reschedule Uncompleted Work To Start After option.

3 Enter the start after date in the box. By default, today's date appears.

You can use this method to reschedule the entire project or just selected tasks. Select either the Entire Project or the Selected Tasks option to specify your choice.

By default, any tasks that were in progress are split so that remaining work is scheduled after the date you specify. If you don't want in-progress tasks to be split, click Tools, Options. Click the Schedule tab. Clear the Split In-Progress Tasks check box.

newfeature! In previous versions of Microsoft Project, when you rescheduled uncompleted work, date constraints were removed and changed to As Soon As Possible or As Late As Possible. Now in Microsoft Project 2002, uncompleted tasks that have a date constraint, such as Must Start On or Finish No Earlier Than, are not rescheduled. This preserves the constraint and gives you the option of deciding how to handle it.

newfeature! Also in previous versions of Microsoft Project, when you rescheduled uncompleted work, you could not enter a date in the past; you could only enter the current or future date. In Microsoft Project 2002, you can enter any reschedule date you want, even one in the past. If a task is in progress, the date does need to be after the task's existing stop date or actual start date.

Chapter 10

Manually Updating Project Costs

If resources are assigned to tasks in your project plan and those resources also have their costs entered in Microsoft Project, costs are updated whenever you enter actual progress information. For example, suppose a $25/hour resource is assigned to 8 hours of work on a task. When you enter that the task is 50 percent complete, $100 of actual cost is recorded for this task.

If you do not want Microsoft Project to calculate costs for you in this manner, you can turn off this option and enter costs yourself. To turn off automatic cost calculation, follow these steps:

1 Click Tools, Options.

2 In the Options dialog box, click the Calculation tab.

3 Clear the Actual Costs Are Always Calculated By Microsoft Project check box.

4 By default, any edits you make to cost will be distributed evenly across the actual duration of a task. If you would rather distribute the costs to the status date, select the Edits To Total Actual Cost Will Be Spread To The Status Date check box.

To enter task costs manually, display a task sheet and click View, Table, Cost to apply the Cost table. Enter total actual costs in the Actual field of the task.

To manually enter timephased costs for tasks or assignments, display the Task Usage view. Click Format, Details, Actual Cost to add the Actual Cost field to the timesheet portion of the view.

> **tip** **Don't enter costs manually**
>
> It can be very cumbersome and tricky to update costs manually. You'll experience more accurate results if you enter resources and their costs in your project plan, along with any fixed costs of tasks. When you assign those resources to tasks, costs are forecasted. When you enter progress on tasks, actual costs are calculated.

Chapter 11

Responding to Changes in Your Project

During the execution phase of your project, your resources are working on their tasks, and you're tracking their progress by entering actuals into your project plan. Those actuals, combined with your baseline information, give you the means to compare your current progress against your original plan. As part of your project control responsibilities, you use this information to keep an eye on project progress. In this way, you can analyze project performance, see how you're doing, and take any corrective action that you might deem necessary.

As you monitor and analyze project performance on a day-to-day basis, occasionally you'll need to make adjustments. Perhaps one task is finished a few days early, and this affects its successors and their assigned resources. Maybe another task took longer than expected and went overbudget. Suppose various changes in the schedule caused a resource to become overallocated and another one to be underutilized.

You might find that you need to adjust your project plan here and there to account for these variances. Sometimes, the differences work in your favor, as might be the case in a task finishing early. Other times, the differences point to a potential problem, which you can prevent if you catch it soon enough.

The nature of the changes you make depends on the priorities of your project. Remember the one fixed side of your project triangle (finish date, budget/resources, or scope), and adjust your project accordingly.

For more information about the project triangle, see Chapter 9, "Checking and Adjusting the Project Plan."

In addition to the day-to-day monitoring and adjusting of a project in progress, sometimes larger modifications are needed because of external changes imposed on the project. For example, your customers might announce that you must move the finish date up six weeks. Or a new corporate edict might cut $8,000 from your budget or reduce your staff by 10 percent.

Also, sometimes wholesale changes to the project are needed because the scheduled finish date, overall cost, or resource allocation has somehow gotten way off track. In this case, radical measures might be needed to bring the project into conformance again.

With large, externally imposed changes or a temporarily derailed project, you might need to *replan* or reschedule the project. The techniques used are similar to those you used to hit your targets when you were first planning the project. You make adjustments to the schedule, costs, resources, or scope in your project plan, and Microsoft Project recalculates your schedule so you can quickly see the results of your replanning.

Baseline, Actual, and Scheduled Project Information

In the course of monitoring project performance, there are four terms to keep in mind:

Baseline. The baseline dates, costs, durations, and so on, are your project plan's values at the time you saved baseline information. This is also referred to as *planned* information.

Actual. The actual progress information includes data such as percent complete, actual work, actual finish date, and so on.

Scheduled. The current project combines the project's actual performance on tasks with the planned schedule for current and future tasks. Together, this forms the current plan as scheduled. This is also referred to as *current* information, or the current plan.

Variance. The difference between baseline information and scheduled information is the variance. Microsoft Project subtracts the baseline value from the scheduled value (which has incorporated any actuals you have entered) to calculate the variance. So a positive variance means you're behind in your schedule or over budget, whereas a negative variance means you're ahead of the game—finishing faster or under budget. A variance of 0 indicates that your baseline and scheduled values are exactly the same. If actuals have been entered, this means that everything went exactly according to plan. If the task is still in the future, this means that projections forecast that the task will still go according to plan.

Whether you're making large adjustments to respond to large issues or small adjustments to keep a healthy project well on its way, you can always keep a close eye on progress. You can analyze the current status of the project and decide on any corrective actions necessary.

InsideOut

It might seem odd that variances are calculated from scheduled values rather than actual values. However, because the scheduled values incorporate any actual values, it makes sense. And by not requiring actual values to make the calculation, you can see variances in future tasks as well. If you see any large variances projected for future tasks or for the project as a whole, you'll still have time to take corrective action and head off the problems.

Monitoring and Adjusting the Schedule

If you're managing a time-constrained project, there are a few pieces of task information you'll want to keep a close eye on, including:

- Project finish date
- Critical path
- Start and finish dates of critical tasks
- Current progress of critical tasks

If actuals have changed task scheduling to the point where your target project finish date is projected to be late, you're going to need to adjust the schedule to bring that finish date back in line.

Monitoring Schedule Progress

Use one or more of the following techniques to help you monitor progress toward your finish date:

- Review finish dates and the critical path.
- Check and adjust task constraints, dependencies, and durations.
- Add resources to tasks.

For more information about monitoring and adjusting the schedule to achieve a specific finish date, see "Bringing In the Project Finish Date" on page 240.

Chapter 11

Another method for monitoring schedule progress is to save a baseline and then compare it with the current schedule. For example, you can see baseline finish dates for tasks next to their scheduled finish dates, based on actuals you've entered. Then you can look at the variances between the baseline and scheduled finish. The finish date variance, for example, is calculated as follows:

(Scheduled/Current) Finish – Baseline Finish = Finish Variance

> **tip** **Evaluate your schedule variances and performance with earned value analysis**
>
> You can use earned value calculations, such as the Schedule Performance Index (SPI) and Schedule Variance (SV) earned value fields to analyze your project performance so far.
>
> For more information, see Chapter 13, "Analyzing Project Information."

Reviewing Overall Schedule Progress

Review your project statistics to get a broad view of how your project status compares with your baseline. Project statistics show your currently scheduled start and finish dates, along with their baseline, actual, and remaining values. To review your project statistics, follow these steps:

1 Click Project, Project Information. The Project Information dialog box appears.

2 Click the Statistics button. The Project Statistics dialog box appears. The current, or scheduled, finish date appears in the Finish column (see Figure 11-1).

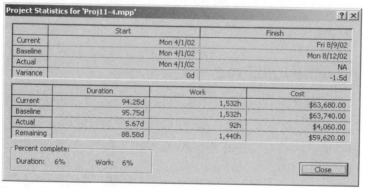

Figure 11-1. The Project Statistics dialog box shows overall project information with its currently scheduled values, baseline values, actual values, and more.

Chapter 11: Responding to Changes in Your Project

Another way to keep your eye on the schedule at all times is to add the project summary task row, as follows:

1 Display the Gantt Chart or other task sheet.

2 Click Tools, Options, and in the Options dialog box, click the View tab.

3 Select the Show Project Summary Task check box.

The project summary task appears at the top of any task sheet view, including the Gantt Chart (see Figure 11-2). Task information is rolled up for the entire project and its summary total displayed in the project summary row. Specifically, the Finish field in the project summary row shows the latest finish date in the project. If you've added additional fields or applied different tables, information is also rolled up for those fields as appropriate.

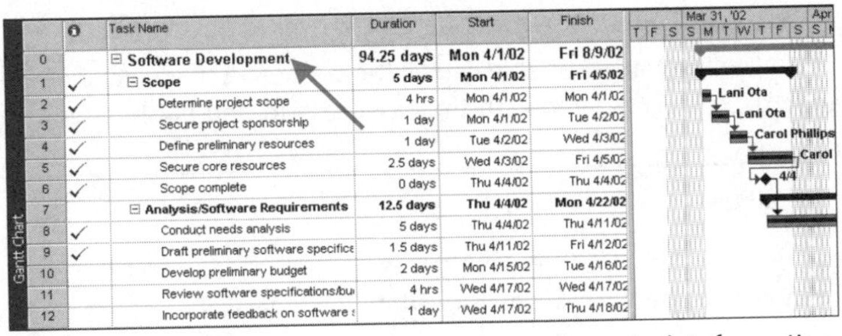

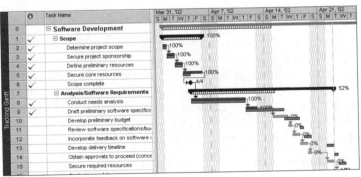

Figure 11-2. The Project Summary row rolls up task information to display the totals for the entire project.

By default, the regular Gantt Chart shows progress as a thin black line through the Gantt bar. To also see percent complete next to the Gantt bars, apply the Tracking Gantt. Click View, Tracking Gantt (see Figure 11-3).

Figure 11-3. The Tracking Gantt view shows progress, percent complete, and the critical path.

Reviewing Schedule Variances

To review the differences between your original baseline plan values and your currently scheduled values, apply the Variance table, as follows:

1 Display the Gantt Chart or other task sheet.

2 Click View, Table, Variance. The Variance table is applied to the current view (see Figure 11-4).

	Task Name	Start	Finish	Baseline Start	Baseline Finish	Start Var.	Finish Var.
0	⊟ Software Development	Mon 4/1/02	Fri 8/9/02	Mon 4/1/02	Mon 8/12/02	0 days	-1.5 days
1	⊟ Scope	Mon 4/1/02	Fri 4/5/02	Mon 4/1/02	Thu 4/4/02	0 days	1.5 days
2	Determine project scope	Mon 4/1/02	Mon 4/1/02	Mon 4/1/02	Mon 4/1/02	0 days	0 days
3	Secure project sponsorship	Mon 4/1/02	Mon 4/1/02	Mon 4/1/02	Tue 4/2/02	0 days	-0.5 days
4	Define preliminary resources	Mon 4/1/02	Tue 4/2/02	Tue 4/2/02	Wed 4/3/02	-1.5 days	-0.5 days
5	Secure core resources	Wed 4/3/02	Fri 4/5/02	Wed 4/3/02	Thu 4/4/02	0 days	1.5 days
6	Scope complete	Thu 4/4/02	Thu 4/4/02	Thu 4/4/02	Thu 4/4/02	0 days	0 days
7	⊟ Analysis/Software Requirements	Thu 4/4/02	Mon 4/22/02	Thu 4/4/02	Wed 4/24/02	0 days	-1.5 days
8	Conduct needs analysis	Thu 4/4/02	Thu 4/11/02	Thu 4/4/02	Thu 4/11/02	0 days	0 days
9	Draft preliminary software specifica	Thu 4/11/02	Fri 4/12/02	Thu 4/11/02	Tue 4/16/02	0 days	-1.5 days

Figure 11-4. The Variance table shows the currently scheduled start and finish dates as compared with the baseline start and finish dates.

tip **Quickly switch tables**

To quickly change to a different table, right-click the Select All box in the upper-left corner of the table in a sheet view. The list of tables appears.

To quickly see the name of the current view and table, position your mouse pointer over the Select All box. A ScreenTip lists the name of the current view and table.

Troubleshooting

Your scheduled values change whenever you enter actuals

Whenever you enter actual progress information, Microsoft Project recalculates your scheduled information based on these actuals. This is so you can see any effect the actual progress information has on the rest of your schedule. This also enables you to continue to see scheduled projections for the project finish date and total cost, based on performance to this point. For example, if Task A was scheduled to be finished on May 15, but it is finished on May 20 instead, you'd need to know how its successor Task B is now scheduled. This is especially important if these are critical tasks.

If you want to keep your scheduled start and finish dates for comparison purposes, save a baseline or interim plan before you enter the actuals.

Reviewing the Critical Path

By viewing the finish date or the critical path, you can easily see whether you're still scheduled to hit your target finish date, given the actuals you've entered. To see the critical path, click View, Tracking Gantt. If you need to bring in the finish date, you might want to focus on the critical tasks. You can filter your task sheet to show only critical tasks by clicking Project, Filtered For, Critical. To show all tasks again, click Project, Filtered For, All Tasks.

> **tip** To select a filter, you can also click the Filter tool on the Formatting toolbar. In the Filter list, click Critical. When finished, click All Tasks in the Filter list.

> For more information about viewing the critical path, see "Viewing the Critical Path" on page 236.

> **note** After a critical task is completed, it becomes noncritical because it can no longer affect the completion of future tasks.

Reviewing Task Progress

Reviewing the progress of critical tasks is the most effective means of learning quickly whether your project is staying on track with its target finish date. The following filters can help you focus on any potential problems with task progress:

- Late/Overbudget Tasks Assigned To
- Should Start By
- Should Start/Finish By
- Slipped/Late Progress
- Slipping Tasks (see Figure 11-5)
- Tasks With Deadlines
- Tasks With Fixed Dates

	Task Name	Start	Finish	Baseline Start	Baseline Finish	Start Var.	Finish Var.
17	⊟ **Design**	**Thu 4/25/02**	**Thu 5/16/02**	**Wed 4/24/02**	**Tue 5/14/02**	**0.5 days**	**1.5 days**
18	Review preliminary software specifications	Thu 4/25/02	Fri 4/26/02	Wed 4/24/02	Fri 4/26/02	0.5 days	0.5 days
19	Develop functional specifications	Mon 4/29/02	Fri 5/3/02	Fri 4/26/02	Fri 5/3/02	0.5 days	0.5 days
20	Develop prototype based on functional spec	Mon 5/6/02	Thu 5/9/02	Fri 5/3/02	Thu 5/9/02	0.5 days	0.5 days
21	Review functional specifications	Fri 5/10/02	Mon 5/13/02	Thu 5/9/02	Mon 5/13/02	0.5 days	0.5 days
22	Incorporate feedback into functional specific	Wed 5/15/02	Wed 5/15/02	Mon 5/13/02	Tue 5/14/02	1.5 days	1.5 days
23	Obtain approval to proceed	Thu 5/16/02	Thu 5/16/02	Tue 5/14/02	Tue 5/14/02	1.5 days	1.5 days
24	Design complete	Thu 5/16/02	Thu 5/16/02	Tue 5/14/02	Tue 5/14/02	1.5 days	1.5 days

Figure 11-5. Apply the Slipping Tasks filter to quickly see which tasks are in jeopardy.

315

Part 3: Tracking Progress

To apply one of these filters, follow these steps:

1 Display the Gantt Chart or other task sheet you want to filter.

2 On the Formatting toolbar, click the arrow in the Filter tool.

Filter

3 In the Filter list, click the filter you want.

4 When you want to show all tasks again, click All Tasks in the Filter list.

You can also run reports that provide information about the progress of tasks such as:

- Unstarted Tasks
- Tasks Starting Soon
- Tasks In Progress
- Completed Tasks
- Should Have Started Tasks
- Slipping Tasks

To run a report, follow these steps:

1 Click View, Reports.

2 Double-click Current Activities.

3 Double-click the report you want.

4 If a dialog box appears asking for more information, enter the information, and then click OK. The report appears in a preview window.

---

tip **Review status indicators**

You can add the Status Indicator field to any task sheet. This field displays icons that indicate whether a task is completed, in progress, or not yet started. The indicators also show whether the task is on schedule or behind schedule.

Select the column heading next to which you want to insert the Status Indicator column. Click Insert, Column. In the Field Name list, click Status Indicator.

Working with Progress Lines

You can add *progress lines* to your Gantt Chart. Progress lines provide a graphic means of seeing whether tasks are ahead of schedule, behind schedule, or exactly on time. Progress lines are shown for tasks that have been completed, are in progress, or are currently due. They are not shown for tasks in the future.

For any given progress date, which you can set as the status date, you can have Microsoft Project draw a progress line connecting in-progress tasks and tasks that should have started (see Figure 11-6).

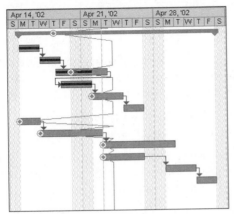

Figure 11-6. The peaks indicate a negative or positive variance, whereas straight lines show tasks that are exactly on time.

Progress lines create a graph on the Gantt Chart that provides valuable progress information, as follows:

- Peaks pointing to the left indicate work that's behind schedule.
- Peaks pointing to the right indicate work that's ahead of schedule.
- Lines straight down the middle of a Gantt bar indicate a task that's right on time.

To add progress lines, follow these steps:

1 Display the Gantt Chart.

2 Click Tools, Tracking, Progress Lines. The Progress Lines dialog box appears (see Figure 11-7 on the next page).

Chapter 11

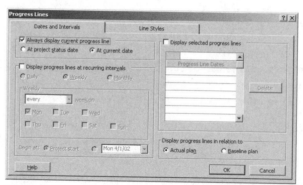

Figure 11-7. Set progress lines in the Gantt Chart using the Progress Lines dialog box.

3 On the Dates And Intervals tab, select the Always Display Current Progress Line check box. Then select whether you want the progress line to be displayed at the project status date or the current date.

4 Under Display Progress Lines In Relation To, select whether you want progress lines to reflect the actual plan or your baseline.

5 Set any other preferences for the way you want dates and intervals of dates to be represented with your progress lines. You can enter specific progress line dates, display progress lines at selected date intervals, and so on.

6 Click the Line Styles tab, and set your preferences for the way you want the progress lines to appear in the Gantt Chart. You can specify the line type and color and the progress point shape and color for the current progress line and other progress lines (see Figure 11-8).

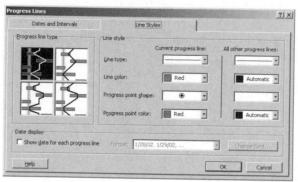

Figure 11-8. Use the Line Styles tab in the Progress Lines dialog box to customize the way progress lines appear in your Gantt Chart.

Chapter 11

To remove progress lines, follow these steps:

1 Click Tools, Tracking, Progress Lines. The Progress Lines dialog box appears.

2 On the Dates And Intervals tab, clear the Always Display Current Progress Line check box.

Correcting the Schedule

Suppose you've reviewed your schedule details and found that your project isn't going as quickly as planned and the finish date is in jeopardy. Or perhaps upper management has imposed a schedule change, and you need to work toward a different finish date.

If you need to take corrective actions in your project plan to bring in the scheduled finish date, you can:

● Check schedule assumptions, such as duration, constraints, and task dependencies, to see if any adjustments can be made.

● Add resources to recover a slipping schedule. This will likely add costs.

● Cut scope to recover a slipping schedule. This will probably require stakeholder approval.

---

tip   **Run a what-if project**

Suppose an external change is being proposed, or you just want to see the effect of a potential change to your project plan. You can save another version of your project plan and make the necessary adjustments to reflect the potential change. You can then examine specifically what the imposed changes will do to your project plan in terms of schedule, cost, and resource allocation.

To do this, click File, Save As. In the File Name box, enter a name for the what-if project, and then click OK.

You can change the what-if project as much as you like. Because you've saved it under a different file name, your working version of the project plan remains intact, but you've been able to gain valuable information about the impact of potential change.

If you or other stakeholders decide to go ahead with the change, you can adopt the what-if project as your new working project.

For more information about adjusting the schedule to meet the current or new finish date, see "Bringing In the Project Finish Date" on page 240.

Chapter 11

Project Management Practices: Schedule Control

It's understood that very few projects run precisely as planned. Tasks take more or less time than planned, resources discover new information, forgotten tasks are remembered, and outside forces influence the project implementation. When changes to the project schedule take place, you might have to revise durations, rearrange task sequences, or analyze what-if scenarios for your project.

Microsoft Project is an excellent tool for schedule control because it can calculate and predict the effects of any schedule changes, whether the change comes as a result of entering actual information or what-if information. Microsoft Project tracks your planned dates against your actual dates (and other schedule information). This variance analysis is key to schedule control. Analyzing variances in dates, durations, and other schedule information helps you detect where the project is diverging from your original plan. You can then predict possible delays in the schedule further down the line and take corrective actions now to offset those delays.

note When you've adjusted your project plan to achieve the finish date you need, be sure to check costs, resource allocation, and scope. You need to know how your changes affect other areas of the project plan.

Monitoring and Adjusting Costs

If your project is a budget-constrained project, you'll want to keep a close eye on the resource and task costs, and on estimated costs for the project as a whole. You'll also want to adjust your project plan if any actuals come in that are likely to blow the budget.

Monitoring Project Costs

Use one or more of the following techniques to monitor and adjust costs to help you work within your budget:

- Display specialized views and tables to review project costs.
- Adjust the schedule to reduce costs.
- Adjust assignments to reduce costs.

> For more information about monitoring and adjusting costs to achieve a specific budget, see
> "Reducing Project Costs" on page 249.

Using baseline information you saved, you can review your current costs and compare them with baseline costs. For example, you can see baseline costs for tasks (including their resource costs) next to their scheduled costs, based on actuals you've entered. Then you can review the variances between the baseline and scheduled cost. The cost variance is calculated as follows:

(Scheduled/Current) Total Cost – Baseline Cost = Cost Variance

> **tip** Evaluate your cost variances and performance with earned value analysis
>
> You can use earned value calculations, such as the Budgeted Cost of Work Scheduled (BCWS) and Cost Variance (CV) earned value fields to analyze your project performance against the budget so far.

> For more information, see Chapter 13, "Analyzing Project Information."

Reviewing Overall Cost Totals

There are two ways to review your overall cost totals, as follows:

- Review project statistics. Click Project, Project Information, and in the Project Information dialog box, click the Statistics button. Under Cost, review the current, baseline, actual, and remaining cost for the project.

- Add the project summary task row. In the Gantt Chart or other task sheet, click Tools, Options, and in the Options dialog box, click the View tab. Select the Show Project Summary Task check box. Summary totals for task information are displayed in the project summary row at the top of the sheet.

Reviewing Cost Variances

To review the differences between your original baseline costs and your currently scheduled costs, apply the Cost table, as follows:

1 Display the Gantt Chart or other task sheet.

2 Click View, Table, Cost. The Cost table is applied to the current view (see Figure 11-9 on the next page).

	Task Name	Fixed Cost	Fixed Cost Accrual	Total Cost	Baseline	Variance	Actual	Remaining
0	⊟ Software Development	$0.00	Prorated	$63,800.00	$63,740.00	$60.00	$4,500.00	$59,300.00
1	⊟ Scope	$0.00	Prorated	$1,840.00	$1,240.00	$600.00	$1,840.00	$0.00
2	Determine project scope	$0.00	Prorated	$200.00	$200.00	$0.00	$200.00	$0.00
3	Secure project sponsorship	$0.00	Prorated	$200.00	$400.00	($200.00)	$200.00	$0.00
4	Define preliminary resources	$0.00	Prorated	$640.00	$320.00	$320.00	$640.00	$0.00
5	Secure core resources	$0.00	Prorated	$800.00	$320.00	$480.00	$800.00	$0.00
6	Scope complete	$0.00	Prorated	$0.00	$0.00	$0.00	$0.00	$0.00
7	⊟ Analysis/Software Requireme	$0.00	Prorated	$4,680.00	$5,220.00	($540.00)	$2,660.00	$2,020.00
8	Conduct needs analysis	$0.00	Prorated	$1,800.00	$1,800.00	$0.00	$1,800.00	$0.00
9	Draft preliminary software spe	$0.00	Prorated	$540.00	$1,080.00	($540.00)	$540.00	$0.00
10	Develop preliminary budget	$0.00	Prorated	$640.00	$640.00	$0.00	$320.00	$320.00
11	Review software specification	$0.00	Prorated	$340.00	$340.00	$0.00	$0.00	$340.00

Figure 11-9. Apply the Cost table to a task sheet to see total planned costs for tasks. With the summary task row also applied, you can see rolled up cost totals as well.

Reviewing Cost Performance Using Earned Value Analysis

If you've saved a baseline and are entering actuals, you can evaluate current cost and schedule performance using earned value calculations. To generate most earned value information, you must have the following items in your project plan:

- A saved baseline

- Resources assigned to tasks

- Costs associated with assigned resources

- Actual progress information

To review earned value information, follow these steps:

1 Display the Gantt Chart or other task sheet.

2 Click View, Table, More Tables.

3 Click Earned Value, Earned Value Cost Indicators, or Earned Value Schedule Indicators, depending on the type of earned value information you want to review (see Figure 11-10).

	Task Name	BCWS	BCWP	CV	CV%	CPI	BAC	EAC	VAC
0	⊟ Software Develop	$6,300.00	$4,440.00	($60.00)	-1%	0.99	$63,740.00	$64,601.35	($861.35)
1	⊟ Scope	$1,240.00	$1,240.00	($600.00)	-48%	0.67	$1,240.00	$1,840.00	($600.00)
2	Determine projec	$200.00	$200.00	$0.00	0%	1	$200.00	$200.00	$0.00
3	Secure project s	$400.00	$400.00	$200.00	50%	2	$400.00	$200.00	$200.00
4	Define preliminar	$320.00	$320.00	($320.00)	-99%	0.5	$320.00	$640.00	($320.00)
5	Secure core reso	$320.00	$320.00	($480.00)	-149%	0.4	$320.00	$800.00	($480.00)
6	Scope complete	$0.00	$0.00	$0.00	0%	0	$0.00	$0.00	$0.00
7	⊟ Analysis/Software	$5,060.00	$3,200.00	$540.00	16%	1.2	$5,220.00	$4,339.13	$880.88
8	Conduct needs a	$1,800.00	$1,800.00	$0.00	0%	1	$1,800.00	$1,800.00	$0.00
9	Draft preliminary	$1,080.00	$1,080.00	$540.00	50%	2	$1,080.00	$540.00	$540.00
10	Develop prelimine	$640.00	$320.00	$0.00	0%	1	$640.00	$640.00	$0.00
11	Review software	$340.00	$0.00	$0.00	0%	0	$340.00	$340.00	$0.00

Figure 11-10. The Earned Value Cost Indicators table displays earned value fields related to budget performance.

> **tip** **See all available earned value fields**
>
> To see all earned value fields available in Microsoft Project, click Help, Reference. Click Fields Reference. At the bottom of the topic, click the See A List Of Field Types link. In the Field Types topic, click the Earned Value Fields link.

Table 11-1 lists the default contents of each of the three earned value tables.

Table 11-1. Earned Value Tables

Table name	Included fields
Earned Value	BCWS (Budgeted Cost of Work Scheduled)
	BCWP (Budgeted Cost of Work Performed)
	ACWP (Actual Cost of Work Performed)
	SV (Schedule Variance)
	CV (Cost Variance)
	EAC (Estimate At Completion)
	BAC (Budget At Completion)
	VAC (Variance At Completion)
Earned Value Cost Indicators	BCWS (Budgeted Cost of Work Scheduled)
	BCWP (Budgeted Cost of Work Performed)
	CV (Cost Variance)
	CV% (Cost Variance Percent)
	CPI (Cost Performance Index)
	BAC (Budget At Completion)
	EAC (Estimate At Completion)
	VAC (Variance At Completion)
	TCPI (To Complete Performance Index)
Earned Value Schedule Indicators	BCWS (Budgeted Cost of Work Scheduled)
	BCWP (Budgeted Cost of Work Performed)
	SV (Schedule Variance)
	SV% (Schedule Variance Percent)
	SPI (Schedule Performance Index)

> For more information about analyzing project performance with earned value, see Chapter 13, "Analyzing Project Information."

Chapter 11

> **Troubleshooting**
>
> **Your earned value fields are all $0.00**
>
> If you've applied an earned value table or inserted an earned value field only to find all the values to be $0.00, it likely that you're missing one or more of the pieces of information needed by Microsoft Project to calculate earned value fields.
>
> For earned value to be calculated, you must have all the following items in your project plan:
>
> - A saved baseline
> - Resources assigned to tasks
> - Costs associated with assigned resources
> - Actual progress information

Reviewing Budget Status

The following filters can help you focus on any potential problems with project costs and budget:

- Cost Greater Than
- Cost Overbudget (see Figure 11-11)
- Late/Overbudget Tasks Assigned To
- Work Overbudget

	Task Name	Fixed Cost	Fixed Cost Accrual	Total Cost	Baseline	Variance	Actual	Remaining
1	☐ Scope	$0.00	Prorated	$1,840.00	$1,240.00	$600.00	$1,840.00	$0.00
4	Define preliminary resources	$0.00	Prorated	$640.00	$320.00	$320.00	$640.00	$0.00
5	Secure core resources	$0.00	Prorated	$800.00	$320.00	$480.00	$800.00	$0.00

Figure 11-11. Apply the Cost Overbudget filter to quickly see which tasks are or are projected to be over budget.

Apply a filter by clicking the arrow beside the Filter tool on the Formatting toolbar. In the Filter list, click the name of the filter you want. To show all tasks again, click All Tasks in the Filter list.

You can also run reports that provide information about costs and budget status, as follows:

- Cash Flow
- Budget (see Figure 11-12)
- Overbudget Tasks
- Overbudget Resources
- Earned Value

Budget Report as of Tue 4/23/02				
Software Development				
Task Name	**Fixed Cost**	**Fixed Cost Accrual**	**Total Cost**	**Baseline**
Develop code	$0.00	Prorated	$7,200.00	$7,200.00
Developer testing (primary debugging)	$0.00	Prorated	$7,200.00	$7,200.00
Develop Help system	$0.00	Prorated	$4,800.00	$4,800.00
Develop user manuals	$0.00	Prorated	$4,800.00	$4,800.00
Develop training materials	$0.00	Prorated	$4,200.00	$4,200.00
Conduct needs analysis	$0.00	Prorated	$1,800.00	$1,800.00
Develop functional specifications	$0.00	Prorated	$1,800.00	$1,800.00
Obtain user feedback	$0.00	Prorated	$1,800.00	$1,800.00
Develop prototype based on functional specifications	$0.00	Prorated	$1,440.00	$1,440.00
Review modular code	$0.00	Prorated	$1,200.00	$1,200.00
Test module integration	$0.00	Prorated	$1,200.00	$1,200.00
Conduct training usability study	$0.00	Prorated	$1,120.00	$1,120.00
Develop unit test plans using product specifications	$0.00	Prorated	$960.00	$960.00
Develop integration test plans using product specifica	$0.00	Prorated	$960.00	$960.00
Review Help documentation	$0.00	Prorated	$960.00	$960.00

Figure 11-12. Run the Budget report to see how you're progressing compared to your budget.

To run a cost report, click View, Reports. Double-click Costs, and then double-click the report you want.

Realigning the Project with the Budget

Suppose you've reviewed your budget details against the current project costs and found that you're going to end up well over budget. Or perhaps upper management has asked you to cut costs by 10 percent, and you need to work toward a different total project cost.

If you need to take corrective actions in your project plan to reduce project costs, you can:

- Recheck your cost assumptions such as resource rates, per-use costs for resources, and fixed costs for tasks.
- Adjust the schedule to reduce costs. Reducing task durations and adjusting task dependencies can help reduce costs.

- Adjust assignments to reduce costs. Add, remove, or replace resources on assignments as appropriate to cut costs.

- Cut scope to reduce costs. This will probably require stakeholder approval.

> **note** When you've adjusted your project plan to achieve the budget you need, be sure to check your finish date, resource allocation, and scope. You need to know how your changes affect other areas of the project plan.

For more information about reducing project costs, see "Reducing Project Costs" on page 249.

Project Management Practices: Cost Control

Cost control is the means for a project to stay within the bounds of the prescribed project budget. This involves continual monitoring of the project plan, tracking actual work and cost information, and taking corrective action where needed. If a task early in the project costs more than expected, costs might have to be trimmed in later tasks. In addition, outside forces might affect the project budget. For example, certain material costs might have gone up from the time you developed your plan to the time you're actually procuring the material. Or your company might undertake a cost-cutting initiative that requires you to cut all project costs by 15 percent.

When changes to project costs take place, you might have to adjust assignments or scope to bring costs in line with the budget. If you have a positive cost variance, the scheduled or current cost is more than your planned baseline cost. If you have a negative cost variance, the scheduled cost is less than your baseline cost. Although you certainly need to know why costs are higher than planned, you also should look into costs that are lower than planned. This can point to potential problems with increased risk, and perhaps with quality issues.

Earned value analysis is particularly useful for cost control. With variances and earned value analysis, you can assess the differences between planned and scheduled costs, determine their causes, and decide if corrective actions are needed.

Monitoring and Adjusting Resource Workload

If you're a resource manager, or if your biggest project priority is to maintain a balanced workload among your resources, monitor your resources' workload and see if anyone is unexpectedly overallocated or underallocated. As you receive information from resources about their assigned tasks and enter actuals, you can see whether you need to take any action to prevent potential resource allocation problems in the near future.

Monitoring Resource Workload

Use one or more of the following techniques to help you monitor and adjust the schedule to achieve a balanced resource workload:

- Review resource workloads.
- Adjust resource availability.
- Adjust assignments.
- Split tasks to reschedule remaining work for when resources have available time.
- Level assignments.

Because work is the measure of resource effort on tasks, you can use the baseline value for work to help review how well resources are utilized according to actual and scheduled values. For example, you can see Maureen's baseline work for tasks next to her values for scheduled work, based on actuals you've entered on her progress. Then you can review the variances between the baseline and scheduled work. Work variance is calculated as follows:

(Scheduled/Current) Work – Baseline Work = Work Variance

If actual work values are a good deal higher than originally planned, you can anticipate some problems with resource overallocation now or in the near future.

> For more information about balancing the resource workload, see "Balancing Resource Workloads" on page 253.

Part 3: Tracking Progress

> **tip** Analyze your work variances and performance with earned value
>
> You can use earned value calculations such as the Budgeted Cost of Work Scheduled (BCWS) and Actual Cost of Work Performed (ACWP) earned value fields to analyze your project performance based on work.
>
> For more information, see Chapter 13, "Analyzing Project Information."

Reviewing Overall Work Totals

There are two ways to review your overall work totals, as follows:

- Review project statistics. Click Project, Project Information, and in the Project Information dialog box, click the Statistics button. Under Work, review the current, baseline, actual, and remaining work for the project.

- Add the project summary task row. In the Gantt Chart or other task sheet, click Tools, Options, and in the Options dialog box, click the View tab. Select the Show Project Summary Task check box. Summary totals for task information are displayed in the project summary row at the top of the sheet.

Reviewing Work Variances

To review the differences between your original baseline work and your currently scheduled work, apply the Work table, as follows:

1 Display the Gantt Chart or other task sheet.

2 Click View, Table, Work. The Work table is applied to the current view (see Figure 11-13).

	Task Name	Work	Baseline	Variance	Actual	Remaining	% W. Comp.
0	⊟ **Software Development**	**1,536 hrs**	**1,532 hrs**	**4 hrs**	**104 hrs**	**1,432 hrs**	**7%**
1	⊟ **Scope**	**44 hrs**	**28 hrs**	**16 hrs**	**44 hrs**	**0 hrs**	**100%**
2	Determine project scope	4 hrs	4 hrs	0 hrs	4 hrs	0 hrs	100%
3	Secure project sponsorship	4 hrs	8 hrs	-4 hrs	4 hrs	0 hrs	100%
4	Define preliminary resources	16 hrs	8 hrs	8 hrs	16 hrs	0 hrs	100%
5	Secure core resources	20 hrs	8 hrs	12 hrs	20 hrs	0 hrs	100%
6	Scope complete	0 hrs	0 hrs	0 hrs	0 hrs	0 hrs	100%
7	⊟ **Analysis/Software Requirements**	**108 hrs**	**120 hrs**	**-12 hrs**	**60 hrs**	**48 hrs**	**56%**
8	Conduct needs analysis	40 hrs	40 hrs	0 hrs	40 hrs	0 hrs	100%
9	Draft preliminary software specificε	12 hrs	24 hrs	-12 hrs	12 hrs	0 hrs	100%
10	Develop preliminary budget	16 hrs	16 hrs	0 hrs	8 hrs	8 hrs	50%
11	Review software specifications/bu	8 hrs	8 hrs	0 hrs	0 hrs	8 hrs	0%
12	Incorporate feedback on software ε	8 hrs	8 hrs	0 hrs	0 hrs	8 hrs	0%

Figure 11-13. Apply the Work table to a task sheet to see work baselines, actuals, and schedule. With the summary task row applied, you can see rolled up work totals as well.

Reviewing Resource Allocation

If a resource is overallocated, his or her name appears in red in any resource view. In resource sheets, a leveling indicator is also displayed next to the resource name, recommending that the resource be leveled.

3		Daniel Penn	Work
4		Kim Yoshida	Work
5		This resource should be leveled based on a Day by Day setting.	k
6		Adam Stein	Work
7		Katherine Inman	Work

To see the extent of overallocation or underallocation for a resource, use the Resource Graph, as follows:

1 Click View, Resource Graph (see Figure 11-14).

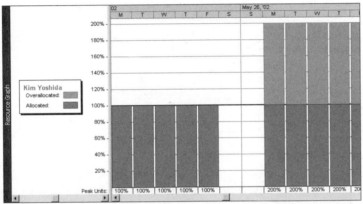

Figure 11-14. The Resource Graph can show whether a resource is fully allocated, overallocated, or underallocated for a selected period of time.

2 Review the allocation for the first resource.

3 On the Standard toolbar, click the Zoom Out button to see the Resource Graph for a longer period of time. Click the Zoom In button to see details about a shorter period of time.

4 By default, the Resource Graph shows peak units for each time period, including the percentage allocated and the percentage overallocated. You can show different types of information in the Resource Graph. Click Format, Details, and then click another type of information, for example, Work or Remaining Availability.

5 To see information for the next resource, press the Page Down key.

The leveling indicator often suggests that the resource be leveled on a Day By Day basis. This is because Microsoft Project has found that this resource is overallocated by at least one minute over the resource availability for a day.

You might find that level of detail too fine for your purposes. It might be more effective to level resources on a Week By Week basis or a Month By Month basis. Although the overallocation is still detected when you're overallocated by just one minute, looking at the entire week or the entire month instead of just one day provides more "wiggle room" for overallocations to take care of themselves.

You can also see the details about which assignments are causing resource overallocations (or underallocations) by using the Resource Usage view, as follows:

1 Click View, Resource Usage (see Figure 11-15).

	ⓘ	Resource Name	Details	May 26, '02						
				F	S	S	M	T	W	T
4	◈	⊟ Kim Yoshida	Work	8h			14h	16h	16h	16h
		Review functional specifications	Work							
		Identify modular/tiered design parameters	Work							
		Assign development staff	Work							
		Develop code	Work	8h			8h	8h	8h	8h
		Developer testing (primary debugging)	Work				6h	8h	8h	8h

Figure 11-15. The Resource Usage view shows how resources are allocated for each time period, as well as the specific assignments that contribute to that allocation.

2 Any resource whose name appears in red or with a leveling indicator is overallocated. Review the timesheet portion of the view to see where the overallocation occurs. You might need to scroll to move to a different time period.

3 On the Standard toolbar, click the Zoom Out button to see the Resource Usage view for a longer period of time. Click the Zoom In button to see details about a shorter period of time.

4 Review the sheet portion of the view to see the assignments for each resource.

5 You can add the Overallocation field to the timesheet portion of the view, which you can use to learn how many hours or days, for example, a resource is overallocated. To do this, click Format, Details, Overallocation (see Figure 11-16).

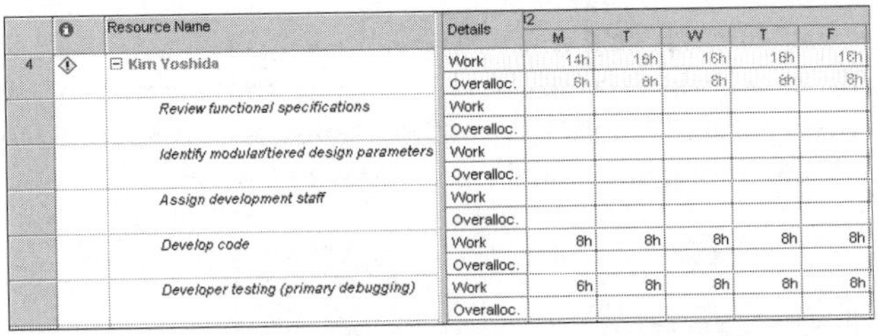

Chapter 11: Responding to Changes in Your Project

Figure 11-16. Add the Overallocation field to the Resource Usage view to see the number of hours (or other time period) by which each resource is overallocated.

---

tip **Apply the Work table to the Resource Usage view**

If you apply the Work table to the Resource Usage view, you can see work details for each resource and assignment, including baseline work, the variance between the baseline and scheduled work, any actual work reported, remaining work, and percent complete.

---

6 To see underallocations or the amount of time that a resource is available for more assignments, add the Remaining Availability field to the timesheet portion of the view. Click Format, Details, Remaining Availability.

Use the Resource Allocation view to see the Resource Usage view in combination with the Tracking Gantt. Click View, More Views. In the More Views dialog box, click Resource Allocation, and then click Apply (see Figure 11-17).

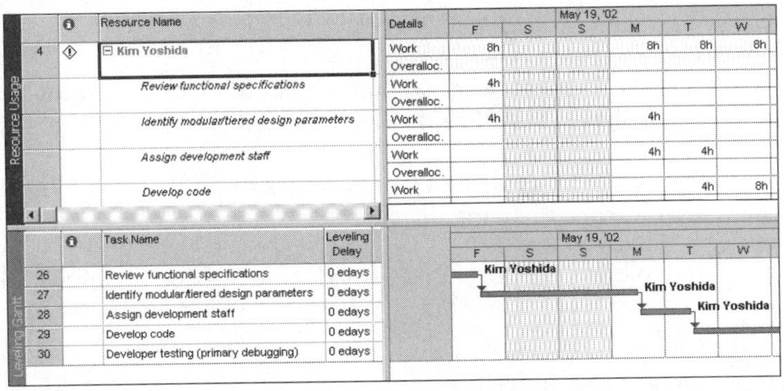

Figure 11-17. With the Resource Allocation view, you can see task information in the lower pane for any assignment you click in the Resource Usage view in the upper pane.

With the Summary table applied to a resource view, you can see the Peak field, which can quickly tell you whether a resource is allocated to their maximum availability (100 percent), overallocated (more than 100 percent), or underallocated (less than 100 percent). Click View, Table, Summary (see Figure 11-18).

	Resource Name	Group	Max. Units	Peak	Std. Rate	Ovt. Rate	Cost	Work
1	Lani Ota	Mgmt	100%	100%	$50.00/hr	$0.00/hr	$2,000.00	40 hrs
2	Carol Phillips	PM	100%	100%	$40.00/hr	$0.00/hr	$4,480.00	112 hrs
3	Daniel Penn	Analyst	100%	100%	$45.00/hr	$0.00/hr	$6,840.00	152 hrs
4	Kim Yoshida	Dev	100%	200%	$60.00/hr	$0.00/hr	$15,840.00	264 hrs
5	Tristan Randall	Test	100%	200%	$30.00/hr	$45.00/hr	$8,400.00	280 hrs
6	Adam Stein	Train	100%	300%	$35.00/hr	$0.00/hr	$8,960.00	256 hrs
7	Katherine Inman	Tech Com	100%	200%	$40.00/hr	$0.00/hr	$13,440.00	336 hrs
8	Deployment team	Deployment	100%	100%	$40.00/hr	$60.00/hr	$3,840.00	96 hrs
9	Contract developers	Dev	300%	0%	$0.00/hr	$0.00/hr	$0.00	0 hrs
10	Trainers	Train	400%	0%	$0.00/hr	$0.00/hr	$0.00	0 hrs

Figure 11-18. By looking at the Peak field for resources, you can quickly see the level of a resource's allocation and whether they're available to take on more assignments.

The following filters can help you focus on any potential problems with overallocated resources:

- Overallocated Resources (see Figure 11-19)
- Work Overbudget
- Resources/Assignments With Overtime
- Slipping Assignments.

	Resource Name	Group	Max. Units	Peak	Std. Rate	Ovt. Rate	Cost	Work
4	Kim Yoshida	Dev	100%	200%	$60.00/hr	$0.00/hr	$15,840.00	264 hrs
5	Tristan Randall	Test	100%	200%	$30.00/hr	$45.00/hr	$8,400.00	280 hrs
6	Adam Stein	Train	100%	300%	$35.00/hr	$0.00/hr	$8,960.00	256 hrs
7	Katherine Inman	Tech Com	100%	200%	$40.00/hr	$0.00/hr	$13,440.00	336 hrs

Figure 11-19. Apply the Overallocated Resources filter to quickly see a list of resources who have more work assigned than time available for that work.

With a resource view displayed, apply a filter by clicking the Filter tool on the Formatting toolbar. In the Filter list, click the name of the filter you want.

You can also run the following reports that provide information about resource usage:

- Who Does What
- Who Does What When
- To-Do List
- Overallocated Resources (see Figure 11-20)
- Task Usage
- Resource Usage

To run an assignments or workload report, click View, Reports. Double-click Assignments or Workload, and then double-click the report you want.

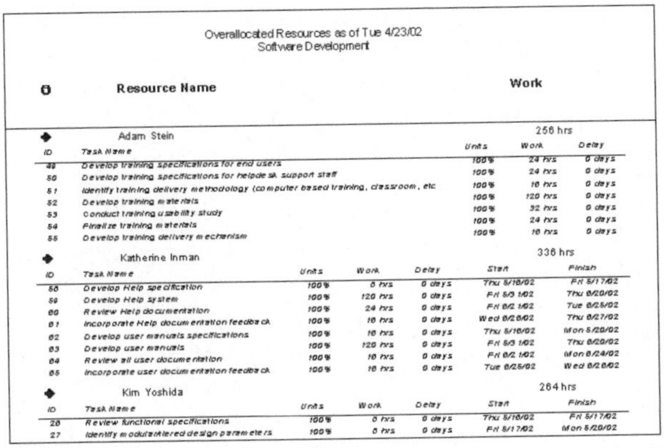

Figure 11-20. Run the Overallocated Resources report to get detailed information about resources who have too much work assigned.

Balancing the Resource Workload

Suppose you've reviewed information about assignments and workload throughout your project plan and you find that some resources are overallocated and others are underallocated. Or perhaps your company has undergone a reduction in force, and your project staffing has been reduced by 15 percent.

If you need to take corrective actions in your project plan to balance the resource workload, you can:

- Adjust resource availability.

- Adjust assignments, for example, add resources, replace resources, delay a task or assignment, or specify overtime.

- Split tasks to balance the workload.

- Use the Microsoft Project leveling feature to balance the workload.

- Adjust scope. This will probably require stakeholder approval.

note When you've adjusted your project plan to achieve the resource allocation levels you need, be sure to check the scheduled finish date, costs, and scope. You need to know how your changes affect other areas of the project plan.

For more information about balancing resource workloads, see "Balancing Resource Workloads" on page 253.

Part 4

Reporting and Analysis

Reporting Project Information

You've built your project plan and you're using it to track progress and display project information. Now that you're executing the plan, you'll want to share the important data with stakeholders. For example, suppose your new test procedure worked better than expected but your materials testing ran into some unanticipated slowdowns. Although it's all reflected in the project plan, you'd like to present your information in a more formal, professional style.

You can print views and generate reports built in to Microsoft Project 2002 and use them as an integral part of your project communication plan. These views and reports leverage the power of Microsoft Project 2002 by providing the clarity and specific focus required by corporate and program departments. By tailoring the views and reports to the interests of different groups (finance, human resources, and procurement, among others), you can keep information flowing freely and avoid misunderstandings. Microsoft Project views and reports are often used for:

● Weekly project team meetings

● Monthly department status conferences

● Quarterly or annual executive reviews

InsideOut

The Microsoft Project preformatted reports are designed to be printed and cannot be saved. You must re-create them each time you want to print them. This ensures that the data generated is always current.

In addition to printing views and generating built-in reports, you can design custom reports to meet your specific project communication needs. You can also publish project information to the Web.

Establishing Your Communications Plan

Reports are instrumental in effective project management. As a part of the initial project planning, you'll determine the requirements for reporting, including:

Report recipients.   Who needs to see them?

Specific content of the reports.   What type of information is included?

Frequency of publication.   How often should you generate them?

The frequency of publication varies due to many factors, including differing requirements of the report recipients and the fluidity of the data. It is important to strike a balance between providing up-to-date information often enough and overloading a stakeholder with too detailed or too frequent reporting.

Establishing your communications strategy for a project helps you effectively point to problems and unexpected changes. Through effective communication you can avoid larger problems, understand root causes, and communicate realistic progress and estimates. Specifically, with reports you can:

- Review status.
- Compare data.
- Check progress on the schedule.
- Check resource utilization.
- Check budget status.
- Watch for any potential problems looming in the future.
- Help stakeholders make decisions affecting the project.

Using the appropriate Microsoft Project views and reports on a regular basis for progress analysis and communication is a key component of effective project management. By implementing a communications plan, including regular presentations of reports to stakeholders, you can keep interested parties aware of crucial information and trends.

Project Management Practices: Communications Management

Communication is a vital element of successful project management. Effective project communication ensures that the appropriate information is generated, collected, and distributed in a timely manner to the appropriate project stakeholders. Different stakeholders need different kinds of project information—from the team members carrying out the project tasks, to customers sponsoring the project, to executives making strategic decisions regarding the project and the organization. Your stakeholders don't just receive project information; they also generate it. When all your stakeholders share project information, people are linked and ideas are generated—all of which contributes to the ultimate success of the project.

The first stage of effective project communications management is communications planning. This should take place in the initiating and planning stage of the project, in conjunction with scope and activity development. As you develop and build your project plan, you also need to determine what types of communication are going to be necessary throughout the life of the project.

Determine what tools you have at your disposal and how your project team communicates most effectively. Examples of communication vehicles include meetings, presentations, e-mail, letters, reports, an intranet site, and so on. It's likely that you'll use a combination of these vehicles as well as other communications means for different aspects of project management. If you're using Microsoft Project Server and Web Access, you have a very effective and targeted means of communicating electronically with your team members and other stakeholders.

Your communications plan might specify that your team will use Microsoft Project Server and Web Access to manage assignments and report on progress. You'll have weekly meetings and weekly status reports. Perhaps you'll also have monthly resource management and cost management reviews. You'll post certain views of the project periodically to Microsoft Project Web Access for all stakeholders to review and you'll print specific reports to disseminate at these various planned meetings.

While the project is being executed, you'll be executing your communications plan. You'll report on current project status, describing where the project stands at that point in time, especially as it relates to the schedule, budget, scope, and resource utilization. You'll also report on overall progress, describing the accomplishments of the project team to date and what is yet to be done. Finally, you'll make forecasts, using project plan information to predict future progress on tasks and anticipating potential problems.

Tasks will be completed, milestones met, deliverables handed off, and phases concluded. As part of your communications management strategy, you'll need to have a means of documenting project results and the receipt of deliverables as each stage of the project is completed.

Setting Up and Printing Views

Suppose you've been tracking and managing your project for some time now, using the Gantt Chart and other Microsoft Project views. By printing views, you can take the information with you and study it at your leisure or share it with team members and stakeholders. When you print a view, it becomes a kind of report that further enhances your ability to manage the project.

> **note** You can't print any form views (Task Form or Resource Form) or combination (split-screen) views. You can print one part of a split screen at a time, but if one part of the split screen is a form (such as Task Entry), it cannot be printed.

To print a view, follow these steps:

1 Open the view, and arrange the data as you want it to appear when printed.

> For more information about working with views, see Chapter 4, "Viewing Project Information."

Print

2 On the Standard toolbar, click Print.

To adjust how the view will look when printed, follow these steps:

1 Open the view, and arrange the data as you want it to appear when printed.

2 Click File, Page Setup to display the Page Setup dialog box. Specify the options you want for the printed view using the controls on the different tabs of this dialog box (see Figure 12-1). When finished, click OK.

Print Preview

3 On the Standard toolbar, click Print Preview. This opens a window showing how the view will appear when printed and the results of the Page Setup options you selected (see Figure 12-2).

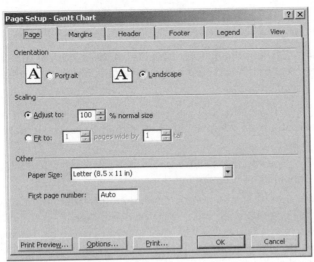

Figure 12-1. Use the Page Setup dialog box to set your margins, legend, headers, and more.

4 To make further adjustments to the print options, click Page Setup.

5 To make further adjustments to the view itself, click Close on the Print Preview toolbar, and work in the view.

6 When finished with your adjustments, click Print on the Standard toolbar.

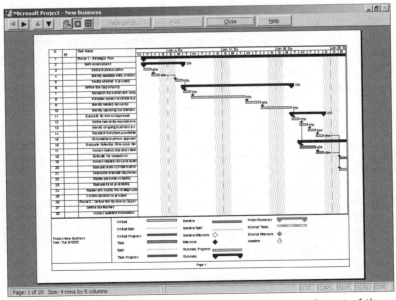

Figure 12-2. The Print Preview window shows the print layout of the current view.

341

Page Setup Options

The following list describes the options available on the six tabs of the Page Setup dialog box, which controls how your view looks when printed. To display this dialog box, click File, Page Setup:

Page tab. Specify whether the view should be printed in portrait or landscape orientation and whether the view should be scaled up or down to fit on a page.

Margins tab. Specify the size of each of the four margins and whether a border should be printed around the page.

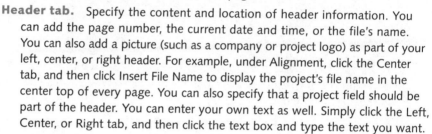

Insert
File Name

Header tab. Specify the content and location of header information. You can add the page number, the current date and time, or the file's name. You can also add a picture (such as a company or project logo) as part of your left, center, or right header. For example, under Alignment, click the Center tab, and then click Insert File Name to display the project's file name in the center top of every page. You can also specify that a project field should be part of the header. You can enter your own text as well. Simply click the Left, Center, or Right tab, and then click the text box and type the text you want.

Insert
Current
Date

Footer tab. Specify the content and location of footer information. The same information available for headers is available for footers. For example, click the Left tab in the Alignment area, and then click Insert Current Date to display the date in the lower-left corner of every page. The Preview box shows what your footer will look like.

Legend tab. Specify the content and location of a view's legend. By default, the project's title and the current date are added as a two-inch legend on every page. The same information available for headers and footers is available for legends. You can also enter your own information.

View tab. Specify what elements you want printed on each page, for example, notes, blank pages, sheet columns, and so on.

InsideOut

The Insert Current Date and Insert Current Time buttons take their information from the computer's system clock. This date and time will change to reflect the date or time that you print the view. If you want a fixed date or time, in the Alignment area of the Page Setup dialog box, simply type the date or time on the Left, Center, or Right tab text box itself.

Setting Up and Printing Reports

For your monthly project status presentation to upper management or customers, use one of Microsoft Project's built-in, preformatted reports. The professional layout of pertinent data makes for a document appropriate in any executive forum held in the boardroom.

The Microsoft Project reports are fast and easy to use. You can generate a new report with a few mouse clicks—a boon for time-constrained project managers. For example, you can print a report that contains the most up-to-date project status minutes before the start of a meeting.

To see the built-in reports available to you, click View, Reports. The Reports dialog box appears, showing the available report categories (see Figure 12-3).

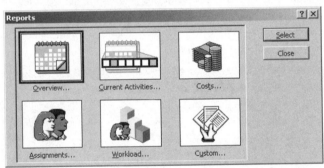

Figure 12-3. There are five report categories for 22 individual reports, as well as a Custom category you can use to design your own report.

tip You can also open the Reports dialog box using the Project Guide. On the Project Guide toolbar, click Report. In the Project Guide pane, click Select A View Or Report, click Print A Project Report, and then click Display Reports.

The following six categories of reports are available:

- Overview
- Current Activity
- Cost
- Assignment
- Workload
- Custom

Each category focuses on a specific type of information. You might find that certain reports are best suited to one type of audience, whereas other reports are better for another type of audience. For example, Cost reports might be most appropriate for meetings with the finance department, whereas you might prefer to distribute Assignment reports to team leads.

To generate these reports, Microsoft Project gathers information from a particular period, from certain tables, and with a particular filter applied as appropriate for the requirements of the specific report. Information is formatted with bands, highlights, fonts, and other layout considerations.

To select and print a report, follow these steps:

1 Click View, Reports.

2 In the Reports dialog box, double-click the report category you want.

3 Double-click the report you want.

4 If a dialog box prompts you for more information, such as a date range, enter it, and click OK.

The report appears in a Print Preview window (see Figure 12-4). Click any portion of the report to zoom in on it. Click a second time to zoom back out again. Click Page Setup to change the page orientation, scaling, margins, header, or footer.

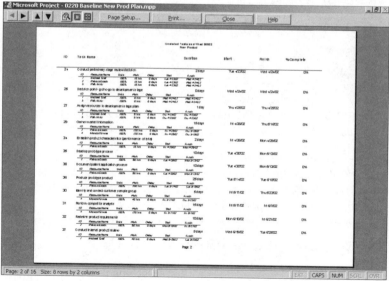

Figure 12-4. A picture of the report shows how it will look when printed.

344

5 When ready to print the report, click Print on the Print Preview toolbar.

6 The Print dialog box appears. Select the page range and number of copies you'd like to print, and click OK.

> **note** Microsoft Project reports all have a set format and are generated from the current project data. Because of this, you cannot save a built-in report—essentially, it's already saved.

You can edit various aspects of a report. The elements available for editing vary by report. In some reports, all you can change is the font. In other reports, you can change the reporting period, filter for specific types of information, specify that information be drawn from a specific table, and more. To edit a report, follow these steps:

1 Click View, Reports.

2 In the Reports dialog box, double-click the report category you want.

3 Click the report you want, and then click Edit. A dialog box appears, showing the options available for this report (see Figure 12-5).

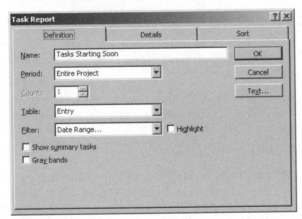

Figure 12-5. You can edit different types of information depending on the report you choose.

4 In many reports, you can click the Text button to further specify the font options you want.

Using Overview Reports

The Overview reports are well suited for executives and upper management, who need more generalized project information and status. The Overview reports provide summary project information at a glance.

To see the available Overview reports, follow these steps:

1 Click View, Reports.

2 In the Reports dialog box, click Overview, and then click Select. The Overview Reports dialog box appears (see Figure 12-6).

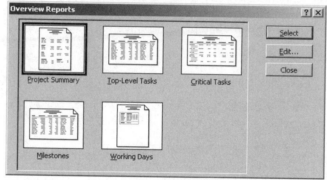

Figure 12-6. The Overview Reports dialog box shows the available summary reports.

3 Double-click the report you want. A preview of the report appears, showing how the report will look when printed.

Using the Project Summary Report

The Project Summary report focuses on the most important information in the project plan and is particularly useful to upper management because of its concise presentation of overall project data.

The Project Summary report includes a high-level summary of dates, duration, work, costs, work and resource status, and notes. The format is designed for easy comparison of planned versus actual data. This information is generated from the Project Statistics dialog box. The header of this report shows the company name, the project title, the date produced, and the project manager's name (see Figure 12-7). The source of this header information is the properties data entered for the project.

> **tip** To enter project properties, click File, Properties. Complete the information on the Summary tab.

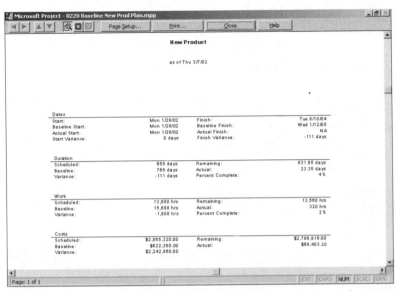

Figure 12-7. The Project Summary report shows overall project duration, dates, and cost.

Using the Top-Level Tasks Report

The Top-Level Tasks report presents information about the project plan's summary tasks. It displays the results of the top summary tasks, rolling up all the data from any subtasks. This is most useful for organizations that are clearly divided into functional groups. If each group has its own section at the same level in the project plan, the Top-Level Tasks report will quickly show the status of each group's efforts (see Figure 12-8).

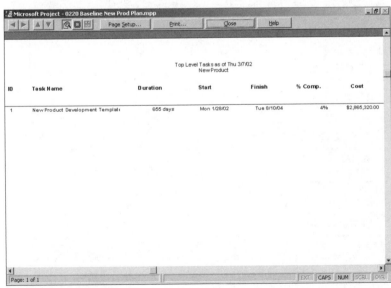

Figure 12-8. The Top-Level Tasks report shows summary task information.

For more information about summary tasks and subtasks, see "Organizing Tasks into an Outline" on page 75.

Using the Critical Tasks Report

The Critical Tasks report filters your project information to show only those tasks that are most likely to affect the project finish date; that is, critical tasks. In addition to displaying task notes, this report provides successor task information, which enables the reader to see what is being affected by the critical task first, assisting with mitigation planning.

InsideOut

This successor task information is in an unusual format that is not used in other standard reports. The successors are placed on a mini-table below the name of the critical tasks, with italic font style. This format takes some getting used to, but it is worth the time because it contains such pertinent and useful information.

Because the information is always changing, it's a good idea to print this report very shortly before presenting it for review. For example, on the day of the report's presentation, a predecessor task to a critical task might finish early, thus allowing the critical task to start earlier and no longer *be* critical. This report also lists any summary tasks to the critical tasks and any indicators from the Task Entry view (see Figure 12-9).

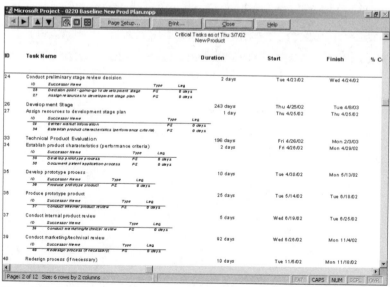

Figure 12-9. The Critical Tasks report shows only critical tasks.

Chapter 12

The Critical Tasks report is typically used to explain why problems are occurring in a project. This report does an excellent job of showing the source of some problems, but it must be used with the understanding that the listing of critical tasks can change easily and often. The inclusion of summary and successor tasks in the report helps present a more expanded description of how the critical tasks relate to other tasks in the project. If the list becomes too lengthy, you can filter it down further:

1 In the Overview Reports dialog box, click Critical Tasks, and click Edit. The Task Report dialog box appears.

2 Click any of the filters in the Filter list to define the type of critical tasks you'd like to see in the report.

> For more information about critical tasks, see "Working with the Critical Path and Critical Tasks" on page 233.

Using the Working Days Report

The Working Days report specifies, for each base calendar used in the project, which days are working days and which are nonworking days (see Figure 12-10). You might use several base calendars to reflect the scheduled working days of different functional groups, or to reflect labor contracts. The format is tabular; there are columns for day of the week, hours of the day, and dates of nonworking days. One table is drawn for each calendar. The data in this report might not change very often, so it would be appropriate to include it in a comprehensive project review or a quarterly or annual report.

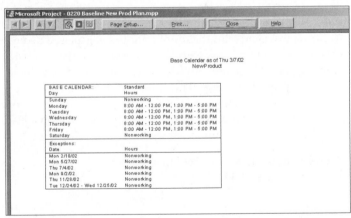

Figure 12-10. The Working Days report shows working days for each base calendar used in the project.

> For more information about calendars, see "Setting Your Project Calendar" on page 58.

Using Current Activity Reports

The Current Activity reports are intended for more frequent usage and geared toward audiences more directly involved with the work of the project. For example, project teams can use these reports at weekly status meetings. Functional groups in a project can use these reports to check quickly how they are doing according to the project plan. Many project managers rely on these reports toward the end of projects, when current status must be monitored frequently. There are six standard reports in the Current Activity category (see Figure 12-11).

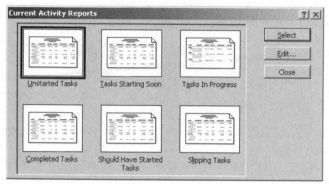

Figure 12-11. The Current Activity Reports dialog box shows the available reports for this category.

Using the Unstarted Tasks Report

Tasks in the project that have not had any actual progress reported are displayed in the Unstarted Tasks report. Generally, the number of tasks displayed decreases as the project progresses. Because of this, this report can be very effective toward the end of the project. You might want to see the number, type, and requirements of all unstarted tasks at any time in the project, however. This information can help with planning expenditures, deploying tools and materials, and assessing quickly the amount of the work yet to be done. This report is also effective for showing functional leads and team members the scope of their required efforts.

Resources associated with the tasks are listed in a mini-table format. Task notes are printed as well (see Figure 12-12).

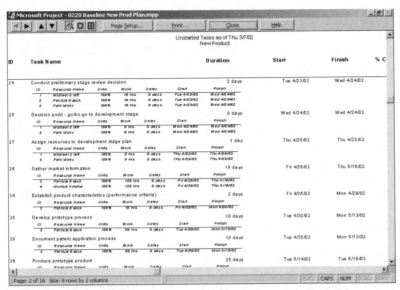

Figure 12-12. The Unstarted Tasks report shows all tasks that have no progress reported on them.

Using the Tasks Starting Soon Report

The Tasks Starting Soon report is actually a subset of the Unstarted Tasks report. The format is the same as the Unstarted Tasks report (see Figure 12-12).

To generate the Tasks Starting Soon report, follow these steps:

1 Click View, Reports.

2 In the Reports dialog box, double-click Current Activities, and then double-click Tasks Starting Soon. The Date Range dialog box appears.

3 In the Show Tasks That Start Or Finish After box, enter the date after which you want to see tasks that are scheduled to start or finish. This is the beginning of the date range of tasks for your report. Click OK.

4 In the And Before box, enter the date before which you want to see tasks that are scheduled to start or finish. This is the ending of the date range of tasks for your report. Click OK to see the results.

> **note** The date range can yield a surprisingly large number of tasks. For example, if there are many summary divisions in a large project plan, each subgroup will have several tasks in a certain date range. The functional managers are aware of all these tasks, but when the entire project is displayed, the total number of tasks in that range can be an eye-opener. Conversely, if a large date range is entered and few tasks reported, this can indicate a high-risk time period.

Chapter 12

351

Using the Tasks In Progress Report

The Tasks In Progress report is a very handy tool that enables project managers to keep close track of work currently being done. This report quickly shows the amount of work that has started; it also points out tasks that are behind schedule. The tasks are grouped by month; each month includes both the tasks started in previous months but that are still in progress, and the tasks started in the current month. Consequently, the number of tasks displayed is larger in the last months of the report. Other than that addition, the report is formatted the same as the Unstarted Task report (see Figure 12-12). Grouping tasks by the month of their start dates helps managers see the longest ongoing tasks that are still unfinished. Using this report regularly helps prevent managers from overlooking (or forgetting) the status updates and long-overdue tasks.

Using the Completed Tasks Report

The other end of the spectrum of status reports about current activities is the report showing all completed activities. The Completed Tasks report is significant for both historical reference and as a record of the team's accomplishment. It provides real data about "lessons learned," helps estimate future project time frames, and gives managers a general idea of how much work is left to do in the current project. Another important use of this report is as a boost team morale, motivation, and pride. Although the project goal is paramount, accomplishments to date can be recognized. This report does that by showing tasks that are 100 percent complete. The data is grouped by month (see Figure 12-13).

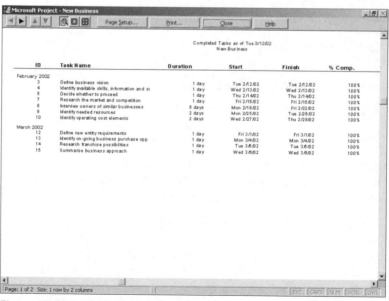

Figure 12-13. The Completed Tasks report shows all tasks that are reported as complete so far.

Chapter 12

Using the Should Have Started Tasks Report

You need to know what the team has accomplished so far, but you need to know what is lagging behind as well. The Should Have Started Tasks report, most effective when used regularly and fairly frequently, alerts project managers to all tasks that have not started yet and their scheduled start dates have passed. Sometimes the data shown in this report reflects missing status updates, and that makes this report an effective tool for optimizing the flow of communication on project progress. Any tasks that do not have an actual start status and that are scheduled to start on or before a given date (usually the current date) are displayed in this report. The format (see Figure 12-14) includes mini-tables for successor tasks information, and summary tasks that show the tasks immediately affected by those starting late.

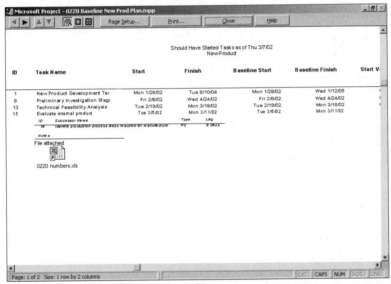

Figure 12-14. The Should Have Started Tasks report shows all tasks that are due to start but have no actual start date reported.

Using the Slipping Tasks Report

The Slipping Tasks report is used only with projects that have a saved baseline. The emphasis of this report is a list of tasks that have started but that will finish after their baseline finish date. This slipping of the finish date can be caused by the start date occurring later than originally planned or by an increase in the duration. This report helps project managers determine which tasks might require added resources, which tasks might require replanning of their duration, and which tasks have become (or might soon become) critical. As with the Should Have Started Tasks report (see Figure 12-14), the format shows summary tasks, tasks notes, and mini-tables of immediate successor tasks. Additionally, the amount of date variance from the baseline start and finish dates is listed.

> For more information about saving and using a baseline, see Chapter 10, "Saving a Baseline and Updating Progress."

Using Cost Reports

The Cost reports in Microsoft Project 2002 are a powerful and very effective means of tracking the fiscal health of a project. By using these reports, project managers can quickly and accurately focus on the pressing cost issues and catch potential problems early.

The Cost reports category provides five reports for reviewing your project's costs and budget (see Figure 12-15).

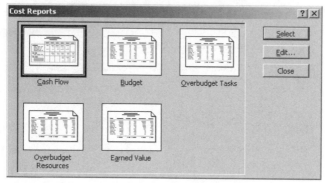

Figure 12-15. Choose one of the available cost-related reports in the Cost Reports dialog box.

Using the Cash Flow Report

The Cash Flow report is a tabular, cross-referenced report that displays the scheduled and actual costs of each task, broken down into one-week periods. The methods of cost accrual defined by the project manager are shown, and all types of costs (human resources, materiel, equipment, fees, and so on) are aggregated for their tasks (see Figure 12-16). Summary tasks are included to aid in grouping costs by type or phase of work being done. Each week and each task is totaled. The information shown enables quick comparisons with baseline budgets or projections. This report is often used in conjunction with others, such as the Overbudget Tasks Report, the Tasks In Progress Report, and the Slipping Tasks Report, both to show cost impacts and to clarify budget and earned value figures.

Cash Flow as of Tue 3/12/02
New Business

	2/10/02	2/17/02	2/24/02	3/3/02	3/10/02
Phase 1 - Strategic Plan					
Self-Assessment					
Define business vision	$560.00				
Identify available skills, information and support	$960.00				
Decide whether to proceed	$560.00				
Define the Opportunity					
Research the market and competition	$400.00				
Interview owners of similar businesses		$5,000.00			
Identify needed resources			$1,280.00		
Identify operating cost elements			$1,200.00		
Evaluate Business Approach					
Define new entity requirements			$560.00		
Identify ongoing business purchase opportunities				$560.00	
Research franchise possibilities				$560.00	
Summarize business approach				$560.00	
Evaluate Potential Risks and Rewards					
Assess market size and stability				$800.00	
Estimate the competition				$400.00	
Assess needed resource availability				$800.00	
Evaluate realistic initial market share					$4(
Determine financial requirements				$800.00	
Review personal suitability					$5(
Evaluate initial profitability					$5(
Review and modify the strategic plan					
Confirm decision to proceed					
Phase 2 - Define the Business Opportunity					
Define the Market					
Access available information					$4(

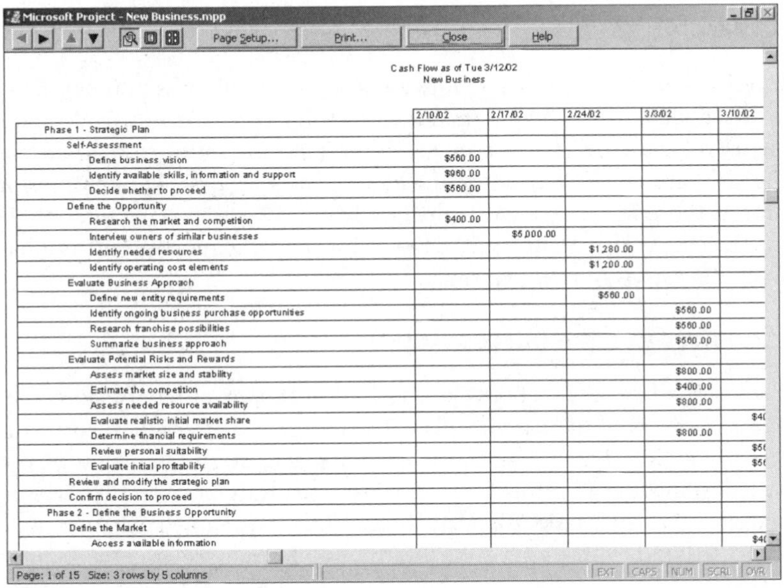

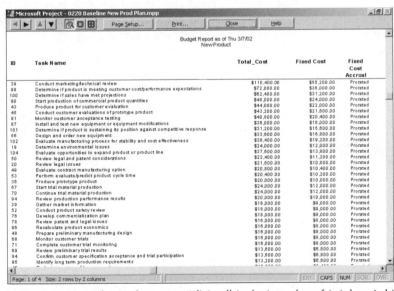

Figure 12-16. The Cash Flow report shows scheduled and actual costs for task by week.

Using the Budget Report

The Budget report lists all project tasks in order of total cost. The actual costs are reflected here, as are the baseline cost, variance, fixed cost, accrual method, and remaining cost. Tasks are listed from highest to lowest cost, so focusing on "big ticket" items is easy. Each column of cost data is totaled (see Figure 12-17).

Budget Report as of Thu 3/7/02
NewProduct

ID	Task Name	Total_Cost	Fixed Cost	Fixed Cost Accrual
39	Conduct marketing/technical review	$110,400.00	$55,200.00	Prorated
99	Determine if product is meeting customer cost/performance expectations	$72,000.00	$36,000.00	Prorated
100	Determine if sales have met projections	$62,400.00	$31,200.00	Prorated
90	Start production of commercial product quantities	$48,000.00	$24,000.00	Prorated
43	Produce product for customer evaluation	$44,000.00	$22,000.00	Prorated
45	Conduct customer evaluations of prototype product	$43,200.00	$21,600.00	Prorated
91	Monitor customer acceptance testing	$40,800.00	$20,400.00	Prorated
87	Install and test new equipment or equipment modifications	$36,000.00	$18,000.00	Prorated
101	Determine if product is sustaining its position against competitive response	$31,200.00	$15,600.00	Prorated
86	Design and order new equipment	$33,600.00	$16,800.00	Prorated
102	Evaluate manufacturing process for stability and cost effectiveness	$38,400.00	$19,200.00	Prorated
19	Determine environmental issues	$24,000.00	$12,000.00	Prorated
104	Evaluate opportunities to expand product or product line	$27,600.00	$13,800.00	Prorated
50	Review legal and patent considerations	$22,400.00	$11,200.00	Prorated
20	Review legal issues	$21,600.00	$10,800.00	Prorated
49	Evaluate contract manufacturing option	$20,800.00	$10,400.00	Prorated
53	Perform evaluate/predict product cycle time	$20,400.00	$10,200.00	Prorated
36	Produce prototype product	$20,000.00	$10,000.00	Prorated
67	Start trial material production	$24,000.00	$12,000.00	Prorated
70	Continue trial material production	$24,000.00	$12,000.00	Prorated
94	Review production performance results	$20,000.00	$10,000.00	Prorated
29	Gather market information	$18,000.00	$9,000.00	Prorated
52	Conduct product safety review	$18,000.00	$9,000.00	Prorated
76	Develop commercialization plan	$18,000.00	$9,000.00	Prorated
78	Review patent and legal issues	$16,000.00	$8,000.00	Prorated
96	Recalculate product economics	$16,000.00	$8,000.00	Prorated
48	Prepare preliminary manufacturing design	$16,000.00	$8,000.00	Prorated
68	Monitor customer trials	$16,000.00	$8,000.00	Prorated
71	Complete customer trial monitoring	$16,000.00	$8,000.00	Prorated
69	Review preliminary trial results	$13,600.00	$6,800.00	Prorated
84	Confirm customer specification acceptance and trial participation	$13,600.00	$6,800.00	Prorated
95	Identify long term production requirements	$13,200.00	$6,600.00	Prorated

Figure 12-17. The Budget report lists all tasks in order of total cost, highest cost to lowest.

Using the Overbudget Tasks Report

The Overbudget Tasks report provides a quick look at all tasks in the project that have actual or scheduled costs higher than their baseline costs. Obviously this report can only be used for projects with saved baselines. The amount of cost variance is listed, and the tasks are sorted in order of the highest variance first. The columns of data are the same as those in the Budget report (see Figure 12-17), but the filter only selects the tasks with costs higher than the baseline. This report is most useful as a basis for analyzing the causes of cost overruns.

Using the Overbudget Resources Report

Like the Overbudget Tasks report, the Overbudget Resources report shows the resources with costs in excess of the baseline plan. The resources with highest cost variances are listed first. The Cost, Baseline Cost, Variance, Actual Cost, and Remaining Cost columns are totaled to include all resources on the list. Usually, the reason these resources are overbudget is that their tasks are taking longer than the planned duration in the baseline. It is formatted in the same way as the Overbudget Tasks report and the Budget report (see Figure 12-17).

Using the Earned Value Report

The Earned Value report is based on the concept of earned value—a comparison of planned and actual costs. To understand the information shown in this report, you'll need to understand the following terms:

- *Earned value* is the analysis of cost performance based on factors of original budget, original schedule, actual costs, and actual schedule performance. The analysis always uses a single point in time as the reference point for the comparisons being made. This point in time is referred to as the *status date*.

- *Budgeted Cost of Work Scheduled* (typically called BCWS) is the cost amount originally defined for a task, up to the status date.

- *Budgeted Cost of Work Performed* (BCWP) is the originally determined cost of a task, multiplied by the calculated percent complete. This is the percent complete of the task as it has been performed, so this figure is calculated against the original expectations.

- *Actual Cost of Work Performed* (ACWP) is defined for this report as the costs incurred from the actual amount of work done on a task and any fixed costs accrued for that task.

- *Schedule Variance* (SV) is the result of subtracting the BCWS from the BCWP. Even though it's called "schedule variance," the variance really calculated is cost resulting from schedule considerations.

- *Cost Variance* (CV) is the result of subtracting the ACWP from the BCWP. If the number is positive, the actual costs are less than what was budgeted.

- *Estimate At Completion* (EAC) is the amount calculated by adding the actual costs of a task so far and the remaining costs of that task, resulting in a composite total of costs.

- *Budgeted At Completion* (BAC) is the full baselined cost of a task, including both resource costs and any fixed costs associated with the task.

- *Variance At Completion* (VAC) is the amount calculated by subtracting the scheduled cost of a task from its baseline cost. The scheduled cost is the cost of completing the task as currently scheduled. Once again, a positive number here shows a cost underrun.

> For more information about earned value analysis, see "Analyzing Progress and Costs Using Earned Value" on page 381.

The format of the Earned Value report (see Figure 12-18 on the next page) is a straightforward listing of every non-summary task in the project with columns for the cost breakdowns along the top of the report.

InsideOut

The Earned Value report is dependent on complete and current status updates. If this report is used formally for presentation to other stakeholders, an Earned Value status date (sometimes referred to as the "cutoff date") is often employed to ensure accurate status in the report. Depending on the requirements of the project, the status date might be monthly or quarterly, but usually not more frequent than that.

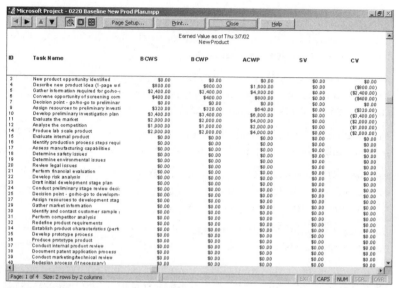

ID	Task Name	BCWS	BCWP	ACWP	SV	CV
3	New product opportunity identified	$0.00	$0.00	$0.00	$0.00	$0.00
4	Describe new product idea (1-page wri	$800.00	$800.00	$1,600.00	$0.00	($800.00)
5	Gather information required for go/no-;	$2,400.00	$2,400.00	$4,800.00	$0.00	($2,400.00)
6	Convene opportunity of screening com	$400.00	$400.00	$800.00	$0.00	($400.00)
7	Decision point - go/no-go to preliminar	$0.00	$0.00	$0.00	$0.00	$0.00
9	Assign resources to preliminary investi	$320.00	$320.00	$640.00	$0.00	($320.00)
10	Develop preliminary investigation plan	$3,400.00	$3,400.00	$6,800.00	$0.00	($3,400.00)
11	Evaluate the market	$2,000.00	$2,000.00	$4,000.00	$0.00	($2,000.00)
12	Analyze the competition	$1,000.00	$1,000.00	$2,000.00	$0.00	($1,000.00)
14	Produce lab scale product	$2,000.00	$2,000.00	$4,000.00	$0.00	($2,000.00)
15	Evaluate internal product	$0.00	$0.00	$0.00	$0.00	$0.00
16	Identify production process steps requi	$0.00	$0.00	$0.00	$0.00	$0.00
17	Assess manufacturing capabilities	$0.00	$0.00	$0.00	$0.00	$0.00
18	Determine safety issues	$0.00	$0.00	$0.00	$0.00	$0.00
19	Determine environmental issues	$0.00	$0.00	$0.00	$0.00	$0.00
20	Review legal issues	$0.00	$0.00	$0.00	$0.00	$0.00
21	Perform financial evaluation	$0.00	$0.00	$0.00	$0.00	$0.00
22	Develop risk analysis	$0.00	$0.00	$0.00	$0.00	$0.00
23	Draft initial development stage plan	$0.00	$0.00	$0.00	$0.00	$0.00
24	Conduct preliminary stage review deci:	$0.00	$0.00	$0.00	$0.00	$0.00
25	Decision point - go/no-go to developm-	$0.00	$0.00	$0.00	$0.00	$0.00
27	Assign resources to development stag	$0.00	$0.00	$0.00	$0.00	$0.00
29	Gather market information	$0.00	$0.00	$0.00	$0.00	$0.00
30	Identify and contact customer sample :	$0.00	$0.00	$0.00	$0.00	$0.00
31	Perform competitor analysis	$0.00	$0.00	$0.00	$0.00	$0.00
32	Redefine product requirements	$0.00	$0.00	$0.00	$0.00	$0.00
34	Establish product characteristics (perf	$0.00	$0.00	$0.00	$0.00	$0.00
35	Develop prototype process	$0.00	$0.00	$0.00	$0.00	$0.00
36	Produce prototype product	$0.00	$0.00	$0.00	$0.00	$0.00
37	Conduct internal product review	$0.00	$0.00	$0.00	$0.00	$0.00
38	Document patent application process	$0.00	$0.00	$0.00	$0.00	$0.00
39	Conduct marketing/technical review	$0.00	$0.00	$0.00	$0.00	$0.00
40	Redesign process (if necessary)	$0.00	$0.00	$0.00	$0.00	$0.00

Figure 12-18. The Earned Value report shows a summary of all task costs, based on your specified status date.

Using Assignment Reports

There are four standard reports in Microsoft Project relating to assignments (see Figure 12-19).

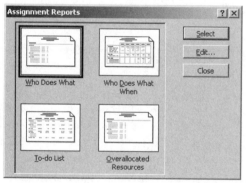

Figure 12-19. The Assignment Reports dialog box lists the reports having to do with resources and their assigned tasks.

Using the Who Does What Report

The Who Does What report lists the tasks assigned to each resource. Task details and the resource's name are displayed in mini-tables on the summary level; indicators for notes and resource leveling are also included in the report. This report can help you or a resource manager plan for coverage when a resource becomes unavailable. It also shows clearly the relative number of assignments for all the resources on the project. Resources are listed by Resource ID number (see Figure 12-20).

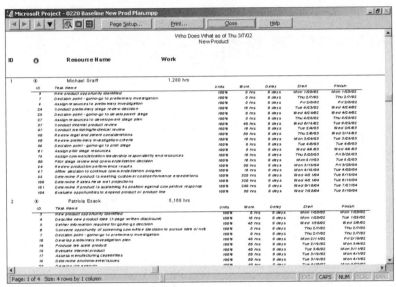

Figure 12-20. The Who Does What report shows which resources are assigned to which tasks.

Using the Who Does What When Report

The Who Does What When report is an amplification of the information given in the Who Does What report, adding the daily breakdowns of hours of work assigned. You can see all the work hours assigned to tasks on any given day in a table layout. You can also easily see when a resource is assigned to excessive amounts of work on a given day. The resource's name and all tasks assigned to him or her are listed on the right of the page, and the columns of individual days are shown on the left (see Figure 12-21 on the next page).

InsideOut

Because it is so detailed, the Who Does What When report requires a large amount of paper when printed. Also, generating the data needed to create the report might take some time. Because of this, it might be best to use this report less frequently than others, or to view it in Print Preview rather than printing it. You cannot print a date range with this report unless you create a new custom report based on the data this report generates.

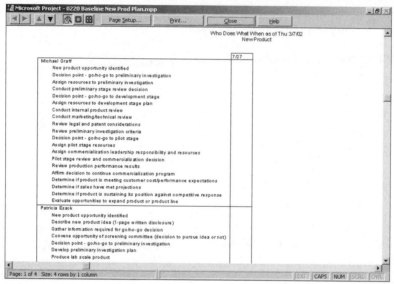

Figure 12-21. The Who Does What When report is a daily accounting of resources and the tasks to which they are assigned.

Using the Overallocated Resources Report

The Overallocated Resources report lists only the resources that have been assigned work in excess of their availability as reflected in their resource calendars. For example, if a resource's availability is based on the Standard calendar, the resource will become overallocated when scheduled for more than eight hours per day, or more than five days per week. This report includes the resource's name and total work hours on the summary level, and information about the tasks assigned to that resource in the mini-table level (see Figure 12-22).

> **note** The list includes every task assigned to a resource, not just the tasks for which the resource is overallocated. An analysis of the start and finish dates of the tasks and the amount of work scheduled during those time spans will point to the periods of overallocation. Resources who are overallocated have an overallocated indicator by their name, but the report does not show which specific tasks are causing the overallocation.

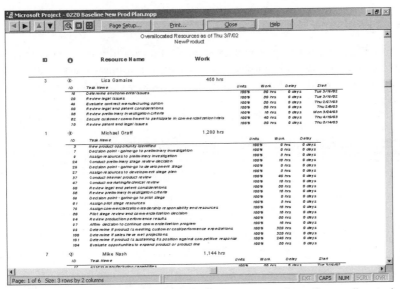

Figure 12-22. The Overallocated Resources report lists all overallocated resources along with their assignments.

> For more information about resolving overallocated resource issues, see "Balancing Resource Workloads" on page 253.

Using Workload Reports

There are two reports in the Workload report category: the Task Usage report and the Resource Usage report (see Figure 12-23 on the next page). These reports are excellent tracking tools for seeing the amount of work per task or per resource, on a daily basis. Both reports have a tabular format with individual weeks of the project in columns on the left and the lists of tasks or resources on the right. This is the same kind of layout as the Who Does What When report, so the same cautions about the size of the printed report are appropriate.

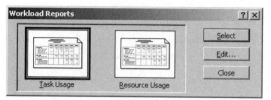

Figure 12-23. The Workload Reports dialog box shows the available reports in this category.

Using the Task Usage Report

The Task Usage report emphasizes a resource's hours and units for each task in the project. Summary tasks are shown so the logical groupings of tasks within the project are easy to follow. Totals are shown for each week and each task. Under the task names are the names of the resources assigned to that task (see Figure 12-24). This is a clear way to show the full extent of work and material being used for every task.

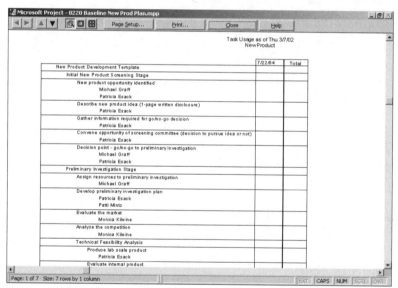

Figure 12-24. The Task Usage report shows assignments by task.

Using the Resource Usage Report

The Resource Usage report emphasizes the work done by each individual resource, so the information is sorted by resource names. For each resource, all assigned tasks are listed along with weekly totals of the hours of work assigned for that task. The format of the page layout is the same as the Task Usage report, with columns for the weeks on the right of the sheet.

Two preformatted variations of this report are available: the Resource Usage (work) and the Resource Usage (material) reports, which filter for the two types of resources. To generate these reports, follow these steps:

1 Click View, Reports.

2 In the Reports dialog box, double-click Custom.

3 Using the scroll bar, find and select Resource Usage (Material) or Resource Usage (Work).

Building Custom Reports

The last category of standard reports is Custom reports. Customizing a report is a useful way to change an existing standard report or to create a new report using a list of report formats.

By customizing reports, project managers can do the following:

● Focus the data in a more specific way.

● Add more detail.

● Change the presentation of information.

● Insert graphics and objects.

Often, after using the standard predefined reports for several reviews and meetings, ideas for customizing the presentation and content will be generated by both project managers and the report's audiences.

There are three methods of creating a custom report:

● Create a new report entirely from scratch. In this case, you choose one of the main report type formats: task, resource, monthly calendar, or crosstab. From there you create the report from the tabs and fields in the resulting dialog box.

● Select and edit an existing report. In this case, you are permanently changing the built-in report itself.

● Copy and edit an existing report. You're creating a new version based on the built-in version of the report, and the latter remains intact with its original settings.

To begin the process of building a custom report, follow these steps:

1 Click View, Reports.

2 In the Reports dialog box, double-click Custom.

3 In the Custom Reports dialog box, click the report you want to build in the Reports list (see Figure 12-25).

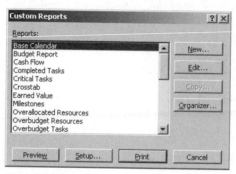

Figure 12-25. The Custom Reports dialog box provides the tools needed to build a new report.

4 Click New, Edit, or Copy, depending on how you want to create your report.

> **tip** Although you can create a custom report from the ground up, you can also simply modify certain details of an existing preformatted report. To customize any built-in report, click the report's name, and then click Edit. A dialog box opens in which you can edit the content of that particular report. Your custom changes to the report are saved automatically.

In addition to the built-in reports and sub-reports, there are four generic formatting options which apply to the types of reports their names specify. You can preview these formats from the Custom Reports dialog box by selecting their names and clicking Preview. The four formatting options are:

- Task
- Resource
- Crosstab
- Monthly Calendar

> **note** *Crosstab* reports are tabular presentations of data with key information fields along the left of the page and a measurement division unit (often units of time, such as days) along the top of the right side of the page.

Microsoft Project enables you to customize reports by taking data from the basic data tables in the Microsoft Project database. When customizing a report or report type, you will specify the content in the categories of Definitions, Details, and Sorting. After you select a report to customize and click the Edit button, a dialog box opens. The Definition tab (see Figure 12-26) presents all the options for altering and defining a custom report.

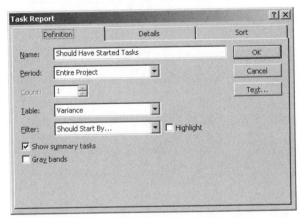

Figure 12-26. Use the Definition tab to design custom reports.

Publishing Project Information to the Web

newfeature! With the pervasive use of the World Wide Web and company intranets, you might find it very useful to publish your project information as a Web page. This is made much easier in Microsoft Project 2002 by the addition of the Export Wizard.

Start with the view of project data that you'd like to publish to the Web; for example, the Gantt Chart or Task Usage view. Follow these steps to publish the view:

1 Open the view and set it up the way you want it to appear on the Web.

2 Click File, Save As Web Page. The Save As dialog box appears.

3 In the Save In box, select the drive or folder in which you keep your HTML files. If you have access to it, select the actual folder for your intranet Web site files.

4 In the File Name box, give your file a name that's clear and easy for you to remember. However, avoid using the project name itself, which is the default. This will prevent confusion in the future when you open your project file.

5 Make sure that Web Page (*.html, *.htm) appears in the Save As Type box.

6 Click Save.

> **note** Project reports cannot be converted to HTML because they are designed for previewing and printing only and cannot be saved. This goes for the built-in reports as well as any custom reports you have created.

newfeature!

At this point, the Export Wizard opens:

1 The Export Wizard's Welcome page explains the process. Click Next.

2 On the Map page, click New Map, and then click Next. The Map Options Page opens (see Figure 12-27).

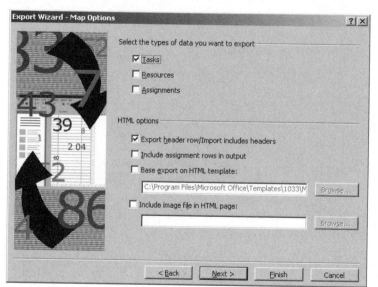

Figure 12-27. Specify how you want data to be published in your Web page with the Export Wizard.

3 Under Select The Types Of Data You Want To Export, select the Tasks check box. Under HTML Options, select Export Header Row/Import Includes Headers. Click Next. The Task Mapping page opens (see Figure 12-28).

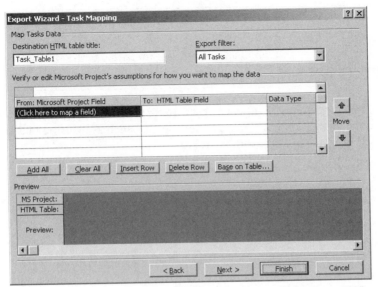

Figure 12-28. On the Task Mapping page, you tell the Export Wizard which fields you want exported to the Web page.

4 In the Destination HTML Table Title box, give the table a name or just use the default, for example, "Task_Table1."

5 In the Export Filter box, click All Tasks.

6 Click the Base On Table button, and then choose the table that you want exported; for example, the Entry table. This fills in the From: Microsoft Project Field and To: HTML Table Field columns. The Preview area shows what the HTML table will look like. When finished, click Next.

7 The End Of Map Definition page opens. If you want to save this map for future use, click Save Map.

8 Click Finish.

Your customized table of the selected view is now saved as an HTML Web page. You can view it with any browser to see how it looks. You'll see that Microsoft Project has added some title and project information, including:

- Project Name
- Project Start Date
- Project Finish Date

> **tip** Summary tasks are shown in bold and tasks retain their indentation as in Microsoft Project. The table is sized to fit the Web page, so task names will be text wrapped as necessary. The column header names are formatted with shading to make them easily distinguishable.

You might need to upload your newly built HTML Web page to a Web server. This can be done by the same process you generally use, such as by using File Transfer Protocol (FTP) or by using Microsoft Front Page.

Analyzing Project Information

As part of your efforts in tracking and controlling your project, you might want to analyze certain aspects of project performance. Project analysis can give you a closer look at the overall execution of the project. For first-time efforts at managing a particular kind of project or new variations on an established project theme, you and the stakeholders might want to see performance indicators and estimates for the remainder of the project. These indicators help assess the effectiveness of the plan and define the amount of corrective action needed to bring actual performance in line with the baseline. Three key factors often examined in performance analysis are:

- Work required for task completion
- Cost required for task completion
- Schedule adherence

In the course of tracking your project, you probably study different views; you might even have created custom views to show specific types of project information, such as schedule slippage. The careful study of the data in those views is a kind of analysis, as is the evaluation of project information in other formats presented by Microsoft Project. There are also techniques you can use with Microsoft Project to analyze project information, including exporting data to Microsoft Excel and performing earned value calculations.

The starting point for any analysis is to decide what you want to evaluate. Do you want to look at schedule performance, resource performance, or cost performance? You also need a good idea of how you'd like to work with the data to get the information you need.

Calculating Project Information in Microsoft Excel

You can easily move portions of the data in the project plan into Microsoft Excel. In Excel, you have unique formatting options and can manipulate the figures using formulas and calculations. Excel can calculate numerical data in sophisticated ways. For example, you can create pivot tables with the data. You can also create graphs, such as S-curves, showing project performance information.

Suppose you'd like to look closely at the efficiency of the work performed so far, to see if the amount of work per task is consistent with the plan, getting further away from the plan, or getting closer to the plan. To analyze your project schedule using Excel, start by displaying the task sheet view that includes the relevant data you want to work with, as follows:

1 Click View, More Views.

2 In the More Views dialog box, click Task Sheet, and then click Apply.

3 Click View, and then click the table whose information you want to export to Excel (see Figure 13-1).

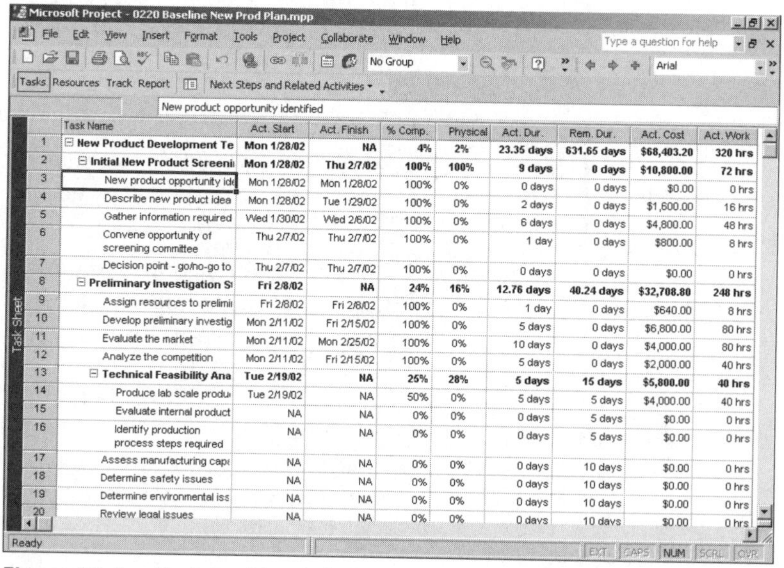

	Task Name	Act. Start	Act. Finish	% Comp.	Physical	Act. Dur.	Rem. Dur.	Act. Cost	Act. Work
1	**New Product Development Te**	**Mon 1/28/02**	**NA**	**4%**	**2%**	**23.35 days**	**631.65 days**	**$68,403.20**	**320 hrs**
2	**Initial New Product Screeni**	**Mon 1/28/02**	**Thu 2/7/02**	**100%**	**100%**	**9 days**	**0 days**	**$10,800.00**	**72 hrs**
3	New product opportunity ide	Mon 1/28/02	Mon 1/28/02	100%	0%	0 days	0 days	$0.00	0 hrs
4	Describe new product idea	Mon 1/28/02	Tue 1/29/02	100%	0%	2 days	0 days	$1,600.00	16 hrs
5	Gather information required	Wed 1/30/02	Wed 2/6/02	100%	0%	6 days	0 days	$4,800.00	48 hrs
6	Convene opportunity of screening committee	Thu 2/7/02	Thu 2/7/02	100%	0%	1 day	0 days	$800.00	8 hrs
7	Decision point - go/no-go to	Thu 2/7/02	Thu 2/7/02	100%	0%	0 days	0 days	$0.00	0 hrs
8	**Preliminary Investigation S**	**Fri 2/8/02**	**NA**	**24%**	**16%**	**12.76 days**	**40.24 days**	**$32,708.80**	**248 hrs**
9	Assign resources to prelimi	Fri 2/8/02	Fri 2/8/02	100%	0%	1 day	0 days	$640.00	8 hrs
10	Develop preliminary investig	Mon 2/11/02	Fri 2/15/02	100%	0%	5 days	0 days	$6,800.00	80 hrs
11	Evaluate the market	Mon 2/11/02	Mon 2/25/02	100%	0%	10 days	0 days	$4,000.00	80 hrs
12	Analyze the competition	Mon 2/11/02	Fri 2/15/02	100%	0%	5 days	0 days	$2,000.00	40 hrs
13	**Technical Feasibility Ana**	**Tue 2/19/02**	**NA**	**25%**	**28%**	**5 days**	**15 days**	**$5,800.00**	**40 hrs**
14	Produce lab scale produ	Tue 2/19/02	NA	50%	0%	5 days	5 days	$4,000.00	40 hrs
15	Evaluate internal product	NA	NA	0%	0%	0 days	5 days	$0.00	0 hrs
16	Identify production process steps required	NA	NA	0%	0%	0 days	5 days	$0.00	0 hrs
17	Assess manufacturing cap	NA	NA	0%	0%	0 days	10 days	$0.00	0 hrs
18	Determine safety issues	NA	NA	0%	0%	0 days	10 days	$0.00	0 hrs
19	Determine environmental iss	NA	NA	0%	0%	0 days	10 days	$0.00	0 hrs
20	Review legal issues	NA	NA	0%	0%	0 days	10 days	$0.00	0 hrs

Figure 13-1. Task tracking information in Microsoft Project can be exported to Excel.

Now you have specific data to work with. You are ready to move this information into Microsoft Excel.

newfeature! With the new Microsoft Project Export Wizard, it is now easier to transfer your data. Before starting the export process, decide on the form you want the project data to take in Excel. You can export the selected data to Excel so that it appears in Excel much as you're seeing it in the Task Sheet. Or you can export your project data as a template, with the different types of project data appearing in different worksheets.

Exporting Selected Data to Excel

You want to export your data to Microsoft Excel as it is now formatted (all on one worksheet). To export the data, follow these steps:

1 Click the Select All cell in the upper-left cell in the view, above the ID number. This selects all the data in this sheet (see Figure 13-2).

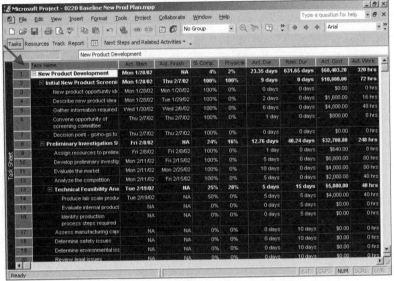

Figure 13-2. Your task information is selected for export.

2 Click File, Save As. The Save As dialog box appears (see Figure 13-3 on the next page).

3 Choose a directory where you want to save your information. The directory location of the Microsoft Project file is the default.

4 Choose a name for your Excel file. The default name is the project file name as it is, but with the *.xls* extension.

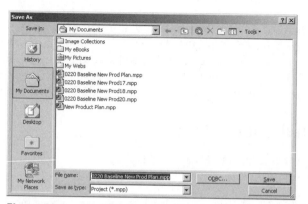

Figure 13-3. To start the export, open the Save As dialog box.

tip   **Naming your Excel file**

Naming conventions are flexible, but for easy reference, you might indicate the date you are creating the file and the original name of the Microsoft Project file. For example, "021502NewProductPrjSchedPerf.xls."

5 In the Save As Type box, select Microsoft Excel Workbook (*.xls).

6 On the Standard toolbar click Save. The new Export Wizard appears (see Figure 13-4).

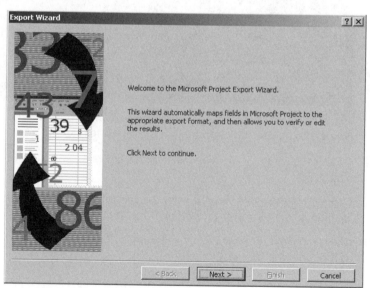

Figure 13-4. The Export Wizard appears.

7 On the Welcome page of the wizard, click the Next button.

8 On the Export Wizard – Data page, the Selected Data option is selected as the default (see Figure 13-5). Click the Next button.

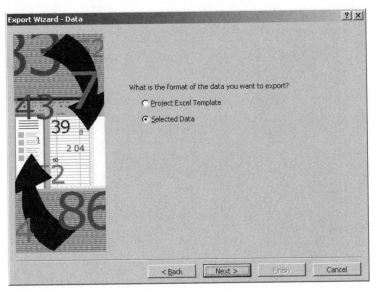

Figure 13-5. Choose to export the selected data.

9 On the Export Wizard – Map page, the New Map option is selected as the default (see Figure 13-6). Click the Next button.

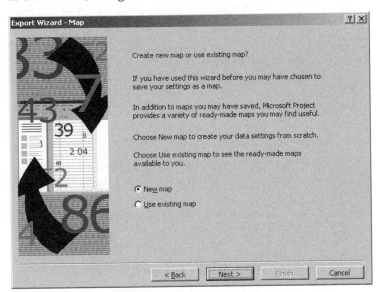

Figure 13-6. You will create a new export map.

10 On the Export Wizard – Map Options page, select the check box for the type of data you want to map (Tasks). Under Microsoft Excel Options, select the Export Includes Headers check box (see Figure 13-7). Click the Next button.

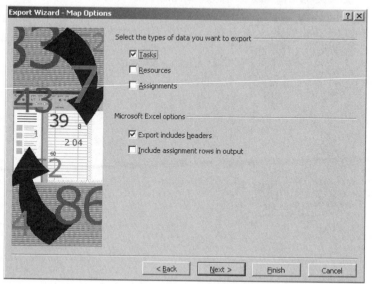

Figure 13-7. You choose to map task data, including headers.

11 On the Export Wizard – Task Mapping page, name the destination worksheet (for example, 021502_SchedTrkg), or use the default of Task_Table1.

12 Choose an export filter. All Tasks is the default.

If you want, use the Verify Or Edit Microsoft Project's Assumptions For How You Want To Import The Data table. This is a very flexible tool that enables you to specify, one data field at a time, how the data should be defined when it is exported to Excel. For example, the Predecessor field could be defined as a numeric data type, although it is normally a text data type. You also can specify the column label for each field of data going to Excel.

Use the buttons below the table to help with the process. If you're not interested in editing fields, click the Base On Table button (see Figure 13-8), and then in the Select Base Table For Field Mapping dialog box, select the appropriate Microsoft Project table, for example, Tracking (see Figure 13-9).

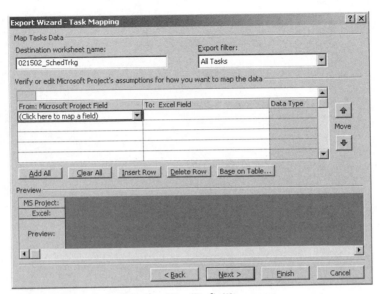

Figure 13-8. Complete the Map Definition page.

Figure 13-9. Choose which Microsoft Project table to use as your data source.

> **note** The Earned Value tables are in this list. These useful cost management tables are well suited to further manipulation within Excel.

The data as it will appear in Excel is presented in the Preview table at the bottom of the Export Wizard – Task Mapping page (see Figure 13-10 on the next page). Use the scroll bar to view all the columns. When ready, click Next.

Chapter 13

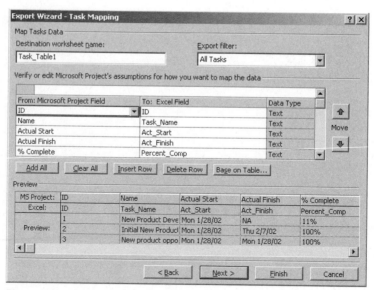

Figure 13-10. The Fields and Preview areas show the information from the table you selected as your data source.

13 On the End Of Map Definition page of the wizard, you can select the Save Map check box to keep the settings you've just specified for future use or complete the process without saving settings. Click the Finish button.

The data you wanted to see has been exported from Microsoft Project to Microsoft Excel, and you've defined the exact layout of the Excel workbook. The possibilities for using this feature are tremendous; you can easily specify data to export, data type conversion, even data labeling from Microsoft Project to Excel, and then save the settings.

InsideOut

After exporting the data to Excel, the first time you open the new workbook and make changes, you might see a prompt upon saving to overwrite with the latest Excel format. Because you exported your data from Microsoft Project into Excel 2002, this might be unexpected. Click the Yes button. Nothing will be lost, and you probably won't see any differences the next time you open the file.

Exporting Project Data to Excel as a Template

For some kinds of analysis, you need to look at your project data by general type. When exporting a template to Excel, Microsoft Project organizes data into Task, Resource, and Assignment types of data. Each data type is presented with its relevant information on its own Excel worksheet. The template is an invaluable aid for viewing a focused presentation of the essential information about each type of data. To make a Microsoft Excel template from your project file, follow these steps:

1 Start with the Microsoft Project view that shows the information you are interested in analyzing, for example, the Task Sheet with the Tracking table applied.

2 Click File, Save As.

3 Change the Save In and File Name settings, if necessary.

4 In the Save As Type box, click Microsoft Excel Workbook (*.xls). Click Save. The Export Wizard appears.

5 On the Welcome page of the wizard, click the Next button.

6 In the Export Wizard – Data page, select Project Excel Template, and then click the Finish button.

The workbook is created with four worksheets of discrete information: Task_Table, Resource_Table, Assignment_Table, and Info_Table for general information (see Figure 13-11).

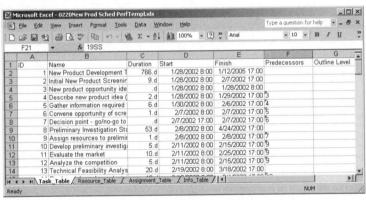

Figure 13-11. When you export project information to an Excel template, four worksheets are created to hold all information from the selected table.

> **tip** When exporting date fields into Microsoft Excel, the format of the target file includes the time of day in the cells. To drop the time portion in Excel, first select the entire worksheet. Then click Format, Cells. The Format Cells dialog box appears. Click the Number tab, and click Date in the Category list. Then choose the date format you prefer.

Exporting Numeric Data

Because Microsoft Excel is such a powerful tool for working with numeric data, you might want to move some of this data from Microsoft Project for more in-depth analyses. The Excel Export Wizard makes this easy. For our purposes, *numeric data* will be defined as any data that can be used in calculations and mathematical operations. Examples of such data include cost and work data. Work data (such as hours) can be converted to numeric fields but is stored in Microsoft Project as text because of the unit names such as hours, days, or weeks. Date data is not numeric, even though it consists mostly of numbers. The first step is to create the view in Microsoft Project that holds the numeric fields you want to export to Excel.

Suppose you've made some progress in your project and you'd like to export the cost performance data to analyze it in Excel. Do the following:

1 Click View, More Views.

2 In the More Views dialog box, click Task Sheet, and then click Apply.

3 Click View, Table.

4 Click Cost, and then click Apply. You now have the numeric data to export to Excel.

Export your numeric data using the same process described in "Exporting Selected Data to Excel" earlier in this chapter. A couple of optional variations, to exclude or modify data types, are as follows:

- On the Export Wizard – Task Mapping page, you can individually select only the fields that contain numeric values.

> **caution** Some data fields calculated in Microsoft Project, for example, BAC and Variance, are not listed in the Map Tasks Data page. You can export them separately from the Earned Value Table or perform the calculations yourself in Excel.

- To change the data type in a column, after exporting, select the column in Excel (don't include headings), and then click Format, Cells (the current data type will be preselected). Then select Number or Currency, choose decimal attributes, and click OK. You might not want to make these kinds of changes because Microsoft Project automatically keeps currency data and number data with their proper data types. If your preferred formatting style is different than the results of the exported version, you might want to make a change.

InsideOut

When data mapping in the Export Wizard, if you choose to export data from Task, Resource, and Assignment data types, you must create different data maps with a unique Destination Worksheet name for each of them. This entails using the Export Wizard once for each type of data.

When you get to the Map Options page of the wizard, you must choose the type of data you want to export: task, resource, or assignment. This choice determines which Microsoft Project tables the wizard maps data from, so if you need to export two or all three of the data types, you will need to use the wizard two or three times.

Analyzing Project Data with Crosstab Tables

Another technique for analyzing project data is using crosstab tables of information. In Microsoft Excel, these are called *pivot tables*. Essentially, these pivot tables are a flexible way to reorganize data in comparative form, with one category of information being filtered and populated into another category of information. Microsoft Project has a built-in means of exporting project data into Excel pivot tables.

Suppose you'd like to analyze the information regarding relative cost performance of different groups of team members, and also see how that performance varies according to the different phases of your project. You can see this using an Excel pivot table, as follows:

1 Click View, Resource Usage.

2 Click Project, Group By, Resource Group.

   This groups your resources by resource group. The groupings appear in the view separated by yellow bars.

3 Click View, Table, Cost. Click the Select All box in the upper-left corner of the table to select all data in the sheet.

4 Click File, Save As. Specify the file name and location if necessary. In the Save As Type box, click Microsoft Excel PivotTable (*.xls), and then click the Save button. The Export Wizard appears.

5 On the Export Wizard Welcome page, click the Next button. On the Map page, click New Map, and then click the Next button.

6 On the Map Options page, click Resources as the type of data. Read the explanation on this page of how PivotTable mapping is done, and then click the Next button.

Chapter 13

7 On the Resource Mapping page, specify the destination worksheet name, the export filter, and each field to export. Remember to put the PivotTable Data field, for example, Cost, at the end of the list. Click the Finish button.

In Microsoft Excel, open your newly created PivotTable workbook. You see that there are two worksheets; one contains the field data specified and the other holds the actual pivot table, which you can now modify. Your choices for working with the PivotTable are extensive, including graphic charting of your results. There is also a handy floating PivotTable toolbar. It is likely that you will want to make some changes to the pre-formatted PivotTable to see different groupings and summaries. You can use the Excel PivotTable Wizard to make these alterations.

Charting Project Data Using S-Curves

Suppose you exported numerical project data into Excel and the worksheets show you what you need to know. Now you'd like to share information, for example, actual cost of work for a task, in a more graphical format. One popular format for graphing performance trends is the *S-Curve graph*. Use the charting and graphing capabilities of Microsoft Excel to build an S-Curve graph of your task cost data, as follows:

1 Click View, More Views, Task Entry.

2 Click the column heading of the Predecessors field. Click Insert, Column. In the Field Name box, click Actual Cost, and then click OK.

3 Click the Select All cell in the upper-left corner of the Task Entry view to select all data in the view.

4 Save the data as an Excel workbook.

5 Open the Excel workbook you just created. Select the columns and rows for Task Name and Actual Cost that have data in them by holding down Ctrl key as you click.

Chart Wizard

6 On the Formatting toolbar in Excel, click Chart Wizard.

7 In Step 1 of 4, click the Custom Types tab, select the Smooth Lines chart type, and then click the Next button.

8 In Step 2 of 4, ensure that the Data Range is the two columns you chose in step 5. You should see the moving lines around your selected columns in the worksheet behind the wizard. Use the Data Range selection button if needed.

9 Next to Series In, click Columns, and then click the Next button.

10 In Step 3 of 4, click the Legend tab, and select the Show Legend check box. Under Placement, click Right, and then click the Next button.

11 In Step 4 of 4, under Place Chart, click As New Sheet. Leave the name as Chart1, and then click the Finish button.

You have created an S-Curve graph showing the costs of each task.

Analyzing Progress and Costs Using Earned Value

Most project information analysis is performed by comparing the actuals to the baseline. Microsoft Project allows many baselines to be established, but only the *current* baseline is used for analysis. The comparison process will either show a consistency between the scheduled or actual work and the baseline, or it will show a *variance*. Variance is a measure of time or cost, or a calculated numerical representation of that measure. Time variance means *schedule variance*, such as days behind schedule, and *cost variance* is measured in monetary units, such as dollars over budget.

For a complete discussion of working with baselines, see "Saving Original Plan Information Using a Baseline" on page 282.

Variance analysis is an effective means of gauging project performance. Some methods of variance analysis available in Microsoft Project are:

- Earned Value calculation
- Cost Performance Indexing
- Schedule Performance Indexing
- Estimate At Complete
- Variance At Complete

Earned Value calculation is a systematic method of measuring these variables of project performance.

The practice of tracking earned value requires a disciplined approach, with consistent data cutoff dates, usually monthly, and accurately reported status. Many companies maintain a separate department for Cost Management and Analysis, using methods such as earned value analysis, because it requires such exacting standards. The benefits come in the form of insightful evaluation of performance versus spending. Microsoft Project, with its powerful earned value calculation tools, provides a great means of making that evaluation.

> **tip** If you've saved multiple baselines, you can specify which baseline to use for earned value analyses. To do this, click Tools, Options, and then click Calculation. Click the Earned Value button. In the Baseline For Earned Value Calculations list, click the baseline you want to use.

Measuring earned value helps you see the adherence to the baseline plan or deviation from it, in terms of cost and schedule. Earned value analysis uses comparisons of the following factors:

Budgeted Cost of Work Scheduled (BCWS). This is the calculated cost of a task according to its schedule. For example, if a task *should be* 50 percent finished according to the schedule, the BCWS would be 50 percent of the originally planned cost of that task. Microsoft Project determines the values by using the baseline dates for the task and today's date for determining scheduled percent complete.

Budgeted Cost of Work Performed (BCWP). This is the cost of the task work *actually* done, according to the original budget. If the task is actually 50 percent complete, the BCWP will be the originally planned cost of the work on the task multiplied by 50 percent. Because this is a measure of actual work costs incurred, BCWP is sometimes called the *earned value* of a task.

Actual Cost of Work Performed (ACWP). This is the sum of all costs actually accrued for a task to date. It will include fixed and incidental costs that are not figured in the BCWP. By default, today's date is used to determine the cutoff of cost accrual. You can set a different status date if you prefer. To do this, click Project, Project Information, and in the Project Information dialog box, click a new date in the Status Date box. Other kinds of costs reflected in this measure are: fixed costs, overtime costs, and any per-use costs.

Cost Variance (CV). This is the measure of the difference between the budgeted costs and the actual costs of a task (ACWP–BCWP).

Schedule Variance (SV). This is the measure of the difference between the cost as planned and the cost as performed (BCWP–BCWS). It shows clearly how much schedule slippage and duration increases affect cost.

Estimate At Completion (EAC). This is the projected cost of a task at its completion. The projection is based on current schedule performance.

Budgeted At Completion (BAC). This is the baseline cost of a task at its completion. The budgeted cost is based on the baseline planned schedule performance.

382

Variance At Completion (VAC). This is the difference between actual cost at completion and baseline cost at completion. This is the cost variance for a completed task.

newfeature! **Cost Performance Index (CPI).** This is a calculated numerical indicator of Earned Value for Cost. The perfect number for this is 1. It represents BCWP divided by ACWP.

newfeature! **Schedule Performance Index (SPI).** This is a calculated numerical indicator of Earned Value for Schedule. The perfect number for this is 1. It represents BCWP divided by BCWS.

newfeature! **Cost Variance Percent (CV%).** This shows the difference between how much a task should have cost and how much it has actually cost to date, displayed in the form of a percentage. It represents the difference in BCWP and ACWP, divided by BCWP, then multiplied by 100, that is, [(BCWP–ACWP)/BCWP]*100. Positive percentages show an under-budget condition, while a negative percentage indicates an overbudget condition.

newfeature! **Schedule Variance Percent (SV%).** This shows, in the form of a percentage, how much you are ahead of or behind schedule for a task. It represents SV divided by BCWS, then multiplied by 100. Positive percentages indicate that you're currently ahead of schedule.

newfeature! **To Complete Performance Index (TCPI).** This shows a ratio of the work yet to be done on a task to the funds still budgeted to be spent on that task. It represents this formula: (BAC–BCWP)/(BAC–ACWP). It helps you estimate whether you will have surplus funds or a shortfall. Values over 1 indicate a potential shortfall.

newfeature! **Physical Percent Complete.** This is a user-entered value that can be used in place of % Complete when calculating Earned Value or measuring progress. It represents a judgment that overrides the calculations based on actual duration. To use this option, click Tools, Options, and then click Calculation. Click the Earned Value button. In the Default Task Earned Value Method list, click Physical % Complete.

Suppose you're using Microsoft Project to keep track of earned value to see how cost-efficient your plan is. To review your earned value information, do the following:

1 Click View, More Views. Click Task Sheet, and click Apply.

2 Click View, Table, More Tables. The More Tables dialog box appears.

3 In the Tables list, click Earned Value, and then click Apply. This displays the earned value data for your project (see Figure 13-12).

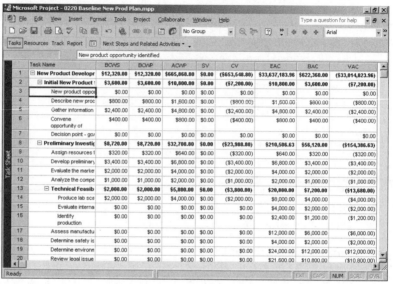

Figure 13-12. Use the earned value table to review earned value fields.

Three earned value tables are available:

- Earned Value
- Earned Value Cost Indicators
- Earned Value Schedule Indicators

The fields they include direct the focus of the information they provide. The Earned Value table contains the following fields:

- Task Name
- BCWS (budgeted cost of work scheduled)
- BCWP (budgeted cost of work performed)
- ACWP (actual cost of work performed)
- SV (schedule variance)
- CV (cost variance)

- EAC (estimate at completion)
- BAC (budget at completion)
- VAC (variance at completion)

These data fields give you a general overall picture of your Earned Value data.

When you display the Earned Value Cost Indicators Table, the differences in fields are the exclusion of SV (schedule variance) and the addition of:

- CV% (cost variance percentage)
- CPI (cost performance index)
- TCPI (total cost performance index)

These new fields focus on the cost details.

When you display the Earned Value Schedule Indicators Table, the fields from the Earned Value Table are Task Name, BCWS (budgeted cost of work scheduled), and BCWP (budgeted cost of work performed), with the addition of:

- SV (schedule variance)
- SV% (schedule variance percentage)
- SPI (schedule performance index)

This enables you to see only the schedule specific factors in your Earned Value calculations.

Part 5

Managing Multiple Projects

Managing Master Projects and Resource Pools

As a project manager, you juggle time, money, resources, and tasks to carry out and complete a project successfully. Often however, you're not juggling just multiple elements of a single project, you're juggling multiple projects, each with its own associated challenges. The following are three typical scenarios involving multiple projects:

- Katherine manages a large project containing many phases or components for which other project managers are responsible. In Microsoft Project, she can set up a master project with subprojects representing those subphases. She can keep an eye on the overall picture while the project managers responsible for the individual phases have complete control over their pieces of the project.

- Frank manages several unrelated projects and keeps the information for each in separate project files. Occasionally, however, he needs to see information about all of them in relation to one other. He might need to print a view or report that temporarily combines the projects. With Microsoft Project, Frank can consolidate information from multiple related or unrelated projects and can do so either temporarily or permanently.

- Sarah, Dennis, and Monique are project managers in the same organization. Although they manage different projects, they use many of the same resources. Sometimes their projects conflict with one another because of demands on the same resources at the same time. In Microsoft Project, they can create a resource pool file that contains the resources they all use. They can then link their individual project files to that resource pool. The resource availability and usage information is available through that resource pool. When one project assigns tasks to a resource in the resource pool, the resource pool is updated with that resource's allocation information.

Structuring Master Projects with Subprojects

With Microsoft Project, you can insert one project into another. Inserted projects look and act like summary tasks in any task view. You can view and change all tasks within that inserted project. The task information is changed in the source project file as well, because by default, the two projects are linked.

Although you might insert projects for a variety of reasons, the most effective use of this capability is to create a *master project* structure with *subprojects* inserted within that master project. This structure is most useful when you have a large project containing a number of subcomponents, especially if those subcomponents are managed by other project managers. If you're managing the overall project, your master project can give you the view you need into the planning and execution of all the subprojects.

> **note** Reviewing multiple projects' information in a master project structure is somewhat analogous to using the enterprise Portfolio Analyzer feature. If you're using Microsoft Project Professional with its enterprise features, you can use the Portfolio Analyzer to see a high-level overview of multiple projects throughout the enterprise. With the Portfolio Analyzer, you can review schedule information, cost performance, and resource allocation, for example.
>
> > **For more information about using the enterprise Portfolio Analyzer, see "Analyzing Multiple Projects Using Project Portfolio" on page 580.**

Even if you're the sole project manager, you might find the master project-subprojects structure helpful for alternating between project details and the overall project picture.

Information in the master project and subprojects are interactively linked to each other. When project managers of the subprojects make changes, by default, you see those changes reflected in your master project. The reverse is true as well—you can change subproject information in your master project and those changes are updated in the source subproject.

Your master project can also contain regular tasks. Tasks and subprojects can be organized in relation to one another, and your inserted subprojects can be part of an outline structure and have dependencies, just like regular tasks.

Setting Up a Master Project

When you want to set up a master project with subprojects, first decide where all the files are going to reside. If you're the sole user of the projects and subprojects, the files can all be stored on your own computer. If you're handling the master project and other project managers are responsible for subprojects, you'll need to store the projects on a central file server or in a shared folder to which all the managers have access.

Inserting Projects into a Master Project

Creating a master project is simply a matter of inserting subordinate projects into what you're designating as the central controlling project, that is, the master project. To insert a subproject into a master project, follow these steps:

1 Open the project that you want to become the master project.

2 Display the Gantt Chart or other task sheet.

3 Click the row below where you want to insert the project. This can be at any level in an existing outline structure. The inserted project adopts the outline level of the task above the location where it's inserted.

4 Click Insert, Project. The Insert Project dialog box appears (see Figure 14-1).

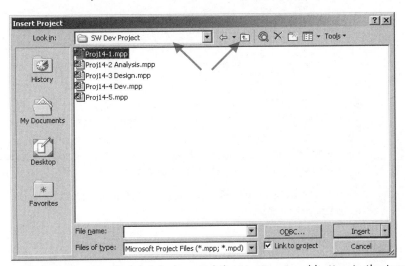

Figure 14-1. Use the Look In box and the Up One Level button in the Insert Project dialog box to find the location of the project you want to insert.

5 In the Insert Project dialog box, browse to the drive and folder in which the subproject is stored.

6 Click the project file, and then click the Insert button. The project is inserted and its name appears in the selected task row. The inserted project icon appears in the Indicators field (see Figure 14-2).

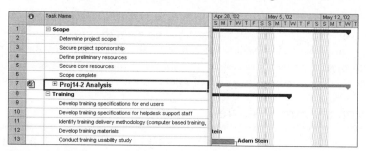

Figure 14-2. The inserted project looks like a summary task among your regular tasks.

7 To see the tasks in the inserted project, click the plus sign next to the project name in the Task Name field. The subproject expands to show all tasks (see Figure 14-3). They look and behave exactly as though you created them in this project.

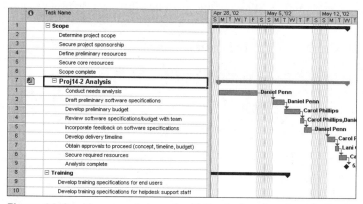

Figure 14-3. You can view and edit the tasks of an inserted project in the same way as those that were originally created in the master project.

To hide the tasks in the inserted project, click the minus sign next to the project name.

Chapter 14: Managing Master Projects and Resource Pools

8 Repeat steps 3-6 for any other projects you want to insert into your master project (see Figure 14-4).

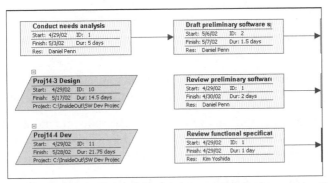

	O	Task Name	Apr 28, '02	May 5, '02	May 12, '02
4		Define preliminary resources			
5		Secure core resources			
6		Scope complete			
7		⊟ Proj14-2 Analysis			
1		Conduct needs analysis	Daniel Penn		
2		Draft preliminary software specifications	Daniel Penn		
3		Develop preliminary budget	Carol Phillips		
4		Review software specifications/budget with team	Carol Phillips,Dani		
5		Incorporate feedback on software specifications	Daniel Penn		
6		Develop delivery timeline	Carol F		
7		Obtain approvals to proceed (concept, timeline, budget)	Lani		
8		Secure required resources	Ca		
9		Analysis complete	5,		
10		⊞ Proj14-3 Design			
11		⊞ Proj14-4 Dev			
12		⊞ Proj14-5 Test			
8		⊟ Training			
9		Develop training specifications for end users			
10		Develop training specifications for helpdesk support staff			

Figure 14-4. This master project contains four subprojects, each one containing the plan for a major project phase.

In the Network Diagram view, the summary task representing the subproject is formatted differently from other tasks and includes the path and name of the source project file (see Figure 14-5). The subproject tasks themselves look the same as regular tasks.

Conduct needs analysis
Start: 4/29/02   ID: 1
Finish: 5/3/02   Dur: 5 days
Res: Daniel Penn

Draft preliminary software s|
Start: 5/6/02   ID: 2
Finish: 5/7/02   Dur: 1.5 days
Res: Daniel Penn

Proj14-3 Design
Start: 4/29/02   ID: 10
Finish: 5/17/02   Dur: 14.5 days
Project: C:\InsideOut\SW Dev Projec

Review preliminary softwar|
Start: 4/29/02   ID: 1
Finish: 4/30/02   Dur: 2 days
Res: Daniel Penn

Proj14-4 Dev
Start: 4/29/02   ID: 11
Finish: 5/28/02   Dur: 21.75 days
Project: C:\InsideOut\SW Dev Projec

Review functional specificat|
Start: 4/29/02   ID: 1
Finish: 4/29/02   Dur: 1 day
Res: Kim Yoshida

Figure 14-5. In the Network Diagram, the node representing the subproject summary task shows the name of the source project file as well as its start and finish dates.

In the Calendar view, the name of the subproject appears with the individual subproject tasks (see Figure 14-6 on the next page). If you don't see the subproject name, drag one of the gray sizing bars along the left edge of the Calendar view to increase the height of the rows in the calendar.

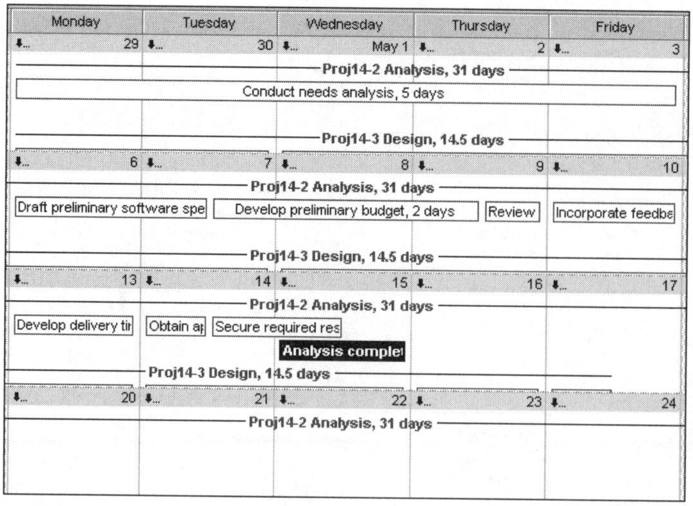

Figure 14-6. The Calendar view displays the subproject name above the individual subproject tasks.

Breaking Up a Large Project into Subprojects

You might know during the preplanning stage of your project that you want your project set up as a master project with subprojects. That makes things easier. On the other hand, you might not know until you're in the middle of project execution that a master project is just the solution you need. You can still set it up without having to significantly rework your project files.

If you already have multiple project files that you want to bring together with a master project, it's pretty simple. Create a new project file, insert the projects, and you're all set.

If you have a single large project file and you want to break it up into more manageable subproject files, it's a little trickier, but still very doable. In this case, you need to do some reverse engineering. The overall process for doing this is as follows:

1 Create a new project file for each new subproject you want to insert.

2 In each new file, set the project start date (or project finish date if you're scheduling from the finish date) for the project.

3 Set the project calendar to match the project calendar in the original file.

> For information about copying calendars and other project elements from one project file to another, see "Copying Project Elements Using the Organizer" on page 423.

4   Move tasks from the large project file into the subproject file using the Cut and Paste commands. Be sure to select all task information by selecting the row headers, not just the task names. This will move all necessary task information, including any actual progress information, to the new project file.

5   After you have all your separate project files set up, as well as the proper project start and finish dates and calendars, you can insert those files as subprojects into your master project.

> **note**   If you're working with Microsoft Project Professional and Microsoft Project Server for enterprise features, only subprojects are published to the enterprise server unless the server has been explicitly set up to accept master projects. You create and maintain your master project on your local computer.

> For more information about publishing projects to the enterprise server, see "Updating Enterprise Project Information" on page 568.

Working with Subproject Information

You can edit any task, resource, or assignment in a subproject. By default, any change you make to subproject information is instantly made in the source project file. Likewise, any change made in the source project file updates the information in your master project. This is because the subproject and source project are *linked*. This is convenient because you never have to worry about whether you're synchronized with the most current subproject information.

> **tip**   **Work with subproject-related fields**
>
> You might find it helpful to add certain subproject-related fields to a task sheet or resource sheet. You can add the Project, Subproject File, and Subproject Read Only fields to a task sheet. You can add the Project field to a resource sheet. For example, if you want to know which project a resource is associated with, add the Project field to the Resource Sheet.
>
> To add a field, click the column heading to the right of where you want the new field to be inserted. Click Insert, Column. In the Field Name list, click the field you want.
>
> You can also sort, group, or filter tasks or resources by these fields.
>
> For more information about the ways you can view project data, see "Rearranging Your Project Information" on page 114.

Troubleshooting

There are duplicated resource names in your master project

Often, your master project contains a set of tasks and a set of resources assigned to those tasks. When you insert a project, the resources from that inserted project are added to your master project. Resource information appears in the resource views, and task information from the subproject appears in the task views just as if you had entered it in the master project originally. You can review and edit the information normally.

If you've inserted a project that contains some of the same resources as your master project, you'll see their names listed twice in your resource sheets. One instance of the resource name is associated with the master project, and the other instance is associated with the subproject. If that resource is a part of other projects you insert, that name could appear additional times.

You can only assign resources from a particular subproject to tasks in that subproject. That is, you cannot assign resources from one subproject to tasks in a different subproject.

If you want to work with a single set of resources across all your projects, consider setting up a resource pool. For more information, see "Sharing Resources Using a Resource Pool" later in this chapter.

Changing Subproject Information to Read Only

In some cases, you might not want to change subproject information. Maybe you only want to view it in the master project. This might be the case when you have several project managers in charge of their own subprojects, and you need only to see the high-level view of all integrated project information. In this case, you can change a subproject to be read-only information in your master project, as follows:

1 Display the Gantt Chart or other task view.

2 Click the summary task that contains the name of the subproject.

3 On the Standard toolbar, click Task Information.

4 In the Inserted Project Information dialog box, click the Advanced tab (see Figure 14-7).

5 Select the Read Only check box. Now, if you make changes to any subproject information and then try to save the master project, you'll see a message reminding you that the subproject is read-only.

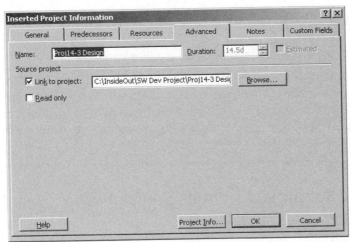

Figure 14-7. Use the Advanced tab in the Inserted Project Information dialog box to change a subproject to read-only or to remove the link to the subproject.

---

tip **Review overall project information for an inserted project**

You can review project information and statistics for a subproject in a master project. Double-click the summary task that contains the name of the subproject. The Inserted Project Information dialog box appears. Click the Advanced tab. Click the Project Info button. The Project Information dialog box appears for the inserted project, showing the project start, finish, and status dates, as well as the name of the project calendar.

To see overall project information, including the project start, finish, and cost, click the Statistics button.

Viewing the Critical Path in a Master Project

By default, Microsoft Project calculates a single critical path across all your projects. If you prefer, you can change your settings to see the critical path for each subproject, as follows:

1 In your master project, click Tools, Options, and in the Options dialog box, click the Calculation tab.

2 Clear the Inserted Projects Are Calculated Like Summary Tasks check box. This results in a critical path being calculated for the master project independent of the subprojects. In addition, the critical path for each subproject is shown.

You can easily see the critical path(s) in the Tracking Gantt chart.

> ## Troubleshooting
>
> **You lose text and bar formatting when you insert projects**
>
> The formatting of the master project is adopted by any inserted projects. This means that if you've changed the styles for text, Gantt bars, or Network Diagram nodes in the subproject, you won't see those customizations in the master project. However, any formatting changes you've made to the master project are adopted by subprojects being inserted.

Unlinking a Subproject from its Source File

You can keep a subproject in a master project but unlink the subproject from its source project file. When you unlink a subproject from its source project file, changes to the source file won't affect the subproject in the master project, and vice versa. To disconnect a subproject from its source, follow these steps:

1 Display the Gantt Chart or other task view.

2 Click the summary task that contains the name of the subproject.

3 On the Standard toolbar, click Task Information.

4 In the Inserted Project Information dialog box, click the Advanced tab.

5 Clear the Link To Project check box. The subproject is now disconnected from its source. The inserted project icon is removed from the Indicators field. Although the project file name still appears in the summary task name field, it's now just a regular summary task—not an inserted project (see Figure 14-8).

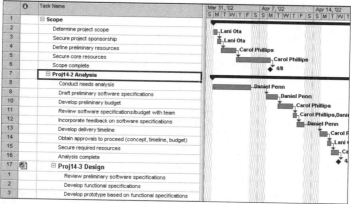

Figure 14-8. The tasks from the disconnected subproject remain in the project, but they no longer have a link to the source project file.

Consolidating Project Information

You can join information from multiple projects into a *consolidated project*. This can be useful if you're managing several unrelated projects at one time. Sometimes you need to see information from several projects in relation to one another, particularly when you want to view, organize, or work with project information from all projects as a single unit.

You can consolidate projects temporarily, for example, to print a specific view based on information in the projects. You can sort, group, or filter the tasks or resources of the combined projects. If this is a combination you use frequently, you can make it permanent and save the consolidated file for future use.

What's the Difference Between a Consolidated Project and a Master Project?

A consolidated project is simply another implementation of the Insert Project feature. The differences are as follows:

- The consolidated project is not necessarily structured as a hierarchy, as are the master project and subprojects. With a consolidated project, you might bring all the projects together at the same outline level. With subprojects, some projects might be subordinate to others, and you're likely to need them to be laid out in a specific sequence.

- The projects might be completely unrelated to one another. The consolidated project might simply be a repository for multiple files.

- The consolidation of projects in a single file might be temporary—just long enough for you to review certain information or generate a report.

To combine multiple projects into a single consolidated project file, follow these steps:

1 On the Standard toolbar, click New. A new project window appears.

2 Click Insert, Project.

3 Select the project files you want to include in the consolidated project.

    If the project files are all stored on the same drive and in the same folder, open that location. Hold down the Shift key to select multiple adjacent project files. Hold down the Ctrl key to select multiple nonadjacent project files.

4 Click the Insert button. The projects are inserted into the new file (see Figure 14-9).

	ⓘ	Task Name	Dura	Jul 28, '02	Aug 4, '02
				T F S S M T W T F S	S M T W T F S
1	📋	⊞ **Office Move**	12.		
2	📋	⊞ **Engineering**	612.2!		
3	📋	⊞ **Database**	9		
4	📋	⊞ **Startup**	12.		

Figure 14-9. The selected projects are inserted into a new window.

5 If you need to consolidate project files located on other drives or folders, repeat steps 2–4 until all the files you want are consolidated into your new project file.

6 To keep this file permanently, click File, Save. Select the drive and folder in which you want to store the consolidated file. Enter a name for the consolidated file in the File Name box, and then click the Save button.

If you're just using this file temporarily, you don't need to save it.

If the project files are already open, you can use the following alternative method to consolidate them:

1 Make sure all the project files you want to consolidate are open.

2 Click Window, New Window.

3 In the Projects list, click the names of the project files you want consolidate (see Figure 14-10). Hold down the Shift key (for adjacent project files) or the Ctrl key (for nonadjacent project files) to select the other projects.

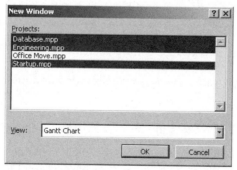

Figure 14-10. Select the projects you want to consolidate in the New Window dialog box.

4 In the View list, click the view in which you want to display the consolidated information initially. After you click OK, a new project window appears with the multiple project files inserted and expanded to show all tasks (see Figure 14-11).

Chapter 14: Managing Master Projects and Resource Pools

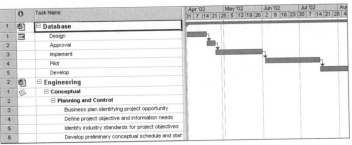

Figure 14-11. The selected projects are inserted into a new window, and consolidated in alphabetical order.

Opening Multiple Project Files as a Set

If you always open the same set of project files, you can put those files together in a project *workspace*. Without creating a master project or consolidating the files into a single project file, you can simply associate the projects together. When you open the workspace file, all projects that are a part of that workspace open at once. To save a project workspace, follow these steps:

1 Open all project files you want to be a part of the workspace.

2 Close any project files you do not want to save in the workspace.

3 Click File, Save Workspace. The Save Workspace As dialog box appears (see Figure 14-12).

Figure 14-12. Use the Save Workspace As dialog box to group project files that should always be opened at the same time.

4 Select the drive and folder in which you want to save the workspace file, and then enter the name for the workspace in the File Name box.

5 Click the Save button. Workspace files are saved with the *.mpw* extension.

Sharing Resources Using a Resource Pool

Typically, when you create a project file, you set up and schedule your tasks and then add resources and assign tasks to them. Often however, resources are assigned to tasks in multiple projects. You might be the manager of these different projects and use the same resources in all of them. Or multiple project managers might share the same resources for their projects.

To prevent conflicts between projects and avoid resource overallocation among multiple projects, you can create a resource pool. A *resource pool* is a project file that's devoted to maintaining information about resources, including their availability, costs, and current usage or allocation.

Any project manager who wants to use the resources in the resource pool file can link the project file to the resource pool file and make the project file a *sharer file*. When you link a project file to the resource pool file, the resource names and other information appear in your project file. You can then assign those resources to tasks as if you originally created them in this project file.

> **note** Using a resource pool for multiple projects is similar to using the enterprise resource pool. If you're using Microsoft Project Professional with its enterprise features, your resource pool is all users identified as part of the enterprise—potentially everyone in the entire organization. With the enterprise resource pool, you can check skill sets, availability, costs, and other resource information to find the right resources for your project.
>
> For more information about using the enterprise resource pool, see "Working with the Enterprise Resource Pool" on page 570.

Setting Up a Resource Pool

Resource pools are easier to manage in the long run if you have a project file whose only job is to serve as the resource pool file. However, if all the resources you need for the pool are already in a project you're executing, for example, you can use that as your resource pool file as well.

To create a resource pool in its own dedicated project file, follow these steps:

1 On the Standard toolbar, click New. A new project window appears.

2 Display the Resource Sheet.

3 If necessary, click View, Table, Entry to apply the Entry table.

4 Enter the information for all work or equipment resources you want to be included in the resource pool. This includes at least the resource name, maximum units, and standard rate.

If different from the default, also enter the cost per use, cost accrual method, and calendar. Enter the initials, group, and overtime rate if applicable to your projects.

5 If you want material resources to be a part of your resource pool, enter at least the material resource names, identify them as material resources, then enter the material labels and the unit costs.

6 After you've entered all resource information, click File, Save. Select the drive and folder in which you want to store the resource pool file. If other project managers will be using this resource pool, make sure you save the file in a location to which you all have access, such as a central file server or a shared folder.

7 Enter a name for the resource pool file in the File Name box, and then click the Save button. Give the resource pool file a name that identifies it as such, for example, *ResPool.mpp*, or *Marketing Resources.mpp*.

For more information about entering resource information, see Chapter 6, "Setting Up Resources in the Project."

If you already have resource information in an existing project file, you can use it to create your resource pool file and cut down on your data entry. One method for doing this is to copy the existing project file and then delete the task information from the new copy. To do this, follow these steps:

1 Open the project file that contains the resource information you want to use.

2 Click File, Save As.

3 Select the drive and folder in which you want to store the resource pool file.

4 Enter a unique name for the resource pool file in the File Name box, and then click the Save button.

5 Display the Gantt Chart or other task sheet.

6 Click the Select All box in the upper-left corner of the sheet, above the row 1 header. The entire sheet is selected.

7 Press the Delete key. All task information is deleted.

8 Display the Resource Sheet and check the resource information. Update any information as necessary, including adding or removing resources.

9 On the Standard toolbar, click Save.

Another method of using existing resource information is to copy and paste information from the existing project files to the new resource pool file. To do this, follow these steps:

1 Open the project file that contains resource information you want to copy.

2 Display the Resource Sheet.

3 Select resource information by selecting the row headers.

To select adjacent resource rows, drag from the first to the last row header. Or click the first row, hold down the Shift key, and then click the last row.

To select nonadjacent resource rows, click the first row header. Hold down the Ctrl key, and then click all other rows you want to select.

Be sure to select the row headers, not just the task names. This will copy all the necessary information, including maximum units and costs, associated with the resource, even if that information isn't displayed in the sheet.

4 On the Standard toolbar, click Copy.

5 On the Standard toolbar, click New. A new project window appears.

6 Display the Resource Sheet.

7 On the Standard toolbar, click Paste. The resource information you copied from the other project file is inserted into the appropriate fields in the Resource Sheet.

8 Click File, Save As.

9 Select the drive and folder in which you want to store the resource pool file. Enter a name for the resource pool file in the File Name box, and then click the Save button.

Linking a Resource Pool to Your Project

After the resource pool is set up, you can link it to your project file. The project file that uses a resource pool is called the *sharer file*. As long as the resource pool and the sharer file are open at the same time, the resources in the resource pool file appear in the sharer file as if they were originally entered there. Even if you have resources in your project file, you can still use resources from the resource pool.

Chapter 14: Managing Master Projects and Resource Pools

To link a resource pool to your project, follow these steps:

1 Open the resource pool file.

2 Open your project file. In your project file, click Tools, Resource Sharing, Share Resources (see Figure 14-13).

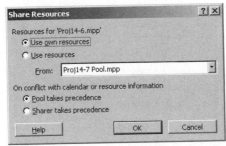

Figure 14-13. Use the Share Resources dialog box to specify that you want to use the resource pool with your project file.

3 Select the Use Resources option.

4 In the From list, click the name of the resource pool file. All open files are displayed in this list.

5 Specify how you want any resource information conflicts to be handled.

If you want the resource pool information to be the final authority in a conflict, select the Pool Takes Precedence option. This is the default.

If you want the resource information in the sharer file (your project file) to be the final authority, select the Sharer Takes Precedence option.

6 Click OK. Your project file is now designated as a sharer file of the resource pool, thereby linking the two. Now all resource information in the resource pool appears in your project file (see Figure 14-14), and any resource information in your project file is added to the resource pool.

	ⓘ	Resource Name	Type	Material Label	Initials	Group	Max. Units	Std. Rate	Ovt. Rate	Cost/Use	Accrue At	Base Calendar	Code
1		Lani Ota	Work		L	Mgmt	100%	$50.00/hr	$0.00/hr	$0.00	Prorated	Standard	
2		Carol Phillips	Work		C	PM	100%	$40.00/hr	$0.00/hr	$0.00	Prorated	Standard	
3		Daniel Penn	Work		D	Analyst	100%	$45.00/hr	$0.00/hr	$0.00	Prorated	Standard	
4		Kim Yoshida	Work		K	Dev	100%	$60.00/hr	$0.00/hr	$0.00	Prorated	Standard	
5		Tristan Randall	Work		T	Test	100%	$30.00/hr	$45.00/hr	$0.00	Prorated	Standard	
6		Adam Stein	Work		A	Train	100%	$35.00/hr	$0.00/hr	$0.00	Prorated	Standard	
7		Katherine Inman	Work		K	Tech Comm	100%	$40.00/hr	$0.00/hr	$0.00	Prorated	Standard	
8		Deployment team	Work		D	Deployment	100%	$40.00/hr	$60.00/hr	$0.00	Prorated	Standard	
9		Contract developers	Work		C	Dev	300%	$0.00/hr	$0.00/hr	$0.00	Prorated	Standard	
10		Trainers	Work		T	Train	400%	$0.00/hr	$0.00/hr	$0.00	Prorated	Standard	

Figure 14-14. With the resource pool and sharer file linked, the resource information for both files is merged.

Troubleshooting

You don't see an open project file in the Share Resources dialog box

Typically, any open project files are shown in the Use Resources From list in the Share Resources dialog box. Sharer files are the exception, however. You are never given the choice to use a sharer file as a resource pool.

You can now work with your project file and the resources as usual, including assigning resources from the pool to tasks. Be sure to save both the sharer file and the resource pool file because you're saving the link between the two. You're also saving any resource information from your sharer file as additional resources in the resource pool.

note You can make a regular project file into a resource pool file. Open the project file you want to use as a resource pool file. Also open the project file that is to become the sharer file. In the sharer file, click Tools, Resource Sharing, Share Resources. Select the Use Resources option, and then select the other project file in the From list.

Although making a regular project file into a resource pool can be convenient at first, keep in mind that when the project ends, the assignments will still be a part of the resource pool file even though they're no longer relevant.

The next time you open your sharer file, you'll be prompted to open the resource pool also (see Figure 14-15).

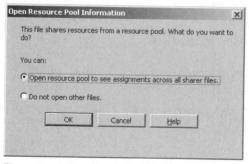

Figure 14-15. If you choose to open the resource file, you'll be able to see all resources, including their assignments, in your sharer file.

Click OK to open the resource file. It's opened with read-only privileges. If you select the Do Not Open Other Files option, the resources you're using from the resource pool do not appear.

If you open a resource pool file before opening any of its sharer files, you are prompted to select whether you want read-only or read-write privileges in the resource pool file (see Figure 14-16).

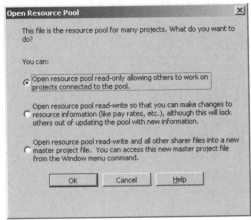

Figure 14-16. You see this alert whenever you directly open a resource pool file. Specify whether you want to open the resource pool as read-only or read-write.

Select the first option to open the resource pool as a read-only file. This is the default, and you should use this option in most cases. You can still update assignment information when working with a read-only resource pool.

Select the second option to open the resource pool as a read-write file. Choose this option when you need to explicitly change basic resource information such as cost or group information. Only one user can open a resource pool as a read-write at a time.

Select the third option to open the resource pool as a read-write file along with all of its sharer files. These files will be combined into a master project file.

Troubleshooting

The resources are missing from your sharer file

Suppose you've already linked your project file to a resource pool, thereby making the file a sharer file. But when you close the resource pool, the resources no longer show up in your sharer file.

Open the resource pool and the resources will appear again.

> **note** If you're working with Microsoft Project Professional and Microsoft Project Server
> for enterprise features, you cannot use a local resource pool when you're logged in
> to the enterprise server. If for some reason you need to use a non-enterprise resource
> pool and sharer file, you can do so when not logged on to the enterprise server.
>
> For more information, see Chapter 24, "Using Enterprise Features to Manage Projects."

Checking Availability of Resource Pool Resources

Display the Resource Usage view or the Resource Graph in the resource pool file to check
the availability of resources across all sharer projects. In these views you can see all the
assignments for all the resources in the resource pool. You can see the amount of time
they're assigned, if they're overallocated, or if they have time available to take on more
assignments.

> For more information about checking resource allocation, see "Monitoring and Adjusting
> Resource Workload" on page 327.

InsideOut

When reviewing assignments across multiple projects in the Resource Usage view
of the resource pool file, there's no way to discern which assignments are from
which projects.

If you want to see the projects responsible for each assignment, add the Project field
to the sheet portion of the Resource Usage view. Click the Work column heading,
for example, and then press the Insert key. In the Field Name box of the Column
Definition dialog box, click Project, and then click OK. The Project field is listed.
The project file name for each assignment is listed.

Updating Resource Pool Information

If you need to change resource-specific information, such as cost information, notes,
maximum units, working time calendar, and so on, you need to open the resource pool
file with read-write privileges and change the information. After you save these changes,
the next time any users of the sharer files open the resource pool or refresh their resource
pool information, they'll see the updated information.

Chapter 14: Managing Master Projects and Resource Pools

If you're changing resource assignments, there's more flexibility. You can open the resource pool file with read-only privileges, access all your resource information, and change assignment information as needed. When you start to save the sharer file, a message appears asking if you want to update the resource pool with your changes (see Figure 14-17). Click OK. Even though the resource pool is read-only, it's updated with your changes at that moment. Any other users of the resource pool will see the changes the next time they open the resource pool or when they refresh the open resource pool.

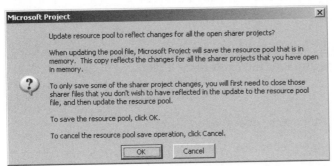

Figure 14-17. This message appears when you're working with a read-only resource pool and you make changes that affect resources in the pool.

Another way to update the resource pool after making assignment changes is to click Tools, Resource Sharing, Update Resource Pool.

If you're working with a sharer file and the resource pool that others also use, it's a good idea to periodically refresh the resource pool to make sure you have the latest changes to resource and assignment information. Click Tools, Resource Sharing, Refresh Resource Pool.

InsideOut

Sometimes project managers find that Microsoft Project works more slowly when there are large resource pools linked with large or complex project files.

If you experience system performance problems like this, open the sharer file without the resource pool file. If you can get by without the resource information, you'll be able to work faster.

Another alternative is to break your project into a master project with subprojects. Then link the resource pool with the smaller subprojects.

Disconnecting a Resource Pool from a Project Plan

If you no longer need the resource pool and the sharer file to be linked, you can disconnect them, as follows:

1 Open both the resource pool and the sharer file.

2 Display the sharer file.

3 Click Tools, Resource Sharing, Share Resources.

4 Select the Use Own Resources option.

The resources assigned to tasks in the sharer project remain in the project file. Any assignment information for these resources is removed from the resource pool file.

You can also disconnect the link from within the resource pool, as follows:

1 Open both the resource pool and the sharer file.

2 Display the resource pool file.

3 Click Tools, Resource Sharing, Share Resources (see Figure 14-18).

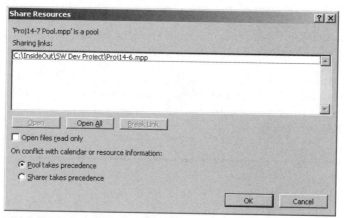

Figure 14-18. In the resource pool, the Share Resources dialog box shows the path of all sharer files.

4 In the Sharing Links box, click the name of the sharer file that you want to disconnect from the resource pool.

5 Click the Break Link button.

Exchanging Information Between Project Plans

You might occasionally find it necessary to share information between project plans. This is particularly true when you're working with multiple projects or adapting information from an old finished project to a new project you're beginning to plan. There are a variety of situations in which you might need to share information, as follows:

- Starting or finishing a task in one project might depend on the start or finish of a task in another project.

- Copying or moving task or resource information or specific fields from one project to another.

- Copying customized project elements, such as views, reports, or calendars from one project to another.

With Microsoft Project, you can easily exchange different types of information between project plans, enabling you not only to model your project appropriately, but also to increase your efficiency by decreasing duplicated entries or development.

Linking Information Between Project Plans

When you link two tasks, you're creating a task dependency or task relationship between them. In the most common link type, Finish-to-Start, as soon as a predecessor task finishes, its successor task can start.

Tasks don't have to be in the same project to be linked. You can have *external links*. An *external predecessor* is a task in another project that must be finished (or started) before the current task can start (or finish). Likewise, an *external successor* is a task in another project that cannot start (or finish) until the current task is finished (or started). Creating task relationships with external tasks like this is also referred to as *cross-project linking*.

Linking Tasks Between Different Projects

To link a task in one project to a task in another project, do the following:

1 Open both projects. Close any other projects.

2 Click Window, Arrange All. This isn't required to link, but it enables you to see the tasks in both projects.

3 In the Task Name field, double-click the task that is to be the successor to the external predecessor.

4 In the Task Information dialog box, click the Predecessors tab.

5 In the ID column, type the project path name and ID number of the external predecessor, separated by a backslash (see Figure 15-1).

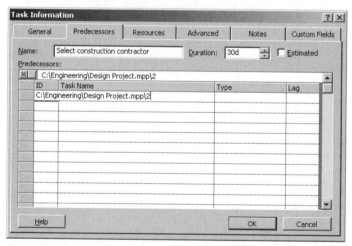

Figure 15-1. On the Predecessors tab in the Task Information dialog box, enter the path, name, and task ID of the external predecessor in the ID field.

For example, suppose the path name of the project containing the predecessor is *C:\Engineering\Design Project.mpp*, and the ID for the predecessor task is 15 (see Figure 15-2). You'd type:

C:\Engineering\Design Project.mpp\15

Then press Enter.

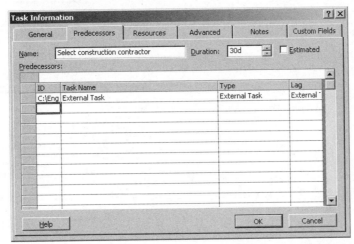

Figure 15-2. After you enter the name and ID of the external task, the other fields contain the words "External Task" and are temporarily not editable.

If you're linking tasks between two enterprise projects, the projects must both be of the same enterprise *version*, for example, "published" or "published1," according to the enterprise version control protocol. Plus, you need to precede the string with two angle brackets: <>. For example:

<>\Design Project.mpp.published\15

> For more information about enterprise project versions, see "Updating Enterprise Project Information" on page 568.

6 Click OK. The name of the external predecessor appears in the current project just above the successor task. By default, table text, Gantt bars, and Network Diagram nodes of external predecessors are formatted in gray (see Figure 15-3 on the next page).

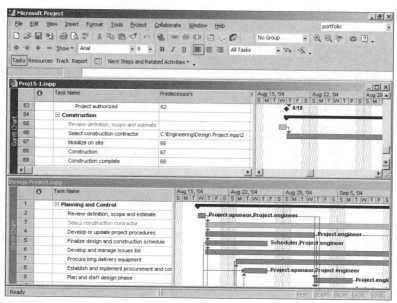

Figure 15-3. Any external predecessors or external successors are displayed in gray.

InsideOut

When you first enter an external predecessor in the Task Information dialog box, you can't immediately change the link type or enter lead or lag time. Those fields contain the words "External Task" and are not editable.

Click OK to close the dialog box, and then open it again. When you click OK, Microsoft Project finds the external task information and checks that it's valid. When you open the dialog box again, the name of the external task appears on the Predecessors tab, and the Type and Lag fields are now editable.

Just as with regular predecessors, you can change the link type from the default finish-to-start to any of the other three link types (finish-to-finish, start-to-start, or start-to-finish). You can also enter lead time or lag time. Again use the Predecessors tab in the Task Information dialog box to do this, as follows:

1 In the Task Name field, double-click the successor task to the external predecessor.

2 In the Task Information dialog box, click the Predecessors tab. The name of the external task appears in the Task Name field, and the Type and Lag fields are now editable (see Figure 15-4).

Chapter 15: Exchanging Information Between Project Plans

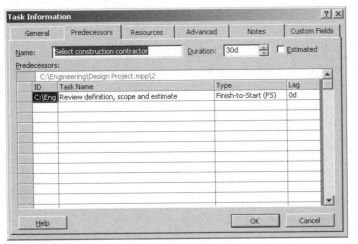

Figure 15-4. The second time you open the Task Information dialog box, the name of the external task appears in the Predecessors table.

3 To change the task dependency to a type other than finish-to-start, select the type in the Type field.

4 To enter any lead or lag time for the dependency, enter the value in the Lag column. Lag time is entered as a positive number, while lead time is entered as a negative number.

For more information about task dependencies in general, including lead and lag time, see "Establishing Task Dependencies" on page 139.

Linking Projects

Sometimes an entire project cannot start or finish until another entire project has finished or started. You can set up this relationship between projects by using a master project and subprojects.

For more information about setting up a master project with subprojects, see "Structuring Master Projects with Subprojects" on page 390.

You can also simply create a task dependency between key tasks in the two projects. For example, if Project1 can't start until Project2 is completely finished, set up a finish-to-start task dependency from the final task or milestone in Project2 with one of the first tasks in Project1.

Chapter 15

> **tip** **Enter external link information in the Predecessor field of the Entry table**
>
> You can enter the information about an external predecessor directly in the Predecessor field of the Entry table or any other table showing the Predecessor field. If you want to change the link type or enter lead or lag time, you can do it all in one step.
>
> For example, for an external task with a finish-to-finish task link and 2 days of lead time, you could enter:
>
> C:\Engineering\Design Project.mpp\15FF-2d
>
> There are no spaces between the task ID, link type, and lead time.

Reviewing Cross-Project Links

You can see your external links in the different views throughout your project. Whether they're external predecessors or external successors, by default external tasks are highlighted in gray in sheets. External tasks are also represented with gray Gantt bars and gray Network Diagram nodes.

If you double-click an external task, the project containing that task opens, and the task is selected. You can then review its task information and current schedule. The other project is still open, and you can return to it by double-clicking the corresponding external task in the second project.

> **tip** **Hide external tasks**
>
> If you don't want external tasks to be visible in your project, you can hide them. Click Tools, Options, and in the Options dialog box, click the View tab. Under Cross Project Linking Options, clear the Show External Successors and the Show External Predecessors check boxes.

To review the details about links throughout your project, click Tools, Links Between Projects. The Links Between Projects dialog box shows information about all external predecessors on the External Predecessors tab (see Figure 15-5). Likewise, the External Successors tab shows information about all external successors.

Chapter 15: Exchanging Information Between Project Plans

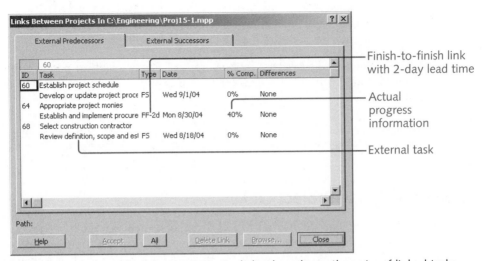

Finish-to-finish link with 2-day lead time

Actual progress information

External task

Figure 15-5. The Links Between Projects dialog box shows the pairs of linked tasks along with their link types, finish dates, current percent complete, and any available updates.

To see the path and name of an external task, click the task name in the Task field. The path and name appear in the lower-left corner of the dialog box.

There are two fields related to external tasks that you can add to a table or use for sorting, grouping, or filtering. The External Task field is a Yes/No (Boolean) field, and simply indicates whether or not the task is external. The Project field contains the name of the project to which this task belongs. For external tasks, the project field also contains the full path (see Figure 15-6).

	Task Name	External Task	Project
55	Evaluate input on feasibility of construction input	No	Proj15-1
56	⊟ Definition Phase Completion	**No**	**Proj15-1**
57	Generate scope document (including infrastructure)	No	Proj15-1
58	Generate project capital estimate	No	Proj15-1
59	Develop or update project procedures	Yes	C:\Engineering\Design Project.mpp
60	Establish project schedule	No	Proj15-1
61	Review definition, scope, and estimate	No	Proj15-1
62	Scope complete/issue cost estimate	No	Proj15-1
63	Establish and implement procurement and contracting plan	Yes	C:\Engineering\Design Project.mpp
64	Appropriate project monies	No	Proj15-1
65	Project authorized	No	Proj15-1
66	⊟ Construction	**No**	**Proj15-1**
67	Review definition, scope and estimate	Yes	C:\Engineering\Design Project.mpp
68	Select construction contractor	No	Proj15-1
69	Mobilize on site	No	Proj15-1
70	Construction	No	Proj15-1
71	Construction complete	No	Proj15-1

Figure 15-6. You can add the External Task or Project fields to a task table to provide information about your cross-project linking.

Chapter 15

Part 5: Managing Multiple Projects

To add a field to a task table, click Insert, Column, and then click the field in the Field Name column.

Whether you add the External Task or Project fields to a table or not, you can sort, group, or filter by these fields. This can be handy when you want to see all your external tasks together.

> For more information about sorting, grouping, or filtering by a particular field, see "Rearranging Your Project Information" on page 114 and Chapter 25, "Customizing Your View of Project Information."

Updating Cross-Project Links

By default, the Links Between Projects dialog box appears whenever you open a project file that contains external links that have changed since the last time you opened the file. The Differences field alerts you to any changed information, such as a changed name, schedule change, new progress information, and so on (see Figure 15-7).

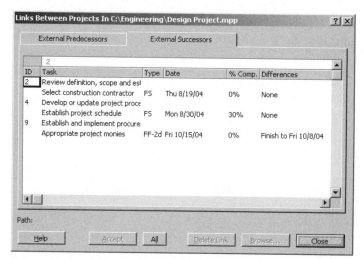

Figure 15-7. The Links Between Projects dialog box appears when you open a project whose external links have changed, and the change is noted in the Differences field.

To incorporate changes from external tasks into your project plan, follow these steps:

1 In the Links Between Projects dialog box, review the change in the Difference field.

2 Click the name of the task that has changed, and then click the Accept button.

To incorporate multiple changes all at once, click the All button.

To close the dialog box without incorporating the changes, click the Close button. As long as there are differences between the linked task information in the two projects, this dialog box will appear every time you open the project.

You can modify how differences between projects are updated, as follows:

1 Open the project containing external links.

2 Click Tools, Options, and in the Options dialog box, click the View tab.

3 Under Cross Project Linking Options, clear the Show Links Between Projects Dialog On Open check box. If this check box is cleared, the Links Between Projects dialog box will not appear when you open the project. Whenever you want to synchronize information between the two projects, you'll need to click Tools, Links Between Projects, and then update links.

4 If you want external task changes to automatically be updated in your project, select the Automatically Accept New External Data check box.

Removing Cross-Project Links

To remove an external link, do the following:

1 Click Tools, Links Between Projects.

2 In the Links Between Projects dialog box, click the External Predecessors tab or External Successors tab.

3 Click the link you want to remove.

4 Click the Delete Link button.

Copying and Moving Information Between Projects

Suppose there's a set of resources in a project you just finished, and you want to use them in a new project you're starting to plan. You can copy the resource information from one project to another using the Copy and Paste commands.

Maybe you're working with a huge project, and you need to break it up into a master project and subprojects. Or maybe several people are managing different pieces of a single project, and you're trying to pull together fragments of different project files related to that one project. You can move task information from one project to another using the Cut and Paste commands.

You can copy or move entire sets of task or resource information. You can also copy individual fields of information, such as task names and durations, or resource names.

Copying and Moving Task and Resource Information

When you want to copy or move all task information, including the task name, duration, predecessors, dates, notes, progress information, resource assignments, and so on, you need to select the entire task. Likewise, you can copy or move all resource information, including maximum units, availability dates, costs, and calendars by selecting the entire resource, not just the resource name.

To copy or move task or resource information from one project to another, follow these steps:

1 In the source project, apply a task sheet or resource sheet. It doesn't matter whether the sheet contains all the information fields you want to copy or move. All information associated with the task or resource will be copied or moved.

2 Click the row heading for all tasks or resources you want to copy or move.

If the tasks or resources are adjacent, simply drag across the row headings to select them. Or click the first row heading, hold down the Shift key, and then click the last row heading (see Figure 15-8).

	Task Name	Duration	Start	Finish
24	Develop specific scope	5 days	Mon 3/1/04	Fri 3/5/04
25	Prepare final conceptual schedule	10 days	Mon 3/8/04	Fri 3/19/04
26	Provide written scope information	5 days	Thu 3/18/04	Wed 3/24/04
27	⊟ **Discipline Support**	**43 days**	**Mon 2/9/04**	**Wed 4/7/04**
28	Create deliverables list	6 days	Mon 2/9/04	Mon 2/16/04
29	Start flow sheets and design criteria	5 days	Tue 2/17/04	Mon 2/23/04
30	Start discipline-specific drawings and equipment list	11 days	Tue 2/17/04	Tue 3/2/04
31	Start conceptual layout	11 days	Tue 2/17/04	Tue 3/2/04
32	Complete flow sheets and design criteria	15 days	Thu 3/18/04	Wed 4/7/04
33	Complete discipline-specific drawings and equipment list	15 days	Thu 3/18/04	Wed 4/7/04
34	Complete conceptual layout	15 days	Thu 3/18/04	Wed 4/7/04
35	⊟ **Conceptual Phase Completion**	**10 days**	**Thu 4/8/04**	**Wed 4/21/04**
36	Prepare conceptual scope and estimate for review	5 days	Thu 4/8/04	Wed 4/14/04
37	Evaluate business plan - rework as needed	5 days	Thu 4/15/04	Wed 4/21/04
38	Conceptual phase complete	0 days	Wed 4/21/04	Wed 4/21/04

Figure 15-8. Drag or use the Shift key to select adjacent tasks.

If the tasks or resources are nonadjacent, click the row heading of the first task or resource you want to select, hold down the Ctrl key, and then click the row headings of all other tasks or resources to be copied or moved (see Figure 15-9).

Chapter 15: Exchanging Information Between Project Plans

	Task Name	Duration	Start	Finish
24	Develop specific scope	5 days	Mon 3/1/04	Fri 3/5/04
25	Prepare final conceptual schedule	10 days	Mon 3/8/04	Fri 3/19/04
26	Provide written scope information	5 days	Thu 3/18/04	Wed 3/24/04
27	⊟ **Discipline Support**	**43 days**	**Mon 2/9/04**	**Wed 4/7/04**
28	Create deliverables list	6 days	Mon 2/9/04	Mon 2/16/04
29	Start flow sheets and design criteria	5 days	Tue 2/17/04	Mon 2/23/04
30	Start discipline-specific drawings and equipment list	11 days	Tue 2/17/04	Tue 3/2/04
31	Start conceptual layout	11 days	Tue 2/17/04	Tue 3/2/04
32	Complete flow sheets and design criteria	15 days	Thu 3/18/04	Wed 4/7/04
33	Complete discipline-specific drawings and equipment list	15 days	Thu 3/18/04	Wed 4/7/04
34	Complete conceptual layout	15 days	Thu 3/18/04	Wed 4/7/04
35	⊟ **Conceptual Phase Completion**	**10 days**	**Thu 4/8/04**	**Wed 4/21/04**
36	Prepare conceptual scope and estimate for review	5 days	Thu 4/8/04	Wed 4/14/04
37	Evaluate business plan - rework as needed	5 days	Thu 4/15/04	Wed 4/21/04
38	Conceptual phase complete	0 days	Wed 4/21/04	Wed 4/21/04

Figure 15-9. Use the Ctrl key to select nonadjacent tasks.

3 On the Standard toolbar, click Copy.

If you're moving the information, on the Standard toolbar, click Cut.

Cut

4 Open the destination project.

5 Display a view compatible with the information you've copied or cut. That is, if you're copying or moving task information, display a task sheet view, such as the Gantt Chart or Task Usage view. If you're copying or moving resource information, display a resource sheet view, for example, the Resource Sheet or Resource Usage view.

6 Click anywhere in the row where you want the first of your selected tasks or resources to be pasted.

When you paste full rows of task information or resource information, they are inserted among any existing tasks or resources. No information will be overwritten.

7 On the Standard toolbar, click Paste. The copied or cut information is pasted into the cells, starting at your anchor cell.

Copying Fields Between Projects

Instead of copying all information about tasks and resources, you can simply copy the contents of a field, such as the task names, resource names, or a custom text field. This can be handy if you just need to copy a set of resource names, for example, or a set of task names with their durations.

note Although you can move (rather than copy) fields from one project to another, it isn't all that useful to do so. For example, if you were to cut resource names from one project, you'd be left with a set of resource information that has no names associated with them.

To copy the contents of a field, do the following:

1 In the source project, apply the view containing the fields you want to copy.

2 Select the fields.

If the fields are adjacent, simply drag to select them. Or click the first field, hold down the Shift key, and then click the last field (see Figure 15-10).

	ⓘ	Resource Name	Type	Material Label	Initials
1		Kim Yoshida	Work		kly
2		Katherine Inman	Work		kmi
3		Adam Stein	Work		ajs
4		Tristan Randall	Work		tsr
5		Daniel Penn	Work		dwp
6		Carol Philips	Work		cdp
7		Lani Ota	Work		lo

Figure 15-10. Drag or use the Shift key to select adjacent fields.

If the fields are nonadjacent, click the first field, hold down the Ctrl key, and then click all other fields to be copied (see Figure 15-11).

	ⓘ	Resource Name	Type	Material Label	Initials
1		Kim Yoshida	Work		kly
2		Katherine Inman	Work		kmi
3		Adam Stein	Work		ajs
4		Tristan Randall	Work		tsr
5		Daniel Penn	Work		dwp
6		Carol Philips	Work		cdp
7		Lani Ota	Work		lo

Figure 15-11. Use the Ctrl key to select nonadjacent fields.

3 On the Standard toolbar, click Copy.

4 Open the destination project.

5 If necessary, apply a table that contains the same or compatible field as the information you're pasting.

For example, if you're pasting text information, such as task names, make sure the Task Name or other editable text field is available. If you're pasting cost information, you need to paste it into an editable currency field, such as Standard Rate or Cost1. If necessary, add a field to a current table. Click a column heading, and then press the Insert key. In the Field Name list, click the name of the field you want.

6 Click the anchor cell, which is the cell in which you want the first of your selected fields to be pasted.

7 On the Standard toolbar, click Paste. The copied information is pasted into the cells, starting at your anchor cell.

The information overwrites any existing information; it does not insert new cells. Because of this, be sure that you have the right number of blank cells in which to paste your information.

Troubleshooting

Your pasted information deleted existing information

When you paste selected fields of task or resource information, those fields flow into any existing cells, starting with the anchor cell and continuing into the cells below. If any of those cells contain information, that information is overwritten.

If this wasn't your intention, and if you haven't done any other operations yet, quickly press Ctrl+Z to undo the paste operation. Your overwritten information returns.

If you've done other work since you pasted, you might have to re-create the over-written information or use your backup project file.

tip   **Copying information between your project plan and other applications**

You can copy and paste project information into other applications, and paste information from other applications into your project plan.

For more information about this, see Chapter 16, "Exchanging Information with Other Applications."

Copying Project Elements Using the Organizer

In the course of working on a project over a year or so, you might have created a number of efficiencies for yourself. For example, you might have modified and saved a view to display all key cost information at a glance, or created a report for a specific meeting you have every other week. Maybe you've created a set of macros to automate a number of repetitive task progress tracking activities.

When you start a new project and you're looking at your new project file, you might think you need to do all that modifying, customizing, and creating all over again. Not so. Just as you can copy task information from one project to another, you can copy customized project elements like tables, calendars, and fields from one project to another. You do this with the Organizer.

Some elements you change in your project also change your Microsoft Project global template, which is applied to all projects on your computer system. Many other elements just stay in the current project. You can use the Organizer to copy elements to the project global template, thereby making them available to all projects. You can also use the Organizer to copy elements from one project to another.

> For information about using the project global template, see Chapter 28, "Standardizing Projects Using Templates." To use the enterprise global template, see "Working with the Enterprise Global Template" on page 564.

With the Organizer, you can copy the following project elements:

- Views
- Tables
- Groups
- Filters
- Reports
- Base calendars

- Custom fields and outline codes
- Toolbars
- Forms
- VBA modules and macros
- Import/export maps

No matter which type of element you copy, the procedure is the same. You select a source file that contains the element that you want to copy, select a destination file into which you want to copy the element, and then copy the element.

Copying an Element from a Project to the Global Template

To copy an element from a project to the project global template, follow these steps:

1 Open the project that contains the element you want to copy.

2 Click Tools, Organizer. The Organizer dialog box appears (see Figure 15-12).

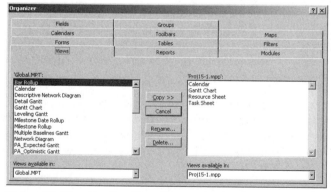

Figure 15-12. Use the Organizer to copy, rename, or delete customized elements between projects, or between a project and the project global template.

3 Click the tab for the type of element you want to copy, for example, Views or Reports.

4 In the <Element> Available In list on the right side of the dialog box, click the project that contains the element that you want to copy. <Element> stands for the name of the current tab.

5 Click the name of the element you want to copy in the list of elements on the right side of the dialog box.

6 Click the Copy button. If an element with the same name already exists in the project global template, a confirmation message appears. Click Yes if you want to replace the element in the project global template with the one from the source project.

To copy the element with a different name, click the Rename button, and then type a new name.

Copying an Element Between Two Projects

To copy an element between two projects, follow these steps:

1 Open both the source and destination projects.

2 Click Tools, Organizer.

3 In the Organizer dialog box, click the tab for the element you want to copy.

4 In the <Element> Available In list on the right side of the dialog box, click the source project.

5 In the <Element> Available In list on the left side of the dialog box, click the destination project.

6 Click the name of the element you want to copy in the list of elements on the right side of the dialog box.

7 Click the Copy button. If an element with the same name already exists in the project global template, a confirmation message appears. Click Yes if you want to replace the element in the project global template with the one from the source project.

To copy the element with a different name, click the Rename button, and then enter a new name.

For more information about working with the Organizer, including renaming and deleting elements, see "Sharing Customized Elements among Projects" on page 636.

Part 6

Integrating Microsoft Project with Other Programs

427

Exchanging Information with Other Applications

You can exchange data in your project file with other applications. Often, someone you need to send information to does not have access to Microsoft Project but has another compatible application. You might want to move project data to a spreadsheet or database application to manipulate the information in certain ways. By the same token, bringing information into Microsoft Project from another application can save an immense amount of time and effort. Here are some other reasons you might want to exchange project data with other applications:

● To prepare a presentation, using a graphics-oriented application

● To add data from Microsoft Project to a spreadsheet for further calculation

● To put your project information into a comprehensive storage repository

● To enable stakeholders without Microsoft Project to work with the data

● To add project information to a larger database

● To add data from another application into Microsoft Project

● To enable direct connectivity between Microsoft Project and other applications with OLE DB

● To make your project data accessible to any application using XML

● To put project information into a text document

● To map your project data to a database using ODBC

Microsoft Project's views, tables, and reports hold a vast amount of data. There are even more fields of data that are not typically visible to the project manager but that can be exchanged with other applications. Because the Microsoft Project database is so large, you'll want to decide in advance how much of the entire project you need to exchange.

Object Linking and Embedding for Databases (OLE DB)

OLE DB was developed by Microsoft as an open specification that is designed to be an interface to all kinds of data within an organization. It provides low-level connectivity between multiple types of data sources.

> For more information about the project database, see Chapter 32, "Working with Microsoft Project Data."

eXtensible Markup Language (XML)

new feature!

Microsoft Project plans can now be saved as XML (eXtensible Markup Language). XML is a type of meta-language that serves to define other languages and their data. With XML, you can:

● Define the structure of data used.

● Have your data be platform-independent.

● Automatically process data defined by XML.

● Define your own unique markup tags that hold your data elements.

The simple and consistent nature of XML makes it very useful for exchanging data between many types of applications.

It's important to keep in mind that some methods of exchanging data move the data and then freeze it, so the information transferred cannot be altered after the exchange. Other methods move the data into the other application and allow it to be dynamically manipulated.

Open Database Connectivity (ODBC)

ODBC is a protocol used to access data in SQL database servers. With ODBC drivers installed, it is possible to connect a Microsoft Project database to SQL databases.

note When referring to the exchange of data between applications, we will use the terms *source* and *destination* to mean the originating application and the receiving application, respectively.

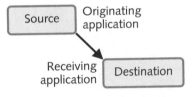

Copying Information

One of the most convenient and effective ways to exchange information between Microsoft Project and other applications is to use the Copy and Paste commands.

Copying from Microsoft Project to Another Application

Suppose you've been asked to put together a basic description of the Technical Feasibility Analysis Phase of your project and put the information into a Microsoft Excel worksheet. Because you'll be dealing with just one phase of your project and you'll want to present a small number of data fields, the best way to move the data from your project file to Excel is by using the Copy and Paste commands. To copy and paste the data, follow the steps on the next page.

Chapter 16

1 In Microsoft Project, display the Task Entry view. Click View, More Views. Click Task Entry, and then click Apply.

2 Select the data that you will be copying (see Figure 16-1).

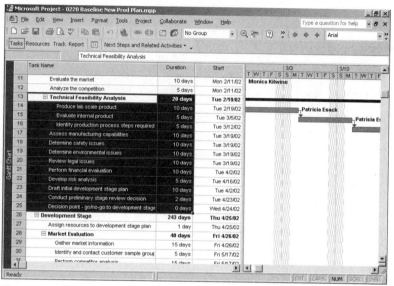

Figure 16-1. Select a small number of fields for copying.

3 Click Edit, Copy Cell. This places a copy of the selected data on the Clipboard.

4 Open Microsoft Excel and the worksheet into which you want to paste project information. Select the cell you want to be the upper-left cell of the data from the source file.

5 Click Edit, Paste. Your data is moved from the Clipboard into this destination file (see Figure 16-2).

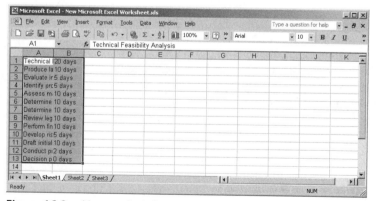

Figure 16-2. Your project data is pasted into Excel.

> **tip** When copying data without column headers, leave room in the destination file to add them.

The exchange of project information using the Copy and Paste commands is done the same way in other applications as well. Unless the workspace of the destination application is normally laid out in columns and rows (as is the case with spreadsheet and database applications), the incoming project information is formatted as a block. You'll need to do some reformatting to restore the columns and rows of your project data.

InsideOut

Microsoft Word does not automatically place Microsoft Project data in table cells. Instead, the project data is pasted as tab-delimited text. To convert the pasted data into a table in Microsoft Word, select the data and click Table, Convert, Text To Table.

Copying information from an application and pasting it into Microsoft Project is performed in the same general manner. You select and copy the source data, select the destination anchor cell in Microsoft Project, and finally paste the data. The anchor cell is the upper-left cell of the block where you're pasting the data.

Because the Copy and Paste commands do not allow for any data mapping after the Paste operation, take care to place data correctly.

There is a special instance in which copying and pasting data from Microsoft Project is the only way you can exchange data. That is when you are copying the *timephased* information into Excel from the Task Usage or Resource Usage views. This is the data from the timesheet portion of the usage views. Timephased information cannot be mapped with the Export Wizard. You must copy it from Microsoft Project and paste it into Excel, as follows:

1 In Microsoft Project, click View, Task Usage. Click Apply. The Task Usage view appears.

2 Click View, Table, Cost. The Cost table data columns appear in the sheet portion of the Task Usage view.

3 In the sheet portion of the view, select the columns of data you want to copy (see Figure 16-3 on the next page).

For more information about using the Export Wizard, see "Calculating Project Information in Microsoft Excel" on page 370.

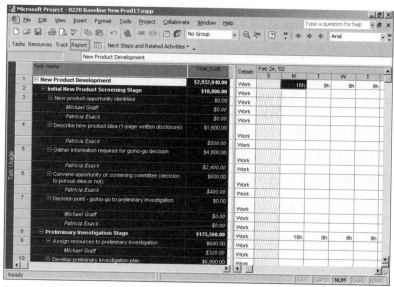

Figure 16-3. Select non-timephased data for copying.

4 Click Edit, Copy Cell.

5 Open the Microsoft Excel worksheet you will use as the destination file. Select a cell that will be the upper-left corner of your block of data, making sure you have an empty row above it. Click Edit, Paste. Your Task Usage data is pasted (see Figure 16-4).

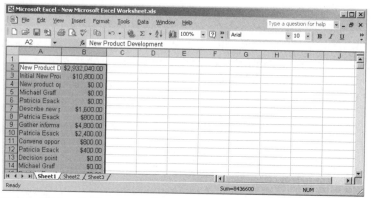

Figure 16-4. Paste your task usage data with an empty row above it.

6 Return to the project file by clicking the Microsoft Project button on your Windows taskbar. In the timesheet portion of the view, set the timescale to the units you prefer. If you want to display days, you might not have to change anything. Scroll to the start date of the data you want to copy. If your timescale is days, you'll need to limit the time span of the data. Select and drag across the headings of the time periods you want to copy (see Figure 16-5).

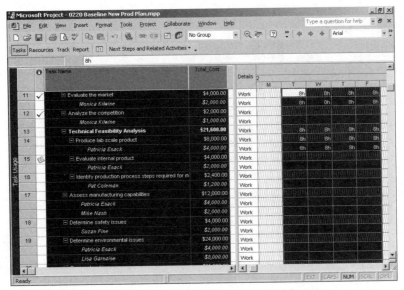

Figure 16-5. Select the timephased data you want to copy.

7 Click Edit, Copy Cell.

8 Return to the Excel destination file by clicking the Microsoft Excel button on your Windows taskbar. Click the worksheet cell that will become the upper-left corner of your cost data. Be sure it is aligned with the rows you just pasted.

9 In Excel, click Edit, Paste Special.

10 In the Paste Special dialog box, select the Paste option. In the As box, select Text, and click OK. The timephased data from the Microsoft Project source file appears alongside the task data that you pasted first (see Figure 16-6). Add the column heading names to complete the process.

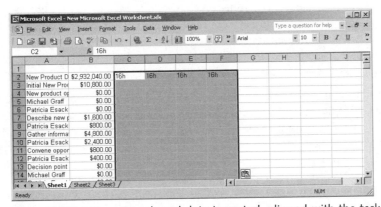

Figure 16-6. Your timephased data is pasted, aligned with the task data rows.

InsideOut

Be careful if you're trying to copy all timephased data. Because the contents of each time period is pasted into its own column, there might be too much data to paste into Excel.

Also, take note of the fields showing in the Details column of the timephased portion of the view. If the Work field is showing (which is the default), Microsoft Project formats the data fields with an "h" after the number. When this is copied into Excel, you'll need to remove that letter from the cells if you want to do numerical calculations of the data.

Copying from Another Application to Microsoft Project

Suppose you asked your manufacturing manager to put together a detailed task list of the process that will be used to manufacture your new product. He completes the list, including tasks and resource assignments, using Microsoft Access. This is an ideal use of the Copy and Paste commands to transfer data into Microsoft Project from another application. To copy the information you need from Microsoft Access into Microsoft Project, follow these steps:

1 Open the Access database that will be the source file. Go to the datasheet view. How you get to this view depends on the structure of the database, but typically you can click View, Datasheet View.

Troubleshooting

Your data isn't being pasted into your destination file correctly

When you exchange data using the Copy and Paste commands, it's important to remember that fields and columns of data will stay in the order and format of their source file. Before you paste data from another application into your project file, first set up the columns in the source file in the order of the corresponding columns into which they'll be pasted in your project file.

Also be careful that data formats, particularly numbers and dates, are the same in the source file as in your project file. If you want to copy and paste data from another application into a project file that has no project field equivalent, insert columns of generic custom fields (for example, Text1 or Number1) to hold the new type of data. These extra columns must match the column order in the source file. This is called manual *data mapping*, and must be done before you give the Paste command. If you paste inappropriate data into Microsoft Project fields, a paste error message will alert you that a mismatch has occurred.

2 Select the rows or columns you want to copy. Click Edit, Copy.

3 Return to your project plan. Apply the view and table that represents the closest match to the types of information you'll be pasting.

4 If you need to add any columns to match the incoming information, click the column to the left of which you want to insert the new field. Click Insert, Column. In the Field Name list, click the name of the field you want, and then click OK.

5 Click the cell where you want the incoming information to begin to be pasted.

6 Click Edit, Paste. The copied information is pasted into the columns you've prepared. Other project data will be automatically populated also, but you'll need to review and adjust that data to make it accurate.

These actions will save a large amount of time and ensure the accuracy of the information you received from the Access source file.

Copying and pasting lists of items is a very effective means of exchanging information with another application.

Form and format are crucial when copying data into Microsoft Project. The data must be arranged in the same order as the Microsoft Project destination file, and the data types (such as numbers or text) must be the same as the destination cells.

Pasting data into Microsoft Project overwrites data in the destination cells. If this is not your intention, first insert the appropriate number of empty rows.

Any information that can be moved to the Clipboard by using the Copy command can be pasted into Microsoft Project, but not all types of views will accept all types of data. For example, the only kind of data you can paste into the chart portion of the Gantt Chart is objects, such as pictures, and you cannot paste anything into the Network Diagram.

InsideOut

When copying lists, be sure the source file uses a type of cell structure, or the data might be pasted into one Microsoft Project cell. Tables in Microsoft Word will work like cells for this function, but tables in other text processor applications might not.

Embedding Information

An *object* is a class or a group of data that gets its format from another application. Embedding objects as a means of sharing information is a further extension of the excellent versatility of Microsoft Project. So even though Microsoft Project cannot create line art, it can receive it and embed it as objects in the Gantt Chart. Graphical illustration is probably the most popular use of embedding with Microsoft Project, but other formats of data can be embedded as well. When referring to the process of embedding objects, the originating application is called the *server application* and the receiving application is called the *client application*.

Embedding from Microsoft Project to Another Application

Suppose your company is preparing for its quarterly review, and the report is being prepared in Microsoft Word. In your portion of the report, you'd like to include information taken directly from your Microsoft Project Gantt Chart. You know you can always copy and paste the material, but for this report, you want the Gantt Chart to look exactly as it does in Microsoft Project. In this case, you would embed the Gantt Chart into the Word document. To do this, follow these steps:

1 In your project plan, display the view you want to embed in the Word document.

2 Manipulate the view to show the information you want.

For example, suppose you want to change the timescale in the Gantt Chart so that it shows more information in a smaller space. Double-click the timescale. The Timescale dialog box appears (see Figure 16-7). Make changes to the timescale definitions to show larger units of time. This contracts the bar chart area.

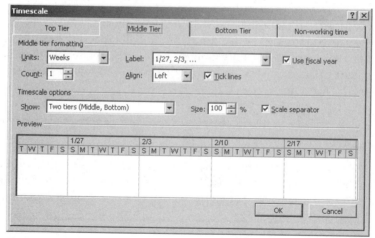

Figure 16-7.   Use the timescale settings to reduce your chart area.

3 Move the screen divider bar to cover all columns except Task Name, and then shrink the indicators column so it can't be seen, by dragging its right margin to the left.

4 Click the Select All box in the upper-left corner of the sheet, above row 1, to select the whole view.

5 Click Edit, Copy Picture. In the Copy Picture dialog box, (see Figure 16-8), select the For Screen, Rows On Screen, As Shown On Screen options, and then click OK.

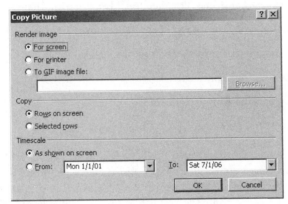

Figure 16-8. Make your copying choices for the Copy Picture function.

6 Open the Microsoft Word document that will be the client application. Click the place on the page where you want to paste the object.

7 Click Edit, Paste Special.

8 In the Paste Special dialog box, select Paste As Picture, and then click OK. The object from Microsoft Project is embedded into the Word document.

If needed, you can resize the object image in the client application.

---

tip **Embed the view as a Microsoft Project Document Object**

One variation on the embedding process is to embed the view as a Microsoft Project Document Object. This is done by the same procedure as embedding from Microsoft Project, except that you use Copy rather than Copy Picture, and Paste Special As Microsoft Project Document Object rather than Paste As Picture. This feature enables you to reopen the entire project from the embedded object by double-clicking it. Of course, Microsoft Project must be installed on the computer where the client application is located. Also, because this embeds the entire project, it uses a very large amount of memory while the project is open. In addition, it makes the client file much larger. Still, it can be very convenient.

Embedding can be done in this manner with all client applications that support the Paste Special functions, for example, Microsoft Excel and Word. This can be especially useful when you're preparing presentations of project status using Microsoft PowerPoint, for example.

Chapter 16

Embedding from Another Application to Microsoft Project

Objects can be embedded into Microsoft Project from other applications, but only in a limited number of places. Usually, objects are embedded in the chart portion of the Gantt Chart. Other available locations for embedding in Microsoft Project are as follows:

- The Notes portion of the Task Form or Task Information dialog box
- The Notes portion of the Resource Form or Resource Information dialog box
- The Notes tab in the Assignment Information dialog box
- The Objects box in the Task Form
- The Objects box in the Resource Form
- Headers, footers, and legends of printable pages

Other objects that are useful for embedding in the Gantt Chart include graphic charts of the data, symbols to show significant points, and even cartoons and drawings. In addition to graphic objects, other media forms can be embedded, too, such as sounds and video. The appropriateness of embedded objects should be considered before proceeding. Suppose you want to place symbols in the Gantt Chart to both draw attention to critical items and show where celebrations are in order. To do this, follow these steps:

1 In the Gantt Chart, click the chart portion of the view.

2 Click Insert, Object. The Insert Object dialog box appears.

3 Select the Create From File option. Click the Browse button, and find the location of the image you want to embed. Click the image file, and click the Insert button.

4 In the Insert Object dialog box, click OK. The picture appears in the Gantt chart. You can move and resize the image as needed.

Occasionally, you might need to embed an object and then work with it in its server application after it has been placed in your project plan. To do this, follow these steps:

1 Open the server application, and select the data you want to embed. Click Edit, Copy.

2 In Microsoft Project, display the Gantt Chart. Click the chart portion of the view.

3 Click Edit, Paste Special.

4 In the Paste Special dialog box, select Paste.

5 In the As box, click the name of the server application (for example, Microsoft Word Document), and then click OK. The object is embedded in the Gantt Chart, and can still be modified in the server application. You can move and resize the embedded object as needed.

6 To open the server application of an object embedded in Microsoft Project, double-click the object. The server application opens, and you can use its commands and tools to work with the object as needed. When finished, on the File menu, click the Close or Exit command. The server application closes, and the object appears in your project file showing the changes you just made.

Importing and Exporting Information

You've now used a few other applications to exchange information with Microsoft Project. There are many more types of programs that can process Microsoft Project data and deliver data that Microsoft Project can import.

Microsoft Project 2002 supports importing and exporting with the file types shown in Table 16-1.

Table 16-1. Supported File Types

Type of file	File name extension
Microsoft Project files	.mpp
Microsoft Project templates	.mpt
Microsoft Project databases	.mpd
Web pages	.html or .htm
Microsoft Access databases	.mdb
Microsoft Excel workbooks	.xls
Microsoft Excel PivotTables	.xls
Text files (tab delimited)	.txt
CSV Text files (comma delimited)	.csv
XML format files	.xml

Information can also be exported to or imported from an ODBC database.

Importing Information into Microsoft Project

To import data to Microsoft Project, such as a portion of an Access database, follow these steps:

1 In Microsoft Project, click File, Open.

2 In the Open dialog box, click the folder where your Access database is located in the Look In box.

3 In the Files of Type list, click Microsoft Access Database (*.mdb). Click the file name of your database, and then click the Open button.

4 On the Import Wizard Welcome page, click the Next button.

5 On the Map page, select the New Map option. Click the Next button.

6 On the Import Mode page, click Append The Data To The Active Project. Click the Next button.

7 On the Map Options page, under Select The Types Of Data You Want To Import, click Tasks. Click the Next button.

8 On the Task Mapping page, click the Access database table you want to use in the Source Database Table Name field. Choose the fields you want to import, using the From: Database Field and the To: Microsoft Project Field table. The unmapped data will appear in red. If it is unmapped, it won't be imported. Click the Next button.

9 On the End of Map Definition page, click the Finish button (without saving). The new data appears in your project plan.

Exporting Information from Microsoft Project

Just as importing enables you to bring information from other applications' file formats into Microsoft Project, exporting converts your Microsoft Project information into the file format for another application. You can then open the converted, or exported, project information directly in that other application, as if it were originally created in that application.

When you export from Microsoft Project, you use the Export Wizard, as follows:

1 In Microsoft Project, open the project that contains the information you want to export.

2 Click File, Save As.

3 In the Save As Type list, click the file type to which you want to export your project information. For example, if you want to export your project information to XML, click XML Format (*.xml).

If you want to export your data to a Microsoft SQL Server or an Oracle Server, click the ODBC button, and then skip to step 5.

4 In the File Name box, enter the name for the exported file.

5 Click the Save button.

The Export Wizard opens and guides you step by step through selecting the specifics of data mapping what you want from Microsoft Project to the destination file. Some of the specific steps and choices of the Export Wizard vary depending on the file type you are exporting to.

6 Work through each page of the Export Wizard, clicking the Next button after making your selections on each page.

7 On the final page, click the Finish button. Microsoft Project exports your project information to the selected file format.

Troubleshooting

Your exported project information contains more data than you wanted

You probably chose to map fields to be exported based on a Microsoft Project data table, not realizing that the table contains more fields of data than you expected.

To export only the project information you want, take some extra time on the Map Data page of the Export Wizard to make sure you specify only the data fields you want to export. On this page, use the Filter box to narrow the data chosen. You can complete the data mapping table with information from only specific Microsoft Project data tables, or select specific individual fields to be mapped.

Linking Information

Linking is another method of transferring data between applications. By linking, you can keep a connection to the server application, and then when a change or update is made there, it will be reflected in the client application. One advantage of linking is that the file size is much smaller than it would be if the information in the linked file were embedded. A potential difficulty with linking is that you need to remain aware of the current location of the linked file and its update status. If the linked file is moved, the link will be broken. If the information in the linked file becomes obsolete, the linked information will also be out of date.

Linking from Microsoft Project to Another Application

You can insert a linked graphical object in another application from Microsoft Project by using the Copy command, rather than using the Copy Picture command. To do this, follow this procedure:

1 Open a graph view in Microsoft Project, such as the Gantt Chart or Resource Graph. If you're linking from the Gantt Chart, select the rows of data you want. If you're linking from the Resource Graph, show the resource you want. Scroll the chart portion of the view to the time period you want to show.

2 Click Edit, Copy or Copy Task.

3 Open the client application, for example, Microsoft Word. Place the mouse pointer where you want to paste the view.

4 Click Edit, Paste Special.

5 In the Paste Special dialog box, select the Paste Link option. In the As box, select Microsoft Project Document Object. Click OK. The linked view appears in the Word document. When changes are made to the server application (Microsoft Project), they will be reflected in the client application (Word).

The two key steps to remember in the procedure are to click Copy rather than Copy Picture, and click Paste Special As A Link.

The graph views that can be copied and pasted as links include:

- Gantt Chart
- Network Diagram
- Resource Graph

Generally, what you see on the screen in Microsoft Project is exactly what gets pasted as the linked object, so set up the view to show only what you want to be seen. This also applies to the rows of data you want to show.

Nongraphical data can also be pasted as links. Most views can be linked. The exceptions are the Calendar view and the form views, such as the Task Form or Resource Form, because they cannot be copied.

To link a view to another application do the following:

1 In your project, set up the view to show all the data you want to copy on screen, and select that data.

2 Click Edit, Copy Task or Edit, Copy Cell.

Depending on what you have selected, the menu might say Copy Task or Copy Cell. For example, if you clicked a Gantt Chart bar, the menu would say Copy Task. Don't choose Copy Picture from the Edit menu.

3 Open the client application, place the mouse pointer where you want to paste the data, and click Edit, Paste Special. In the Paste Special dialog box, select the Paste Link option. In the As box, click Microsoft Project Object, and then click OK. The view appears in the client application as it was when you copied it, and it's linked to the project.

Linking from Another Application to Microsoft Project

The data connection of a linked object can be made using another application as the server and Microsoft Project as the client. This can be a handy way to show currently updated information from a different origin. As with all objects, linked objects can only be pasted within a few places in Microsoft Project. The favorite site for pasting objects, as we've seen, is the Gantt chart.

To link data from another application, follow these steps:

1 In Microsoft Project, open the Gantt Chart. Click the chart portion of the view.

2 Click Insert, Object. The Insert Object dialog box appears (see Figure 16-9).

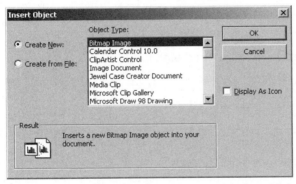

Figure 16-9. Select the object you want to insert into your project plan.

3 Select the Create From File option, and then click the Browse button to locate the file you will link.

4 In the Browse dialog box, navigate to the file you want to link, and then click the Insert button.

5 In the Insert Object dialog box, select the Link check box, and then click OK. The linked object appears in the Gantt Chart. Move and size the object in the Gantt Chart as you like. Double-click the object to open it in the server application for editing.

---

note The Display As Icon check box in the Insert Object dialog box is useful when you are linking to a large document. When the linked object is displayed as an icon, you just double-click the icon to open the linked file. With files such as databases and worksheets, this is the most efficient way to place a linked object into Microsoft Project. The file name is included with the icon, as well as the shortcut arrow symbol.

Another efficient use of linked objects is to place them in the Notes fields of tasks or resources. Not only is this less intrusive to people viewing your project, but it is often the more specific place for supporting documentation about a task or resource. For example, you can link a spreadsheet of cost performance numbers from another project into the notes for a current task. To do this, follow these steps:

1 In the Gantt Chart or other task view, click the task to which you want to link an object.

2 On the Standard toolbar, click Task Information.

3 In the Task Information dialog box, click the Notes tab.

4 Under Notes, click the Insert Object button.

5 In the Insert Object dialog box, select the Create From File option. Click the Browse button to locate your server application file.

6 Click the file, and click the Insert button.

7 Select the Link and Display As Icon check boxes, and then click OK.

8 The linked file icon appears in the Task Notes box.

> **note** Bear in mind that adding links to your project will change the way you open the file. You will be prompted each time you open the file (see Figure 16-10) to choose whether to re-establish the links or open the file without them. If you do not want to see the reminder about the links, click Tools, Options, and then click the View tab. Clear the Show OLE Links Indicators check box.
>
>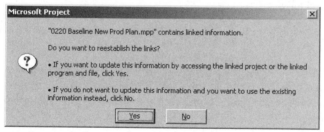
>
> **Figure 16-10.** Each time you open a linked document, you are prompted to re-establish the link.

Using Microsoft Visio with Microsoft Project

Many of the processes and structures reflected in your project plan can be represented in a graphical format and illustrated to help readers visualize them. You already are using a Gantt chart and network diagram for depiction of your project work. By using

Microsoft Visio, you can create more extensive visual graphic representations of the flows, concepts, structure and organization involved with your project. The unique capabilities of Microsoft Visio to generate clear illustrations of various systems, processes, structures, and organizations make it a great tool to use in conjunction with Microsoft Project. You can use Microsoft Visio as a stand-alone tool, providing visual depiction of your project information, or as a source of embedded illustrations within your project plan.

For example, in Microsoft Visio you can generate a Work Breakdown Structure (WBS) chart of your project. Using the Copy command in Microsoft Visio and the Paste Special, Paste As Picture command in Microsoft Project, you can embed the diagram in a vacant area of your Gantt Chart to illustrate the organization of your work. Using the same commands, you can also build an organization chart in Microsoft Visio and embed it in the Notes box of the Resource Information dialog box for a resource you want to show in a hierarchy.

Hyperlinking Information

Suppose one of your managing stakeholders has asked you to put a link to your project information on his department's intranet Web page. With Microsoft Project, this is done quite easily. You can also efficiently insert hyperlinks into your project file from Web pages or HTML files.

Hyperlinking from Microsoft Project to Another Application

To create a hyperlink from Microsoft Project to another application, follow these steps:

1 In Microsoft Project, open the view that shows the information you want to link.

2 Click File, Save As Web Page.

3 In the Save In list, click the folder on your intranet Web server. Make a note of the full path to the file, including server name, folder name, file name.

4 In the File Name box, enter a name for the Web page you're creating from this project view, and then click the Save button.

5 The Export Wizard opens. On the Welcome page, click the Next button.

6 On the Map page, choose New Map, and click the Next button.

7 On the Map Options page, click Tasks as the type of data, and click Export Header Row/Import Includes Headers, and then click the Next button.

8 On the Task Mapping page, select and map the fields you want to be displayed.

Two quick ways to map data fields here are with the Add All button or with the Base On Table button. The Add All button populates the data mapping table with all Microsoft Project fields and maps them to the HTML Table fields. The Base On Table button populates the data mapping table with fields from the Task table or Resource table.

9 When you've included the data you want to map to HTML, click the Next button. On the End of Map Definition page, click the Finish button.

10 Open the intranet Web page in an HTML editor, and insert the link to the file name you just created, using the full path and the following format:

<a href=http://servername.com/foldername/filename.html>The New Product's Gantt Chart</a>.

This step might be more appropriately done by the Webmaster, but it is necessary to complete the process.

Hyperlinking From Another Application to Microsoft Project

You might come across very relevant reference material for some tasks on the Internet. You can make a hyperlink in Microsoft Project to the Web pages you would like to include. The process is quick and efficient:

1 In Microsoft Project, display the view that contains the task to which you want to add a hyperlink.

2 Click the task name.

3 On the Formatting toolbar, click the Insert Hyperlink button. The Insert Hyperlink dialog box appears.

4 Under Link To, click Existing File Or Web Page.

5 In the Text To Display box, type a short description of the Web page.

6 In the Look In list, locate the source file. Click OK. The Web link icon appears in the Indicators column of the current view. If you rest your mouse pointer over the hyperlink indicator, the Web page name appears.

7 To open the hyperlink, right-click the hyperlink indicator, click Hyperlink, and click Open. Your Web browser is launched, you connect to the Internet if necessary, and then the hyperlinked Web page appears. Alternatively, you could double-click the hyperlink indicator.

caution As with many sites on the Internet, the Web page you hyperlink to is subject to change or removal. Periodically check your hyperlinks to ensure they are still accurate.

Integrating Microsoft Project with Microsoft Excel

There are many file formats and applications that can be used to share information with Microsoft Project 2002. One of the most convenient and useful is Microsoft Excel.

To transfer information between Microsoft Project and Excel, you might use one of the following methods:

● Copy and paste the information as you would in other Microsoft Office applications.

● Copy and use the Paste Special command to place the selection in Microsoft Project as an object.

● Import information from Excel into Microsoft Project or from Microsoft Project into Excel.

● Export information from Excel into Microsoft Project by using one of the new Excel-to-Microsoft Project templates.

● Export information using the Export Wizard in Microsoft Project.

● Link information between the Microsoft Project and Excel files.

449

Copying Information Between Microsoft Excel and Microsoft Project

You can easily copy and paste information in columns and rows between Microsoft Project and Microsoft Excel. You can also paste a portion of an Excel worksheet or chart into certain areas of Microsoft Project as an embedded object.

When using the Copy and Paste commands to transfer sheet data from Excel into Microsoft Project, be careful to:

● Set up the specific Microsoft Project view into which you want to paste Excel data.

● Arrange the columns in Excel in the same order as the columns in Microsoft Project.

● Format the data in Excel the same way it is formatted in Microsoft Project.

● Paste the data in the specific rows and columns intended.

Copying and Pasting Sheet Information

After the columns are set up the way you need, copy and paste the information by following these steps:

1 In Microsoft Excel, select the cells or columns to be copied.

2 On the Standard toolbar, click Copy.

3 In Microsoft Project, display the view in which you want to paste the copied information. Make sure the columns are in the order in which you copied them in Excel. If columns are not in the right order, information might be pasted into fields you didn't intend. Also, if columns are the wrong data type, you might get unexpected results or error messages. For example, if you try to paste currency information into a date field, you might get a paste error message.

4 Select the "anchor" cell, which will become the upper-left corner of the cells you are pasting.

5 On the Standard toolbar, click Paste.

---

tip **Copy sheet information from Microsoft Project to Microsoft Excel**

You can follow these steps to copy and paste sheet information from Microsoft Project to Excel as well. However, you don't have to worry about setting up the columns properly in Excel, because Excel columns can take any kind of data.

Copying and Pasting Objects

You can insert a portion of an Excel worksheet or chart into Microsoft Project as an *object*. An object is a self-contained piece of information that is moved as a single item. This can be anything from a picture to a selected portion of a worksheet.

Objects can be pasted into Microsoft Project only in specific locations, as follows:

- Chart portion of the Gantt Chart
- Notes tab of the Task Information, Resource Information, and Assignment Information dialog boxes
- Objects details of the Task Form or Resource Form with the Objects details applied

To simply copy and paste an object into Microsoft Project, do the following:

1 In Microsoft Excel, select the chart or set of cells to be copied.

2 On the Standard toolbar, click Copy.

3 In Microsoft Project, display the view or form in which you want to paste the copied object.

4 On the Standard toolbar, click Paste. If the Paste command is not available, press Ctrl+V.

To paste Excel information as an object, use the Paste Special command as follows:

1 In Excel, select the data or chart you will be pasting into Microsoft Project.

2 Click Edit, Copy.

3 Open the Microsoft Project file into which you'll be pasting your information.

4 Display the location where you want to place the object, for example, the Gantt Chart or the Notes tab of the Task Information dialog box.

5 Click Edit, Paste Special. The Paste Special dialog box appears, (see Figure 17-1).

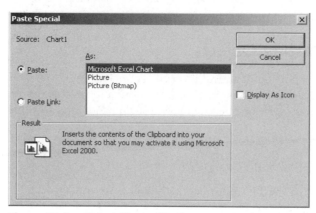

Figure 17-1. Select the application name in the Paste Special dialog box.

6 Select the Paste option. In the As box, click Microsoft Excel Worksheet.

If you've copied a set of cells from Excel, clicking Microsoft Excel Worksheet ensures that the cells are pasted as an object rather than table data.

7 Click OK. The data or chart is pasted in Microsoft Project. The Excel information is pasted into your project file.

Other options in the Paste Special dialog box enable you to do the following:

Paste Link. Any changes made to the object in Excel will be reflected in the project file each time you open it. If you choose this option, every time you open your file in Microsoft Project, you will be prompted to reconnect the links or open the file without enabling the links.

Picture. The worksheet data from Excel, even though it's not a chart, will be pasted as if it were a graphic. In the Paste Special dialog box, select the Paste option. In the As box, select Picture or Picture (Bitmap). While the picture object will not be editable, it can still be resized.

Display As Icon. If you select this check box in the Paste Special dialog box, only the Microsoft Excel icon will appear in the project file. When you double-click the icon, the object opens. When you close the object, you're back in Microsoft Project. This can help save space on the Gantt Chart or Notes boxes.

Troubleshooting

Your pasted object is covering up bars in the Gantt Chart

When pasting objects into your Gantt Chart, plan ahead to be sure the object you are pasting will be easy to see without covering up the existing bars and labels. For example, pasting a portion of a worksheet as a picture can easily take up the space of dozens of task rows on the Gantt Chart. Finding that much empty space could mean pasting the object so far into the right or left portion of the Gantt Chart that viewers would not normally see your pasted object.

Estimate the size requirements, place the pasted item as close to existing bars as possible, and try to be consistent in your placements; for example, always to the right of associated bars, or always above associated bars.

tip   **Periodically review pasted objects for timeliness**

If you paste objects into Microsoft Project, periodically review them for timeliness. It is easy for a chart or table of statistics to become outdated as the project moves forward.

Importing and Exporting with Microsoft Excel

In many project teams, you're likely to be the only one using Microsoft Project. However, certain team members might maintain and track extensive plan information using Microsoft Excel. You might need to exchange that data regularly between the two applications, and you need the process for doing so to be quick and easy.

You can *import* information from Excel into Microsoft Project, and *export* information from Microsoft Project into Excel. When you import information, you're bringing information in a foreign file format (for example, the Excel .xls file format) into the current application (for example, Microsoft Project, which uses the .mpp file format). When you export information, you're saving information in the current application in a different file format, so that it can be easily opened by another application. In both cases, the information will look as though it had been created originally in the destination application.

Importing a Project Task List from Excel

newfeature!

You can get a task list from an Excel workbook and quickly incorporate it into Microsoft Project, using the new Microsoft Project Task List template in Excel. This is especially helpful when you integrate the suggestions of team members and stakeholders into the project plan to make it more inclusive or more accurate.

For example, suppose that the marketing department suggested an addition to the project plan that will provide more detail for their test marketing efforts. They've developed a list of tasks for this in Excel, and you've reviewed and accepted their additions. You'd now like to integrate the Excel data into your project plan. The best way to accomplish this is by using the new Microsoft Project Task List Template in Excel. Follow these steps:

1 In Microsoft Excel, click File, New.

2 In the New Workbook task pane, click General Templates.

3 In the Templates dialog box, click the Spreadsheet Solutions tab.

4 Click Microsoft Project Task List Import Template, and then click OK.

   If the template is not in the Templates dialog box, close the dialog box, and then click File, Open. Browse to the Office template directory, which is typically \Program Files\Microsoft Office\Templates\1033. In the Files Of Type list, click Templates. Double-click the Tasklist.xlt file.

   Note the two worksheets that are set up in this workbook (see Figure 17-2): Task_Table and Info_Table. The task list data will be put in the Task_Table sheet.

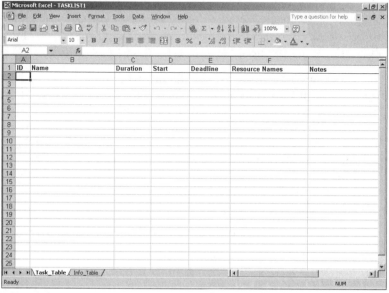

Figure 17-2. Enter project data in the Microsoft Project Task List Import Template in Excel.

4 Enter the data into the template (see Figure 17-3).

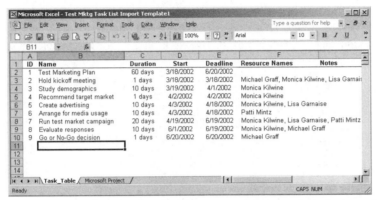

Figure 17-3. The completed Task List template is ready to be exported.

5 Save the Task List template as an Excel workbook (*.xls), as usual in Excel. You will later import this Excel workbook into Microsoft Project.

---

note The functions of this Excel template are specifically built for integration with Microsoft Project. They include automatic addition of *days* as the unit of Duration, automatic formatting of dates with the year, and automatic numbering of the task ID cells. Also, the second worksheet, labeled "Info_Table" or "Microsoft Project," contains a brief explanation of how Microsoft Project can use and augment the template.

At this point, the new task list is ready to be imported and integrated with the existing Microsoft project plan, as follows:

1 In Microsoft Project, open your project plan.

2 Display the Gantt Chart or Task Sheet view.

3 Click File, Open. The Open dialog box appears.

4 In the Files Of Type box, click Microsoft Excel Workbooks (*.xls).

5 In the Look In box, find the folder that contains the Excel file.

6 Click the file, and then click the Open button.

7 On the Welcome page of the Import Wizard, click the Next button.

8 On the Data Type page, select Project Excel Template, and click the Next button.

9 On the Import Mode page, select Append The Data To The Active Project, and click the Finish button. The worksheet information is placed in your project (see Figure 17-4).

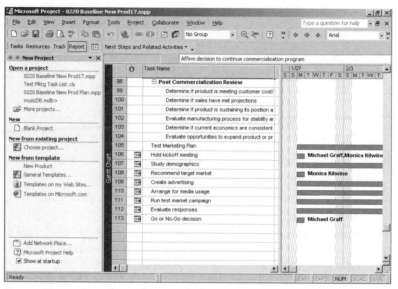

Figure 17-4. Data from the template is appended to the project.

If you scroll to the right, you see that the resources have all been placed in the proper column, but the Predecessors column is empty. Imported tasks need to be linked and summarized or subordinated as necessary. You might decide to place the list, as a group of tasks, somewhere within your project tasks. This can be done easily with the Insert New Task command.

> For more information about inserting and organizing tasks, see Chapter 3, "Starting a New Project."

> **note** Be aware of the dates assigned to imported task lists. They have been given a start date of the first day of the project and Start No Earlier Than constraints by default.

The task dates will have to be added in the project file to complete the data integration. To change the date constraint to the As Soon As Possible constraint, do the following:

1 Select the names of all tasks with date constraints.

2 On the Standard toolbar, click Task Information.

3 In the Multiple Task Information dialog box, click the Advanced tab. In the Constraint Type box, click As Soon As Possible (see Figure 17-5).

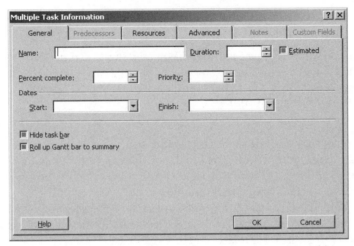

Figure 17-5. Set the Constraint type to As Soon As Possible.

> For more information about setting constraints, see "Scheduling Tasks to Achieve Specific Dates" on page 147.

You might want to compare your Excel worksheet with your results in Microsoft Project to be sure that all the information is accurate.

> **note** Both the Microsoft Project Task List Import Template and the Project Plan Import Export Template are installed with Microsoft Project. If you have Microsoft Excel installed on the same computer as Microsoft Project, those templates then become available in Excel.

Working with the Excel Import Export Template

If you or someone else on the team is doing more than just building a task list in Excel, you can use the Microsoft Project Import Export Template. This template can be used in Excel to build a project with tasks, resources, and assignments. Then you have a properly formatted worksheet for many of the essential elements of a plan for importing into Microsoft Project.

To use this template, follow these steps:

1 In Microsoft Excel, click File, Open.

2 In the Templates dialog box, click the Spreadsheet Solutions tab.

3 Click Microsoft Project Plan Import Export Template, and then click OK.

> **note** If the Template is not in the Templates dialog box, close the dialog box, and then click File, Open. Browse to the Office template directory, which is typically \Program Files \Microsoft Office\Templates\1033. In the Files Of Type list, click Templates. Double-click the Projplan.xlt file.

This template has worksheets for tasks, resources, and assignments. There is also a worksheet for overall information. The key data fields are set up so that when you fill in the worksheets and export them into Microsoft Project, you don't need to map your data. If you decide to add data in extra columns (fields), Microsoft Project will map that data to an appropriate field in the Microsoft Project data tables for you. The fourth worksheet in the template is labeled Info_Table and is a useful explanation of the best uses of this template with Microsoft Project.

When you've populated the fields in the template with your data, click the Save As command to save the data as an Excel Workbook (*.xls) as usual. This workbook will become the source file when you import the data into Microsoft Project. To import the information from this new Excel workbook into Microsoft Project, do the following:

1 Start Microsoft Project.

2 Click File, Open.

3 In the Look In list, find the location of the Excel workbook you want to import.

4 Click the file, and then click the Open button. The Microsoft Project Import Wizard opens to the Welcome page.

5 Click the Next button.

6 On the Data Type page, click Project Excel Template, and then click the Next button.

7 On the Import Mode page, click As A New Project, and then click the Finish button. The new project opens with all the data populated from the template.

InsideOut

If there are any inconsistencies in the format or content of the template data from what Microsoft Project expects to see, error messages will appear. Often, you can click Continue The Import With Error Messages, and Microsoft Project will make corrections to the data as it builds the new project file.

---

note Predecessors and links are not created when you import from this template, but the dates that are imported are accurate. The dates are constrained with a Finish No Earlier Than type of constraint. If you want to remove the constraint, add the links between tasks first, select all the tasks, and then remove the constraints using the Task Information button. Then, if necessary, reset the dates by constraining just one of them (usually the task that starts the earliest).

Exporting from Microsoft Project to Microsoft Excel

Suppose one of the managers in your company's accounting department wants to analyze your project information along with that of other projects. The department uses Excel for project data, so you'll need to export your Microsoft Project information to an Excel workbook.

When exporting from Microsoft Project, you will use an export template that is even more easily accessible than the template used by Excel. The procedure is as follows:

1 In Microsoft Project, click File, Save As.

2 In the Save As File Type list, click Microsoft Excel Workbook (*.xls).

3 Click the Save button.

newfeature!

4 On the Export Wizard Welcome page, click the Next button.

5 On the Data page, click Project Excel Template, and click the Finish button.

6 Your data is saved as a complete Excel workbook, keeping the data's original file name.

7 In Microsoft Excel, open the Excel file. It should be in the same directory as your project file.

8 Resize and reformat the date fields, if you want. Note the Smart Tags on some cells, and the formatting of durations like "53.d."

9 Click File, Save. You might be prompted that the file is in the Excel 5.0/95 format. Save your Excel file as the latest Excel format.

Troubleshooting

You have to convert the Excel version format

When you export Microsoft Project data to Microsoft Excel, the data is interpreted by Excel as an old Excel format. This does not cause a problem, but upon saving the Excel file, you will see a prompt stating that the file is in an older format, and asking if you want to update to the latest Excel format.

This message is somewhat confusing, since the data is not actually from an older version of Excel. It is advisable to always save to the latest format when prompted to do so.

Linking Between Microsoft Project and Microsoft Excel

The Project Excel templates are the most efficient means to integrate information between the two applications, but other methods exist. We've looked at Copy and Paste techniques, but one that deserves further explanation is pasting as a link. In this process, you use the Paste Special command to paste the object as a link.

The procedure is the same when you paste data from Microsoft Project. The information from the view you pasted will be updated in the Excel file to reflect any changes in your Microsoft Project file.

In both applications, when you open the file that contains links, you will see a dialog box prompting you to update the file using the link (see Figure 17-6).

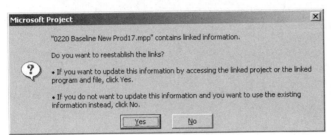

Figure 17-6. You will see this prompt when opening the project with links.

Linking documents can be an excellent means of maintaining comprehensive and current information.

---

tip   **Use linked documents with caution**

You might not have control over what happens to the document you've linked into Microsoft Project; it might become obsolete or erroneous, or even get deleted. The users of the file your project is linked to might not understand how their data will be processed by Microsoft Project, and they might cause a problem by formatting or positioning data incorrectly.

A linked Excel workbook can be placed in the Gantt Chart or in the Notes boxes within the Task, Resource, or Assignment Information forms (see Figure 17-7 on the next page). If you insert the link there, a Note indicator appears in the task sheet, but no text appears when you rest the mouse pointer over it. To create a note label, do the following:

1   In the Task Information dialog box, click the Notes tab.

2   Click inside the Notes text box.

3   Type in a brief label such as *Attachment* to remind yourself about the linked workbook being there.

4 Click OK. The label on the Note indicator will appear when you hover the mouse pointer over it.

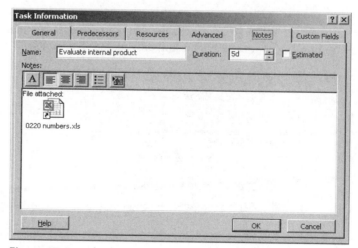

Figure 17-7. The linked worksheet icon is placed in the Task Information Notes box.

Integrating Microsoft Project with Microsoft Outlook

Microsoft Outlook has well-focused features for managing e-mail, tracking short-term tasks, and maintaining your calendar of appointments. If the people in your company use Outlook, you can take advantage of the integration capabilities between Outlook and Microsoft Project. Microsoft Project interfaces quickly and easily with Outlook to help you communicate with team members and stakeholders, and maximize your efficiency.

newfeature!

Importing Microsoft Outlook Tasks into Microsoft Project

One of the key features of Microsoft Outlook is the personal task list (see Figure 18-1).

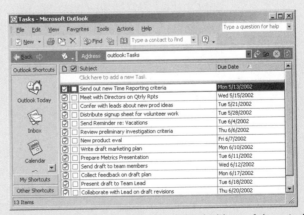

Figure 18-1. The Outlook Task list holds useful reminders of work to do.

463

Microsoft Project makes it easy for you to grab your Outlook Task list and add it to your project plan. To do this, follow these steps:

1 Open your project plan in Microsoft Project, and display the Gantt Chart (see Figure 18-2).

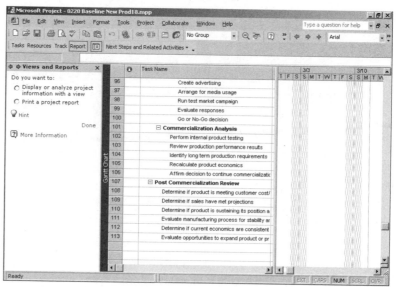

Figure 18-2. The Gantt Chart can be used to import Outlook Task lists.

2 Click Tools, Import Outlook Tasks. The Import Outlook Tasks dialog box appears.

3 Use the check boxes in the dialog box to select which tasks you want to import (see Figure 18-3), or click the Select All button. Usually, you will not want to import the items with the darker background and a hyphen to the left of their names; those are just labels. If you have tasks in the Outlook list that aren't relevant to your project plan, make sure those tasks are not selected. When you've selected the appropriate tasks, click OK.

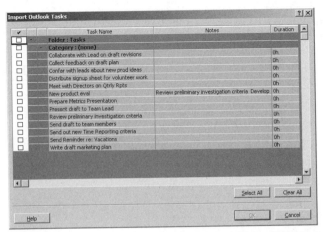

Figure 18-3. Select tasks to import into Microsoft Project.

4 The tasks you selected are appended to your Gantt chart. These new tasks retain any notes from Outlook, but their durations will read "1 day?" (see Figure 18-4). The question mark in the duration helps remind you to set the tasks' true durations. By default, tasks imported from Outlook display the project's start date, and don't have predecessors or resources.

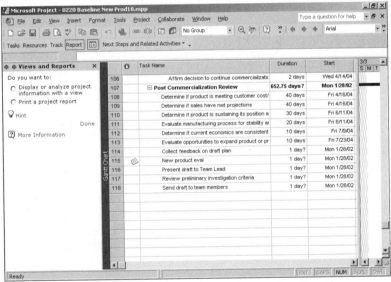

Figure 18-4. The imported Outlook Task list includes notes.

You can import Task lists from Outlook to a project with no tasks entered yet. If the tasks you will be tracking in Microsoft Project are already in Outlook, importing Outlook Task lists is a great timesaver.

> **caution**   If a task in Outlook is 100 percent complete, it will not be imported into Microsoft Project. Also, some Outlook tasks might be saved in multiple folders, so when importing be careful not to add the same task to the project more than once.

If you would like to import tasks from Microsoft Project into Outlook, use the Copy and Paste commands to move one task at a time.

newfeature!

Adding Microsoft Outlook Web Parts on the Digital Dashboard

A Microsoft *digital dashboard* is a preconfigured Web page designed to convey key information efficiently to a team or small organization. The digital dashboard's design groups and positions all key information logically and consistently; the information is accessed through hyperlinks. In addition, Microsoft digital dashboards can be enhanced and customized to suit the user's needs.

> For information about building a digital dashboard, refer to the Microsoft Project Software Development Kit (SDK) article "Building a Digital Dashboard." To access the SDK, go to *http://msdn.microsoft.com/project*, and then click the Microsoft Project 2002 SDK link.

The principal components that make up a digital dashboard are called *Web Parts*, and Outlook 2002 can be used to make them. Web Parts are self-contained, reusable components that consist of types of information varying from sophisticated dynamic Web page content embedded in a frame to concise text messages in HTML. You can include a document, such as a project plan, in a Web Part. Generally, most features and content that can be seen on a Web page can be included in a Web Part.

To use a digital dashboard in your organization, you'll need to have a computer that can access a folder on a server that's running either Microsoft Exchange 2000 Server with Service Pack 1 (SP-1) or Microsoft SharePoint Portal Server. Choose the folder that you'll use for your organization's digital dashboard, and label it.

To create a digital dashboard for use with Microsoft Outlook, you can use the Digital Dashboard Resource Kit (DDRK), version 2.2 that you can download from the Microsoft Developer Network site at *http://www.msdn.microsoft.com/downloads/*.

Depending on your needs, the system requirements for Digital Dashboards will vary. Consult with your system administrator and refer to the DDRK for guidance.

Troubleshooting

You're having problems building a Digital Dashboard

If you are trying to build a Digital Dashboard starting in Microsoft Outlook, you are supposed to be able to begin the process by locating a folder containing the Digital Dashboard template. Because this is a very new feature, and requires an exact setup, you might not be able to find this folder. If this occurs, consult your system administrator.

Because you can use virtually any type of Web page in a Web Part, you can place any Microsoft Project view, for example, the Task Sheet or Network Diagram, on your digital dashboard. Of course, your computer must meet the requirements for accessing a digital dashboard's server folder. To publish a Microsoft Project view as a Web Part, do the following:

1 In Microsoft Project, display the view you want to publish as a Web Part.

2 Click File, Save As Web Page.

3 In the Save As dialog box, locate and select your digital dashboard folder, and then click Save. At this point you might be prompted to log on to the server that contains your digital dashboard folder. After you've connected to the server, the Web File Properties form appears.

4 In the Name box, enter the name you want for this Web Part, for example, "March 15 NP Project."

5 In the Description box, enter a clear, short definition of this Web Part, for example, "Current project status as of March 15, 2002, from Microsoft Project."

6 Select Include This Web Part On The Dashboard.

7 Define the default position of the Web Part on the digital dashboard page, and click OK. Your Microsoft Project view is now a Web Part of your digital dashboard as you can see by clicking the name of the Web Part you created in step 4.

> **note** After it has been created, a digital dashboard and all its Web Parts can be opened from Outlook 2002 or by using a browser on the same server network and entering the URL of the digital dashboard in the Location box. Be sure to include the folder names for both the overall digital dashboard repository and your individual digital dashboard: for example, *http://widgets.com/orgdigidashbds/mydigidash/*.

Building Your Resource List with Microsoft Outlook

One technique that can save time and improve accuracy when you're building a project plan is to use the Microsoft Outlook Address Book or Contacts list as the source of the resource names list in Microsoft Project.

You can use the following procedure as long as you have a resource's name and e-mail address stored somewhere in Microsoft Outlook—either in the Address Book or your Contacts list:

1 In Microsoft Project, open a new, blank project.

2 Click View, Resource Sheet. Select the first blank cell in the Resource Name column.

3 Click Insert, New Resource From, Address Book. The Select Resources dialog box appears (see Figure 18-5). In the Show Names From The list, choose the name of the area where you've stored the contact information for the resources you want to add.

4 On the left side of the Select Resources dialog box, select the names of resources you want to add to your project. Hold down the Shift key to select multiple adjacent resources or the Ctrl key to select multiple nonadjacent resources. Click the Add button to copy the resources to your project.

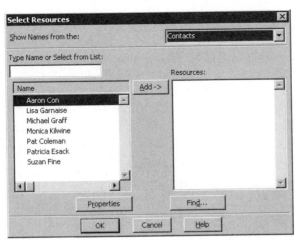

Figure 18-5. You can copy resources from your Outlook Contacts list as long as the contacts have e-mail addresses.

> **tip** It's unlikely that you would have a name stored in your Contacts list without an e-mail address, but if you do, that name won't be accessible using the preceding method. If you want to add a resource without an e-mail address, you can first open that person's contact information in Microsoft Outlook and add a dummy e-mail address, such as ?@?.com.

Collaborating with Team Members through E-Mail

If you use Microsoft Project Server, you can integrate it with Microsoft Outlook to collaborate with your project team members in multiple ways. If you choose to transmit information with Microsoft Project Server in this way, set up the connection as follows:

1. Open a Microsoft Project 2002 file.

2. Click Collaborate, Collaboration Options.

3. On the Collaborate tab, in the Collaborate Using list, click E-Mail Only. This will connect Microsoft Project Server with your Outlook e-mail system. Any changes, updates, task assignments, and messages regarding the project will be communicated through e-mail with Outlook.

> For more information about how to communicate project information using your e-mail system, see Chapter 20, "Collaborating Using E-Mail."

Chapter 18

Sending Updates Directly to Recipients

To send refined project updates directly to targeted recipients, follow these steps:

1 After working in your project plan and saving your changes, display the Gantt chart and select the tasks you have changed. Click File, Send To.

2 In the submenu, choose one of the four options: Mail Recipient (as Attachment), Mail Recipient (as Schedule Note), Routing Recipient, or Exchange Folder (see Figure 18-6). All four options utilize Outlook.

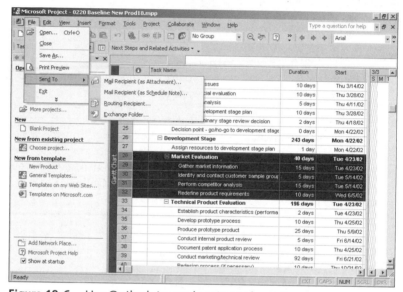

Figure 18-6. Use Outlook to send project information.

3 If you choose to send the update as a schedule note, the Send Schedule Note dialog box is displayed (see Figure 18-7). Choose the recipient of the e-mail message by selecting the appropriate check box.

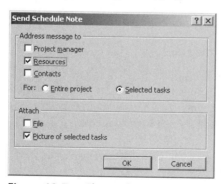

Figure 18-7. Choose how you want to send project information to Outlook recipients.

4 Click the Selected Tasks option, select the Picture Of Selected Tasks check box, and then click OK.

5 Your browser opens, connecting you to your e-mail system and automatically sending the specific note you've defined.

Project Management Practices:
Communications Management

Using Microsoft Outlook can be part of your project's communications management plan. For example, you can communicate with the project team with the Microsoft Project message handler, in which project status messages are reviewed and responded to in Microsoft Outlook. You can use Web Parts on a digital dashboard so that everyone can simultaneously see views published at specified intervals. And you can use the routing feature of Microsoft Project and Outlook to send the project plan for review on a quarterly basis among certain managing stakeholders.

However you decide to work with Microsoft Outlook, work with your system administrator to make sure the servers and permissions are set the way you need.

Part 7

Collaborating as a Team

Chapter 19

Evaluating Team Collaboration Solutions

Communication is a critical component of effective project management. Establishing an effective two-way information flow can prevent problems from occurring. A good communication plan for your project addresses all the essential aspects of keeping information flowing and describes the methods envisioned for enabling that flow. Microsoft Project 2002 has powerful features for collaboration within a project team and an enterprise.

Suppose you are beginning a project that brings a completely new product to market. Based on your experience and the nature of this project, you know there will be an even greater need than usual for team members to collaborate. As the project progresses, there will be new ideas, methods, and resources required. To keep all these unpredictable changes from bringing a halt to everything else, you'll need to have constant contact with the team members. Team members will also need continual communication among themselves. This kind of project will require intensive collaboration, and Microsoft Project 2002 can enable that in multiple ways.

The means of collaboration you choose will depend on many factors, including the availability of specific computer applications to team members, the network set up in your enterprise, and the comfort level of team members with certain tools. Sometimes a less sophisticated application can be more effective because it enables you to get everyone up to speed with a minimal learning curve.

Part 7: Collaborating as a Team

Collaborating with your project team by using Microsoft Project can be done in a variety of ways, but these are the three primary methods:

- E-mail system

- Microsoft Project Web Access with Microsoft Project Server

- Integration of project information, such as issues lists or Gantt Charts, with an intranet site using a digital dashboard, such as SharePoint Team Services

Each of these Microsoft Project-enabled team collaboration methods has its advantages. In general, e-mail systems are the easiest to understand and Microsoft Project Web Access is the most powerful.

Using E-Mail for Collaboration

Suppose you've decided to use e-mail as the collaboration solution for your new project. In addition to being able to attach project plans, views, and selected elements to your e-mail messages, you can easily send project information directly from your project plan using the Send To command.

newfeature! You can access and enable e-mail team collaboration through the new Collaborate menu. The e-mail collaboration method is designed for use with MAPI-based e-mail programs, so it supports many e-mail systems, including Microsoft Outlook. You can specify exactly who should be on your Microsoft Project e-mail list, what kinds of information and notifications are to be sent, and when certain types of project-related e-mail messages are to be sent to your team. You can also receive notifications, updates, and information from team members and then integrate that information directly into your project.

There are a wide variety of ways that e-mail collaboration can be customized to suit the way you want to use it. For example, you can use e-mail to exchange project information with some of your project team members, and use Microsoft Project Web Access for the rest. You can also automatically transmit project assignment information to only the resources involved through e-mail.

Working with e-mail collaboration, you can send assignments to resources, and they, in turn, can accept or decline them. Team members must reply to these messages. If a resource does not reply, that is regarded as an acceptance of an assignment. The response goes to your e-mail inbox, and you can reply, save, or integrate the information in the update message directly into your project plan.

Chapter 19: Evaluating Team Collaboration Solutions

If you want to make e-mail your primary means for project team collaboration and communication, you can set that as your default for all new projects. You can also specify a label to identify project-related e-mail messages so team members can easily identify project-related communications.

You can choose which assignment information fields you want to publish in your e-mail messages. You can also customize the order in which the fields are presented.

One of the essential pieces of information involved in tracking your project is the hours worked. You can set up a time-tracking system that can even track overtime hours separately.

For team members who use Outlook as their e-mail system, task assignments can automatically be incorporated into their Outlook task lists.

For special communications through e-mail, you can use the Send As command to designate your message routing. This is particularly helpful when you're transmitting project files by e-mail; you can carefully target just the key individuals who need to know that information.

> For more information about setting up e-mail to communicate project information, see Chapter 20, "Collaborating Using E-Mail."

newfeature! Using Microsoft Project Server and Web Access for Collaboration

The most powerful solution for collaborating and communicating with your project team is Microsoft Project Server and Web Access. These tools work directly with your project plan, and enable a broad range of instantaneous information exchange. Microsoft Project Server is the repository of the database, and Microsoft Project Web Access is the interface for the team members or other stakeholders who are reviewing or communicating project information. The purpose of this system is to make a seamless connection between your project plan and your team members. The data interchange is truly dynamic, and it is directly driven by your project plan.

With Microsoft Project Web Access, the team members can see all the relevant project information for their assignments and more. The Web site that is their Microsoft Project Web Access page (see Figure 19-1 on the next page) has an easy-to-navigate layout that makes receiving and sending project information efficient.

Part 7: Collaborating as a Team

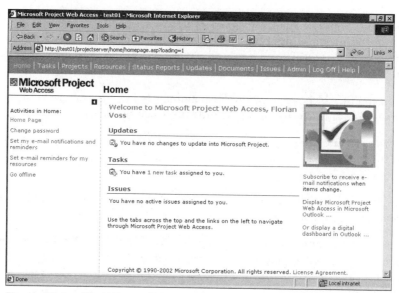

Figure 19-1. The Microsoft Project Web Access Home page is easy to navigate.

With Microsoft Project Web Access, team members can do the following:

- Update task information

- Change tasks

- Delegate assignments

- Add activities

- Make comments that will be incorporated into the project plan

Information updated or changed by team members is stored initially in the Microsoft Project Server database. As project manager, you can accept or reject changes. If you accept an update, you can incorporate it immediately into your project plan. The files in Microsoft Project Server are then updated to show that the change has been accepted, and team members who review the project plan through Microsoft Project Web Access can see the updates.

The Microsoft Project Web Access intranet site itself is very versatile and filled with project information. Team members can see different views of the project data, enter time reports, update tasks, see assignments, view summary project plans, send information to the project manager, see notifications of interest to them in particular, and more. Each Microsoft Project Web Access user can individually customize the site and make it more effective for the way he or she works.

As with the e-mail solution, you can send tasks to the assigned resources (see Figure 19-2).

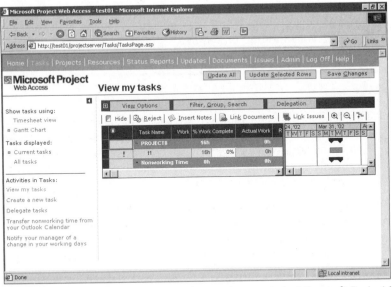

Figure 19-2. Team members see their assignments in Microsoft Project Web Access.

Any required updates can be sent in the same manner. Unlike the e-mail solution, however, the team member will see information beyond his or her own assignments and be able to interface directly with the project data. As the project manager, you still approve all changes to the project plan, but that approval step makes instant updates to both your project plan and the Microsoft Project Server database, which everyone using Microsoft Project Web Access can view. Although there are limitations on the levels of information that team members can change, resources still can view virtually the entire project and keep informed of the latest progress as it happens.

Microsoft Project Server and Web Access provide a vastly accelerated process for exchanging task assignments and updates for the project plan. Any changes you make in your project plan are incorporated into Microsoft Project Server. Send notifications regarding critical tasks or other items of interest, for example, and the Microsoft Project Web Access users can respond immediately not only with task updates, but with status reports in narrative text as well. As the project manager, you can also view data directly from Microsoft Project Server while you are working in your project plan. This enables you to accept changes and make alterations to the project plan based on those changes—all without leaving your project plan.

Setting up Microsoft Project Server and Web Access with Microsoft Project is not difficult, and there are aids within Microsoft Project to make the process clear and easy. Most of these settings are on the new Collaborate menu.

Also built into Microsoft Project 2002 is a Collaborate toolbar with convenient buttons for the most-used collaboration procedures.

InsideOut

You still have the flexibility of saving your work in Microsoft Project 2002 without publishing the changes to Microsoft Project Server. For example, you might have an extensively revised plan, involving new and altered links to numerous tasks, and you would need to spend a couple of days to confirm that the changes were valid before publishing them to Microsoft Project Server.

Whether or not you use a backup copy of your plan (which is a good practice for re-planning), the project plan would not be ready for dissemination to your team until your verification process was complete. You would simply save the plan without using any of the collaboration options until you've finished validating the revised plan.

For more information about working with Microsoft Project Server and Web Access to communicate project information, see Chapter 21, "Managing Your Team Using Microsoft Project Web Access." For setup guidelines, see Appendix A, "Installing Microsoft Project 2002."

Understanding Microsoft Project Server and Web Access

The relationship between Microsoft Project, Microsoft Project Server, and Microsoft Project Web Access is very effective. The key component is your Microsoft Project 2002 database. This is populated with data from your views, tables, and forms in the project plan. All the project information that you entered, as well as other data that works "behind the scenes," is found in the Microsoft Project database. When you set up your Microsoft Project Server and Web Access system, the Microsoft Project Server (itself holding a database) will extract some of the data from your Microsoft Project database tables. It converts and rearranges this information using XML. After this "translated" database is established, the Microsoft Project Web Access site is populated with information from the Microsoft Project Server. Both Microsoft Project Server and Web Access use XML to pass data, and Microsoft Project Web Access uses HTML to present that data and build interactive features. Other technologies, such as ActiveX controls, contribute to the capabilities of the Microsoft Project Web Access interface.

The transactional process is fairly simple. When you make a change to the data in your Microsoft Project database and publish it to Microsoft Project Server, the relevant data is parsed into XML formats, read into the Microsoft Project Server database, and transmitted to the Microsoft Project Web Access site where it is converted back from XML into HTML-rendered text. Not all the data from the project plan is used. The time span for all this data movement is very short; it will vary by network configuration and database size, but the process is efficient.

The Microsoft Project Web Access component is essentially a URL with unique capabilities to work specifically with Microsoft Project Server.

The Microsoft Project Server component is essentially a database and server custom-designed to convert data to and from your project plan and to interface with Microsoft Project Web Access using that data.

The Microsoft Project 2002 component is the origin of all data, and it interfaces with Microsoft Project Server through the Microsoft Project 2002 database.

For more information about the Microsoft Project database and the Microsoft Project Server database, and the two interact, see Chapter 32, "Working With Microsoft Project Data."

Together, these components help keep everyone on your project team simultaneously and instantaneously informed of the project's progress. It also enables two-way communication and valuable timely input from the team members who are fulfilling the project.

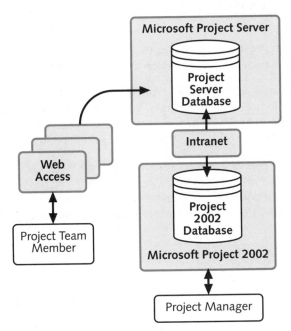

Both Microsoft Project Server and Web Access can be used with Microsoft Project 2002 Standard or Microsoft Project 2002 Professional for team collaboration and communication. If your enterprise is likely to need a larger-scale tool for monitoring numerous projects, Microsoft Project 2002 Professional is the appropriate application.

Creating Custom Collaboration Solutions

There are other possible means of creating a collaborative environment for your project team. Two that might be useful for your project are Microsoft SharePoint Team Services and a custom-built digital dashboard.

SharePoint Team Services is an effective and highly focused central Web site for exclusive use by a predefined group; in this case, your project team. The SharePoint team Web site is designed carefully to contain key information, including complete documents and lists of issues. SharePoint Team Services is designed to hold these information lists; virtually all you need to do to get the benefit of these brilliantly designed Web sites is connect to their URLs. If you are using Microsoft Project Server with SharePoint Team Services, you can take advantage of the Issues Tracking and Document Library features in Microsoft Project Web Access.

Then you could post your project files to the Documents area. You could use the site to coordinate your project team's Issues List with the larger organization's lists. If you're not using Microsoft Project Server, you can still establish a connection to an existing SharePoint team Web site and arrange for the required permissions to post and use documents.

If you create your own SharePoint team Web site, in addition to Issues and Documents, you use the wide range of categories of information that are supported on the page.

The SharePoint team Web sites are built on the foundation of Web Parts, which are reusable components that can hold a great variety of Web-capable information. You can make a Web Part with simple HTML text or with dynamic data contained in a frame. Another more elemental Web page built with Web Parts is a digital dashboard.

A digital dashboard is not as prefabricated as a SharePoint team Web page. A digital dashboard basically provides a place to put Web Parts. As such, it can be specifically focused on only one subject if you like. You could choose your project as that subject and build your own interactive digital dashboard to hold Web Parts consisting of the following:

- Project views
- A critical issues list

- Notice boards

- A calendar

- Task lists

- Rosters

- Charts

- Presentations

- Photos

If you can put an item in a Web page, it can go into a Web Part, and from there into a digital dashboard. You can use graphics, text, charts, tables, frames, dynamic page features, hyperlinks, and any other item that can be included in a Web page.

Deciding on the Right Solution for Your Team

With so many possible methods of project team collaboration, it's important for you to take time to analyze your project team's needs, preferences, and assets. The most powerful and effective collaboration solution is Microsoft Project Server and Web Access. But your team might not have the infrastructure or working style to make that a realistic choice for you.

First consider factors in your communications plan, such as:

- What are your highest-priority types of information?

- Who are the stakeholders and team members who need the most constant contact?

- How often and where will you communicate project plan changes?

Other factors to consider include:

- What type and size is your e-mail system?

- How familiar and comfortable are your team members with the Internet?

- Do your functional leads prefer to be (or have) a single point of contact?

- Do you have a skilled Web developer at your disposal?

- Will your executives want to see your team status communications?

- Do you have resources who work off-site or from home?

- What hardware and network resources do you have?

- Is your project information likely to be "time-critical"?

- How much time will team members have for communication each day?

The answers to these questions and an analysis of your communication plan will go a long way toward determining the ideal collaboration solution for your team. If time for communicating is scarce and the IT environment is adequate, consider Microsoft Project Server and Web Access.

If you have a Web-savvy department but Microsoft Project Server and Web Access aren't appropriate, consider a digital dashboard or SharePoint Team Services.

If you need to communicate often and can do so effectively with somewhat limited amounts of information, consider using the e-mail collaboration solution.

Chapter 20

Collaborating Using E-Mail

Suppose you've been chosen to manage a new product launch, from concept to market. You know from experience that new product projects require especially close collaboration and input from everybody on the team. You've selected the best resources to be your team for this project but some of them can't use Microsoft Project Server and Web Access to collaborate. With Microsoft Project, you can collaborate and keep project communication flowing freely by using e-mail.

E-mail can be a very effective communication medium; it is often the best collaboration solution for a project team. The benefits of using e-mail include:

Universality.   It's almost always installed and available. Your team members might use vastly differing software applications, but they all will usually be connected to an e-mail system.

Familiarity.   Team members already use and understand e-mail. All the team members will be comfortable using e-mail and they will require no training time.

Speed.   A message will be delivered moments after it is sent. The limitation is that e-mail isn't always read right away. As part of the planning process, you can set some expectations for e-mail use; opening and reading all project messages twice daily might be a reasonable requirement. You can make decisions and take action based on that expectation. For example, if you've sent a new assignment through e-mail and haven't received a rejection of it after a full business day, you can proceed on the understanding that it was accepted by the resource.

485

Flexibility. Distribution lists and attachments add to the range of capabilities. E-mail can transfer many types of information including text, attached documents, and dynamic HTML pages. Microsoft Project takes advantage of this flexibility through the predefined collaboration functions.

Accessibility. Team members can often send and receive e-mail from many locations.

Traceability. A written record will exist of project communications.

Integration with the Communications Plan. Organizations often use e-mail as an official means of communicating many types of information, so it's already integrated with team members' work habits.

Integration with Microsoft Project. Many features are built into Microsoft Project that enable fast, accurate two-way collaboration using e-mail.

Whether your e-mail system is set up through your organization's intranet or the Internet, you can use Microsoft Project to communicate project information with all team members through e-mail. Either way, you need to know how your e-mail setup might affect "outside" team members, such as vendors or contractors.

One often-overlooked benefit of using e-mail as your collaboration method is that it creates a written record of your project communications. This is very helpful when you need to trace the origins of ideas, tasks, and assignments. For example, you can trace the date that you made a new task assignment, and demonstrate that it was timely and avoided work delays. This written record can also contribute to establishing your "lessons learned" file after project completion.

You might have already alluded to using e-mail in your project's communication plan or even in the project scope document. Collaborating using Microsoft Project's unique e-mail capabilities is an excellent way to implement your plan.

The ability to collaborate using e-mail is designed into Microsoft Project. You don't need to leave your project file to use the e-mail collaboration features. This chapter details the e-mail collaboration features you can use to assign tasks, update projects, transmit documents, and send notifications.

The following are a few examples of e-mail collaboration:

- You are the project manager, and you've had to re-plan a portion of the project plan due to the loss of a piece of needed equipment. After the changes are made, you use the project e-mail collaboration solution to send new assignments to the resources who will be doing the work.

- You are a project team member, and you've just completed an important assignment ahead of schedule. You know this should allow other tasks to have an earlier start, though you might not know every other task affected. Using the project e-mail collaboration solution, you send your update to the project manager and it's reflected in the project plan immediately.

- You're a project team member, and you've just found out that you can use a slightly different method for one of your future tasks and thereby achieve cost and schedule savings. You use the e-mail collaboration solution to propose a task change for the project plan. Your message gets to the project manager and the change is implemented directly in the project plan as soon as the project manager accepts your message.

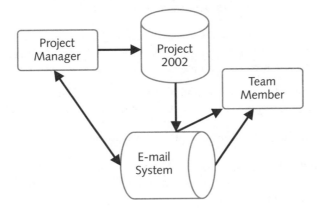

Setting Up and Administering E-Mail for Your Team

If you're a small group or company without a great deal of technical support at your disposal, you might need to set up and administer e-mail with Microsoft Project yourself. Otherwise, you can pass this task off to your system administrator.

Understanding System Requirements

The system requirements for enabling the team e-mail collaboration solution are as follows:

- The project manager must have Microsoft Project 2002 installed on his or her computer.

● A network must be in place that can be used to transmit e-mail messages. Most often in businesses, this is a *Local Area Network* (LAN).

● The e-mail system must be compliant with the *Messaging Application Programming Interface* (MAPI) and it must be a 32-bit system. Microsoft Outlook is an example of a MAPI-compliant system.

Setting Up E-Mail Collaboration

To set up your e-mail collaboration solution, you first need to ensure that the system you're using will support the system requirements. If Microsoft Outlook, Microsoft Exchange, or Microsoft Mail is being used on the system, you meet these requirements. For individual team members and the project manager, the setup entails the following:

1 Run the Files\Support\WGsetup\WGsetup.exe file from the Microsoft Project 2002 CD. This will install, among other files, the Workgroup Message Handler, which enables the preformatted messages in your e-mail system.

2 Confirm or establish the connection to the MAPI-compliant e-mail system. If needed, you can connect to the network drive using Windows Explorer.

You or your system administrator need to do the following:

1 Copy the entire WGsetup folder to the network drive. This is a network location that is accessible to all team members and has the MAPI-compliant 32-bit e-mail system.

2 From the WGsetup folder, open the WGsetup.exe file, and follow the instructions as prompted.

After the network is set up, you can use e-mail collaboration within Microsoft Project. If you haven't done so already, add the e-mail addresses for all the team members. To do this, follow these steps:

1 Click Collaborate, Collaboration Options. The Options dialog box appears with the Collaborate tab displayed.

2 In the Collaborate Using list, select E-Mail Only. If you get a warning message, close it. Click OK to close the Options dialog box.

3 Display the Resource Sheet.

Chapter 20: Collaborating Using E-Mail

4 Select the column to the left of where you want the Email Address column to be inserted.

5 Click Insert, Column. The Column Definition dialog box appears.

6 In the Field Name box, click Email Address, and then click OK (see Figure 20-1).

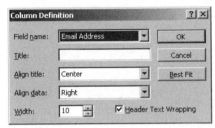

Figure 20-1. Choose Email Address in the Column Definition dialog box.

7 In the Resource Sheet, enter the resources' e-mail addresses in their corresponding Email Address fields (see Figure 20-2).

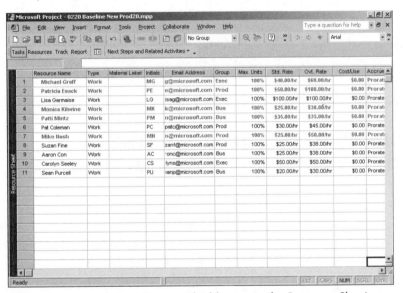

Figure 20-2. You can enter e-mail addresses in the Resource Sheet.

8 Click File, Save.

Entering E-Mail Addresses Automatically

If you haven't added resource names or other information yet, you can add resource names along with their e-mail addresses automatically. You can do this through the Address Book if you use Microsoft Outlook, or you can have your system set up for access to the Active Directory.

If you use Microsoft Outlook, enter resources and their e-mail addresses as follows:

1 Display the Resource Sheet.

2 Click Insert, New Resource From, Address Book. Your Outlook Address Book opens.

3 Select the names of the resource(s) you want to add to your project plan, and then click the Add button. When done, click OK.

If you use the Active Directory, enter resources and their e-mail addresses as follows:

1 Display the Resource Sheet.

2 Click Insert, New Resource From, Active Directory. Your Outlook Address Book opens.

3 Select the names of the resource(s) you want to add to your project, and then click the Add button. When done, click OK.

In either case, the selected resources are added to your project plan, along with their e-mail addresses.

Sending Assignments and Updates to Team Members

After entering all the e-mail addresses of the project resources, send each resource his or her assignments. This *publishing* of assignments is a primary function of e-mail collaboration. When you publish a task, you're sending the task details through e-mail to each assigned resource. The resources can reply to the assignment notice with an acceptance or rejection and add explanatory comments.

As you work through the project, you publish any tasks that have been added or changed so that team members always have the up-to-date assignment information they need.

You can also request task updates for assigned tasks, in which resources provide actual progress information such as number of hours worked or percent complete. For example, you might establish a weekly update schedule for your team members to send you e-mail progress reports with their hours worked per task. You can then incorporate this information into the project plan to facilitate your project tracking and monitoring efforts.

For more information about entering actual progress information on tasks, see "Updating Task Progress" on page 291.

Troubleshooting

When publishing e-mail tasks, you get a message about Microsoft Project Server

In the course of publishing tasks to your team members, you might see a message stating, "After publishing to Microsoft Project Server, your project will be saved. Do you want to proceed?" If you see this message, click OK.

This message applies only to publishing tasks to team members using Microsoft Project Web Access. However, this message might appear when you publish assignments through e-mail.

Sending Assignments to Team Members

To send all task information to the assigned resources, follow these steps:

1 Click Collaborate, Publish, New And Changed Assignments.

2 The Publish New And Changed Assignments dialog box appears (see Figure 20-3).

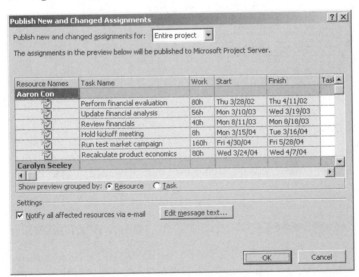

Figure 20-3. Send all project assignments to their assigned resources.

3 In the Publish New And Changed Assignments For list, click Entire Project.

4 Under the task table, select the Resource option next to Show Preview Grouped By.

5 Be sure that the Notify All Affected Resources Via E-Mail check box is selected.

6 If you want to revise the introductory note that will be sent with all the assignments, click the Edit Message Text button. Because this is the initial assignment publication, some explanation of the process is appropriate. Click OK. If you're not already connected to the e-mail network, your browser will automatically launch. If you are actively set up on your e-mail network, you will receive a confirmation message.

After your messages are sent, the Gantt Chart will show Unconfirmed indicators (see Figure 20-4) next to each task that was assigned through e-mail. These indicate that an assignment has been published for that task but that you have not yet received a response.

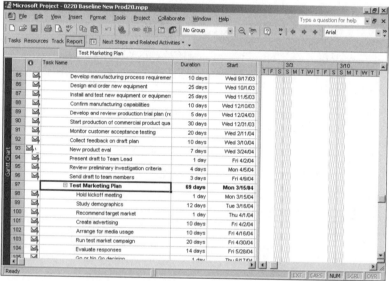

Figure 20-4. Unconfirmed indicators (envelopes with question marks) designate assignments that have been sent through e-mail, but that have not yet been acknowledged by the resource.

Receiving Acknowledgments from Team Members

When a team member responds to an assignment, you receive an e-mail message from the team member in your e-mail inbox. The subject line indicates your published Microsoft Project information—either new assignments or all information. Depending on the e-mail program you use, the information might be contained in a special e-mail form or in an attachment (see Figure 20-5).

Chapter 20: Collaborating Using E-Mail

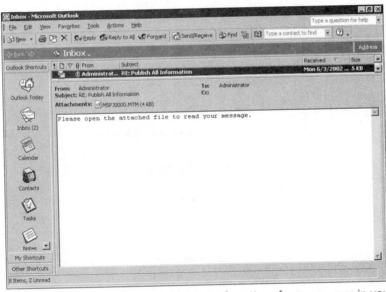

Figure 20-5. You receive assignment confirmations from resources in your e-mail inbox.

To review and incorporate your team members' responses to their assignments, follow these steps:

1 If necessary, open the e-mail attachment. The team member's response to your assignment appears (see Figure 20-6).

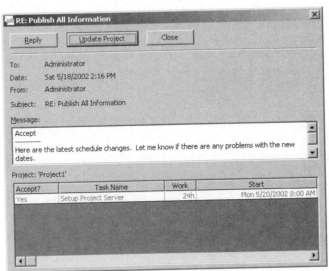

Figure 20-6. The message indicates whether the resources accepts or declines the assignment.

2 If you want to incorporate the team member's response into your project plan, click the Update Project button.

In your project plan, the Unconfirmed indicator for the assignment disappears.

> **note** You receive messages regarding task updates and progress information from team members in the same way.

Sending Task Updates to Team Members

If you add new tasks or change assigned tasks in any way, you need to publish those specific tasks to the assigned resources. Follow these steps to publish selected tasks to the assigned resources:

1 On the Gantt Chart or other task sheet, click the tasks you want to publish (see Figure 20-7).

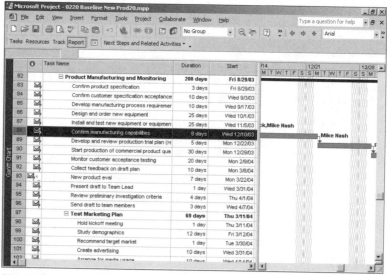

Figure 20-7. Click the task you want to send to the assigned resources.

2 Click Collaborate, Publish, New And Changed Assignments. If you see a message regarding Microsoft Project Server, just click OK.

3 The Publish New And Changed Assignments dialog box appears (see Figure 20-8). Confirm your task selections. Since you chose specific tasks, Selected Items is the default selection in the Publish New And Changed Assignments For list. Confirm your chosen assignments, and then click OK. If you're not already connected to the e-mail network, your browser will launch.

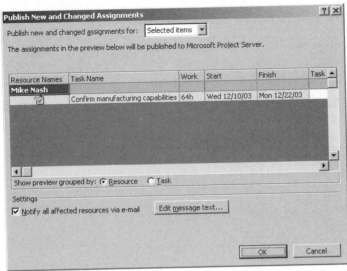

Figure 20-8. Use the Publish New and Changed Assignments dialog box to confirm and send assignments to the resources.

---

tip   **The Unconfirmed indicator**

If you publish a change to an assignment that has been sent but not responded to, the Unconfirmed indicator remains unchanged. If the assignment change has been responded to before the current change, the Unconfirmed indicator will be displayed until the resource has responded to the current change.

Requesting Progress Information

You can quickly send an e-mail to resources requesting information about an assignment. To do this, follow these steps:

1   In your project plan, display the Gantt Chart or another task view.

2   Select the tasks for which you want progress information.

To select adjacent tasks, drag across them. To select nonadjacent tasks, click the first task, hold down the Ctrl key, and then click all the other tasks you want to select.

3   Click Collaborate, Request Progress Information.

4   In the message that appears, click OK.

---

tip   You can also quickly request project information by right-clicking a selected task's name, clicking Request Progress Information, and then clicking OK.

Publishing Complete Project Information

Another capability of e-mail collaboration is publishing all the project information. This would be most useful at the initial stages of the plan or whenever there is a change to the baseline that should be understood by all the team members.

To publish all information, open your project plan. Click Collaborate, Publish, All Information. The project plan is e-mailed to all resources, and a confirmation message appears (see Figure 20-9).

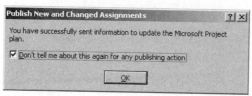

Figure 20-9. A confirmation message indicates that you have successfully sent all project information.

Resending Task Assignments

Occasionally, it might be necessary to republish task assignments to the team members. You might want to do this as an extra reminder, to confirm crucial tasks about to be performed, or because a resource lost the original assignment e-mail. To republish assignments, follow this sequence:

1 In the Gantt Chart or other task sheet, select the tasks you want to republish.

2 Click Collaborate, Publish, Republish Assignments.

3 If the Microsoft Project Server message appears, click OK. The Republish Assignments dialog box appears.

4 In the Publish New And Changed Assignments For box, click Selected Items.

5 Your browser launches if necessary, and the assignment changes are sent through e-mail to the resources assigned to the selected tasks.

Receiving Assignments from the Project Manager

> **note** This section describes the process of working with e-mail collaboration messages received from the project manager. Team members should read this section.

As the member of a project team, you can use e-mail to exchange information about your tasks and current status with your project manager. With special e-mail messages from Microsoft Project, you obtain fast notification of changes regarding your tasks. Just as quickly, you can send assignment and status updates back to the project manager.

Receiving and Responding to Assignments

You receive new or changed assignment messages in your e-mail inbox. The subject box of these special e-mails contains a brief description of the assignment action (see Figure 20-10). This lets you know that you have important project information to open. Depending on which e-mail application you're using, the assignment e-mail might show the assignment form directly, or it might include an attachment containing the assignment form.

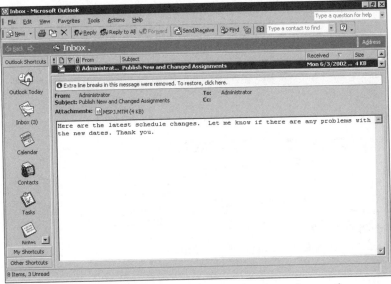

Figure 20-10. An assignment notification sent through e-mail.

If there is not an attachment, the e-mail form itself will contain preformatted features enabling quick and direct communication back to the project manager. To read and respond to a Microsoft Project e-mail message, do the following:

1 Double-click the e-mail message to open it. A special e-mail form generated by Microsoft Project appears (see Figure 20-11 on the next page).

Chapter 20

Part 7: Collaborating as a Team

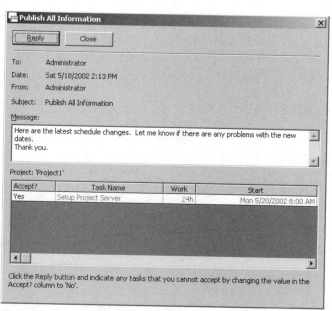

Figure 20-11. Use this special e-mail form to quickly acknowledge your assignments.

2 Click Reply. The Reply form opens (see Figure 20-12).

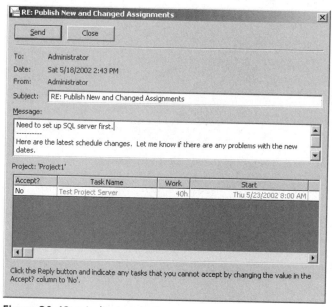

Figure 20-12. Indicate whether you accept or decline the assignment, and add any comments as necessary.

3 In the Accept? field, keep the default Yes to accept the assignment, or double-click on the word Yes to change it to No if you decline the assignment.

4 If necessary, enter a comment in the Message box.

5 Click the Send button. The message is sent to the project manager's e-mail inbox.

You might receive this message when the project manager sends the initial set of assignments to you. You might also receive it when the project manager adds one or two new assignments, or when there's been a change to assignments you're already working on.

> **tip** **Add or update tasks in your Outlook Task list**
>
> If you are using Microsoft Outlook, you can add or update the tasks in your Outlook task list. Click the Update Task List button in the Microsoft Project e-mail form.

Providing Assignment Status Updates

Throughout the project, you will need to communicate your current progress on tasks with the project manager. The project manager sends you a status request e-mail message, to which you can respond as follows:

1 In your e-mail program, double-click the status request message.

2 Click the Reply button.

3 In the appropriate fields, enter the information as applicable to your individual assignments.

Depending on how the project manager has customized the status request form, you might be asked to provide percent complete, hours worked, actual start and finish dates, and so on.

4 Enter any comments you want in the Message box.

5 Click the Send button.

Exchanging Project Information Using E-Mail

In addition to exchanging specific assignment and status information through your e-mail system, you can also use e-mail to send information to team members, stakeholders, and other interested parties.

Sending an Entire Project File with E-Mail

You can quickly send an entire file to selected recipients directly from within your project file. To do this, follow these steps:

1 Click File, Send To, Mail Recipient (As Attachment).

2 If not already running, your e-mail application is launched, opening the e-mail message form with your project file already attached and the name of the project in the Subject field.

3 Using the usual procedures appropriate for your e-mail system, add the e-mail addresses of the recipients and any comments.

4 Click the Send button. The message with the entire project file attached will be sent to the specified recipients.

Routing a Project File

Sometimes you need specific information from certain individuals regarding the project. Maybe one team member is developing the task list, someone else is adding the resources, and someone else is assigning those resources to tasks. Or perhaps you want various leads to update progress on their segments of the project. One very effective way to give a comprehensive picture of your work is to *route* your project plan through e-mail to a list of individuals. These recipients will get your e-mail message either one person at a time or all at once, at your choice. To do this, follow these steps:

1 In Microsoft Project, click File, Send To, Routing Recipient. The Routing Slip dialog box appears (see Figure 20-13).

2 To enter the names of the individuals you want to be on the project's distribution list, click the Address button. The Address Book dialog box appears (see Figure 20-14).

Chapter 20: Collaborating Using E-Mail

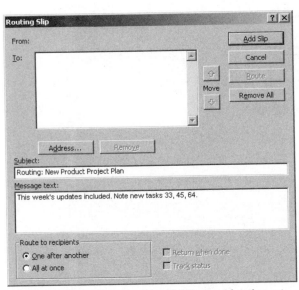

Figure 20-13. Add the e-mail addresses for those to whom you want to route the project.

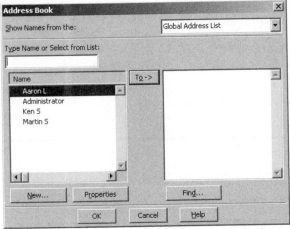

Figure 20-14. Use your e-mail system's address book to help you compile your routing distribution list.

3 Click names in the left window, and then click the To button to specify your routing recipients (see Figure 20-15 on the next page).

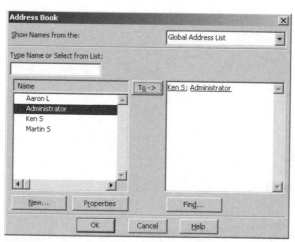

Figure 20-15. Select the routing recipients you want.

4 If you're routing the project one recipient at a time, designate the order of recipients by rearranging their names on the list using the Move buttons.

5 In the Subject field, change the subject if you want.

6 In the Message Text box, enter any comments or instructions to accompany the attached project file.

7 Under Route To Recipients, accept the One After Another option (the default) or the select the All At Once option.

8 Click the Route button. The message with the project file is routed to your designated recipients through e-mail.

InsideOut

The routing function is enabled for Microsoft Outlook and Exchange Server, but does not work with other e-mail applications.

For more information about how Microsoft Project works specifically with Microsoft Outlook, see Chapter 18, "Integrating Microsoft Project with Microsoft Outlook."

There are more optional features available when you're using a Routing Slip. Notification of routing is a useful capability. If you have chosen to route your e-mail message to one recipient after another, you can opt to receive notification after every new routing of the message takes place. This helps you track where the message and the project file are every step of the way. Of course, routing to recipients one after the other is time-consuming and not practical for urgent information. For review and evaluation purposes, however, sequential routing is ideal. Each recipient can add comments

Chapter 20

to the message and make changes to the project file before sending it along. As the project manager and the originator of the message and the file, you will want to see the results of these evaluations, and by using a Routing Slip, you can have the e-mail returned to you when it's done moving through its route.

If the project file is being routed to one person after another, each recipient opens the project file and reviews or adds the information as requested. The recipient moves it along to the next designated recipient by clicking File, Send To, Next Routing Recipient, and OK in the Routing Slip dialog box.

Sending Schedule Notes from Microsoft Project

You might need to transmit the project file to a specific group other than your routing list, or you might want to send a selected portion of the project plan to certain resources. These requirements are handled best by using the Schedule Note e-mail feature in Microsoft Project.

The best uses for the Schedule Note feature are when you have a small group of tasks you would like to show to specific resources and when you would like to send a reminder about a select group of tasks to all resources on the project. For example, if you wanted to draw attention to a critical path, sending a Schedule Note would be an effective and convenient method of doing so.

To send a Schedule Note, do the following:

1 Choose File, Send To, Mail Recipient (As Schedule Note).

2 The Send Schedule Note dialog box appears (see Figure 20-16). Select the check boxes for the recipients, and specify the attachment. Click OK.

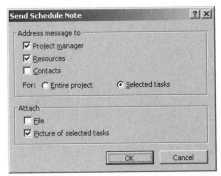

Figure 20-16. You can transmit a selected update with a Schedule Note.

3 If you are using Microsoft Outlook, the e-mail message form appears with address information filled in and the title bar reflecting the name of the project file. The specified attachment is included. You can add comments, fill in the Subject line, revise the addressees, or simply click Send and transmit your schedule note.

4 If you are not using Microsoft Outlook, after step 3, your Web browser launches (if necessary), and you can use the appropriate methods for sending e-mail with attachments.

> **note** The recipients of schedule notes must be identified in your project plan's Resource Sheet together with their e-mail addresses.

Sending the Project File to an Exchange Folder

You can send your project file to one of your Microsoft Exchange or Outlook folders. This can be useful if you would like to organize, categorize, or sort your file along with other files in your Exchange folder. It also provides you with another means of accessing the project file: through Outlook. To send the file to an Exchange folder, do the following:

1 Click File, Send To, Exchange Folder.

The Send To Exchange Folder dialog box appears, displaying the folders available to you, including Calendar, Inbox, Notes, Contacts, Tasks.

2 Click the folder to which you'd like to send the project file.

3 Click OK. Your project file is copied into the selected folder.

> **note** You can also create a new folder from the Send To Exchange Folder dialog box. This is helpful when you want to organize your project files in a specially designated folder.

Chapter 21

new feature!
Managing Your Team Using Microsoft Project Web Access

As a project manager, one of your most important duties is to facilitate communication. Your project communications plan should include the methods to be used, the different media, the intended audiences, the frequency, and the purposes for communicating. Of all these communication requirements, perhaps the most crucial is internal project team collaboration. In all projects, the team members need to know what is going on and how they are progressing.

For team collaboration using Microsoft Project, the most robust solution is to use Microsoft Project Server and Web Access. This flexible and versatile tool enables a wide range of information sharing between project team members and you, the project manager. The content and the format of the information are expansive and can be customized to fit your project team's needs ideally. You assign and update tasks and send project information to team members and selected project stakeholders. The team members can view their assignments and project information, and send updates, task changes, and status information back to you.

> **note** In Microsoft Project 2002, the Microsoft Project Server and Web Access solution is the next generation of Microsoft Project Central, which you might have used with Microsoft Project 2000.

505

In addition to these functions, Microsoft Project Server with Web Access enables you to work with project issues, project reports, graphic views, and specialized content available to team members who are using Microsoft Project Web Access. Microsoft Project Web Access can also be integrated with SharePoint Team Services for additional functionality. With Microsoft Project Server and Web Access, your team members and stakeholders can provide updates to multiple managers, view the entire project, customize their Microsoft Project Web Access information display, sort, filter, and group project information, and more.

This chapter provides an overview of Microsoft Project Server and Web Access, the system administrator's role, and the functions used by the project manager.

For information about functions used by team members and other stakeholders using Microsoft Project Web Access, see Chapter 22, "Communicating Information Using Microsoft Project Web Access." For guidelines for setting up Microsoft Project Server and Web Access, see Appendix A, "Installing Microsoft Project 2002."

Understanding Microsoft Project Server and Web Access

The primary purpose of Microsoft Project Server and Web Access is to enable instant and rich information exchange from the project plan to the team members, stakeholders, and other interested parties. As such, the Microsoft Project Server side of the implementation becomes the crucial nexus of the communication flow. The Microsoft Project Server receives data from Microsoft Project 2002 as specified by the project manager, reformats the data, and transmits it to designated Microsoft Project Web Access users, who can then view the information in their preferred styles. In turn, Microsoft Project Web Access users can send information as well as view it.

In addition, if the team members are using Microsoft Outlook accounts, the project manager and the team members can make automated changes to their Outlook Task Lists and other folders. The complete Microsoft Project Web Access team is communicating with an integrated system comprised of Microsoft Project 2002, Microsoft Project Server, Microsoft Project Web Access, and optionally, the Microsoft Outlook e-mail system and SharePoint Team Services.

The amount of information that can be shared, the variety of formats in which it can be sent, the speed of transmittal, and the connectivity of all team members are immense. The intent of Microsoft Project Server and Web Access is to increase the level of shared knowledge within a project team, and to do this in a manner that makes collaboration easy and quick. The vast amounts of information involved could require complicated methods to retrieve and respond to it all. Microsoft Project Server and Web Access expand the knowledge base available while shrinking the difficulty of sharing it.

Either Microsoft Project 2002 Standard or Professional can be used with Microsoft Project Server and Web Access. The information for each project file is stored in the project database, and that database is the source of the information that is sent to Microsoft Project Server. The data tables from Microsoft Project 2002 are converted and reorganized by Microsoft Project Server into its own data tables.

In Microsoft Project Server, the data is transformed to XML format, which in turn facilitates very flexible usage within Microsoft Project Web Access, the Web-based client. From Microsoft Project Server, data is selectively transmitted to specified Microsoft Project Web Access users (see the diagram) and is displayed in various formats within the Microsoft Project Web Access sites.

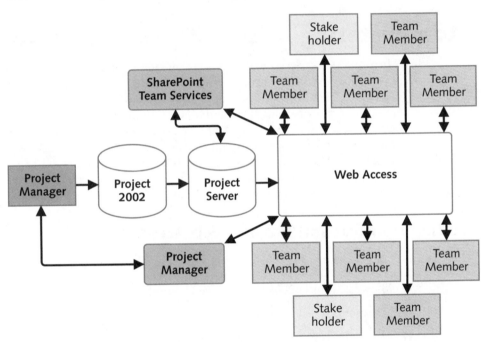

Microsoft Project Web Access is actually an intranet Web site with features and capabilities customized for each user. The chief feature is the project data in many representations, but there are also sections of the Microsoft Project Web Access pages for issues, documents, notices, reminders, password maintenance, and more. From within the Microsoft Project Web Access site, a user can change views, delegate tasks, send status reports, report time, view entire projects, send messages, make notifications, integrate information with Outlook, and more.

From Microsoft Project Web Access, the data is sent back to the Microsoft Project Server, which processes it as XML, and then converts and transmits the information to the Microsoft Project 2002 database.

The project manager has immediate access to this new data and can choose to automatically update the project plan with it or view it without making changes to the project plan. Other custom options for handling incoming data are also available.

This process, though cyclical, does not necessarily have to start with the project manager. Although the project manager must initially publish the project and assignments, team members and stakeholders can send information, updates, and status reports on their own initiative. User privileges for information access and processing are set by the project system administrator working with the project manager. The various types of privileges can be set for all users at once or customized for each user according to his or her individual responsibilities.

Administering Microsoft Project Server

In a Microsoft Project Server and Web Access implementation, a project system administrator is required. While the project manager can perform this role, it's more effective to assign a specialist to set up and administer Microsoft Project Server. Establishing system settings, permissions, roles, and other options is a crucial action for getting the best performance for your team's unique needs. After system setup is complete, Microsoft Project Server system administration requires special skills for providing the highest level of service and performance to the project team. Whenever a team member or the project manager needs to change options, permissions, and roles within the system, the change can be made by the project system administrator.

Setting Up Microsoft Project Web Access

The components of a Microsoft Project Web Access setup are as follows:

- Microsoft Project 2002 Standard or Microsoft Project 2002 Professional
- Microsoft Project Server
- Microsoft Project Web Access client

First Microsoft Project is installed on the project manager's computer. Then the project system administrator sets up the Microsoft Project Server, either on the same computer or on one to which the project manager has access. The first link in the systematic communication chain is from the Microsoft Project 2002 application database to the Microsoft Project Server database, so the project manager will need to be connected with the computer running the Microsoft Project Server.

> **note** Guidelines for setting up Microsoft Project Server can be found in Appendix A, "Installing Microsoft Project 2002."

When Microsoft Project Server is installed, it's tested with the Microsoft Project 2002 application to check out the settings. Then the project system administrator sets up and configures the Microsoft Project Web Access intranet site that connects with Microsoft Project Server. The server hosting the Microsoft Project Web Access site must be running with Internet Information Server (IIS) to process the intranet data.

After these installations and tests are successful, the project system administrator can use Microsoft Project Server to perform all the remaining elements of setting up the team's system. To begin this setup process, the project system administrator does the following:

1 On the Windows taskbar, click Start.

2 Point to Programs, point to the Microsoft Project Server, and then click Configure Microsoft Project Server. The Administration Overview page in Microsoft Project Server appears. If a different page appears, click the Admin menu at the top of the page.

Confer with your project system administrator about the roles, requirements, and permissions you want to assign to your individual team members and any other users of the Microsoft Project Web Access site. Specify which groups you'll be using and inform the project system administrator of any special options you want individual users to have for their Microsoft Project Web Access accounts. To set up the project team's accounts on the system, do the following:

1 In the left pane of the Microsoft Project Web Access window, click the Manage Users And Groups link. The Users page appears (see Figure 21-1 on the next page).

Part 7: Collaborating as a Team

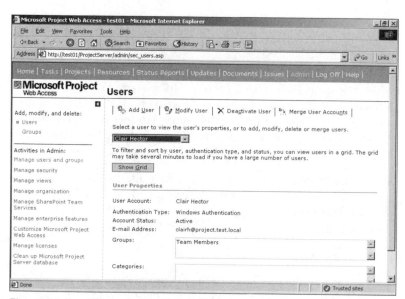

Figure 21-1. The project system administrator sets up team member accounts in Microsoft Project Server.

2 Click Add User. The Add User page appears (see Figure 21-2).

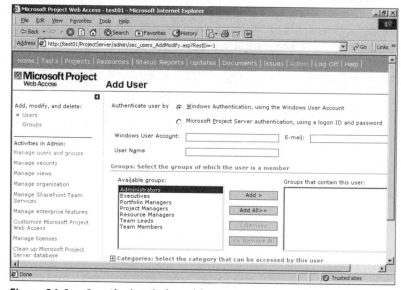

Figure 21-2. Specify details for adding a user to Project Server.

3 Choose the authentication method for the user: Windows User authentication or Microsoft Project Server authentication.

Chapter 21: Managing Your Team Using Microsoft Project Web Access

---

tip Add a new group

To add a group, on the Administration Overview page, click Manage Users And Groups. The Users page appears. In the left pane, under Add, Modify And Delete, click the Groups link. Then on the Groups page (see Figure 21-3), click Add Group. The Add Group page appears (see Figure 21-4).

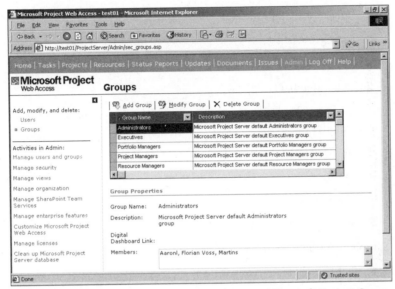

Figure 21-3. Decide which groups need to use Microsoft Project Server.

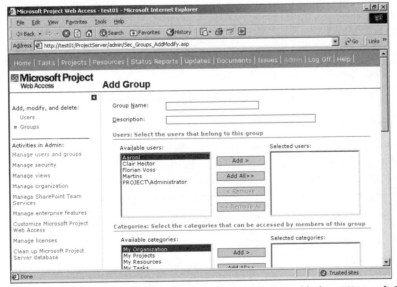

Figure 21-4. Specify the details of the groups to be added to Microsoft Project Server.

Chapter 21

4 Select the group(s) to which the user will be assigned as a member. The predefined choices are:

- Administrators

- Executives

- Portfolio Managers

- Project Managers

- Resource Managers

- Team Leads

- Team Members

5 Choose which categories of data will be available for access by this user. The categories are:

- My Organization

- My Tasks

- My Projects

- My Resources

6 Set the permissions for this user. Allow or deny permission to do the following:

- Edit Enterprise Resource Data

- Open Project

- Save Project

- See Enterprise Resource Data

- See Projects In Project Center

- See Projects In Project Views

- See Resource Associations In Assignment Views

- View Documents And Issues

note You can quickly set permissions using predetermined templates provided on this page. They allow permissions generally appropriate to the user's role.

7 Set the user's global permissions, manually or with a template, by role.

8 Click Save Changes.

The project system administrator should then create or modify security categories, templates, and authentications. To do this, click the Manage Security link in the left pane of the Administrative Overview page.

Setting Microsoft Project Web Access Options

Your project system administrator can specify and customize the views that are available in Microsoft Project Web Access. As part of this specification, the administrator can designate view types:

- Project view
- Project Center view
- Assignment view
- Resource Center view

By using the Manage Organization functions, the administrator can decide which features of Microsoft Project Web Access to make available to the users. The features include:

- Collaboration
- Enterprise Portfolio Management
- Status Reports
- Tasks
- To-Do List
- Transactions
- Views

Also within the Manage Organization function, the administrator can add, change, or delete menus that will be seen by the Microsoft Project Web Access users.

Setting Up SharePoint Team Services Connections

The project system administrator sets up the connections to enable team members to use SharePoint Team Services to work with project-related documents and issues. The administrator does this by building and addressing subwebs to contain specified information for inclusion in SharePoint Team Services, and by giving team members automatic access to those subwebs.

By integrating Microsoft Project Server and Web Access with SharePoint Team Services, you and your project team can post and view documents and issues that are hosted on the SharePoint server. The link is from Microsoft Project Web Access, and adds another dimension for document management and integrated team communication.

To enable this feature, the project system administrator logs on to Microsoft Project Server to access the Administrative Overview page. Do the following to set up SharePoint Team Services:

1 In the left pane, click the Manage SharePoint Team Services link.

2 On the Connect To Servers page, click Add Server, and type in the proper information for the IIS server. When finished, save the settings, and your setup appears (see Figure 21-5).

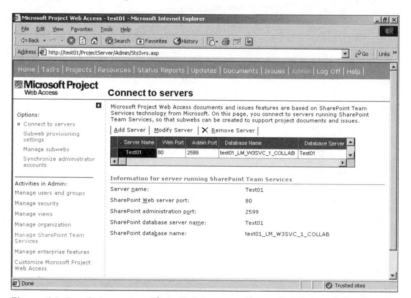

Figure 21-5. Set up your SharePoint access through Microsoft Project Server.

Setting Up Advanced Options

Through the Administrative Overview page, the project system administrator can also do the following tasks:

- Manage enterprise features, such as resource and project analysis, for users of Microsoft Project Professional with the enterprise features.

- Customize Microsoft Project Web Access formats, categories, and content.

- Manage the Client Access Licenses.

- Clean up the Microsoft Project Server database.

These options and settings are all accessed from the links in the left pane of the Administrative Overview page.

> **note** Setup guidelines for Microsoft Project Server and Web Access are found in Appendix A, "Installing Microsoft Project 2002." For comprehensive step-by-step installation instructions, refer to Pjsvr10.chm, which can be found on the Microsoft Project Server CD or the installation point for Microsoft Project Server.

Assigning Tasks

After Microsoft Project Server and Web Access are set up, you, as project manager, can now populate your team members' Microsoft Project Web Access sites with their individual assignment information, as well as views of overall project information.

First confirm that your collaboration option in Microsoft Project is set for using Microsoft Project Server and Web Access, as follows:

1 Microsoft Project, click Collaborate, Collaboration Options. The Options dialog box appears with the Collaborate tab displayed (see Figure 21-6).

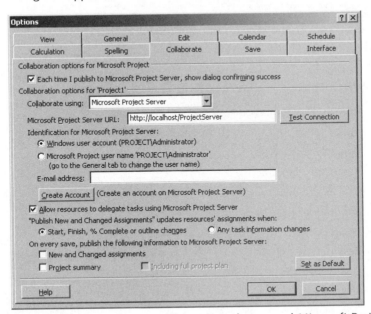

Figure 21-6. Specify your collaboration choices and Microsoft Project Server location.

2 Under Collaboration Options for <Project Name>, click Microsoft Project Server in the Collaborate Using list.

Chapter 21

3 In the Microsoft Project Server URL box, type the URL of your Microsoft Project Server.

4 Click the Test Connection button. After the test runs properly, a success message appears.

5 If necessary, establish an account with your user name and password. To do this, click the Create Account button and enter your account information.

Sending Assignments to Team Members

You begin by sending, or *publishing*, all the assignments to all your resources. After the initial transmittal, you'll only need to publish new and changed assignments as they occur.

The Collaborate Toolbar

Microsoft Project 2002 includes a new Collaborate toolbar (see Figure 21-7), which includes buttons as shortcuts to various team collaboration functions.

Figure 21-7. Use the new Collaborate toolbar to quickly access various team collaboration functions.

If the Collaborate toolbar is not already showing, display it by clicking View, Toolbars, Collaborate. The buttons, from left to right, are as follows:

- Publish All Information
- Publish New And Changed Assignments
- Publish Project Plan
- Republish Assignments
- Update Project Progress
- Request Progress Information
- Project Center
- Resource Center
- Portfolio Analyzer
- Portfolio Modeler
- Documents
- Issues

Chapter 21: Managing Your Team Using Microsoft Project Web Access

To send the initial set of assignments, do the following:

1 Display the Gantt Chart or another task sheet.

2 Click the Select All box at the upper-left corner of the sheet, above the row 1 heading.

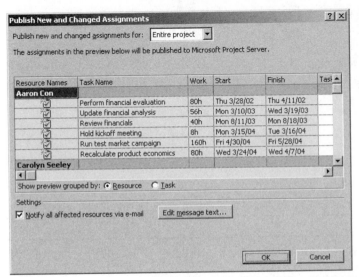

Publish New And Changed Assignments

3 Click Collaborate, Publish, New and Changed Assignments. Alternatively, you can click Publish New And Changed Assignments on the Collaborate toolbar. Because this is the first publication, every assignment is new.

4 In the message box asking if you want to proceed after the project is saved, click OK. The Publish Assignments dialog box appears (see Figure 21-8).

Figure 21-8. You can preview the assignments you are publishing.

5 In the Publish New And Changed Assignments For list, click Entire Project.

6 If you want to provide more information or edit your e-mail notification statement, click Edit Message Text, and make the changes you want.

Part 7: Collaborating as a Team

---

tip **Group assignments by task**

The Publish Assignments dialog box displays the assignments grouped by resources. You can group assignments by tasks instead, if you prefer. In the Show Preview Grouped By area, click Task (see Figure 21-9).

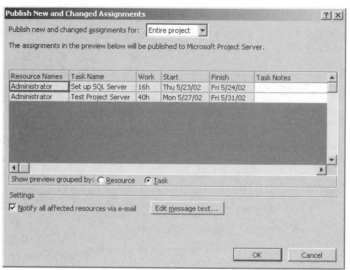

Figure 21-9. You can group your assignments by task in the Publish New And Changed Assignments screen.

---

tip **Send notification e-mail to team members**

You can send an e-mail notice to team members when new assignments are published. In the Publish New And Changed Assignments dialog box, select the Notify All Affected Resources Via E-Mail check box. You'll want to select this check box if every resource assigned in the project has a valid e-mail address entered your project plan.

If any team members do not have access to e-mail, clear this check box. Regardless of whether team members receive an e-mail notification, the assignments will still be published to Microsoft Project Web Access.

Accepting Assignment Confirmations

After you publish the new assignments, your team members can view them on their Microsoft Project Web Access sites. When they accept or reject their new assignments, Microsoft Project Server and the project plan are updated.

In the Indicators column of the project plan, the icon for published assignments changes from the red exclamation point to the check mark, indicating that the assignment has been received and accepted or rejected by the assigned resource.

Accepting New Tasks

Using Microsoft Project Web Access, your team members can create new tasks and send them to you for inclusion in the project plan, if you approve.

You will be able to review any newly created tasks by logging on to Microsoft Project Web Access, seeing a notice that there is a new or changed assignment, and then opening the Tasks page of your Microsoft Project Web Access site. The new task will be identified by a plus sign. Accept new tasks by doing the following:

Project Center

1   Log on to Microsoft Project Web Access. To do this quickly, click Project Center on the Collaborate toolbar.

2   Review the Home page of your Microsoft Project Web Access site for notices of new or changed assignments. Click the new task notice and view the information from the team member about the new task.

3   Click Update to accept the proposed addition and incorporate it into the project plan in Microsoft Project.

Setting Assignment Options

As the project manager, you need to be informed of all activity on the project and some options within Microsoft Project Web Access enable you to speed up this process. Along with accepting tasks and updates and incorporating them into your project plan, you can reject proposed new tasks quickly, and easily allow delegation of existing tasks.

Project Management Practices: Delegating Tasks

The project manager should develop and practice firm guidelines about appropriate reasons and procedures for delegating work. As a general practice, prior approval is expected from at least one person at a management level above that of the delegator.

With Microsoft Project Web Access, the rules might be more flexible because the project manager can see the proposed delegation action and approve or deny it quickly. If such rules are not in place, you might want to establish guidelines with your project team about the delegation process to avoid overuse or mistaken assumptions.

You can reject proposed new tasks on the Tasks page in your Microsoft Project Web Access site.

You can specify whether you want to allow team member delegation authority from Microsoft Project. To do this, click Collaborate, Collaboration Options, and then select or clear the Allow Resources To Delegate Tasks Using Microsoft Project Server check box.

Updating Task Information

Communicating with your team using Microsoft Project Server and Web Access speeds the complete and accurate sharing of changes and updates you make to the project plan through the sending and receiving of progress updates and status reports.

Establishing Update and Status Options

To set up your update and status options, do the following:

1 In Microsoft Project, click Collaborate, Collaboration Options.

2 Under "Publish New And Changed Assignments" Updates Resources' Assignments When, select the Any Task Information option if you want your resources to receive updates every time you change a task.

If you want to send updates only when you change critical task or scheduling information, select the Start, Finish, % Complete, Or Outline Changes option.

3 Under On Every Save, Publish The Following Information To Microsoft Project Server, specify which information you'd like to have automatically published whenever you save the project. Select or clear the New And Changed Assignments check box, the Project Summary check box, and the Including Full Project Plan check box.

The predictability and consistency of reports governed in this way keeps the level and accuracy of information you have high. By working with your project system administrator, you can specify reporting settings for the following:

- The default method for reporting progress
- The default reporting requirements
- The time periods covered in each report

Sending Task Updates to Team Members

It is typical to have numerous changes involving task scheduling. Microsoft Project Server and Web Access assist in making these updates accessible and easy to transmit to team members. When task information has significantly changed in your project plan, you can send those updates reflecting those changes to your project team as follows:

Publish All
Information

1 Click Collaborate, Publish, All Information, or click Publish All Information on the Collaborate toolbar.

2 A message box appears, warning you that your project will be saved after you publish it. Click OK in the message box.

The published task update information is sent to your team members' Microsoft Project Web Access sites. They receive a notice on their Home page that a new or updated assignment has been sent to them (see Figure 21-10). When they open their Project page, they can review the changes.

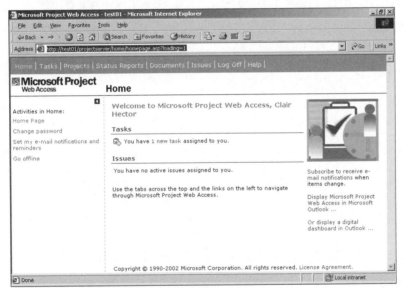

Figure 21-10. Team members receive notifications in Microsoft Project Web Access regarding new and changed assignments.

Receiving Task Updates from Team Members

Just as you send task updates to your team members regarding changes to their assignments, team members need to send you updates regarding progress on those assignments.

With your team, establish how often you want to receive updates about actual task progress from them. You might want them to send you a task update every Friday, for example. They can also send you a task update whenever they have a significant change they want you to know about, or whenever they complete a major milestone.

Request Progress Information

You can also request task updates at any time from within Microsoft Project. To do this, click Request Progress Information on the Collaborate toolbar. A message is sent to the team members requesting information about current percent complete, remaining work, or other progress information on assigned tasks.

Incorporating Task Updates into the Project Plan

When a team member updates progress information on one or more assigned tasks, he or she sends the update to you, and you're alerted to it on the Home page of your Microsoft Project Web Access site. You can view the update by clicking the notification link. If you accept it, simply click the Update button.

Update Project Progress

If you open your project plan and see update pending indicators next to certain tasks, this means that updates have been sent from Microsoft Project Web Access and are now pending incorporation into the project plan. Any progress information previously accepted by you in Microsoft Project Web Access is in the server, and affected tasks are marked with the update pending indicator. Click Collaborate, Update Project Progress to complete the process. Or click Update Project Progress on the Collaborate toolbar. When you click Update Project Progress, the accepted information is sent from the server and incorporated into your project plan. The update pending indicator then disappears.

Requesting and Compiling Text-Based Status Reports

Often the progress updates and task change information is not enough to tell the whole story about what is happening on the project. You can use Microsoft Project Web Access Status Reports to help team members add detail that explains causes and circumstances surrounding the updates, and to provide a narrative overview of current project status.

You can request these text-based status reports as follows:

1 In your Microsoft Project Web Access site, click the Status Reports menu.

2 In the Status Reports page, click Request Status Report.

3 Choose the specifics of the report type, from whom, and how often you would like it to be sent.

4 Send the request.

On the Status Reports page, you can either view individual status reports that have been submitted per your request or you can group the status reports into one. If you choose Group, you'll see a list of report information including who the report is from and what time period the report covers. You can apply a filter to view status reports for certain time periods. You can then select and open the individual reports on the list or see a compiled summary report.

Publishing Project Views to Microsoft Project Server

You can publish specific project views to Microsoft Project Server. Users of Microsoft Project Web Access can then access these views. This can be helpful for team members who want to see the big picture, that is, the overall context of their tasks. Project views are also essential for other stakeholders, especially executives or others involved in specific aspects of the project, such as accounting or procurement, because you can publish specific views that highlight the information they're most interested in. Work with your project system administrator to learn the options you have for customizing the views.

You can publish project views every time you save your project plan. Or, if you prefer, you can publish views only at your discretion, as follows:

1 Click Collaborate, Publish, Project Plan.

2 In the message that appears, click OK.

3 Select the Project Plan With Summary option or the Summary Only option.

Publish
Project
Plan

You can also publish a project view by clicking Publish Project Plan on the Collaborate toolbar.

These views of the project plan are sent to Microsoft Project Server. Team members can see these views, modified for Microsoft Project Web Access, when they open the Project Center and the Project page.

Chapter 21

Working with Manager Information in Microsoft Project Web Access

As the project manager, you have a Project Manager account in Microsoft Project Web Access. You can access this account by doing the following:

1 Open Internet Explorer on your computer.

2 In the Internet Explorer Address box, enter the Microsoft Project Web Access URL. Press Enter.

3 Depending on your configuration, you might need to enter your user name and password. The Welcome page for Microsoft Project Web Access appears.

Resource Center

With your Project Manager account, you can view team information and access additional features. These are helpful for keeping abreast of all the developments in your project and for communicating new and changing requirements to your team members and stakeholders. On your Microsoft Project Web Access site, you have the Project Center, in which you can view charts of your project plans, and the Resource Center, in which you can view your project resource's assignment information. You can directly access these pages from within Microsoft Project by clicking Project Center or Resource Center on the Collaborate toolbar.

Working with the Updates Page

In Microsoft Project Web Access, you have an Updates page, (see Figure 21-11), which provides information about the transactions you need to be aware of that have been reported through Microsoft Project Server and Web Access. This information is excellent for confirming what has transpired, what information is available from resources, and what you need to watch closely. If no current updates are shown, a description of the methods of transacting updates with your resources is given on this page. You have options to see a history of update transactions, insert your own notes, review resource calendar changes, and apply grouping and filtering.

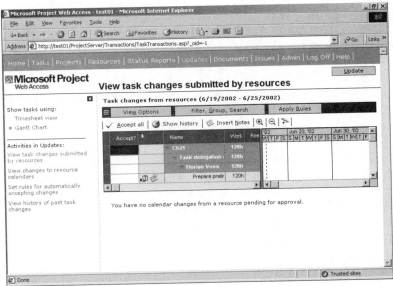

Figure 21-11. Information and transactions from your resources is shown on the Updates page.

Viewing the Timesheet

On your Microsoft Project Web Access site, the Tasks page contains a Timesheet view. At the top of the view are three tabs:

- The View Options tab contains the formatting and content options available for viewing the timesheet.

- The Filter, Group, Search tab contains options for arranging the tasks in the timesheet.

- The Delegation tab presents options for assigning tasks to team members.

On the toolbar below the tabs, six buttons offer additional ways to present data. You can:

- Hide the selected task in the timesheet.

- Reject the selected task.

- Insert notes pertinent to tasks.

- Create links to relevant documents stored in the Document Library.

- Create links to relevant issues that are stored in the Issues Tracker.

- Specify the time period for the timesheet listings.

Working with Task Lists

If you or your team members use Microsoft Outlook, your task lists can be integrated with Microsoft Project Server and Microsoft Web Access. You or a team member can update, add to, and synchronize your task list through Web Access. Settings and permissions from your project system administrator are required to fully enable this capability.

Compiling Resource Comments

Comments received from team members can be viewed in Microsoft Project. Comments that team members add to their task acceptance or task update messages are incorporated into assignment notes. Assignments with notes show the note indicator in the Task Usage or Resource Usage view in Microsoft Project, grouped by task or by resource. Double-click the indicator to open and read the note.

Setting Message Rules

You can define certain limitations for Microsoft Project Web Access messaging. In cooperation with your project system administrator, you can set the addressing options and other parameters of the messages that can be sent from within your team's Microsoft Project Server and Web Access system. This is done by your project system administrator in the Administrative Overview page of Microsoft Project Server.

Tracking Issues and Storing Documents

If you set up your system to accommodate SharePoint Team Services, you can use the issues and documents management tools integrated with Microsoft Project Server and Web Access. Of course, your entire team must be able to access the SharePoint server for this. Your project system administrator sets up the permissions and defines the other settings that enable this service.

Working with the Issues Tracker

Issues tracking is integral to project management and team communication because most issues either arise from task activity or will affect task activity. By tracking issues related to a project, you can improve communication on project-related issues, and ensure that problems are handled before they become crises.

Depending on privileges, you and your team members can create an issue, set its priority, and assign responsibility. The issue page includes a due date, discussion of the issue, and date of resolution. Issues can be associated with affected tasks, documents in the document library, or other related issues.

After the project system administrator sets up and configures SharePoint Team Services and the Issues Tracker, you can see issues directly from your Microsoft Project Web Access site. To add, edit, and review issues, click the Issues menu. The Issues page appears.

You can also open the Issues Tracker from your project plan. In Microsoft Project, click Collaborate, Issues. Or click Issues on the Collaborate toolbar.

Issues

Working with the Document Library

A document library can be an excellent repository for project-related documents such as the scope statement, product specifications, team contact information, change control plan, and more. By creating a central location for public documents related to the project, you can enhance collaboration and the project management process, ensuring that all team members and other stakeholders have all essential information at their disposal.

Depending on privileges, you and your team members can add a document, view documents, and search for documents in the document library. When adding a new document, you enter the file name and location for the document, specify the owner and status (for example, Draft, Reviewed, Final, and so on), and enter any pertinent comments. You can also associate a document with specific tasks if you want.

After the project system administrator sets up and configures SharePoint Team Services and the Document Library specific to your team, you can see documents directly from your Microsoft Project Web Access site. To add or review documents, click the Documents menu. The Documents page appears.

You can also open the Document Library from your project plan. In Microsoft Project, click Collaborate, Documents. Or click Documents on the Collaborate toolbar.

Documents

Customizing Microsoft Project Web Access

You can focus your Microsoft Project Web Access sites on just the type and format of information you need the most. The following list indicates the various aspects of Microsoft Project Web Access that can be customized to fit the way your team works:

E-mail notification. This can be set to be automatically sent to selected members at specific times and for specific purposes.

Views. The Microsoft Project Web Access users, the project manager, and the project system administrator can customize the views. The content, format and size of views, such as the Gantt charts, is primarily set by the project system administrator, but the order and some formatting of content can be set by the team members too.

Menus. By working with the project system administrator, you can specify changes, additions, and deletions to the menus shown on your team's Microsoft Project Web Access pages.

Templates. There are customizable templates for some of the content, particularly the graphics, shown on the Microsoft Project Web Access pages. The project system administrator can use these templates to create the style that you prefer.

Additional content. You can add content and specify where it will be shown on your team's Microsoft Project Web Access pages. The project system administrator performs this in concert with your needs. This added content can be virtually anything that can be put onto a Web page.

> **note** Because the dimensions of the portion of the page in which the added content appears are limited, smaller items are more easily useful.

Communicating Information Using Microsoft Project Web Access

This chapter is intended for project team members, resource managers, interested executives, and other stakeholders who will be using the Microsoft Project Web Access interface to review and exchange project information. If you're interested in the project manager or project system administrator roles and uses of Microsoft Project Server and Web Access, see Chapter 21, "Managing Your Team Using Microsoft Project Web Access."

Team members, resource managers, team leads, stakeholders, and executives can use Microsoft Project Web Access to view and manage information from the Microsoft Project plan, which is disseminated by the project manager. Each role brings with it a different focus and group of priorities for information access, and Microsoft Project Web Access provides a broad range of data to aid each user. Microsoft Project Web Access can also be customized to further focus the view of information available.

Certain features of Microsoft Project Web Access are more useful to some user roles than to others. A note at the beginning of each section in this chapter identifies the roles that might benefit the most from the information in that section.

> **note** In Microsoft Project 2002, Microsoft Project Web Access is the next generation of Microsoft Project Central, which you might have used with Microsoft Project 2000.

529

Project Management Practices: Implementing Your Communication Plan

An essential ingredient of good project planning is the development of a comprehensive communication plan that describes the planned channels, intentions, and audiences for communicating project information. The many facets of communicating information that Microsoft Project Web Access provides make it a primary asset to project communications.

The type of information that is shared, the frequency and scope of the information, the formats, the senders and receivers, and even the types of responses can all be clearly defined for the Microsoft Project Web Access team, including stakeholders and executives. Other methods of sending information might become obsolete because the information can be transmitted more efficiently using Microsoft Project Web Access.

Furthermore, the connections between Microsoft Project Web Access and other communications channels, such as SharePoint Team Services and Microsoft Outlook e-mail and online calendars, can expand the range and capability of your project's communication processes.

Getting Started with Microsoft Project Web Access

Your project manager and project system administrator are responsible for setting up Microsoft Project Web Access user accounts for all team members and other stakeholders on the project team. Access your account by doing the following:

1   Open Internet Explorer on your computer.

2   In the Internet Explorer Address box, enter the Microsoft Project Web Access URL that your project manager or project system administrator has provided for you. Press Enter.

3   Depending on your configuration, you might need to enter your user name and password and then click the Log In button. Your Microsoft Project Web Access Home page appears (see Figure 22-1).

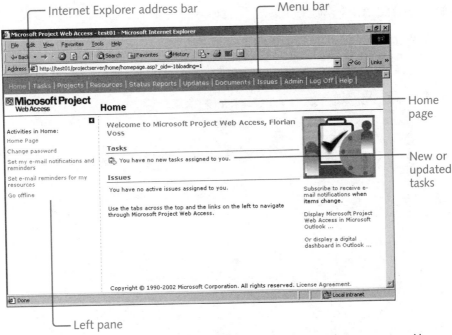

Figure 22-1. As soon as you log on to Microsoft Project Web Access, your Home page appears.

On this page, you can click a link to learn more about new or updated tasks, click a link in the left pane, or click a menu to display a different page.

When you're ready to end your Microsoft Project Web Access session, click the Log Off menu.

Reviewing Assignments in Microsoft Project Web Access

note This section is designed for project team members, who are the individuals executing the assignments.

When the team is set up and the project plan is developed, the project manager sends, or *publishes*, all assignments to their assigned resources. As a team member, you can see your assignments in your view of Microsoft Project Web Access. With Microsoft Project Web Access, you can therefore collaborate with your project manager on the proposed new or changed assignments by accepting or declining them with explanatory comments.

Reviewing and Accepting Tasks

When you log on to Microsoft Project Web Access, you see a notification of any new task assignments directly on the Home page (see Figure 22-2). From there, you just click the notification link to view the assignment information on the Tasks page.

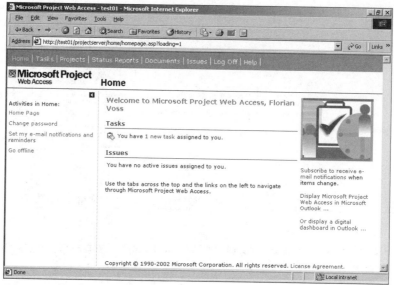

Figure 22-2. New assignments are posted on the Home page.

The Tasks page (see Figure 22-3) shows a Gantt Chart of your assignments, including a table containing the following information:

- Task indicators, such as the new assignment indicator (the red exclamation point)

- Task name

- Work assigned, in hours

- Percent of the work complete

- Actual work performed, in hours

- Remaining work to be done, in hours

Chapter 22: Communicating Information Using Microsoft Project Web Access

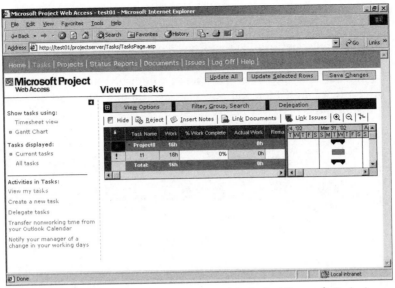

Figure 22-3. You can view your assigned tasks in Microsoft Project Web Access.

This is the default information provided. Your project manager might customize the information depending on project requirements.

The right side of the Gantt Chart displays the Gantt bars. This area displays:

- A four-week view of the daily timescale

- The current date, seen as a dashed vertical line

- Summary task bars

- Individual task bars, with progress lines as applicable

---

tip   **Switch to a timesheet view of tasks**

If you prefer to view your task information in a timesheet instead of the Gantt Chart, in the left pane, click the Timesheet View link.

Part 7: Collaborating as a Team

Creating and Submitting New Tasks

Suppose you're performing significant work that doesn't fit the definition of any of your assigned tasks, yet is necessary to the completion of the project and should be tracked. To keep your project manager informed, and to ensure your work on the project is accounted for, you can create and submit a new task to the project manager using the Tasks page (see Figure 22-4).

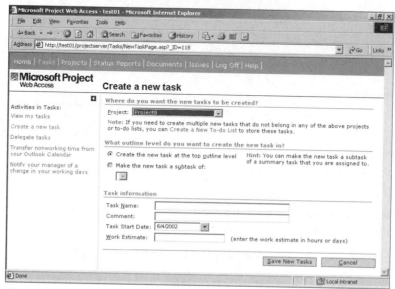

Figure 22-4. Specify the basic definition of your new task.

To create and submit a new task, do the following:

1 Click the Tasks menu to display the Tasks page.

2 In the left pane of the Tasks page, click the Create a New Task link.

3 On the Create A New Task page, specify the options associated with the task, as follows:

- The project in which the new task belongs

- The outline level in which the task belongs, such as under a specific summary task

- The task name

- Comments to associate with this task

- The task start date

- A work estimate, in terms of hours or days

4 After selecting your specifications, click Save New Tasks.

---

tip **Create a to-do list**

In the course of carrying out your assignments, you might have a number of smaller activities that aren't big enough to be tasks. You can create a to-do list for yourself, using the Create A New Personal Or Shared To-Do List link on the Projects page (see Figure 22-5). A to-do list is a collection of smaller activities that support the project and that you don't want to overlook, for example, "Get director's signature on change request by April 30." The to-do lists are only stored in your own Microsoft Project Web Access site, and are not included in the overall project plan.

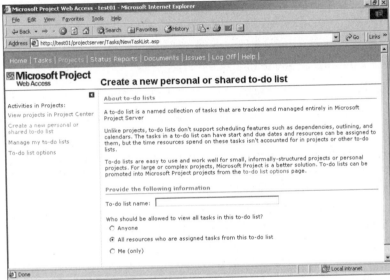

Figure 22-5. Add small project activities on a To-Do List.

Delegating Tasks

note The ability to delegate tasks to other team members is a function that is enabled with permission of the project manager and set by the system administrator. The persons who might need to delegate tasks are team leads, resource managers, and the team members. Stakeholders and executives do not require task delegation authority.

The reasons why a task might need to be delegated vary, but the option to allow it is necessary to avoid schedule difficulty or even work stoppage.

Project Management Practices: Delegating Tasks

The project manager should develop and practice firm guidelines about appropriate reasons and procedures for delegating work. As a general practice, prior approval is expected from at least one person at a management level above that of the delegator.

With Microsoft Project Web Access, the rules might be more flexible because the project manager can see the proposed delegation action and approve or deny it quickly. If such rules are not in place, the project manager might want to establish guidelines with the project team about the delegation process to avoid overuse or mistaken assumptions.

Do the following to delegate a task:

1 Click the Tasks menu to display the Tasks page.

2 In the left pane of the Tasks page, click the Delegate Tasks link.

3 Select the task or tasks you would like to delegate, and click the Delegate Task button. The Delegate Tasks wizard appears.

4 Specify the resource to whom you are delegating the task. Also specify whether you are assuming the lead role on the task and whether you want to keep tracking it on your timesheet. Click the Next button.

5 In Step 2 of the Delegate Tasks wizard, confirm your changes and click the Send button to send them to your project manager.

Updating Tasks in Microsoft Project Web Access

note This section applies to team members who are performing assigned work on project tasks.

Sending Task Updates

The tasks assigned to you are shown on the Tasks page in Microsoft Project Web Access. You can view and update your tasks in either the Gantt Chart or Timesheet view. With the Timesheet view, you can enter specific data about hours worked per week and nonworking time.

To update your task information and send the update to the project manager, follow these steps:

1 Click the Tasks menu to display the Tasks page.

2 In the left pane of the Tasks page, click the Gantt Chart or Timesheet link to display your tasks the way you want.

3 Update your tasks by editing the following fields:

- Percent of the task's work that is complete

- The actual work performed on the task, in hours

- The remaining work to do on the task, in hours

> **note** These are default fields. Your project manager might customize your Timesheet or Gantt Chart to include other fields to be updated.

4 When finished, click the Update All, Update Selected Rows, or Save Changes button. The following explains when each button is applicable:

- The Update All button sends updates of any changed assignments to the Microsoft Project Server and then to your project manager.

- The Update Selected Rows button sends updates of just those tasks you've selected.

  To select multiple adjacent rows, click the first row, hold down the Shift key, and then click the last row you want to select.

  To select multiple nonadjacent rows, click the first row, hold down the Ctrl key, and then click all the other rows you want to select.

- The Save Changes button saves the information you've changed but will not send the updates to your project manager. This is helpful if you haven't finished entering information, or if your manager likes to receive updates on a particular day of the week.

> **tip** **Update multiple managers**
>
> Your system administrator can set team members' Microsoft Project Web Access sites to send updates to selected multiple managers. Microsoft Project Server will direct updates to each of the recipient project managers.

Creating and Submitting Text-Based Status Reports

> **note** Status reports are useful to team members, team leads, and resource managers who share their information and interpretations of the project's progress. The requirement for status reports is often defined in the project communications plan and is expected to be well understood by all team members.

To create a status report, click the Status Reports menu. You can choose transmission and recipient options and write textual status reports on several kinds of work progress. You also can add comments about any of the progress reported.

When finished filling in the text fields, send or save the status report. Sending it will transmit it to your project manager. Saving it will make it available for further editing, but will not transmit the report to your project manager.

Viewing Information in Microsoft Project Web Access

> **note** Viewing information is useful for everyone who uses your team's Microsoft Project Web Access: resource managers, team members, team leads, stakeholders, and executives.

The ability to display project information in numerous formats, and to make pertinent information available to all team members and stakeholders, is a chief strength of Microsoft Project Web Access.

Viewing the Entire Project

On the Projects page, you can view the entire team's detailed project plan or summary level project information. You can also view filtered and grouped project information.

To see the entire project plan, do the following:

1 Click the Projects menu.

2 In the left pane of the Projects page, click View Projects In Project Center. This opens the page with both complete and summarized project information. The formats and content of the views depend on the custom settings made by your system administrator, the project manager, and you.

The content in the Project Center page is variable according to your needs and role and the permissions set by your system administrator and project manager. If you're an executive, for example, your Project Center page might best be used for summary-level project information and top-level data on all projects under your responsibility. On the other hand, if you're a team member, your Project Center might best be used for more detailed and comprehensive views of your individual project plan.

Viewing the entire project plan is an option available to all Microsoft Project Web Access users, but resource managers and team leads often need to do so more than executives. The Project Center page often contains a mixture of summary information on several related projects and complete information on one project. This provides context and clarity of information for stakeholders and team members alike. The presentation of the data is similar to the Gantt Chart on the Tasks page.

Because much project information is sensitive, the system administrator, in cooperation with the project manager, can set permissions to include viewing of filtered data, read-only access for the tables and fields presented, and predefined summarization criteria.

Rearranging Project Information

The project information displayed in the Project Center can be further sorted, filtered, and grouped.

The Filter, Group, And Search tab, located directly above the tables and graphs of the project data, opens when you click it to give you options for sorting, filtering and grouping. You can choose the following settings:

- Sort by resource or task
- Filter information using up to three criteria
- Group information by specified groupings

Integrating with Microsoft Outlook

Microsoft Project Web Access is designed to work with Microsoft Outlook as an added dimension of its communication functions. This enables you to see items that are in your Outlook folders while you're using Microsoft Project Web Access. You can also add certain types of Microsoft Project Web Access information into Outlook.

Two of the handiest methods of integrating Microsoft Project Web Access with Outlook can be set up from your Microsoft Project Web Access Home page.

Use the following links in the right pane of the Home page (see Figure 22-6), to start setting up connections with Outlook:

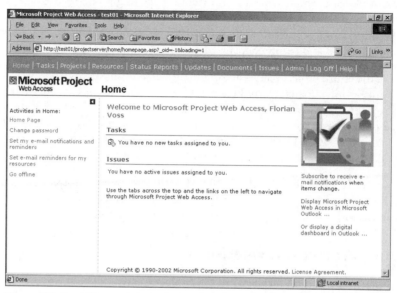

Figure 22-6. You can integrate Microsoft Project Web Access with Microsoft Outlook.

- The Display Microsoft Project Web Access In Microsoft Outlook link will get you started on enabling interconnection.

- The Or Display A Digital Dashboard In Outlook link is a method of showing Microsoft Project Web Access data in Outlook that uses digital dashboard technologies, such as Web Parts. For details on system requirements for digital dashboards, consult your project system administrator.

Both of these features enable you to see your Microsoft Project Web Access information from anyplace you can use Microsoft Outlook.

Managing Information in Microsoft Project Web Access

> **note** The need to manage your project information in Microsoft Project Web Access is shared by team members, team leads, resource managers, and other stakeholders. Regardless of your role, you each have distinct requirements, and you can tailor Microsoft Project Web Access to meet those information requirements effectively.

Working with Your Updates Page

The Updates page contains a listing of incoming notices, assignments, and information, as well as outgoing status reports, tasks proposed or delegated and other communications. This page is useful to help you recall what data and information exchanges have taken place through your Microsoft Project Web Access site, and perhaps to remind you what is still to be finished, responded to, reported, or resolved.

Viewing Your Timesheet

Your timesheet is an integral part of the Microsoft Project Server and Web Access system. It provides schedule and work information that goes directly into your team's Microsoft Project plan. This gives accurate and timely progress updates for your manager's tracking needs.

To view and update your timesheet, do the following:

1 Click the Tasks menu. The View My Tasks page appears (see Figure 22-7).

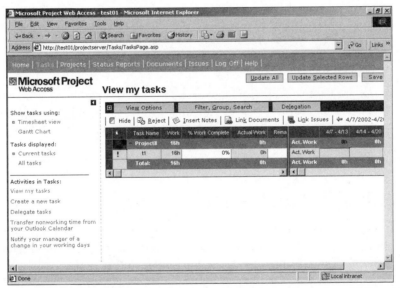

Figure 22-7. You can see your list of tasks in the Task section of Microsoft Project Web Access.

2 In the left pane, click the Timesheet View link.

3 Click the blue arrows (Go To Previous Period and Go To Next Period) along the top right of the timesheet to find the week for which you want to enter information.

4 Click the appropriate field cell, such as % Complete or Actual Work, and enter updated information, using the proper units.

5 Click one of the buttons at the top of the page: Update All, Update Selected Rows, or Save Changes. The update buttons will send the data to your project manager through Microsoft Project Server.

Working With Your Task Lists

Microsoft Project Web Access makes it easy to track your tasks, and to see your own task list. You are always notified of new assignments directly on the Home page when you log on to Microsoft Project Web Access. You also see indicators on your task list to show changes and notes associated with individual tasks.

To view all your assignments, including any new ones, do the following:

1 Click the Tasks menu. The View My Tasks page appears.

2 In the left pane, under Tasks Displayed, click the All Tasks link.

3 In the left pane, under Show Tasks Using, click the Timesheet View or the Gantt Chart link.

---

tip   **Using task indicators**

In your task list, indicators are displayed for some tasks in the Indicators column of the task table. For example, the red exclamation point is the indicator that this task is new and requires your attention and acceptance or rejection. The yellow notepad indicator shows that there is a comment associated with that task.

Tracking Issues and Storing Documents

Depending on your Microsoft Project Web Access configuration, your team might be set up to use the issues and documents management tools. Your project system administrator sets up the permissions and defines the other settings that enable this service.

Working with the Issues Tracker

Issues tracking is integral to project management and team communication because most issues either arise from task activity or will affect task activity. By tracking issues related to a project, your team can easily communicate project-related issues, and ensure that problems are handled before they become crises.

Depending on privileges, the project manager and team members can create an issue, set its priority, and assign responsibility. The issue page includes a due date, discussion of the issue, and a comment about the resolution. Issues can be associated with affected tasks, documents in the document library, or other related issues.

To add, edit, and review issues, click the Issues menu. The Issues page appears.

Working with the Document Library

A document library can be an excellent repository for project-related documents such as the scope statement, product specifications, team contact information, change control plan, and more. By creating a central location for public documents related to the project, your team can enhance collaboration and the project management process, ensuring that the project manager, all team members, and other stakeholders have all essential information at their disposal.

Depending on privileges, the project manager and team members can add a document, view documents, and search for documents in the document library. When adding a new document, you enter the file name and location for the document, specify the owner and status (for example, Draft, Reviewed, Final, and so on), and enter any pertinent comments. You can also associate a document with specific tasks if you want.

To add or review documents, click the Documents menu. The Documents page appears.

Part 8

Managing Projects Across Your Enterprise

Understanding the Enterprise Features

The enterprise features of Microsoft Project Professional extend the power of Microsoft Project beyond the individual project to the mid-size to large-size multiple-project business. The enterprise features are available with Microsoft Project Professional and function as a superset of Microsoft Project 2002. The enterprise features can provide information about dozens of projects and thousands of resources. It holds data from multiple project plans that were built using Microsoft Project Professional. It can give information about every resource and every project in the entire company. The enterprise features are implemented through Microsoft Project Professional together with Microsoft Project Server and Web Access, as well as with SQL Server.

> For detailed system requirements for Microsoft Project Server and the enterprise features, see Appendix A, "Installing Microsoft Project 2002."

Why Use Enterprise Features?

For any business that works on multiple projects, the benefits of using the enterprise features are great. The enterprise features essentially enable executives, owners, and top-level managers to see and analyze information on all the projects in their organization. This universal view is ideal for gaining a comprehensive understanding of the nature and progress of the activity within the entire organization. Executives can see and evaluate information about all the resources in their enterprise and all the projects going on in their organization. The enterprise features also help individual project managers plan and control their projects within the context of their entire organization.

Standardizing Projects in an Enterprise

A key element of effective management and control systems is standardization. The purpose of standardization is to ensure that one project is operating with the same ground rules as any other project. In many kinds of businesses, specific templates for project phases and activities can be applied in standardized formats. The chief advantage of consistent standardized project plans is that all the projects can be measured by the same rules. Measuring performance in discrete portions of a business, such as departments or functional divisions, for use in making executive decisions is known as applying metrics. The areas of performance typically tracked using management metrics are cost, schedule, and personnel utilization. Metrics are meaningful and fair when standardized practices are in place. Management and executive evaluation and direction are enhanced when decisions can be made based on predictable guidelines.

The Microsoft Project enterprise features provide a standardized model of project plans and thus of management metrics. The executive who analyzes company-wide information using the enterprise features of Microsoft Project Professional, such as Portfolio Modeler and Portfolio Analyzer, can be confident that the structure and elements of all the project plans are standardized. An executive can be sure that there is a true comparison of "apples with apples." The techniques and data used in Microsoft Project to calculate progress, such as the enterprise global template, are consistent, and the resulting reports use the same metrics. This predictability and clarity of content are a primary advantage of standardization. The enterprise features further standardize the projects' data by applying specific and clear-cut templates that define how the information is presented.

Customizing Projects throughout an Enterprise

Although the data and analysis methods in the Microsoft Project enterprise features are structured and standardized, you can customize the way that data is organized and presented. One useful means of customization is to specify the level of detail and the amount of information that will be available for executive analysis. Another kind of customization can be done for the graphical format of the data presentation. You can customize the kind of analysis performed on the project and resource data as well.

More than an interesting possibility, customization at this summary level of data is indispensable for executives who need to see specific information quickly and in the format that is most clear and convenient. Using the enterprise features of Microsoft Project Professional, you can create custom fields for use with the enterprise global template to bring the right information to your upper management.

Managing Enterprise Resources

In large organizations, particularly those that have multiple work locations, resource management can be difficult. The allocation and utilization of resources can be done in many ways depending on the practices of the organization, but the need to see enterprise-wide resource information is crucial to performance. The lack of a skilled worker for a job can cause serious delays or loss of business. Likewise, having underutilized resources can be an unnecessary drain on the business treasury and reduce profits.

Microsoft Project Professional can provide valuable insight into resource utilization, allocation, and availability throughout the enterprise. Although it's not a human resources management tool, the enterprise features do help executives and upper managers utilize resources by showing information about all the resources in all the projects. Some enterprise features that aid in resource usage are:

- The Team Builder Wizard
- The enterprise resource pool
- The Resource Substitution Wizard
- Generic resources
- Resource availability graphs

> For further information about enterprise features for resource usage, see Chapter 24, "Using Enterprise Features to Manage Projects."

Using this information, decision makers can avert performance reductions that can result from inefficient usage of resources.

Reviewing Project Portfolios

A key benefit of using Microsoft Project Professional is that the enterprise features provide company-wide views of project information, or *portfolio*, and present this comprehensive data in a clearly understandable form in a single location. Executives can see at a glance their entire portfolio of projects, note their progress to date, and compare one with another.

An executive can also use the Portfolio Analyzer to perform analysis of the information about the projects and resources in his or her organization. Through these analyses, the executive can find available resources, compare costs of projects, see currently active work, and view the data in a variety of different ways in projects throughout the enterprise. The primary tool for analyzing the information is the OnLine Analytical Processing (OLAP) Cubes, used for both projects and for resources. This tool enables the user to "mine" the enterprise data for specific kinds of information drawn from the entire organization.

Users of the Microsoft Project Professional enterprise features can set up portfolios to show specified projects or all projects in their company. In cooperation with the project system administrator, users can customize their portfolios. The projects in the portfolio view are in summary form, which presents information in a way that makes multiple projects easy to scan and compare. By using the features of Portfolio Analyzer and Portfolio Modeler, executives can evaluate and compare the projects they need to see. In fact, it is the ability to compare projects quickly in the portfolio view that makes it so useful to executives and upper managers.

Understanding Enterprise Implementations

You can better understand what the enterprise features do and how they do it by understanding how they're implemented and how they fit into the project management system of Microsoft Project Professional.

Processing Enterprise Projects

The following describes the process of working with multiple projects in an enterprise environment:

1 The project system administrator sets up the *enterprise global template*, an overall template for project plans to be created throughout the enterprise. This global template contains any standardized information, custom fields, views, formulas, and other types of custom information pertinent to the organization.

2 Project managers throughout the organization use the enterprise global template in Microsoft Project Professional to build and maintain their individual project plans.

3 The project plans are sent, or *checked in*, to Microsoft Project Server as enterprise projects. Microsoft Project Server interfaces with SQL Server, on which the enterprise data is based. Microsoft Project Server also interfaces with Microsoft Project Web Access, which provides a Web-based view of project information (see Figure 23-1).

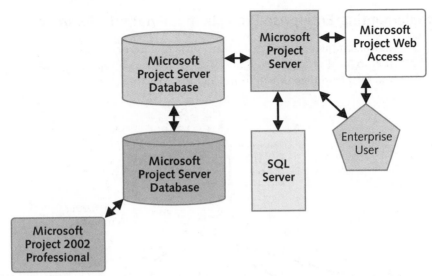

Figure 23-1. The enterprise system consists of several interdependent components.

4 Project managers use the enterprise resource pool to find resources in the organization who have the right skill set and availability for their individual project requirements.

5 Executives can view multiple projects in the organization using the portfolio view in Microsoft Project Web Access. The executive can also log on directly to Microsoft Project Server and see project and resource data through that tool. Using the Portfolio Analyzer, executives can review a high-level summary of projects throughout the enterprise, including information about scheduling, costs, resources, and more. Using the Portfolio Modeler, executives, as well as project managers, can run what-if scenarios on various possibilities having to do with schedule, budget, resources, and scope.

For more information about using the enterprise global template, custom fields, the enterprise resource pool, the Portfolio Analyzer, and the Portfolio Modeler, see Chapter 24, "Using Enterprise Features to Manage Projects."

Modeling Enterprise Implementations

There are probably hundreds of ways your organization can implement the enterprise features of Microsoft Project Professional. The components are designed to be flexible and scalable. This section includes three implementation examples, based on modern organizational structures.

Chapter 23

Implementing Enterprise Projects in a Pyramid Hierarchy

One example of a straightforward project enterprise implementation is the classic hierarchical model (see Figure 23-2) with a single top point and more connections the further you go down, from CEO to project team member.

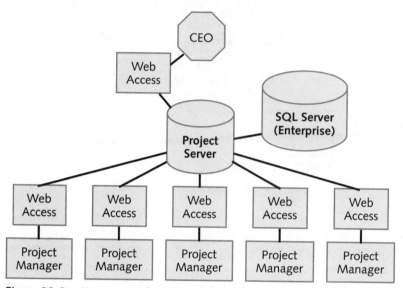

Figure 23-2. You can implement enterprise projects in a classic pyramid hierarchy.

For example, imagine a software development company with five different projects in progress at the same time. Each of the project managers uses Microsoft Project 2002 Professional to manage his or her projects. Microsoft Project Server is installed in the central data systems office, along with SQL Server 2000. Each of the five projects has ten Microsoft Project Web Access user accounts connected to it through the Microsoft Project Server. The CEO of the company has an executive account set up to work with Microsoft Project Server with Web Access.

The five project managers publish their enterprise project and resource information through Microsoft Project Server. Their team members and stakeholders use Microsoft Project Web Access to see their pertinent project information and collaborate effectively. The CEO can use the enterprise account to see and evaluate all the projects in the company in a standardized form, and view and analyze all the resources in the company.

Implementing Enterprise Projects in a Tapered Block Hierarchy

A second example involves larger organizations that have dozens of projects being worked on at a given time. This type of implementation is more of a "tapered block" model of information exchange and access. There are multiple sources of information at the project level and multiple, though fewer, connections at the upper enterprise level. This model is effective for large, discretely organized firms, like telecommunications companies, that make executive decisions based on input from department heads.

For example, suppose each of the projects is using Microsoft Project Professional and is connected to Microsoft Project Server. Microsoft Project Server is set up for enterprise features and all the project managers publish their enterprise project and resource data to Microsoft Project Server. At the enterprise account level, ten vice presidents connect to their enterprise accounts, in which they view and analyze project and resource information, focusing on the projects that are most important to them. They then advise and inform the company president.

Implementing Enterprise Projects in a Straight Block Hierarchy

A third enterprise implementation example is a company that uses a pure project management model for their organization. Some construction companies are set up in this way. This model would be more of a "straight block." The next level of authority and responsibility below the president is the project manager. All the work in the company is planned, performed, and tracked as projects.

For example, suppose that there are 12 different projects being done, each independent and equal in importance to the company. The 12 project managers all use Microsoft Project Professional and all are connected to Microsoft Project Server, which is set up for enterprise features. All the project managers and the company president have enterprise accounts. They see the resource and project information about all or selected projects among the 12. They are able to quickly resolve prioritization and utilization issues by using the enterprise features. The president is also able to see the entire company's work and resources in a standardized manner.

Under some circumstances, there might be multiple Microsoft Project Servers with multiple SQL Servers. Although this would not allow for total enterprise data evaluation, it could be useful, for example, for a very large company that is divided into divisions that use their individual instances of Microsoft Project Professional with enterprise features.

The style of the implementation depends on the structure and management practices of your company. The primary factor is having multiple projects working simultaneously— a situation common to most enterprises.

Chapter 23

> **note** If the implementation is likely to include a single Microsoft Project Server and several users who would be accessing the system at the same time, the project system administrator can set up a companion view server to ease some of the processing load of the primary Microsoft Project Server.

Administering Enterprise Features

Project managers interact with the project system administrator and publish their project data to the enterprise repository. They need to understand the enterprise requirements and options that the project system administrator controls. It is equally important that the executives and upper-level managers understand the enterprise options the project system administrator controls.

Setting Up Enterprise Features and Options

To use enterprise features, the following setup is required:

- Microsoft Project Professional

- Microsoft Project Server connected to the instances of Microsoft Project Professional

- SQL Server connected to the Microsoft Project Server

Furthermore, all enterprise account holders need a connection to Microsoft Project Server.

> **caution** The setup of the SQL Server is essential to the Microsoft Project enterprise features. Particular attention should be given to the connection for building OLAP cubes. The Decision Support Objects (DSO) file is a key requirement that must be located properly.

Project managers can connect to Microsoft Project Server to access their enterprise accounts either through the use of Microsoft Project Web Access, or through a direct Internet connection to the Microsoft Project Server while they are working in Microsoft Project Professional.

The project system administrator can also set up the enterprise features so that users can access them through Microsoft Project Server or through Microsoft Project Web Access to SharePoint Team Services for the Issues Tracker or Document Library (see Figure 23-3). SharePoint is a helpful information source, but the project system administrator must create subwebs with Microsoft Project Server for the clients to use. The information in SharePoint Team Services can complement the enterprise data, but it cannot be stored in the same data repository.

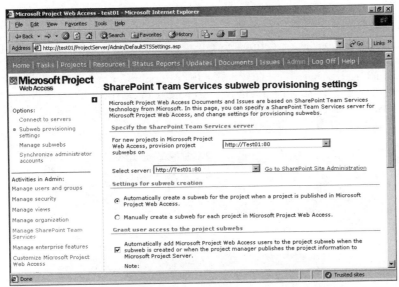

Figure 23-3. The project system administrator can add SharePoint Team Services to the Microsoft Project Server.

> For specific guidelines about setting up Microsoft Project Professional for enterprise features, refer to Appendix A, "Installing Microsoft Project 2002." For detailed installation procedures, see the Pjsvr10.chm help file on the Microsoft Project Server CD.

Administering Enterprise

One of the primary features of an enterprise account is the enterprise portfolio, which is set up and customized by the project system administrator. This permission is granted within Microsoft Project Server in the Manage Users And Groups pages of the Admin section.

With such sensitive and all-inclusive enterprise data, security is very important. The project system administrator, working with company executives and project managers, sets several access filters, groupings, permissions, login parameters, and the authentication option.

As situations change and personnel join and leave the organization, the project system administrator will need to consult with resource managers and project managers to change the permissions in Microsoft Project Server accordingly.

The project system administrator handles the provision of special views, analysis tools for executives, and differing access levels for enterprise data.

Developing Templates

There are a number of predefined enterprise templates. These templates can be set by the project system administrator and customized to suit the requirements of the individual users. These templates define the presentation of information about projects and resources. Styles and content of bar charts can be specified (see Figure 23-4). Formats, such as outlining conventions and content of resource list tables, can also be tailored through templates and customizations.

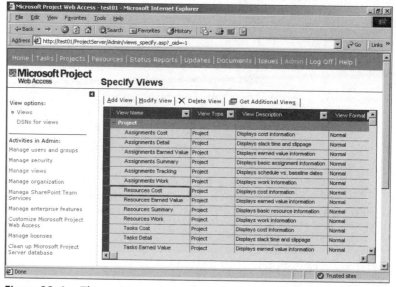

Figure 23-4. The project system administrator uses Microsoft Project Server to define what is shown in views.

Additionally, the project system administrator can set up specific custom fields to be included in the enterprise information screens. This is useful for seeing a high-level summary of a data field not included in the standard enterprise templates.

The project system administrator can tailor enterprise data by implementing the following optional setups:

- Define custom views
- Apply formulas to enterprise data
- Design reports
- Build and apply macros to enterprise data
- Set up custom calendars
- Define and customize information tables

The enterprise global template is the basic template for organizing and storing the data that is used by enterprise account holders. Enterprise information can be viewed and analyzed in its standard formats without the need for any extra customization.

The most convenient and flexible means of viewing, analyzing, and accessing enterprise data is through the use of Microsoft Project Web Access with an executive level set of permissions set by the project system administrator.

Using Microsoft Project Web Access, you can view all enterprise resource information, see your entire portfolio of projects in one place, and perform some analytical functions to compare and evaluate data.

The Microsoft Project enterprise features provide unmatched visibility into a whole company's project work efforts and the resources used to make it happen. They give clear and easy-to-use access to vital status information and can help you avoid trouble and ensure smooth operations. With their many large-scale capabilities, the enterprise features help executives and managers to see the big picture, plan for the future, and use their resources wisely.

newfeature!

Using Enterprise Features to Manage Projects

The enterprise features of Microsoft Project Professional are designed to be used with multiple project plans and by multiple managers and executives across the enterprise. As such, it is a management tool in the *super* class; it facilitates management of multiple projects and great numbers of resources. It functions on a higher level than Microsoft Project Standard, the management tool for the individual projects, in that it can store and provide data from many individual projects. It also can work as a planning tool for project and resource managers who need to see information about projects and resources across the entire enterprise. Because there is so much enterprise information to manage, standardizing the information so it can be compared and contrasted is very important.

Executives and upper-level managers use the enterprise features as a method of monitoring and measuring the work and resources in their entire organization. They can see information about dozens of projects and thousands of resources, presented in a way that is most relevant to their requirements. Each executive can have a unique set of views and presentations of the enterprise information. There is no need to sift through extraneous data to get to what he or she really needs to know. And as the needs and preferences of an individual user change, his or her access and views of the enterprise information can change as well.

At the heart of the system is the individual project plan, created and controlled by a project manager using Microsoft Project Professional, which is the edition that provides the enterprise features. The project manager accesses the enterprise features through Microsoft Project Server and Web Access, and is

559

responsible for regularly checking in enterprise updates. The enterprise project files are different from those of the stand-alone desktop application, but are easily built from them. The project manager continues to use Microsoft Project Professional for project planning, and can continue to send and receive updates through Microsoft Project Web Access, if applicable. The transmittal of the enterprise project information to Microsoft Project Server is done with special operations that are built into Microsoft Project Professional.

> For more details about how the enterprise features work with Microsoft Project Professional, Microsoft Project Server, and Microsoft Project Web Access, see Chapter 23, "Understanding the Enterprise Features."

Defining Your Enterprise User Profile

Your project system administrator initially sets up permissions and access for work with the enterprise features. When that's done, you can define your user profile in Microsoft Project Professional and Microsoft Project Server. To do this, follow these steps:

1 Start Microsoft Project Professional and open the project you will be making an enterprise project. You can create new enterprise projects or transform existing projects created locally into enterprise projects.

2 Click Tools, Enterprise Options, Microsoft Project Server Accounts.

3 In the Microsoft Project Server Accounts dialog box, click Add.

4 Enter a name for your account and the URL for your Microsoft Project Server. Be careful to use the format *http://servername/virtualdirectoryname*. Click the Test Connection button to test the connection.

5 Choose the kind of account access to Microsoft Project Server you have: Windows User or Microsoft Project Server account. If you chose Microsoft Project Server account, enter your user name for that account.

InsideOut

A Windows User account is more versatile and convenient than a Microsoft Project Server account. You use the same password and identification as for your Windows system, and that integrates well with Microsoft Project Server; saving time and enhancing security by enabling quick password changes. Logging on and saving your project files is easier, and you'll have more permissions potentially available for enterprise features.

6 Select the Set Default Account check box if you want this account to be your default for Microsoft Project Professional startup.

> **note** Setting this account as the default is a great convenience if you expect to use Microsoft Project Server and the enterprise features regularly. You will be connected to this account each time you launch Microsoft Project Professional.

Working with Enterprise Projects

You can turn an existing project plan into an enterprise project by importing it to Microsoft Project Server. You can also create an enterprise project from scratch. Either way, enterprise projects are based on the enterprise global template. Once they are imported, enterprise projects are then checked in and out of the Microsoft Project Server.

The project system administrator, with input from project managers throughout the organization, can develop custom enterprise fields that become a part of the enterprise global template. This way, all enterprise projects use the same fields, which ensures standardization and tailors the projects to the manner in which the organization manages and analyzes projects.

Importing a Project Plan as an Enterprise Project

After you have an active account on Microsoft Project Server that opens when you start Microsoft Project Professional, you can import any existing project plans as an enterprise project. To import your project as an enterprise project, do the following:

1 In Microsoft Project Professional, close the project you want to import as an enterprise project, and save it as a file on your local drive.

2 Open any other project in Microsoft Project Professional.

> **tip** **Close the project file to be imported**
>
> When importing an existing project as an enterprise project, the project file you want to import must be closed, and some other project file must be open. Save the project file to be imported to an easy to locate place on your local drive. You can, for example, create a folder named ImportProjects.

3 Click Tools, Enterprise Options, Import Project to Enterprise. The Import Projects Wizard appears (see Figure 24-1 on the next page).

561

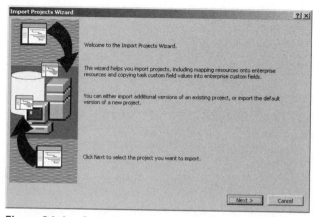

Figure 24-1. Post your project to Microsoft Project Server using the Import Projects Wizard.

4 On the first wizard page, click the Next button. The Import Project page of the wizard appears. Navigate to the folder containing the project you want to import. Click the file, and then click the Import button.

5 On the following page of the wizard (see Figure 24-2), you can change the enterprise standardization settings if you need to:

- Name
- Version
- Type
- Calendar
- Custom enterprise fields and their values

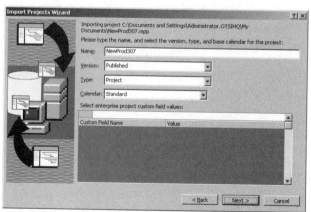

Figure 24-2. Review and accept default values for identification.

However, these settings are important for configuration and document control in the enterprise. They are all preset in this wizard to the standard enterprise values. It's best to retain the default values in these fields to maintain enterprise standardization.

6 Click the Next button.

7 On the third wizard page, match resource names if necessary (see Figure 24-3). This is only necessary if you are importing to a previously checked-in project. Then any newly added resources need to be matched with resources in the enterprise resource pool. For a first-time import, this is not necessary. Click the Next button.

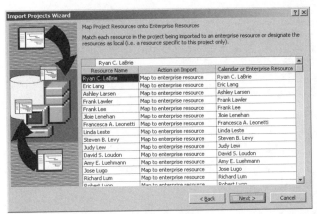

Figure 24-3. For previously imported projects, associate any unmatched resources between your project and the enterprise resource pool.

8 On the fourth wizard page, click the fields you want to import as enterprise custom fields. Click the Next button.

9 On the next page, a status report of the import process appears (see Figure 24-4). Make any necessary corrections. When finished, click the Import button.

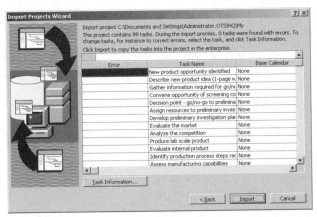

Figure 24-4. If your data has imported properly, you see the information reported here.

10 The final page of the wizard appears (see Figure 24-5), indicating that the import process has completed. If you need to import other projects, click the Import More Projects button. Otherwise, click the Finish button.

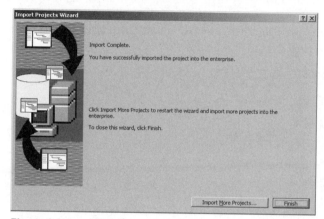

Figure 24-5. Click the Import More Projects button if you have additional projects to import.

Working with the Enterprise Global Template

Enterprise projects that are checked in to Microsoft Project Server are based on the *enterprise global template*. This is the structural and functional program that takes the data from your project plan and stores it on the Microsoft Project Server when you are working with enterprise projects. The enterprise global template is nearly identical to the project global template (the global.mpt file) in appearance, content, and usage. In addition to enterprise-specific information, the enterprise global template contains enterprise project standards, such as calendars, views, fields, tables, and filters, all of which make up the Microsoft Project interface.

As soon as you log on and connect to Microsoft Project Server, the enterprise global template is sent to your computer and loaded into memory. When you open your enterprise project, you're also checking out the enterprise global template, even though you can't make changes to it. When you save your enterprise project, you're checking the template back in to the Microsoft Project Server.

The enterprise global template has a complete structure ready to be filled in, but the data is not already populated. When working with your project plans, you still use the project global template; when you save a project plan as an enterprise project, the data is copied into the enterprise global template and it loads the file in the Microsoft Project Server.

To see the enterprise global template, click Tools, Enterprise Options, Open Enterprise Global. The appearance is identical to the project global template, so to confirm what you are seeing, you might want to check the title bar, which should read "Microsoft Project – Checked-Out Enterprise Global." Also, of course, there is no data in the enterprise global template's fields.

Although you can view the enterprise global template by opening it this way, don't attempt to enter data directly into it. Continue to use your project global template that you have populated already. When you save your project, the enterprise global template is populated with your data before being checked in to the Microsoft Project Server.

Only the project system administrator or other users with the proper permissions can change the enterprise global template, for example, to add a toolbar, a set of custom fields, or a newly designed view. Most organizations give this responsibility solely to the project system administrator because any change to the enterprise global template affects all projects throughout the enterprise. A good practice is to have enterprise project managers submit requests and samples to the project system administrator. If the changes should be made, the project system administrator makes the change to the enterprise global template. The next time users check out a project file, they will use the new version of the enterprise global template.

> For more information about working with the project global template, see Chapter 28, "Standardizing Projects Using Templates."

Customizing Enterprise Fields

There is a set of enterprise custom fields that can be added to the enterprise global template to hold special information such as specific type of currency, date, or text information.

The enterprise custom fields are as follows:

- Enterprise Cost1 through Enterprise Cost10
- Enterprise Date1 through Enterprise Date30
- Enterprise Duration1 through Enterprise Duration10
- Enterprise Flag1 through Enterprise Flag20
- Enterprise Number1 through Enterprise Number40
- Enterprise Resource Outline Code1 through Enterprise Resource Outline Code29
- Enterprise Task Outline Code1 through Enterprise Task Outline Code30
- Enterprise Text1 through Enterprise Text40

---

tip **Use regular custom fields**

Only the project system administrator or another user with the proper privileges can save custom enterprise fields to the enterprise global template.

As an enterprise user and project manager, if you need custom fields for your own project plans that don't affect the enterprise, you can define your own custom fields. Instead of using the enterprise custom fields, you can use Cost1-10, Date1-10, Text1-30, and so on.

For more information about regular custom fields, see "Customizing Fields" on page 613.

To work with custom fields, follow these steps:

1 Check out the enterprise global template by clicking Tools, Enterprise Options, Open Enterprise Global. The template opens.

2 Click Tools, Customize, Enterprise Fields. The Customize Enterprise Fields dialog box opens.

3 On the Custom Fields tab (see Figure 24-6), you see a list of available custom fields. By default, the enterprise custom fields for tasks are listed.

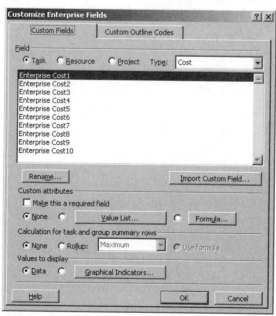

Figure 24-6. You can add customized fields for your enterprise global template.

To display enterprise custom fields for resources, select the Resource option.

To display enterprise custom fields for the project, select the Project option.

4 Under Custom Attributes, specify whether the field is required and whether you want to define a value list or formula for the field.

> For more information about defining custom fields, including setting up value lists, rollup values, and graphical indicators, see "Customizing Fields" on page 613.

To create a drop-down list of values for your custom field, click the Value List button. The Value List dialog box appears (see Figure 24-7). When you're finished defining the value list, click OK to return to the Custom Fields tab.

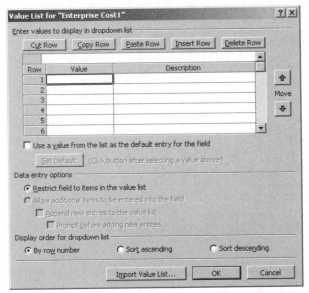

Figure 24-7. Make your own value list to show what you require in your custom field.

5 Define additional options for your custom field under Calculation For Task And Group Summary Rows and Values to Display.

6 To define custom outline codes, click the Custom Outline Codes tab (see Figure 24-8 on the next page). Define your choices for Outline Code and Enterprise Attributes, and click OK. The custom enterprise fields are now set up for you to use.

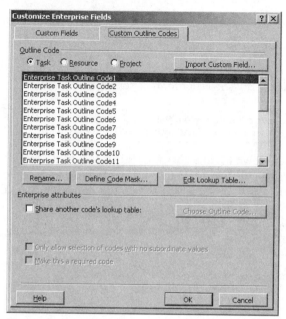

Figure 24-8. Define your preferred breakdown structures or outlining codes for enterprise projects.

For more information about defining and assigning outline codes, see "Working with Outline Codes" on page 631.

Updating Enterprise Project Information

When you open an enterprise project, you're *checking out* the project. Likewise, when you save a project as an enterprise project, you're *checking in* the project. You can set up alternate versions of a published enterprise project. You can also work offline if necessary.

Checking Enterprise Projects In and Out

While you're working with a checked-out enterprise project, no other enterprise account users can access that project.

After you save and check in the project again, it becomes accessible to other enterprise account users. Upon checking in your project, a message states that your project calendars will be saved with the standard enterprise calendars.

Similarly, if you've imported more than one project as an enterprise project, either by the initial import or by checking them in to the server, you can check out any of them from the system. To check out a file while connected to the server, open the project plan in Microsoft Project Professional by using File, Open, and then click the name of the enterprise project.

After updating the project, click Save, and check it back in. To check in a project, you must be online, that is, connected to Microsoft Project Server, and the project you're checking in must have already been imported as an enterprise project.

Working with Published Versions of Enterprise Projects

When you check in a project to the Microsoft Project Server, it's renamed with the suffix "published." Perhaps you significantly changed your project plan, gave it a new baseline, or even reconfigured the work to comply with company directives. In such situations, you need to establish a new *version* of your project. Version control is very important for enterprise projects and is set up by the project system administrator. This is to avoid having multiple versions of the same project, and to prevent any linked projects being "orphaned" by losing contact with a project that has a new version.

The project system administrator can archive, delete, add, and link or unlink versions of project plans. If you need to post a new version of your project, contact your project system administrator. Generally, the replaced version is archived, so it can still be worked with and viewed but not saved to Microsoft Project Server. The new version will be added and named differently from the old one, and any links to other project will be re-established. You might notice a difference such as the suffix being "published2" in your project's name.

Working Offline with Enterprise Projects

You can save an enterprise project and work with it offline if needed. This is handy if you are physically away from the network or want to try some contingency scenarios with the enterprise project. When you are ready to reconnect, simply log onto the server, open your enterprise project file, and then save it. Because you are back online and connected to the system, your file will be checked in when you save it.

Troubleshooting

How do you know which projects you can convert to enterprise?

When converting projects to enterprise projects, you can choose only Microsoft Project Professional files that have been saved locally, and not the file that is open. It is recommended that you save such project files locally to a folder that is easily identified as containing projects for use with enterprise features.

Chapter 24

Working with Microsoft Project Professional in stand-alone mode is convenient in many circumstances and enables more mobility. The ability to then re-establish the connection is an indispensable advantage.

Working with the Enterprise Resource Pool

With the enterprise features, resources throughout an entire organization can now be managed effectively as part of project management efforts. This is enabled by means of the *enterprise resource pool,* which can include all resources from all projects in the enterprise or even all employees in the organization.

With the enterprise resource pool, high-level visibility of resource availabilities, skills, roles, and utilization is now possible. Executives can see when additional staff is needed and where there are underutilized resources. They also can view the basic data for all project resources in one place.

Furthermore, project managers can plan for project staffing needs with accurate and current resource information from the entire enterprise, instead of from just their own team or group. The advantages of the multiple project resource pool, such as resource sharing between project managers, are magnified when applied to the entire enterprise.

Resource managers can use the enterprise resource pool to staff, plan, and budget with more accuracy and confidence. They can see resources by skill level and definition, availability, and organizational hierarchy. In addition, they can assist project managers with current and anticipated resource requirements by analyzing the enterprise resource database. In concert with the project managers, resource managers can work with generic resources in the enterprise resource pool to perform planning and contingency analyses.

With the Resource Substitution Wizard, a project manager or resource manager can quickly find and substitute resources who are required for specific project work, or who need to be transferred. Of course, company policies regarding authorizing work must be followed when assigning resources from outside one's own department.

Within individual projects, using Microsoft Project Web Access also integrates well with the enterprise resource pool. Project-level resource managers, team leads, and team members can plan their work needs, assignment possibilities, and availabilities cooperatively with the project manager.

> For more information about how Microsoft Project Web Access helps project teams collaborate, see Chapter 21, "Managing Your Team Using Microsoft Project Web Access."

> **note** When connected to the Microsoft Project Server, you cannot use the regular resource pool features. If you need to work with the regular resource pool, disconnect from the server, and the features become available again.
>
> For more information about working with the resource pool, see "Sharing Resources Using a Resource Pool" on page 402.

Importing Resource Information to Enterprise

You and other project managers throughout the organization initially import resources to Microsoft Project Server when you import your existing project plans as enterprise projects. When many project plans have been imported, and multiple resource lists have been imported, you can import additional resources from several other project plans at once, as follows:

1 In your checked-out enterprise project, click Tools, Enterprise Options, Import Resources To Enterprise.

2 The Import Resources Wizard appears. On the wizard's first page, click the Next button.

3 The Open From Microsoft Project Server page appears. Click the name of the project whose resources you want to import, and then click the Open button.

4 On the next page, map any custom resource fields from your original project to the enterprise project (see Figure 24-9). If you have none to map, do not click in the table. Click the Next button.

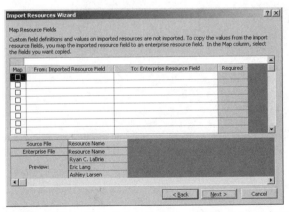

Figure 24-9. Map the project resources you are importing.

5 On the next page, you will see a list of your project resources. If the check boxes are not already selected, click the Select/Deselect All button to designate the resources you want to import (see Figure 24-10). If the check boxes are already selected, click the Next button.

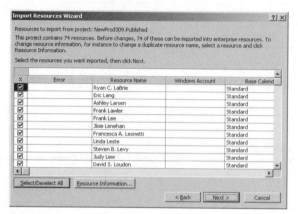

Figure 24-10. Choose the resources in your plan you want to import.

6 On the Import Complete page (see Figure 24-11), click the Import More Resources button if you need to import resources from other enterprise projects or those saved as files on your local computer. This is a handy way to be sure all your project resources are included in the enterprise resource pool. When done, click the Finish button.

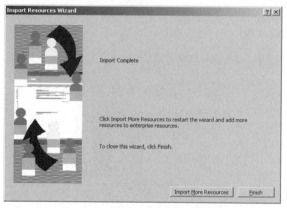

Figure 24-11. You can continue importing resources using the Import Resources Wizard.

Troubleshooting

You can't get any resources to match for importing

Suppose you're trying to import resources and you see an error message stating "This project contains a certain number of resources. Before changes, 0 of these can be imported into enterprise resources."

This error message often appears if you selected a check box in the Map Resource Fields page of the Import Resources Wizard, and did not have any custom resource fields to map. Often you do not need to map custom resource fields to the enterprise resource database. If this is the case, on the Map Resource Fields page simply examine the preview of your resources and click the Next button.

Another common cause of this error message is that you've inadvertently deselected the resource names on the next Import Resources Wizard page. Normally, all resources are automatically selected on this page, and there is no need to change that. If you click the Select All/Deselect All button, you might accidentally deselect your list of resources. Usually, all you need to do on this page is click the Next button. The exception is when you do not want to include specific resources in the import. In that case, individually clear those resources' check boxes.

You might also receive this error message if the resources in your project file are not correctly defined.

Building a Project Team

As a project manager, you can use enterprise resource management features to help build your project team. The enterprise resource pool helps you see all the potential resources you can use.

Using Generic Resources

A *generic resource* is typically a resource defined by role or skill set, such as *VB Programmer Expert*. In Microsoft Project, you can add generic resources to your project plan. With the proper permissions, you can add generic resources to the enterprise resource pool. These generic resources can then be used for planning and contingency purposes by project managers, resource managers, and executives. Because they're applied to your entire company, it's good practice to confirm that your description of the generic resource is acceptable and understandable to all. It's also good practice to review the resource pool to be sure that there is not already a generic resource that matches the one you are about to create.

Chapter 24

Generic resources are not associated with any availability status. They're intended to be placeholders. They can be checked out of the enterprise pool multiple times by multiple project managers.

You can also create generic resources directly in your project plan. Then you can use the Resource Substitution Wizard, which searches the enterprise resource pool for resources that meet the skill and availability criteria for that generic resource.

Substituting Resources

The enterprise resource pool gives managers a great tool for finding skilled people for their requirements within the entire organization. When a manager finds a resource who is not in his project team, he can do a resource substitution. Again, the guidelines and rules for sharing and authorizing resources must be set by your company. Typically you need to negotiate with a resource's manager if you want to use the resource in your project. Before doing resource substitution, be sure to identify which resource in your own project will be substituted. Often, this is best accomplished by creating a generic resource, with specific availability calendars equal to that of the resource you want to obtain.

To perform a resource substitution, do the following:

1 Log on to Microsoft Project Server to establish your enterprise connection.

2 In Microsoft Project Professional, open the project in which you're doing your resource planning.

3 Click Tools, Substitute Resources. The Resource Substitution Wizard starts.

4 On the first page, click the Next button.

5 On the Choose Projects page (see Figure 24-12), select the projects for which you need to substitute resources. This list includes all the active enterprise projects that are not checked out at the time. Click the Next button.

6 On the Choose Resources page, select the work resources you want the wizard to assign to tasks.

7 On the Choose Related Projects page, include any other projects you want to be considered when substituting resources. Enter any related projects' details, such as name and relationship to your project. Click the Next button.

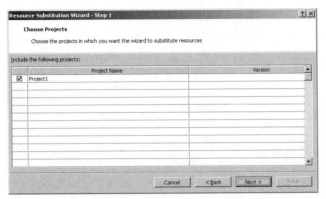

Figure 24-12. Select the check boxes for the projects in which you want the Wizard to substitute resources.

8 On the Choose Scheduling Options page, define other options you want to be applied. The defaults set the Priority at 500 and the Scheduling Option is set to use all the resources in your project. You can change the scheduling priority to a higher value, such as 700, if needed to be consistent with your project. Click the Next button.

9 On the Substitute Resources page, review the configuration based on the selections you have specified so far, and then click the Run button.

10 Click the Next button. On the Review Results page, check the results of the substitution. For the resources that were found, this page shows:

- Tasks
- Skill profiles
- Assigned resources
- Requested resources
- Request/demand status

You can manipulate the list shown by sorting, filtering, or grouping them to better see what you are interested in. If no resources are found based on your criteria, all fields will show but the table will be empty. Click the Next button.

11 On the Choose Update Options page, decide whether to update the other projects with the results of the wizard or to save the results of the wizard to a folder you specify. Click the Next button.

12 The Finish page (see Figure 24-13) includes reminders about what to do to complete the overall resource substitution process. Click the Finish button.

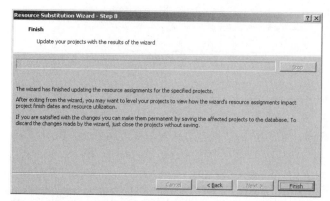

Figure 24-13. Read and heed the suggestions given on the Resource Substitution Wizard's Finish page.

Using the Team Builder

Using the Team Builder is an effective way to use the enterprise resource pool to create your project team while still in the planning phase. Team Builder can be used after a plan is built, but is most effective in the initial planning phase. This feature is enabled with proper permissions set up for you by your project system administrator.

To use the Team Builder, follow these steps:

1 Click Tools, Build Team From Enterprise. If this is your first use of the feature, you will see a message box reminding you that enterprise standard calendars are required (see Figure 24-14). Additionally, if there are more than 1000 resources in the enterprise database, you will be prompted to filter the list by outline codes.

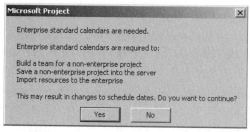

Figure 24-14. You must use standard enterprise calendars with the Team Builder.

The Build Team page appears (see Figure 24-15). It should have a full list of enterprise resources in the left pane.

Chapter 24

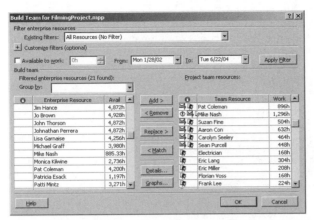

Figure 24-15. Enterprise resources and the current project resources appear in the Build Team page.

A list of the enterprise resources appears in the left pane, and a list of the open project's resources appears in the right pane. If you're building a team for a new project, there might be no resources shown in the Team Resource pane.

2 If you want to narrow the list of enterprise resources to choose from, choose from the list of existing resource filters (see Figure 24-16). You can also build a custom filter.

Figure 24-16. Choose a filter to narrow the list of enterprise resources.

You can also group the enterprise resources by predetermined criteria or by custom enterprise outline codes, if any have been created by your project system administrator (see Figure 24-17).

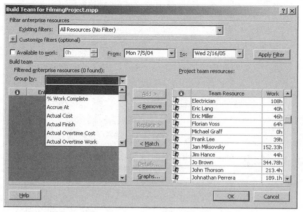

Figure 24-17. You can choose enterprise resources using many grouping criteria.

3 When your resource list is the way you want, associate resources using one of the following methods:

- Choose enterprise resources, and add them to your project team with the Add button.

- Choose any of your project resources you will not need, and move them into the enterprise list by clicking the Remove button.

- Choose a specific enterprise resource and a specific project team resource, and switch them by clicking the Replace button.

- Choose a generic resource under Team Resource, and find if any exist in the enterprise resource database by clicking the Match button.

- Choose a resource, and click the Details button to get more information about that resource.

- Choose a resource, and click Graphs to see that resource's availability graph (see Figure 24-18). This feature is a great means of forecasting needs and availabilities of resources, and it enables you to see quickly if a resource has time to work during the times you require.

Chapter 24

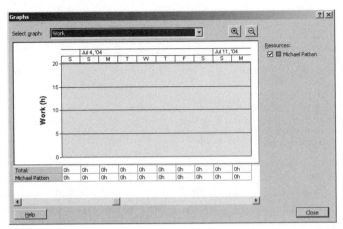

Figure 24-18. You can view availability graphs of resources when using Team Builder.

4 When finished choosing and adding resources, click OK. Your project team is built.

Viewing and Updating Resource Information

With enterprise resources in your project plans, you can review resource information in a variety of ways as enabled by enterprise features.

Reviewing Resource Availability Graphs

Availability graphs for enterprise resources are enabled in the Team Builder, and on the Microsoft Project Server in the Resource View, with the proper permissions set by your project system administrator. They can also be accessed in Microsoft Project Professional in the Assign Resources dialog box. With these graphs, you can see:

● Timephased work assignments of one or multiple resources

● Timephased availability and remaining availability of one or more resources

● Timephased resource data grouped by project

Using Resource Outline Codes

You can use *resource outline codes* to view resource information in different groupings that are pertinent to how your organization does business.

Your project system administrator can create custom resource outline codes to help group resources in various ways, for example, to create the Organizational Breakdown Structure (OBS) used by your organization. Resource outline codes can assist you in finding and reviewing resources in Team Builder or when you open the enterprise resource pool.

For more information about defining, assigning, and grouping by resource outline codes, see "Working with Outline Codes" on page 631.

Updating Resource Information

When you import a project for the first time, the resource information is automatically checked in to the enterprise resource pool.

Those with permission to check out resources from the enterprise resource pool can update basic resource information, such as names, cost information, maximum units, and so on. To do this, open the enterprise project and then click Tools, Enterprise Options, Open Enterprise Resource Pool. You then have access to the enterprise resources and you can make modifications to their information. When you save your project, the resources are checked back in.

Analyzing Multiple Projects Using Project Portfolio

One of the primary capabilities of the Microsoft Project Professional enterprise features is that it can show information about every project in the entire organization. In large organizations, or those that have very large numbers of active projects, it's generally not practical to review the details of every project throughout the organization. However, it's highly advantageous to see a high-level summary of project tasks, schedules, costs, and resource utilization. It's also helpful to be able to roll information from multiple projects together, and to make comparisons among them.

With Microsoft Project Professional and the enterprise features, there are three methods that executives can use to review, analyze, and manipulate high-level project summary information, as follows:

- The Portfolio view in Microsoft Project Web Access
- The Portfolio Analyzer through Microsoft Project Server
- The Portfolio Modeler

In Microsoft Project Web Access, you can set up a personal Portfolio view of just the enterprise projects you want to see. Your project system administrator sets the permissions and selects the projects and details for your portfolio. This is similar to setting up the Project Center for Microsoft Project Web Access, but with many more projects to choose from. Having this large, carefully tailored Portfolio view available leverages the power of the enterprise features.

Also, executives can be set up with a Portfolio Analyzer view in Microsoft Project Server that provides summary information in three formats:

- Pivot table
- Chart, such as line graphs
- A combination of both

Portfolio
Analyzer

The Portfolio Analyzer is valuable to senior managers and executives who require special evaluation and analysis of enterprise projects and resources. If you're working in Microsoft Project Professional and want to quickly switch to the Portfolio Analyzer, click Portfolio Analyzer on the Collaborate toolbar.

Portfolio
Modeler

In the same way, you can open the Portfolio Modeler by clicking Portfolio Modeler on the Collaborate toolbar.

> **note** If the Collaborate toolbar is not showing, in Microsoft Project, click View, Toolbars, Collaborate.

OnLine Analytical Processing (OLAP) cube is an analytical tool intended to selectively locate and organize task or resource data from a Microsoft SQL Server. For Microsoft Project Server enterprise features, they are designed to serve as means to selectively examine different aspects of the databases. OLAP capabilities are set up by the project system administrator for individual users (see Figure 24-19 on the next page).

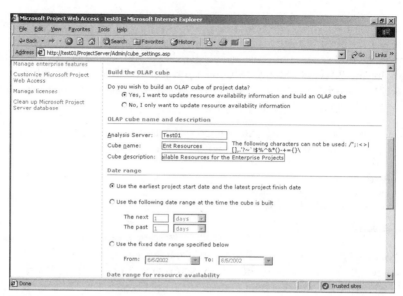

Figure 24-19. The parameters of your OLAP cube are set in Microsoft Project Server.

OLAP cubes use the SQL Server 2000 Analysis Services and the Decision Support Objects file to facilitate their operations. Ranges and types of information to be included in the OLAP cube are defined by the project system administrator in concert with the executive user. Such data items as date ranges and resource fields are used to define the cube. You can have OLAP cubes set up for either project or resource data, or both. The OLAP cubes are the means by which the data is analyzed; they are not the actual user interface. The user interface is the Portfolio Analyzer View page in Microsoft Project Server.

Part 9

Customizing and Managing Project Files

Chapter 25

Customizing Your View of Project Information

Organizations are as unique as people, and each project that an organization manages has its own particular needs. The solution to each new challenge requires a specific set of information, just as each step in managing a project does. You can control what information you see and how it is formatted, whether you want to satisfy your own preferences or meet the specialized needs of a particular project. Almost every aspect of Microsoft Project can be molded to your specifications, including:

- Views
- Tables
- Fields
- Groups
- Filters
- Reports

If you or your organization use outline codes, such as accounting codes to categorize tasks or skill codes to categorize resources, you can customize outline codes in Microsoft Project for this purpose. You can adapt these codes to your organization's standards; apply them to project tasks and resources; and then sort, group, or filter information using your custom outline codes.

You can use these customized elements in one project or every project you create. This chapter describes how to customize all these elements and use them in your projects.

Part 9: Customizing and Managing Project Files

Customizing Views

Each view gives you a different perspective on your project information. The right view with pertinent data can simplify your project management tasks or uncover potential problems. You can specify which views you see, change the tables and fields that appear in a view, and control how information is categorized and displayed so you can look at your project information the way you want.

Changing the Content of a View

Microsoft Project includes a variety of standard views that present task, resource, and assignment information. When these standard views don't meet your needs, you can customize their content or create new views that are more suitable. For combination views, you can change which views appear in the top and bottom pane; and in single pane views, you can specify which view, table, group and filter to apply when the view appears.

To customize the content of an existing combination view, follow these steps:

1 Click View, More Views.

2 In the More Views dialog box, click the view's name in the Views list (see Figure 25-1).

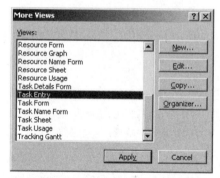

Figure 25-1. You can edit an existing view, copy an existing view, or create a completely new view.

3 To change the existing view, click the Edit button. To create a new view based on the existing view, click the Copy button.

4 The View Definition dialog box appears. In the Name box, you can type a new name for the view.

5 In the Top box, click the view that you want to appear in the top pane (see Figure 25-2).

6 In the Bottom box, click the view that you want to appear in the bottom pane.

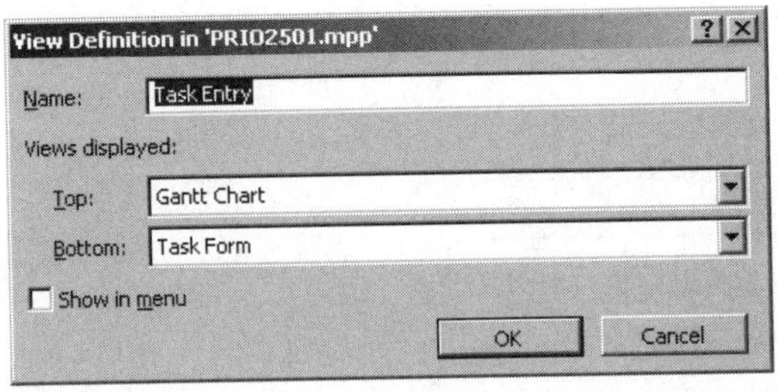

Chapter 25: Customizing Your View of Project Information

Figure 25-2. Specify which views are displayed in the top and bottom panes of a combination view.

InsideOut

The View menu and the View bar include the views used most frequently by the majority of Microsoft Project users. However, if you prefer other views such as the Task Details Form or one of your customized views, you might get tired of clicking More Views every time you want to use them.

You can replace the default views with your favorites on the View menu and View bar. Click View, More Views. Click the view you want to add to the View menu, and then click Edit. In the View Definition dialog box, select the Show In Menu check box. To remove a view that you don't use from the list, clear its Show In Menu check box.

You can also modify the order in which views appear. By default, task views appear first and in alphabetical order, followed by resource views in alphabetical order. In the More Views dialog box, click the view you want to move, and then click Edit. In the Name box, add a number in front of the name to move it to the top of its respective list. If you prefix all the displayed views with a sequential number, they'll appear in numerical order.

You can prefix a view name with text to differentiate customized views from standard ones. For example, if you add the prefix "C-" at the beginning of the name of each customized view, the list will segregate your customized and standard views.

To customize the content of an existing single pane view, do the following:

1 Click View, More Views.

2 In the More Views dialog box, click the view's name in the Views list.

3 Click the Edit button. The View Definition dialog box appears (see Figure 25-3 on the next page). If you want to create a new view that is similar to the selected view, click the Copy button and type a new name in the Name box.

Part 9: Customizing and Managing Project Files

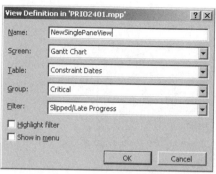

Figure 25-3. You choose a table, group, and filter when you customize a single pane view.

---

tip   **Create customized elements before you reference them**

If you plan to use customized tables, groups, or filters in a view, you must create those elements before you use them in a customized view. You must also create customized single pane views before you can include them in a combination view.

---

4 In the Table box, click the table that you want to appear in the customized view.

5 In the Group box, click the group that you want to use.

6 In the Filter box, click the filter that you want to apply.

7 If you want to highlight filtered tasks, select the Highlight Filter check box.

InsideOut

Changing the table that appears in a view also changes the table in the definition of that view. That table appears the next time you display that view. However, applying a group or filter to a view does not change the group or filter selected in the View Definition dialog box. The view uses the group and filter you chose when you customized the view.

When you customize an existing single pane view, the View Definition dialog box displays the type of view used, but you can't modify it. However, when you create a new single pane view, you can choose which type of view to use.

If none of the existing views come close to meeting your needs, you can create a new single pane or combination view. To do this, follow these steps:

1 Click View, More Views.

2 In the More Views dialog box, click New.

3 In the Define New View dialog box, select either the Single Pane View or Combination View option, and then click OK. The View Definition dialog box for the type of view you selected appears.

4 Specify the contents of the view, as described in the section "Changing the Content of a View," earlier in this chapter.

---

tip **Applying a view quickly**

You can use the keyboard to choose a view from the View menu by assigning a keyboard shortcut. Type an ampersand (&) before the letter that you want to use for the shortcut. After you save the customized view, click View, and then press the shortcut letter to apply the view.

Use a different letter for each keyboard shortcut. If you choose a letter that is already in use by another menu entry, you might have to press the letter more than once to choose the view you want.

Formatting a Gantt Chart View

The chart portion of the Gantt Chart view provides a graphical representation of your project schedule. You can emphasize information in your schedule by formatting individual Gantt bars or all Gantt bars of a certain type. Similarly, you can apply formatting to different categories of text or only to the text that is selected. Link lines and gridlines communicate information but they can also clutter the Gantt Chart. Layout options and formatting for gridlines control how much you see of these elements.

Using the Gantt Chart Wizard

If you would rather not format each element in a Gantt Chart view, you can use the Gantt Chart Wizard to specify what information you want to see and how to format the Gantt Chart's elements. You can choose a standard type of Gantt Chart such as Critical Path or Baseline, choose from several predefined Gantt Chart styles, or create a custom Gantt Chart. If you opt for a customized Gantt Chart, you can control which types of Gantt bars appear and customize the color, pattern, and end shapes for each type. You can choose to display resources and dates on the taskbars and choose exactly the fields you want to display. Finally, you can show or hide the link lines between dependent tasks.

Formatting the Appearance of Gantt Bars

You can modify the shape, fill pattern, and color of individual bars or all Gantt bars of a particular type. You can also customize the marks that appear at the beginning and end of those bars. For example, you might want to accentuate critical tasks that aren't complete by making them red with red stars at each end.

To change the appearance of all Gantt bars of a particular type, follow these steps:

1 Click View, Gantt Chart or click another Gantt chart view.

2 Click Format, Bar Styles. The Bar Styles dialog box lists all the Gantt bar types for the current view with the settings for their appearance (see Figure 25-4). For example, Gantt bars appear as a blue bar for normal tasks, whereas summary Gantt bars are solid black with black end marks at both ends.

> **tip** **Open the Bar Styles dialog box quickly**
>
> You can also open the Bar Styles dialog box by double-clicking the background of the chart portion of a Gantt chart.

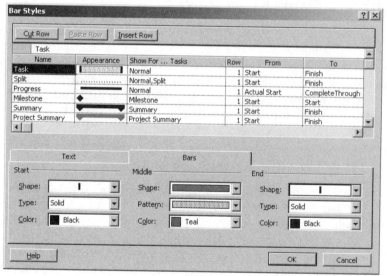

Figure 25-4. You can customize the appearance of the Gantt bar as well as markers at its start and end.

3 To change the look of a specific type of Gantt bar, click its name in the list.

4 Click the Bars tab, and then make the changes you want to the Start, Middle, and End of the bar. The settings for the start and end determine the appearance of the markers at the beginning and end of the bar, whereas the settings for the middle control the appearance of the bar itself.

To change the pattern, color, and shape of the Gantt bar for individual tasks, do the following:

1 In the sheet portion of the view, click the task or tasks whose Gantt bars you want to change.

2 Click Format, Bar, and in the Format Bar dialog box, click the Bar Shape tab.

3 On the Bar Shape tab, make the changes you want to the Start (beginning marker), Middle (the bar itself), and End (ending marker).

Troubleshooting

Changing the bar style for one task changes the Gantt bars for all tasks

The Bar and Bar Styles commands on the Format menu sound similar, but they operate quite differently. The Bar command applies the changes you make to only the tasks that are currently selected. The Bar Styles command applies changes to all Gantt bars of a particular type, for example, critical tasks, incomplete tasks, or milestones.

This distinction is analogous to changing the formatting in a word processing document. You can select an individual paragraph and change the formatting to Arial 14, Bold. But if you want all headings to use this formatting, you can save time by creating a style and applying it to each heading paragraph.

In addition to changing the styles of Gantt bars, you can also define new types of Gantt bars. To do this, follow these steps:

1 Apply a Gantt chart view.

2 Click Format, Bar Styles.

3 Scroll to the end of the list of Gantt bar types or click a row above where you want to insert your new Gantt bar type, and then click Insert Row.

4 In the Name field, type the name of your new Gantt bar.

5 Click the cell in the Show For … Tasks column.

6 Click the down arrow in the box, and then click the category of task for which this bar should be displayed. For example, if you're creating a style for tasks that aren't finished, click Not Finished.

> **tip**   **Create a Gantt bar style for multiple conditions**
>
> If you want a Gantt bar style to appear when more than one condition exists, click the first condition, type a comma, and then click the second condition, such as "Critical, Not Finished." You can also create a Gantt bar that appears when a condition is not true. Type the word "Not" in front of a selected task condition, such as "Not Milestone," or "Critical, Not In Progress."

7   In the From and To columns, click the date fields that determine the beginning and end of the Gantt bar. For example, you might draw a progress bar from the Start date to the Complete Through date, or a bar from the Actual Start date to the Deadline date for critical tasks that aren't yet finished.

8   Click the Bars tab, and then specify the appearance for the Start, Middle, and End of the bar.

9   Click the Text tab, and then click the box for the position, such as Left or Right, depending on where you want text to appear for the Gantt bar.

10   Click the down arrow in the box, and then click the name of the task field whose content you want to appear for this Gantt bar type.

> **tip**   **Create a bar style for flagged tasks**
>
> If you want to call attention to tasks that don't meet any of the task conditions listed in the Show For ... Tasks field, you can create a new bar style that applies only to marked or flagged tasks. When you mark or flag tasks, they appear in that bar style.
>
> You can add the Marked field to the sheet portion of your Gantt Chart, and then set the value to Yes for each task you want to mark. If you are already using the Marked field, you can insert a column for one of the custom flag fields, such as Flag1, and set it to Yes for those tasks. In the Bar Styles dialog box, create a new bar style to show for the Marked or the custom flag field and specify its appearance and associated text.

Troubleshooting

A Gantt bar doesn't appear in the chart

A Gantt chart displays bars in the order that they appear in the Bar Styles dialog box. If Gantt bars with a narrower shape such as progress bars appear above the normal Gantt bars in the list, the wider Gantt bars hide the narrower ones.

If you rearrange the order so the narrower Gantt bars appear below the wider ones in the Bar Styles list, you will be able to see both bars.

InsideOut

Some tasks might meet the conditions for several types of Gantt bars. If this occurs, Microsoft Project draws a Gantt bar for the task for each condition that it satisfies. These bars might overlap each other and obscure some of the information you want to see.

To avoid this, you can stack up to four Gantt bars, one above the next, so they're all visible. To do this, in the Bar Styles dialog box, specify 1, 2, 3, or 4 in the Row field for each overlapping Gantt bar.

Formatting the Appearance of Gantt Bar Text

Displaying task field values next to the Gantt bars makes it easy to correlate task information with bars in the chart. By displaying text next to Gantt bars, you can often reduce the number of columns needed in the sheet portion of the Gantt Chart and display more of the chart portion.

To change the text for all Gantt bars of a particular type, follow these steps:

1 Click Format, Bar Styles.

2 Click the name of the Gantt bar type whose text you want to change.

3 Click the Text tab.

4 Click the box for the position, such as Left or Right, where you want the text to appear for the Gantt bar.

5 Click the down arrow in the box, and then click the name of the task field whose content you want to appear for this Gantt bar type.

   For example, if you want text to appear inside the Gantt bar, click the Inside box, click the down arrow, and then click the name of the field whose content you want to appear inside this Gantt bar type.

To change the text accompanying the Gantt bar for selected tasks, do the following:

1 In the sheet portion of the view, click the task or tasks whose Gantt bar text you want to change.

2 Click Format, Bar, and in the Format Bar dialog box, click the Bar Text tab.

3 On the Bar Text tab, click the box for the position, such as Left, Right, Top or Bottom, where you want the text to appear for the Gantt bar.

4 Click the down arrow to the right of the box, and then click the name of the task field whose content you want to appear for this Gantt bar (see Figure 25-5).

For example, if you want text to appear to the right of the Gantt bar, click the Right box, click the down arrow, and then click the name of the field whose content you want to appear on the right end of this task.

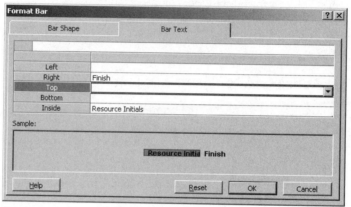

Figure 25-5. You can specify fields to display as text for selected Gantt bars.

Although you can change the text position and content for individual Gantt bars, you can't change the font, style, or color of the text. To change the text style for all Gantt bars of a particular type, follow these steps:

1 Click Format, Text Styles.

2 In the Item To Change box, click the type of task whose text style you want to change.

For example, if you want the text accompanying all critical tasks to be 16-point red type, click Critical Tasks in the Item To Change box.

3 Make the changes you want in the Font, Font Style, Size, and Color boxes.

Formatting Text Styles and Individual Text

The Text Styles command on the Format menu formats the text for tasks of a particular type. To change the attributes of only the selected text, use the Font command instead. Click Format, Font, and then choose the font, font style, size, and color.

Formatting the Layout of Gantt Bars

Link lines between dependent tasks show how tasks are related to each other. However, too many link lines can obscure the information you are trying to communicate. You might want to modify the appearance of link lines, the height of Gantt bars, or whether splits and rolled up bars are displayed if the schedule is too cluttered. To change the layout of links and bars in a Gantt chart, do the following:

1 Click Format, Layout.

2 In the Layout dialog box, select the option for how you want the links between dependent tasks to appear.

For example, you can hide the link lines, draw them as S-shapes between the ends of tasks, or display them as L-shapes from the end of one task to the top of another task.

3 Choose a date format to use when a date field is associated with a Gantt bar.

4 If necessary, choose the height of the Gantt bar.

5 Choose other layout options to roll up Gantt bars, draw the bar width in increments of whole days, or show splits.

For example, if you roll up Gantt bars, summary tasks display information about their subordinate tasks. If you are fine-tuning your project schedule, you might want to view where splits occur or see the duration of tasks down to the hour.

Formatting the Appearance of Gridlines

Gridlines separate elements such as columns and rows in the sheet portion of a Gantt chart or the dates and tasks in the chart portion. For example, you might want to add horizontal lines to the chart to help correlate Gantt bars with their associated tasks in the sheet portion. To change the gridlines in a Gantt chart, follow these steps:

1 Click Format, Gridlines.

2 In the Line To Change box, click the element whose gridlines you want to add, remove, or change.

Elements for both the sheet portion and chart portion of the Gantt chart appear in the Line To Change list. The current style appears in the Normal area.

3 Change the line type in the Type box and the color in the Color box.

4 If you want to display lines at certain intervals, such as after every fourth item, click the interval in the At Interval area.

For information about modifying the timescale in the Gantt Chart, see "Modifying the Timescale," later in this chapter.

Changing the Format of a View

Changes you make to formatting within a view apply to only the active view. For example, modifications you make to the chart, bar or text styles, individual Gantt bars, or text formatting in the Tracking Gantt appear only when you display the Tracking Gantt. You can customize the formatting for each view without worrying about modifying all the others.

Also, changes you make to views in one project file apply only to that project file. When you create a new project file, it uses the default views. If you want to make customized views available to other project files, see "Sharing Customized Elements among Projects" later in this chapter.

Modifying a Network Diagram

Network diagrams display tasks as boxes, or nodes, with link lines showing the task dependencies. Because a network diagram doesn't include a task sheet like the Gantt Chart, it's important to specify the information that you want to appear inside the boxes. You can customize the appearance of the boxes or how they are arranged within the diagram.

Formatting the Content and Appearance of Boxes

Just as you can change the appearance of Gantt bars for different types of tasks, you can modify the boxes in a network diagram depending on the task type. You can also control what task information appears inside those boxes.

To change the appearance and content for all boxes of a particular type, do the following:

1 Click View, Network Diagram.

2 Click Format, Box Styles. The Box Styles dialog box lists all the box types for the current view and the settings for their appearance (see Figure 25-6).

3 To customize a specific type of box, click its name in the list.

4 To change the fields that appear within the box, click a data template in the Data Template box. A preview of the box using the selected data template appears.

Chapter 25: Customizing Your View of Project Information

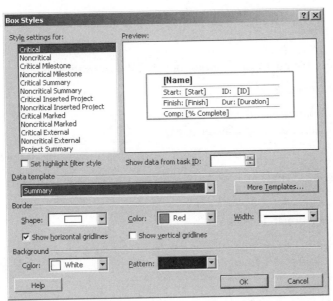

Figure 25-6. You can customize the appearance of a network diagram
box as well as specify what task information appears inside each box.

---

tip   **Showing other information in a network diagram**

newfeature!

You can also modify or create new data templates for the boxes in the Network
Diagram. For example, you might want to include a custom field in a data template.
Click More Templates, click a template name, and then click Edit or Copy. To create
a new template, click New. To insert a field into the data template, click the cell where
you want to insert the field, click the down arrow, and then click the name of the
field in the list.

You can also add fields that display graphical indicators to the template.

---

5   If necessary, change the shape, color, and width of the box border.

6   If you want to display horizontal or vertical gridlines between the fields
inside a box, select the Show Horizontal Gridlines and Show Vertical
Gridlines check boxes.

7   If necessary, choose a background color and pattern.

---

caution   Although you can select different colors and patterns for the box background,
any combination other than solid white makes it difficult to read the task information.

To change the displayed fields and border appearance for individual boxes, follow
these steps:

1 Choose the boxes you want to format in the Network Diagram.

2 Click Format, Box.

3 Click a data template in the Data Template box. A preview of the box using
the selected data template appears.

4 Make the changes you want to the shape, color, and width of the border.

5 Make the changes you want to the background color and pattern for the box.

---

tip   **Accessing the Format dialog box**

You can open the Format Box dialog box by double-clicking the border of a box.
Double-clicking the background of a Network Diagram opens the Box Styles dialog box.

Formatting the Layout of Boxes

The Network Diagram is much like a flowchart of the tasks in a project. The layout
options for the Network Diagram control how boxes are positioned and aligned,
the distance between the boxes, the appearance of links, and other settings.

To change the layout of a Network Diagram, do the following:

1 Click Format, Layout. The Layout dialog box appears.

2 To position boxes manually, select the Allow Manual Box Positioning option.

3 Choose the order in which boxes are placed on the diagram in the Arrangement box. For example, you can arrange the boxes from the top left down
to the bottom right of the diagram. You can choose to place critical tasks
before others.

4 Choose the alignment, distance between rows and columns, and the width
and height of the boxes.

5 Select link options such as whether to draw lines orthogonally or directly
between boxes, whether to include arrows and link labels.

6 If necessary, choose link colors.

> **tip** **Fine-tune the display of the Network Diagram**
>
> If you select the option to position boxes automatically, it's a good idea to select the Adjust For Page Breaks check box also. Otherwise, boxes located across a page break are printed on two pages in the diagram.
>
> Summary tasks are difficult to distinguish in a network diagram, so you might want to clear the Show Summary Tasks check box. If you display summary tasks, you should select the Keep Tasks With Their Summaries check box.

Modifying the Resource Graph

The Resource Graph presents resource allocation, cost, or work over periods of time. The horizontal axis represents time, whereas the vertical axis represents units such as availability, cost, or work. You can choose the fields that you want to appear in the graph. You can also modify the appearance of bars and text of particular types and change the gridlines in the graph. However, you can't modify the appearance of individual bars or text.

newfeature! The Resource View displays the resources that comprise the enterprise resource pool. This view enables you to view, group, and edit enterprise resource information, and also to inspect resource availability across multiple projects.

> For more information about working with enterprise resources, see "Working with the Enterprise Resource Pool," on page 570.

Modifying the Appearance of Resource Graph Bars

The Bar Styles dialog box for the Resource Graph contains four areas, each of which controls the appearance of bars for different sets of information. For example, if you graph overallocations, the two top areas display overallocations, whereas the bottom areas display allocations less than or equal to the maximum available units. The areas on the left side of the dialog box control how group data appears. The areas on the right side of the dialog box control the appearance of data for one selected resource.

Follow these steps to modify the appearance of Resource Graph bars of a particular type:

1 Click View, Resource Graph.

2 Click Format, Bar Styles. The bars in the Resource Graph represent information that you don't see in the Gantt Chart. The Bar Styles dialog box (see Figure 25-7 on the next page) contains different settings than the Gantt Chart Bar Styles dialog box.

Part 9: Customizing and Managing Project Files

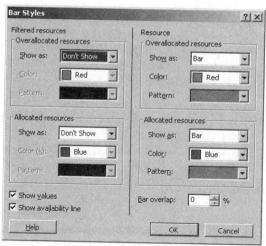

Figure 25-7. You can choose which field to display in the Resource Graph for individual resources and groups of resources.

3 In the Bar Styles dialog box, choose the method for displaying the data, color, and pattern.

InsideOut

When the Resource Graph appears in the bottom pane below a task view, the graph shows the values for only one resource. When the Resource Graph appears below a resource view or in the top pane, it displays the values for all tasks. It can display the data for one resource, a group of resources; or compare data for one resource to a group. If you want to see only the data for the selected resource, click Don't Show in the Show As box for Filtered Resources. However, if you want to compare the values of the selected resource to other resources in a filter, click one of the other graph methods in the Filtered Resources area. To differentiate overallocations from regular assignments, choose methods, colors, or patterns in the Overallocated and Allocated areas of the dialog box.

In addition, when you view any of the fields that relate to work or resource availability, you can select the Show Availability Line check box to display resource availability on the graph.

Changing the Information that Appears in the Resource Graph

To choose which values you want to see in the Resource Graph, click Format, Details. A shortcut menu appears with the following choices:

Peak Units. Represents the highest percentage of units assigned to a resource during each period on the graph. Units that exceed the maximum units for the resource appear as an overallocation.

---

caution **Peak units can be misleading**

Peak units are helpful for analyzing the allocation of a resource that represents more than one person, such as Painters, which might have maximum units of 400 percent for a four-person painter pool. However, if one resource is assigned full time to two 2-day tasks during one week, Peak Units equals 200 percent (two tasks multiplied by 100 percent allocation) even though the person can complete 4 days of work during one week.

Work. Displays the amount of work assigned to a resource during the period. If the hours exceed the number of hours available for the resource, the excess hours appear as an overallocation. The hours available for a resource take into account the resource calendar and the resource's maximum units.

Cumulative Work. Displays the total work assigned to the resource since the project began.

Overallocation. Includes only the hours that the resource is overallocated during the period, not work hours that fit in the resource's workday.

Percent Allocation. Represents the work assigned to a resource as a percentage of their available time.

Remaining Availability. Shows the number of hours that the resource is available. This graph is helpful when you are trying to find someone to work on a new task.

Cost. Displays the labor cost and per-use cost of a resource for the period. The total cost of a task appears in the period in which the task begins or ends, if resource costs accrue at the start or end.

Cumulative Cost. Shows the running total of the cost since the start of the project. This choice can show the total cost of a project when you display the value for a group that includes all the project resources.

Work Availability. Represents the number of hours that a resource could work based on his or her maximum units and resource calendar. It doesn't take into account any existing assignments.

Unit Availability. Displays the same information as Work Availability, formatted as a percentage.

Chapter 25

> **tip** **Modifying field formats**
>
> The settings in the Options dialog box control how information is formatted in the
> Resource Graph. To change the unit for work, click Tools, Options. Click the Schedule
> tab, and then change the units in the Work Is Entered In box. To change the currency
> format for costs, click Tools, Options. Click the View tab, and change the options
> in the Currency section.

To modify which information appears in the Resource Graph, follow these steps:

1 Right-click the background of the Resource Graph, and then click the field
to display.

For example, if you are trying to eliminate the overallocations for a resource,
click Overallocation or Percent Overallocation. However, if you are looking
for an available resource, click Remaining Availability.

2 If necessary, right-click the background of the Resource Graph, and then
click Bar Styles to adjust the appearance of the information. For example,
you can view overallocations for the selected resource and others in the
same resource group (see Figure 25-8).

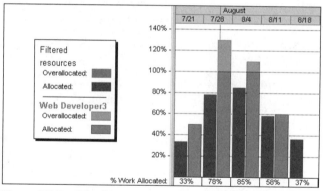

Figure 25-8. The Resource Graph can show information for one selected
resource and a group of resources.

> For information about modifying the text styles or gridlines in the Resource Graph, follow the
> steps described in "Formatting Text Styles and Individual Text" and "Formatting the Appearance
> of Gridlines," earlier in this chapter.

Modifying the Calendar View

You can customize the bar styles, text styles, layout, gridlines, and timescale for the Calendar view.

To modify the bar styles for a particular type of task, do the following:

1 Click View, Calendar.

2 Click Format, Bar Styles. The Bar Styles dialog box lists all the task types for the calendar.

3 To change the appearance of a specific type of Calendar bar, click its name in the list.

4 Choose the Bar Type, Pattern, Color, and Split Pattern for the bar.

5 Choose the fields that you want to appear inside the Calendar bar. For example, if you want to see the task name and resource initials, type "Name, Resource Initials" in the Field(s) box.

To modify the arrangement of tasks in the Calendar, follow these steps:

1 Click Format, Layout. The Layout dialog box for the Calendar view appears.

2 To display as many tasks as you can in the Calendar boxes, select the Attempt To Fit As Many Boxes As Possible option. This sorts tasks by Total Slack and then by Duration. Otherwise, tasks appear in the current sort order.

3 Select the Automatic Layout check box to reapply the layout options as you add, remove, or sort tasks.

To modify the timescale in the Calendar, do the following:

1 Click Format, Timescale.

2 In the Timescale dialog box, click the Week Headings tab, and then choose the titles that you want to appear for months, weeks, and days in the calendar.

3 Select the 5 Days or 7 Days option to display the work days or all days in a week.

4 Select the Previous/Next Month Calendars check box to preview the previous and following months.

5 Click the Date Boxes tab to specify the information you want to appear in the heading for each date box.

6 Click the Date Shading tab to customize how working and nonworking time for base and resource calendars appear on the calendar.

> For information about modifying the text styles or gridlines in the Calendar, follow the steps described in "Formatting Text Styles and Individual Text" and "Formatting the Appearance of Gridlines," earlier in this chapter.

Modifying a Sheet View

The Resource Sheet and the Task Sheet display information about your project resources and tasks in a tabular layout. You can change the table that appears in the sheet view along with the height of rows and width of columns.

> For more information about customizing text, see the sidebar, "Formatting Text Styles and Individual Text," earlier in this chapter.

Follow these steps to change the table in the sheet view:

1 Click View, More Views. Click Task Sheet, or another sheet view.

2 Right-click the Select All box in the upper-left corner of the table (above row 1). A shortcut menu appears with tables for the sheet view. Click the name of the table that you want to appear.

For example, to see costs in the Task Sheet, click Cost on the shortcut menu. If the table you want doesn't appear on the shortcut menu, click More Tables, and in the More Tables dialog box, double-click the table you want in the Tables list.

To resize a column in the sheet, use one of the following methods:

● Position the mouse pointer between two column headings until it changes to a two-headed arrow, and then double-click the column edge to resize the column to fit all the values in the column.

● Position the mouse pointer between two column headings until it changes to a two-headed arrow, and then drag the column on the left to the desired width.

● Double-click the column heading to display the Column Definition dialog box. Click the column width in the Width box or click Best Fit.

---

newfeature!

tip   **Display column headings the way you want**

Microsoft Project 2002 provides text wrapping for header cells in a table as well
as manual header row height adjustment. To adjust the row height automatically
to display the entire column title, click View, Table, and then click More Tables.
Click the table you want to modify, and then click Edit. In the Table Definition dialog
box, select the Auto-Adjust Header Row Heights check box.

You can change the height of one or more rows in a sheet.

For information about resizing all rows in a table, see "Customizing Tables," later in this chapter.

Do the following to resize individual rows in a sheet:

1 Click the rows you want to resize in the sheet view.

2 To make the selected rows taller, position the mouse pointer beneath
the ID number of one of the selected rows and drag downward. To make the
selected rows shorter, position the mouse pointer above the ID number of
a selected row and drag upward.

For information about inserting, deleting, moving, and copying rows and columns in a table,
see "Customizing Tables" later in this chapter.

Modifying a Usage View

Usage views, such as the Resource Usage and Task Usage view, display information
divided across time periods. Usage views include a sheet view in the left pane and a timephased grid (the timesheet) with the field details in the right pane. You can customize
the sheet and the timescale for the timesheet as you can in the Gantt Chart and other
views. You can also choose which fields you want to see in the timesheet.

To select and format the timephased fields shown in the timesheet in a usage view,
follow these steps:

1 Click View, Resource Usage, or choose another usage view.

2 Right-click the timesheet, and then click Detail Styles.

3 The Detail Styles dialog box lists the different timephased fields you can
display in the timesheet, such as Work, Actual Work, Overtime Work,
and Cost (see Figure 25-9 on the next page).

4 Click the Usage Details tab to specify which fields you want to see.

Part 9: Customizing and Managing Project Files

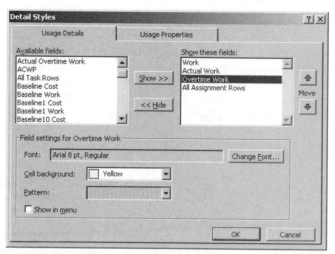

Figure 25-9. Choose the fields to display and their formatting in the Detail Styles dialog box.

5 Click the fields you want to add in the Available Fields list, and then click Show to add them to the timesheet. You can also click fields in the Show These Fields list, and then click Hide to remove fields from the timesheet.

6 To change the order in which fields appear, click a field in the Show These Fields list, and then click the up or down arrows.

7 Choose the font, color, and pattern for the selected field if you want to change its appearance in the timesheet.

---

tip **Adding fields in the timesheet**

To quickly add a field, right-click the timesheet, and then click the field you want to add on the shortcut menu. A check box appears in front of the field name on the shortcut menu and another row of timephased information appears in the timesheet for each task.

newfeature! To remove a field from the timesheet, right-click the grid, and on the shortcut menu, click the field you want to remove.

The Usage Properties tab in the Detail Styles dialog box includes the following options for formatting the detail headers and the data within the timesheet:

● If you want to align the data in the timesheet cells, click Right, Left, or Center in the Align Details Data box.

● If you can't see the field names on the left side of the timesheet, click Yes in the Display Details Header Column box.

● If the field names are missing in some of the rows, select the Repeat Details Header On All Assignment Rows check box.

● If the field names take up too much space, select the Display Short Detail Header Names check box.

For information about modifying the text styles or gridlines in a Usage view, follow the steps described in "Formatting Text Styles and Individual Text" and "Formatting the Appearance of Gridlines," earlier in this chapter. For information about formatting the sheet portion of the Usage view, see "Modifying a Sheet View" and "Customizing Tables," later in this chapter. For information about formatting the timescale, see "Modifying the Timescale," later in this chapter.

The values in the timesheet often exceed the width of the columns. Instead of adjusting the width of columns in the Timescale dialog box, you can resize them in the Usage view timesheet with the mouse. To resize columns in the timesheet, follow these steps:

1 Position the mouse pointer between two column headings in the timesheet until it changes to a two-headed arrow.

2 Drag the pointer to the left or right until the columns are the desired width.

If the current view displays a timesheet in both panes, changing the column width on one pane changes the width in the other pane so the timesheet columns always line up. You can press Ctrl+Z to reset the width to its previous size.

Modifying the Timescale

The timescale is a prominent feature in many Microsoft Project views, such as the Gantt chart and usage views. You can display up to three timescales in a view. For each time-scale, you can customize the units, the labels for time periods, and label alignment. You can also display a calendar or fiscal year. In addition, you can choose how many timescales you want to use as well as the width of each period in the timescale.

Changes you make to the timescale apply only to the active view, but those changes become a permanent part of that view definition. Your timescale customizations appear each time you display that view.

To set the options for one or more tiers in the timescale, do the following:

1 Display a view that contains a timescale, such as Gantt Chart, Task Usage, or Resource Graph.

2 Right-click the timescale heading, and then click Timescale on the shortcut menu. The Timescale dialog box appears.

newfeature!

3 The Timescale dialog box has four tabs (see Figure 25-10): Top Tier, Middle Tier, Bottom Tier, and Non-Working Time. The Middle Tier tab is displayed by default. In the Show list under Timescale Options, click the number of tiers you want to display (one, two, or three).

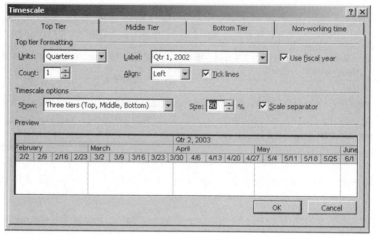

Figure 25-10. Customize the time periods that appear in a Gantt Chart, Task Usage, or Resource Graph view.

4 To change the width of the timescale columns, click a percentage in the Size box.

5 Select the Scale Separator check box to draw lines between each timescale tier.

To set the options for each timescale tier, follow these steps:

1 In the Timescale dialog box, click the tab for the timescale tier you want to customize.

2 In the Units box, specify the time unit you want to display for the current tier. For example, you might choose Quarters for the top tier if your organization's financial performance depends on this project.

> **caution** The time unit in a lower tier must be shorter than the unit for the tier above it. For example, if the top tier time unit is months, the middle tier can't be years.

Chapter 25: Customizing Your View of Project Information

3 To display the fiscal year in the timescale, select the Use Fiscal Year check box.

4 To display an interval of more than one unit, choose the number of units in the Count box. For example, to display two-week intervals, click Weeks in the Units box and 2 in the Count box.

5 To change the label format, choose a format in the Label box, for example, 1st Quarter, Qtr 1, 2002, or 1Q02.

6 Click Left, Right, or Center in the Align box to position the label in the timescale.

7 If you chose to display more than one tier, click the tabs for the other tiers and repeat steps 2 through 6.

caution   When you click the Zoom In or Zoom Out buttons on the Standard toolbar or click Zoom on the View menu, changes you make to the labels in the timescales disappear.

You can also control how nonworking time appears in the timescale. To set the nonworking time options in the timescale, do the following:

1 In the Timescale dialog box, click the Non-Working Time tab.

2 To display nonworking time using the same format as that for working time, select the Do Not Draw check box.

3 If you display the nonworking time, choose the color and pattern for the nonworking time shading.

4 Choose the calendar whose nonworking time you want to display in the Calendar box.

tip   **Changing nonworking time**

The Non-Working Time tab in the Timescale dialog box changes the appearance of nonworking time. To modify the schedule for nonworking time, click Tools, Change Working Time, or right-click the timescale heading, and then click Change Working Time.

For more information about changing working and nonworking time, see "Setting Your Project Calendar" on page 58.

Customizing Tables

Sheet views, such as Gantt Chart, Task Usage, and Resource Sheet, display a table of data. If the information you want doesn't appear in the current table, you can switch tables or modify the table contents. You can customize the contents of a table directly in the view or through the Table Definition dialog box.

For information on modifying a table in the view, see "Using Tables" on page 102.

InsideOut

Table changes you make in the view change the table definition. If you insert or remove columns, modify the column attributes in the Column Definition dialog box, or adjust the column width using the mouse, the table definition changes to reflect those modifications.

Because it is so easy to make changes to a table in a view, it's important to remember that those changes become a permanent part of that table's definition. If you want to keep the current table the way it is, make a copy of it, and then make your modifications to the copy.

Modifying the Columns in a Table

You can add, move, remove, or modify columns in any table. To modify the definition of an existing table, follow these steps:

1 Right-click the Select All cell in the upper-left corner of the sheet, above row 1, and then click More Tables on the shortcut menu to open the More Tables dialog box with the current table selected.

2 Click the Edit button.

---

tip **Create a table quickly**

To use the current table as a template for a new table, click Copy instead of Edit. To use a different table as a template, click that table's name, and then click Copy.

---

3 The Table Definition dialog box shown in Figure 25-11 appears. If necessary, type a descriptive name in the Name box.

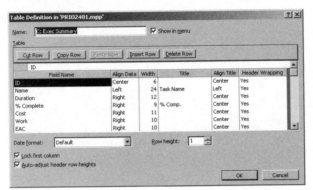

Figure 25-11. Customize the columns for a table in the Table Definition dialog box.

4 If you want this table to appear on the Table menu, select the Show In Menu check box.

To move a column in the table, move fields in the rows in the Table Definition list by doing the following:

1 Click the field name you want to move, and then click Cut Row.

2 Click the row above where you want to insert the field.

3 Click Paste Row to insert the field at the new location.

You can add columns to the end of the field list or insert them where you want. To insert a column into the table, follow these steps:

1 Click the row above where you want to insert the field.

2 Click Insert Row to insert a blank row in the list.

3 Click the Field Name cell, and click the field name you want in the list.

---

caution Pressing Enter is the same as clicking OK; either action will close the Table Definition dialog box. To complete the row with default entries, press Tab or click another cell in the list.

4 Specify the alignment of the data and the column heading as well as the
width of the column.

If you want the column heading text to wrap, click Yes in the Header
Wrapping cell.

5 To display text other than the field name in the column header, type the text
you want to appear in the column header in the Title cell.

Troubleshooting

You can't find the field you want to add in the Field Name list

When you're editing a task table, only task fields appear in the Field Name list. Likewise,
when you edit a resource table, you can add only resource fields. Assignment fields
appear only when you edit Usage views.

Similarly, if you can't find the table you want to modify, you might have the wrong type
of view displayed. In the More Tables dialog box, select the Task or Resource option
to display the list of task or resource tables.

To remove a column in a table, follow these steps:

1 Click the field name for the column you want to remove.

2 Click Delete Row.

Modifying Other Table Options

You can customize other properties of a table in the Table Definition dialog box.
For example, you can specify the format of dates or set a row height for all rows.

To set other table options, do the following:

1 In the Table Definition dialog box, click the format you want for any date
fields in the table in the Date Format box. If you don't change this setting,
the table uses the default date format for the entire project.

2 To change the height of the rows in the table, click a number in the Row
Height box. This number represents a multiple of the standard row height.

3 To adjust the height of the header row to make room for the full column
title, select the Auto-Adjust Header Row Heights check box.

InsideOut

If a table includes numerous columns, you might have to scroll in the sheet portion of the view to see them. But it's difficult to enter data in the correct cells when you can't see the task name column. You can keep a column in view by moving it to the first column and then selecting the Lock First Column option in the Table Definition dialog box.

To lock the Task Name column, in the Table Definition dialog box, click Name in the Field Name column, and then click Cut Row. Click the first row in the Field Name list, and then Click Paste Row to insert the Name field in the first row in the list. Select the Lock First column check box. The Task Name appears in the first column and does not disappear as you scroll.

Creating a New Table

If none of the existing tables even come close to meeting your needs, you can create a completely new table. To do this, follow these steps:

1 Click View, Table, and then click More Tables.

2 In the More Tables dialog box, select the Task or Resource option to create a task or resource table, respectively.

3 Click New. The Table Definition dialog box appears with a default name in the Name box.

4 Enter a new descriptive name in the Name box.

5 If you want this table to appear in the View menu and View bar, select the Show In Menu check box.

6 Continue by adding the fields you want to appear in the table.

> For information about how to add fields to a table, see "Modifying the Columns in a Table," earlier in this chapter.

Customizing Fields

The project database comes with a complete set of fields of varying data types. You can modify a few attributes, such as the title or alignment, for some of these built-in fields. Or you might change the font of the fields that appear in a row for a particular task. You can't change what those fields represent or how they are calculated.

> For a complete list of Microsoft Project fields and their descriptions, see Appendix B, "Field Reference."

newfeature!

If you want to track information that Microsoft Project doesn't monitor, you can create your own custom fields and add them to tables in your views. For example, you might want to track overhead costs that are calculated based on some combination of task duration, number of resources, and material resources consumed.

Microsoft Project provides several custom fields of each type for tasks and additional custom fields of each type for resources. In addition, there are sets of custom outline codes for both tasks and resources. Microsoft Project Professional provides similar sets of enterprise-level custom codes and custom outline codes. With Microsoft Project Professional, you can define project-related custom fields in addition to task and resource fields.

The custom fields are as follows:

Cost.   Cost1 through Cost10 expressed in currency

Date.   Date1 through Date10 expressed as a date

Duration.   Duration1 through Duration10 expressed as time

Finish.   Finish1 through Finish10 expressed as a date

Flag.   Flag1 through Flag20 expressed as Yes/No flags

Number.   Number1 through Number20 expressed as numeric data

Start.   Start1 through Start10 expressed as a date

Text.   Text1 through Text30 expressed as alphanumeric text up to 255 characters

Outline Code.   Outline Code1 through Outline Code10. (The outline code format is defined by a code mask.)

---

caution   Even though the Start and Finish fields appear in the custom field list, Microsoft Project uses these fields to store the dates for interim baseline plans. If you intend to save interim baselines in your project, don't use the custom Start and Finish fields. Information in those fields will be overwritten when you save an interim baseline. Instead, use custom Date fields for your customized dates.

Customizing a Field

Custom fields already exist; you can't introduce new fields into the project database. Unlike the standard fields in the Microsoft Project database, you can modify the valid values for custom fields or specify how their values are calculated. You can control how their summary values are determined. If you don't want to display the values for a custom field, you can substitute graphical indicators.

Follow these steps to customize a field:

1 Click Tools, Customize, and then click Fields. The Customize Fields dialog box appears.

2 Click the Custom Fields tab to display the options for a custom field (see Figure 25-12).

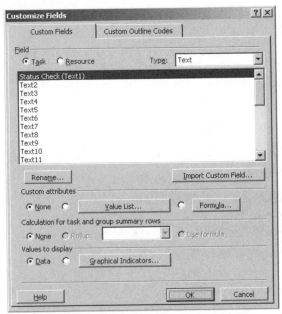

Figure 25-12. Create an alias, a list of values, a formula for calculation, or set additional options for a custom field.

3 Select the Task or Resource option to customize a task or resource field. The field names for both task and resource custom fields are the same.

4 Choose the type of custom field you want to customize in the Type box.

Troubleshooting

The custom field name isn't informative as a column heading in a table

You can change the title that appears in a column heading by clicking the heading and typing text for the heading in the title box. For example, you might use a title such as Overhead Cost instead of Cost1 in the column heading. Changing the title in this way affects the heading only in that table. If you include the Cost1 field in another table, the column heading reverts to the field name.

You can create an alias for a custom field so the alias appears instead of the field name each time you use the field. In the Customize Fields dialog box, click Rename. Enter a descriptive name for the field. The alias and the original field name both appear in field lists.

Specifying the Values for a Custom Field

You can control the values that a custom field accepts. You can specify a list of valid values for a custom field or define a formula to calculate the result. If you do not specify a list of values or a formula, the custom field will accept any entry as long as it meets the requirements for the data type.

To specify a list of values that appears in a custom field list, do the following:

1 In the Customize Fields dialog box, click Value List. The Value List dialog box appears (see Figure 25-13).

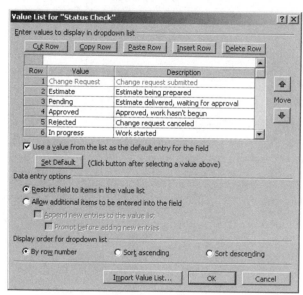

Figure 25-13. Specify the values to appear in a list for a custom field.

2 Click a blank cell in the Value column, and then type the value. In the Description cell in the same row, add the corresponding description.

tip   **Modifying custom field values**

You can insert new values, remove existing values, or rearrange the values by clicking Cut Row, Copy Row, Paste Row, Insert Row, or Delete Row. You can also rearrange the order of the values by clicking the up and down arrows.

3 To specify one of the values as the default, select the Use A Value From The List As The Default Entry For The Field check box. Click the cell that contains the default value, and then click Set Default. The default value appears in red.

4 To prevent users from entering values not in the list, select the Restrict Field To Items In The Value List option.

   If you choose to allow other entries in the custom field, you can add them to the value list automatically by selecting the Allow Additional Items To Be Entered Into The Field option and Append New Entries To The Value List check box. It's good practice to also select the Prompt Before Adding New Entries check box to prevent typographical errors from creating new values in the list.

5 Select one of the options to order the values. The By Row Number option displays the values in the order you enter them in the list. You can also sort the values in ascending or descending order.

tip   **Using existing values in a new custom field**

If you have already created a value list that contains the entries you want in another custom field or in another project, click Import Value List. Click the project that contains the value list; select the option for the type of field (Task, Resource, or Project), and then click the name of the custom field that contains the value list.

Creating a Calculated Field

You can calculate the value of a custom field by defining a formula made up of functions and other fields in the Microsoft Project database.

To define a formula for a calculated field, follow these steps:

1 In the Customize Fields dialog box, click the Formula option.

2 Click the Formula button. The Formula dialog box appears and displays the custom field name followed by an equal sign above the formula edit box (see Figure 25-14 on the next page).

Chapter 25

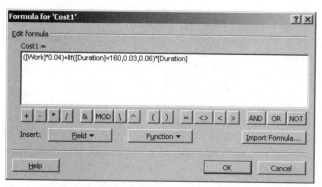

Figure 25-14. Build a formula using numerous functions and any field in the Project database.

3 To add a field to the formula, click Field, point to the field category, and then click the field you want to add.

4 To type a value in the formula, click the location in the formula where you want to insert the value, and then type the text or number.

5 To add a function to the formula, click one of the function buttons or click Function, point to the function category, and then click the function you want to add.

6 To direct the order that functions execute, insert parentheses in the formula.

Sharing Formulas with Other Projects

You can share most customized elements between projects by copying them with the Organizer. Although the Organizer has tabs for most elements, a tab for formulas doesn't exist. To copy a formula between projects, you have to copy the custom field whose definition contains the formula.

For more information about sharing elements, see "Sharing Customized Elements among Projects" later in this chapter.

You can also import the formula from a custom field in another project into a custom field in the active project. In the Formula dialog box, click Import Formula. In the Import Formula dialog box, click the project that contains the formula; select the option for the type of field (Task, Resource, or Project), and then click the name of the custom field that contains the formula.

Calculating Group and Summary Values

By default, Microsoft Project does not calculate values for custom fields for summary tasks or for the rows containing rolled up values for groups. However, you can specify how to calculate a value for summary rows. To use the same formula that you defined for the custom field, select the Use Formula option in the Calculation For Task And Group Summary Rows section. If you select the Rollup option, you can choose from several simple calculations including the following:

Average.   The average of all nonsummary values underneath the summary task or group.

Average First Sublevel.   The average of all the values of tasks one level below.

Maximum.   The largest value of all nonsummary values.

Minimum.   The smallest value for all nonsummary values.

Sum.   The sum of all nonsummary values underneath the summary task or group.

When you work with a custom number field, the following calculations also appear when you select the Rollup option:

Count All.   The number of summary and nonsummary tasks one level below the summary task or group.

Count First Sublevel.   The number of nonsummary and summary tasks one level below the summary task or group.

Count Nonsummaries.   The number of nonsummary tasks below the summary task or group.

Do the following to pick a mathematical function for a rollup value:

1 Select the Rollup option.

2 Click one of the functions in the Rollup list.

Working with Graphical Indicators

You can use graphical indicators to represent the text or values of a custom field. You can use these indicators to make values easier to understand or to hide numeric values from some audiences. For example, you might want to display a green light when a task is ahead of schedule; a yellow light when a task is slightly behind schedule; and a red light when a task is more than two weeks late.

Part 9: Customizing and Managing Project Files

To display graphical indicators instead of values for nonsummary rows, follow these steps:

1 Under Values To Display in the Customize Fields dialog box, select the Graphical Indicators option, and then click the Graphical Indicators button. The Graphical Indicators dialog box appears.

2 To assign graphical indicators to nonsummary rows, select the Nonsummary Rows option.

3 To choose the indicators to display and the conditions under which to display them, click the first empty cell in the Test column, click the down arrow, and then click the test you want to apply for an indicator.

4 Type the value for the test in the Value(s) cell. For example, to display an indicator when a custom number field has a negative value, click Is Less Than in the list in the Test cell, and then type 0 in the Value(s) cell.

5 Click the Image cell, click the down arrow, and then click the graphical indicator to display when the condition is true.

6 To define graphical indicators when other conditions are true, repeat steps 3, 4, and 5 in the next blank row in the dialog box.

---

tip   **Display summary rows differently than nonsummary rows**

By default, summary rows and the project summary row both inherit the same conditions that you specify for nonsummary rows. If you want to use different conditions for summary rows, select the Summary Rows option, and then clear the Summary Rows Inherit Criteria From Nonsummary Rows check box. Define the tests and indicators for summary rows as you would for nonsummary rows. To specify different conditions for the project summary row, select the Project Summary option, and then clear the Project Summary Inherits Criteria From Summary Rows check box. Define the tests and indicators for the project summary row.

For information about enterprise fields, see "Customizing Enterprise Fields" on page 565.

Customizing Groups

newfeature!

You can group tasks, resources, or assignments that meet a set of conditions. For example, you might group tasks by their schedule variance so you can concentrate on the ones furthest behind schedule. You might group resources by their level of availability so you can assign the resources with the most free time. You can also choose to group assignments instead of tasks or resources, for example to see which assignments are running over budget on hours. Group headings show subtotals for the values in the numeric fields for the group. For example, you might display assignments grouped by salaried and hourly employees and contractors so you can see the total hours of work performed by each group. When you group these elements, subtotals for the groups appear in the Task and Resource Sheet as well as in the timesheet in Usage views.

Modifying a Group

If one of the existing groups doesn't meet your needs, you can modify it or copy and then modify it if you want to keep the original group intact. Do the following to customize a group:

1 Click Project, Group by, More Groups.

2 In the More Groups dialog box, click either the Task or Resource option to display the task or resource groups.

3 To modify an existing group, click the group you want to modify in the list, and then click Edit or Copy. The Group Definition dialog box appears (see Figure 25-15).

4 If necessary, change the name of the group in the Name box.

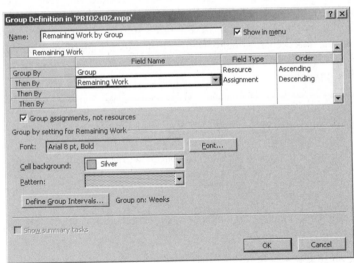

Figure 25-15. Group tasks, resource, or assignments by one or more fields.

5 Click the first empty cell in the Field Name column, click the down arrow, and then click the name of the field by which you want to group. The category for the field (Task, Resource, or Assignment) appears in the Field Type cell.

6 If necessary, change the grouping order. For example, you might want to use descending order to locate the resources with the most availability more easily.

7 To group assignments instead of tasks or resources, select the Group Assignments, Not Tasks check box for a task group or Group Assignments, Not Resources check box for a resource group.

8 To change the font, click Font. In the Font dialog box, choose a font, font style, font size, and color.

9 To change the background color, click a color in the Cell Background box.

10 To change the pattern for the group headings, click a pattern in the Pattern box.

Troubleshooting

You can't change the calculation for the value that appears in the group heading row

The group heading rows for standard fields display the sum of the values for the entries in the group. However, you might want to use a different calculation for the group heading row, such as the largest value or the average.

Although you can't change the calculation for a standard field group summary, you can create a custom field equal to the standard field. Then you can calculate the group summary for the custom field using the other summary calculations. To do this, first create a calculated custom field. Then set the custom field equal to the standard field. Select the Rollup option, and choose the calculation you want to use for the rolled-up value.

Groups often display elements in small sets, one set for each discrete value that exists in the field that you grouped. This works well for fields such as Milestones that only have two values. For groups based on cost or work, the number of discrete values can seem endless. However, you can define intervals for groups. To do this, follow these steps:

1 In the Group Definition dialog box, click the field for which you want to define intervals.

2 Click Define Group Intervals. The Define Group Interval dialog box appears (see Figure 25-16). The default selection for Group On is Each Value.

Chapter 25: Customizing Your View of Project Information

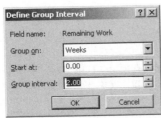

Figure 25-16. Set the starting value and size for group intervals.

3 Click the down arrow in the Group On box, and then click the interval you want to use in the list.

The intervals listed depend on the type of field. For example, the intervals for a field that represents work include units in which work is measured, such as hours, days, weeks, and months.

4 To start the interval at a specific number, type the number in the Start At box.

5 To define the interval size, type the number in the Group Interval box. To group assignments in intervals of two weeks worth of work, type 2.

Creating a New Group

When no groups exist that are similar to what you want, you can create a new group. To create a new group, do the following:

1 Click Project, Group By, More Groups.

2 In the More Groups dialog box, select the Task or Resource option to create a task or resource group, and then click New.

3 Type a descriptive name for the group in the Name box.

4 Click the first empty cell in the Field Name column, click the down arrow, and then click the name of the field by which you want to group. The category for the field (Task, Resource, or Assignment) appears in the Field Type cell.

5 To group assignments instead of tasks or resources, select the Group Assignments, Not Tasks check box for a task group or the Group Assignments, Not Resources check box for a resource group.

6 Change the order of the grouping to Descending if necessary.

InsideOut

There are several types of groups in Microsoft Project. Each one serves a different purpose, so it's important to choose the correct one. A group resource represents several interchangeable resources. For example, you might define a resource called Carpenters, which represents five carpenters who can do basic carpentry. The Maximum Units for this resource would be the sum of the maximum units for each individual in the group resource, or 500 percent in this example.

A resource group represents a category of individual resources. You might define a resource group for employees and another for contractors so you can sort, filter, and view assignments using these categories.

Finally, a group that you apply using the Group By command on the Project menu categorizes and sorts tasks, resources, or assignments based on the values in any field in Microsoft Project.

Customizing Filters

Projects contain so much information that the data can simply get in the way when it's not pertinent. Filters restrict the tasks or resources that appear so you can more easily analyze your situation. Microsoft Project provides a number of standard filters that you can use as is to weed out certain kinds of information and use as templates for your own customized filters. For example, the Cost Overbudget filter displays tasks in which the estimated cost for the task is greater than the baseline cost.

caution   You might expect the Work Overbudget filter to behave in a similar fashion, displaying tasks in which the estimated work for the task is greater than the baseline work. However, the Work Overbudget filter compares actual work on a task to the baseline work. This filter only warns you that a task is overbudget when the actual work exceeds the baseline work—long after the problem arose. You can modify the Work Overbudget filter to replace the Actual Work field with the Work field so that it displays tasks that are forecast to exceed the work budget.

Modifying a Filter

You can modify an existing filter or copy and then modify it if you want to continue to use the original. To customize a filter, follow these steps:

1 Click Project, Filtered For, More Filters.

2 In the More Filters dialog box, select the Task or Resource option to display the task or resource filters.

3 To modify an existing filter, click the filter you want to modify in the list, and then click Edit or Copy.

4 Click the Field Name cell you want to change, click the down arrow, and then click the name of the field by which you want to filter (see Figure 25-17).

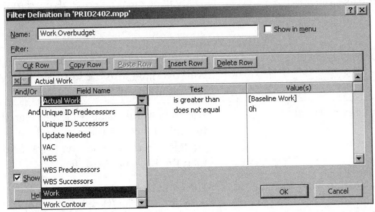

Figure 25-17. Modify the fields, tests, and values for a filter to display only the tasks that meet your criteria.

5 Click the Test cell, click the down arrow, and then click the name of the test you want to use for the filter.

6 Specify the value you want to use for the filter test in the Value(s) cell. You can type a value, click a field name from the list, or type a prompt to define an interactive filter.

For information about creating an interactive filter, see "Creating Interactive Filters" later in this chapter.

7 To display the summary tasks for tasks that pass the filter criteria, select the Show Related Summary Rows check box.

Troubleshooting

A filter doesn't display the correct tasks

Making changes to your project can cause what appear to be incorrect filter results. If you make changes to your project after a filter is applied, elements that no longer meet the filter criteria won't disappear until you reapply the filter. You can reapply the current filter by pressing Ctrl+F3.

Table 25-1 describes the tests you can use within a filter and provides an example of each.

Table 25-1. Filters

Filter test	How you can use it
Equals	The values must be equal. For example, to filter for milestones, test whether the Milestone field equals Yes.
Does Not Equal	The values are different. For example, to show tasks with overtime, use the test Overtime Work field does not equal 0h.
Is Greater Than	The Field Name value is greater than the entry in the Value(s) cell. For example, to show tasks that are late, check whether the Finish field is greater than the Baseline Finish field.
Is Greater Than Or Equal To	The Field Name value is greater than or equal to the entry in the Value(s) cell. For example, to show tasks at least 50 percent complete, test whether the % Complete field is greater than or equal to 50 percent.
Is Less Than	The Field Name value is less than the entry in the Value(s) cell. For example, to show tasks that are ahead of schedule, check whether the Finish field is less than the Baseline Finish field.
Is Less Than Or Equal To	The Field Name value is less than or equal to the entry in the Value(s) cell. For example, to show tasks that are under budget, test whether the Cost Variance field is less than or equal to 0.
Is Within	The Field Name value is between or equal to the boundary values in the Value(s) cell. For example, to find the tasks within a range, test whether the ID is within the range specified in the Value(s) cell. To specify a range, type the starting value, type a comma, and then type the last value, such as 100,200.
Is Not Within	The Field Name value is outside the boundary values in the Value(s) cell. For example, to find the tasks that are not in progress, test whether the % Complete is not within 1%,99%.

Filter test	How you can use it
Contains	The Field Name value is text that contains the string in the Value(s) cell. For example, to find the tasks to which a resource is assigned, test whether the Name field contains the resource name.
Does Not Contain	The Field Name value is text that does not contain the string in the Value(s) cell. For example, to find resources not in a resource group, check whether the Resource Group does not contain the name.
Contains Exactly	The Field Name value is text that must exactly match the string in the Value(s) cell. For example, to find tasks to which only a particular resource is assigned, check whether the Resource Name field contains exactly the resource's name.

Creating Filters

If you can't find a filter similar to what you want, you can create one. To do this, follow these steps:

1 Click Project, Filtered For, More Filters.

2 In the More Filters dialog box, select the Task or Resource option to create a task or resource filter, and then click New.

3 In the Filter Definition dialog box, type a descriptive name for the filter in the Name box.

4 If you want the new filter to appear on the Filtered For menu, select the Show In Menu check box.

5 Click the field, test, and values for each test you define for the filter.

6 To include the summary rows for the tasks or resources that meet the filter criteria, select the Show Related Summary Rows check box.

---

tip **Use wildcard characters to locate the text you want**

You can compare a text field value to a string with wildcard characters when you use the Equals or Does Not Equal tests. Wildcard characters include:

● * represents one or more characters.

● ? represents any single character.

For example, DB* would match DB Developer, DB Administrator, and DB Designer. Des??? Would match Design, but not Describe.

Calculated Filters

You can define filter tests that compare the values in two different fields for the same task or resource. For example, to see whether a task started according to plan, you can test whether the Actual Start date is equal to or less than the Baseline Start date.

To define a test that compares two fields, do the following:

1 Click the Field Name cell, click the down arrow, and then click the name of the field by which you want to filter.

2 Click the Test cell, click the down arrow, and then click the name of the test you want to use.

3 Click the Value(s) cell, click the down arrow, and then click the name of the field with which you want to compare the first field. A field name in the Value(s) cell is enclosed in square brackets [ ].

Creating Filters with Multiple Tests

Sometimes it takes more than one or two tests to filter the list to your satisfaction. You can create filters in which tasks or resources must meet at least one of the criteria.

To define multiple tests in a filter, follow these steps:

1 In the Filter Definition dialog box, type a descriptive name for the filter in the Name box.

2 Click the field, test, and values for each test you define for the filter.

3 If you want to add a test to the filter, click the And/Or cell in the first blank row, and click And or Or.

If you click And, the filter only displays elements that meet both criteria. The filter displays tasks that meet one or both of the criteria when you click Or.

4 Repeat steps 2 and 3 to define the field, test, and values for an additional test.

When there are more than two tests, filters evaluate tests in the order they occur in the filter definition. The filter displays elements based on the results of the first two tests. It then compares those results to the outcome of the next test. The filter continues until there are no further tests to evaluate.

In some cases, you might want to adjust the order in which the tests are evaluated. For example, you might want to filter tasks first for those that use a particular resource and that aren't yet complete. Then you want to further filter the list for tasks that start and finish within a particular date range. You can group the filter criteria by clicking And or Or in the And/Or cell of an otherwise empty row.

Do the following to group criteria within a filter:

1 Define one or more criteria for the first group of tests within the filter.

2 Click the And/Or cell in the next blank row, click the arrow, and then click And or Or (see Figure 25-18).

3 Define the criteria for one or more additional tests in the rows below the grouping row.

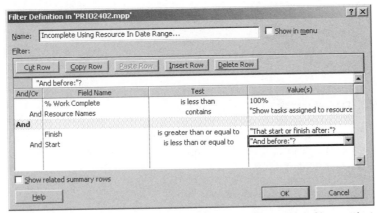

Figure 25-18. Control the order of test evaluation for a filter with And or Or operators.

Creating Interactive Filters

In many cases, you want to supply different values to a filter each time you use it. Interactive filters request values and then filter based on the values you provide.

To create an interactive filter, follow these steps:

1 In the Filter Definition dialog box, type a descriptive name for the filter in the Name box.

2 Click the field and test for the filter.

3 In the Value(s) cell, type a text string followed by a question mark (see Figure 25-19). When you apply the filter, the text string appears as a prompt in a dialog box. The question mark instructs Microsoft Project to pause until the user enters the value.

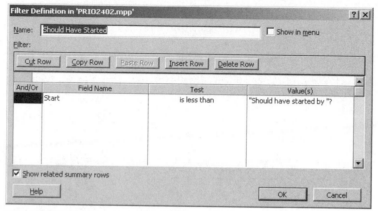

Figure 25-19. Create a filter that waits for user input.

Customizing AutoFilter Criteria

AutoFilter is an easy way to filter by values in one or more fields. In addition, you can quickly create custom filters by saving an AutoFilter test. However, AutoFilter operates on only one field at a time.

To create a custom filter using AutoFilter:

1 Display the sheet view whose rows you want to filter.

2 Click AutoFilter on the Formatting toolbar. The AutoFilter arrows appear in the column headings for each field in the sheet view.

3 Click the arrow in the column whose information you want to filter by, and then click Custom. The Custom AutoFilter dialog box appears with the field set to the current column (see Figure 25-20).

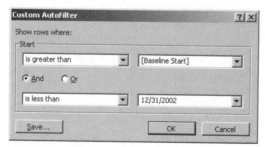

Figure 25-20. Customize and save an AutoFilter.

4 Click the arrow in the first test box, and click the test you want to apply.

5 In the first value box, click the arrow, and then click a value or a field name. You can also type a value in the box if the one you want doesn't appear in the list.

6 To add a second test, select the And or Or option.

7 Click the test and value for the second test.

8 To save the AutoFilter test, click Save, which displays the Filter Definition dialog box. You can enter a filter name and make other changes before you save the filter.

Working with Outline Codes

By default, the task outline delineates a hierarchy of tasks. A work breakdown structure (WBS) is a special hierarchy that separates the work for your project into manageable pieces that you can assign to project resources. The work breakdown structure isn't the only hierarchy you might need. Your organization's resource manager might want to review the resource breakdown structure, whereas the procurement manager might require a bill that itemizes the materials for the project. The accounting department might have another set of codes for tracking income and expenses by business unit.

You can create up to 10 sets of custom task and resource codes for these purposes, in much the same way you set up WBS codes. You can then sort, group, or filter your tasks or resource by any of these outline codes as your needs dictate.

> For information about setting up a task outline of summary tasks and subtasks, see "Sequencing and Organizing Tasks" on page 71. To set up and apply work breakdown structure codes, see "Setting Up Work Breakdown Structure Codes" on page 79.

Setting Up Outline Codes

Outline codes are customizable alphanumeric codes that provide a method of categorizing tasks and resources in your project. Microsoft Project does not recalculate custom outline codes as you modify the location or indentation of a task or resource because only you know the structure of tasks or resources you want to represent. To help others use your custom outline codes properly, you can create a lookup table so users can choose values from a list. You can eliminate invalid codes by restricting users to choosing only the predefined values.

An outline code can consist of several levels of uppercase or lowercase letters, numbers, or characters, along with a symbol to separate the levels of the code. The maximum length for an outline code is 255 characters.

> For information about working with enterprise outline codes, see "Customizing Enterprise Fields" on page 565.

Follow these steps to set up a custom outline code:

1 Click Tools, Customize, Fields, and in the Customize Fields dialog box, click the Custom Outline Codes tab.

2 Select the Task or Resource option to display task or resource outline codes, and then click the name of the code that you want to modify in the code list.

3 To rename the custom outline code, click the Rename button, and then type the new name in the Rename Field dialog box. This name and the original field name appear in lists where the outline code appears.

Defining a Code Mask

The code mask is the template that delineates the format and length of each level of the outline code as well as the separators between each level. To define the code mask, do the following:

1 On the Custom Outline Codes tab of the Customize Fields dialog box, click the outline code for which you want to define a code mask.

2 Click the Define Code Mask button. The Outline Code Definition dialog box appears.

3 In the Sequence field of the first row, choose whether the first level of the code (or hierarchy) is a number, uppercase letters, lowercase letters, or alphanumeric characters.

4 In the Length field of the first row, specify the length of the first level of the code.

A number in the Length cell indicates a fixed length for that level. If the level can contain any number of characters, click Any in the list.

5 In the Separator field of the first row, specify the character that separates the first and second level of the code.

6 Repeat steps 1, 2, and 3 until all the levels of your custom outline code are set up (see Figure 25-21).

As you enter the code mask for each succeeding level, the Code Preview box shows an example of the code.

Chapter 25: Customizing Your View of Project Information

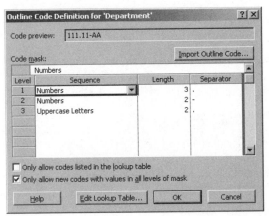

Figure 25-21. Define a custom outline code to display alternate hierarchies for tasks and resources.

Controlling Outline Code Values

You can define settings to help users enter the correct values and format for outline codes. To do this, follow these steps:

1 To restrict codes to only those listed in a lookup table, select the Only Allow Codes Listed In The Lookup Table check box.

2 If users can enter codes not in a lookup table, you can make sure they enter values in each level of the code by selecting the Only Allow New Codes With Values In All Levels Of Mask check box.

Defining a Lookup Table

A lookup table comprises a list of values for the outline code. To define a lookup table, do the following:

1 In the Customize Fields dialog box, click the outline code for which you want to create a lookup table.

2 Click the Edit Lookup Table button.

---

tip **Access the lookup table quickly**

When you define a code mask, you can also click Edit Lookup Table in the Outline Code Definition dialog box.

---

3 To make the hierarchy levels more apparent as you define lookup values, select the Display Indenting In Lookup Table check box.

The values are indented according to their level in the hierarchy. In addition, you can click the plus and minus signs that precede higher level values to expand or collapse the outline levels as demonstrated in Figure 25-22.

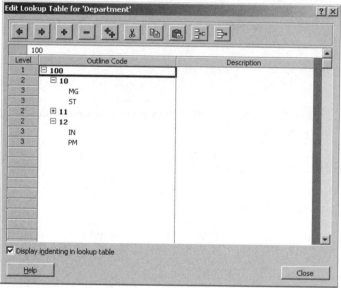

Figure 25-22. Define values in a lookup table to simplify outline code data entry.

4 Click the first blank cell in the Outline Code column.

5 Type a value in the Outline Code cell.

6 Click the Description cell, and type a meaningful description of the entry.

7 To demote an entry to the next level of the code, click the entry, and then click the Indent button at the top of the dialog box. To promote the entry one level higher in the code, click the Outdent button.

The outline code level appears in the Level column. If the value you enter doesn't conform to the mask defined for that outline level, the entry appears in red with a warning indicator.

8 Repeat steps 4 through 7 to define additional values in the lookup table.

---

tip **Modify values in a lookup table**

To insert a value in the outline, click the Insert Row button. You can also use the Delete Row, Cut, Copy, and Paste buttons to edit the values that already exist in the list.

Assigning Outline Codes

You can assign outline code values to tasks and resources as you would enter values for any other fields in Microsoft Project. You can type the values or, if you created a lookup table, choose one from a list.

To assign values for a custom outline code, follow these steps:

1 If your custom outline code doesn't appear in the current table, right-click a column heading, and then click Insert Column on the shortcut menu.

2 Click the outline code field in the Field Name box, and then click OK.

3 Click a cell in the custom outline code column.

4 If no lookup table exists, type the value in the cell. When a lookup table exists, click the down arrow in the cell, and then click an entry in the list.

---

tip   **Determining the correct format for an outline code**

Without a lookup table, there is no way to identify the format for the outline code. However, if you enter a value that doesn't conform to the code mask, an error message appears that includes the correct format.

Reviewing Your Tasks or Resources by Outline Code

Grouping, filtering, and sorting by outline codes is similar to changing the order of tasks and resources based on values in other fields. You simply apply a group, filter, or sort criteria that uses the custom outline code.

To quickly group tasks or resources using a custom outline code, do the following:

1 Click Project, Group by, Customize Group By.

2 In the Customize Group By dialog box, click the down arrow in the Field Name cell, and then click the name of the outline code.

3 If necessary, change the value in the Order cell, the color and pattern of the group, and other group settings.

For information about customizing a group and creating a permanent group using a field, see "Modifying a Group," earlier in this chapter.

Chapter 25

To quickly filter tasks or resources using a custom outline code, follow these steps:

1 Display the sheet view whose rows you want to filter.

2 On the Formatting toolbar, click AutoFilter. The AutoFilter arrows appear in the column heading for each field in the sheet view.

3 Click the arrow in the outline code column.

4 Click the value by which you want to filter or click Custom if you want to create a custom filter based on the outline code.

> For information about customizing a filter, see "Customizing Filters," earlier in this chapter.

To sort your tasks or resource using an outline code, do the following:

1 Click Project, Sort, Sort By.

2 In the Sort By dialog box, click the down arrow in the Sort By box, and then click the name of the outline code in the list.

3 If necessary, select the Ascending or Descending option to change the sort order.

Sharing Customized Elements among Projects

If you customize elements, such as tables, views, fields, or filters in one project, you will probably want to use those elements in a new project. Customized elements are stored in the project in which you create them, but you can copy these elements to other projects or templates using the Organizer. If you want a customized element available to every new project, use the Organizer to copy the element to the global template. In addition, you can use the Organizer to rename or remove elements from a project or template.

> For information about using the global template, see "Working with the Project Global Template" on page 671. To use the enterprise global template, see "Working with the Enterprise Global Template" on page 564.

Working with the Organizer

The Organizer includes tabs for every type of customizable element in Microsoft Project. By clicking a tab, you can see the elements of that type that are available in two project files. These project files can be active projects or templates, so you can copy customized elements between active projects, from a project to a template, or even restore the original element from a template to a project.

You can copy, delete, or rename customizable elements including the following:

- Views
- Toolbars
- Forms
- Groups

- Calendars
- Modules
- Fields
- Filters

- Reports
- Maps
- Tables

To open the Organizer, click Tools, Organizer. An Organizer button to open
the Organizer dialog box is also available in the following dialog boxes:

- More Views
- More Tables
- More Filters

- More Groups
- Custom Reports
- Customize Forms

For information about customizing reports, see "Building Custom Reports" on page 363.

Copying Customized Elements

No matter which type of element you copy, the procedure is the same. You choose
a source file that contains the element you want to copy, choose a destination file
into which you want to copy the element, and then copy the element.

Follow these steps to copy an element from a project to the global template:

1 Open the project that contains the element you want to copy.

2 Click Tools, Organizer to open the Organizer dialog box (see Figure 25-23).

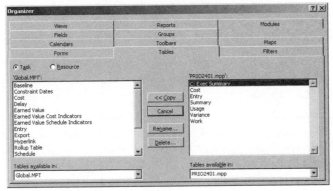

Figure 25-23. Copy customized elements between projects and templates,
or rename and delete existing elements.

3 Click the tab for the type of element you want to copy.

4 In the <Element> Available In box on the right side of the dialog box, click the project that contains the element you want to copy. <Element> stands for the name of the current tab.

5 Click the name of the element you want to copy from the list of elements on the right side of the dialog box.

6 Click Copy. If an element with the same name already exists in the global template, Project asks you to confirm that you want to replace the element in the global template. Click Yes to replace the element in the global template with the one from the source project.

To copy the element with a different name, click Rename, and then type a new name.

To copy an element between two projects, do the following:

1 Open both the source and destination projects.

2 Click Tools, Organizer to open the Organizer dialog box.

3 Click the tab for the type of element you want to copy.

4 In the <Element> Available In box on the right side of the dialog box, click the source project.

5 In the <Element> Available In box on the left side of the dialog box, click the destination project.

6 Click the name of the element you want to copy from the list of elements on the right side of the dialog box.

7 Click Copy. If an element with the same name already exists in the destination, Microsoft Project asks you to confirm that you want to replace the element in the destination project. Click Yes to replace the element in the destination project with the one from the source project.

To copy the element with a different name, click No. Then click Rename, and enter a new name.

---

caution You can't rename some built-in elements. In addition, you can't rename fields in the Organizer. You must change field names in the Customize Fields dialog box.

InsideOut

Microsoft Project treats toolbars differently than other customizable elements. Toolbars apply to the application instead of a particular project, so they are stored in the global template by default. When you modify a toolbar, the modified version appears no matter which project you open.

If you want to share a customized toolbar with someone else, copy it from the global template to a project file, and then send the project file to that person. They can use the Organizer to copy the toolbar to their global template.

Removing Customized Elements

Customized elements can simplify your work but extraneous elements in projects and templates can be distracting. When you copy a customized element to the global template, you no longer need it in the project in which you created it. If you created a customized element by accident, you can remove it using the Organizer. To do this, follow these steps:

1 Open the project that contains the element you want to delete.

2 Click Tools, Organizer to open the Organizer dialog box.

3 Click the tab for the type of element that you want to delete.

4 In the <Element> Available In box on the right side of the dialog box, click the project that contains the element you want to delete. <Element> stands for the name of the current tab.

5 Click the name of the element you want to remove from the list of elements on the right side of the dialog box.

6 Click Delete. In the confirmation box, click Yes to delete the element.

Renaming Customized Elements

You can rename customized elements using the Organizer. For example, you should rename a customized element in your project if you want to copy it to the global template without overwriting the original element in the global template. You can't rename some built-in elements. Fields are renamed in the Customize Fields dialog box.

Do the following to rename a customized element:

1 Open the project that contains the element that you want to rename.

2 Click Tools, Organizer to open the Organizer dialog box.

3 Click the tab for the type of element that you want to rename.

4 In the <Element> Available In box on the right side of the dialog box, click the project that contains the element you want to rename. <Element> stands for the name of the current tab.

5 Click the name of the element in the list of elements on the right side of the dialog box.

6 Click Rename. The Rename dialog box appears.

7 Type the new name for the element.

Restoring Customized Elements to their Default State

If you forget that changes you make to a table in a view modify that table's definition, you might customize a standard table accidentally. You can reverse the changes you made, but if you made a lot of changes before you realized your mistake, it's easier to restore the standard table. You can restore standard elements by copying them from the global template into your active project using the Organizer.

Follow these steps to restore a standard element:

1 Open the project to which you want to restore a standard element.

2 Click Tools, Organizer to open the Organizer dialog box.

3 Click the tab for the type of element that you want to restore.

---

tip **Restoring the table that appears in the current view**

You can't restore a table if it appears in the current view. Either switch to a view that does not use that table or right-click the blank cell above the ID numbers, and click another table name on the shortcut menu.

---

4 In the <Element> Available In box on the right side of the dialog box, click the project to which you want to restore the standard element. <Element> stands for the name of the current tab. The global template appears on the left side of the dialog box by default.

5 Click the name of the element you want to restore in the list of elements in the global template on the left side of the dialog box.

6 Click Copy. When the confirmation dialog box appears asking you to confirm that you want to replace the element in the project, click Yes.

Chapter 26

Customizing the Microsoft Project Interface

Microsoft Project offers a plethora of commands to assist project managers with every aspect of managing a project. Menus, toolbars, and keyboard shortcuts provide easy access to commonly used features. However, you might find that commands you use frequently are not easily available or don't appear on a menu at all, whereas commands you never use stake a prime position. As you use Microsoft Project and identify the commands you use the most, you can customize the menus and toolbars to display your favorites. You can also assign keyboard shortcuts to access commands without removing your hands from the keyboard.

Microsoft Project provides forms for entering data into fields. Some forms, such as the Task Entry and Task Details Forms, are off limits—you can't change them. However, there are several predefined forms you can modify or copy to fit your data entry requirements. You can also build your own forms if your needs are quite specialized.

Creating and Customizing Toolbars

Toolbars display commands without taking up much space. However, if you display several toolbars and each one includes commands you don't use, you give up screen area that you might prefer to use for a Gantt Chart or other project information. You can keep the space that toolbars take to a minimum by customizing existing toolbars or creating your own.

641

> **tip** Display toolbars on one row
>
> You can display the Standard and Formatting toolbars on one line to reduce the space that these toolbars use. Right-click a toolbar, and then click Customize. In the Customize dialog box, click the Options tab. Clear the Show Standard And Formatting Toolbars On Two Rows check box. If some of the commands you want don't appear when these toolbars share a row, click the Toolbar Options arrow on the right end of the toolbar, and then click the toolbar button you want.

Customizing Toolbars

If the built-in toolbars have most of what you need, it might be easier to customize those toolbars than to create your own. You can add, remove, or rearrange toolbar buttons. For example, you might add a few buttons to the Standard toolbar from the Resource Management and Tracking toolbars. You can also specify how toolbars display their command and the appearance of buttons.

Adding and Removing Buttons on a Toolbar

To add a button to an existing toolbar, follow these steps:

1 If the toolbar you want to customize is not visible, click View, Toolbars, and then click the name of the toolbar you want to display.

2 Click Tools, Customize, Toolbars. The Customize dialog box appears (see Figure 26-1).

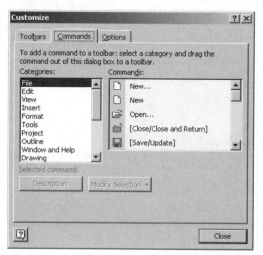

Figure 26-1. You can drag commands from the list in the Customize dialog box to a toolbar or menu.

3 Click the Commands tab. Categories of commands, such as File, Format, or Tracking, appear on the left side of the dialog box. The commands within the selected category appear on the right side of the dialog box.

4 Click the category of the command you want to add. If you don't know the category to which it belongs, select a generic category, such as All Commands or All Macros.

---

tip **Add a menu to a toolbar**

To add a built-in menu to a toolbar, open the Customize dialog box, and click the Commands tab. Click Built-In Menus, and then drag the menu you want from the Commands box to its new position on the toolbar.

To add a custom menu to a toolbar, click New Menu in the Categories box, and drag the menu name from the Commands box to the toolbar. Right-click the new menu on the toolbar, type a name in the Name box on the shortcut menu, and then press Enter. After naming the menu, you can drag commands or menus to the new menu. Right-click a menu entry to modify the button images and text.

---

5 Drag the command you want to add from the command list to the toolbar. The mouse pointer changes to an I-beam to indicate where the command will be placed. Move the mouse pointer until the I-beam is in the right location, and then release the mouse button.

Working with Personalized Toolbars

Microsoft Project personalizes toolbars and menus by displaying only the commands you use most frequently. Initially, Microsoft Project loads menus and toolbars with commands popular with the majority of users. As you select commands on menus and toolbars, those commands appear near the top of a menu, whereas commands you rarely use disappear.

To access hidden toolbar buttons, click the Toolbar Options button at the end of the toolbar, and then click the button you want. To access hidden commands on a menu, click the double arrows at the bottom of the menu, and then click the command you want.

If you prefer to see all commands on a toolbar or menu at all times, you can turn off personalized menus. To do this, right-click any menu or toolbar and click Customize in the shortcut menu to display the Customize dialog box. In the Customize dialog box, click the Options tab. Select the Always Show Full Menus check box.

To remove a button from a toolbar, do the following:

1 If the toolbar you want to customize is not visible, click View, Toolbars, and then click the name of the toolbar you want to customize.

2 Click Tools, Customize, Toolbars. The Customize dialog box appears.

3 On the toolbar, right-click the command you want to remove, and then click Delete in the shortcut menu.

Quickly Customize Toolbars

You can customize toolbars without using the Customize dialog box. If you want to hide or display buttons that appear on a toolbar by default, click the Toolbar Options button, point to Add Or Remove Buttons, and then point to the name of the toolbar you want to customize. A list of all the buttons associated with the toolbar appears. Commands that are dimmed are not on the toolbar by default. Commands that do not have a check mark are hidden. Commands that are preceded by a check mark are currently shown in the toolbar. If you add a button to a toolbar, you can remove it only by using the Customize dialog box.

Clicking a command in the list toggles the command between hidden and visible.

To rearrange the buttons on a toolbar, follow these steps:

1 Display the toolbar you want to customize by clicking View, Toolbars, and then clicking the toolbar's name.

2 Click Tools, Customize, Toolbars. The Customize dialog box appears.

3 Drag the button along the toolbar until the I-beam is in the location you want and then release the mouse button.

Troubleshooting

You can't remove buttons on a toolbar

The Add Or Remove Buttons command doesn't remove custom buttons you added to a built-in toolbar or any buttons on a custom toolbar. A custom toolbar's name is dimmed in the Add Or Remove Buttons shortcut menu, so you must click Customize to remove buttons from it. Buttons added to a built-in toolbar are dimmed on the shortcut menu. To remove custom buttons on a built-in toolbar or any buttons on a custom toolbar, drag the buttons off the toolbar while the Customize dialog box is open.

Changing the Properties of a Toolbar

When you right-click a toolbar button while the Customize dialog box is open, a shortcut menu with commands for changing the contents and properties of a toolbar appears. The commands on this shortcut menu include the following:

Reset.   Restores the original button, command associated with the button, and settings for the button on a built-in toolbar.

Delete.   Removes the button.

Name.   Displays a box in which you can enter a new name that appears in the ToolTip for the button.

Copy Button Image.   Copies the selected button image to the Clipboard so you can paste it to another button.

Paste Button Image.   Pastes the image on the Clipboard to the selected button. You can copy graphics from other applications or images from other buttons.

Reset Button Image.   Restores the button image to the default.

Edit Button Image.   Opens the Button Editor dialog box in which you can edit the image.

Change Button Image.   Displays a menu of images from which to select a new image.

Default Style.   Displays only a button image on a toolbar and the button image and text on a menu.

Text Only (Always).   Displays only text for the command in toolbars and menus.

Text Only (In Menus).   Displays a button image on a toolbar and only text on menus.

Image And Text.   Displays a button image and text in toolbars and menus.

Begin A Group.   Adds a group divider to the toolbar.

Assign Macro.   Opens the Customize Tool dialog box in which you can select a command for the button.

Troubleshooting

The toolbar doesn't appear where I want it

Toolbars might appear docked at the top, sides, or bottom of the screen or float in their own window in the middle of the screen. To change the location of the toolbar, drag the toolbar to the top, side, or bottom of the screen. To float the toolbar, drag it into the middle of the screen. Double-click the toolbar to toggle between docking and floating.

Creating Toolbars

If the commands you use most are scattered across several built-in toolbars, creating a toolbar of your favorite commands might be the best solution. You can also use the Organizer to copy an existing toolbar as a template.

To create a new toolbar, follow these steps:

1 Click Tools, Customize, Toolbars. The Customize dialog box appears.

2 Click the Toolbars tab, and then click New.

3 In the New Toolbar dialog box, type the name of the toolbar. After you click OK, the toolbar name appears in the toolbars list in the Customize dialog box and the empty toolbar appears on the screen.

4 In the Customize dialog box, click the Commands tab.

5 Click the category of the command you want to add.

6 Drag the command you want to add from the command list to its location on the new toolbar. The command appears on the toolbar (see Figure 26-2).

Figure 26-2. You can create a toolbar with the commands in any category you use frequently.

You can use the Organizer to make a copy of a toolbar so you can modify it to meet your needs. Because Microsoft Project saves toolbars and menus in the global template by default, you must copy the toolbar to your active project, rename it, and then copy the new toolbar back into the global template for editing.

For more information about the global template, see Chapter 28, "Standardizing Projects Using Templates."

To use an existing toolbar as a template for a new toolbar, do the following:

1 Click Tools, Organizer.

2 In the Organizer dialog box, click the Toolbars tab. Elements in the global template appear on the left side of the dialog box.

3 In the list for the global template, click the name of the toolbar you want to use as a template.

4 Click Copy to copy the toolbar to your active project.

5 Click the toolbar you just copied to the list for your active project, and then click Rename.

6 In the Rename dialog box, type a unique name for the toolbar.

7 Click Copy again to copy the renamed toolbar back to the global template.

8 Click the toolbar in the list for your active project, and then click Delete so the toolbar appears only in the global template list.

9 Follow the steps in the section "Customizing Toolbars," earlier in this chapter, to make changes to the new toolbar.

Troubleshooting

You can't find the custom toolbar you built

Customized menus belong to the application, not the active project, and are stored in the global template so that they are available whenever you use Project on your computer. If you open the project that was open when you created the custom toolbar on another computer, the toolbar does not appear on the Toolbars menu. To see the custom toolbar on another computer, you must either copy the global template to this computer or use the Organizer to copy the toolbar. See the tip "Share modified toolbars and menus" later in this chapter for the steps to follow.

Deleting Toolbars

You can't delete built-in toolbars. You can only delete toolbars that you created. Follow these steps to delete a user-defined toolbar:

1 Click Tools, Customize, Toolbars. The Customize dialog box appears.

2 Click the Toolbars tab, and then click the name of the user-defined toolbar you want to delete.

3 Click the Delete button. Click OK in the dialog box that prompts you to confirm the deletion.

> **tip** **Use the Organizer to delete toolbars**
>
> To delete one or more toolbars without displaying each one, click Tools, Organizer. Click the Toolbars tab. Click the name of the toolbar you want to delete, and then click Delete.

Troubleshooting

You can't delete a toolbar

You can't delete the toolbars that are built into Microsoft Project but you can reset them to their original configuration. The Delete button is dimmed when you select a built-in toolbar in the Customize dialog box. To reset a built-in toolbar, click the toolbar in the list, and then click Reset. Click OK in the dialog box that prompts you to confirm your actions.

Resetting a toolbar removes any customizations you make including any custom buttons you created. To save custom buttons, copy them to another toolbar before you reset the current one.

Modifying Button Images

You can modify the image of a button on a toolbar. For example, if you created several Print buttons, each of which prints to a different printer, you can modify a button's image to indicate which printer it uses. You can move the image around within the boundaries of the button or change the colors of the cells that make up the image.

Do the following to modify a button image:

1 Right-click a toolbar, and then click Customize. The Customize dialog box appears.

2 Right-click the button you want to edit, and then click Edit Button Image. The Button Editor dialog box appears (see Figure 26-3).

Chapter 26: Customizing the Microsoft Project Interface

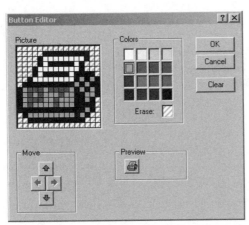

Figure 26-3. You can modify the image that appears on a toolbar button.

3 To modify the image, click a color in the Colors area. If you want to erase
colored boxes in the image, click the Erase box.

4 In the Picture area, click individual cells or drag the mouse pointer over
cells to change their color.

As you change the image, you can see what the image looks like in the
Preview area.

5 To move the image within the picture area, click a directional arrow
in the Move area. If the image fills the picture area in one or more
directions, the directional arrows might be dimmed.

Creating and Customizing Menus

Menus are simply toolbars with a different presentation style. Menus can contain
commands or other menus. Although toolbars are thriftier with space, menus can
display a description of the commands or submenus.

---

tip **Share modified toolbars and menus**

Toolbars and menus belong to the entire Microsoft Project application, not just a
particular project. They are stored in the global template by default. When you modify
a toolbar or menu, the modified version is available no matter which project you open.
To share a customized toolbar with someone else, copy it from the global template to
a project file, and then send the project file to that person. He or she can use the
Organizer to copy the toolbar to their global template.

Customizing Menus

You can add, remove, or rearrange commands and submenus on a menu. You can also specify whether the menu displays buttons or text, and change the appearance of buttons as you do for toolbars.

To add a menu to another menu, follow these steps:

1 Click Tools, Customize, Toolbars. The Customize dialog box appears.

2 Click the Commands tab. Scroll to the bottom of the Categories list, and click New Menu. New Menu is the only command in the New Menu category.

3 Drag the New Menu command to the location where you want to insert it (see Figure 26-4).

Figure 26-4. You can insert a menu or command on a menu bar.

Creating Keyboard Shortcuts

You can assign a keyboard shortcut to any command on a menu. With the Customize dialog box open, right-click the menu or command for which you want to define a keyboard shortcut. In the Name box on the shortcut menu, type an ampersand (&) before the letter you want to use as the shortcut.

Use a different letter for each keyboard shortcut. If you choose a letter that is already in use by another menu entry, you might have to press the letter more than once to select the command you want.

To choose a command using a keyboard shortcut, click a menu to display its commands. Press the shortcut letter for the command you want to select.

To add a command to an existing menu, follow these steps:

1 Click the Commands tab in the Customize dialog box.

2 Click the category of the command you want to add to the menu.

3 Drag the command from the command list to its new location.

---

tip   **Drag menus and commands where you want them**

When you drag New Menu or any other command to a menu bar, an I-beam pointer appears. Drag the command until the I-beam is where you want to place the command or menu, and then release the mouse button. If you want to insert a command in a menu on the menu bar, drag the command to the menu where you want to insert it. When the commands for that menu appear, drag the mouse pointer to its new location and release the mouse button.

To remove a command from a menu, do the following:

1 Click Tools, Customize, Toolbars. The Customize dialog box appears.

2 Right-click the command you want to remove from the menu bar, and then click Delete. If you want to remove a command from a pull-down menu underneath the menu bar, navigate to the command you want to remove, right-click it, and then click Delete.

---

tip   **Rearrange commands on a menu**

You can rearrange the commands on a menu and modify their properties in the same way that you customize buttons on a toolbar. With the Customize dialog box displayed, drag a command or menu to its new location. To modify the properties of a command or menu, right-click it, and then click the command you want on the shortcut menu, as described in the section "Changing the Properties of a Toolbar" earlier in this chapter.

Creating and Customizing Forms

Custom forms are dialog boxes that display Microsoft Project fields for data entry. These forms don't behave like built-in forms such as Task Entry. To use a custom form, you first select the tasks or resources you want to edit with the form. Then you open the form and enter values into the fields. When you click OK on the form, the changes are applied to the selected tasks or resources, and the form disappears.

---

tip   **Enter field values using a table**

If you want to enter field values without having to open and close a custom form, you can add the fields you want to a table. You can then edit the values in the sheet portion of a view.

Creating Forms

You can create a new custom form or copy an existing form and then edit it. You can add fields, text, and buttons to the form. You can also add group boxes to separate items within the form.

Follow these steps to create a new form:

1 Click Tools, Customize, Forms. The Customize Forms dialog box appears.

2 To create a new custom form, click New. If you want to use an existing form as a template, click the form in the list, and then click Copy.

3 In the Define Custom Form dialog box, type a new name for the form. If you want to open the form with a keyboard shortcut, type the letter in the Key box.

> **caution** Microsoft applications use many letters of the alphabet for other commands, such as C for copy, X for cut, and P for paste. If you select one of these reserved characters for a shortcut key, a warning appears that instructs you to select another letter.

4 When you click OK, the Custom Form Editor opens (see Figure 26-5).

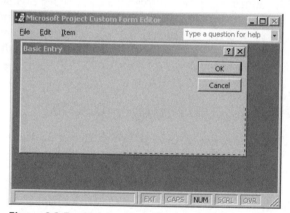

Figure 26-5. You can specify the size and position of the dialog box for a custom form as well as its contents.

5 To change the size of the form, drag a corner or one of its edges until the form is the size you want.

6 To change where the form appears when it loads, move the mouse pointer to the title bar of the form until a four-headed arrow appears. Drag the form to the new location.

If you want to specify an exact size and location for the form, double-click the form. In the Form Information dialog box, enter values in the X and Y boxes to specify the form's location. Enter values in the width and height boxes to specify the form's size.

---

tip   **Specify the size of your form**

The values in the X and Y boxes represent pixels on your screen. If your screen resolution is 1280 by 1024, a form with a width of 640 and height of 512 would take up half the screen.

Adding Fields

Custom forms display fields that contain information about the selected tasks or resources. By default, you can view or edit any of the fields in a form. However, you can restrict a field so that it can't be edited.

To add a field to a form, follow these steps:

1   In the Custom Form Editor window, click Item, Fields. The Item Information dialog box appears (see Figure 26-6).

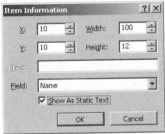

Figure 26-6.   You can specify the size, position, and field name as well as whether users can edit the field value.

2   To specify the location of the field, enter values in the X and Y boxes.

3   To specify the size of the field box, enter values in the Width and Height boxes.

---

tip   **Resize a field box by dragging**

You can resize a field box by dragging one of its edges or corners. You can move the field box by dragging the center of the box to the new location.

---

4 Click the arrow in the Field box, and then click the field that you want
   to appear in the box.

5 To prevent users from editing the field, select the Show As Static Text check
   box. A value appears in the field, but users can't edit those values.

Adding Text

You can add text to label the fields or convey other information to the user.

To add text to a form do the following:

1 In the Custom Form Editor window, click Item, Text. A new, blank text box
   appears within the form you are editing.

2 Double-click the text box to display the Item Information dialog box.

3 Type the text you want to appear on the form in the Text box.

Follow these steps to modify text:

1 To change the size of the text box, drag one of its edges or corners.

2 To reposition the text box in the form, drag the center of the text box to the
   location you want.

Adding Buttons

A new form includes OK and Cancel buttons by default. However, if you removed
one of these buttons earlier and want to replace it, you can add buttons to the form.
To do this, follow these steps:

1 In the Custom Form Editor window, click Item, Button. The New Button
   dialog box appears.

2 Select the option for the button that you want to add to the form. You can
   add only an OK or Cancel button.

3 Click OK in the New Button dialog box to add the button to the form.

4 Drag the button where you want it to appear in the form.

---

tip   **Forms can't contain more than one OK or Cancel button**

A form includes an OK and Cancel button by default. You can't add another OK or
Cancel button to the form. The only time you can exercise the Item, Button command
is after you delete one of those buttons.

Adding a Group Box

If a form contains a lot of fields, you can make the form more readable by grouping the related fields. You can add a group box to the form and then move the items you want to group into it.

To add a group box to a form do the following:

1 In the Custom Form Editor window, click Item, Group Box. The group box appears in the custom form.

2 Drag the group box to the location you want in the form.

3 To resize the group box, drag one of its edges or corners.

4 To change the text that appears at the top of the group box, double-click the group box. The Item Information dialog box appears. Type the new label in the Text box.

5 Move any other items you want into the group box.

For information about creating forms using Visual Basic for Applications, see "Creating UserForms" on page 756.

Editing Forms

Follow these steps to edit an existing form:

1 Click Tools, Customize, Forms. The Customize Forms dialog box appears.

2 Click the name of the form you want to edit, and then click Edit.

3 Make the changes you want in the Custom Form Editor window, as described in the section "Creating Forms," earlier in this chapter.

4 Click File, Save to close the Custom Form Editor window and save the changes to the form.

Renaming Forms

Do the following to rename an existing form:

1 Click Tools, Customize, Forms. The Customize Forms dialog box appears.

2 Click the name of the form you want to rename, and then click Rename.

3 Type the new name in the Define Custom Form dialog box.

Displaying Custom Forms

It's not easy to access the command to display a custom form. However, if you plan to use a custom form frequently, you can add a button to a toolbar or assign a shortcut key to open it.

To open a custom form from the Microsoft Project menus, follow these steps:

1 Select the tasks or resources you want to edit.

2 Click Tools, Customize, Forms. The Customize Forms dialog box appears (see Figure 26-7).

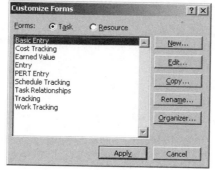

Figure 26-7. Select the tasks or resources you want to edit, and then click Apply to display the form.

3 Click the name of the form you want to display, and then click Apply.

To open a form from a toolbar, follow these steps:

1 Click Tools, Customize, Toolbars. The Customize dialog box appears.

2 Click the Commands tab. Click the All Forms category.

3 Drag the form you want to add from the command list to the toolbar.

> For more information about adding buttons to toolbars, see "Adding and Removing the Buttons on a Toolbar" earlier in this chapter. For information on defining a keyboard shortcut for a form, see "Creating and Customizing Forms" earlier in this chapter.

Chapter 27

Automating Your Work with Macros

One of the easiest ways to increase your day-to-day productivity with Microsoft Project is to use macros. Macros can automate repetitive, tedious, or complex tasks, freeing your time for more important tasks like managing your projects.

This chapter focuses on macros you might use to automate tasks that you need to do frequently. Typically, macros are created by recording the steps in a task, which means that little (if any) programming is required.

> For more information about advanced macro tasks such as using them as part of larger solutions to customize or extend Microsoft Project's interface and functionality, see Part 10, "Programming Custom Solutions."

Understanding Macros

Washing the dishes—what a chore. Pick up a dirty plate, wash it with soapy water, rinse it off, and then dry it. It's the same every time. But with a dishwasher, all the tedium of washing, rinsing, and drying is automatically handled by the machine, leaving you free to do better things with your time. (Now if you could only get the kids to empty it without being told...) Similarly, you don't want to perform the same tedious series of commands week after week; you just want a specially formatted report to print every Friday. What you need is a macro.

What Is a Macro?

Basically, a macro is a shortcut that performs a series of commands. Rather than manually performing each step necessary to complete a task, you simply tell the software what each step is, what needs to be accomplished in each

657

step, and in what order the steps must occur. Then you designate some way to set this series of commands in motion.

In the past, creating a macro usually involved one of the following two problems:

- The macro language was powerful but arcane, which resulted in a complicated process that took a lot of time to learn.

- The macro language was easier to understand but limited in the range of tasks it could perform, making for a very frustrating experience.

In Microsoft Project, however, you have the best of both worlds with Visual Basic for Applications (VBA). A subset of the highly popular Visual Basic programming language, VBA is both powerful and easy to understand. What's more, the tools available in Microsoft Project make creating macros about as easy as can be. Most macros can be created without ever seeing, much less writing, VBA code.

Why Use Macros?

When you use Microsoft Project (or any other business productivity software) you use it because it makes doing your job easier and more efficient. One of the reasons that software can make you more productive is that the features it has are, in a sense, a collection of macros that accomplish tasks that the software designers feel can be accomplished more effectively by using a computer. More importantly for this discussion, these "macros" perform tasks that the designers learned their customers want. But what the designers can't do is create *all* the features that *every* customer wants. This is where macros can prove so useful.

Because individual users can create a macro to accomplish some particular task, you can essentially customize the software by adding "features" that support the particular way you do your job.

For example, let's say that you do have to print a certain report every Friday. Before you can print anything, you have to do the following:

- Choose the right view of your project data.

- Choose among several filters to exclude unwanted tasks.

- Choose how and in what way you will sort the data.

- Choose the report format you need.

After you've opened the right project, you might have to click your mouse well over a dozen times before you can print the report. With a macro to perform all those steps for you, printing the report would be reduced to only a few mouse clicks.

Just because macros can be used to perform a complex series of steps doesn't mean that every macro has to be elaborate. Maybe you have certain simple things you do in Microsoft Project all the time, such as creating WBS code masks. By recording a macro and creating a new toolbar button for it, you have a convenient one-click method of opening the WBS Code Definition dialog box.

> For more information about creating new toolbar buttons to run macros, see "Creating Toolbar Buttons" later in this chapter.

Creating Macros

The easiest and quickest way to create a macro, especially one that is going to be used to automate a lengthy series of steps, is to record the steps that make up a task. Recording a macro is just what it sounds like: Start the macro recorder, perform the series of actions you want the macro to do, and then stop the recorder. In most cases, there's no need to edit the VBA code generated by the recorder.

> For more information about creating macros by writing VBA code directly, including how to edit macros, see Chapter 31, "Writing Microsoft Project Code with Visual Basic for Applications."

Understanding the Record Macro Dialog Box

Before you can record a macro, you must first get your project environment ready for recording by setting the conditions that are required for the steps in the macro to occur. This might include something obvious like opening a particular project, but can also include steps like selecting a certain task or resource. You should also have a clear plan for what you want to record; any mistakes you make while the macro recorder is running will be included in the macro. Now you're ready to begin recording.

● <u>R</u>ecord New Macro...

Click Tools, Macro, Record New Macro. This displays the Record Macro dialog box (see Figure 27-1 on the next page), in which you can enter information about the macro (such as a name and a description) and assign it a shortcut key.

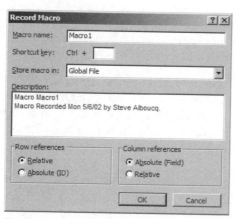

Figure 27-1. The decisions you make in the Record Macro dialog box determine not only when you can use a macro but aspects of how it will behave when it runs as well.

> For more information about assigning keyboard shortcuts to macros, see "Creating Keyboard Shortcuts" later in this chapter.

There are three settings in the Record Macro dialog box that are even more important than the name of the macro or the keyboard shortcut you might use to run it. These are:

Store Macro In. Use the choices in the drop-down list to specify where the macro will be stored. If you choose This Project, the macro is stored in the file with the project that is currently open and will be available only when that project is open. If you choose Global File, the macro is stored in the global file (Global.mpt) and is available whenever Microsoft Project is running, regardless of whether a particular project (or any project at all) is open.

Row References. Accept the default setting of Relative if you want Microsoft Project to record relative row references. This means that when the macro is run, it will always attempt to move the same number of rows from the selected cell after the macro encounters the command to select a new cell.

For example, say a cell in row 1 is selected and, while recording the macro, you select a cell in row 4. From then on, every time the macro is run and encounters the command to select a new cell, it will always move three rows from whatever cell was selected before the macro was run.

Select the Absolute option if you want be certain that a particular row—based on the selected cell's row ID—will be selected when a macro runs. In the example just given, your macro will always select a cell in row 4, regardless of which cell is selected before the macro is run.

Column References. Unlike row references, the default setting for column references is Absolute, based on the selected field. No matter where fields are positioned, absolute column references select the same column every time. Relative column references work just like relative row references.

InsideOut

Most of the macros you record should be stored in the project where you will use them, rather than in the global file. The main reason for this is that your macro won't work unless a certain set of conditions are met, and these conditions are usually particular to the file in which you created the macro. For example, you might need to select a particular task before running your macro, or perhaps a varying group of resources.

What is probably more important from a practical standpoint is the shared nature of the global file. Because all the macros in a particular project must share the available keyboard shortcuts, toolbar buttons, and names, only one macro in a project can use Ctrl+A as a keyboard shortcut, for example. This rule also applies to the Microsoft Project global file, which is open whenever Microsoft Project is running. If you use Ctrl+A as a keyboard shortcut in the global, no other macro in the global file can use that shortcut. If you store your Ctrl+A macro in the project file, however, you can have another macro, stored in another project, that also uses Ctrl+A as its keyboard shortcut.

Finally, macros stored in a specific project are available if you send the project to someone else. The Microsoft Project global file, on the other hand, is local to a particular computer.

Absolute Column References Can Be Tricky

The decision to use absolute column references might seem like a no-brainer, but absolute column references are based on the selected field. Because fields can be moved, you might sometimes get unexpected results.

For example, suppose you recorded a macro using absolute column references in a project you share with someone else. When you recorded the macro, you selected the third column, which contained the Start field. At some point, however, your co-worker opened the project and inserted the Duration field as the third column.

The next time you run the macro, the fourth column gets selected, because that's the new location of the Start field. If you assumed that the third column would always be selected, because absolute column references are "safe" and that's where you always put the Start field, your macro is now broken.

Knowing When to Say "When"

Knowing when to stop the recorder can be as important as the recording environment itself. For an automatic procedure like a macro to be truly trustworthy—and therefore useful—it should have an ending point that is intuitive or at least easy to remember.

For example, the Bold button on the formatting toolbar is basically a macro to automate clicking Font on the Format menu and then clicking Bold in the Font Style list. If you have already selected a word, you know that clicking the Bold button will format the word a certain way and then stop. If you haven't selected a word, you know that the Bold button will turn on a certain kind of formatting for anything you type until you click it again to turn that formatting off. Both endings are so easy to remember that they've probably become intuitive for you.

The same should be true for any macro you record. It should be easy for you to remember what conditions must be met before you can run the macro, what the macro will do, and when it will stop. A macro that performs a 20-step procedure for you is no good if you're afraid to run it because you can't remember what it might do along the way.

Adding the Visual Basic Toolbar

If you record new macros frequently or prefer to run macros by selecting them by name rather than using a keyboard shortcut or a toolbar button, you might find it convenient to use the Visual Basic toolbar:

To display the Visual Basic toolbar, simply right-click any toolbar or toolbar button, and then click Visual Basic on the shortcut menu. The same commands that are available by pointing to Macro on the Tools menu are available here.

Recording a Macro

Let's return to the idea of a weekly report, as described earlier in this chapter. The report that you print every Friday requires you to do the following:

- Change the view to the Tracking Gantt.
- Apply a filter to display only incomplete tasks.
- Sort the tasks by finish date in ascending order.
- Print the results using the Slipping Tasks report.

Chapter 27: Automating Your Work with Macros

You've decided to automate these tasks by recording them in a macro. Follow these steps to record the macro:

1 Click Tools, Macro, Record New Macro to open the Record Macro dialog box.

2 Click This Project in the Store Macro In list.

Enter a name like *Friday_Report* in the Macro name box. Change the first line of the Description box to a descriptive name like *Weekly task report*.

3 Because the macro won't be selecting cells, leave the default settings for row and column references, and then click OK to begin recording.

> **note** Remember, everything you do when recording will be written into the macro that you are creating, including any mistakes.

4 Click View, Tracking Gantt.

5 Click Project, Filtered For, Incomplete Tasks.

6 Click Project, Sort, By Finish Date.

7 Click View, Reports.

8 Double-click Current Activities, double-click Slipping Tasks, and then click Print.

9 Click OK in the Print dialog box, and then click Close in the Reports dialog box.

10 Stop the recorder by clicking Tools, Macro, Stop Recorder:

> **note** We've chosen to store this macro in the open project, but it's a good example of a macro that could be stored in the global file as well. Because all it does is change the way the data in a particular project is displayed and then print a report, you could record the steps to open the right project at the beginning of the macro. You could then print the report anytime Microsoft Project is running without having to manually open the project first.

Troubleshooting

Why doesn't your macro select the right cell?

If your macro is supposed to select cells as it runs, but selects the wrong ones or even causes an error, one of the following items may be the cause:

● The macro was recorded using one combination of settings for absolute or relative column or row references, but the actual conditions under which the macro is run require a different combination.

You can either rerecord the macro, using a combination that better suits the situation under which the macro is run, or you can edit the macro code in the Visual Basic Editor and change it manually.

If you change the reference settings manually, the following table shows the different values that should be used when changing the type of column and row references:

Reference	Absolute	Relative
Column	The value for the Column argument is the name of the field in quotes.	The value for the Column argument is a positive number, indicating the number of the column.
Row	The value for the Row argument is a positive number, indicating the number of the row, and the RowRelative argument is False.	The value for the Row argument may be either a negative or positive number. The RowRelative argument is either True or is missing (the default value is True).

note The columns for the row number and the Indicators field (if showing) are both counted when using relative column references. The first "normal" column is actually column 3 when manually editing column references in a macro.

● The macro assumes that a particular cell or item has been selected before the macro is run.

You could always try to remember that the proper cell is selected before running the macro, but rerecording the macro (or editing it in the Visual Basic Editor) to select the proper cell before it does anything else will solve the problem and also makes the macro more robust.

Troubleshooting *(continued)*

● The column (or row, if it is for a subtask) containing the cell to select may have been hidden, or the row may have been deleted.

Most of the solutions to this problem involve writing complicated Visual Basic code, so the best solution, until you're more comfortable working with the Visual Basic Editor to edit your macros, is to simply make sure that the proper conditions are met before running your macro. Using column references can also help you spot this problem early on, because your macro will cause an error on the line that refers to the missing column and make it easier for you to guess at what the problem is.

Looking at Macro Code

For many people, knowing how to record and play back a macro is sufficient for most of their needs. But what if you made a minor mistake while recording a macro? What if you recorded a complex macro that referenced a project by file name, and then the file name was changed? Although you might not ever need to know how to write VBA code, much less create an entire macro with it, the first step to making simple changes or corrections is understanding how simple and logical the macro code can be.

For more information about the Visual Basic Editor, see "Using the Visual Basic Editor" on page 734.

If you were to start the Visual Basic Editor that is included as part of Microsoft Project and open the *Friday_Report* macro, this is the code you would see:

```
Sub Friday_Report()
' Macro Weekly task report
' Macro Recorded Tue 3/5/02 by Steve Alboucq.
    ViewApply Name:="Tracking Ga&ntt"
    FilterApply Name:="I&ncomplete Tasks"
    Sort Key1:="Finish", Ascending1:=True
    ReportPrint Name:="Slipping Tasks"
End Sub
```

It's quite short and reasonably simple. You might already have made some guesses about what different sections of the code mean, such as information that also appears in the Microsoft Project interface. Table 27-1 gives descriptions of each line in the VBA code.

Table 27-1.   Breakdown of Code in the Friday_Report Macro

Macro code	What it means
`Sub Friday_Report()`	The beginning of the macro. *Sub* is short for subroutine, which is what a macro really is. The text that follows is the name of the macro.
`' Macro Weekly task report` `' Macro Recorded Tue 3/5/02 by Steve Alboucq.`	Any line that starts with an apostrophe is a comment and is ignored by Visual Basic. You can use comments anywhere in a macro to remind yourself of what the different parts do.
`ViewApply Name:="Tracking Ga&ntt"`	This line changes the view to the Tracking Gantt. The ampersand (&) comes before the letter that acts as an access key on the View menu.
`FilterApply Name:="I&ncomplete Tasks"`	This line applies a filter to display only incomplete tasks.
`Sort Key1:="Finish", Ascending1:=True`	This line sorts the tasks by finish date in ascending order.
`ReportPrint Name:="Slipping Tasks"`	This line prints the Slipping Tasks report.
`End Sub`	The end of the macro, like the period at the end of a sentence.

If, after recording the macro, you decide that you'd prefer to sort the tasks in descending order, it wouldn't take that much time or trouble to record the macro all over again. But it would take even less time to simply edit the macro and change `True` to `False` in the line `Sort Key1:="Finish", Ascending1:=True`.

Follow these steps to start the Visual Basic Editor:

1 Click Tools, Macro, Macros.

> **tip** Pressing Alt+F8 is another way to display the Macros dialog box.

2 In the Macro Name list, click the name of the macro you want to edit.

3 Click the Edit button to start the VBE and begin editing the macro code.

Running Macros

Run Macro

There are three standard methods for running a macro. First you can run a macro by selecting it from the list of available macros in the Macros dialog box. In the Macros dialog box, select the name of the macro you want to run, and click the Run button.

The other two methods are to press a keyboard shortcut assigned to a macro and to click a toolbar button created for a macro.

Creating Keyboard Shortcuts

Key commands such as Ctrl+C are the oldest and most common shortcuts to access software features, especially displaying dialog boxes or performing some quick action. Unfortunately, as more and more keyboard shortcuts are assigned to software features, fewer of these simple combinations are left over to be used for macros.

In Microsoft Project, a keyboard shortcut for a macro must be a combination of the Ctrl key and a letter. Because Microsoft Project has many built-in keyboard shortcuts, the only letters available for macro shortcuts are A, E, J, M, Q, T, and Y.

You can assign a keyboard shortcut to a macro when you record it, as described in the section titled "Creating Macros" earlier in this chapter. You can also assign a keyboard shortcut to a macro any time after you've created it by opening the Macro Options dialog box (see Figure 27-2).

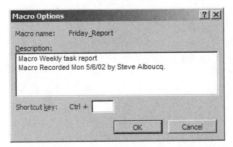

Figure 27-2.   Change a macro's description or shortcut key with the Macro Options dialog box.

667

Follow these steps to open the Macro Options dialog box:

1 Click Tools, Macro, Macros.

2 Click the name of the macro you want to modify from the Macro Name list.

3 Click the Options button to edit the shortcut key combination or macro description.

> **tip** To gain the most advantage of the quick access provided by keyboard shortcuts, assign them to frequently used macros that perform simple tasks such as opening a dialog box.

Creating Toolbar Buttons

The most common shortcut for running a macro is to create a toolbar button for it. This is true for the following reasons:

- You don't have to memorize a key combination.

- You can display the name of the macro as part of the button.

- You can add it to both a menu and a toolbar, and you can group it with other buttons that are related in some way.

> **tip** Beginning with Microsoft Project 2000, menus are treated just like toolbars; you can add, modify, or even delete menus and menu commands as desired.

A macro is not associated with a toolbar button when you record it. Instead, you actually customize the Microsoft Project interface by using the Customize dialog box (see Figure 27-3).

Follow these steps to create a new toolbar button for a macro:

1 Right-click any toolbar or toolbar button, and then click Customize on the shortcut menu to open the Customize dialog box.

2 On the Commands tab, click All Macros in the Categories list.

3 Click the name of a macro in the Commands list, and then drag it to the desired location on any toolbar or menu.

Chapter 27: Automating Your Work with Macros

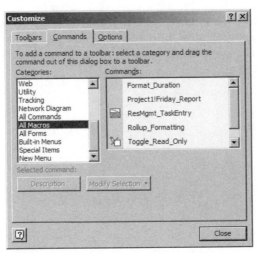

Figure 27-3. Open the Customize dialog box to choose a macro to add as a toolbar button.

InsideOut

The Description button on the Commands tab of the Customize dialog box is not very useful for the macros you create because there is no way to control what it displays. If the macro isn't one that comes with Microsoft Project (these macros display graphics next to the macro name in the Commands list), clicking the Description button just displays a generic description of how to access the Macros dialog box.

tip To see the description for any macro, open the Macros dialog box and click the name of the macro in the Macro Name list.

Part 9: Customizing and Managing Project Files

When you create a toolbar button for a macro, the button initially displays just the name of the macro. You can modify the new button in many ways including renaming it, assigning an image to it, or changing its display style. You can even edit the image used for a button or draw your own.

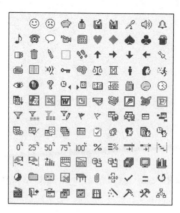

Follow these steps to assign an image to the button (the caption will be displayed as a ScreenTip):

1 Right-click any toolbar or toolbar button, and then click Customize on the shortcut menu to open the Customize dialog box.

2 Click the toolbar button on which you want to display an image. When the Customize dialog box is displayed, clicking a toolbar button doesn't run the macro or command; instead, it selects the button. When selected, the button has a black border.

3 Click the Modify Selection button on the Commands tab in the Customize dialog box.

4 On the shortcut menu, point to Change Button Image, and then click the graphic you want to use.

5 Click the Modify Selection button again, and then click Default Style. The button will display the image you selected, but the name of the macro will appear only as a ScreenTip when you move the mouse pointer over the button.

tip The Name box on the shortcut menu for the Modify Selection button is used for both the caption and the ScreenTip of the button you're modifying. You can change this text to whatever suits you without also changing the name of the macro itself.

Chapter 28

Standardizing Projects Using Templates

With each project you manage, you learn more and more. You practice effective project management methods and see what works and what doesn't. You gain more knowledge about project management in your specific discipline or industry. Likewise, as you continue to manage projects with Microsoft Project, you increase your proficiency with it as a productivity tool for planning, tracking, and communicating your project information.

You can record some of the knowledge you gained from hard-won project management experience by using Microsoft Project *templates*. As you enter the closing phase of a project, saving the project file as a template for future use can be one of your most valuable project closing activities. Templates are special project files in which various types of project information can be stored for use with future projects, either by you or by other project managers.

You can also use templates to save yourself from reinventing that old wheel. Obtain project templates already developed by industry experts and adapt them for your own project requirements, thereby saving time and giving yourself a leg up on planning your next project.

Whether a template is based on your project experiences or someone else's, it can contain the following types of information:

- Tasks
- Sequences and task dependencies
- Durations
- Resources

671

Templates are also a great means of setting standards. If your organization follows a specific methodology in each project, if certain review processes are required at certain stages, or if a specific format is mandated for progress reports, those requirements can all be reflected in the template. Similarly, any custom features that reflect organization standards or that you've designed to make your project work more effective can also become a part of your template.

Understanding the Template Types

There are three types of templates in Microsoft Project:

The project template.   The project template might contain task and resource information that you can use as a basis for starting a new project. It's often based on past project experiences in the organization or in the industry. For example, there are software project templates, commercial construction templates, product development templates, and so on.

There are a wide variety of project templates available, both within Microsoft Project and from third-party sources. You can use such a project template as the basis for a new project you're creating. If you're closing a project, you can save and adapt your plan as a project template file for you or others to use and benefit from your experience.

The global template.   The *global template*, also referred to as the *global.mpt file*, is a template that contains elements and settings pertinent to how you use Microsoft Project. Such elements include views, tables, groups, filters, and reports for customized ways of looking at project information. The global template can include calendars, macros, and toolbars, for specific methods of executing Microsoft Project commands and functions. The global template can also include general Microsoft Project program settings to set defaults for editing, scheduling, and calculations, to name a few.

The global template is automatically attached to every project file you work with. As the user and project manager, you have control over the content of your global template, although you can share it with others if you want.

The enterprise global template.   If you use enterprise features with Microsoft Project Professional, the *enterprise global* template is also automatically attached to every enterprise project you check out. Think of it as a global template over the project global template, or the "global global." This template dictates standards being enforced and customizations made available throughout the enterprise. These standards make it possible for project information throughout the enterprise to be compared and analyzed in relation to one another.

Because the enterprise global template affects all projects throughout
the enterprise, only users who have certain permissions can check out
and modify the enterprise global template. Many organizations give that
responsibility to one or two project system administrators.

For more information about the enterprise global template, see "Working with the Enterprise
Global Template" on page 564.

Working with the Project Global Template

The project global template, or *global.mpt*, is an integral part of every project file.
Essentially, it's a collection of default settings for a variety of elements throughout
a project file. These elements include the following:

- Views
- Tables
- Groups
- Filters
- Reports
- Base calendars

- Custom fields and outline codes
- Toolbars
- Forms
- VBA modules and macros
- Import/export maps

As you alter settings in your project by, for example, customizing your view and calendar
settings, modifying tables, and creating sets of custom fields, those changes initially
apply to just the current project. If you want your custom settings available to any
project opened on your local computer, you can add them to the global template using
the Organizer (see Figure 28-1). Those new settings become your new defaults.

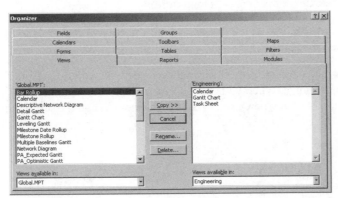

Figure 28-1. Use the Organizer to copy customized elements to the project global
template to make those elements available to other projects.

Chapter 28

> For more information about the Organizer, see "Sharing Customized Elements among Projects" on page 636.

The project global template also contains your Microsoft Project-wide settings, which you access by clicking Tools, Options. In the Options dialog box, various categories of options are available, like View, Schedule, Calculation, and so on. Certain settings apply just to the current project file; others apply to Microsoft Project as a whole, and change the project global template. You can use the Set As Default button to add current project settings to your project global template (see Figure 28-2).

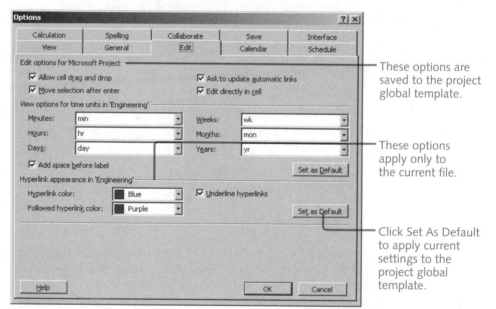

These options are saved to the project global template.

These options apply only to the current file.

Click Set As Default to apply current settings to the project global template.

Figure 28-2. Any group of options specified as being for the current file applies only to that file unless you click the Set As Default button.

Settings that do not specify that they apply only to the current file apply to Microsoft Project in general (see Figure 28-3).

When you change a Microsoft Project setting, every new file you open from that point on will reflect that change. When you change a local project setting and then set it as a default, it will apply to any new projects but it will not change the setting for other existing projects.

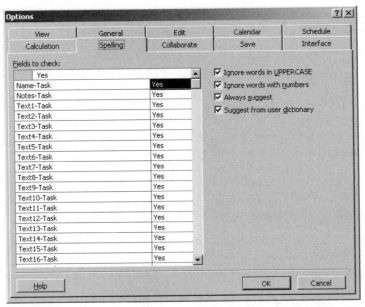

Figure 28-3. The settings on the Spelling tab apply to your spelling checker options in Microsoft Project in general. Changes here update the project global file.

Working with Project Templates

A project template is a standardized starting point for a new project. A template can contain task information, resource information, or both. It might be very broad in scope, showing just major phases and generic resource names, for example. Or the template can be highly detailed, with multiple outline levels of tasks, their durations, task dependencies, and specific resource information.

Microsoft Project comes with a set of built-in templates for a variety of industries and applications. Microsoft Project templates are available from third-party sources as well, such as professional societies and standards organizations. You can also create your own templates based on previous projects you have completed. It's a good practice to adapt and save the plan of a completed project as a template for future use in your organization, either for yourself or for others.

For more information about using a project plan as template, see "Creating Your Own Project Template," later in this chapter.

Part 9: Customizing and Managing Project Files

Microsoft Project Built-in Templates

The following templates are supplied with Microsoft Project:

- Commercial construction
- Engineering
- Home move
- Infrastructure deployment
- New business
- New product

- Office move
- Project office
- Residential construction
- Software development
- Software localization

There are additional built-in templates for the deployment in your organization of specific Microsoft products, such as Windows XP, Exchange Server, and more.

Microsoft Project online Help provides comprehensive details about each template provided. In the Help box, type *templates*, and then click the Templates Included With Microsoft Project link.

You can find additional templates on the Microsoft Project Web site. Click File, New. In the Project Guide, click the Templates On Microsoft.com link.

A project template serves as a knowledge base for a certain type of project. It is meant to save you time in planning your new project and to let you build on past project experiences. The project template can also help set and enforce organizational standards. It can disseminate custom features and elements, such as specially designed reports, company-specific base calendars, modified views, and so on.

Starting a New Project using a Template

Whenever you start a new project, you're given the opportunity to choose a template. If you start a project with a template, your new project file is populated with information from that template. You then adapt that information to meet your project's specific requirements. When you save the file, you're saving a new project file, rather than overwriting the existing template file. This way the template remains available for use in its more generic format.

Creating a New Project with a Template

To create a new project from a template, follow these steps:

1 Click File, New.

> **note** If you just click the New button on the Standard toolbar, you won't get the choices you need in the Project Guide.

Chapter 28: Standardizing Projects Using Templates

2 In the Project Guide, under New From Template, click the General Templates link.

3 In the Templates dialog box, click the Project Templates tab (see Figure 28-4).

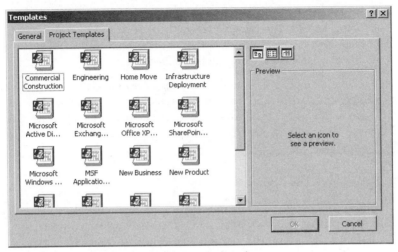

Figure 28-4. All built-in templates are listed.

4 Click the project template you want to use, and then click OK (see Figure 28-5).

If this is the first time you've chosen a template, Microsoft Project might need to install it. This just takes a few moments.

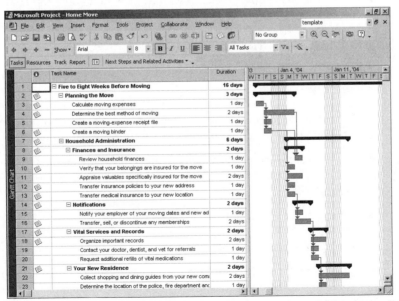

Figure 28-5. A new project file is created based on your selected template.

Chapter 28

Create a New Project from an Existing One

Even if an existing project has not been used to create a new project template, you can still use that project as the basis for a new project. To do this, click File, New. In the Project Guide, under New From Existing Project, click the Choose Project link. Browse to find the project you want to use as the basis for your new project, and then open it. When you save this file, Microsoft Project makes sure you give it a different name, so the original file remains intact.

When you use a project file as the basis for a new project plan, you might need to do a little more adaptation than with a regular template. For example, you'd probably need to remove all date constraints and any actuals. You might need to remove resource information as well.

Saving Your New Project

The original template file has an extension of *.mpt*, indicating that it is a Microsoft Project template file type. When you save a new project file based on a template, by default your new project file is saved as a normal *.mpp* (Microsoft Project plan) file. To save a project based on a template do the following:

1 On the Standard toolbar, click Save.

2 In the Save As dialog box, choose the drive and folder in which you want to save the new project.

3 In the File Name box, enter a descriptive name for your project, and then click the Save button.

Adapting the Template to Your Project

Review your new project file for the types of information included and the level of detail. Review as follows:

- In the Gantt Chart or other task sheet, review the list of tasks. Determine whether you need to add more tasks or remove extraneous ones.

- Check to see whether durations are filled in for the tasks. If they are, see if they seem close to the durations you're going to be expecting in your new project.

- Review the chart portion of the Gantt Chart or the Network Diagram and see whether task dependencies have been set up. Review their appropriateness and their complexity.

- Display the Resource Sheet and see if there is any resource information. There might be generic resources. If you're using a template generated within your organization, you might see names of actual individuals.

Based on this review, you can see how much adaptation you'll need to do to tailor this template to your project.

Creating Your Own Project Template

After you've planned and tracked a few projects to completion using Microsoft Project, you'll see that you're recording valuable information in your project plans. Of course you'll archive your project plan for historical purposes. However, you can also use an existing or completed project plan as the basis for a template that will save you and others a great deal of time in planning future projects.

By creating your own template, you can save task and resource information, format settings, project-specific options, calendars, macros, and other elements that you've used successfully in other projects. Any Microsoft Project file can be saved as a template.

To save an existing project file as a template for future use by you or other project managers, follow these steps:

1 Open the project file you want to save as a template.

2 Click File, Save As.

3 In the Save As Type list, click Template (*.mpt). The file name changes from the *.mpp* extension to *.mpt*, indicating that a copy of the regular project plan file will be saved as a template file. Also, the file is moved to the Templates folder. As long as your template is stored in this folder, it will appear in the Templates dialog box.

4 Click the Save button. The Save As Template dialog box appears (see Figure 28-6).

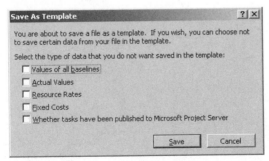

Figure 28-6. The file might include tracking and other specific information not appropriate for a template. Select the information you want to exclude from the template.

5 Select the check box for any item you do *not* want to be saved as part of the template, and then click the Save button. The file is saved as a template in your Microsoft Templates folder on your computer's hard disk.

tip   **Copy templates that others have created**

If you want to use templates that others in your organization have created, or if you've obtained templates from a third-party source or an industry standards organization, copy the file into your Microsoft Templates folder. This ensures that you'll see the templates in the Templates dialog box.

If you're using Windows XP or Windows 2000, the path is C:\Documents and Settings \<Name>\Application Data\Microsoft\Templates.

If you're using Windows 98, the path is C:\Windows\Application Data\Microsoft \Templates.

By default, the Application Data folder is hidden in Windows XP and Windows 2000. To show hidden files and folders, in Windows Explorer, click Tools, Options. Click the View tab. In the Advanced Settings box, double-click Hidden Files And Folders if necessary to show its options. Select the Show Hidden Files And Folders option.

To check that your new template appears in the Templates dialog box, do the following:

1 Click File, New.

2 In the Project Guide, under New From Template, click the General Templates link. Your new template should be listed on the General tab (see Figure 28-7).

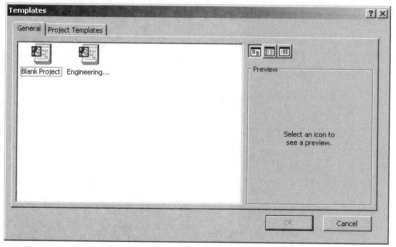

Figure 28-7.   The General tab of the Templates dialog box contains any templates you've created.

> **tip** **Change the location where templates are stored**
>
> By default, templates stored in the Microsoft Templates folder appear in your Templates
> dialog box. You can store templates in a different folder, however, and direct the
> Templates dialog box to find them in the new location. This can be useful if a set
> of templates has been developed for your organization and they've been placed
> on a file server for multiple project managers to use and perhaps update.
>
> To change the location of the Microsoft Templates folder, click Tools, Options, and in
> the Options dialog box, click the Save tab. Under File Locations, click User Templates,
> and then click the Modify button. Browse to the new location, and then click OK.

Review the new template file and see if there is any other information that should
be removed. Here are some suggestions:

- Display the task sheet and apply the Constraints table. See if there are any
  date constraints that should be changed to As Soon As Possible or As Late
  As Possible.

- Review the task dependencies shown in the template. Determine whether
  they're useful or should be removed.

- Review the Resource Sheet. Decide whether you want to keep specific
  resource information or replace it with generic resource names. Also decide
  whether you should change maximum units and other availability information, and whether the cost information should be retained or deleted.

- Review tasks, resources, and assignments and see if there are any notes that
  should be removed.

When you're finished adapting the template, click Save on the Standard toolbar.
Your changes are made to the template.

Updating an Existing Template

If you find you need to update the information in an existing template, you cannot
simply open the template and save it. This will save a copy of the template as a
regular project (*.mpp*) file. To update and save information in the template itself,
follow these steps:

1 Click File, New.

2 In the Project Guide, under New From Template, click the General
Templates link.

3 In the Templates dialog box, double-click the template you want to update.

4 Make the changes you want to the template.

5   On the Standard toolbar, click Save. The Save As dialog box appears,
showing the contents of the Templates folder.

6   In the Save As Type list, click Template (*.mpt). Your template should
appear in the list of files.

7   Click the template, and then click the Save button. A prompt appears
indicating that you're about to replace the existing file (see Figure 28-8).

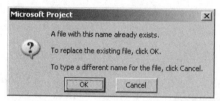

Figure 28-8.   Microsoft Project warns you that you're about to replace
the existing template file, but that's exactly what you want to do.

8   Click OK. The Save As Template dialog box appears.

9   Click the Save button. Your changes are saved to the template file.

> **note**   If several project managers use the same project template, be careful when you're
> updating templates, as your changes can affect many projects.

Closing a Project

After the planning, executing, and controlling phases of the project, the final phase is
the closing of the project. At this point you've fulfilled the goals of the project and it's
now complete. In the closing phase of the project, you can analyze project performance
with concrete data about schedule, cost, and resource utilization. You can also identify
lessons learned and save acquired project knowledge.

Analyzing Project Performance

Review your overall project and compare your baseline plan to your actual plan.
You can review variances in the schedule, in costs, and in assignment work. Any large
variances can help point out problem areas in the project. Some helpful reports for
such analysis include the following:

- Project Summary
- Top-Level Tasks
- Milestones
- Budget
- Overbudget Tasks
- Overbudget Resources
- Earned Value

To generate one of these reports, click View, Reports. Then double-click Overview or Costs.

For more information about generating reports, see Chapter 12, "Reporting Project Information."

Recording Lessons Learned

Whether or not you're going to continue to be involved in this type of project, others are likely to benefit from the experience and knowledge you've gained. At the end of your project, gather your team together and conduct a "postmortem" session in which you can objectively discuss what went well with the project and what could be improved next time.

It's often helpful to have team members prepare notes in advance. In larger projects, you might find it more practical to conduct a series of meetings with different groups of team members and stakeholders, perhaps those who were responsible for different aspects of the project.

Be sure to have a concrete method for recording the discussion points. After the session, compile the lessons learned report, including solutions to identified problem areas.

Project Management Practices: Administrative Closure

As you completed each major milestone or phase, you've probably been getting formal acceptance of that phase by the sponsor or customer. The sponsor reviews the deliverables and checks that the scope and quality of work are completed satisfactorily, and then signs off his or her acceptance of that phase.

When you reach the end of the project, you get your final acceptance and signoff, which at this point should be a formality because the sponsor has been involved and signing off on the interim deliverables all along.

This final project acceptance is part of the *administrative closure* of the project. Administrative closure also includes analyzing project success and effectiveness, and archiving documents and results. At this point, contracts are closed and budget records are archived. Employees should be evaluated, and their skills in your organization's resource pool should be updated to reflect the increase in skills and proficiencies they've gained as a result of working on this project.

A complete set of project records should make up the project archives, and these archives should be readily available for reference for future like projects.

If the project plan is your repository for project-related documents, add your lessons learned report to the closed project. You can embed the document in the plan, create a link to the document, or add it to the document library through Microsoft Project Server and Web Access.

For more information about adding a document to a project, see "Attaching Project Documentation" on page 62.

In addition to archiving the document with the rest of the project historical records, include it with your planning materials for the next project. Be sure to keep your solutions in the forefront so you can continue to improve your project management processes.

Saving Acquired Project Knowledge

Through the planning and tracking of your project, it's likely that you've recorded a mass of valuable information about the following:

- Task durations

- Task and resource costs

- Work metrics (units per hour completed, and the like)

You might want to collect information about planned or actual durations, work, and costs to use as standards for planning future projects.

These durations and work metrics can be included in a project template based on the closing project. Save the project plan as a project template for future use by you or other project managers in your organization who will be working on a similar type of project. In your template, you can remove actuals, resource names, and constraint dates, for example. But the tasks, durations, task dependencies, base calendars, and generic resources can be invaluable in a project template. In addition, any custom solutions you've developed, such as views, reports, filters, and macros, can also become a part of your template. Through the efficiencies you've built into your project plan, you're laying the groundwork for future efficiencies.

Chapter 29

Managing Project Files

It's a very basic concept: when you save a project file, you're ensuring it'll be there when you need to open and work on it again. In a nutshell, managing project files involves saving, finding, and opening your project files. The majority of the time, that's all there is to it. But you can't open a file if you can't find it. You want to be sure you know where you put your files, and if you're at a loss, you need to know the best techniques for searching and finding them quickly.

You also want to guard against data loss in the event of a system crash by saving your file often enough and having a recent backup file handy. Another safeguard is password protection. These are all aspects of sound file management, which are covered in this chapter.

Opening Project Files

After you save a project, you can open it again and continue working. You can open a file stored on your own computer or on a network drive. If you're working in an enterprise environment, you can open your project file from the Microsoft Project Server.

You can open many different types of files in Microsoft Project 2002, including database, spreadsheet, or text files. For more information about the different types of files that you can open in Microsoft Project, see "Saving and Opening with Different File Formats" later in this chapter.

For information about creating a new project file, including using the new Project Guide, see "Creating a New Project Plan" on page 51.

Opening a Saved Project

You can open files from your local machine as well as from a network drive. If you're running Microsoft Project Professional, you can also open a project file from a project stored in the Microsoft Project Server database.

Opening a Project from Your Local Computer or a Network Drive

To open a project from your local computer or a network drive, do the following:

Open

1 On the Standard toolbar, click Open. The Open dialog box appears with your default folder selected (see Figure 29-1).

Figure 29-1. The Open dialog box shows the list of available project files in the selected location.

> **tip** You can also click File, Open to display the Open dialog box.

2 In the Look In box, click the drive or folder where the project file resides.

3 If necessary, double-click the folder that contains the project file.

4 Double-click the project file you want to open. You can also click the project and then click Open.

Open Options

When you open your project, you have three options for how the file is opened: Read-Write, Read-Only, or Copy. In the Open dialog box, click the arrow to the right of the Open button to choose which option you want in the list:

Open.   Opens the project file normally, that is, in Read-Write mode. This mode is selected by default when you simply click the Open button (rather than the Open arrow).

Open Read-Only.   Opens the project in Read-Only mode. You can view the project but you can't save it. To save any changes you make to a Read-Only project file, you will need to save the file with a different name, using the File, Save As command.

Open as Copy.   Opens a copy of the project file you selected. "Copy (1) of" is added in front of the file name. If you open a second copy, it will be named "Copy (2) of," and so forth. Any changes you make appear only in the copy of the file, not in the original file.

Opening a Project from Microsoft Project Server

To open an enterprise project file, you must open the project from Microsoft Project Server. Opening an enterprise project is also referred to as *checking out* the file. This prevents anyone else from changing the file while you are working on it. However, others can still view the read-only file.

note   This section applies only if you're working with Microsoft Project Professional set up for an enterprise environment.

To open a project stored in the Microsoft Project Server database, follow these steps:

1   Click File, Open.

2   Enter your user ID and password if prompted, and then click OK.

3   The Open From Microsoft Project Server dialog box appears (see Figure 29-2 on the next page). Make sure the Read/Write To Check Out option is selected.

Chapter 29

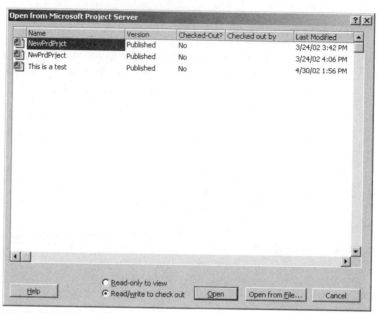

Figure 29-2. The Open From Microsoft Project Server dialog box shows the projects stored on the Microsoft Project Server that you are authorized to check out or view.

4 Double-click a project's name. The project file opens in Microsoft Project.

If you want to work with the project while not connected to Microsoft Project Server, click File, Save Offline, and specify the location where you want to save the project. If there are other users with accounts on the same server, they will not be able to edit the file until you click File, Save Online (which saves it to Microsoft Project Server).

> For more information about working with enterprise projects, see Chapter 24, "Using Enterprise Features to Manage Projects."

Opening Projects Created in Previous Versions of Microsoft Project

In Microsoft Project 2002, you can easily open project files created in earlier versions of Microsoft Project. If the file was created in Microsoft Project 2000 or Microsoft Project 98, it can be opened directly in Microsoft Project 2002 with no additional steps required.

If the project file was created in a version of Microsoft Project earlier than Microsoft Project 98, it must first be saved as an MPX file before Microsoft Project 2002 can open it as a project file. The MPX file format is a record-based ASCII text file format available in Microsoft Project.

> **note** In addition to the MPX file format, you can open a variety of file formats other than the standard MPP file format. For more information, see "Opening and Saving with Different File Formats" later in this chapter.

newfeature!
Searching for Files

Have you ever been unable to find a file? The search can be frustrating and painful, and it is often a big waste of time. A new file-finding feature is built into Microsoft Project 2002 that simplifies finding lost files.

To search for a file, do the following:

1 On the Standard toolbar, click Open.

2 If you are logged in to Microsoft Project Server, the Open From Microsoft Project Server dialog box appears. Click the Open From File button to display the Open dialog box. (If you're not logged in to Microsoft Project Server, skip this step.)

3 In the Open dialog box, click Tools, and then click Search. The Search dialog box appears (see Figure 29-3).

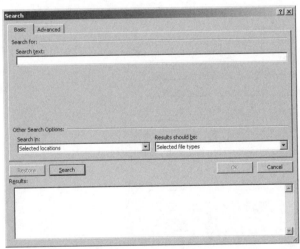

Figure 29-3. Use the Search dialog box to enter and execute basic or advanced search parameters.

4 Make sure the Basic tab is displayed.

5 In the Search Text box, type a portion of the file name you want to search for. For example, if you know your file name contains the word "software" or "deployment," as in "Software Deployment Project," enter one or more of those words.

6 In the Search In box, select the check boxes for the drives, network drives, and folders in which you want to search for the file.

7 In the Results Should Be box, select the check boxes for the types of files you want to search for, for example, Project Files and Web Pages.

Adding Project Summary Information

All projects can have a title, subject, author, manager, and other information associated with them. When you add project summary information to your project, you are adding levels of detail that can be used for reports and searches. For example, if you search for a project's author and the author has indeed been identified for a project, that project is returned as a result of the search. You can also use these fields when creating customized reports. For example, if you want to create a set of reports about projects managed by a specific project manager, the Manager field would need to be completed for each project.

To add project summary information to your project, do the following:

1 Click File, Properties. The Properties dialog box appears (see Figure 29-4).

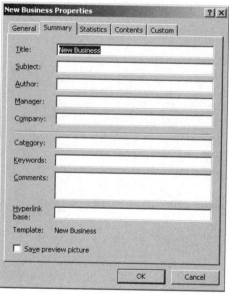

Figure 29-4. Information you add to the Properties dialog box can be used in reports and searches.

2 If necessary, click the Summary tab.

3 Enter any summary information in the fields provided, for example, Title, Subject, Author, Manager, and Company.

Chapter 29: Managing Project Files

InsideOut

You might find that the size of your project file has ballooned. This can happen if you select the Save Preview Picture check box. If you experience trouble with enormous file sizes, look in the Properties dialog box and clear the Save Preview Picture check box.

Sometimes the basic search on the file name doesn't return the file you need, or it returns too many files. You can perform an advanced search, which includes a specific property and value for the file. The properties in an advanced search are the ones you can enter in the file's Properties dialog box. Properties include author, comments, company, creation date, manager, subject, and more. For example, you can search for a project file by the name of its author or by its creation date.

To perform an advanced search for a file, follow these steps:

1 In the Search dialog box, click the Advanced tab.

2 In the Property box, click the property of the file for which you want Microsoft Project to search.

3 In the Condition box, click the condition of the property you have selected, corresponding with the value you will select. Examples of conditions are: Is (Exactly), Includes, Equals, More Than, At Most, and so on.

4 In the Value box, type the value of the property and condition you've selected.

5 Click the Add button.

---

tip   **Narrow the search**

Add more than one set of criteria and use the And and Or options to include or exclude an additional set of criteria from the previous set.

---

6 In the Search In box, select check boxes for the drives, folders, and network drives in which you want to search for the file.

7 In the Results Should Be box, select the check boxes for the types of files you want to search for, for example, Project Files and Web Pages.

8 Click Search.

Saving Files

Saving a project file ensures that it's stored on a hard disk for future access. The hard disk might be on your own computer, on your company's network, or on the Microsoft Project Server for an enterprise project. Saving files to a consistent location can make finding your primary and backup files very easy.

Saving a New Project to Your Local Computer or Network Drive

Do the following to save a project file to a drive on your local computer or to a network drive:

1 On the Standard toolbar, click File, Save As. The Save As dialog box appears (see Figure 29-5).

Figure 29-5. The Save As dialog box displays the contents of the default folder.

2 In the Save In box, click the drive or folder where you want to save the file.

3 If necessary, double-click the folder in which you want to save the file.

4 In the File Name box, type the name of the file.

5 Click Save.

After saving a file with a name and in a specific location, be sure to save continually during your work session. A good rule of thumb is to save about every five minutes, or anytime after you make significant changes that you wouldn't want to lose in the event of a system failure or power outage. On the Standard toolbar, click the Save button or press Ctrl+S.

> **tip** You can have Microsoft Project automatically and periodically save your file so you don't have to remember to do so. See "Saving Project Files Automatically" later in this chapter.

Save Options

Depending on what you're trying to do, there are different ways to save your project file:

Save. When you click File, Save, Microsoft Project displays the Save As dialog box, in which you name the file and select the location where it is to be saved. For projects that are already saved, the Save command simply saves your changes to the existing file.

Save As. When you click File, Save As, the Save As dialog box appears, in which you name the file and select the location where it is to be saved. This can be used to save new project files as well as create an alternate or backup copy of your project or save it as a different file type.

Save as Web Page. When you click File, Save As Web Page, the Save As dialog box appears with Web Page (*.html; *.htm) selected as the file type. Saving the current view as a Web page enables you to post to your project's Web site on the Internet or your intranet. Select the location of the Web page to be saved, enter the name, and click Save.

Save Workspace. When you open all the projects that you want to save and open together, and then click File, Save Workspace, you can combine individual projects into a group that's always opened together. The Save Workspace As dialog box appears with Workspace (*.mpw) selected as the file type. Select the location of the workspace to be saved, enter the name, and click Save. Now whenever you open a workspace file, all the projects saved in this workspace are opened at the same time.

Saving a Project to Microsoft Project Server

When working with an enterprise project, you first open the project from Microsoft Project Server. To do this, follow the procedure on page 687. When you are finished with the project, you save and *check in* the file to the Microsoft Project Server database.

note This section applies only if you're working with Microsoft Project Professional set up for an enterprise environment.

To save a file to Microsoft Project Server, follow these steps:

1 If you are already connected to Microsoft Project Server, click File, Save. If you are not connected to Microsoft Project Server, click File, Save Online. The Save To Microsoft Project Server dialog box appears (see Figure 29-6 on the next page).

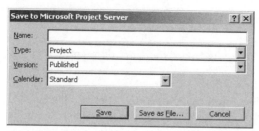

Figure 29-6. The Save To Microsoft Project Server dialog box enables you to save project plans in an enterprise environment.

2 Indicate whether the project is a Project or a Template.

3 Select a Version. Published is the default version.

4 Select the Calendar associated with the project. Standard is the default calendar.

What's in a File Name?

In Microsoft Project, you can name a project just about anything you want, as long as the name doesn't exceed 255 characters. Any combination of upper-case and lower-case letters can be used because Microsoft Project does not recognize case in file names. The following symbols cannot be used in a file name:

- Asterisk (*)
- Backward slash (\)
- Colon (:)
- Forward slash (/)
- Greater-than symbol (>)

- Less-than symbol (<)
- Question mark (?)
- Quotation mark (")
- Pipe symbol (|)
- Semi-colon (;)

5 Click Save. The project is now saved on Microsoft Project Server and will be available for others to open. Note that you must close the project on your computer before others will be able to open this project.

tip If you want to save the project offline, click Save As File. Other users will not be able to open this project until you save it to Microsoft Project Server.

Specifying the Default Save Location

If you have a drive or folder dedicated to your project management files, you might want to make that your default save location. This will be the folder that is presented first whenever you open or save a project file. To set the default folder, do the following:

1 Click Tools, Options.

2 In the Options dialog box, click the Save tab (see Figure 29-7).

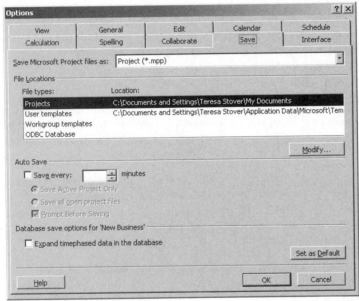

Figure 29-7. Use the Save tab in the Options dialog box to set defaults for saving project files.

3 Under File Locations, click the Modify button. The Modify Location dialog box appears.

4 Browse to the drive and folder where you want your new project files to be saved by default. Click OK.

5 In the Options dialog box, click OK.

---

tip **Set the default file type**

If you regularly save your project files as something other than an MPP file (for example, a Microsoft Project Database or Microsoft Project 98 file) you can change the default file type from MPP to your file type of choice. Click Tools, Options, and in the Options dialog box, click the Save tab. In the Save Microsoft Project Files As box, select the file type you want to use as the default.

Saving and Opening
with Different File Formats

A file format is an arrangement of data in a file that specifies the file type and defines the file in a way that allows any application that can open the file to open it correctly. When you create and save a regular project file, it's saved as an MPP (Microsoft Project Plan) file, with the *.mpp* extension. The *.mpp* extension indicates that this is indeed a regular project file.

However, you can save project files in other file formats. You can also open files with other file formats in Microsoft Project. Table 29-1 details the file formats supported by Microsoft Project for saving, opening, or both.

Table 29-1. Supported File Formats

File format	Extension	Notes
Microsoft Project plan	*.mpp*	Saves the file as a Microsoft Project Plan file. This is the default file type for projects being saved or opened.
Microsoft Project template	*.mpt*	Saves the file as a Microsoft Project Template file. The template can then be used as a basis for new projects. When you open a file based on a template, you can change and save those changes to the template file.
Microsoft Project workspace	*.mpw*	Saves open project files as a Microsoft Project Workspace file. When you open a MPW file, all associated projects are opened in a single step.
Microsoft Project Exchange	*.mpx*	Opens a file created in a version of Microsoft Project earlier than Microsoft Project 98. This is a record-based ASCII text file format that Microsoft Project 2002 can read, allowing early Microsoft Project files to be converted to Microsoft Project 2002 files.
Microsoft Project database	*.mpd*	Saves the project file as a Microsoft Project Database. This file type can be opened in Microsoft Access or any other application that can open the MPD file format. This replaces the older MPX file format as the standard interchange format for Microsoft Project data.
Web page	*.html*	Saves the current view as a Web page. The file can then be published to an Internet or intranet Web site.

File format	Extension	Notes
Microsoft Project 98	.mpp	Saves the Microsoft Project 2002 file so that it can be opened by Microsoft Project 98. Any feature in Microsoft Project 2002 that is not in Microsoft Project 98 (for example, enterprise fields and additional baselines) is not saved in this format.
Microsoft Access database	.mdb	Saves the file as a Microsoft Access database. The file can then be opened in Microsoft Access. You can also open Access files in Microsoft Project. To save a Microsoft Project file in an ODBC format, click the ODBC button in the Save dialog box and follow the instructions in the Select Data Source dialog box.
Microsoft Excel workbook or PivotTable	.xls	Saves the file as a Microsoft Excel workbook or as a Microsoft Excel PivotTable. The file can then be opened in Microsoft Excel. A *PivotTable* is a table that combines and compares large amounts of data, and in which you can rotate columns and rows to modify the source data to create different views. You can also open an Excel file in Microsoft Project.
Text (Tab delimited)	.txt	Saves the file as a text file using tabs to separate the data. This is ideal for using the project information in a third-party application or on another operating system. You can also open a text file in Microsoft Project.
Text (comma delimited)	.csv	Saves the file as a text file using commas to separate the data. This is ideal for using the project information in a third-party application or on another operating system. You can also open a CSV file in Microsoft Project.
eXtensible Markup Language	.xml	Saves the file as XML data. When Microsoft Project saves data as XML, the structure is determined by the Microsoft Project XML schema. You can also open an XML file in Microsoft Project. An XML file must conform to the Microsoft Project XML schema for Microsoft Project to understand and open it. For more information about the Microsoft Project XML Schema, see Projxml.htm on the Microsoft Project 2002 installation CD.

newfeature!

Chapter 29

> **note** When you open a file from a different file format in Microsoft Project, this can be referred to as *importing* the file. Likewise, when you save a project file with a different file format, this can be referred to as *exporting* the file. There's often more to the import and export process than simply opening or saving the file. Sometimes you need to create an *import/export map*.
>
> For more information about importing and exporting, see "Importing and Exporting Information" on page 441.

Safeguarding Your Project Files

After your hard work creating, updating, and tracking your project file, you want to make the file as secure as possible. The further you get into the life cycle of the project, the more information you have in the project plan. The more information stored there, the more devastating a file loss can be.

Saving Project Files Automatically

Although it's not hard to remember to click the Save button every few minutes while working, you can also have Microsoft Project remember for you. You can set Microsoft Project to automatically and regularly save your file every few minutes. This can decrease your risk of losing recent work.

To have Microsoft Project automatically save active and open projects, follow these steps:

1 Click Tools, Options.

2 In the Options dialog box, click the Save tab.

3 Under Auto Save, select the Save Every check box, and then enter how often (in minutes) you want Microsoft Project to automatically save your active or open projects.

4 If you want Microsoft Project to save only the active project, select the Save Active Project Only option.

5 If you want Microsoft Project to save the active project along with any other open projects, select the Save All Open Project Files option.

It can be handy to be notified when your application is going to perform an action that you might not otherwise be aware of. However, you might find the Prompt Before Saving feature annoying. You've already instructed Microsoft Project to save your file at a frequency that you specified. If you don't want to be asked whether or not you want to save at every specified interval, clear the Prompt Before Saving check box. However, if you frequently experiment with what-if scenarios in your project file, you might want to be prompted before it saves one of your experiments.

Backing Up Your Project Files

It's always a good policy to have at least two copies of any important computer file. This way, if the file is inadvertently deleted or somehow is corrupted, or if you get a little crazy with your what-if scenarios, you have another file to go back to.

> **note** You cannot create backups of project files if the project is stored on Microsoft Project Server or if you are running Microsoft Project Professional in online mode.

To automatically create backups of active project files, do the following:

1 Click File, Save As.

2 In the Save As dialog box, click Tools, and then click General Options. The Save Options dialog box appears (see Figure 29-8).

Figure 29-8. Use the Save Options dialog box to set up file backups and passwords.

3 Select the Always Create Backup check box.

Chapter 29

The backup copy adopts the same file name as the original project file, but has a different extension. BAK is appended to the file name of all backup copies. For example, the backup file of "deployment.mpp" is "deployment.bak."

To restore a backup file as a regular project file, follow these steps:

1 On the Standard toolbar, click the Open button.

2 In the Open dialog box, browse, if necessary, to the drive and folder where the backup file is stored.

3 Be sure that All Files (*.*) is selected in the Files Of Type box. Otherwise, files ending in .bak will not appear in the list.

4 Find the backup file, and double-click it. Microsoft Project opens the backup file.

5 Click File, Save As.

6 The Save As dialog box appears. If necessary, browse to the location where you want to save the restored backup project file.

7 Enter a new file name for the restored backup file.

8 Make sure that Projects (*.mpp) is selected in the Save As Type box.

9 Click Save.

---

tip   **Keep a backup on a separate drive**

Your project BAK file is a great contingency in case your project file is accidentally deleted or corrupted. However, if both the project and the backup are saved on the same drive and that drive crashes, your backup will be lost as well. Remember to periodically save a backup to an alternate drive.

Protecting Your Project Files with a Password

If you are not using Microsoft Project Server as a central location for your company's project files, saving your project files to a public network folder is one way to have centralized project files. This enables your company to back up critical files more regularly and reliably. It also provides a convenient location for your co-workers to collaborate on projects. However, it can also allow unauthorized individuals access to files with sensitive or confidential information. Perhaps your project is in its initial phase and you aren't ready to share it with the rest of the company. Or maybe a project has information that should only be seen by a small group of people in your organization. If this is the case, consider assigning a password to prevent unauthorized access to sensitive project files.

> **note** You cannot protect a project file with a password if it is stored on Microsoft Project Server or if you are running Microsoft Project Professional in online mode.

There are two types of passwords, Protection and Write Reservation. To assign a password to a project, do the following:

1 Click File, Save As.

2 In the Save As dialog box, click Tools, and then click General Options.

3 In the Save Options dialog box, enter the password in either the Protection Password or Write Reservation Password text box.

   With a protection password, users can open the project file only if they know the password.

   With a write-reservation password, users can view the project file, but they cannot change it.

4 Click OK.

5 In the Confirm Password dialog box, type the password again. Click OK.

> **tip** **The Read-Only Recommended option**
>
> If you want to remind users to open the project as Read-Only without locking out users who might have forgotten the password, consider the Read-Only Recommended check box. If you select this check box, the next time a user goes to open this file, a message suggests that the user open the file as read-only unless they need to save changes to the file. It then provides the option of opening the file as Read-Only or not.

Responding to a Microsoft Project Problem

newfeature!

If you encounter a problem with Microsoft Project, such as the program freezing or experiencing a "fatal error," you can send the details of the problem to the Microsoft Project development team. When the error happens, a dialog box is displayed, providing the option to restart Microsoft Project and view the details of the error report. If you want to provide information on the problem to Microsoft, click Send The Report To Microsoft. If you don't want to provide the information, click Don't Send.

Depending on the severity of the error, you might be able to continue working in Safe mode, at least to get to the point where you can save your file.

InsideOut

Depending on the nature of the error you encounter, your entire project file could be sent to the Microsoft Project development team. If your project contains confidential information, be sure to click Don't Send.

Part 10

Programming Custom Solutions

Understanding the Visual Basic Language

Before discussing the Microsoft Project object model, the Visual Basic Editor, and other aspects of and tools for creating and editing code-based solutions in Microsoft Project, you must first understand some of the elements and principles of Visual Basic:

- Objects, properties, methods, and events
- Data types
- Variables
- Decision and loop structures
- Procedures
- Scope

As you develop your Visual Basic skills and move on to writing more advanced code, there are some general principles of software development that make writing code easier, faster, and less prone to error:

- Using naming conventions for procedures and variables
- Writing modularized code
- Writing formatted code
- Writing efficient code
- Trapping errors

Finally, although much of the discussion presented here is necessarily at a relatively high level, given the overall focus of this book, the intent of this chapter is to provide an overview

705

of the Visual Basic concepts you'll need to take full advantage of VBA in Microsoft Project without being forced to look for a separate reference. After you're comfortable with the information presented here, you should find that most of what remains to be learned in Visual Basic is simply an extension of what you already know.

> **note** Although *Visual Basic for Applications* is used to collectively describe the programming language and environment included with Microsoft Project, the language itself is Visual Basic. For the remainder of this chapter, *Visual Basic* is used to refer to the language and its elements.

> For more information about these and many other Visual Basic concepts, see the topics under the heading "Visual Basic Conceptual Topics" in the table of contents of Microsoft Visual Basic's Help files.
>
> The Microsoft Developer Network (MSDN) at *http://msdn.microsoft.com/* is also an excellent resource for programming guidelines, tips, and examples.

Installing VBA Help

By default, the Help files for VBA are automatically installed the first time you use them. Follow these steps if you want to install them now:

1 Insert the Microsoft Project 2002 CD-ROM into your computer's CD-ROM drive.

2 Open the Control Panel, and then double-click Add/Remove Programs.

> **note** The name of this item might be slightly different for your operating system.

3 Click Microsoft Project in the list of installed programs, and then click Change.

4 Click Add Or Remove Features, and then click Next.

5 Expand the Office Shared Features item and then expand the Visual Basic for Applications item.

6 In the Visual Basic Help list, click Run From My Computer.

7 Click the Update button.

This installs several Help files, including those for the Microsoft Project object model, concepts and language reference specific to VBA in Microsoft Office and related programs, general Visual Basic concepts and language reference, and Microsoft Forms.

Understanding Objects, Properties, Methods, and Events

Objects, properties, methods, and events, along with variables and procedures, form the core of how you interact with Microsoft Project, whether it's by using a macro or creating an entire VBA program within Microsoft Project.

> **tip** Standard Visual Basic and general programming terms are italicized the first time they are discussed in this chapter.

Objects

An object is a discrete, identifiable thing. It can be something generic, like a window or a toolbar, or it can be something specific to Microsoft Project, like a project or a resource. Most objects have at least three common *properties*, such as:

Name. This is the name of the object, like "project" or "calendar."

Application. This is a way to access the object that represents the software itself.

Parent. This is a way to access the object that precedes the object in the *object model*.

Objects also usually have properties specific to its type. For example, a Task object has properties that return the start and finish dates. Because objects form the basis of how you interact with Microsoft Project, they also have *methods* and *events*.

A *collection* is a group of objects, almost always of the same type: A Tasks collection, not surprisingly, is made up of Task objects. Collections typically have the following features:

An Add method. This is a way to add a new object to the collection.

An Item property. This is a way to access a particular object in the collection.

A Count property. This is the number of objects in the collection.

Perhaps confusingly, a collection is also an object, which means a collection can have all the same features of an object, including properties (such as Name, Application, and Parent) and methods.

Chapter 30

Parents and Children:
The Object Model Hierarchy

An object model is a system of objects that provides a programmatic model for interacting with an application. Object models in VBA are represented in a hierarchical "tree" fashion, with the Application object (the object representing the program itself) as the root. All other objects and collections are *children* of the root object.

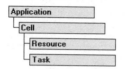

In Microsoft Project, for example, collections like the Windows, Projects, and Tables collections, as well as the Cell and Selection objects (and others) are *child objects* of the Application object. For each of those child objects, then, the Application object is not only the root of the object model, but the *parent object*.

Other than the Application object, which has no parent, every object and collection has a parent object. Objects usually have child objects (the Project object has Resources and Tasks collections, for example), and collections always have children: Each object in the collection is a child of the collection itself.

Properties

A property is an aspect or characteristic of an object. A property can be simple, such as the name of the object. A more complex property might be a collection of child objects. Properties are either *read-only*, which means they only provide information, or *read/write*, which means they can also be changed as needed.

For example, the Name property of a Project object is read/write, because you can always rename a project. The Parent property, though, which returns a reference to the Application object, is read-only.

Methods

A method is just a way of telling an object to do something. The Application object, for example, has an AppMinimize method. When you *call* (or "invoke") the AppMinimize method, you're telling Microsoft Project, represented by the Application object, to minimize its window.

Many methods return information about the results of the action, such as when the AppMinimize method returns a value of True or False to tell you if Microsoft Project was minimized successfully.

Some methods can accept *arguments*, which are ways of supplying additional information to the method. The Tasks collection's Add method, for example, has optional Name and Before arguments, so that you can specify a name and position for the new task as you create it. For example, the following code creates a task called "Write chapter" as the third task (the new task is inserted before what was the third task) in a collection of tasks:

```
ActiveProject.Tasks.Add "Write chapter", 3
```

For more information about working with optional arguments, see "Named Arguments" later in this chapter.

Calling Methods that Return Values

If a method returns a value, you can call the method with parentheses or without them:

- Calling a method with parentheses returns either a value or a reference to an object, so you must do something with the result or an error will occur. The following code returns a *reference* to the Task object it just created:

```
ActiveProject.Tasks.Add("Write chapter", 3)
```

By itself, this code will result in a syntax error.

- Calling a method without parentheses means that the method takes action and discards the return value. The following code creates a task:

```
ActiveProject.Tasks.Add "Write chapter", 3
```

For more information about methods that return values (*functions*), see "Understanding Procedures" later in this chapter.

Events

An event can occur (*fire*) when an object does something as the result of a method or user action, which can *trigger* the event. Sometimes, several events can fire in sequence. Events can contain calls to methods, which can then cause even more events to fire.

For example, when the following code creates a new task, it triggers the Application object's ProjectBeforeTaskNew event:

```
ActiveProject.Tasks.Add "Write chapter", 3
```

If you wanted to prevent the task from being created, you could use the event's Cancel argument to do so.

In another example, closing Microsoft Project with an unsaved project file open causes several events of the Project object to fire:

Project_BeforeSave.   This fires just before Microsoft Project asks if you want to save the project.

Project_BeforeClose.   This fires just before the project closes.

Project_Deactivate.   This fires as the closing project is about to *lose focus*.

---

note Several Application-level events also fire in this example.

Understanding Data Types

When you create (*declare*) a variable or function by specifying a data type, you are letting Visual Basic know that the variable will always contain a certain kind of data. This is known as an *explicit declaration*. Although not technically required in Visual Basic, it is an excellent programming practice because:

- *Implicit declarations* (creating a variable without specifying its data type) result in the Variant data type. Whereas each of the other data types use varying amounts of memory, Variants always use the same comparatively large amount of memory regardless of the data they store. This can result in an inefficient use of memory. For example, storing True or False information in a Variant instead of a Boolean variable uses eight times as much memory.

- If you always use explicit declarations and mistype the name of a variable, Visual Basic recognizes that it's a mistake and gives you a warning. If you use an implicit declaration, Visual Basic just assumes it's a new variable. This can cause unexpected results in your code that are hard to fix because you might not notice the typo.

- Using the functions included with Visual Basic when converting data from one type to another makes your code easier to understand and maintain.

---

tip Put the following line at the beginning of every class, user form, or code module to have Visual Basic warn you if you accidentally make an implicit declaration:

```
Option Explicit
```

To make sure that you always use explicit declarations, you can select the Require Variable Declaration check box in the Visual Basic Editor. This check box is on the Editor tab of the Options dialog box, which you can open by clicking Tools, Options.

Table 30-1 lists data types. Although it is not a complete list, it is probably sufficient for the majority of code you will write in VBA.

Table 30-1. Data Types

Type	Description
String	Used to store any kind of alphanumeric information.
	Numbers stored in Strings are treated as text, so sorting numbers in a String variable means that 10 comes before 2.
Long	Used to store numbers in the range -2,147,483,648 to 2,147,483,647.
Integer	Used to store numbers in the range -32,768 to 32,767. Integers use half as much memory as Longs.
Boolean	Used to store True or False information.
	If you pass a nonzero number to a *Boolean* variable, the variable becomes *True*. If you pass a *Boolean* value of *True* to a numeric variable, the variable becomes -1.
	False always becomes 0, and vice versa, when you pass values between *Boolean* and numeric variables.
Object	Used to store references to objects.
	Object variables declared as Object are referred to as being *late-bound*. Late-bound variables are sometimes necessary, such as when your code must work with several different types of object. Code that uses late-bound references, however, runs slower than references declared for a specific *class*, like a Project, Resource, Task, and so on. This is known as *early binding*.
	(The term "object variable" is sometimes used to generically describe a variable that stores a reference to an object, even if the variable was declared as a specific class of object.)

For more information about declaring variables, including prefixes and other naming conventions, see "Naming Conventions" later in this chapter.

Understanding Variables

Variables are simply places where information is temporarily stored while a program is running. A variable has a value only when you *assign* one to it, either through direct interaction (clicking a button on a dialog box, for example) or by the action of code in your program.

Variables are used when interacting with users, tracking details while the program is running, and passing information among different parts of the program. They are also used to represent individual items in a collection of items, such as when working one-by-one through a collection of tasks in a project.

A Boolean variable, for example, is declared as the following:

```
Dim blnStatus As Boolean
```

An *array* is a special type of variable that can store many related values at one time. (Because an array has to be declared like any other variable, all the data in an array has to be the same data type. The exception, of course, would be an array declared as Variant.) In fact, an array can store a nearly unlimited number of values—limited primarily by the amount of memory in your computer—in up to 60 dimensions.

Arrays are a lot like temporary spreadsheets, where each "cell" (*element*) in a "column" (*dimension*) is a single piece of data. Each time you add a dimension, it's like adding another column to your "spreadsheet." The final dimension in an array declaration (or the only dimension in a one-dimension array) is essentially the number of rows in your spreadsheet.

note By default, the dimensions in an array are 0-based, which means that the first element is numbered 0 instead of 1. When you declare the size of the array, you essentially subtract 1 from the *upper bound* of the array.

Examples of array declarations are shown in Table 30-2.

Constants are similar to variables in that they store data, but the value of a constant is specified when you declare it and never changes while your code is running. In this sense, they are like read-only properties.

At first glance, constants might not appear very useful, but they are valuable tools for writing *self-documenting code*. For example, the Microsoft Project constant "pjFinishToStart" is a much more meaningful description of the link type for a task than 1, which is the value it represents.

A typical String constant might be declared as:

```
Const c_strName As String = "Some text"
```

Table 30-2. Array Declarations

Description	Declaration
One-dimension Long array of fixed size (1 column with 5 rows)	`Dim lngOneDArray(4) As Long`
Two-dimension Integer array of fixed size (5 columns with 10 rows)	`Dim intTwoDArray(4, 9) As Integer`
Two-dimension Integer array of fixed size using 1-based (not zero-based) dimensions	`Dim intTwoDArray(1 To 5, 1 To 10) As Integer`

One-dimension String array of variable size	Initial declaration:
	`Dim strVarArray() As String`
	Specification of initial size:
	`ReDim strVarArray(4)`
	Specification of new size, while retaining existing data:
	`ReDim Preserve strVarArray(9)`

Two-dimension String array of variable size	Initial declaration:
	`Dim strVarArray() As String`
	Specification of initial size:
	`ReDim strVarArray(4, 9)`
	Specification of new size, while discarding existing data:
	`ReDim strVarArray(4, 19)`

> For more information about self-documenting code, see "Writing Code that is Easily Understood" later in this chapter.

Understanding Procedures

For all intents and purposes, everything that happens in your code happens in procedures. *Functions* and *subroutines* ("subs") are both types of procedures you can write. Both contain Visual Basic code (*statements*) and both can accept input (*arguments*).

The only real difference between functions and subroutines is that functions can directly return information to the *calling procedure* by assigning a value to the name of the function. This means you can use functions like variables, so functions should be declared as a certain data type, just like any other variable.

For example, the following code has a sub AddTask that calls a function strNewTask:

```
Function strNewTask(strName As String, intBefore As Integer) As String
    ActiveProject.Tasks.Add strName, intBefore

    If ActiveProject.Tasks(intBefore).Name = strName Then
        strNewTask = "Success!"
    Else
        strNewTask = "Failed to create task!"
    End If
End Function

Sub AddTask()
    MsgBox strNewTask("Write chapter", 3)
End Sub
```

The Sub and End Sub, Function and End Function statements define the boundaries of the sub or function. As you can see, the statement declaring the function declares it as a particular data type, whereas the sub does not.

This code contains several other items worth noting:

- The function has two arguments, strName and intBefore, which are declared just like any other variables, even though they are part of the function declaration.

- To return a value from a function, you must first assign a value to the name of the function, as in the line

  ```
  strNewTask = "Success!"
  ```

- The MsgBox function (It is itself a function because it can return information about which button the user clicked; by calling it without parentheses, we're discarding the Integer value that it would otherwise return.) takes several arguments, one of which is a String that contains the text to display in the dialog box. Instead of being supplied as text in quotes (a *string literal*) or even as a "traditional" variable, the argument is supplied as the return value of the function strNewTask.

Understanding Scope

Scope is a term used to describe when and where a variable or procedure is available. There are three levels of scope:

Procedure. Variables declared at this level (using the *Dim* keyword) are only available within the procedure. Also referred to as *local*.

Module. Variables and procedures declared at this level (using the *Dim* keyword or, for improved readability, the *Private* keyword) are available anywhere within a form, class, or module. Also referred to as *private*.

> **note** Declaring a variable with module-level scope should not be confused with the idea of simply declaring a variable in a module. By default, variables declared in a module are available only within the module (module scope), but declaring a variable with the *Public* keyword makes it available everywhere (global scope).

Global. Variables and procedures declared at this level (using the *Public* keyword) are available throughout your program. Also referred to as *public*.

The value stored in any variable is temporary, dependent upon where it was declared. When a variable *goes out of scope* it is reset to its default value, such as 0 for numeric variables. In the case of a local variable, for example, it goes out of scope when the procedure in which it is declared has been completed.

Understanding Decision Structures

Decision structures control whether other statements *execute*, according to the results of *conditional statements*. In the function strNewTask, for instance, there was an If...Then...Else decision structure that determined what to set for the function's return value, based on the results of a test.

There are four different decision structures, each suitable for different situations, but they are all very similar:

If...Then. The simplest of all decision structures, the If...Then statement takes just one action if just one condition is met. If the condition is not met, the statement does nothing:

```
If ActiveProject.Tasks(1).PercentComplete = 100 Then MsgBox "Task complete!"
```

If the first task's PercentComplete property is not 100, the line is skipped.

> **note** Unlike the other decision structures, If...Then can either be a statement or a *block*. An If...Then statement is one test, one action, and one line of code. An If...Then block is still one test, but it can perform many actions over several lines of code.
>
> Because a decision block is essentially a miniature procedure, it must have some sort of ending statement. The End If statement at the end of a decision block works just like the End Sub or End Function at the end of a procedure.

If...Then...Else. A more common form of decision structure is the one used in the function strNewTask, If...Then...Else. Unlike the If...Then statement, this structure performs a test to determine not if it should take action, but which action it should take. Something will always happen, because meeting the condition results in one action, and anything else results in the second:

```
If ActiveProject.Tasks(1).PercentComplete = 100 Then
    MsgBox "The task is complete!"
Else
    MsgBox "The task is not finished."
End If
```

In this situation, if the task's PercentComplete property is 100, the dialog box appears just like for the If...Then statement. The difference here is that anything less than 100 also displays a dialog box.

If...Then...ElseIf. A variation on the If...Then...Else type is the If...Then...ElseIf block. In this variation, there can be any number of ElseIf statements, each of which performs a further refinement of the test defined in the original If...Then statement. For example:

```
If ActiveProject.Tasks(1).PercentComplete = 100 Then
    MsgBox "The task is complete!"
ElseIf ActiveProject.Tasks(1).PercentComplete >= 50 Then
    MsgBox "The task is more than half finished."
ElseIf ActiveProject.Tasks(1).PercentComplete > 0 Then
    MsgBox "The task has started, but is less than 50% complete."
Else
    MsgBox "The task has not started!"
End If
```

Select Case.   This is another way to test for a large number of conditions, but in a more readable way than an If...Then...ElseIf block.

```
Select Case ActiveProject.Tasks(1).PercentComplete
    Case Is = 100
        MsgBox "The task is complete!"
    Case Is >= 50
        MsgBox "The task is more than half finished."
    Case Is > 0
        MsgBox "The task has started, but is less than 50% complete."
    Case Is = 0
        MsgBox "The task has not started!"
End Select
```

> **note**   The *Is* keyword used here is only required because these Case statements are also comparisons, which means they have to be compared with something. Typically, the Select Case statement contains a reference to a variable and each Case statement represents a different possible value.

As you can see, using the Select Case structure makes it much easier to find the different conditions for displaying a dialog box. In fact, the statement

```
Case Is = 0
```

is even more explicit than is strictly necessary, because we've already eliminated every other possible value for the PercentComplete property. In this instance, a simple

```
Case Else
```

would have been sufficient, and probably just as readable.

> **tip**   The value in using an explicit construction instead of the Case Else statement can be shown by simply asking this question: What if you didn't know that the range of possible values for the PercentComplete property was 0–100?

Understanding Loop Structures

Unlike decision structures, which control *whether* other statements execute, loop structures control *how often* other statements execute.

Chapter 30

There are just three loop structures, even though the last in this list has several variations:

For...Next.   A For loop is used to work through a known number of items. The number of times the loop should run is specified by means of a counter variable, which typically increments by 1 each time the loop repeats.

The following code loops through a task's resource assignments and displays the name of each resource in its own dialog box:

```
Dim intCount As Integer

For intCount = 1 To ActiveProject.Tasks(1).Assignments.Count
    MsgBox ActiveProject.Tasks(1).Assignments(intCount).ResourceName
Next intCount
```

> **tip**   Even though the number of items in a For loop must be known, that number doesn't have to be known by you, the programmer. In this code, the Assignments collection's Count property is used to supply the value for intCount.

You can use the Step argument to increment by values greater than 1, or you can use it to decrement the counter. If you decrement your loop, of course, the initial value of the counter must be set to the number of items, instead of to one. This code works like the previous example, but in reverse order:

```
Dim intCount As Integer

For intCount = ActiveProject.Tasks(1).Assignments.Count To 1 Step -1
    MsgBox ActiveProject.Tasks(1).Assignments(intCount).ResourceName
Next intCount
```

For Each...Next.   This is essentially a For loop for objects, although it can also be used for items in an array. In this case, the code behaves identically to the first For example, but uses an object variable instead of a numeric counter:

```
Dim objAssign As Assignment

For Each objAssign In ActiveProject.Tasks(1).Assignments
    MsgBox objAssign.ResourceName
Next objAssign
```

Quite often, loop structures contain decision structures. The following code loops through every task in a project and displays a dialog box stating whether the task is complete:

```
Dim objTask As Task

For Each objTask In ActiveProject.Tasks
    If objTask.PercentComplete = 100 Then
        MsgBox "The task is complete!"
    Else
        MsgBox "The task is not finished."
    End If
Next objTask
```

Do...Loop.   A Do loop is really a combination of an If...Then statement and a For loop for which you don't know how many items there are. It executes code an undetermined number of times, but is limited by the results of a test it performs for each repetition.

The two most common forms of a Do loop are the Do While...Loop and Do Until...Loop structures. A Do While loop runs code as long as the condition is true, whereas the Do Until loop runs code only when the condition is false (that is, until it's true). Compare the following two examples:

```
Sub WhileTest()
    Dim intCount As Integer

    intCount = 1
    Do While intCount <= 10
        MsgBox intCount
        intCount = intCount + 1
    Loop
End Sub

Sub UntilTest()
    Dim intCount As Integer

    intCount = 1
    Do Until intCount > 10
        MsgBox intCount
        intCount = intCount + 1
    Loop
End Sub
```

In each case, 10 dialog boxes appear, incrementing from 1 to 10. The difference is that the Do While loop runs while the variable is less than or equal to 10. The Do Until loop runs until the variable is greater than 10.

> **note** Unlike a For loop, it's possible that the statements in a Do loop won't be executed because the result of the conditional test might never be true. If the variable intCount in the two procedures had been set to 11 instead of 1, neither loop would run.

The other two variations of a Do loop are the Do...Loop While and Do...Loop Until structures. Whereas the more "traditional" Do loops test the condition statement before proceeding, these variants perform their actions and then test to see if a condition is true. The following code always displays a dialog box, even though the condition is never true:

```
Dim intCount As Integer

intCount = 100
Do
    MsgBox intCount
    intCount = intCount + 1
Loop While intCount <= 10
```

Writing Code that is Easily Understood

Recording a simple macro here or there might not seem much like programming, but after you start creating them by hand, recording and editing more complex macros, or even writing what amount to full-fledged computer programs, some general principles of software development become more important. One of these is using a consistent system of coding conventions.

Coding conventions result in code that is *self-documenting*, which is to say, written in such a way that it describes what it is and what it's used for. Different aspects of self-documenting code can be accomplished through several methods, some of which have been touched on earlier in this chapter:

- Naming conventions for procedures and variables
- Constants
- Explicit declarations
- Modularized code
- Named arguments
- Formatted code

You know that your coding conventions work when someone unfamiliar with your code can rely upon the code itself to "explain" what procedures do, what type of data they accept or return, which variables have local or global scope, and so on.

> **tip** **Use comments**
>
> Use comments liberally throughout your code. Strictly speaking, of course, comments have nothing to do with self-documenting code, but they are used to make your code as readable and easy to understand as possible.
>
> Comments in Visual Basic begin with an apostrophe ('). Anything that comes after the comment character, even if it's in the middle of a line of code, is considered a comment and ignored by Visual Basic.

Naming Conventions

Using a system of naming conventions is one of the easiest things you can do to make your code self-documenting. Using naming conventions means doing two things: using descriptive names for procedures and variables and using prefixes that describe the data type, scope, and function of the procedure or variable.

Assigning descriptive names to procedures and variables doesn't have to mean that names will be long and complicated. All that is required is that the name indicate roughly what the procedure is used for or the type of information represented by the variable. Mixed case should be used to make the name easier to read, such as AddTask, FormatTableForPrinting, or TaskName.

Prefixes can be used to describe many things about the procedure or variable, such as type, scope, and function. In fact, there is a commonly used system of prefixes for Visual Basic, some examples of which are shown in Tables 30-3 through 30-6.

Table 30-3 shows prefixes that describe data types, such as strTaskName.

Table 30-3. Data Types

Prefix	Type of variable
bln	Boolean
str	String
int	Integer
lng	Long
obj	Object
var	Variant

Chapter 30

Table 30-4 shows prefixes that describe controls, such as cmdOK and txtTaskName.

Table 30-4. Controls

Prefix	Type of control
chk	Check box
cmd	Command button
frm	Form
lbl	Label
lst	List box
mnu	Menu
opt	Option button
txt	Text box

Table 30-5 shows prefixes that describe scope, such as the local variable strTaskName and the global gstrTaskName.

Table 30-5. Scope

Prefix	Type of scope
no prefix	Procedure (local)
m	Module (private)
g	Global (public)

Table 30-6 shows prefixes that describe function, such as c_gstrTaskName for a global String constant and a_intTaskList to describe a local Integer array.

Table 30-6. Function

Prefix	Type of function
c_	A constant
a_	An array

The following example of a sub and a function, taken from the discussion on procedures earlier in this chapter, illustrates the use of prefixes and descriptive names:

```
Function strNewTask(strName As String, intBefore As Integer) As String
    ActiveProject.Tasks.Add strName, intBefore

    If ActiveProject.Tasks(intBefore).Name = strName Then
        strNewTask = "Success!"
    Else
        strNewTask = "Failed to create task!"
    End If
End Function

Sub AddTask()
    MsgBox strNewTask("Write chapter", 3)
End Sub
```

Suppose that you were reading the code for the first time, the two procedures weren't right next to each other, and all you saw was AddTask. Suppose further that AddTask was written as follows:

```
Sub AddTask()
    MsgBox strNewTask(strTaskName, intTaskNum)
End Sub
```

Because of a consistent pattern of naming conventions, you can infer a lot about strNewTask:

- strNewTask is a function.

  Functions use a prefix and subs do not.

- The function returns a String.

  The prefix *str* denotes a String variable.

- The function takes at least two arguments.

  You do not know, however, if either argument (or both) is optional.

- The first argument requires a String representing the name of a task.

  The prefix *str* denotes a String variable and the name of the variable indicates the type of information it contains.

- The second argument requires an Integer representing the position of the new task in the task list.

  The prefix *int* denotes an Integer variable and the name of the variable indicates the type of information it contains.

Chapter 30

723

Declarations

As described earlier in this chapter in the discussion on data types, variables (including functions, which you can think of as a special type of variable) can be declared implicitly or explicitly. Although there's nothing fundamentally "wrong" with using implicit declaration, explicit declaration is generally a good idea because:

● Using the right data type is simply a matter of using the right tool for the job. The smaller a data type is (the less memory it uses), the faster it runs.

> **note** Although there might be situations in which you don't know the data type returned by a called procedure, which might make you inclined to rely upon implicit declaration, you should still explicitly declare the variable as Variant. Doing this doesn't create any performance gains, but you still get the other benefits of explicit declaration.

● Explicit declaration means if you mistype a variable name, Visual Basic recognizes the error and warns you of the mistake. Implicit declarations mean that any variable name not already known by Visual Basic results in a new variable.

● If you want to declare a variable with module-level or global scope, you have to explicitly declare the variable with the Dim, Private, or Public keywords.

● It's easier to find and understand the uses for variables that are explicitly declared, especially if they are consistently grouped at the beginning of a module or procedure.

Named Arguments

When supplying arguments for a method, each argument is separated from the next with a comma, for example:

```
ActiveProject.Tasks.Add "Write chapter", 3
```

When it comes to self-documenting code, however, that code isn't especially descriptive. You can probably guess that "Write chapter" is the name of the new task, but it's harder to guess what the 3 is for. This is one way in which *named arguments* can be valuable.

Using named arguments means that, instead of supplying just the values for each argument, you precede each value with the name of the argument. The argument name is then separated from the argument value with a colon and an equal sign:

```
ActiveProject.Tasks.Add Name:="Write chapter", Before:=3
```

It is now clear that the name of the new task is "Write chapter" and that it appears before the task that is currently third in the task list.

Named arguments are also used for methods that have many optional arguments, some of which you aren't using. Without named arguments, you must supply a comma as a placeholder for each optional argument, so that the arguments you are using appear in the expected order and position. This results in code that can be quite cryptic:

```
Application.WBSCodeMaskEdit , , , 2, "-"
```

The only way to find out what the two values are being used for is to look up the method in Help. If you use named arguments, however, you don't need to use placeholder commas and the code is very descriptive:

```
Application.WBSCodeMaskEdit Length:=2, separator:="-"
```

> **tip** When you use named arguments, you can specify them in any order you choose. The code in the previous example could have been written with the two arguments in reverse order:
>
> ```
> Application.WBSCodeMaskEdit separator:="-", Length:=2
> ```

Constants

Constants are an important and useful feature of Visual Basic that makes code self-documenting. In fact, Visual Basic is full of constants, including what is probably the most common constant of all, vbCrLf. This constant represents a carriage-return and linefeed and is used to format text for display. The following code displays a sentence in two lines:

```
MsgBox "Here is a long sentence, " & vbCrLf & "broken into two lines."
```

The vbCrLf constant is much more user-friendly, not to mention convenient, than the old method of using Chr$(13) & Chr$(10) to do the same thing.

As mentioned earlier in this chapter, constants are frequently used to represent fixed numeric data, such as the Microsoft Project constant "pjFinishToStart." The name of the constant, especially when you know that it's a member of the PjTaskLinkType *enumeration* ("enum"), is very effective at describing what kind of link is being applied with the LinkPredecessors method, for example. Using just the numeric value of pjFinishToStart doesn't provide you with any real information at all.

You can create your own constants much like you would a variable, except you use the Const keyword and immediately assign a value to it:

```
Const c_lngMyFinishToStart As Long = 10
```

Modularized Code

When you record a macro, all the code generated by the macro recorder is written into one procedure. As you learn to write code by hand and begin to write more complex procedures, you might be inclined to continue this practice. Breaking your code into separate components for easily identifiable tasks, however, makes reading, debugging, maintaining, and modifying your code much simpler.

For example, and looking again at the AddTask and strNewTask procedures, you can see that there's no reason the functions of the two procedures couldn't have been combined into one. Keeping them separate means that AddTask could be modified to perform additional tasks by simply calling new procedures in addition to strNewTask, such as SearchForUnassignedResources and AssignResources.

Another aspect of modular code is that it makes writing new code faster and easier. A procedure that searches for overallocated resources, for instance, could be called from many other procedures rather than rewriting the same code for every procedure that needed it.

Formatted Code

Part of what makes something easy to read, whether it's a book, a Web site, or computer code, is its layout. Formatting your code for readability doesn't just make things easier on your eyes, it makes writing and debugging your code easier, too. As with naming conventions, there are some practices that have been standardized for Visual Basic:

- Indenting, typically 4 spaces, is used to help differentiate the "contents" of a construct from the statements that define the construct. For example, the contents of a sub are indented from the Sub and End Sub statements. Similarly, the contents of a decision structure are indented from, for example, the If...Then and End If statements.

- Grouping declarations of variables and constants at the beginning of modules and procedures makes them easier to find.

- Using blank lines before and after procedures, variable declarations, and decision and loop structures makes them easier to find and read.

- Using multiple, indented lines for If...Then statements not only makes it easier to differentiate the condition from the action taken when the condition is met, but simplifies the work necessary to add additional actions.

  For example, the line

  ```
  If ActiveCell.Task.PercentComplete = 100 Then MsgBox "Task complete!"
  ```

  from the discussion of If...Then statements could have been written as

  ```
  If ActiveCell.Task.PercentComplete = 100 Then
      MsgBox "Task complete!"
  End If
  ```

  Although Visual Basic supports placing multiple statements on one line, each separated from the others with a colon (:), doing so makes your code much harder to read.

- Breaking long lines into multiple lines with an underscore (_) prevents excessive horizontal scrolling. The line continuation character can only be used after an operator, such as the &, +, And, and Or operators, or between arguments of a procedure. For example:

  ```
  ViewEditCombination Name:="Check Resources View", Create:=True, _
      TopView:="Gantt Chart", BottomView:="Resource Sheet"
  ```

  and

  ```
  If blnThis = True And blnThat = True And blnThose = False And _
      blnOthers = True Then
          MsgBox "Hey!"
  End If
  ```

> **tip** When using the line continuation character, it's customary to indent the continued lines by two characters.

When breaking long lines of quoted text into multiple lines, the & operator and the line continuation character must be used outside of the quotation marks or they will be considered as part of the text:

```
MsgBox "This is a very long line of text and would scroll " & _
    "horizontally for quite a ways, which is why it was broken " & _
        "into several lines of code."
```

Writing Efficient Code

There are some people who would say that in this age of cheap computer memory and stunningly fast processors, efficient code isn't as important as it used to be. Perhaps they're right in a strict sense, but the idea of efficient code is more than just code that doesn't require much memory and uses as few processor cycles as possible. Efficient code also means using the best data type for the job, using object references wisely, and writing "smart" code.

InsideOut

Visual Basic is a compiled language, which means that what you write is converted by a *compiler* into machine code for use by the computer. Modern compilers are amazingly good at optimizing the compiled code, but you are (in theory, at least) giving up some level of efficiency by not writing machine code directly. The trade-off is that it is much, much faster and easier to write in a compiled language.

Visual Basic is also what's known as a high-level language, which means that it doesn't support methods for working with memory and the computer's processor that are available in a low-level language like C.

Writing efficient code is as much an art as a science, and a full discussion of it is far beyond the scope of this book. There are, however, some simple things you can do to make your code more efficient:

● When working with objects, use early-binding as much as possible.

As discussed earlier in this chapter, early-binding means declaring object variables of a specific class, like Project, Resource, Form, or CommandBar. Object variables that are early-bound run faster than those that are late-bound, or that are declared simply As Object.

● When you're done working with an object variable, get rid of it. When you're finished with an object variable, set it equal to the keyword *Nothing*. This clears the object reference and frees up memory. For example:

```
Dim objAssign As Assignment

For Each objAssign In ActiveProject.Tasks(1).Assignments
    MsgBox objAssign.ResourceName
Next objAssign

Set objAssign = Nothing
```

---

tip   Object variables that are local in scope will be automatically cleared when the procedure ends and they go out of scope.

● When making multiple calls to an object, use the With and End With statements.

This code makes the Office Assistant feature visible and causes it to perform an animation action:

```
Assistant.Visible = True
Assistant.Sounds = True
Assistant.Animation = msoAnimationGetAttentionMajor
```

As you can see, there are three calls to the Assistant object. Each time Visual Basic encounters one of those calls, it has to create another internal reference to the Assistant object. The following construction performs the same action, is much more readable, and Visual Basic only has to create one internal object reference:

```
With Assistant
    .Visible = True
    .Sounds = True
    .Animation = msoAnimationGetAttentionMajor
End With
```

● Always close connections to external objects.

When working with connections to data sources or other applications, you should always be sure to close the connection when you are finished with it. The reasoning behind this is at its most obvious when working with other applications programmatically. When you use Automation to access Microsoft Excel's object model from Microsoft Project, for example, you are actually starting Excel invisibly. If you fail to close the connection when you are done, Excel continues to run—and take up memory—until the computer is shut down.

For more information about Automation and working with other applications programmatically, see Chapter 31, "Writing Microsoft Project Code with Visual Basic for Applications."

● Increase the upper bound of a dynamic array in chunks.

When you redimension the upper bound of a dynamic array, avoid doing so individually for each new element. Instead, make a reasonable guess of how many additional elements are likely to be necessary and enlarge the array accordingly.

Chapter 30

> **tip** To know when you're running out of available elements from the last time the array was redimensioned, you'll need to create a variable that tracks how many elements are already in use. If you don't, and you assign a value to an element that hasn't been created, you'll receive a "subscript out of range" error message.

- When determining which data type to use, choose the best one for the job.

  As discussed earlier in this chapter, in a general sense, using a specific data type is faster and almost always uses less memory than when using a Variant. More specifically, there are several different numeric data types, each suitable for a different range of values, and each using more or less memory than the others.

> **note** You need to be aware of the individual limitations of each numeric data type when determining which type to use. For example, assigning a value greater than 32,767 to an Integer or assigning any negative value to a Byte causes an overflow error.

Trapping Errors

Try as you might to be perfect, you will introduce errors into your code. Many of these will be simple typing or syntax errors that will be caught by Visual Basic. Still others will be errors of action, in which your code works differently than you intended, that you will catch when testing your code. The remainder consists of situations that you didn't think would arise or actions you didn't think your users would take. It is for this last class of errors that error trapping is so important.

Take the following procedure, for example:

```
Sub DisplayTaskNames()
    Dim objTask As Task

    For Each objTask In ActiveProject.Tasks
        MsgBox objTask.Name
    Next objTask
End Sub
```

It seems harmless enough because it just iterates through the tasks in the current project and displays each task name in a dialog box. But the code has a fatal flaw, assuming that there is a task on each line of the Gantt Chart, Task Sheet, or other task view. If there is a blank line, Visual Basic raises an error because there is no Task object where it expects to find one.

In this instance, there are two ways to handle the situation. The first solution is to plan for this quirk of Microsoft Project by testing for a Task object before attempting to act upon it. The If...Then statement in the following code avoids the assumption:

```
Sub DisplayTaskNames()
    Dim objTask As Task

    For Each objTask In ActiveProject.Tasks
        ' When an object Is Nothing, there is no object.
        ' If an object isn't Nothing, there must be
        '    an object.
        If Not (objTask Is Nothing) Then
            MsgBox objTask.Name
        End If
    Next objTask
End Sub
```

This is an example of code being "smart." By testing for a known but only potential problem, you have effectively trapped an error before it happens.

The following code is more representative of error trapping because it uses the On Error statement and features an actual error handler, although the fact that it knows what error might occur makes it a little artificial:

```
Sub DisplayTaskNames()
    Dim objTask As Task

    ' If an error arises, execution of the code skips
    '    ahead to the label "ErrorHandler."
    ' If the error is handled successfully, execution
    '    returns to the line that follows the line
    '    where the error occurred.
    On Error GoTo ErrorHandler

    For Each objTask In ActiveProject.Tasks
        MsgBox objTask.Name
    Next objTask

ErrorHandler:
    ' Knowing that a blank line instead of a Task object results
    '    in error code 91, you can clear the error and move on.
    If Err.Number = 91 Then
        Err.Clear
        Resume Next
    End If
End Sub
```

> For more information about error handling and the Err object, see the "On Error Statement" topic in Microsoft Visual Basic Help.

Error trapping doesn't necessarily mean writing error handlers that allow your code to fail gracefully, usually by telling the user about a problem and asking them to fix it. Instead, error trapping can be thought of in the larger context of "preemptive debugging." If you do a good job of planning ahead, true error handlers are sometimes unnecessary. Trapping errors can be as simple as writing code that enforces rules.

Suppose part of your code queries the user for a number between 1 and 10. What if the user doesn't provide a number? Will your code fail because it expects an answer, or will it test for a blank value and re-query the user for a response? What if the user enters a letter or other invalid character, instead of a number? By thinking about the potential situation and planning ahead, you have avoided an error condition.

> **tip** Humans being human, and therefore unpredictable, code that interacts with a user typically requires the most planning and error handling.

Although there is much still to learn about Visual Basic, you should now have a solid base of knowledge upon which you can further develop your skills in Microsoft Project or anywhere else that supports a Visual Basic-based language.

> For more information about using Visual Basic in Microsoft Project, see Chapter 31, "Writing Microsoft Project Code with Visual Basic for Applications."

Writing Microsoft Project Code with Visual Basic for Applications

If you've read Chapter 27, "Automating Your Work with Macros," or if you've ever created a macro in Microsoft Project, you already know that Visual Basic for Applications is one of the most powerful features of Microsoft Project. But there is much more to VBA (as it is more commonly called) than creating macros to automate repetitive, tedious, or complex tasks.

> **note** Although *Visual Basic for Applications* is used to collectively describe the programming language and environment included with Microsoft Project, the language itself is Visual Basic. For the remainder of this chapter, *Visual Basic* is used to refer to the language and its elements.

> For additional information about Visual Basic, see Chapter 30, "Understanding the Visual Basic Language."

After reading this chapter, you will be able to:

- Edit or expand upon macros you have recorded.
- Find and fix errors in your macro code.
- Create your own forms and dialog boxes for user interaction.

- Access Microsoft Project features from other programs, such as Microsoft Office and Visio, or even from Web pages.

- Use external libraries to provide additional capabilities to your macros.

> For more information about working with external data and other items outside the VBA environment, see Chapter 32, "Working with Microsoft Project Data."

Before you can tap into the power of Visual Basic for Applications, though, you need to learn more about the Visual Basic Editor and development environment.

Using the Visual Basic Editor

One of the major components of VBA is the Visual Basic Editor. The editor is the development environment you use when writing, editing, and debugging code. It is also where you create forms (*UserForms* in the context of VBA) for interacting with the users of your code, and create references to external objects and libraries.

The discussion in this section is focused on just two aspects of the Visual Basic Editor: The windows and the Tools menu. Other elements of the editor are described as part of larger discussions later in the chapter.

> **tip** Standard Visual Basic and general programming terms are italicized the first time they are discussed in this chapter.

Windows

When you open the editor either by clicking Tools, Macro, Visual Basic Editor, or by pressing Alt+F11, just two windows are visible:

- The Project Explorer shows all the modules, UserForms, and other items in your VBA project, including references to other projects.

> **note** Unless otherwise noted, *project* in this chapter means VBA project, whereas *plan* is used to refer to Microsoft Project plan files.

When you open the editor, two VBProject objects are listed. The first object, the ProjectGlobal project, contains all the code, UserForms, and modules associated with the Global file. The second object, the VBAProject project ("VBAProject" is the default name of any new project), contains the same items associated with the open Microsoft Project plan.

Initially, the ThisProject object is selected in the Project Explorer. This Project represents the plan itself, including events associated with the plan (see Figure 31-1).

Figure 31-1. View all of the items in your project by using the Project Explorer.

For more information about plan-level events, see "Working with Events" later in this chapter.

- The Properties window lists the properties for the selected item (see Figure 31-2). You can use the Properties window to easily change *design-time* properties, such as the name or style of an object, which can only be modified by using the editor.

tip Some of the properties listed in the Properties window are also *run-time* properties, which means they can be changed by your code while it is running.

Figure 31-2. The Properties window shows the properties of the selected project and each of the items (UserForms, modules, and so on) contained in it.

Also of major importance is the Code window, where you spend the majority of your time when using the editor. All Visual Basic code attached to a plan or a UserForm, or in a module or class, appears in the Code window. To open the Code window, simply double-click an item in the Project Explorer. (To view code for a UserForm, right-click, and click View Code.)

There are four controls associated with the Code window:

The Objects box. For all items in the Project Explorer, this box displays the word (General). For VBProject objects and UserForms, it also displays the name of the object (Project or UserForm). Finally, for UserForms, the Objects box also displays the name of each control on the UserForm.

Objects

The Procedures/Events box. For all items in the Project Explorer, this box displays the word (Declarations) and the names of procedures. For VBProject objects and UserForms, it also displays the names of events associated with the object selected in the Objects box.

Procedures/Events

The Procedure View button. Displays just one procedure at a time in the Code window.

Procedure View

The Full Module View button. Displays all procedures in the Code window, each separated by a horizontal line. Full Module is the default view for the Code window.

Full Module View

The following windows are also part of the editor, but will be discussed in more detail later in this chapter:

Immediate. Any code entered in this window is immediately evaluated and run. Code entered in the Immediate window is not saved. It is frequently used as a sort of scratch pad, especially when debugging.

Locals. Displays information about all local (procedure) variables and their values. Used when debugging.

Watch. Displays information about *watches* that have been created. A watch is any expression that can be evaluated to produce a value. Used when debugging.

UserForm. Displays a UserForm. Used when creating or editing the visual elements of a UserForm.

Toolbox. Displays controls that can be placed on a UserForm, including ActiveX controls and other insertable objects you might have added to your project from external sources. Used when creating or editing the visual elements of a UserForm.

Object Browser. Displays information about the objects, properties, methods, events, and constants (the object model) that are available in *type libraries* referenced by your project or that you create in procedures. (Type libraries are files with the *.olb*, *.tlb*, or *.dll* extension.) Used when writing code or learning about the features of an object model.

Tools Menu

One of the most powerful functionalities of the VBA environment is its ability to extend itself beyond the bounds of the host program. Two of the commands that provide this functionality, adding references to other object models and additional controls for UserForms, are found on the Tools menu. Also on the Tools menu are the following commands for customizing the editor and adding Help files, password protection, and digital signatures to your project:

References. Opens the References dialog box (see Figure 31-3), where you make connections to external libraries, including the object models of other applications.

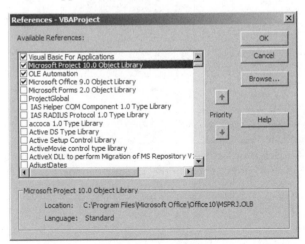

Figure 31-3. The References dialog box controls which objects are available to your project. Selections here determine which object models display in the object browser.

Libraries that are referenced by a project are indicated by the check box next to the library name. Clearing the check box of any library that you are not using in your project results in faster compilation of your project because unused object references must otherwise be verified.

> **note** The "Visual Basic for Applications" and "Microsoft Project 10.0 Object Library" libraries are always referenced by Microsoft Project and cannot be removed.

The Priority buttons change the order in which libraries are searched for objects. You should only change the priority of a reference if the same object name is used in more than one referenced library.

> **note** References are specific to each project.

Additional Controls.   Opens the Additional Controls dialog box (see Figure 31-4), where you select additional custom controls to use on your UserForms. This command is only available when creating or editing the visual elements of a UserForm.

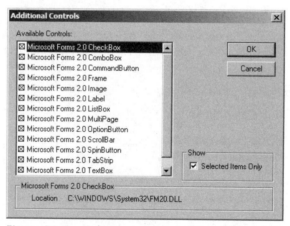

Figure 31-4.   Selections made in the Additional Controls dialog box determine which controls appear in the Toolbox window.

> **note** Although any control that appears in the Available Controls list can be added to the Toolbox, not all controls are authored in such a way that they can be used outside their intended environment.

Options. Opens the Options dialog box (see Figure 31-5), where you select visual, behavior, and other options for the editor that suit your needs or preferences.

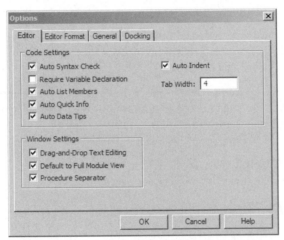

Figure 31-5. Selecting the Require Variable Declaration check box on the Editor tab of the Options dialog box enforces explicit declaration of variables.

VBAProject Properties. Opens the Project Properties dialog box (see Figure 31-6). Do not confuse the Project Properties dialog box with the Properties window. You can use the Project Properties dialog box to modify the properties of a VBProject object, including giving it a description and connecting it to a Help file.

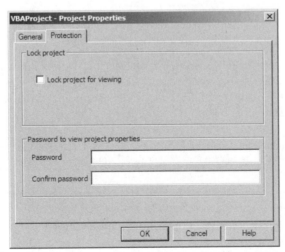

Figure 31-6. Specifying a password without also selecting the Lock Project For Viewing check box protects the Project Properties dialog box only.

> **tip** The project name and description also appear in the object browser, which can be especially useful when searching for specific procedures in larger projects.

You can prevent other people from viewing or modifying your project by clicking the Protection tab, selecting the Lock Project For Viewing check box, and then providing a password.

> **note** The name of this command changes according to the name of the selected project. "VBAProject" is the default name of any new project.

Digital Signature. Displays the Digital Signature dialog box (see Figure 31-7), where you can digitally sign a project with a certificate.

Figure 31-7. The Digital Signature dialog box for a project signed with a certificate created by using SelfCert.exe is shown here.

Digitally signing a project lets other users of your project know that it originated with the signer and has not changed since it was signed. You can use the SelfCert program, found in the Program Files\Microsoft Office \Office10 folder, to create your own certificate.

> For more information about digital signatures, including how to obtain a digital certificate from a commercial Certificate Authority, search for "About digital signatures" in Microsoft Project Help.

> **note** In an environment where the macro security level is set to High on all computers, a self-signed project can be deployed but cannot be run because it does not have a secure enough certificate. You must use a certificate issued by a Certificate Authority in this situation.

> **tip** One way to deploy a project in a High security environment is to send the source code to users as text, instruct them how to paste it into the Visual Basic Editor, and then use SelfCert to certify the code using their own local certificate.

Finding the Right Help

Microsoft Project includes four different Help systems for VBA, and it might not always be clear where the content you're reading originated. Sometimes you might know which Help system contains the information you need but you might not be able to figure out how to open that specific Help file.

To get assistance with	Do the following
General Visual Basic concepts and language reference	Click Help, Microsoft Visual Basic Help in the editor.
Concepts and language reference common among Microsoft Office and related programs (including Microsoft Project)	Click a Microsoft Office-specific item in code or in the object browser and then press F1.
Members of the Microsoft Project object model	Click a Microsoft Project-specific item in code or in the object browser and then press F1.
UserForms	Click a UserForm, a control on a UserForm, or an item in the Properties window, and then press F1.

Understanding the Microsoft Project Object Model

Now that you have a foundation in Visual Basic concepts and know your way around the development environment, you're almost ready to begin creating customized solutions in Microsoft Project. The final piece of the VBA puzzle to familiarize yourself with is the object model.

But how do you familiarize yourself with an object model? Should you just dive in and start writing code, trusting that you'll figure out the object model as you go? Should you start reading the Help files that are included with Microsoft Project? Or should you use the object browser to (literally) browse the object model? The answer to all three of these questions is Yes. Choose the one that best suits your particular requirements and situation.

741

What Is an Object Model?

As described in Chapter 30, "Understanding the Visual Basic Language," an object model is a system of objects that provide a programmatic model for interacting with an application. That's a bit of a mouthful, but what it means is the object model is your portal to the features of Microsoft Project. The features of the object model, in concert with the power of Visual Basic, provide you with the ability to make Microsoft Project do virtually anything you want.

InsideOut

The object model is amazingly full-featured, but it is important to understand that it's not the Visual Basic "version" of all the features in Microsoft Project. As with every program that exposes one to programming, the object model does not always have a one-to-one correlation to what you can see or do in the user interface. It is just those portions of the program that seem useful for macro writers and other developers. This is why, even though new items have been continually added as the programming environment in Microsoft Project has developed, you can still occasionally find features that are not fully accessible (or not available at all) through the object model.

Learning a mature object model like that of Microsoft Project is made easier by relationships, both in the object model and in the Microsoft Project interface:

- Items that are important in the program are important in the object model, too. For example, the most important objects in the object model, aside from the Application, are the Project, Task, Resource, and Assignment objects.

- Relationships between items in the object model match those same relationships in the program itself.

- The hierarchical nature of the object model makes finding these relationships much simpler.

For more information about working with Microsoft Project's object model from another program, see "Extending and Automating Microsoft Project" later in this chapter.

Useful Tools When Learning the Object Model

Although there are many different ways to learn your way around the object model, there are three tools that can make doing so much easier:

Auto List Members. This option for the Visual Basic Editor (enabled by default) automatically lists all methods, properties, events, and children for an object as you type your code.

Besides saving additional typing—you can just select the item you want from the list—this option can help you learn about a relevant portion of the object model as you work (see Figure 31-8).

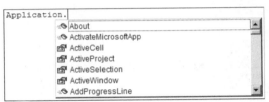

Figure 31-8. The Auto List Members box, shown here displaying part of the list for the Application object, is great way to learn about the object model as you work.

---

tip **How object-oriented code relates to the object model**

When you see a period between two object names in Visual Basic code, such as Application.Projects or ActiveCell.Task.Assignments, you have "branched" from one section of the object model to another.

If you think of the object model as a tree with the Application object as its root, this "dot syntax" of *object-oriented* code is not only a useful reminder that you've moved from one "branch" to another, but it can actually help you understand the relationships between items in the object model.

Microsoft Project Visual Basic Reference. Whether you use it with the object browser, while writing code, or if you just browse its contents, the Visual Basic reference for Microsoft Project contains everything you need to know about the object model.

There are graphical representations of the object model hierarchy, full explanations of the members of the Microsoft Project object model—including links to Help topics about the other object models automatically referenced by a project—and many examples showing the object model "in action."

Object Browser. The object browser (see Figure 31-9 on the next page) displays all the items (properties, methods, event, and so on) in every object model that is referenced by your project. Open it by pressing F2 or clicking the Object Browser button.

Object
Browser

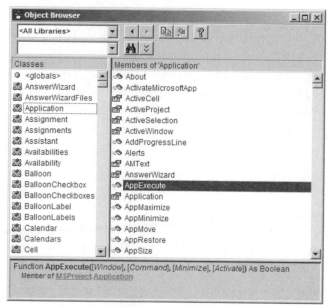

Figure 31-9. The object browser displays information about the libraries referenced by your project.

The object browser has three panes. The pane on the left is a list of *classes*. A class can be one of several things, including an object, collection, module, *type* (a user-defined data type), or enumerated data type (a collection of constants; usually referred to as an *enum*).

Clicking a class displays a list of members for the class in the pane on the right. In the figure just shown, one of the members of the Application object is selected.

Finding the Default Member of a Class

The icons next to a class or member name provide information about the item, such as whether it's a method or a property. A method with the ⚞ icon, or a property with the ⚞ icon, is the default member of its class.

Although default members can be used simply by referring to their class, doing so can sometimes make your code less readable. For example, although CostRateTable(2) is much less readable than CostRateTable.Index(2), because the default property for most objects is Name, using Tasks(4) (or any collection name) instead of Tasks.Item(4) is a common practice.

The Details pane (see Figure 31-10) lists specifics about the selected item, such as whether a property is read-only or read/write, the numerical value for a constant, or the arguments for a method.

Figure 31-10. For properties or methods that return objects, the name of the object is a link in the Details pane.

It can be useful, especially if several libraries are referenced by your project, to filter the list of items shown in the object browser. You might also want to search for specific items by name or by part of a name. Use the Library and Search Text boxes (see Figure 31-11) to filter the list of items referenced by your project and search for specific items, respectively.

Figure 31-11. Use the Library box to filter items in the object browser and the Search Text box to find specific items.

> **note** By default, the Search Text box performs "loose" searches, which means that searching for *task* returns items like Task, TaskDependency, ExternalTask, DefaultTaskType, and so on.
>
> To return only exact matches for a search, right-click anywhere in the Object Browser window, and then click Find Whole Word Only.

Creating Macros

Chapter 27, "Automating Your Work with Macros," described how to create a macro by recording the steps that make up a task. Although creating macros that way is easy enough and does work, it's not the most effective way to write Visual Basic, especially as your development skills grow. Creating macros in the Visual Basic Editor also enables you to use many more tools to develop Visual Basic solutions than are provided by recording actions in the Microsoft Project interface.

Writing a Macro in the Editor

Writing macros directly in the editor can seem a little daunting if you don't have much experience with programming or if you aren't comfortable with the object model. There are few tools to help you start (other than the Add Procedure window, which you can find by clicking Insert, Procedure), so one way to begin is to simply record a macro and then edit it in the Visual Basic Editor.

For the purposes of this discussion, though, you can simply follow these steps to create a macro in the editor directly:

1 Create a new project, and then open the Visual Basic Editor by pressing Alt+F11.

2 Double-click the ThisProject object in the Project Explorer.

The Code window opens with the cursor in the upper-left corner.

3 Type the following code in the Code window:

```
Function strNewTask(strName As String, intBefore As Integer) As String
    ActiveProject.Tasks.Add strName, intBefore

    If ActiveProject.Tasks(intBefore).Name = strName Then
        strNewTask = "Success!"
    Else
        strNewTask = "Failed to create task!"
    End If
End Function
```

> **note** Be sure to capitalize variable names exactly as they are shown here.

As you enter the code, you will notice some things that the editor does:

■ As you type `strName As` in the function definition, a list displays classes and data types. As you start typing `String`, the list scrolls until String is selected (see Figure 31-12). You can continue typing the word, select String from the list, or press Ctrl+Space to complete the word.

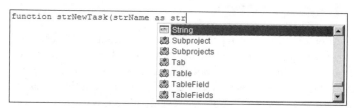

Figure 31-12. The Auto List Members feature scrolls through an alphabetical list of possible matches for data types and constants as you type.

■ When you press Enter at the end of the line containing the function definition, several things happen at once: as the word "function" is capitalized, a blank line and End Function are inserted, and Visual Basic keywords (Function, String, Integer, and so on) are colored blue.

■ When you press Enter at the end of a line containing an equals sign (=), the editor puts spaces around the equals sign.

4 Type the following code in the Code window:

```
Sub AddTask()
    Dim strTaskName As String
    Dim intTaskNum As Integer

    strTaskName = InputBox$("Type a name for the new task:")
    intTaskNum = CInt(InputBox$("Type the position for the new " & _
      "task in the task list:"))

    MsgBox strNewTask(strTaskName, intTaskNum)
End Sub
```

As you enter this code, the same actions occur as when you entered code for the function, but also something really interesting also happens: Typing `strnewtask(` causes the Quick Info feature to list information about the arguments and return value for strNewTask (see Figure 31-13).

```
    MsgBox strnewtask(|
End Sub       strNewTask(strName As String, intBefore As Integer) As String
```

Figure 31-13. The Quick Info feature lists details about procedures you create and about items in the object model.

Returning to the Microsoft Project interface and opening the Macros dialog box (click Tools, Macro, Macros) shows the AddTask procedure as a new macro.

> **tip** After the Visual Basic Editor has been opened, Alt+F11 toggles between Microsoft Project and the editor.

Deciding Where to Create and Store Procedures

The discussion so far has been about creating procedures in the ThisProject object for the VBAProject project, but that might not always be the best place to create procedures. In deciding where to create procedures, you should think about what the code is meant to do and whether you want to distribute your code to other people.

Depending upon your needs and the type of code you're writing, you should create procedures in the following areas:

● The ProjectGlobal project, if you want your procedures available for every plan you work with. Procedures in the ProjectGlobal project are associated with the Global file, which is opened every time you start Microsoft Project.

- The VBAProject project, if the procedures are only used for that particular plan. Procedures in the VBAProject project are associated with that particular plan and are available to anyone who opens the plan.

- A code module, if you want to be able to easily distribute the code to other people. Modules can be easily distributed because they are not associated with any particular plan and can be imported into a project as needed. Also, because they are not associated with any plan, modules are a good place to store general "utility" code.

> **note** To add an existing module to a project, right-click the project in the Project Explorer, click Import File, and then browse to the file that you want to insert.

Working with Events

Macros require user action to start, but you might occasionally need code to start automatically. For example, every time a shared plan is saved, you might want to store information about the person who saved it. In a situation like that, you need code that is run from an *event procedure*.

An event procedure is any code that is tied to an event, such as when a plan is saved or a task is deleted. When the event *fires*, the code is activated. Anything you can do in a "regular" procedure you can also do in an event procedure, including calling other procedures and making references to other object models.

> For more information about events in UserForms, such as Click events for buttons, see "Creating UserForms" later in this chapter.

In Microsoft Project, there are events attached to the Application and Project (representing an open plan) objects. You can find the events by looking for the event icon in the object browser or by expanding the Events item in the Contents tab of the Microsoft Visual Basic Reference.

> **tip** To sort items in the object browser by type instead of simply alphabetically, right-click anywhere in the object browser, and then click Group Members.

Creating Application Event Procedures

Creating Application event procedures is a three-step process. The first step is to create a class module that contains an Application object variable declared with events. *WithEvents* is a Visual Basic keyword that means the variable should respond to events. You can only use WithEvents in class modules.

The second step is to *bind* the class containing your event procedure to the Application object. You do this by first declaring a variable that represents the class module and then writing a procedure that assigns the variable to the Application object.

For the last step, you need to decide how to run the code that binds the class to the Application object. You can either write the binding code directly in a project-level event procedure or if you want to keep your code more modular, you can write it anywhere you like and then simply call it from a project-level event.

Follow these steps to create an event procedure for the Application object:

1 Right-click anywhere in the Project Explorer, and then click Insert, Class Module.

2 In the Code window for the new class, enter the following code:

```
Public WithEvents objMSProjectApp As Application
```

---

note The variable represented here by objMSProjectApp can be named anything you like.

---

3 In the Objects box, select objMSProjectApp.

The editor creates a blank procedure for the NewProject event. If you want to write a procedure for a different event, click it in the Procedures/Events box.

4 Write your event code as you would for any other procedure.

For example, the following code prevents a particular resource from being assigned to tasks. (Note that the procedure declaration must be entered on one line in the Visual Basic Editor, not on three as shown here.)

```
Private Sub objMSProjectApp_ProjectBeforeAssignmentChange(ByVal asg As
Assignment, ByVal Field As PjAssignmentField, ByVal NewVal As Variant,
Cancel As Boolean)

    If Field = pjAssignmentResourceName And _
      NewVal = "Patricia Brooke" Then
        MsgBox "Patricia is no longer available for assignment!"
        Cancel = True
    End If
End Sub
```

5 Change the Name field in the Properties window for the class from **Class1** to **clsAppEventProcedures**.

6 In any module except the class module where you wrote the event procedure, enter the following code in the Code window:

```
Dim clsAppEvents As New clsAppEventProcedures

Sub BindEventToApplication()
    Set clsAppEvents.objMSProjectApp = Application
End Sub
```

7 Double-click ThisProject in the Project Explorer to open the Code window, click Project in the Objects box, and then type the following code in the Project object's Open event:

```
BindEventToApplication
```

Creating Project Event Procedures

To create an event procedure for the Project object, the code must be written in the ThisProject object, rather than in a code module. Events for the Project object are attached to the plan, which ThisProject represents.

Follow these steps to create an event procedure for the Project object:

1 Double-click ThisProject in the Project Explorer to open the Code window.

2 In the Objects box, click Project.

The editor creates a blank procedure for the Open event. If you want to write a procedure for a different event, click it in the Procedures/Events box.

3 Write your event code as you would for any other procedure.

For example, the following code adds information to the plan's summary task about who saved the plan and when, each time it is saved:

```
Private Sub Project_BeforeSave(ByVal pj As Project)
    Dim strName As String

    strAlias = InputBox("Please enter your name: ")
    pj.ProjectSummaryTask.AppendNotes vbCrLf & "Saved by " & _
        strName & " on " & Date$ & " at " & Time$ & "."
End Sub
```

Debugging Macros

You will occasionally make mistakes in your code. Many will be simple syntax or typing errors that are caught by the Visual Basic compiler. Most of the rest become obvious when you examine your code (the "duh" factor). Sometimes, however, you'll find a situation in which something is going wrong and you can't immediately figure out why. Your next step is to use the debugging tools available in the editor.

> For more information about debugging, including some concepts and general principles, see "Trapping Errors" on page 730.

Although most of the features discussed here are true debugging tools like breakpoints, there are other features of the editor that are useful when debugging but that also have uses outside a debugging situation.

Using Breakpoints

A *breakpoint* is a place in your code where you want to temporarily break out of the run-time environment without actually ending your program, so that you can examine the code during execution. A breakpoint (and you can have as many as you want at one time) is a lot like a Pause button.

The F9 key toggles a breakpoint for the selected line of code, which is marked (using the default colors) by a brown dot in the margin and brown background for the line of code (see Figure 31-14). You can only create breakpoints in lines of executable code, which excludes blank lines, comments, and even lines where you declare a variable.

```
Function strNewTask(strName As String, intBefore As Integer) As String
    ActiveProject.Tasks.Add strName, intBefore

    If ActiveProject.Tasks(intBefore).Name = strName Then
        strNewTask = "Success!"
    Else
        strNewTask = "Failed to create task!"
    End If
End Function
```

Figure 31-14. If a new task is successfully created in this function, this breakpoint never gets hit and execution proceeds normally.

> **tip** Press Ctrl+Shift+F9 to clear all breakpoints from your code.

Tracing Execution

After your program has been paused, you need to see what's going wrong with your code. This can mean watching your code run line by line (*tracing*) to see where, for example, it takes a different path through a decision structure than what you expected.

The following tools are available when tracing code:

- The F8 key *steps into* a procedure, which is the most detailed mode of tracing. If the procedure you're tracing makes a call to another procedure, execution transfers to the called procedure just as it would normally, but in break mode.

- After you've stepped into a procedure and have decided that you no longer need to trace through it, you can *step out* (Ctrl+Shift+F8) to return to the calling procedure.

- *Stepping over* (Shift+F8) is to treat a call to another procedure as a stand-alone statement; that is, to trace the code that calls another procedure without actually tracing the code in the called procedure.

- Using the Run To Cursor option (Ctrl+F8) essentially creates a temporary breakpoint. Code runs from the current location to the cursor, where it reenters break mode. This is useful if you've stepped into a procedure and want to skip over large sections of it without stepping out of it, but don't want to create an actual breakpoint.

> **note** Pressing F5 while tracing execution returns to normal execution, unless another breakpoint is encountered before the program ends.

Using Watches

Watches are used to keep track of values automatically while debugging. A watch is anything that can be evaluated to produce a value, which means it can be an expression like ActiveProject.Tasks(intBefore).Name = strName, or simply the name of a function or variable (see Figure 31-15).

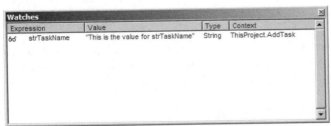

Figure 31-15. The Context column shows that the scope for the variable is local, existing in the AddTask procedure of the current module. If the active statement were in another procedure, the Value column would display <Out of context>.

> **tip**
> The Auto Data Tips option (enabled by default) works like an ad hoc watch by providing information about the value of a variable (including the value of properties) when you move the mouse pointer over it while in break mode.

You can use watches in two ways:

- To simply watch the value of an expression while debugging.

- To define a condition, rather than simply a line of code, that should force entry into break mode.

You can add watches while in design mode or break mode. Although you can manually enter the expression you want to watch in the Add Watch window (see Figure 31-16), it's easier to simply highlight the variable or expression by right-clicking in the Code window, and then clicking Add Watch.

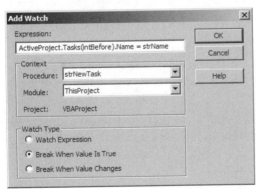

Figure 31-16. Set the Watch Type to specify whether you want to watch the expression or test its value to determine when to enter break mode.

Using the Locals Window

The Locals window acts like a dynamically generated list of watches for the current procedure. As execution moves from one procedure to another in break mode, the Locals window is updated to show a list of local variables and their values (see Figure 31-17).

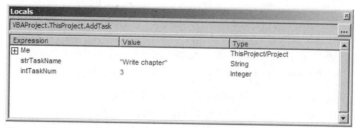

Figure 31-17. Click the plus sign (+) next to the expression "Me" to see the value of every property, variable, and function referenced by or defined in your project.

If a variable can be assigned a value in more than one location in a procedure (such as when a different value is assigned to the same variable, depending upon which path is taken through a decision structure), it is listed once for each possible assignment. Assuming the procedure runs successfully, only one of these occurrences will have an entry in the Value column by the time execution moves out of the procedure.

Unlike the Watches window, which is read-only, you can modify items in the Value column to test different actions taken by your code. If you had a decision structure in your code, for example, that took different actions according to the value of a local variable, you could do the following:

1 Insert a breakpoint at the beginning of the structure, and then run your macro.

2 When execution enters break mode, step through the decision structure to see the results.

3 At the end of the decision structure (or at any time before execution moves to a different procedure), change the value of the variable in the Locals window to something else.

4 Select the line with the breakpoint, use Ctrl+F9 to force execution to return to that line, and then step through the decision structure again.

Using the Immediate Window

The Immediate window (Ctrl+G), which can be used when debugging or at design-time, is a very versatile feature of the editor: Think of it as a "scratch pad" for code.

In design mode, you can enter a question mark (?) and any expression into the Immediate window to be evaluated. Typing ?8*7 and pressing Enter, for example, returns 56 just below the expression in the Immediate window. You can even enter small procedures to be evaluated, although they must be entered as one line, such as:

```
for x = 1 to 3: msgbox x: next x
```

In break mode, you can do anything you can in design mode, plus you can do the following:

- Find the value of variables:

  ```
  ?strname
  ```

> **tip** Capitalization in the Immediate window doesn't matter unless you have multiple variables with the same name but different capitalization.

- Assign new values to any local, module-level, or global variable:

  ```
  strname="some new value"
  ```

- Evaluate expressions:

  ```
  ?ActiveProject.Tasks(intBefore).Name = strName
  ```

> **tip** You can edit an existing expression in the Immediate window and then press Enter to reevaluate it, without having to type the expression anew.

Using Navigation Tools While Debugging

There are a few other features in the editor that, although frequently used while debugging, are actually tools for navigating within your code. They are most useful in modules that contain many procedures, in which finding a particular item can sometimes be difficult.

Bookmarks (see Figure 31-18) can be used to mark a location in your code. Unlike breakpoints, bookmarks can be used anywhere, including blank lines.

Figure 31-18.   Use the bookmark controls on the Edit toolbar to toggle, move between, or delete all bookmarks.

The Definition command (press Shift+F2 or right-click the Code window) moves focus to the location where the procedure or variable under the mouse pointer is defined. If the item is a member of a type library referenced by your project and not defined in your code, focus moves to the appropriate location in the object browser.

The Last Position command (press Ctrl+Shift+F2 or right-click in the Code window) returns focus to the previous location after using the Definition command or changing code. The Last Position command loops through as many as eight locations.

Creating UserForms

Writing macros and other code to accomplish things you need to do is a major part of using VBA, and UserForms are another. UserForms are the visual counterpart to Visual Basic procedures and provide you with the ability to interact with your users as if your creation was part of Microsoft Project itself.

> **note** All the normal rules and principles for working with Visual Basic code, including events and debugging, also apply to working with UserForms.

Creating a Simple Form

To begin designing a UserForm, right-click anywhere in the Project Explorer, and then click Insert, UserForm. A blank UserForm appears (see Figure 31-19) in place of the Code window (if showing) with the Toolbox window floating somewhere near it (see Figure 31-20). At the same time, the information in the Properties window changes to show properties for the new UserForm.

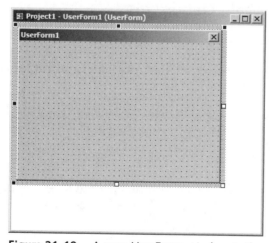

Figure 31-19. A new UserForm window is the visual counterpart to a blank Code window.

Figure 31-20.   Use the Toolbox to place visual components on your UserForm. You can use Tools, Additional Controls to place more "tools" in the Toolbox.

Follow these steps to change some of the default properties of the form:

1   In the Properties window, change the value for the Name field from **UserForm1** to **frmWelcome**.

This changes the name of the form in the Project Explorer and is how you refer to the form, when necessary. Also, if you export it, frmWelcome.frm will be the file name of the form.

2   Change the value for the Caption field from **UserForm1** to **Welcome!**.

This is what appears in the title bar of the form when it is running.

3   Click the Font field, and then use the Browse button to change the base font for the form from 8 point Tahoma to 10 point Arial.

Although changing the font in the form doesn't have any visible effect, any controls you add to the form will use the font you specified as their default font. Changing the font now is quicker and easier than changing it for each control individually later.

Now that you've created a form and modified some of its properties, the next task is to add controls. Follow these steps to add two buttons, a label, and a text box:

1   In the Toolbox window, click the TextBox button, and then draw a rectangle on the form.

2   In the Properties window, change the value for the Name field from **TextBox1** to **txtName**.

3   In the Toolbox window, click the Label button, and then draw a rectangle just above the text box.

Browse

TextBox

Label

4 In the Properties window, change the value for the Name field from **Label1** to **lblName**.

5 Change the value for the Caption field from **Label1** to **Enter your name:**.

CommandButton

6 In the Toolbox window, click the CommandButton button, draw a rectangle to the right of the label and the text box, and then click the CommandButton button again to draw another button just below the first.

7 Click the first button, change the value for Name from **CommandButton1** to **cmdOK**, and then change the value for Caption from **CommandButton1** to **OK**.

8 Click the second button, and give it the name **cmdCancel** and the caption **Cancel**.

9 Adjust the position of the controls and the size of the form (see Figure 31-21).

Figure 31-21. This is what the completed frmWelcome should look like after the controls have been positioned and the form sized appropriately.

Adding Code to Your Form

Before your new form can be used to do anything, you must write event procedures for the controls on it. For the form created in the previous section, you only need to write code for the two buttons.

The button cmdCancel needs code to close the form's window, in case the user doesn't want to use the form. The quickest way to open the Code window for a form or control is to double-click the item while in design mode. If you double-click the Cancel button on the form, the Code window opens to the cmdCancel_Click() event procedure. Type the following code into the Cancel button's Click event:

```
frmWelcome.Hide
```

> **tip** The *Me* keyword always refers to the class (a form is a kind of class) in which it is used. Instead of frmWelcome.Hide, for example, you could simply use Me.Hide.

The cmdOK button is where all the action is for this form. The OK button takes the name the user entered in the txtName box and adds it to the status bar at the bottom of the Microsoft Project window.

With the Code window open, click cmdOK in the Objects box to gain access to the cmdOK_Click() event. Type the following code into the OK button's Click event:

```
Application.StatusBar = "What would you like to do now, " & _
  txtName.Text & "?"
```

This code sets the Application object's StatusBar property to be the text in quotes, plus the value of the txtName box's Text property.

Because you want the form to close after the user clicks the OK button, add the same code you added to the Cancel button's Click event:

```
Me.Hide
```

Integrating Your Form with Microsoft Project

You now have a form with controls and event procedures that perform actions when the controls are used, but no one will ever see the form until you determine how the form is activated. With many types of forms, it's enough that the user runs a macro, which then displays one or more forms as it runs.

For this form, though, you want to automatically display the form every time a particular plan is opened. Follow these steps to create an event procedure for the Project object that will display your form every time the plan is opened:

1 Double-click ThisProject in the Project Explorer to open the Code window.

2 In the Objects box, click Project, and then type the following code into the Project object's Open event:

```
frmWelcome.Show
```

3 In the Procedure/Events box, click BeforeClose, and then type the following code into the Project object's BeforeClose event:

```
Application.StatusBar = False
```

Because code tied to the Project object is changing an application-level property, you need this additional code to "clean up" the effects of using the form by resetting the StatusBar property to its default value (see Figure 31-22 on the next page).

For more information about Project events, see "Creating Project Event Procedures" earlier in this chapter.

Chapter 31

> What would you like to do now, Mr. Jones?

Figure 31-22. This figure shows the Microsoft Project status bar after someone has used the form.

> **note** The first form your users see when opening the plan is actually the macro virus security dialog box. If a user selects the Disable Macros button, none of the event procedures run and your form doesn't display.

Three Birds, One Stone

If you like the idea behind the example of displaying a form every time a specific plan was opened but want something a little more robust, you can avoid three of its potential detractions by working with the Global file (the ProjectGlobal project) instead of a particular plan (the VBAProject project):

● To make the code `frmWelcome.Show` run every time Microsoft Project starts, expand the ProjectGlobal project, and double-click the ThisProject object instead of the ThisProject object under the VBAProject project.

● Because the StatusBar property is reset to its default when Microsoft Project closes, you don't need the BeforeClose event code.

● Because of the special nature of the Global file, users don't see the macro virus security dialog box, which means there's no chance they will choose to disable macros and, consequently, the code to display your form.

A more sophisticated version of this example would be one that added a new menu item or toolbar that could be used to access the forms you have created. This method integrates your forms with the Microsoft Project interface even more closely, although you probably wouldn't bother doing so for a simple, limited-use form like the one you just created.

Follow these steps to create two Project event procedures that add a new item to the View menu (see Figure 31-23) that, when clicked, displays the frmWelcome form:

1 Double-click ThisProject in the Project Explorer to open the Code window.

760

2 In the Objects box, click Project, and then type the following code into the Project object's Open event:

```
Dim objViewBar As CommandBar
Dim objNewItem As CommandBarButton
Dim intTotalItems As Integer

Set objViewBar = Application.CommandBars("View")
intTotalItems = objViewBar.Controls.Count

If objViewBar.Controls(intTotalItems).Caption <> "Show my UserForm" Then
    Set objNewItem = objViewBar.Controls.Add(Type:=msoControlButton)
    objNewItem.Caption = "Show my UserForm"
    objNewItem.BeginGroup = True
    objNewItem.OnAction = "frmWelcome.Show"
End If

Set objNewItem = Nothing
Set objViewBar = Nothing
```

3 In the Procedures/Events box, click BeforeClose, and then type the following code into the Project object's BeforeClose event:

```
Dim objViewBar As CommandBar
Dim intTotalItems As Integer

Application.StatusBar = False

Set objViewBar = Application.CommandBars("View")
intTotalItems = objViewBar.Controls.Count

If objViewBar.Controls(intTotalItems).Caption = "Show my UserForm" Then
    objViewBar.Controls(intTotalItems).Delete
End If

Set objViewBar = Nothing
```

Because code tied to the Project object is changing two application-level items, you need this additional code to "clean up" when the plan is closed by resetting the StatusBar property to its default value and removing the Show My UserForm command from the View menu. This ensures that Microsoft Project is in its default state when other plans are opened.

> **note** Until the plan is closed, the new View menu item is visible from every other open plan. Clicking it from one of those plans, however, results in an error.

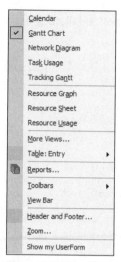

Figure 31-23. The new Show My UserForm command appears at the bottom of the View menu.

Extending and Automating Microsoft Project

As mentioned in the discussion of the Tools menu earlier in this chapter, one of the most powerful functionalities of the VBA environment is its ability to extend itself beyond the bounds of the host program. This can be done in two main ways:

● Referencing external type libraries (files with the *.olb*, *.tlb*, or *.dll* extension) or ActiveX controls (files with the *.ocx*, *.dll*, or *.exe* extension) to provide additional functionality to your code and forms.

● Using *Automation* to run other programs from Microsoft Project or to run Microsoft Project from other programs.

note The Microsoft Project Developer Center at *http://msdn.microsoft.com/project/* contains a great deal of useful information about advanced programming with Microsoft Project, including links to the Microsoft Project Software Development Kit.

Working With External References

Working with external references usually means either adding ActiveX controls to your forms or using external type libraries to do things that aren't part of the object model for the program you're using. The Microsoft Web Browser control, for example, is an ActiveX control commonly added to forms, whereas a reference to one of the Microsoft ActiveX Data Objects (ADO) libraries might be used to provide easy access to data sources.

Using ActiveX Controls

Working with ActiveX controls is probably the easiest way to use external references. Controls that have been *registered* on your computer (this happens automatically when controls are installed on your computer) appear in the Additional Controls dialog box (click Tools, Additional Controls) and can be added to the Toolbox. After a control appears in the Toolbox, you can use it just as you would any of the *intrinsic controls* in the Microsoft Forms library that is included with Microsoft Project.

All ActiveX controls have common properties for a name, physical dimensions and position, tab order, and so on, in addition to whatever properties and methods they supply as part of their specialized functionality. All the general information you know from working with the intrinsic controls also applies to new controls, enabling you to concentrate on working with the new abilities the control provides.

> **note** Many ActiveX controls also have type libraries associated with them, which appear in the object browser. These libraries might be listed in the Library box by the file name of the library instead of by the name of the control as it appears in the Additional Controls dialog box.

Using External Libraries

An external type library (sometimes called a "helper library") is really nothing more than an object model that doesn't have a visual element and doesn't represent the Visual Basic aspect of another program. Type libraries are installed in association with a program or the operating system.

After you add a reference to a library (click Tools, References), the objects, methods, properties, events, and constants defined in the library appear in the object browser. There are no special rules for working with an external type library and you can use its members as you would the members of the Microsoft Project object model.

The following code is an example of working with an external type library. It uses the Microsoft ActiveX Data Objects 2.6 Library to access the values of certain fields for each record in a Jet (Microsoft Access) database:

```
Sub ReadDataFile(strFileName As String)
    ' The Connection object is found in the ADO library
    ' The New keyword in a variable declaration creates an object
    '  reference at the same time as the variable is declared
    Dim conData As New Connection
    ' The Recordset object is found in the ADO library
    Dim rstTopic As New Recordset
    Dim strSelect As String
    Dim bytCount As Byte

    ' Connect to data source
    ' ConnectionString is a property of the Connection object
    conData.ConnectionString = "Provider=Microsoft.Jet.OLEDB.4.0;Data Source= "& _
        strFileName
    ' This Open method is for the Connection object
    conData.Open

    ' Select the records and open a recordset
    strSelect = "SELECT * FROM Topic"
    ' This Open method is for the Recordset object
    rstTopic.Open strSelect, conData

    ' Move to the first record in the Recordset object
    rstTopic.MoveFirst

    ' Read through each record to find the values I want
    For bytCount = 1 To rstTopic.Fields!byt1.Value
        rstTopic.MoveNext

        ' gudtText is a global, user-defined collection object
        gudtText.blnNumbered.Add rstTopic.Fields!byt1.Value
        gudtText.bytMatchNode.Add rstTopic.Fields!byt2.Value
        gudtText.bytNumber.Add rstTopic.Fields!byt3.Value
        gudtText.strText.Add rstTopic.Fields!str2.Value
    Next bytCount

    ' Close the reference to the Connection object
    conData.Close

    ' Clean up the object references
    Set rstTopic = Nothing
    Set conData = Nothing
End Sub
```

Automating Microsoft Project

Automating a program like Microsoft Project means that you control the program remotely, even invisibly, as if you were actually using the interface. This means, for example, that you can use the Spelling Checker feature of Microsoft Word in Microsoft Project or the math functions of Microsoft Excel from within Microsoft Project. In fact, you can even automate Microsoft Project from a Web page.

Automating With a Library Reference

Programs that support making references to the Microsoft Project object model, such as Microsoft Word, provide the easiest access to Automation:

● Setting a reference to a library by using the References item on the Tools menu automatically provides the connection between the *host application* and Microsoft Project.

● Many of the tools available when writing Visual Basic code in Microsoft Project are typically available in the host's development environment, such as the Auto List Members option. (Obviously, writing Automation code from a VBA-enabled program provides all the tools available from Microsoft Project, because they both use the Visual Basic Editor.)

Follow these steps to create a simple example of automating Microsoft Project from any Microsoft Office program:

1 Press Alt+F11 to start the Visual Basic Editor.

2 In the References dialog box, scroll through the Available References list, and then click the Microsoft Project 10.0 Object Library.

3 Create a new procedure and type the following code into it:

```
MSProject.Visible = True
MSProject.FileNew

MSProject.ActiveProject.Tasks.Add "task 1"
MSProject.ActiveProject.Tasks.Add "task 2"
MsgBox MSProject.ActiveProject.Tasks.Count

MSProject.Quit pjDoNotSave
```

An obvious difference from typing this code in Microsoft Project itself is the MSProject class, which represents the Microsoft Project Application object. In every other respect, though, writing code that uses members of the Microsoft Project object model in another application looks and "feels" just as it would in Microsoft Project.

Automating Without a Library Reference

Automating Microsoft Project when you can't directly link to the object model, such as when using Automation from a Web page or some similar environment, follows the same principles as when using a reference. It does, however, require more code and, more importantly, more research.

The additional code is necessary because the host application doesn't have the connection provided by the library reference. You must write code that creates a new *instance* of Microsoft Project as an object reference before you can use the members of the object model.

The additional research is necessary because the host application doesn't know anything about the Microsoft Project object model. This affects your code in two major ways:

- The code you're typing will essentially be treated like text (there's no link to the object model to verify members of objects or automatically list arguments for methods, for example), so you must be reasonably comfortable with the object model, or at least have easy access to information about it.

- You must use the numeric values of any constants defined in the Microsoft Project object model because the host application can't know what values the constants map to without an active reference to the object model. (In this situation, it's common to redefine the constants so your code is as readable as it would be if you did have a library reference.)

Follow these steps to create a simple example of automating Microsoft Project from any program that supports Visual Basic or Visual Basic Scripting edition (VBScript):

1 Define an object variable, and then use the CreateObject method from the Visual Basic (or VBScript) core object library to make a connection to Microsoft Project:

```
Dim Proj As Object

Set Proj = CreateObject("MSProject.Application")
```

> **note** This is an example of a *late-bound* object reference. For more information about late-binding, see Chapter 30, "Understanding the Visual Basic Language."

2 Enter the code that provides the functionality for your procedure, replacing "Application" (writing a procedure in Microsoft Project) or "MSProject" (Automation with a library reference) with the object variable defined in step 1:

```
Proj.Visible = True
Proj.FileNew

Proj.ActiveProject.Tasks.Add "task 1"
Proj.ActiveProject.Tasks.Add "task 2"
MsgBox Proj.ActiveProject.Tasks.Count
```

3 When entering the code for the Quit method, use the numeric value of the pjDoNotSave constant:

```
Proj.Quit 0
```

4 Discard the object variable's reference to Microsoft Project:

```
Set Proj = Nothing
```

---

tip   **Using the Visual Basic Editor**

If it is more convenient, you can enter this code in the Visual Basic Editor of any Microsoft Office program and it will behave just as it would in a Web page or the like. If you do use the Visual Basic Editor, make sure the project doesn't have a reference to the Microsoft Project library.

Working with Microsoft Project Data

Okay, so you're well-versed in using Microsoft Project to create projects, delegate tasks, set up resources and assignments, work with calendars, customize project fields and global settings, and more. What you might not know yet is how Microsoft Project keeps track of all this information, including where and how it is stored. You also might not know the ways in which you can view or use this information outside of Microsoft Project, like opening the database in Microsoft Access or displaying project details in a Data Access Page. This chapter introduces some key concepts about the project database, including the types of tables they include, the types of data contained in the database, and the different ways you can view data that is stored in the Microsoft Project database.

Microsoft Project data can be found in the following locations:

Microsoft Project database. This database is the primary storage location for Microsoft Project data. It is an integral part of any Microsoft Project file and it contains all of the data associated with a project. Data stored in this database can be accessed by opening any file that Microsoft Project can open (depending on the type of file, it might need to be converted to a Microsoft Project 2002 file), by opening a file from Microsoft Project Server, or by opening the project file in another application that can open the file, for example a Microsoft Project Database file opened in Microsoft Access. If you are using the enterprise features with Microsoft Project Professional, this database also stores enterprise project information.

Microsoft Project Server database.   The Microsoft Project Server database stores settings for Microsoft Project Web Access, including security settings, resource views, and enterprise project data. The entire database can be viewed by an authorized Microsoft SQL Server 2000 or Microsoft Data Engine (MSDE) 2000 user. Some settings stored in this database can be accessed by authorized users of Microsoft Project Web Access. Data and settings stored in this database can only be accessed by administrators with permission to access the database. Almost every other person who accesses data stored in this database will access it indirectly when using Microsoft Project Web Access, or when checking projects into or out of Microsoft Project Server.

> For more information about Microsoft Project Web Access, see Chapter 21, "Managing Your Team Using Project Web Access." For more information about working with the Microsoft Project enterprise setup, see Chapter 24, "Using Enterprise Features to Manage Projects."

OLE DB.   Object Linking and Embedding (OLE) is an object-based technology that can be used to share information by providing a uniform approach to how the data is stored and accessed between applications. OLE DB is a set of COM objects that provide database functionality by providing uniform access to data stored in an information container (a Microsoft Project file, for example). OLE DB allows you to access the data in the file (using an OLE DB Provider) much in the same way that you access data in a database. OLE DB provides many of the benefits of a database without requiring the existence of a database to use the data.

In this context, OLE DB is a provider of data, a Microsoft Project file contains the actual data, and Microsoft Access is a tool that you can use to access the data. This chapter is not an attempt to discuss comprehensive OLE DB solutions for Microsoft Project. This chapter is designed to show you one way you can easily access OLE data using Microsoft Access. See "Understanding Microsoft Project OLE DB Data" later in this chapter for more information about OLE DB and how to create a Data Access Page in Microsoft Access that uses the OLE DB Provider to connect to a Microsoft Project file. Once connected, you can access data in the Microsoft Project file in many of the same ways you can access data in a Microsoft Project database.

There are thousands of other ways you could use OLE technology with a Microsoft Project file. For example, you can use ActiveX Data Objects (ADO) to access specific fields in a Microsoft Project file using an OLE DB Provider.

> If you want to know more about OLE DB, see "Working with External References" on page 763. You can also visit *www.msdn.microsoft.com* (for starters, read "What OLE Is *Really* About"). If you need more information about working with Data Access Pages, see Microsoft Access Help.

Introducing Common Database Elements

A database is a collection of information broken into groups of data that have predefined relationships to each other. Each group of data, in turn, is a collection of specific details that is distinct from other groups of data; for example, task information is distinct from resource information. If you can imagine a project as a set of tasks, a set of resources, and a set of assignments, you're already on your way to understanding how the Microsoft Project database fits together.

All the databases used by Microsoft Project share some common elements, including general types of data that are stored in each database. All Microsoft Project databases contain information about the following:

Projects. Project tables link all related information (tasks, resources, assignments, and so on) to a specific project. Project tables also define unique information related to a particular project. In addition, project tables store some global settings like those found in the Options dialog box (Tools, Options) and the Properties dialog box (File, Properties).

Tasks. Task tables define all the fields and relationships in Microsoft Project that make up a task, like start times, finish times, durations, and assigned resources.

Resources. Resource tables define all the fields and relationships that make up a resource, like resource names, costs, amounts of work performed, and cost rate tables.

Assignments. Assignment tables link tasks and resources and other related information, in addition to defining unique information related to a particular assignment.

Calendars. Calendar tables contain all calendars used by projects, resources, tasks, or assignment availability in a project.

Custom Field Information. Each database has a different way of storing customized information. In general, you can create custom fields, including code, date, duration, flag, number, and text fields, for basic projects and enterprise projects.

Application Settings. Global settings, like those stored in the global template and enterprise global template, are stored in various tables in the database, usually project-related tables and in the case of the Microsoft Project Server database, a specific table that tracks administrative preferences.

Each of the databases has a number of unique tables. Some of these unique tables track data that can be accessed only from within that database: for example, the security and view tables in the Microsoft Project Server database. Some just track data in a different way than another database does; for example, the custom fields in the Microsoft Project Server database are separated out into their own individual tables but are included within the Task, Resource, Assignment, and Project tables in the OLE DB.

In addition to the types of information just described, the Microsoft Project database and Microsoft Project Server database also track the following information:

Internal Tables.   These tables store strings of data, for example, the words that appear in the user interface in Microsoft Project or Microsoft Project Web Access. Internal tables are also used by Microsoft Project to link information that is generally used behind the scenes in Microsoft Project.

Security Tables.   These tables are used to determine which users have access to Microsoft Project Web Access and which specific areas they can view. Security tables are also used to help determine whether a user can log on to Microsoft Project Server to check out a project.

Display Settings.   These settings are used in Microsoft Project Web Access to control the appearance of Gantt charts and other display elements. These settings are similar to those you can control with the Microsoft Project global template. The difference is that information stored in this database is modified using Microsoft Project Web Access. Note that the enterprise project global template is an actual project stored in the database. If you checked out the enterprise global template and made changes, you would be changing these display settings in the database.

Notifications and Reminders.   Microsoft Project Web Access has automated notifications and reminders that are tracked with unique tables in the Microsoft Project Server database.

Enterprise Views.   Microsoft Project Web Access can be used to create, store, and display project views. This is the administrative table that stores the settings used to create the views and a large number of dedicated view tables. In general, the type of information stored in these view tables is very similar to the type of information contained in the Microsoft Project OLE DB.

Storing Data in a Database

Information in a database is stored in a set of predefined tables, each made up of a set of predefined columns. A table can have an unlimited number of rows. Think of columns as all the individual components that make up a collection of data, also known as *fields*. Think of rows as a collection of data with a set of individual components, also known as *records*. For example, a task record is made up of the times, dates, assigned resources, and other fields. In a database, a task is the row of data. The times, dates, assigned resources, and other fields are represented by columns.

To view your project information as a Microsoft Project database, follow these steps:

1 Open any project that you have been working on, or create a simple project that has at least two tasks. If you create a simple project, give each task a different name, for example, Start and Finish (see Figure 32-1) and make sure that one of the tasks has an estimated duration and the other doesn't.

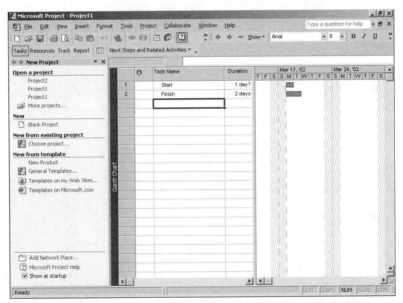

Figure 32-1. This project sample has two tasks: Start and Finish. The Start task has an estimated duration.

2 Save the project as a Microsoft Access Database. The Export Wizard will walk you through the steps. Be sure to select the A Full Project option on the wizard's second page (see Figure 32-2 on the next page).

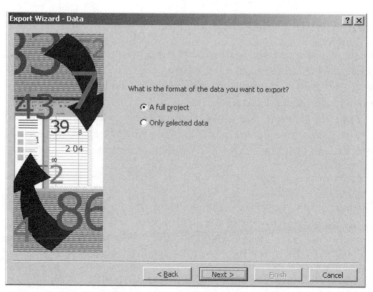

Figure 32-2. The Microsoft Project Export Wizard walks you through the process of exporting a project in a database format. Step 2 enables you to specify whether you want to export a full project or a part of one.

3 Start Microsoft Access, and open the project database you just saved (see Figure 32-3). If you don't see the database listed in the Open dialog box in Microsoft Access, be sure to select All Files (*.*) in the Files of Type box.

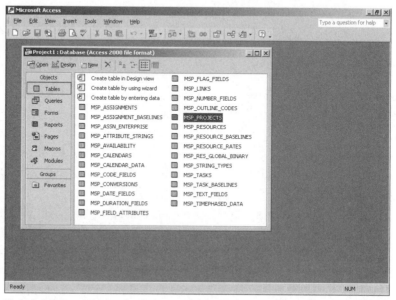

Figure 32-3. Microsoft Access automatically opens to the Database window displaying each table in the database.

4 Find the table marked MSP_TASKS, and double-click it to open the table (see Figure 32-4).

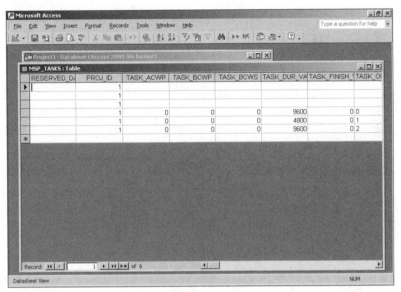

Figure 32-4. Columns in the MSP_TASKS table are the vertical divisions. Rows are the horizontal divisions. Every unique task in your project will have its own row in the MSP_TASKS table.

For more information about exporting Microsoft Project files to other applications such as Microsoft Access, see "Importing and Exporting Information" on page 441.

Notice that each column (scroll to the right to see all of them) has a different name, like TASK_NAME or TASK_DUR_IS_EST. Each separate task occupies a different row in the table. If you locate the TASK_NAME column, you should see the names of the tasks from your project. Find the TASK_DUR_IS_EST column. The task row with the estimated task duration should have a 0 value, and the other task should have a -1 value.

InsideOut

Using -1 and 0 in a database is a simple way to define an either/or situation. If a column contains data that can be either true or false, yes or no, or any other choice between two options, often the database will display a 1 or a 0, or a 0 or a -1, depending on how the database is set up. In this case, Microsoft Access displays 0 and -1 for either/ or values. The higher number represents the positive or true value, the lower number the negative or false value.

Notice also the TASK_UID column. This column assigns each task a unique ID number. No other task in the entire database can share this value. Obviously, a project with hundreds of assignments and resources and thousands of tasks will be a very large table in Microsoft Access. Giving a unique ID number to each row in each table in the database is the simplest way to keep everything organized. The unique ID number is also used to identify relationships in the database, for example, which tasks and resources are part of an assignment. If your database has dozens of projects, the unique ID number is used to identify which tasks and assignments are part of a specific project.

You can open any of the tables in the Microsoft Project database. You can also change information in your project plan and see it instantly reflected in the Microsoft Project database. To do this, follow these steps:

1 In the Project database opened in Microsoft Access, open the MSP_PROJECTS table (see Figure 32-5).

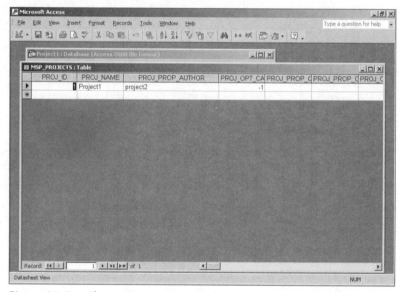

Figure 32-5. The MSP_PROJECTS table is used to store all project-related data.

2 Find the PROJ_PROP_AUTHOR column. Your name might be there, depending on how Microsoft Project is set up.

3 Go to Microsoft Project and make sure the same file is open.

4 Click File, Properties. Enter or modify your name in the Author field.

5 Save the project. If you had closed the project, you might need to use Save As and export the project again. In this case, be sure to replace this new exported file over the original.

6 Go back to Microsoft Access and close and then reopen the MSP_PROJECTS table to refresh it. The name you entered in step 4 should appear in the PROJ_PROP_AUTHOR field.

It might seem that you could change your name in this field, save it, and then have it appear in Microsoft Project. You can try this if you want to, but it doesn't work that way in this instance because the project saved as a Microsoft Access Database acts as a read-only data source, not a read/write data source; Microsoft Access provides read-only access to a Microsoft Project file saved as a database.

Measuring Data in the Database

A database is made up of lots of little pieces of data. In the case of Microsoft Project, there are task names, task durations, calendars, resource costs, and so on. Each of these pieces of data that has a column in a database table also has a *data type* associated with it. Data types are used to define the way the data is stored in the database. For example, a resource cost field needs to hold a number that might not be a whole number, so it needs a data type that allows a number like 20.50. A task name field needs to hold whatever name the project manager gives it, so this field needs to be able to accept normal text (alphanumeric) data, just like what is typed in this paragraph.

There are generalized types of data. Basically, four major areas are required: numbers, dates, text, and yes/no data. The OLE DB uses just these basic data types because it's a relatively simple database when compared to the Microsoft Project and Microsoft Project Server databases, which use more than four data types. For example, the OLE DB uses Number for all fields that store non-date numbers; in the Microsoft Project and Microsoft Project Server databases, numbers are represented by more specific data types like Int (integer, requires 4 bytes of storage), Decimal, Float (approximate numbers), Smallint (integer, requires 2 bytes of storage), or Tinyint (integer, requires 1 byte of storage), and so on.

A data type restricts the type of data allowed in that field in the database and helps keep the right data in the right place. The following sections describe general data types; specific data types are mentioned also.

Yes/No Data

The Yes/No data type is used when you must choose between two options. Examples include the following:

- True or False
- Yes or No
- Schedule From Start or Schedule From Finish

Fields in OLE DB use the Boolean data type to define this data. In the Microsoft Project and Microsoft Project Server databases, the fields that contain the same data are either Bit, Smallint, or Tinyint data types. These three data types are used to represent small amounts of data. Smallint can store integers ranging from -32,766 to 32,766. Tinyint can store integers ranging from 0 to 255. Bit stores either a 0 or a 1.

Dates and Times

Dates and times are stored in either Date (OLE DB) or Datetime (Microsoft Project and Microsoft Project Server databases) fields. They both display their data like this: mm/dd/yy hh:mm:ss AM/PM. For example: 06/01/02 12:00:00 AM for midnight, June 1, 2002.

> **note** If you want to see an example of this field, use Microsoft Access to take a look at the TASK_EARLY_FINISH field in the MSP_TASKS table.

Text Data

Text data is, quite simply, text, including letters and numbers. It can be the name of a project, a resource, or a task. It can be the text that describes an option in the user interface. In the OLE DB, Text is the data type that stores this data. In the Microsoft Project database, the data types Char, Varchar, and Text are used to store this data. In the Microsoft Project Server database, the data types Char, Nvarchar, and Text are used to store this data.

Typically, the Text data type allows the maximum number of characters (up to 2,147,483,647), whereas Char, Varchar, and Nvarchar have their maximum allowable characters defined in the database using (n) to define the maximum length. For example, the Project Name field cannot store more than 255 characters. In the Microsoft Project database, the data type for this field is Varchar(255).

Specific Values

This is information that contains a specific value that is predetermined by Microsoft Project. It could be an integer that represents a selection you have made in the user interface. It could be a single number or a large, seemingly random number that represents a duration or an amount of work.

InsideOut

If the field stores a duration value, it will store the duration as the result of a calculation: minutes x 10. For example, 10 hours would be stored as 10 hours x 60 minutes x 10, or 6000. A work value is stored as minutes x 1000. So 2 hours worked would store as 2 hours x 60 minutes x 1000, or 120,000.

In the OLE DB, the Number data type is used to represent these types of data. In the Microsoft Project Server database, the data types Decimal, Integer, Smallint, and Tinyint are used to represent these types of data.

In the Microsoft Project Server database, the data types Decimal, Float, Integer, Smallint, and Tinyint are used.

How the Microsoft Project Database Stores Values

If you want to see an example of how the Microsoft Project database stores specific values based on settings you choose in the user interface, do the following:

1 In Microsoft Project, open the project you've exported as the database.

2 Click Tools, Options.

3 On the View tab of the Options dialog box, change Decimal Digits to 1 and Placement to something other than the default.

4 Save this project as a Microsoft Access Database.

5 Open the project in Microsoft Access.

6 Open the MSP_PROJECTS table.

7 Find the PROJ_OPT_CURRENCY_DIGITS and PROJ_OPT_CURRENCY_ POSITION fields. Notice the values in the database. Notice the values in the View tab of the Options dialog box. In the case of PROJ_OPT_ CURRENCY_DIGITS, the value corresponds to the value shown in the Options dialog box (0, 1, or 2). In the case of PROJ_OPT_CURRENCY_ POSITION, the value is either 0, 1, 2, or 3, representing $1 (before), $1 (after), $ 1 (before, with space), or $ 1 (after, with space), with 0 being the first item available in the list.

Miscellaneous Data

There are some data types that store unique types of data. These data types are used sparingly. Image data types are used to store binary data in the Microsoft Project and Microsoft Project Server databases. There is also a Uniqueidentifier data type in the Microsoft Project Server database that tracks globally unique IDs.

Understanding Microsoft Project OLE DB Data

You can use the Microsoft Project 10.0 OLE DB Provider to access OLE data stored in a Microsoft Project file. Once connected, you can use this data across a wide variety of data sources, including relational databases, spreadsheets, and the Internet.

You can use Microsoft Access to take advantage of the capabilities of the OLE DB. After you use the Microsoft Project 10.0 OLE DB Provider to connect to a project file in Microsoft Access, you can use Microsoft Project data to create custom reports, break out specific pieces of data, and create Data Access Pages (DAP) reports that can be viewed through Microsoft Internet Explorer.

> For more information about Data Access Pages, see "Creating a Data Access Page Using Microsoft Access" later in this chapter.

Microsoft Project Server uses an OLE DB add-on called *OLE DB for Online Analytical Processing (OLAP)*. This allows Project Web Access to present data using Microsoft Office Web PivotTable and PivotChart reports. You can create your own PivotTable and PivotChart reports by connecting a Microsoft Access DAP to a Microsoft Project MPP file. If you want to create PivotTable or PivotChart reports frequently or have them automatically generated in a Microsoft Project environment, you should consider using the enterprise suite of applications for Microsoft Project (Microsoft Project Professional, Microsoft Project Server, and Microsoft Project Web Access).

> For more information about working with OLAP, see "Analyzing Multiple Projects using Project Portfolio" on page 580.
>
> There are many other ways to use OLE DB. For more information, see Microsoft Access XP and Microsoft Excel XP integrated help. You might also find *Microsoft OLE DB 2.0 Programmer's Guide and Software Development Kit* (published by Microsoft Press) helpful. Or visit *www.microsoft.com/data/oledb*.

Understanding OLE Database Tables

All the data you enter in your project plan can be exposed using the Microsoft Project 10.0 OLE DB Provider. The presentation of this data can vary, depending on the application you use to expose it, but it will always break out into a consistent grouping of data.

The following tables are exposed by the Microsoft Project 10.0 OLE DB Provider:

Assignments.   This table contains all assignment information in the project, including references to all related tasks and resources.

Availability.   This table stores the amount of time, start time, and end time for each time period that each resource is available to work. Each unique time period is stored as a separate row. For example, say a resource is available for 4 hours on Monday and all day Friday. In this case, there would be two rows for this resource, one for the time period on Monday and one for the time period on Friday. If the resource was only available for 2 hours in the morning and 2 hours at the end of the day on Monday, these two time periods would be broken into two separate rows as well.

Calendar.   These three tables store all calendar-related information, including the time periods the calendars cover, whether a calendar is a working calendar or a base calendar, and exceptions.

Cost Rates.   This table stores the costs associated with resources and assignments.

Custom Field tables.   These tables store date, duration, number, text, field, and flag information that has been customized. Some of this information is available only for enterprise projects.

Predecessors.   This table links tasks to their predecessor tasks, including the amount of lead or lag time, the duration of the lead or lag time, and whether the task is start-to-start, finish-to-start, start-to-finish, or finish-to-finish.

Project.   This table stores all project-related information, including project-level settings available in the Properties and Options dialog boxes.

Resources.   This table stores all information about each resource in the project.

Successors.   This table links tasks to their successor tasks, including the amount of lead or lag time, the duration of the lead or lag time, and whether the task relationship is start-to-start, finish-to-start, start-to-finish, or finish-to-finish.

Tasks.   This table stores all information about each task in the project.

Task Splits.   These tables track the start and finish dates for a task that has been split. There is also a separate table for baseline task splits.

newfeature!
Timephased tables.   These are 15 unique timephased tables, five each for assignments, resources, and tasks. Each table is broken down by minute, hour, day, week, and month.

Creating a Data Access Page Using Microsoft Access

A Data Access Page (DAP) can be created when you connect a project file as a data source to Microsoft Access. You can use the DAP to create dynamic Web page reports that can be viewed in Microsoft Internet Explorer.

> **note**   To create a DAP, you must be using Microsoft Project Standard or Microsoft Project Professional with Microsoft Access 2000 or later to create the data connection. To view the DAP in a browser, you need to use Microsoft Internet Explorer 5.0 or later.

To create a DAP, do the following:

1   Create a project with multiple tasks. Save it as a standard project.

2   Open Microsoft Access.

3   On the Standard toolbar, click New. Select Blank Data Access Page. The Select Data Source dialog box appears (see Figure 32-6).

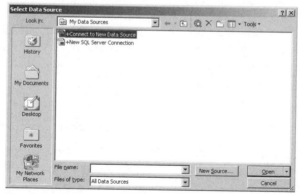

Figure 32-6.   Opening the Select Data Source dialog box is the first step in creating a Data Access Page. You can also open an existing Data Access Page from this dialog box by navigating to its location and clicking the Open button.

4 Click +Connect To New Data Source, and click the Open button. The Data Connection Wizard appears (see Figure 32-7).

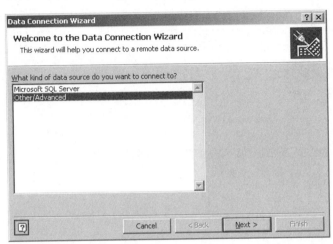

Figure 32-7. Always select Other/Advanced when creating a Data Access Page from a Microsoft Project MPP file.

5 Click Other/Advanced, and click the Next button. The Data Link Properties dialog box appears (see Figure 32-8).

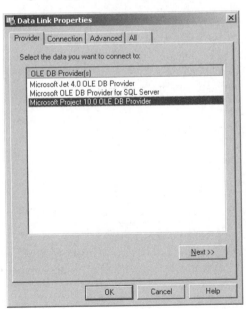

Figure 32-8. The Provider tab lists all available OLE DB providers in Microsoft Access.

6 On the Provider tab, click Microsoft Project 10.0 OLE DB Provider. You will not see this in the list if Microsoft Project is not installed on your local computer.

7 Click the All tab (see Figure 32-9). Select Project Name. Click Edit Value, and then enter the path name to the project file you want to connect the DAP to in the Edit Property Value dialog box (see Figure 32-10). Click OK.

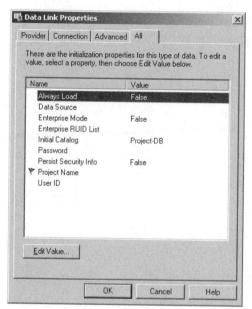

Figure 32-9. The All tab contains properties for the initial state of the Data Access Page when opened in Microsoft Access. If you are running Microsoft Project Professional, you can set Enterprise Mode to True to see all the enterprise fields.

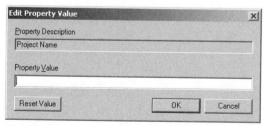

Figure 32-10. Enter the path to the Microsoft Project MPP file you want to open, for example C:\Documents and settings\Desktop\myproject.mpp.

8 Click OK to close the Data Link Properties dialog box. The Data Connection Wizard – Choose Data page appears (see Figure 32-11). Even though the wizard says you can choose the data you want, you shouldn't actually be able to choose anything but all the data.

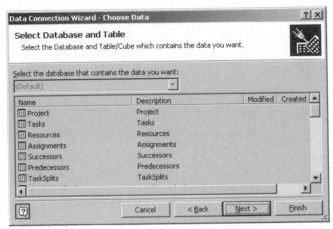

Figure 32-11. The Choose Data page of the Data Connection Wizard enables you to choose which pieces of data you want displayed in the Field List bar in Microsoft Access. You must choose all fields for a Microsoft Project Data Access Page.

9 Click the Next button. The Data Connection Wizard – Finish page appears (see Figure 32-12).

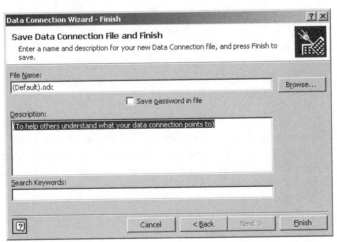

Figure 32-12. The Finish page gives you a chance to enter a description of the Data Access Page and provide keywords that you can later use to search for the file.

10 Enter the name of the DAP in the File Name field. Be sure to leave the ODC file extension. Click the Finish button. Microsoft Access will open the DAP in Design View (see Figure 32-13). This is the working environment for a DAP.

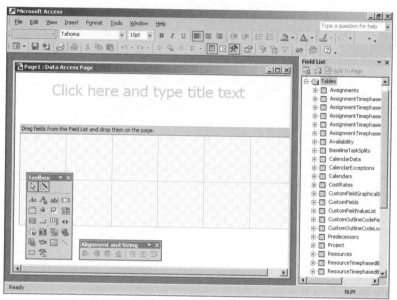

Figure 32-13. Design View has your workspace on the left. The list of fields appears in the Field List bar on the right.

One of the first things you notice in the DAP Design View is the Field List bar on the right. Click the Page Connection Properties button in the upper-left corner of the Field List bar to display the Connection tab of the Data Link Properties dialog box. The third box on this tab should display the path to the project file you entered in Step 8 of the previous procedure. Also in the Field List bar is a folder icon called Tables, and underneath that is a table for every table exposed by the Microsoft Project 10.0 OLE DB Provider.

Click the plus sign next to the Tasks table. You should now see all the fields in the Tasks table. Although it looks different from the MSP_TASKS table in Microsoft Access, much of the information is the same. The only significant difference is that custom field information for tasks is stored in the Tasks table and broken down into separate tables in the Microsoft Project database.

InsideOut

With all the earlier information about rows and columns, you might be a little surprised not to see any rows or columns here in the Field List. All the field names in each list, for example, TaskUniqueID in the Tasks table, represent every column in the table for each row. When you add a field to the DAP, all the rows become available.

newfeature!

The OLE DB Provider uses *friendly names*, which is another way of saying that the OLE DB Provider uses full English words to describe the data contained in the database. For example, the TaskName field contains the name of the task. In the Microsoft Project database, this field is called TASK_NAME. It's usually fairly easy to find the right tables based on their names.

What about the fields that represent the difference between a task's baseline duration and current duration, which is called a task's *duration variance*? In the field exposed by the OLE DB Provider, the field is named TaskDurationVariance, but in the Microsoft Project database, this field is TASK_DUR_VAR.

Fortunately, sensible abbreviations are used in the Microsoft Project database and they are generally intuitive. Even better, all field names exposed by the OLE DB Provider are spelled out even if they are very long: for example, TaskIgnoreResourceCalendar or CustomFieldGraphicalIndicator.

InsideOut

Field names in the Microsoft Project database can get difficult at times. For example RES_RTYPE is used to indicate whether a resource is a normal or generic, as well as whether the resource is active. How would you know?

Microsoft Project includes documentation for each database that goes over the details of every field in each database. These documents can be found on the Microsoft Project 2002 installation CD. Their titles are prjoledb.htm (OLE DB), projdb.htm (Microsoft Project database), and svrdb.htm (Microsoft Project Server database).

To add Microsoft Project field information to the DAP, do the following:

1 Drag each item that you created in your project file from the expanded Tasks table in the Field List bar to the shaded box under the gray bar that says "Drag Fields From The Field List And Drop Them On The Page." For example, all the tasks you've created have a TaskUniqueID, TaskName, and TaskStart, so drag those three fields (see Figure 32-14).

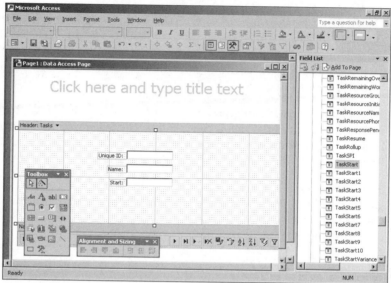

Figure 32-14. A Data Access Page with three elements from the Field List placed on it.

---

tip **Data Access Pages and Visual Basic**

If you've ever worked with Visual Basic, the layout and behavior of this page might seem familiar. If you haven't worked with Visual Basic, right-click any element in the DAP to access commands to change its style and appearance.

For example, right-click TaskUniqueID on the DAP. Click Element Properties for individual fields on the shortcut menu. You can change the background colors; border styles, sizes, and colors; fonts; and data source details.

For information about Visual Basic, see Chapter 30, "Understanding the Visual Basic Language."

---

2 The Layout Wizard will appear if you try to add an entire table, such as the Tasks table, to the DAP (see Figure 32-15). You can choose from Columnar, Tabular, PivotTable, PivotChart, or Office Spreadsheet.

> **note** As you add information to the DAP, Microsoft Access creates a Structured Query Language (SQL) query that controls the behind-the-scenes relationships for the DAP. If you add a field to the DAP that cannot automatically be assigned a SQL relationship, you will be asked to specify the relationship in the Relationship Wizard dialog box.

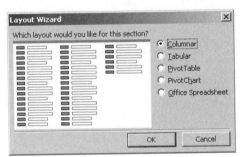

Figure 32-15. The Layout Wizard enables you to choose the way the data will be organized in the Data Access Page.

3 As you drag items, they will be placed on the DAP in the spot where you drop them. Microsoft Access automatically adds data controls for the fields. If you drag an entire table, this could take a few minutes.

4 When you are finished adding data to the DAP, click Save on the Standard toolbar to save the DAP. The Save As Data Access Page dialog box will appear (see Figure 32-16). Enter a name for the DAP, and then click the Save button.

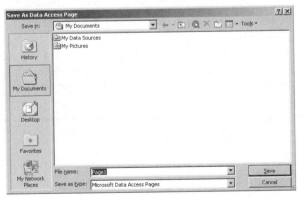

Figure 32-16. The Save As Data Access Page dialog box opens already set to save your file as a DAP.

5 Open Microsoft Internet Explorer. Open the HTML file with the name of the DAP you saved in Step 4. The DAP appears in Internet Explorer (see Figure 32-17).

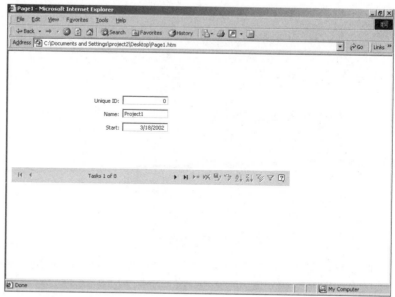

Figure 32-17. Use the navigation tools (left and right arrows) on the Data Access Page to scroll through the data.

6 Click the right and left arrows to browse through the information. Notice that the fields that you selected appear in the DAP.

---

tip **Updating your DAP**

When you create a DAP, you are connecting the project to the DAP as a data source. This means that this is an active, live link from the project to the DAP and if you save your project with new data and refresh the DAP, you will see the updated information in the DAP. To see this in action, go to your project file and add a couple of new tasks. Save the project. Go back to the DAP in Internet Explorer and refresh the page. You should see your new tasks in the DAP.

At this point, you should have a basic understanding of how to connect a project to a DAP using Microsoft Access. A DAP is a simple way to create dynamic reports for others to view outside of Microsoft Project. There are a number of options available to you that you can use to make them more useful and more sophisticated. Perhaps the best way to learn more about creating a DAP is simply to play around with creating them and see how they turn out. Repeat what you like and discontinue what you don't like.

> For more in-depth information about creating and working with a DAP, take a look at the Data Access Pages section of integrated Microsoft Access Help or *Microsoft Access Inside Out*, published by Microsoft Press.

Understanding the Microsoft Project Database

The Microsoft Project Database can be viewed in Microsoft Access or Microsoft Excel if you open a project file saved in the proper format. The Microsoft Project database, when viewed in either Microsoft Access or Microsoft Excel, has more tables than you would see in a project file that has been accessed using OLE DB. Nevertheless, whether you view project data through the Microsoft Project database or OLE DB, you're seeing almost exactly the same set of data.

If you open a project in Microsoft Access, you see a group of tables (see Figure 32-3, earlier in this chapter). The Microsoft Project database includes the following tables:

MSP_ASSIGNMENTS.   This table stores all assignment-related details. A separate table is used for summary assignments (called MSP_ASSN_ENTERPRISE). This is the same type of information stored in the Assignments table in the OLE DB.

MSP_AVAILABILITY.   This table stores the amount of time, the start time, and the end time for each time period that a resource is available to work. This is the same type of information stored in the Availability table in the OLE DB.

MSP_CALENDARS and MSP_CALENDAR_DATA.   These tables store all calendar-related information, including the time periods for the calendars, whether a calendar is a working calendar or a base calendar, and exceptions (see Figure 32-18 on the next page).

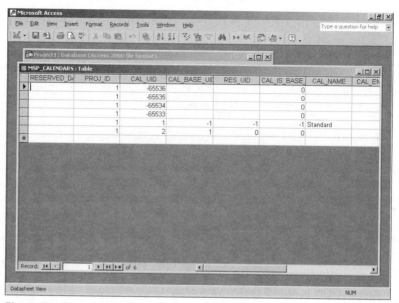

Figure 32-18. The MSP_CALENDARS table is used to store all calendar-related data.

MSP_n_FIELDS. These tables store custom field information related to dates, durations, flag, number, text, code, and more. Substitute CODE, DATE, DURATION, FLAG, NUMBER, or TEXT for the "n" in the table name. Some of this information is available only for enterprise projects.

MSP_n_BASELINES. These tables store baseline data related to assignments, resources, and tasks. Substitute ASSIGNMENT, RESOURCE, and TASK for "n" in the table name.

MSP_LINKS. This table stores predecessor and successor task information, including links to other enterprise projects. This is the same type of information that is stored in the Predecessor and Successor tables in the OLE DB.

MSP_OUTLINE_CODES. This table stores custom information related to outline codes. This is the same type of information that is available when you click Tools, Customize, Fields, and then click the Custom Outline Codes tab in the Customize Fields dialog box.

MSP_PROJECTS. This table stores data related to the project as a whole, including information set in the Properties and Options dialog boxes.

MSP_RESOURCES. This table stores all information about each resource in the project.

MSP_RESOURCE_RATES. This table stores the costs associated with each resource or assignment.

MSP_TASKS. This table stores all information about each task in the project.

MSP_TIMEPHASED_DATA. If you choose to expand timephased data in Microsoft Project (click Tools, Options, the Save tab in the Options dialog box, and select the Expand Timephased Data In The Database check box), the expanded timephased data is saved to this table.

To view the contents of any of the tables, just double-click the table you want to view.

Understanding the Microsoft Project Server Database

The Microsoft Project Server database is used to store data that helps enable collaboration between project managers and team members, manage Microsoft Project Web Access administrative settings, manage users and set their security privileges for accessing Microsoft Project Web Access and Microsoft Project Server, and store the data used to create project and resource view tables.

You can access information stored in the Microsoft Project Server database by connecting Microsoft Project Professional to Microsoft Project Server or by logging on to Microsoft Project Web Access.

For more information, see "Activating Enterprise Features" on page 819 in Appendix A or Chapter 21, "Managing Your Team Using Microsoft Project Web Access."

Once Microsoft Project Server is installed and running, its administration is done mainly through the Admin link in Microsoft Project Web Access. The project system administrator can create new users and groups of users, set permissions for users, create views, and manage the default settings for all users of Microsoft Project Web Access. If you are a general user and need to use certain administrative features of Microsoft Project Web Access, talk to your project system administrator about obtaining appropriate permissions.

If you would like to know more about the individual tables and fields in this database, see Svrdb.htm on the Microsoft Project 2002 installation CD.

Chapter 32

Part 11

Appendixes

Installing Microsoft Project 2002

Microsoft Project now has two editions: Microsoft Project Standard 2002 and Microsoft Project Professional 2002. This appendix includes procedures and guidelines for setting up Microsoft Project as a stand-alone desktop tool.

Microsoft Project 2002 includes two new server-based solutions. If you set up Microsoft Project Server with either edition, you can use the workgroup collaboration features of Microsoft Project Web Access.

If you set up Microsoft Project Server with Microsoft Project Professional, you can also use the enterprise features, which include enhanced project standardization, resource management, and project analysis across an entire organization. This appendix will explain some guidelines regarding the setup of Microsoft Project Server and Microsoft Project Web Access, and connecting Microsoft Project Professional to Microsoft Project Server. For specific Microsoft Project Server and Microsoft Project Web Access setup assistance, refer to the Pjsvr10.chm file that can be accessed from Microsoft Project Server Setup.

Installing Microsoft Project 2002

This section includes information and procedures for setting up Microsoft Project Standard 2002 or Microsoft Project Professional 2002 as a stand-alone desktop project management solution.

Microsoft Project System Requirements

Before you install Microsoft Project Standard 2002 or Microsoft Project Professional 2002, make sure your system meets the minimum requirements. The system requirements for a computer running Microsoft Project include:

- Intel Pentium 133 MHz (minimum) or higher processor. Intel Pentium III class processor (or better) is recommended.

- 48 MB of additional RAM beyond the requirements of your operating system (minimum). 192 MB of RAM is recommended for Microsoft Project Standard 2002. 256 MB of RAM is recommended for Microsoft Project Professional 2002.

- 55–310 MB of available hard disk space, depending on how many optional components are installed. A typical installation (the group of components installed if you do not select a custom or full installation) on a computer that does not have Microsoft Office XP installed requires 105 MB. A full installation (installing all available Microsoft Project files) on the same computer requires 310 MB. If Microsoft Office XP is already installed, only 55 MB is required for a typical installation. Users without Microsoft Windows 2000, Microsoft Windows Millennium Edition, Microsoft Office 2000 Service Release 1, Microsoft Office XP, or Microsoft Project 2000 will require an extra 50 MB of hard disk space for the system files update.

> **note** If you want to use workgroup project collaboration or enterprise project and resource management, you will need to connect Microsoft Project to Microsoft Project Server. See "Enterprise Setup Issues" later in this appendix for more information.

You can run Microsoft Project on any of the following operating systems:

- Microsoft Windows XP Professional (recommended)
- Microsoft Windows XP Home
- Microsoft Windows 2000 Professional
- Microsoft Windows NT 4.0 Service Pack 6.0 (or higher)
- Microsoft Windows Millennium Edition
- Microsoft Windows 98 Second Edition
- Microsoft Windows 98

Setting Up Microsoft Project for the First Time

To set up Microsoft Project on a computer where there is no previous version of Microsoft Project, follow these steps:

1 Close any other applications that are running.

2 Place the Microsoft Project CD in your computer's CD-ROM drive.

 If Microsoft Project Setup doesn't start automatically, click the Start button on the Windows taskbar, and then click Run. Type X:\setup.exe (where X is the name of your CD-ROM drive), and then click OK.

 After Microsoft Project Setup is running, continue through the following steps to complete installation.

> **note** If you are upgrading from a previous version of Microsoft Project, follow the steps detailed in "Upgrading To Microsoft Project," later in this appendix.

3 In the Microsoft Project Setup User Information window, enter your user information and the 25-character product key in the Product Key boxes (see Figure A-1). Click the Next button.

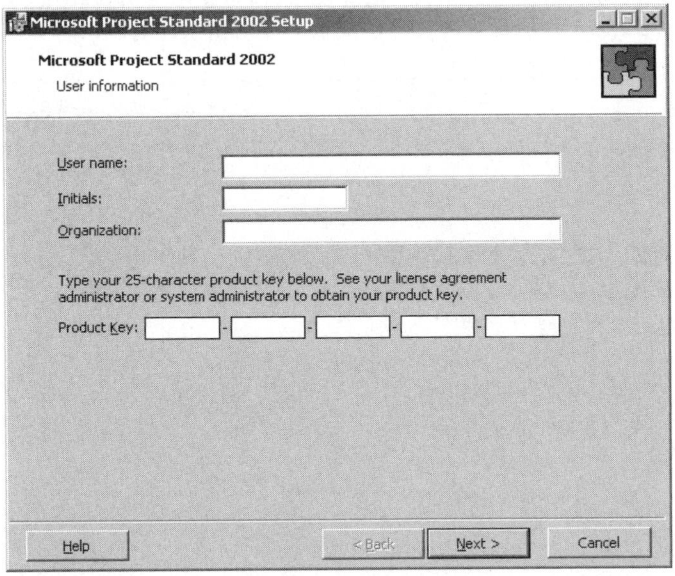

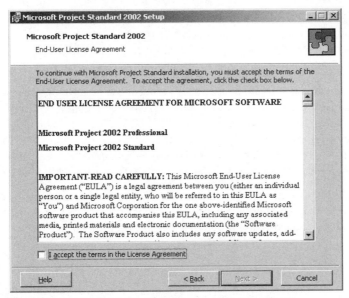

Figure A-1.   First, enter your user information.

4 In the End-User License Agreement window, review the agreement, and then select the I Accept The Terms In The License Agreement check box (see Figure A-2). Click the Next button.

Figure A-2.   Review the End-User License Agreement.

5 In the Choose The Type Of Installation You Need window, select the installation option you want: Install Now, Complete, or Custom (see Figure A-3). Select the Install Now option to install Microsoft Project Standard with the default settings and most commonly used components. Click the Next button. Skip to Step 7 if you selected either Install Now or Complete.

> **note** If this window says Upgrade Now, there's a previous version of Microsoft Project already installed on this computer. Refer to "Upgrading To Microsoft Project 2002" later in this appendix.

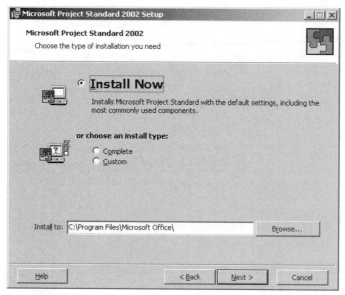

Figure A-3. Specify whether you want to install Microsoft Project with a default, custom, or complete installation.

6 If you choose a Custom installation, the Choose Installation Options For Microsoft Project Standard window appears (see Figure A-4). Click the plus or minus signs to expand or collapse the tree. Click the down arrow next to the component to change its installation status to Run From My Computer, Run All From My Computer, Install On First Use, or Not Available (which means the item is not installed—you can install it later). Click the Next button.

The hard disk space required by the customized installation of Microsoft Project is updated in the lower right corner of the Microsoft Project Setup window when you add or remove features from the installation.

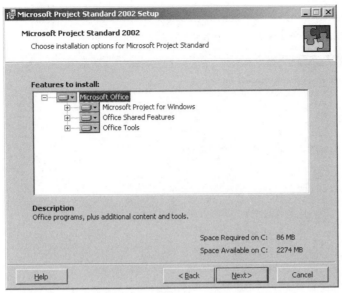

Figure A-4. Specify the installation status of a component by clicking the arrow next to the feature and clicking Run From My Computer, Run All From My Computer, Install On First Use, or Not Available.

7 The Begin Installation page of the Microsoft Project Setup dialog box appears (see Figure A-5). Click the Install button.

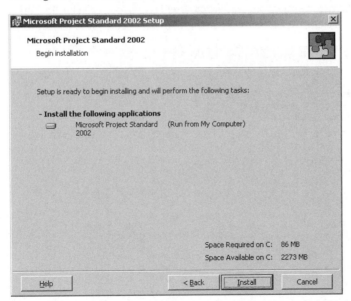

Figure A-5. Click the Install button when you are ready to install Microsoft Project.

The Now Installing Microsoft Project window appears (see Figure A-6). This window tracks the progress of the installation.

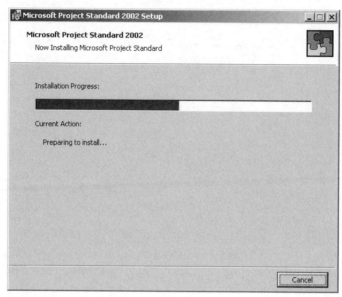

Figure A-6. The installation of Microsoft Project is shown in the progress bar.

When the installation is finished, you will be notified, as shown in the Microsoft Project message box (see Figure A-7). Click OK. You can now run Microsoft Project by clicking Start, Programs, Microsoft Project.

Figure A-7. Microsoft Project has been installed successfully.

Installation Options

You have five ways to install Microsoft Project: Install Now, Upgrade Now, Typical, Complete, and Custom. Any custom component can be added or removed later by placing your Microsoft Project CD-ROM into your CD drive and running Setup.exe. The five installation options do the following:

- **Install Now** installs all the files that are used most commonly by Microsoft Project.
- **Upgrade Now** is available if you have a previous version of Microsoft Project installed on your computer. You will have the option to keep the previous version or replace it when upgrading to Microsoft Project.
- **Typical** is only available if you have a previous version of Microsoft Project installed on your computer. Selecting Typical performs the same installation steps as choosing Install Now.
- **Complete** installs all files available to be installed, including components that are not normally used during the day-to-day use of Microsoft Project by the majority of users.
- **Custom** enables you to install components of Microsoft Project that are not normally installed by selecting from the following options: Run From My Computer, Run All From My Computer, Installed On First Use, and Not Available.

Components that are set to Run From My Computer with Install Now, Upgrade Now, or Typical include Microsoft Project Program Files and the following add-ins:

- Adjust Dates
- Analyze Timescaled Data
- PERT Analysis
- Help For Microsoft Project
- Microsoft Project Templates
- System Information
- Spelling Checker
- Office Assistant (Clippit only)
- Web Publishing
- Core Files For International Support
- Find Fast Control Panel

Components that are set to Installed On First Use with Install Now, Upgrade Now, or Typical include:

- Digital Signature
- Language Settings tool
- Seven additional Office Assistant characters
- Help for Visual Basic for Applications
- Remaining International Support files

Components that are set to Not Available with Install Now, Upgrade Now, or Typical include:

- Extended international support files
- Universal font (an Arial Unicode MS font that contains all the characters, ideographs, and symbols defined in the Unicode 2.1 standard)

Upgrading from a Previous Version of Microsoft Project

How is upgrading from a previous version of Microsoft Project different from a clean installation? If you choose to replace your old version of Microsoft Project when upgrading to Microsoft Project 2002, you might not be able to open project files created in versions of Microsoft Project earlier than Microsoft Project 2000 because the database in Microsoft Project 2002 has been enhanced and expanded with new fields and details. This means that older versions of Microsoft Project will not be able to read a file created in Microsoft Project 2002. Files created in Microsoft Project 2000 can be opened in Microsoft Project 2002 because the databases are compatible; files created in versions of Microsoft Project earlier than Microsoft Project 2000 must be saved as an MPD file format before you can open them in Microsoft Project 2002.

For more information about saving a project file as an MPD file format, see "Saving and Opening with Different File Formats" on page 696.

If you have a previous version of Microsoft Project installed on your computer when you run Microsoft Project 2002 Setup, you will have some choices that are different than the steps described in "Installing Microsoft Project Standard."

To upgrade an older version of Microsoft Project to Microsoft Project 2002, run Microsoft Project 2002 Setup. Be sure to close down any other applications that you might have running. Place the Microsoft Project 2002 CD in your computer's CD-ROM drive. If Microsoft Project 2002 Setup doesn't start automatically, open the contents of the CD-ROM and double-click Setup.exe. After Microsoft Project 2002 Setup is running, continue through the following steps to complete installation:

1 Steps 1 and 2 of the upgrade process are identical to Steps 1 and 2 of the install process described in the section "Installing Microsoft Project 2002," earlier in this appendix.

   The Choose The Type Of Installation You Need page of the Microsoft Project Setup Wizard appears (see Figure A-8). You have four installation options: Upgrade Now, Typical, Complete, and Custom.

2 Select the Upgrade Now option to upgrade your older version of Microsoft Project to Microsoft Project 2002. If you select the Upgrade Now option, Microsoft Project Setup removes your previous version and installs Microsoft Project 2002.

   If you would like to keep your previous version of Microsoft Project, select the Typical, Custom, or Complete option. A Typical installation installs Microsoft Project 2002 with all the default components. The Custom option enables you to select which components you want installed. The Complete option installs all components. See the section called "Installation Options" earlier in this appendix for more information about these options.

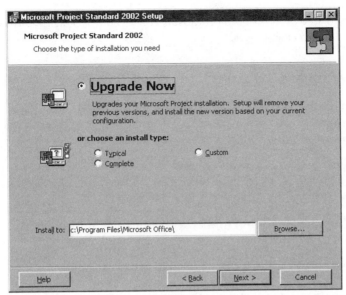

Figure A-8. Upgrade your version of Microsoft Project to Microsoft Project 2002.

3 The Remove Previous Versions Of Microsoft Project page appears (see Figure A-9). Select Remove Previous Version or Keep Previous Version. Click the Next button.

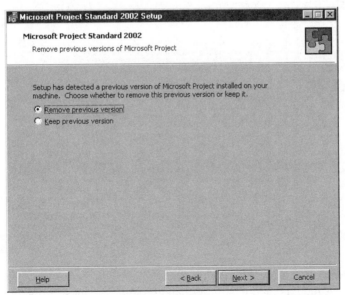

Figure A-9. If you have a previous version of Microsoft Project, you can keep or replace it.

4 Go to step 5 of "Installing Microsoft Project 2002" earlier in this appendix for the remaining steps.

Activating Microsoft Project

Microsoft Project will run in Reduced Functionality Mode until it is activated. The Microsoft Project Activation Wizard will run the first time you run Microsoft Project, and it will guide you through the activation process.

Several functions of Microsoft Project are unavailable when running in Reduced Functionality Mode, including creating new projects, saving projects, printing projects, changing settings in the global template, and more.

You can activate Microsoft Project over the Internet or by phone. If you choose to activate by the phone, the activation process could take longer.

To activate Microsoft Project using the Internet, do the following:

1 Start Microsoft Project. The Microsoft Project Activation Wizard will appear if you have not yet activated Microsoft Project.

2 On the Welcome page of the Microsoft Project Activation Wizard, select either Activate By Using The Internet or Activate By Using The Telephone (see Figure A-10). Click the Next button.

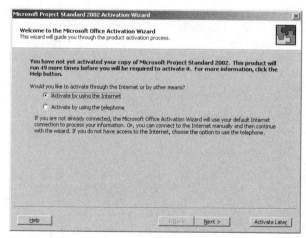

Figure A-10. You can activate Microsoft Project over the Internet or by telephone.

3 Review the Microsoft Office Privacy Policy. This policy tells you what information is required and what information is optional (most of the information is optional). Click the Next button.

4 Enter your information in the Customer Information page. Note that only the country you live in is required. You can register your copy of Microsoft Project by entering the remaining information on this page. Click the Next button.

5 In the Special Offers page, indicate if you would like to receive notifications of product updates or special offers. These are initially set to No. If you want to receive a specific update, you must select a box and enter your e-mail address. Click the Submit button.

6 When the Activation Complete page is visible, you are almost finished. Click the Finish button. You might be asked to restart your computer. Click Yes to restart your computer.

Running Maintenance Mode

After Microsoft Project has been installed successfully, you can add or remove optional features, perform repairs, or uninstall the entire application using Maintenance Mode. To use Maintenance Mode, place your Microsoft Project CD-ROM in your CD-ROM drive to run Microsoft Project Setup. The Maintenance Mode Options window appears (see Figure A-11).

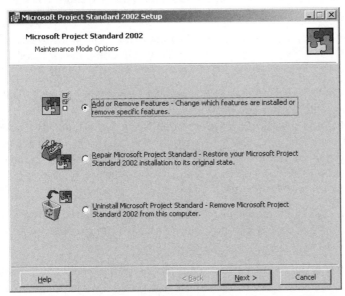

Figure A-11. In the Maintenance Mode Options window, you can add or remove features, and repair or uninstall Microsoft Project.

You can now add or remove features, make repairs, or uninstall Microsoft Project by selecting one of the following options:

- Add Or Remove Features
- Repair Microsoft Project
- Uninstall Microsoft Project

The following sections detail each of these options.

Adding or Removing Features

To add or remove features of Microsoft Project do the following:

1 Place your Microsoft Project CD-ROM in your computer's CD-ROM drive. The Maintenance Mode Options window appears. If this window does not automatically appear, browse to your Microsoft Project CD-ROM and run setup.exe.

2 Select Add Or Remove Features.

3 Click the Next button. The Installation Options For Microsoft Project dialog box appears.

4 To add a feature, click the arrow next to the feature you want to add, and change Not Available to either Run From My Computer or Installed On First Use.

Installed On First Use will make the feature available, and you will be able to run this feature from Microsoft Project at a later date. You might be required to insert the Microsoft Project CD-ROM or access the network drive from which you originally installed Microsoft Project to use the added feature. Because of this, you should only select the Installed On First Use option if you will have access to the Microsoft Project CD-ROM or network location at the time you run this feature.

Run From My Computer will install the feature on your computer's hard disk. You will not be asked to provide the Microsoft Project CD-ROM when you first run this feature.

5 To remove a feature, click the arrow next to the feature you want to remove and change the Run From My Computer or Installed On First Use setting to Not Available. Click the features you want to add or remove, and click the Update button. Microsoft Project Setup will perform the actions you indicated. Setting a feature to Not Available will remove the feature entirely. You will not be able to use this feature until you add it using the steps described earlier.

Repairing Microsoft Project

Occasionally, you might notice that Microsoft Project isn't running as well as it should. This can be caused by many factors, including frequently installing or uninstalling software or continuously using an application.

You can repair your Microsoft Project installation by running Maintenance Mode and selecting the Repair Microsoft Project option. To repair your copy of Microsoft Project, do the following:

1 Place your Microsoft Project CD-ROM in your computer's CD-ROM drive. The Maintenance Mode Options window appears. If this window does not automatically appear, browse to your Microsoft Project CD-ROM and run setup.exe.

2 Select Repair Microsoft Project.

3 Click Next. The Reinstall Or Repair Microsoft Project Installation window appears (see Figure A-12).

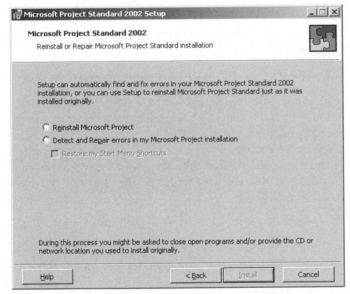

Figure A-12. Choose whether to reinstall Microsoft Project or to detect and repair errors.

4 Select Reinstall Microsoft Project to restore your copy of Microsoft Project to its original settings.

5 Select Detect And Repair Errors In My Microsoft Project Installation to search for the source of the problems you might be experiencing with your current installation of Microsoft Project.

6 Click Install to restore your copy of Microsoft Project to its original settings or to detect and repair errors.

Uninstalling Microsoft Project

You can use Maintenance Mode to uninstall Microsoft Project from your computer. To uninstall Microsoft Project, do the following:

1 Place your Microsoft Project CD-ROM in your computer's CD-ROM drive. The Maintenance Mode Options window appears. If this window does not automatically appear, browse to your Microsoft Project CD-ROM and run setup.exe.

2 Select Uninstall Microsoft Project.

3 Click the Next button.

Troubleshooting

Your computer doesn't have the correct version of Microsoft Windows Installer

If your computer does not have the version of Microsoft Windows Installer required by Microsoft Project 2002, you might receive an error message during installation. The error message might be identified with the number "2355" or with text that says "Corrupt Cabinet." If you receive an error message with either of these indicators and are running Microsoft Windows 98, Microsoft Windows Millennium Edition, or Microsoft Windows NT 4.0, you need to update the version of Microsoft Windows Installer on your computer.

To update the version of Microsoft Windows Installer, do the following:

1 Insert your Microsoft Project CD-ROM into your CD-ROM drive.

2 Open the Files folder and the Support folder, and then find the INSTMSI.exe file.

3 Double-click the INSTMSI.exe file to run it. This updates your version of Microsoft Windows Installer.

4 When the update is finished, restart your computer.

5 Run Microsoft Project Setup.

4   Click Yes to uninstall Microsoft Project or No to cancel (see Figure A-13).

Figure A-13.   Click Yes to uninstall Microsoft Project.

Working with an Administrative Installation Point

If you need to make Microsoft Project available for installation by multiple users on a network, consider creating an administrative installation point. This provides any user who needs to install a copy of Microsoft Project with a way to install it by finding the location on the network and running Setup.exe.

Creating an Administrative Installation Point

To create an administrative installation point, do the following:

1   Click Start, Run.

2   Enter your CD-ROM drive letter.

3   Type Setup.exe.

4   Enter /a.

For example, if your CD-ROM drive letter is D, the line you would enter to create an administrative installation point would be d:\setup.exe /a. You will then specify the location to use as an administrative installation point. Anyone who runs Setup.exe from the administrative installation point will be able to install Microsoft Project.

This feature is only available for versions of Microsoft Project that have one of the following MSI files in the root directory of the CD-ROM:

● prjstde

● prjproe

Adding Your Company Name to the Default Installation

You can add your company's name to the Microsoft Project Setup program in an administrative installation point by adding COMPANYNAME="xx" (where "xx" is your company's name, including the quotation marks) to the command line when creating an administrative installation point. For example:

```
D:\Setup.exe /a COMPANYNAME="Microsoft"
```

> **note** There are many command line options available in Microsoft Project Setup. For a complete list, see Prjsetup.htm, included on the Microsoft Project 2002 installation CD or in the Microsoft Project Resource Kit at *http://www.microsoft.com/office /project/prk/2000*.

Microsoft Project Server Setup Issues

If you want to store projects in a database, use Microsoft Project Web Access, or take advantage of enterprise features, you need to install Microsoft Project Server. To properly install Microsoft Project Server, you should have a solid working knowledge of Microsoft SQL Server 2000 and know how to configure your computer as an administrator.

The Microsoft Project Server CD-ROM includes a Help file called Pjsvr10.chm. If you need to install Microsoft Project Server and its associated applications, you should read through this file very carefully and take good notes of all information you enter during the installation, like Microsoft SharePoint Team Services database information, user names, and so on, so that you will have this information handy for later. In addition, take a look at the Readme.htm file on the Microsoft Project Server CD-ROM and the Readme.htm file on the Microsoft Project Professional 2002 CD-ROM before installing Microsoft Project Server.

Microsoft Project Server provides timesheet, reporting, collaboration, and analysis tools, and stores this information in a database that includes global settings for Microsoft Project Web Access and Microsoft Project. Microsoft Project Server is protected by a security layer that restricts access to only those authorized to send and receive data from the database. Most users will either connect to Microsoft Project Server directly through Microsoft Project 2002 or by using Microsoft Project Web Access.

> For additional information about configuring Microsoft Project Server and Microsoft Project Professional after you have installed both applications, see "Activating Enterprise Features" later in this appendix.

The following applications are used along with Microsoft Project Server:

Microsoft Project Web Access.   This is required for online workgroup project collaboration. Microsoft Project Web Access provides a Web interface to information stored in Microsoft Project Server. Users log onto Microsoft Project Web Access with a user name and password that is stored in Microsoft Project Server. There are different permission levels.

Team members can work with their individual assigned task information and view overall project information. Resource managers and team leads can maintain resource information and delegate tasks. Managing stake-holders can view overall project information. Administrators can set up and modify Microsoft Project Server user accounts and settings.

For more information about using Microsoft Project Web Access, see Chapter 21, "Managing Your Team Using Microsoft Project Web Access."

Microsoft SharePoint Team Services. This enables the document library and issues tracking features of Microsoft Project Server and Web Access. Documents and issues can be accessed from the Documents and Issues pages in Microsoft Project Web Access. This information is stored in a different database from Microsoft Project Server and can be managed from within the Admin area of Microsoft Project Web Access.

Microsoft SQL Server 2000. This is the database application commonly used with the Microsoft Project Server database (you can also use Microsoft Data Engine). All the database tables and stored procedures used by Microsoft Project Server are stored here. Some users of Microsoft Project data will need permission to create, update, or modify data stored in a database stored in Microsoft SQL Server 2000. For more information about the contents of the database, see Svrdb.htm, located on the Microsoft Project 2002 installation CD.

Microsoft SQL Server Analysis Services. This must be installed in order to use the enterprise Portfolio Analyzer features of Microsoft Project Professional. Microsoft SQL Analysis Services must have the same Service Pack updates as those installed for Microsoft SQL Server 2000.

For more information about using Portfolio Analyzer, see "Analyzing Multiple Projects Using Project Portfolio" on page 580.

Microsoft Office Web Components (OWC). This is required to use the View features of Microsoft Project Web Access. If the user's computer doesn't have OWC already installed, Microsoft Project will install a version of OWC that will enable any user of Microsoft Project to use the View features in Microsoft Project Web Access. OWC is already available for users who have Microsoft Office 2000 or Microsoft Office XP installed on their computer. If you want to create or modify a view, a fully licensed version of Microsoft Office XP is required.

Microsoft Project Server System Requirements

The following are the system and feature requirements for Microsoft Project Server. Note that these requirements do not include requirements for Microsoft Internet Information Server, Microsoft SQL Server 2000, Microsoft Active Directory, or Microsoft SharePoint Team Services (including subweb and database requirements):

- Intel Pentium 500 MHz (minimum) or higher processor. Intel Pentium 700 MHz or higher is recommended.

- 128 MB RAM (minimum). 512 MB RAM or higher is recommended.

- 70 MB or more hard disk space.

- Microsoft Windows 2000 Server Service Pack 1 or higher. Microsoft Internet Information Server (IIS) version 5.0 and the Microsoft Management Console (MMC) snap-in for IIS must be installed.

Making Decisions about Your Microsoft Project Server Setup

Before your system administrator sets up Microsoft Project Server, you need to make a few decisions. Your administrator will need to know the following:

- How many people do you expect to use Microsoft Project Server and Microsoft Project Web Access?

- Will users be able to use Microsoft Project Server authentication, Microsoft Windows NT authentication, or both?

- Will users from outside your corporate intranet require access to Microsoft Project Web Access or Microsoft Project Server?

- Are you going to be using Microsoft Project Web Access for team collaboration?

- Are you going to be using the Document Library and Issues Tracker as part of your Microsoft Project Web Access setup?

- Are you and your team members going to use Data Access Pages through Microsoft Project Web Access?

- What are the user names and passwords for your team members and other users of Microsoft Project Web Access?

- What is the user ID that you'll be using to log on to Microsoft Project Server?

- Are you going to be using enterprise features?

- How often do you want to build or update OLAP cubes?

- If you're using enterprise features, do you want to set up Analysis Services for the Portfolio Modeler feature?

Advanced Resources for Microsoft Project

The Microsoft Project Resource Kit is an online resource that contains information about installing, configuring, and supporting Microsoft Project in a large organization. If you are a system administrator, consultant, Microsoft Certified Solutions Provider (MCSP), or an advanced user, you should take a look at the Microsoft Project Resource Kit for advanced topics like setting up Microsoft Project on a terminal server or customizing calls to the Portfolio Data Service (PDS) security layer in Microsoft Project Server.

The Microsoft Project 2002 Project Resource Kit is available at
http://www.microsoft.com/office/project/prk/

Microsoft Project Web Access Setup Issues

Microsoft Project Web Access can be administered by any user who can log on with Administrator privileges. Users with administrative privileges can select the Admin tab and access the following major administrative areas:

Manage Users And Groups. Enables you to add, modify, or deactivate individual user accounts and to create, modify, or delete groups of users.

Manage Security. Enables you to manage security-related aspects of Microsoft Project Web Access.

Manage Views. Enables you to create new project and resource views for users to view project and resource data.

Manage Organization. Enables you to create categories of users to apply permissions to: for example, administrators, project managers, or team members.

Manage SharePoint Team Services.   Enables you to manage the servers running Microsoft SharePoint Team Services. These servers store the content that can be viewed in the Documents and Issues sections of Microsoft Project Web Access.

Manage Enterprise Features.   Enables you to manage enterprise-related features of Microsoft Project Web Access and Microsoft Project Professional. Enterprise features must be enabled in Microsoft Project Web Access for users to perform enterprise-related activities in either Microsoft Project Web Access or Microsoft Project Professional.

Customize Microsoft Project Web Access.   Enables you to set preferences for certain areas of Microsoft Project Web Access, add links or content to your Microsoft Project Web Access Home page, and more.

Manage Licenses.   Enables you to track the number of Microsoft Project Web Access users in your organization and compare this to the number of licenses your organization currently has.

Clean Up Microsoft Project Server Database.   Enables you to inactivate user records from the database that are no longer needed.

> **note**   If you need assistance while using Microsoft Project Web Access, click Help in the top right of the browser window to open Microsoft Project Web Access Help. The Help pane appears on the right side of the Microsoft Project Web Access browser window.

Microsoft Project Web Access System Requirements

To use Microsoft Project Web Access, you need Microsoft Project Server set up in conjunction with Microsoft Project Standard or Microsoft Project Professional. In addition, to use specific Microsoft Project Web Access features, you need the following components installed with Microsoft Project Server:

- SharePoint Team Services from Microsoft. This is required if your team is going to be using the Documents Library and Issues Tracking features. SharePoint Team Services is included with Microsoft Project Server.

- Microsoft Office Web Components (OWC)

- Microsoft Internet Explorer, version 5.0 or higher

- 5-15 MB of available hard disk space

Creating New Users in Microsoft Project Web Access

All users of Microsoft Project Web Access or enterprise features must have a user account created in Microsoft Project Web Access. To create a new user account in Microsoft Project Web Access, do the following:

1 Log on to Microsoft Project Web Access.

2 Click Admin to access the Microsoft Project Web Access administrative features. Only users with Administrator privileges will be able to access this section of Microsoft Project Web Access.

3 Click Manage Users And Groups.

4 Click Add User. The Add User page in Microsoft Project Web Access appears (see Figure A-14).

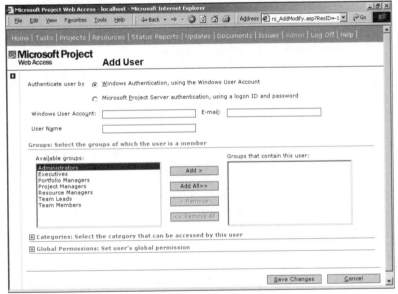

Figure A-14. To create a new user account, you must enter the information in the Add User page in Microsoft Project Web Access.

5 If you choose Windows Authentication, complete the Windows User Account, User Name, and E-mail fields. If you choose Microsoft Project Server Authentication, enter the User Name, Company E-mail Address, and Password. Note that you might not need to enter a company e-mail address if you have already entered this information in the Notifications And Reminders section of Microsoft Project Web Access.

6 Next you need to choose the groups, categories, and global permissions that will be associated with the user. Each group and category has a specific set of permissions associated with it. Global permissions can be set individually or by using a template. To set permissions with a template, select a template from the list (see Figure A-15), and then click the Set Permissions With Template button (see Figure A-16).

Administrator	▼
Administrator	
Executive	
Portfolio Manager	
Project Manager	
Resource Manager	
Team Lead	
Team Member	

Figure A-15. Select a template from the list.

Permissions	Allow	Deny
Edit Enterprise Resource Data	☐	☐
Open Project	☐	☐
Save Project	☐	☐
See Enterprise Resource Data	☐	☐
See Projects in Project Center	☐	☐
See Projects in Project Views	☐	☐
See Resource Assignments in Assignment Views	☐	☐
View Documents and Issues	☐	☐

Set Permissions with Template	Administrator ▼

Figure A-16. After you have selected a template, click the Set Permissions With Template button.

After you set up the user accounts, team members just need to use Internet Explorer to go to the designated URL for the Microsoft Project Web Access location, and then enter a valid user name and password.

Microsoft Project Web Access Permissions

Microsoft Project Web Access has dozens of different permissions. Each permission can be set to Allow or Deny at several levels: user, group, template, organization, or category. If a user has a permission set to Deny at any level, this permission will be set to Deny for all levels, even if it is set to Allow somewhere else. For example, if Create Accounts When Delegating Tasks is set to Allow as part of a user's organization, but this permission is set to Deny at an individual user level, this user will never be allowed to create user accounts when delegating tasks to resources.

For more information about permissions and Microsoft Project Web Access, see the topic "Understanding Microsoft Project Web Access Permissions" in the Admin section of Microsoft Project Web Access Help.

Before assigning groups, categories, and permissions to users, spend some time familiarizing yourself with their capabilities. If you aren't sure which permission, category, or global permission to choose, consider using the default settings provided in Microsoft Project Web Access. You can access Microsoft Project Web Access Help at any time by clicking Help in the top right corner of the browser window.

Enterprise Setup Issues

With the enterprise features of Microsoft Project Professional, you have access to powerful standardization, customization, resource management, and executive analysis capabilities across an entire organization.

Enterprise System Requirements

To be able to use enterprise features in Microsoft Project Professional, you need to have Microsoft Project Professional and Microsoft Project Server set up. In addition, you need the following additional components:

- Microsoft SQL Server 2000 Service Pack 1 or later, or Microsoft Desktop Engine (MSDE) 2000 or later. This must be installed before installing Microsoft Project Server.

- Microsoft SQL Server Analysis Services. This is required for the enterprise Portfolio Analyzer feature.

Activating Enterprise Features

After you have Microsoft Project Professional and Microsoft Project Server set up, along with all user names and passwords, you have the pieces in place to activate the enterprise features.

---

tip   **Create Microsoft Project Server accounts first**

All user names and passwords must first exist in Microsoft Project Server before they can be used to connect Microsoft Project Professional 2002 to Microsoft Project Server. To learn more about creating user names and passwords, see the section "Creating New Users In Microsoft Project Web Access" earlier in this appendix.

To connect Microsoft Project Professional to Microsoft Project Server, follow these steps:

1 Click Tools, Enterprise Options, Microsoft Project Server Accounts. The Microsoft Project Server Accounts dialog box appears (see Figure A-17).

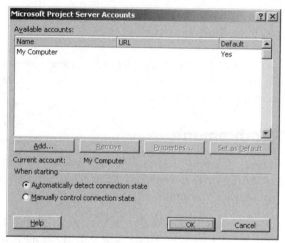

Figure A-17. Use the Microsoft Project Server Accounts dialog box to add, remove, and maintain the settings used to connect to Microsoft Project Server.

2 Click the Add button. The Account Properties dialog box appears (see Figure A-18).

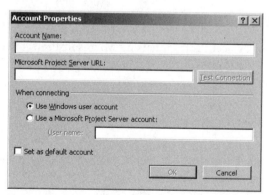

Figure A-18. In the Account Properties dialog box you can enter the account name, type of account, and the URL needed to connect to Microsoft Project Server.

3 Complete the Account Name and Microsoft Project Server URL text boxes.

4 Click Test Connection to verify whether or not you have connected successfully to Microsoft Project Server. If the connection is successful, you will be notified with a message box (see Figure A-19).

Figure A-19. This message box appears when you have successfully tested a connection to Microsoft Project Server.

5 If the connection is not successful, a message box notifies you that the URL is incorrect (see Figure A-20). If you receive an error message, check the URL or ask your administrator for the correct URL for the server to which you want to connect.

Figure A-20. If you receive an error message, check with your administrator to get the correct URL for Microsoft Project Server.

6 In the Account Properties dialog box, specify whether you want to use a Windows user account name or a Microsoft Project Server account name to access Microsoft Project Server. Regardless of the type of account name, it must be registered on Microsoft Project Server before you can use it to connect to Microsoft Project Server from Microsoft Project Professional 2002.

7 Indicate whether you want to use this connection and logon setup as the default account. If you choose this option, Microsoft Project Professional 2002 will automatically connect to Microsoft Project Server using the information specified in steps 4 and 6. If this computer is a shared network computer, you might want to consider not using an automatic method unless the user name and the associated permissions are appropriate for multiple users.

8 Click OK to return to the Microsoft Project Server Accounts dialog box.

9 In the Microsoft Project Server Accounts dialog box, indicate whether you want to automatically detect the connection state or manually control the connection state. If you choose Automatically Detect Connection State, Microsoft Project Professional 2002 will automatically connect to Microsoft Project Server using the specified default account shown in Available Accounts. If you choose Manually Control Connection State, users of this computer will be presented with the Microsoft Project Server Accounts dialog box (see Figure A-21 on the next page). Click Connect to connect to Microsoft Project Server using the highlighted user account, or click Work Offline to open Microsoft Project Professional without connecting to Microsoft Project Server.

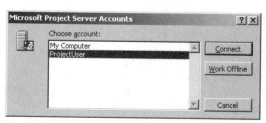

Figure A-21. Connect to Microsoft Project Server or work offline.

10 When you are finished, exit Microsoft Project Professional 2002 and then restart.

When you restart Microsoft Project Professional 2002, you will need to add the Microsoft Project Server URL as a trusted site in Internet Explorer. If the URL is not listed as a trusted site, when you restart Microsoft Project, the Microsoft Project Server Security Login dialog box appears. Follow these steps to make the URL a trusted site in Internet Explorer:

1 In the Microsoft Project Server Security Login dialog box, click Make Server Trusted (see Figure A-22). The Microsoft Project Server URL is added to the list of trusted sites in Internet Explorer.

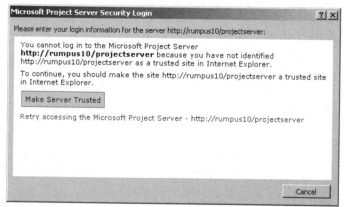

Figure A-22. The URL for Microsoft Project Server must be listed as a trusted site in Microsoft Internet Explorer. You will receive this dialog box when the Microsoft Project Server URL is not listed as a trusted site.

2 You will be prompted to confirm adding the Microsoft Project Server URL to the list of trusted sites (see Figure A-23). Click Yes to add the URL to the list of trusted sites.

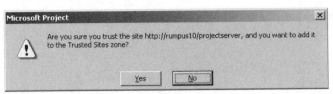

Figure A-23. Click Yes to add the Microsoft Project Server URL to the list of trusted sites in Microsoft Internet Explorer.

3 If the URL for Microsoft Project Server is incorrect, you will not be able to continue and you will be returned to the Microsoft Project Server Security Login dialog box (see Figure A-24). At this point, it is recommended that you click Cancel to quit logging on to Microsoft Project Server, and then choose to run Microsoft Project Professional 2002 offline. Verify the URL for Microsoft Project Server with your administrator and then reenter the information in the Microsoft Project Server Accounts dialog box as described earlier in this section.

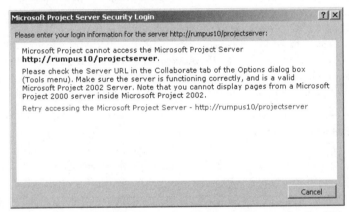

Figure A-24. Check with your administrator to verify the URL for Microsoft Project Server if you see this dialog box.

4 After the Microsoft Project Server URL is listed as a trusted site in Internet Explorer, you can log on to Microsoft Project Server. The Username And Password page of the Microsoft Project Server Security Login dialog box appears (see Figure A-25 on the next page).

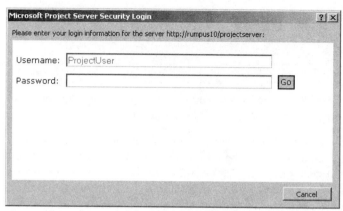

Figure A-25. Enter your password and click the Go button to connect Microsoft Project Professional 2002 to Microsoft Project Server.

5 The user name listed here is the default user name specified in the Account Name field in the Account Properties dialog box. This user name and password must also be created in Microsoft Project Server before you can log on. Enter the password and click Go. If everything is properly set up, you will connect to Microsoft Project Server. If you were unable to connect to Microsoft Project Server, check with your administrator or project manager to make sure you have the correct user name and password.

note If you have added an incorrect URL to the list of trusted sites in Internet Explorer, you can remove it. Click Tools, Internet Options. In the Internet Options dialog box, click the Security tab. Click the Trusted Sites icon, then click Sites. The Trusted Sites dialog box appears. Highlight the URL you want to remove, and then click Remove.

Appendix B
Field Reference

This appendix lists all the fields available in Microsoft Project, broken down by type of data:

- Currency
- Date
- Duration
- Enumerated
- Indicator
- Integer
- Outline Code
- Percentage and Number
- Text
- Yes/No

In addition, the following special categories of fields are grouped together for your reference toward the end of this appendix:

- Custom fields
- Earned Value
- PERT Analysis

Each row in the following tables contains the name of a field in Microsoft Project and the category in Microsoft Project to which the field belongs, for example, tasks, resources, and so on. Each row contains a description of the field, and the name of the field when it's exposed using the Microsoft Project 10.0 OLE DB Provider. Each row also includes the name of the field when you open a project as a database, for example, when you save a project as a Microsoft Access Database and open it in Microsoft Access.

Fields are listed in this appendix if the field in the database contains the same data entered or added through Microsoft Project. Some fields listed in this appendix that can be accessed using the Microsoft Project 10.0 OLE DB Provider do not have a corresponding field in the Microsoft Project database. These "missing" fields are actually the results of calculations based on values stored in other fields. For example, the Cost Variance field contains the difference between a baseline cost and total scheduled cost. The Cost Variance field can be assigned in Microsoft Project and exposed using the OLE DB Provider, but it doesn't have its own field in the Microsoft Project database because Cost Variance is the result of a calculation (Cost – Baseline Cost).

Most fields in Microsoft Project can be found in the following OLE DB Provider or Microsoft Project database tables:

Assignment.   Fields are stored in the Assignments table in OLE DB and in the MSP_ASSIGNMENTS table in the Microsoft Project Database.

Assignment (Timephased).   Fields are stored in the Minute, Hour, Day, Week, and Month assignment-timephased tables in OLE DB.

Resource.   Fields are stored in the Resources table in OLE DB and in the MSP_RESOURCES table in the Microsoft Project Database.

Resource (Timephased).   Fields are stored in the Minute, Hour, Day, Week, and Month resource-timephased tables in OLE DB.

Task.   Fields are stored in the Tasks table in OLE DB and in the MSP_TASKS table in the Microsoft Project Database.

Task (Timephased).   Fields are stored in the Minute, Hour, Day, Week, and Month task-timephased tables in OLE DB.

Custom.   Fields are stored in the tables they are associated with in OLE DB, for example, custom assignment cost fields are in the Assignments table.

---

note   In the MSP_PROJECTS database, however, custom fields are stored in the following tables: MSP_ASSIGNMENT_BASELINES, MSP_DATE_FIELDS, MSP_DURATION_FIELDS, MSP_FLAG_FIELDS, MSP_NUMBER_FIELDS, MSP_OUTLINE_CODES, MSP_RESOURCE_BASELINES, MSP_TASK_BASELINES, and MSP_TEXT_FIELDS. Data stored in these tables isn't as easy to use as the custom fields in the OLE DB Provider because custom fields in the Microsoft Project database are defined by multiple fields, and the tables can contain data for assignments, resources, and tasks.

For more information about these tables, the fields in these tables, and how to understand the data in these tables and how it links to assignments, resources, or tasks, see Projdb.htm included on the Microsoft Project 2002 installation CD.

---

note   Each of the five timephased tables for assignments, resources, and tasks are named "nTimephasedByX" where "n" is assignments, resources, or tasks, and "X" is Minute, Hour, Day, Week, or Month.

For more information about working with fields and adding them to tables, see "Using Tables" on page 102 and "Using Fields" on page 110. For more information about custom fields, see "Customizing Fields" on page 613 and "Working With Outline Codes" on page 631.

> **note** For detailed information about each individual field, including calculations, best uses, and examples, refer to the Fields Reference section of Microsoft Project Help. To do this, open Help. Click Microsoft Project Reference. Click the Fields Reference link, and then click See A List Of Field Types.

Field Types

The fields listed in the following tables (Currency, Date, Duration, Enumerated, Indicator, Integer, Outline Code, Percentage and Number, Text, and Yes/No) are grouped by data type.

Currency Fields

Table B-1 on page 829 lists all currency and currency rate fields available in Microsoft Project.

> For more information about working with costs, see Chapter 8, "Planning Resource and Task Costs," and "Monitoring and Adjusting Costs" on page 320. For more information about analyzing project information with earned value, see Chapter 13, "Analyzing Project Information."

Date Fields

Table B-2 on page 834 lists all date fields available in Microsoft Project.

> For information about working with the project schedule and associated date fields, see Chapter 9, "Checking and Adjusting the Project Plan," and "Monitoring and Adjusting the Schedule" on page 311.

Duration Fields

Table B-3 on page 840 lists all duration fields available in Microsoft Project.

> For more information about durations, see "Setting Task Durations" on page 128.

Enumerated Fields

Table B-4 on page 847 lists all fields that store enumerated values in Microsoft Project.

Indicator Fields

Table B-5 on page 850 contains information about indicator fields, which are used to provide additional information about assignments, tasks, and resources, using a simple visual icon.

Integer Fields

Table B-6 on page 850 lists all integer fields available in Microsoft Project.

Outline Code Fields

Table B-7 on page 852 lists all outline code fields available in Microsoft Project.

Percentage and Number Fields

Table B-8 on page 852 lists all percentage and number fields available in Microsoft Project.

Text Fields

Table B-9 on page 858 lists all text fields available in Microsoft Project.

Yes/No Fields

Table B-10 on page 862 lists all yes/no fields available in Microsoft Project. Yes/no fields are set either by the user or by Microsoft Project, and they indicate the state of a task, resource, or assignment as being on or off, or being true or false. Yes/No fields are also referred to as *Boolean* fields.

Table B-1. Currency Fields

Field	Available categories	OLE DB provider	Microsoft Project database	Description
Actual Cost	Assignment Assignment (Timephased) Resource Resource (Timephased) Task Task (Timephased)	AssignmentActualCost AssignmentTimeActualCost ResourceActualCost ResourceTimeActualCost TaskActualCost TaskTimeActualCost	ASSN_ACT_COST RES_ACT_COST TASK_ACT_COST	The actual costs associated with resource work or fixed costs for tasks.
Actual Fixed Cost	Task (Timephased)	TaskTimeActualFixedCost		The actual fixed cost expenses charged over time.
Actual Overtime Cost	Assignment Resource Task	AssignmentActualOvertimeCost ResourceActualOvertimeCost TaskActualOvertimeCost	ASSN_ACT_OVT_COST RES_ACT_OVT_COST TASK_ACT_OVT_COST	The actual over-time costs.
ACWP	Assignment Assignment (Timephased) Resource Resource (Timephased) Task Task (Timephased)	AssignmentACWP AssignmentTimeACWP ResourceACWP ResourceTimeACWP TaskACWP TaskTimeACWP	ASSN_ACWP RES_ACWP TASK_ACWP	The earned value actual cost of work performed (ACWP).
BAC	Assignment Assignment (Timephased) Resource Resource (Timephased) Task Task (Timephased)	AssignmentBaselineCost AssignmentTimeBaselineCost ResourceBaselineCost ResourceTimeBaselineCost TaskBaselineCost TaskTimeBaselineCost	ASSN_BASE_COST RES_BASE_COST TASK_BASE_COST	The earned value Budget At Completion (BAC). Same as the Baseline Cost field.

(continued)

Table B-1. *(continued)*

Field	Available categories	OLE DB provider	Microsoft Project database	Description
Baseline Cost	Assignment Assignment (Timephased) Resource Resource (Timephased) Task Task (Timephased)	AssignmentBaselineCost AssignmentTimeBaselineCost ResourceBaselineCost ResourceTimeBaselineCost TaskBaselineCost TaskTimeBaselineCost	ASSN_BASE_COST RES_BASE_COST TASK_BASE_COST	The total planned cost for work performed, plus fixed costs.
Baseline1-10Cost	Assignment Assignment (Timephased) Resource Resource (Timephased) Task Task (Timephased)	AssignmentBaseline1Cost10 AssignmentTimeBaseline1Cost-10 ResourceBaseline1Cost10 ResourceTimeBaseline1Cost-10 TaskBaseline1Cost-10 TaskTimeBaseline1Cost-10		The baseline costs for Baseline 1 through Baseline 10.
BCWP	Assignment Assignment (Timephased) Resource Resource (Timephased) Task Task (Timephased)	AssignmentBCWP AssignmentTimeBCWP ResourceBCWP ResourceTimeBCWP TaskBCWP TaskTimeBCWP	ASSN_BCWP RES_BCWP TASK_BCWP	The earned value budgeted costs of work performed (BCWP) costs.
BCWS	Assignment Assignment (Timephased) Resource Resource (Timephased) Task Task (Timephased)	AssignmentBCWS AssignmentTimeBCWS ResourceBCWS ResourceTimeBCWS TaskBCWS TaskTimeBCWS	ASSN_BCWS RES_BCWS TASK_BCWS	The earned value budgeted cost of work scheduled (BCWS) costs.

Field	Entities	Field Names	Field IDs	Description
Cost	Assignment Assignment (Timephased) Resource Resource (Timephased) Task Task (Timephased)	AssignmentCost AssignmentTimeCost ResourceCost ResourceTimeCost TaskCost TaskTimeCost	ASSN_COST RES_COST TASK_COST	The total scheduled cost for an assignment, including expected costs and those already incurred.
Cost Per Use	Resource	ResourceCostPerUse	RES_COST_PER_USE	The cost for each unit of work performed by a resource.
Cost Variance	Assignment Resource Task	AssignmentCostVariance ResourceCostVariance TaskCostVariance		The difference between the baseline cost and total scheduled cost.
Cost1-10	Assignment Resource Task	AssignmentCost1-10 ResourceCost1-10 TaskCost1-10		The values for the custom Cost1 through Cost10 fields.
Cumulative Cost	Assignment (Timephased) Resource (Timephased) Task (Timephased)	AssignmentTimeCumulativeCost ResourceTimeCumulativeCost TaskTimeCumulativeCost		The cumulative cost for all work performed on all assigned tasks, as distributed over time.

(continued)

Table B-1. *(continued)*

Field	Available categories	OLE DB provider	Microsoft Project database	Description
CV	Assignment Assignment (Timephased) Resource Resource (Timephased) Task Task (Timephased)	AssignmentCV AssignmentTimeCV ResourceCV ResourceTimeCV TaskCV TaskTimeCV		The earned value cost variance (CV), which is the difference between the budgeted (baseline) cost and the actual cost of work performed.
EAC	Task	TaskEAC	TASK_EAC	The earned value estimate at completion (EAC), which is the expected total cost of a task.
Fixed Cost	Task Task (Timephased)	TaskFixedCost TaskTimeFixedCost	TASK_FIXED_COST	The expense for a non-resource task.
Overtime Cost	Assignment Resource Task	AssignmentOvertimeCost ResourceOvertimeCost TaskOvertimeCost	ASSN_OVT_COST RES_OVT_COST TASK_OVT_COST	The total scheduled overtime cost for an assignment, resource, or task.

Field	Objects	Field names	Field codes	Description
Remaining Cost	Assignment Resource Task	AssignmentRemainingCost ResourceRemainingCost TaskRemainingCost	ASSN_REM_COST RES_REM_COST TASK_REM_COST	The costs associated with completing remaining scheduled work.
Standard Rate	Resource	ResourceStandardRate	RES_STD_RATE	The standard rate for non-overtime work performed by a resource.
SV	Assignment Assignment (Timephased) Resource Resource (Timephased) Task Task (Timephased)	AssignmentSV AssignmentTimeSV ResourceSV ResourceTimeSV TaskSV TaskTimeSV		The earned value schedule variance (SV), which is the difference between BCWP and BCWS measured in cost terms.
VAC	Assignment Resource Task	AssignmentVAC ResourceVAC TaskVAC	TASK_VAC	The earned value variance at completion (VAC), which is the difference between BAC and EAC, measured in cost terms.

Table B-2. Date Fields

Field	Available categories	OLE DB provider	Microsoft Project database	Description
Actual Finish	Assignment Resource Task	AssignmentActualFinish ResourceActualFinish TaskActualFinish	ASSN_ACT_FINISH RES_ACT_FINISH TASK_ACT_FINISH	The actual date and time when a task is completed.
Actual Start	Assignment Resource Task	AssignmentActualStart ResourceActualStart TaskActualStart	ASSN_ACT_START RES_ACT_START TASK_ACT_START	The actual date and time when a task began.
Available From	Resource	ResourceAvailableFrom	RES_AVAIL_FROM	The start date that a resource is available to start work on a project.
Available To	Resource	ResourceAvailableTo	RES_AVAIL_TO	The end date that a resource is no longer available to work on a project.
Baseline Finish	Assignment Resource Task	AssignmentBaselineFinish ResourceBaselineFinish TaskBaselineFinish	ASSN_BASE_FINISH RES_BASE_FINISH TASK_BASE_FINISH	The originally planned completion date for assignments or tasks.
Baseline Start	Assignment Resource Task	AssignmentBaselineStart ResourceBaselineStart TaskBaselineStart	ASSN_BASE_START RES_BASE_START TASK_BASE_START	The planned beginning date for an assignment or task.

Baseline 1–10Finish	Assignment Resource Task	AssignmentBaseline1Finish-10 ResourceBaseline1Finish-10 TaskBaseline1Finish-10		The baseline finish values for Baseline1Finish through Baseline10Finish.
Baseline 1–10Start	Assignment Resource Task	AssignmentBaseline1Start-10 ResourceBaseline1Start-10 TaskBaseline1Start-10		The baseline start values for Baseline1Start through Baseline10Start.
Complete Through	Task	TaskCompleteThrough		The most recent date that actuals have been reported on a task.
Constraint Date	Task	TaskConstraintDate	TASK_CONSTRAINT_DATE	The date associated with a task constraint.
Created	Task	TaskCreated	TASK_CREATION_DATE	The date and time that a task was first added to this project.
Date1–10	Assignment Resource Task	AssignmentDate1-10 ResourceDate1-10 TaskDate1-10		The values for the custom Date1 through Date10 fields.

(continued)

Table B-2. *(continued)*

Field	Available categories	OLE DB provider	Microsoft Project database	Description
Deadline	Task	TaskDeadline	TASK_DEADLINE	The date by which a task must be completed.
Early Finish	Task	TaskEarlyFinish	TASK_EARLY_FINISH	The earliest date that a task can finish, based on predecessor and successor tasks, constraints, and delays.
Early Start	Task	TaskEarlyStart	TASK_EARLY_START	The earliest date that a task can start, based on predecessor and successor tasks, constraints, and delays.
Expected Finish	Task	TaskFinish2		The expected finish date of a task for PERT Analysis calculations.
Expected Start	Task	TaskStart2		The expected start date of a task for PERT Analysis calculations.

Field	Level	Name	Database	Description
Finish	Assignment Resource Task	AssignmentFinish ResourceFinish TaskFinish	ASSN_FINISH RES_FINISH TASK_FINISH	The date that a task is scheduled to be completed.
Finish1-10	Assignment Resource Task	AssignmentBaseline1Finish-10 ResourceBaseline1Finish-10 TaskBaseline1Finish-10		The values for the custom Finish1 through Finish10 fields.
Late Finish	Task	TaskLateFinish	TASK_LATE_FINISH	The latest date that a task can finish, based on predecessor and successor tasks, constraints, and delays.
Late Start	Task	TaskLateStart	TASK_LATE_START	The latest date that a task can start, based on predecessor and successor tasks, constraints, and delays.
Optimistic Finish	Task	TaskFinish1		The optimistic finish date of a task for PERT Analysis calculations.

(continued)

Table B-2. *(continued)*

Field	Available categories	OLE DB provider	Microsoft Project database	Description
Optimistic Start	Task	TaskStart1		The optimistic start date of a task for PERT Analysis calculations.
Pessimistic Finish	Task	TaskFinish3		The pessimistic finish date of a task for PERT Analysis calculations.
Pessimistic Start	Task	TaskStart3		The pessimistic start date of a task for PERT Analysis calculations.
Preleveled Finish	Task	TaskPreleveledFinish	TASK_PRELEVELED_FINISH	The finish date for a task before resource leveling.
Preleveled Start	Task	TaskPreleveledStart	TASK_PRELEVELED_START	The start date for a task before resource leveling.
Resume	Task	TaskResume	TASK_RESUME_DATE	The date that the remaining portion of a split task is scheduled to resume.

Start	Assignment Resource Task	AssignmentStart ResourceStart TaskStart	ASSN_START RES_START TASK_START	The date that a task or assignment is scheduled to begin.
Start1-10	Assignment Resource Task	AssignmentStart1-10 ResourceStart1-10 TaskStart1-10		The values for the custom Start1 through Start10 fields.
Stop	Task	TaskStop	TASK_STOP	The date a split task is to temporarily stop. This is associated with a subsequent Resume date field.
Summary Progress	Task	TaskSummaryProgress		The progress made on a summary task.

Table B-3. Duration Fields

Field	Available categories	OLE DB provider	Microsoft Project database	Description
Actual Duration	Task	TaskActualDuration	TASK_ACT_DUR	The amount of time that actual work has been performed on a task, up to the current date.
Actual Overtime Work	Assignment Assignment (Timephased) Resource Resource (Timephased) Task Task (Timephased)	AssignmentOvertimeWork AssignmentTimeOvertimeWork ResourceOvertimeWork ResourceTimeOvertimeWork TaskOvertimeWork TaskTimeOvertimeWork	ASSN_OVT_WORK RES_OVT_WORK TASK_OVT_WORK	The amount of overtime work already completed by a resource on a task.
Actual Work	Assignment Assignment (Timephased) Resource Resource (Timephased) Task Task (Timephased)	AssignmentActualWork AssignmentTimeActualWork ResourceActualWork ResourceTimeActualWork TaskActualWork TaskTimeActualWork	ASSN_ACT_WORK RES_ACT_WORK TASK_ACT_WORK	The amount of work already completed by a resource on a task.
Assignment Delay	Assignment	AssignmentDelay	ASSN_DELAY	The amount of time between when a resource is assigned work and when a resource begins work.
Baseline Duration	Task	TaskBaselineDuration	TASK_BASE_DUR	The amount of time originally planned to complete a task.

Baseline Work	Assignment Assignment (Timephased) Resource Resource (Timephased) Task Task (Timephased)	AssignmentBaselineWork AssignmentTimeBaselineWork ResourceBaselineWork ResourceTimeBaselineWork TaskBaselineWork TaskTimeBaselineWork	ASSN_BASE_WORK RES_BASE_WORK TASK_BASE_WORK	The amount of work resource hours originally planned for a task.
Baseline1-10 Duration	Task	TaskBaseline1Duration-10		The baseline duration values for Baseline 1 through Baseline 10.
Baseline1-10 Work	Assignment Assignment (Timephased) Resource Resource (Timephased) Task Task (Timephased)	AssignmentBaseline1Work-10 AssignmentTime Baseline1Work-10 ResourceBaseline1Work-10 ResourceTimeBaseline1Work-10 TaskBaseline1Work-10 TaskTimeBaseline1Work-10		The baseline work values for Baseline 1 through Baseline 10.
Cumulative Work	Assignment (Timephased) Resource (Timephased) Task (Timephased)	AssignmentTimeCumulativeWork ResourceTimeCumulativeWork TaskTimeCumulativeWork		The amount of work over a period of time.
Duration	Task	TaskDuration	TASK_DUR	The amount of working time between a task's start and finish dates.

(continued)

Table B-3. *(continued)*

Field	Available categories	OLE DB provider	Microsoft Project database	Description
Duration Variance	Task	TaskDurationVariance	TASK_DUR_VAR	The difference between a task's baseline duration and total scheduled duration.
Duration1-10	Assignment Resource Task	AssignmentDuration1-10 ResourceDuration1-10 TaskDuration1-10		The values for the custom Duration1 through Duration10 fields.
Finish Slack	Task	TaskFinishSlack		The difference between a task's early start and late finish dates.
Finish Variance	Assignment Task	AssignmentFinishVariance TaskFinishVariance	ASSN_FINISH_VAR TASK_FINISH_VAR	The difference between the baseline start date of a task or assignment and its current finish date.
Free Slack	Task	TaskFreeSlack	TASK_FREE_SLACK	The amount of time that a task can be delayed before it will delay a successor task.

Leveling Delay	Assignment Resource Task	AssignmentLevelingDelay TaskLevelingDelay	ASSN_LEVELING_DELAY TASK_LEVELING_DELAY	The amount of delay caused by resource leveling.
Negative Slack	Task			The amount of time that a task is behind schedule. This time must be recovered to prevent delays for successor tasks.
Optimistic Duration	Task	TaskDuration1		The optimistic task duration for PERT Analysis calculations.
Overallocation	Assignment (Timephased) Resource (Timephased) Task (Timephased)	ResourceTimeOverallocation		The amount of work that exceeds the amount of time a resource is available.
Overtime Work	Assignment Assignment (Timephased) Resource Resource (Timephased) Task Task (Timephased)	AssignmentOvertimeWork AssignmentTimeOvertimeWork ResourceOvertimeWork ResourceTimeOvertimeWork TaskOvertimeWork TaskTimeOvertimeWork	ASSN_OVT_WORK RES_OVT_WORK TASK_OVT_WORK	The amount of work assigned to a resource that is charged at a resource's overtime rate.

(continued)

Table B-3. *(continued)*

Field	Available categories	OLE DB provider	Microsoft Project database	Description
Pessimistic Duration	Task	TaskDuration3		The pessimistic task duration for PERT Analysis calculation.
Regular Work	Assignment Assignment (Timephased) Resource Resource (Timephased) Task Task (Timephased)	AssignmentRegularWork AssignmentTimeRegularWork ResourceRegularWork ResourceTimeRegularWork TaskRegularWork TaskTimeRegularWork	ASSN_REG_WORK RES_REG_WORK TASK_REG_WORK	The amount of work assigned to a resource that is charged at a resource's standard rate.
Remaining Availability	Resource (Timephased)	ResourceTimeRemainingAvailability		The amount of available resource time not currently allocated to any task in a given time period.
Remaining Duration	Task	TaskRemainingDuration	TASK_REM_DUR	The amount of time required to complete a task.
Remaining Overtime Work	Assignment Resource Task	AssignmentRemainingOvertimeWork ResourceRemainingOvertimeWork TaskRemainingOvertimeWork	ASSN_REM_OVT_WORK RES_REM_OVT_WORK TASK_REM_OVT_WORK	The amount of scheduled overtime work remaining on unfinished tasks.
Remaining Work	Assignment Resource Task	AssignmentRemainingWork ResourceRemainingWork TaskRemainingWork	ASSN_REM_WORK RES_REM_WORK TASK_REM_WORK	The amount of work remaining on a task.

Start Slack	Task	TaskStartSlack		The amount of of time that a task can be delayed without affecting a successor task's start date or a project's finish date. Calculated by measuring the difference between a task's early start and late start dates.
Start Variance	Assignment Task	AssignmentStartVariance TaskStartVariance	ASSN_START_VAR TASK_START_VAR	The difference between the baseline start date and the current scheduled start date.
Total Slack	Task	TaskTotalSlack	TASK_TOTAL_SLACK	The amount of of time that a task can be delayed without affecting the project's finish date.

(continued)

Table B-3. *(continued)*

Field	Available categories	OLE DB provider	Microsoft Project database	Description
Work	Assignment Assignment (Timephased) Resource Resource (Timephased) Task Task (Timephased)	AssignmentWork AssignmentTimeWork Resource ResourceTimeWork TaskWork TaskTimeWork	ASSN_WORK RES_WORK TASK_WORK	The total scheduled amount of work assigned to a resource.
Work Availability	Resource (Timephased)	ResourceTimeWorkAvailability		The maximum amount of time that a resource is available to be assigned work during a specified time period.
Work Variance	Assignment Resource Task	AssignmentWorkVariance ResourceWorkVariance TaskWorkVariance		The difference between baseline work and scheduled work.

Table B-4. Enumerated Fields

Field	Available categories	OLE DB provider	Microsoft Project database	Description
Accrue At	Resource	ResourceAccrueAt	RES_ACCRUE_AT	The way in which resource costs are accrued: at the start, end, or prorated across the span of the project.
Base Calendar	Resource	ResourceBaseCalendar	RES_CAL_UID	The base calendar to be used with a particular resource.
Workgroup	Resource	ResourceWorkgroup	RES_WORKGROUP_MESSAGING	The collaboration method used to communicate with resources on a project team.
Constraint Type	Task	TaskConstraintType	TASK_CONSTRAINT_TYPE	The type of constraint applied to a task.
Cost Rate Table	Assignment	AssignmentCostRateTable	ASSN_COST_RATE_TABLE	The cost rate table used for a particular assignment.

(continued)

Table B-4. *(continued)*

Field	Available categories	OLE DB provider	Microsoft Project database	Description
Earned Value Method	Task		TASK_EVMETHOD	The method (Percent Complete or Physical Percent Complete) used to calculate earned value budgeted cost of work performed (BCWP).
Fixed Cost Accrual	Task	TaskFixedCostAccrual	TASK_FIXED_COST_ACCRUAL	The way in which fixed costs are accrued: at the start, the end, or prorated across the task duration.
Priority	Task	TaskPriority	TASK_PRIORITY	The relative importance of the task scheduling; used to determine priority for task leveling.

Resource Type	Assignment	AssignmentResourceType	ASSN_RES_TYPE	The type of resource (work or material) assigned.
Status	Task	TaskStatus		The current status of a task: Complete, On Schedule, Late, or Future Task.
Task Calendar	Task	TaskCalendar	TASK_CAL_UID	The base calendar to be used with a particular task.
(Resource) Type	Resource	ResourceType	RES_TYPE	The type of resource, either work or material.
(Task) Type	Task	TaskType	TASK_TYPE	The type of task: fixed work, fixed units, or fixed duration.
Work Contour	Assignment	AssignmentWorkContour	ASSN_WORK_CONTOUR	The way in which work is distributed over the length of an assignment

Table B-5. Indicator Fields

Field	Available categories	OLE DB provider	Microsoft Project database	Description
Indicators	Assignment Resource Task	Various Various Various	Various Various Various	Indicators that provide additional information about assignments, tasks, and resources.
StatusTask Indicator				Indicators that provide information about whether a task is complete, on schedule, late, or planned.

Table B-6. Integer Fields

Field	Available categories	OLE DB provider	Microsoft Project database	Description
ID	Resource Task	ResourceID TaskID	RES_ID TASK_ID	The position of a task or resource in relation to other tasks or resources.
Outline Level	Task	TaskOutlineLevel		The task's location within the project outline.

Predecessors	Task	TaskPredecessors		The Task ID for a predecessor task.
Resource ID	Assignment			The position of the resource within the project, in relation to other resources.
Successors	Task	TaskSuccessors		The Task ID of a successor task.
Task ID	Assignment			The position of the task within the project, in relation to other tasks.
Unique ID	Assignment Resource Task	AssignmentUniqueID ResourceUniqueID TaskUniqueID	ASSN_UID RES_UID TASK_UID	The unique ID of an assignment, resource, or task.
Unique ID Predecessors	Task	TaskUniqueIDPredecessors		The unique ID of a predecessor task.
Unique ID Successors	Task	TaskUniqueIDSuccessors		The unique ID of a successor task.

(continued)

Table B-6. (continued)

Field	Available categories	OLE DB provider	Microsoft Project database	Description
WBS Predecessors	Task	TaskWBSPredecessors		The work break-down structure code of the pre-decessor tasks.
WBS Successors	Task	TaskWBSSuccessors		The work break-down structure code of the successor tasks.

Table B-7. Custom Outline Codes

Field	Available categories	OLE DB provider	Microsoft Project database	Description
Outline Code 1-10	Resource Task	ResourceOutlineCode1-10 TaskOutlineCode1-10		The values for the custom OutlineCode1 through OutlineCode10 fields.

Table B-8. Percentage and Number Fields

Field	Available categories	OLE DB provider	Microsoft Project database	Description
Assignment Units	Assignment	AssignmentUnits	ASSN_UNITS	The number of resource units assigned to a task, expressed as a percentage of a resource's total availability.

Field	Applies To	Field ID	Description
CPI	Task Task (Timephased)	TaskCPI	The earned value cost performance index, which is the ratio of the difference between BCWP and ACWP.
Cumulative Percent Complete	Task (Timephased)		The progress of a task measured as a percentage of the total work required to finish the task, as distributed over time.
CV Percent	Task Task (Timephased)	TaskCVP	The earned value cost variance percent (CV %), which is the ratio of CV to BCWP, expressed as a percentage.
Max Units	Resource	ResourceMaxUnits RES_MAX_UNITS	The maximum number of units a resource is available to be assigned to tasks in the project.

(continued)

Table B-8. *(continued)*

Field	Available categories	OLE DB provider	Microsoft Project database	Description
Number1-20	Assignment Resource Task	AssignmentNumber1-20 ResourceNumber1-20 TaskNumber1-20		The values for the custom Number1 through Number20 fields.
Objects	Resource Task	ResourceObjects TaskObjects	RES_NUM_OBJECTS TASK_NUM_OBJECTS	The number of objects, such as an inserted graphic or a linked file, associated with either a task or resource.
Peak	Assignment Resource	AssignmentPeakUnits ResourcePeakUnits	RES_PEAK	The number of units that represents a resource's largest assignment (in units), or the number of units required to complete an assignment.

Field	Category	Field Name	Field Code	Description
Peak Units	Assignment (Timephased) Resource (Timephased)	AssignmentTimePeakUnits ResourceTimePeakUnits		The number of units that represents a resource's largest assignment (in units), or the number of units required to complete an assignment, shown for a specific time period.
Percent Allocation	Assignment (Timephased) Resource (Timephased)	AssignmentTimePercentAllocation ResourceTimePercentAllocation		The percentage of a resource's total available units compared to assigned units.
Percent Complete	Task Task (Timephased)	TaskPercentComplete	TASK_PCT_COMP	The ratio of a task's total duration to completed duration.
Percent Work Complete	Assignment Resource Task	TaskPercentWorkComplete	TASK_PCT_WORK_COMP	The ratio of a task's total work to completed work.

(continued)

Table B-8. *(continued)*

Field	Available categories	OLE DB provider	Microsoft Project database	Description
Physical Percent Complete	Task		TASK_PHY_PCT_COMP	A percent complete value that can be used as an alternative to regular percent complete for the purposes of calculating BCWP and other earned value fields.
SPI	Task Task (Timephased)	TaskSPI		The earned value schedule performance index (SPI), which is the ratio of BCWP to BCWS.
SV Percent	Task Task (Timephased)	TaskSVP		The earned value schedule variance (SV %), which is the ratio of SV to BCWS.
Task Outline Number	Assignment	TaskOutlineNumber	TASK_OUTLINE_NUM	Indicates a task's position in the outline.

| TCPI | Task | TaskTCPI | The earned value To Complete Performance Index (TCPI), which is the ratio of remaining work to remaining funds. |

| Unit Availability | Resource (Timephased) | ResourceTimeUnitAvailability | The number of units a resource is available to be assigned work, expressed as a percentage of a resource's total units. |

Table B-9. Text Fields

Field	Available categories	OLE DB provider	Description
Code	Resource	ResourceCode	The information about a resource entered as a code, abbreviation, or number.
Contact	Task	TaskContact	The name of the person responsible for a task.
E-mail Address	Resource	ResourceEmailAddress	The e-mail address for a resource.
Group	Resource	ResourceGroup	The name of the group that a resource is part of.
Hyperlink	Assignment Resource Task	AssignmentHyperlink ResourceHyperlink TaskHyperlink	The title of a hyperlink associated with an assignment, resource, or a task.
Hyperlink Address	Assignment Resource Task	AssignmentHyperlinkAddress ResourceHyperlinkAddress TaskHyperlinkAddress	The hyperlink address of a hyperlink associated with an assignment, resource, or a task.

Term				Description
Hyperlink Href	Assignment Resource Task	AssignmentHyperlinkHref ResourceHyperlinkHref TaskHyperlinkHref		The combination of the Hyperlink Address and the Hyperlink SubAddress fields.
Hyperlink SubAddress	Assignment Resource Task	AssignmentHyperlinkSubAddress ResourceHyperlinkSubAddress TaskHyperlinkSubAddress		The location within a document associated with the Hyperlink Address field.
Initials	Resource	ResourceInitials	RES_INITIALS	The abbreviation of a resource's name.
Material Label	Resource	ResourceMaterialLabel	RES_MATERIAL_LABEL	The name of the unit of measurement associated with a material resource.
Name	Resource Task	ResourceName TaskName	RES_NAME TASK_NAME	The name of a resource or task.
Notes	Assignment Resource Task	AssignmentNotes ResourceNotes TaskNotes	ASSN_RTF_NOTES RES_RTF_NOTES TASK_RTF_NOTES	The notes about an assignment, resource, or task.

(continued)

859

Table B-9. (continued)

Field	Available categories	OLE DB provider	Microsoft Project database	Description
Outline Number	Task	TaskOutlineNumber	TASK_OUTLINE_LEVEL	The number that identifies a task's position in a project's outline; this number is entered automatically by Microsoft Project.
Phonetics	Resource	ResourcePhonetics	RES_PHONETICS	The phonetic information about a resource name; used only in the Japanese version of Microsoft Project.
Project	Assignment Resource Task	Projects Projects Projects	The PROJ_NAME field in the MSP_PROJECTS table contains the name of a project. Match the PROJ_UID in the MSP_ASSIGNMENTS, MSP_RESOURCES, or MSP_TASKS tables to the PROJ_UID in the MSP_PROJECTS table to identify the project name.	The name of the project.

Appendix B: Field Reference

Field	Category	Field Name	Database Field	Description
Resource Group	Assignment Task	ResourceGroup ResourceGroup		The name of a group to which a resource belongs.
Resource Initials	Assignment Task	ResourceInitials in the Resources table ResourceInitials in the Resources table	RES_INITIALS in the MSP_RESOURCES table RES_INITIALS in the MSP_RESOURCES table	The initials of a resource assigned to a task.
Resource Names	Assignment Task	ResourceName in the Resources table ResourceName in the Resources table	RES_NAME in the MSP_RESOURCES table RES_NAME in the MSP_RESOURCES table	The name of a resource assigned to a task.
Subproject File	Task	TaskSubprojectFile		The name of an inserted project, including the path to the project.
Task Name	Assignment	TaskName	TASK_NAME	The name of a task.
Task Summary Name	Assignment	AssignmentTaskSummaryName		The name of a summary task.
Text1-30	Assignment Resource Task	AssignmentText1-30 ResourceText1-30 TaskText1-30	MSP_TEXT_FIELDS MSP_TEXT_FIELDS MSP_TEXT_FIELDS	The values for the custom Text1 through Text30 fields.

(continued)

Table B-9. (continued)

Field	Available categories	OLE DB provider	Microsoft Project database	Description
WBS	Assignment Task	TaskWBS	TASK_WBS	The work break-down structure codes used to represent a task's position within the project.
Windows User Account	Resource	ResourceNTAccount		The Microsoft Windows user name for a work resource.

Table B-10. Yes/No Fields

Field	Available categories	OLE DB provider	Microsoft Project database	Description
Assignment	Assignment Resource Task			Indicates whether this is an assignment.
Can Level	Resource	ResourceCanLevel	RES_CAN_LEVEL	The setting that specifies whether leveling can be performed on the resource.

Field	Type	Constant	Enum	Description
Confirmed	Assignment Resource Task	AssignmentConfirmed ResourceConfirmed TaskConfirmed	ASSN_IS_CONFIRMED	The setting that specifies whether a resource has accepted an assignment using an electronic team collaboration method.
Critical	Task	TaskCritical	TASK_IS_CRITICAL	The setting that specifies whether the task is on the critical path.
Effort Driven	Task	TaskEffortDriven	TASK_IS_EFFORT_DRIVEN	The setting that specifies whether the task is effort-driven.
Estimated	Task	TaskEstimated	TASK_DUR_IS_EST	The setting that specifies whether a task's duration is estimated.
External Task	Task	TaskExternalTask	TASK_IS_EXTERNAL	The setting that specifies whether the task is an external task.
Flag1-20	Assignment Resource Task	AssignmentFlag1-20 ResourceFlag1-20 TaskFlag1-20		The setting that specifies whether the custom fields Flag1 through Flag20 are on or off.

(continued)

Table B-10. *(continued)*

Field	Available categories	OLE DB provider	Microsoft Project database	Description
Group By Summary	Resource Task	TaskSummary	TASK_IS_SUMMARY	The setting that specifies whether a task is a summary task.
Hide Bar	Task	TaskHideBar	TASK_BAR_IS_HIDDEN	The setting that specifies whether Gantt and Calendar bars are hidden for a task.
Ignore Resource Calendar	Task	TaskIgnoreResourceCalendar	TASK_IGNORES_RES_CAL	The setting that specifies whether a resource's calendar is taken into account in conjunction with a task calendar.
Inactive	Resource			The setting that specifies whether an enterprise resource has been made inactive.

Level Assignments	Task	TaskLevelAssignments	TASK_LEVELING_ADJUSTS_ASSN	The setting that specifies whether assignments can be split or delayed to resolve resource overallocations.
Leveling Can Split	Task	TaskLevelingCanSplit	TASK_LEVELING_CAN_SPLIT	The setting that specifies whether resource leveling can cause a task split on the remaining work on a task.
Linked Fields	Assignment Resource Task	AssignmentLinkedFields ResourceLinkedFields TaskLinkedFields	ASSN_HAS_LINKED_FIELDS RES_HAS_LINKED_FIELDS TASK_HAS_LINKED_FIELDS	The setting that specifies whether an assignment, resource, or task has OLE links to it from within the project, another project, or an external application.
Marked	Task	TaskMarked	TASK_MARKED	The setting that specifies whether a task is identified, or *flagged*, as requiring further attention.

(continued)

Table B-10. *(continued)*

Field	Available categories	OLE DB provider	Microsoft Project database	Description
Milestone	Task	TaskMilestone	TASK_MILESTONE	The setting that specifies whether a task is a milestone.
Overallocated	Assignment Resource Task	AssignmentOverallocated ResourceOverallocated TaskOverallocated	ASSN_IS_OVERALLOCATED RES_IS_OVERALLOCATED TASK_IS_OVERALLOCATED	The setting that specifies whether resources have been assigned work beyond their work capacity or availability.
TeamStatus Pending	Assignment Resource Task	AssignmentTeamStatusPending ResourceTeamStatusPending TaskTeamStatusPending	ASSN_TEAM_STATUS_PENDING	The setting that specifies whether a response to a progress request has been received through an electronic team collaboration method.
Recurring	Task	TaskRecurring	TASK_IS_RECURRING	The setting that specifies whether a task is recurring.

Response Pending	Assignment Resource Task	AssignmentResponsePending ResourceResponsePending TaskResponsePending	ASSN_RESPONSE_PENDING	The setting that specifies whether a response to an update has been received through an electronic team collaboration method.
Rollup	Task	TaskRollup	TASK_IS_ROLLED_UP	The setting that specifies whether information on the subtask Gantt bar is rolled up to the summary task bar.
Subproject Read Only	Task	TaskSubprojectReadOnly		The setting that specifies whether a subproject of a task is read-only.
Summary	Task	TaskSummary	TASK_IS_SUMMARY	The setting that specifies whether the task is a summary task.
Text Above	Task			The setting that specifies whether text appears above or below the summary Gantt bar.

(continued)

Table B-10. *(continued)*

Field	Available categories	OLE DB provider	Microsoft Project database	Description
Update Needed	Assignment Resource Task	AssignmentUpdateNeeded ResourceUpdateNeeded TaskUpdateNeeded	ASSN_UPDATE_NEEDED	The setting that specifies whether an update message should be sent to resources to notify them of updates to their assigned tasks through an electronic team collaboration method.

Special Field Categories

The fields listed in the following tables (Custom Fields and Custom Outline Codes, Earned Value, and PERT Analysis) are all included in the tables found earlier in this chapter. In this case, these fields are listed by their function in the project plan.

Custom Fields and Custom Outline Codes

Custom fields can be used to create your own cost, date, duration, finish, flag, number, outline code, start, and text fields in Microsoft Project. The number of customizable fields of a given type can range from 10 to 30. When using Microsoft Project or the OLE DB Provider, you will see the fields listed with the type and the number of the custom field. When you're viewing the custom fields using Microsoft Access or Microsoft Excel, each custom field is stored in a unique table that contains all the data required to identify the custom field or custom outline code and where it is being used within a project. The table name is listed in the Microsoft Project Database column. Table B-11 on page 870 shows custom fields.

> For more information about working with custom fields, see "Customizing Fields" on page 613 and "Working With Outline Codes" on page 631.

Earned Value Fields

Earned value fields are used to measure the cost of work and are based on a task's baseline cost. Table B-12 on page 872 shows earned value fields.

> For information about working with earned value, see Chapter 13, "Analyzing Project Information."

PERT Analysis Fields

PERT Analysis is a technique used to evaluate task durations using best-case (optimistic), expected-case (expected), and worst-case (pessimistic) scenarios based on a task's duration, start date, or finish date. All PERT analysis fields use custom fields to store the information. Table B-13 on page 876 shows PERT Analysis fields.

> For information about working with PERT Analysis, see "Setting Task Durations" on page 128.

Table B-11. Custom Fields

Field	Available categories	OLE DB provider	Microsoft Project database	Description
Cost1-10	Assignment Resource Task	AssignmentCost1-10 ResourceCost1-10 TaskCost1-10		The currency values for the custom Cost1 through Cost10 fields.
Date1-10	Assignment Resource Task	AssignmentDate1-10 ResourceDate1-10 TaskDate1-10		The date values for the custom Date1 through Date10 fields.
Duration1-10	Assignment Resource Task	AssignmentDuration1-10 ResourceDuration1-10 TaskDuration1-10		The duration values for the custom Duration1 through Duration10 fields.
Finish1-10	Assignment Resource Task	AssignmentFinish1-10 ResourceFinish1-10 TaskFinish1-10		The date values for the custom Finish1 through Finish10 fields.
Flag1-20	Assignment Resource Task	AssignmentFlag1-20 ResourceFlag1-20 TaskFlag1-20		The Yes/No values for the custom Flag1 through Flag20 fields.

Number1-20	Assignment	AssignmentNumber1-20	The numeric
	Resource	ResourceNumber1-20	values for
	Task	TaskNumber1-20	the custom
			Number1
			through
			Number20
			fields.
OutlineCode1-10	Resource	ResourceOutlineCode1-10	The values for
	Task	TaskOutlineCode1-10	the custom
			OutlineCode1
			through
			OutlineCode10
			fields.
Start1-10	Assignment	AssignmentStart1-10	The date values
	Resource	ResourceStart1-10	for the custom
	Task	TaskStart1-10	Start1 through
			Start10 fields.
Text1-30	Assignment	AssignmentText1-30	The text values
	Resource	ResourceText1-30	for the custom
	Task	TaskText1-30	Text1 through
			Text30 fields.

Table B-12. Earned Value Fields

Field	Available categories	OLE DB provider	Microsoft Project database	Description
ACWP	Assignment Assignment (Timephased) Resource Resource (Timephased) Task Task (Timephased)	AssignmentACWP AssignmentTimeACWP ResourceACWP ResourceTimeACWP TaskACWP TaskTimeACWP	ASSN_ACWP RES_ACWP TASK_ACWP	The earned value actual cost of work performed (ACWP).
BAC	Assignment Assignment (Timephased) Resource Resource (Timephased) Task Task (Timephased)	AssignmentBaselineCost AssignmentTimeBaselineCost ResourceBaselineCost ResourceTimeBaselineCost TaskBaselineCost TaskTimeBaselineCost	ASSN_BASE_COST RES_BASE_COST TASK_BASE_COST	The earned value Budget At Completion (BAC). Same as the Baseline Cost field.
BCWP	Assignment Assignment (Timephased) Resource Resource (Timephased) Task Task (Timephased)	AssignmentBCWP AssignmentTimeBCWP ResourceBCWP ResourceTimeBCWP TaskBCWP TaskTimeBCWP	ASSN_BCWP RES_BCWP TASK_BCWP	The earned value budgeted costs of work performed (BCWP) costs.
BCWS	Assignment Assignment (Timephased) Resource Resource (Timephased) Task Task (Timephased)	AssignmentBCWS AssignmentTimeBCWS ResourceBCWS ResourceTimeBCWS TaskBCWS TaskTimeBCWS	ASSN_BCWS RES_BCWS TASK_BCWS	The earned value budgeted cost of work scheduled (BCWS) costs.

Field	Entities	Examples	Description
CPI	Task Task (Timephased)	TaskCPI	The earned value cost performance index, which is the ratio between BCWP and ACWP.
CV	Assignment Assignment (Timephased) Resource Resource (Timephased) Task Task (Timephased)	AssignmentCV AssignmentTimeCV ResourceCV ResourceTimeCV TaskCV TaskTimeCV	The earned value cost variance (CV), which is the difference between the budgeted (baseline) cost and the actual cost of work performed.
CV Percent	Task Task (Timephased)	TaskCVP	The earned value cost variance percent (CV %), which is the ratio of CV to BCWP, expressed as a percentage.

(continued)

Table B-12. *(continued)*

Field	Available categories	OLE DB provider	Microsoft Project database	Description
EAC	Task	TaskEAC	TASK_EAC	The earned value estimate at completion (EAC), which is the expected total cost of a task.
Earned Value Method	Task		TASK_EVMETHOD	The method (Percent Complete or Physical Percent Complete) used to calculate BCWP.
Physical Percent Complete	Task		TASK_PHY_PCT_COMP	The percent complete value, also known as earned value percent complete; an alternative to BCWP.
SPI	Task Task (Timephased)	TaskSPI		The earned value schedule performance index (SPI), which is the ratio of BCWP to BCWS.

SV	Assignment Assignment (Timephased) Resource Resource (Timephased) Task Task (Timephased)	AssignmentSV AssignmentTimeSV ResourceSV ResourceTimeSV TaskSV TaskTimeSV	The earned value schedule variance (SV), which is the difference between BCWP and BCWS measured in cost terms.
SV Percent	Task Task (Timephased)	TaskSVP	The earned value schedule variance (SV %), which is the ratio of SV to BCWS.
TCPI	Task	TaskTCPI	The earned value To Complete Performance Index (TCPI), which is the ratio of remaining work to remaining funds.

(continued)

Table B-12. *(continued)*

Field	Available categories	OLE DB provider	Description
VAC	Assignment Resource Task	AssignmentVAC ResourceVAC TaskVAC	The earned value variance at completion (VAC), which is the difference between BAC and EAC, measured in cost terms.

Table B-13. PERT Analysis Fields

Field	Available categories	OLE DB provider	Description
Expected Finish	Task	TaskFinish2	The expected finish date of a task for PERT Analysis calculations.
Expected Start	Task	TaskStart2	The expected start date of a task for PERT Analysis calculations.
Expected Duration	Task	TaskDuration2	The expected duration of a task for PERT Analysis calculations.

Optimistic Finish	Task	TaskFinish1	The optimistic finish date of a task for PERT Analysis calculations.
Optimistic Start	Task	TaskStart1	The optimistic start date of a task for PERT Analysis calculations.
Optimistic Duration	Task	TaskDuration1	The optimistic duration of a task for PERT Analysis calculations.
Pessimistic Finish	Task	TaskFinish3	The pessimistic finish date of a task for PERT Analysis calculations.
Pessimistic Start	Task	TaskStart3	The pessimistic start date of a task for PERT Analysis calculations.
Pessimistic Duration	Task	TaskDuration3	The pessimistic duration of a task for PERT Analysis calculations.

Appendix C
Online Resources for Microsoft Project

This appendix includes links to resources on the World Wide Web related to Microsoft Project and project management.

Microsoft-Sponsored Resources

The following is a list of Microsoft Web sites that can provide further assistance and information in your work with Microsoft Project:

Microsoft Project Home page
http://www.microsoft.com/office/project
Official site for Microsoft Project. Includes sales information, product specifications, deployment kits, and downloads. It also includes links to other resources for Microsoft Project and project management and developer resources.

Microsoft Office Update Template Gallery
http://officeupdate.microsoft.com/templategallery/
In addition to the project template files supplied with Microsoft Project, additional templates are continually being added to the Microsoft Project Web site. To see these templates, in Microsoft Project, click File, New. On the New Project page of the Project Guide, click Templates On Microsoft.com. To navigate to the Web site yourself, enter the Web site address, click the Meetings, Events, And Projects link, and then click the Project Management link.

Microsoft Project Knowledge Base
http://www.microsoft.com/office/support/searchKB.asp
Microsoft Product Support Services maintains a knowledge base of articles about Microsoft Project. You can search this knowledge base to find answers to your specific questions about Microsoft Project, or to troubleshoot a problem you're experiencing.

Microsoft Project newsgroup
news://msnews.microsoft.com/microsoft.public.project
Use any newsreader software, such as Microsoft Outlook Express, to view or subscribe to this official Microsoft Project newsgroup. This newsgroup offers help and discussion with other Microsoft Project users, including Microsoft Most Valuable Professionals (MVPs).

Microsoft Project Solution Providers

http://www.msprojectpartner.com

This site helps you find companies worldwide that can help you develop and implement custom project management solutions for your organization, as well as project management training services. You can search this site for a specific solution provider by name, by type of service provided, by country, by category, and more.

Microsoft Developer Network

http://msdn.microsoft.com/project

The Microsoft Project center within the Microsoft Developer Network (MSDN) Web site contains programming guidelines, tips, and examples for developing solutions for Microsoft Project. The site includes articles of interest to developers, code samples, downloads, links to user groups and newsgroups, and more. Also included are links to the Microsoft Project Software Development Kit (SDK) and Project Resource Kit (PRK).

Microsoft Project 2002 Software Development Kit (SDK)

http://msdn.microsoft.com/project

At this URL, click the Microsoft Project 2002 SDK link.

The Microsoft Project 2002 Software Development Kit contains tools and information for Microsoft Project solution providers, value-added resellers, and other developers interested in extending and customizing the features of Microsoft Project 2002, Microsoft Project Server and Web Access, and the enterprise features. The SDK also includes articles regarding the use of the Component Object Model (COM) add-ins, digital dashboards, the OLAP cube, and more.

Microsoft Project 2002 Resource Kit (PRK)

http://www.microsoft.com/office/project/prk

The Microsoft Project 2002 Resource Kit contains tools and techniques for Microsoft Project administrators, information technology professionals, and support staff who need to deploy and support Microsoft Project 2002, Microsoft Project Server and Web Access, and the enterprise features.

Microsoft OLE DB

http://www.microsoft.com/data/oledb

The Microsoft OLE DB Web site provides product information, technical material, documentation, and downloads related to OLE DB. It also includes links to sites about ADO and ODBC.

For additional Microsoft Project online resources, see the Microsoft Project Readme.htm file. This is included on the Microsoft Project 2002 installation CD.

Independent Resources

The following is a list of independent Web sites that can provide further assistance and information in your work with Microsoft Project and project management:

Project Management Institute (PMI)

> *http://www.pmi.org*
> Project Management Institute is a nonprofit professional organization for project managers. PMI establishes industry-recognized project management standards and provides training. PMI also sponsors the Project Management Professional (PMP) certification, which is the most recognized professional credential for project managers. PMI publishes *A Guide to the Project Management Body of Knowledge (PMBOK)*, which details generally accepted project management standards, practices, knowledge areas, and terminology.

Microsoft Project Users Group (MPUG)

> *http://www.mpug.org*
> The Microsoft Project Users Group is an independent users group formed with the support and recognition of Microsoft. The Web site offers information about a variety of Microsoft Project and project management resources, with a goal to improve the understanding and use of Microsoft Project and related products. It includes a calendar of MPUG events as well as a directory of Microsoft Project user groups around the world.

Microsoft Project Most Valuable Professionals (MVPs)

> *http://www.mvps.org/project*
> This is a Web site maintained by Microsoft Project MVPs, who are "super-users" recognized by Microsoft as providing exceptional service to the Microsoft Project user community. The site includes frequently asked questions and links to information about third-party project management products, including Microsoft Project add-ons and templates.

4PM

> *http://www.4pm.com*
> This Web site includes a variety of project management resources, including articles for beginning and experienced project managers, a project management knowledge base, an online project management bookstore, and distance learning project management courses, including preparation for the PMI certification examination.

Microsoft Project Training Consultancy and Solutions

http://www.msproject.com

This independent Web site includes articles, tips, tricks, case studies, and macros for Microsoft Project users. There are also discussion forums and links to information about third-party products.

Project Connections

http://www.projectconnections.com

The Project Connections Web site offers support, articles, tools, training, templates, and checklists for project and resource management. It includes a vendor directory, a newsletter, and discussion forums. Different levels of content are available for guests, members, and premium subscribers.

Gantthead

http://www.gantthead.com

The Gantthead.com Web site provides support for information technology (IT) project managers. It includes a schedule of relevant events, articles, process information, and downloads including plans, presentations, templates, and checklists. You can review the site as a guest, or you can become a subscribing member for additional content.

> **note** For more Microsoft Project resources, look at the Companion CD to this book. It includes files and instructions that facilitate use of the e-mail workgroup functions, Microsoft Project Server, and Microsoft Project Web Access.

Appendix D
Keyboard Shortcuts

This appendix lists Microsoft Project keyboard shortcuts for commonly used commands and operations you might otherwise carry out using the mouse.

Table D-1.   Working with Files

Action	Keyboard shortcut
New	Ctrl+N or F11
Open	Ctrl+O
Print	Ctrl+P
Save	Ctrl+S
Save As	F12 or Alt+F2
Close	Ctrl+F4
Exit	Alt+F4

Table D-2.   Working with Views and Windows

Action	Keyboard shortcut
Activate the other pane in a combination view	F6
Activate the next project window	Ctrl+F6
Activate the previous project window	Ctrl+Shift+F6
Activate the split bar	Shift+F6
Close the project window	Ctrl+F4
Zoom in	Ctrl+/
Zoom out	Ctrl+Shift+*
Close the program window	Alt+F4
Open a new window	Shift+F11 or Alt+Shift+F1

Table D-3.   **Navigating in a Project View**

Action	Keyboard shortcut
Move to the next task or resource	Enter or down arrow
Move to the previous task or resource	Shift+Enter or up arrow
Move the timescale to the beginning of the project	Alt+Home
Move the timescale to the end of the project	Alt+End
Move left one page	Ctrl+Page Up
Move right one page	Ctrl+Page Down
Move the timescale left	Alt+Left Arrow
Move the timescale right	Alt+Right Arrow
Move the timescale one screen left	Alt+Page Up
Move the timescale one screen right	Alt+Page Down
Move to the first field of the first row	Ctrl+Home
Move to the last field in a row	End or Ctrl+Right Arrow
Move to the last field of the last row	Ctrl+End
Move to the last field in a window	End
Move to the last row	Ctrl+Down Arrow
Move left, right, up, or down to view different pages in the Print Preview window	Alt+Arrow Keys

Table D-4.   **Opening and Working in Dialog Boxes**

Action	Keyboard shortcut
Open the Task Information, Resource Information, or Assignment Information dialog box	Shift+F2
Open the Assign Resources dialog box	Alt+F10
Open the Column Definition dialog box	Alt+F3
Open the Macros dialog box	Alt+F8
Open the Visual Basic Editor	Alt+F11
Move to the next tab in a tabbed dialog box (the tabs must already have focus)	Arrow keys

Action	Keyboard shortcut
Move to the next box, group, option, button, or tab	Tab
Move to the previous box, group, option, button, or tab	Shift+Tab
Move to the next option in group	Right Arrow or Down Arrow
Move to the previous option in a group	Left Arrow or Up Arrow
Show a list in a drop-down list	Alt+Down Arrow
Show the next item in a drop-down list	Down Arrow
Show the previous item in a drop-down list	Up Arrow
Select an option, check box, or button	Spacebar

Table D-5.   Editing

Action	Keyboard shortcut
Cut selection	Ctrl+X
Copy selection	Ctrl+C
Paste contents of Clipboard	Ctrl+V
Fill down	Ctrl+D
Insert task, resource, field	Insert
Delete task, resource, field	Delete
Find	Ctrl+F or Shift+F5
Find again	Shift+F4
Go to	F5 or Ctrl+G
Check spelling	F7
Undo last action	Ctrl+Z

Table D-6. Outlining

Action	Keyboard shortcut
Indent	Alt+Shift+Right Arrow
Outdent	Alt+Shift+Left Arrow
Hide subtasks	Alt+Shift+Minus Sign (Hyphen)
Show subtasks	Alt+Shift+ =
Show all tasks	Alt+Shift+*

Table D-7. Giving Special Commands

Action	Keyboard shortcut
Link tasks	Ctrl+F2
Unlink tasks	Ctrl+Shift+F2
Reset sort to ID order	Shift+F3
Remove a filter and show all tasks or all resources	F3
Insert hyperlink	Ctrl+K
Calculate scheduling changes in all open projects	F9
Calculate scheduling changes in the active project	Shift+F9
Switch between automatic and manual calculation	Ctrl+F9
Open the Office Assistant or the online Help window	F1
Activate the context-sensitive Help pointer in a dialog box	Shift+F1

---

tip   **Find more keyboard shortcuts**

To find additional keyboard shortcuts, you can use Microsoft Project online Help. In the Ask A Question box in the menu bar, type *keyboard shortcut* and then press Enter. Click the Keyboard Commands link.

Index to Troubleshooting Topics

Index to Troubleshooting Topics

Index

Special Characters

24 hours calendar, 159
4PM Web site, 881

A

abbreviations for task duration
time period units, 131
absolute, in project triangle, 232
absolute column references, 661
accelerating finish dates, 234
accepting
assignments, 476, 499, 518
changes, from external tasks, 418
changes, in Web Access team
collaboration, 478
task updates, 522
tasks, 519
tasks, in Web Access, 519, 532
Access
copying from, 436
copying from, maintaining
column order, 437
databases, importing, 441
databases, saving projects
as, 697
datasheet view, opening, 436
pasting from, 437
pasting lists from, 437
viewing Project database in, 791
accessing
e-mail team collaboration, 476
enterprise accounts, 554
enterprise data, with Web
Access, 557
hidden toolbar buttons, 643
lookup tables, quickly, 633
macros, with keyboard
shortcuts, 667
project information, 85
Project Manager account,
in Web Access, 524
Project Server database, 770, 793
project-wide settings, 674
resource availability graphs, 579
Software Development Kit, 466
SQL server data, 431
toolbar buttons, hidden, 643
Web Access account, 530

Account Properties dialog box, 821
accounts
enterprise, accessing, 554
Project Manager (see Project
Manager account)
Project Server, adding, 560
Project Server, creating, 516
Project Server, naming, 560
Project Server, setting
as default, 560
Project Server, vs. Windows
User, 560
Web Access, accessing, 530
Web Access, setting up, 509
accrual, fixed cost, 226
Accrue At field, 847
accruing costs, 224
activating
enterprise features, 819
next project window, keyboard
shortcut for, 883
other pane in combination view,
keyboard shortcut
for, 883
previous project window,
keyboard shortcut for, 883
Project, 806
Project, over the Internet, 806
split bar, keyboard shortcut
for, 883
UserForms, 759
Active Directory
adding resources from, 195
inserting resources from, 490
Active View bar, switching views
with, 86
ActiveX controls, 763
adding to Toolbox, 763
common properties, 763
registering, 763
type libraries, 763
Actual Cost field, 829
actual cost of work performed, 357
actual costs
comparing to planned, 217
for overtime, 829
viewing, 354

actual duration, 299
Actual Duration field, 840
Actual Finish field, 834
Actual Fixed Cost field, 829
Actual Overtime Cost field, 829
Actual Overtime Work field, 840
Actual Start field, 834
Actual Work field, 840
actuals, 283
entering, 293, 300
entering, allowing time for, 293
entering, detail necessary
when, 293
entering, with timesheets, 305
most recent date reported, 835
stopping automatic recalculation
after entering, 314
tracking, 294
ACWP, 357, 382
ACWP field, 829
adapting
base calendars, 160
base calendars, from
Standard, 179
templates, 678, 681
Add method, 707
Before argument, 709
Name argument, 709
adding
ActiveX controls, to Toolbox, 763
assignment delay, 263
authors, to projects, 690
baseline fields, to tables, 287
code modules, to projects, 748
code, to UserForms, 758
columns, to tables, 611
commands, to menus, 650
commands, to toolbars, 643
company name, to administrative
installation point, 811
controls, to UserForms, 757
detailed information to
resources, 181
documents, to document
libraries, 527, 543

About the Authors

Teresa Stover first encountered formal project management in 1986: As the technical publications supervisor for a startup technology company, she had to figure out how she and her staff could complete seven documentation projects at once. Using an early version of Apple's MacProject, PERT charts papered her office walls, and light bulbs went off in her head about the wonders of project management. In 1987, she started Stover Writing Services and managed documentation projects for multiple clients, including Apple Computer, National Semiconductor, Boeing, MetLife, Unisys, and most significantly, the Microsoft Project User Assistance team. For these clients she has developed books, online help, tutorials, and multimedia productions. Having won seven Society for Technical Communications awards, including a Best In Show, Teresa's other books include titles on Windows, Office, Team Manager, and Microsoft Money. When not writing in her Victorian home office in southern Oregon, Teresa conducts workshops on computer, business, and project management topics. She also volunteers for the American Red Cross, and "plays store" Saturdays at her husband's shop, Stovepipe Antiques. Teresa can be reached at sws@echoweb.net.

Stephen T. Adams has been writing Basic since it was an acronym, back in the 1970s. Originally trained to be an intelligence analyst with the CIA, he changed directions in 1990 and began a career in the software industry. He has worked in product support, software testing, and as both an editor and a writer, publishing his first book in 1992. Steve was an award-winning technical writer for Microsoft Project from 1996 until 2002, when he took a developer position at Microsoft. An avid auto racing fan, Steve can occasionally be found tearing it up at the local track, where he likes to pretend he's the next Ayrton Senna.

Bonnie Biafore has always been able to get things done. When she started using Gantt charts, she realized the term for what she did was "project management." In 1996, she started a project management consulting company, MonteVista Solutions, Inc., and soon added writing to her offerings. Exploiting her lifelong habit of redlining others' writing and documenting how to use software tools, she authored *Complete Idiot's Guide to Online Personal Finance* and *Troubleshooting Microsoft Project 2002*. She writes a monthly column about investing using the Internet for *Better Investing* magazine and is finishing a stock study handbook for the National Association of Investors Corporation (NAIC). When she isn't working, she roams the nearby mountains with her husband, Pete, and their two Bernese Mountain Dogs, Emma and Shea.

James A. Scott is a rare case of a history major done good. A strong fascination with computer technology and software development quickly pulled him back from the dark side in the mid-1990s and led him down the path toward technical writing. Since then he has been involved with technical writing, creating Web sites (both copy and code), working with XML when it was almost brand new, and finding ways to enjoy being handed increasingly difficult subjects to write about. During off-times, James can usually be found somewhere in the vicinity of a football (soccer) field.

Ken Speer has been involved with project management since the mid-1980s, when mainframe-based project management systems were the cutting edge. He has experienced the evolution of project management technology firsthand, through the use of Microsoft Project version 1.0 to the present. Ken has been a project management consultant since 1996, with experience in government contracting, aerospace, finance, software development, and telecommunications projects. In addition to using it himself, Ken has mentored other professionals in the use of Microsoft Project. An English teacher and gymnastics coach in a previous life, currently Ken's biggest extracurricular interests are music and bicycling, followed closely by hiking and traveling.

The manuscript for this book was prepared and galleyed using Microsoft Word 2000. Pages were composed by Online Training Solutions, Inc. (OTSI) using Adobe PageMaker 6.52 for Windows, with text in Minion and display type in Syntax. Composed pages were delivered to the printer as electronic prepress files.

coverdesigner
GIRVIN/Strategic Branding & Design

interiorgraphicdesigner
James D. Kramer

coverillustration
Daman Studio

OTSIteam
Jan Bednarczuk
R.J. Cadranell
Liz Clark
Joyce Cox
Nancy Depper
Aaron L'Heureux
Martin Stillion
Lisa Van Every
Nealy White

contactOTSIat
E-mail: info@otsiweb.com
Web site: *www.otsiweb.com*

Work smarter—
conquer your
software *from the inside out!*

Hey, you know your way around a desktop. Now dig into Office XP applications and the Windows XP operating system and *really* put your PC to work! These supremely organized software reference titles pack hundreds of timesaving solutions, troubleshooting tips and tricks, and handy workarounds in a concise, fast-answer format. They're all muscle and no fluff. All this comprehensive information goes deep into the nooks and crannies of each Office application and Windows XP feature. INSIDE OUT titles also include a CD-ROM full of handy tools and utilities, sample files, an eBook links to related sites, and other help. Discover the best and fastest ways to perform everyday tasks, and challenge yourself to new levels of software mastery!

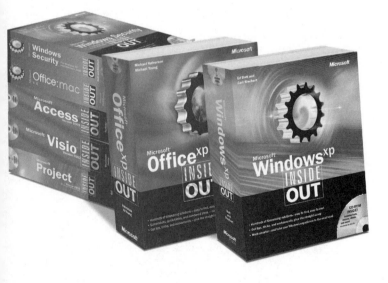

MICROSOFT® WINDOWS® XP INSIDE OUT
ISBN 0-7356-1382-6

**MICROSOFT WINDOWS SECURITY INSIDE OUT
FOR WINDOWS XP AND WINDOWS 2000**
ISBN 0-7356-1632-9

MICROSOFT OFFICE XP INSIDE OUT
ISBN 0-7356-1277-3

MICROSOFT OFFICE V. X FOR MAC INSIDE OUT
ISBN 0-7356-1628-0

MICROSOFT WORD VERSION 2002 INSIDE OUT
ISBN 0-7356-1278-1

MICROSOFT EXCEL VERSION 2002 INSIDE OUT
ISBN 0-7356-1281-1

MICROSOFT OUTLOOK® VERSION 2002 INSIDE OUT
ISBN 0-7356-1282-X

MICROSOFT ACCESS VERSION 2002 INSIDE OUT
ISBN 0-7356-1283-8

MICROSOFT FRONTPAGE® VERSION 2002 INSIDE OUT
ISBN 0-7356-1284-6

MICROSOFT VISIO® VERSION 2002 INSIDE OUT
ISBN 0-7356-1285-4

MICROSOFT PROJECT VERSION 2002 INSIDE OUT
ISBN 0-7356-1124-6

Microsoft Press® products are available worldwide wherever quality computer books are sold. For more information, contact your book or computer retailer, software reseller, or local Microsoft® Sales Office, or visit our Web site at microsoft.com/mspress. To locate your nearest source for Microsoft Press products, or to order directly, call 1-800-MSPRESS in the United States (in Canada, call 1-800-268-2222).

Prices and availability dates are subject to change.

Microsoft
microsoft.com/mspress

Target your problem and
fix it yourself—
fast!

When you're stuck with a computer problem, you need answers right now. TROUBLESHOOTING books can help. They'll guide you to the source of the problem and show you how to solve it right away. Get ready solutions with clear, step-by-step instructions. Go to quick-access charts with *Top 20 Problems* and *Prevention Tips*. Find even more solutions with *Quick Fixes* and handy *Tips*. Walk through the remedy with plenty of screen shots. Find what you need with the extensive, easy-reference index. Get the answers you need to get back to business fast with TROUBLESHOOTING books.

Self-paced
training that works
as hard as you do!

Information-packed STEP BY STEP courses are the most effective way to teach yourself how to complete tasks with the Microsoft Windows operating system and Microsoft Office applications. Numbered steps and scenario-based lessons with practice files on CD-ROM make it easy to find your way while learning tasks and procedures. Work through every lesson or choose your own starting point—with STEP BY STEP'S modular design and straightforward writing style, *you* drive the instruction. And the books are constructed with lay-flat binding so you can follow the text with both hands at the keyboard. Select STEP BY STEP titles also prepare you for the Microsoft Office User Specialist (MOUS) credential. It's an excellent way for you or your organization to take a giant step toward workplace productivity.

Microsoft Press also has STEP BY STEP titles to help you use earlier versions of Microsoft software.

- **Home Networking with Microsoft® Windows® XP Step by Step**
  ISBN 0-7356-1435-0

- **Microsoft Windows XP Step by Step**
  ISBN 0-7356-1383-4

- **Microsoft Office XP Step by Step**
  ISBN 0-7356-1294-3

- **Microsoft Word Version 2002 Step by Step**
  ISBN 0-7356-1295-1

- **Microsoft Project Version 2002 Step by Step**
  ISBN 0-7356-1301-X

- **Microsoft Excel Version 2002 Step by Step**
  ISBN 0-7356-1296-X

- **Microsoft PowerPoint® Version 2002 Step by Step**
  ISBN 0-7356-1297-8

- **Microsoft Outlook® Version 2002 Step by Step**
  ISBN 0-7356-1298-6

- **Microsoft FrontPage® Version 2002 Step by Step**
  ISBN 0-7356-1300-1

- **Microsoft Access Version 2002 Step by Step**
  ISBN 0-7356-1299-4

- **Microsoft Visio® Version 2002 Step by Step**
  ISBN 0-7356-1302-8

Microsoft Press® products are available worldwide wherever quality computer books are sold. For more information, contact your book or computer retailer, software reseller, or local Microsoft Sales Office, or visit our Web site at microsoft.com/mspress. To locate your nearest source for Microsoft Press products, or to order directly, call 1-800-MSPRESS in the United States. (in Canada, call 1-800-268-2222).

Prices and availability dates are subject to change.

Microsoft®
microsoft.com/mspress

Work anywhere, anytime
with the Microsoft guide to
mobile technology

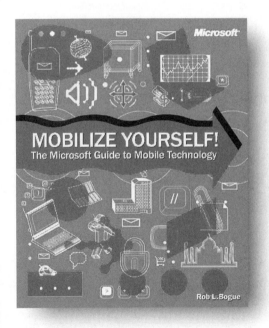

U.S.A. **$29.99**
Canada $43.99
ISBN: 0-7356-1502-0

Okay. You're at the airport but your flight has been delayed. For four hours. No worries—you've got your laptop so you're ready to work. Or are you? Can you connect to the Internet? What about reliable battery power? Here's the answer: MOBILIZE YOURSELF! THE MICROSOFT GUIDE TO MOBILE TECHNOLOGY. This comprehensive guide explains how to maximize the mobility of the technology you have today. And it provides smart answers about the mobile technologies and services you might be considering. From PDAs to the wireless Web, this book packs the insights and solutions that keep you—and your technology—up and running when you're out and about.

microsoft.com/mspress

Get a **Free**
*e-mail newsletter, updates,
special offers, links to related books,
and more when you*

register on line!

Register your Microsoft Press® title on our Web site and you'll get a FREE subscription to our e-mail newsletter, *Microsoft Press Book Connections.* You'll find out about newly released and upcoming books and learning tools, online events, software downloads, special offers and coupons for Microsoft Press customers, and information about major Microsoft® product releases. You can also read useful additional information about all the titles we publish, such as detailed book descriptions, tables of contents and indexes, sample chapters, links to related books and book series, author biographies, and reviews by other customers.

Registration is easy. Just visit this Web page and fill in your information:

http://www.microsoft.com/mspress/register

Microsoft·

- -

MICROSOFT LICENSE AGREEMENT

Book Companion CD

IMPORTANT—READ CAREFULLY: This Microsoft End-User License Agreement ("EULA") is a legal agreement between you (either an individual or an entity) and Microsoft Corporation for the Microsoft product identified above, which includes computer software and may include associated media, printed materials, and "online" or electronic documentation ("SOFTWARE PROD-UCT"). Any component included within the SOFTWARE PRODUCT that is accompanied by a separate End-User License Agreement shall be governed by such agreement and not the terms set forth below. By installing, copying, or otherwise using the SOFTWARE PRODUCT, you agree to be bound by the terms of this EULA. If you do not agree to the terms of this EULA, you are not authorized to install, copy, or otherwise use the SOFTWARE PRODUCT; you may, however, return the SOFTWARE PROD-UCT, along with all printed materials and other items that form a part of the Microsoft product that includes the SOFTWARE PRODUCT, to the place you obtained them for a full refund.

SOFTWARE PRODUCT LICENSE

The SOFTWARE PRODUCT is protected by United States copyright laws and international copyright treaties, as well as other intellectual property laws and treaties. The SOFTWARE PRODUCT is licensed, not sold.

1. **GRANT OF LICENSE.** This EULA grants you the following rights:

   a. **Software Product.** You may install and use one copy of the SOFTWARE PRODUCT on a single computer. The primary user of the computer on which the SOFTWARE PRODUCT is installed may make a second copy for his or her exclusive use on a portable computer.

   b. **Storage/Network Use.** You may also store or install a copy of the SOFTWARE PRODUCT on a storage device, such as a network server, used only to install or run the SOFTWARE PRODUCT on your other computers over an internal network; however, you must acquire and dedicate a license for each separate computer on which the SOFTWARE PRODUCT is installed or run from the storage device. A license for the SOFTWARE PRODUCT may not be shared or used concurrently on different computers.

   c. **License Pak.** If you have acquired this EULA in a Microsoft License Pak, you may make the number of additional copies of the computer software portion of the SOFTWARE PRODUCT authorized on the printed copy of this EULA, and you may use each copy in the manner specified above. You are also entitled to make a corresponding number of secondary copies for portable computer use as specified above.

   d. **Sample Code.** Solely with respect to portions, if any, of the SOFTWARE PRODUCT that are identified within the SOFT-WARE PRODUCT as sample code (the "SAMPLE CODE"):

      i. **Use and Modification.** Microsoft grants you the right to use and modify the source code version of the SAMPLE CODE, *provided* you comply with subsection (d)(iii) below. You may not distribute the SAMPLE CODE, or any modified version of the SAMPLE CODE, in source code form.

      ii. **Redistributable Files.** Provided you comply with subsection (d)(iii) below, Microsoft grants you a nonexclusive, royalty-free right to reproduce and distribute the object code version of the SAMPLE CODE and of any modified SAMPLE CODE, other than SAMPLE CODE, or any modified version thereof, designated as not redistributable in the Readme file that forms a part of the SOFTWARE PRODUCT (the "Non-Redistributable Sample Code"). All SAMPLE CODE other than the Non-Redistributable Sample Code is collectively referred to as the "REDISTRIBUTABLES."

      iii. **Redistribution Requirements.** If you redistribute the REDISTRIBUTABLES, you agree to: (i) distribute the REDISTRIBUTABLES in object code form only in conjunction with and as a part of your software application product; (ii) not use Microsoft's name, logo, or trademarks to market your software application product; (iii) include a valid copyright notice on your software application product; (iv) indemnify, hold harmless, and defend Microsoft from and against any claims or lawsuits, including attorney's fees, that arise or result from the use or distribution of your software application product; and (v) not permit further distribution of the REDISTRIBUTABLES by your end user. Contact Microsoft for the applicable royalties due and other licensing terms for all other uses and/or distribution of the REDISTRIBUTABLES.

2. **DESCRIPTION OF OTHER RIGHTS AND LIMITATIONS.**

   - **Limitations on Reverse Engineering, Decompilation, and Disassembly.** You may not reverse engineer, decompile, or disassemble the SOFTWARE PRODUCT, except and only to the extent that such activity is expressly permitted by applicable law notwithstanding this limitation.

   - **Separation of Components.** The SOFTWARE PRODUCT is licensed as a single product. Its component parts may not be separated for use on more than one computer.

   - **Rental.** You may not rent, lease, or lend the SOFTWARE PRODUCT.

   - **Support Services.** Microsoft may, but is not obligated to, provide you with support services related to the SOFTWARE PRODUCT ("Support Services"). Use of Support Services is governed by the Microsoft policies and programs described in the user manual, in "online" documentation, and/or in other Microsoft-provided materials. Any supplemental software code provided to you as part of the Support Services shall be considered part of the SOFTWARE PRODUCT and subject to the terms and conditions of this EULA. With respect to technical information you provide to Microsoft as part of the Support Services, Microsoft may use such information for its business purposes, including for product support and development. Microsoft will not utilize such technical information in a form that personally identifies you.

- **Software Transfer.** You may permanently transfer all of your rights under this EULA, provided you retain no copies, you transfer all of the SOFTWARE PRODUCT (including all component parts, the media and printed materials, any upgrades, this EULA, and, if applicable, the Certificate of Authenticity), **and** the recipient agrees to the terms of this EULA.

- **Termination.** Without prejudice to any other rights, Microsoft may terminate this EULA if you fail to comply with the terms and conditions of this EULA. In such event, you must destroy all copies of the SOFTWARE PRODUCT and all of its component parts.

3. **COPYRIGHT.** All title and copyrights in and to the SOFTWARE PRODUCT (including but not limited to any images, photographs, animations, video, audio, music, text, SAMPLE CODE, REDISTRIBUTABLES, and "applets" incorporated into the SOFTWARE PRODUCT) and any copies of the SOFTWARE PRODUCT are owned by Microsoft or its suppliers. The SOFTWARE PRODUCT is protected by copyright laws and international treaty provisions. Therefore, you must treat the SOFTWARE PRODUCT like any other copyrighted material **except** that you may install the SOFTWARE PRODUCT on a single computer provided you keep the original solely for backup or archival purposes. You may not copy the printed materials accompanying the SOFTWARE PRODUCT.

4. **U.S. GOVERNMENT RESTRICTED RIGHTS.** The SOFTWARE PRODUCT and documentation are provided with RESTRICTED RIGHTS. Use, duplication, or disclosure by the Government is subject to restrictions as set forth in subparagraph (c)(1)(ii) of the Rights in Technical Data and Computer Software clause at DFARS 252.227-7013 or subparagraphs (c)(1) and (2) of the Commercial Computer Software—Restricted Rights at 48 CFR 52.227-19, as applicable. Manufacturer is Microsoft Corporation/One Microsoft Way/Redmond, WA 98052-6399.

5. **EXPORT RESTRICTIONS.** You agree that you will not export or re-export the SOFTWARE PRODUCT, any part thereof, or any process or service that is the direct product of the SOFTWARE PRODUCT (the foregoing collectively referred to as the "Restricted Components"), to any country, person, entity, or end user subject to U.S. export restrictions. You specifically agree not to export or re-export any of the Restricted Components (i) to any country to which the U.S. has embargoed or restricted the export of goods or services, which currently include, but are not necessarily limited to, Cuba, Iran, Iraq, Libya, North Korea, Sudan, and Syria, or to any national of any such country, wherever located, who intends to transmit or transport the Restricted Components back to such country; (ii) to any end user who you know or have reason to know will utilize the Restricted Components in the design, development, or production of nuclear, chemical, or biological weapons; or (iii) to any end user who has been prohibited from participating in U.S. export transactions by any federal agency of the U.S. government. You warrant and represent that neither the BXA nor any other U.S. federal agency has suspended, revoked, or denied your export privileges.

DISCLAIMER OF WARRANTY

NO WARRANTIES OR CONDITIONS. MICROSOFT EXPRESSLY DISCLAIMS ANY WARRANTY OR CONDITION FOR THE SOFTWARE PRODUCT. THE SOFTWARE PRODUCT AND ANY RELATED DOCUMENTATION ARE PROVIDED "AS IS" WITHOUT WARRANTY OR CONDITION OF ANY KIND, EITHER EXPRESS OR IMPLIED, INCLUDING, WITHOUT LIMITATION, THE IMPLIED WARRANTIES OF MERCHANTABILITY, FITNESS FOR A PARTICULAR PURPOSE, OR NONINFRINGEMENT. THE ENTIRE RISK ARISING OUT OF USE OR PERFORMANCE OF THE SOFTWARE PRODUCT REMAINS WITH YOU.

LIMITATION OF LIABILITY. TO THE MAXIMUM EXTENT PERMITTED BY APPLICABLE LAW, IN NO EVENT SHALL MICROSOFT OR ITS SUPPLIERS BE LIABLE FOR ANY SPECIAL, INCIDENTAL, INDIRECT, OR CONSEQUENTIAL DAMAGES WHATSOEVER (INCLUDING, WITHOUT LIMITATION, DAMAGES FOR LOSS OF BUSINESS PROFITS, BUSINESS INTERRUPTION, LOSS OF BUSINESS INFORMATION, OR ANY OTHER PECUNIARY LOSS) ARISING OUT OF THE USE OF OR INABILITY TO USE THE SOFTWARE PRODUCT OR THE PROVISION OF OR FAILURE TO PROVIDE SUPPORT SERVICES, EVEN IF MICROSOFT HAS BEEN ADVISED OF THE POSSIBILITY OF SUCH DAMAGES. IN ANY CASE, MICROSOFT'S ENTIRE LIABILITY UNDER ANY PROVISION OF THIS EULA SHALL BE LIMITED TO THE GREATER OF THE AMOUNT ACTUALLY PAID BY YOU FOR THE SOFTWARE PRODUCT OR US$5.00; PROVIDED, HOWEVER, IF YOU HAVE ENTERED INTO A MICROSOFT SUPPORT SERVICES AGREEMENT, MICROSOFT'S ENTIRE LIABILITY REGARDING SUPPORT SERVICES SHALL BE GOVERNED BY THE TERMS OF THAT AGREEMENT. BECAUSE SOME STATES AND JURISDICTIONS DO NOT ALLOW THE EXCLUSION OR LIMITATION OF LIABILITY, THE ABOVE LIMITATION MAY NOT APPLY TO YOU.

MISCELLANEOUS

This EULA is governed by the laws of the State of Washington USA, except and only to the extent that applicable law mandates governing law of a different jurisdiction.

Should you have any questions concerning this EULA, or if you desire to contact Microsoft for any reason, please contact the Microsoft subsidiary serving your country, or write: Microsoft Sales Information Center/One Microsoft Way/Redmond, WA 98052-6399.